NOTHING IS TOO BIG TO FAIL

Contents

Nothing Is

Too Big to Fail

*How the Last Financial
Crisis Informs Today*

Kerry Killinger and Linda Killinger

RosettaBooks®
NEW YORK 2021

First edition published 2021 by RosettaBooks

Cover design by Mimi Bark
Interior design by Jay McNair

ISBN-13 (print): 978-1-9481-2276-4
ISBN-13 (ebook): 978-0-7953-5303-1

Library of Congress Cataloging-in-Publication Data

Names: Killinger, Kerry, author. | Killinger, Linda, author.
Title: Nothing is too big to fail : how the last financial crisis informs
   today / Kerry Killinger and Linda Killinger.
Description: First edition. | New York : RosettaBooks, 2021. | Includes
   bibliographical references and index.
Identifiers: LCCN 2020052416 (print) | LCCN 2020052417 (ebook) |
   ISBN 9781948122764 (hardcover) | ISBN 9780795353031 (ebook)
Subjects: LCSH: Global financial crisis, 2008-2009. | Banks and
   banking--Moral and ethical aspects--United States. | Monetary
   policy--United States. | Financial crises--United States. |
   Equality--United States.
Classification: LCC HB3717 2008 .K55 2021 (print) | LCC HB3717 2008
   (ebook) | DDC 330.973/0931--dc23

www.RosettaBooks.com
Printed in Canada

RosettaBooks®

Introduction

On a cold day in November 2009, Federal Reserve chair Ben Bernanke sat facing the newly appointed members of the Financial Crisis Investigation Commission (FCIC), who were investigating the causes of the financial crisis. Bernanke was one of the first people interviewed by the FCIC. It was a private interview, so only part of it was released, but in a rare moment of humility and veracity, Bernanke confessed the truth, "The crisis was caused by macroeconomic events I did not foresee." When asked if the Fed's lack of aggressiveness in regulating the mortgage market was a failure, Bernanke responded, "It was, indeed. I think it was the most severe failure of the Fed."[1]

Treasury Secretary Paulson in his 2010 book also shared a moment of remorse when he said, "I see that, in the middle of a panic, [the seizure of Washington Mutual] was a mistake. As the sixth biggest bank in the country, it was systemically important."

Former New York Fed chair Geithner confessed in his book, "We didn't examine the possibility that the initial fears associated with subprime mortgages and the fall in housing prices could trigger a classic financial crisis, followed by a collapse in the broader economy." He said he didn't require the banks he was overseeing to raise more capital because his staff didn't see a downturn coming.

These three officials may not have anticipated the financial crisis, but they can't say they weren't warned. In the years before the crisis, a number of Nobel Laureate economists warned them about the exploding debt and asset bubbles growing in the economy. Other industry experts, including Kerry Killinger, warned Bernanke and others about the rising risks from an inflated housing market and the massive unregulated shadow subprime system and its heavy trillion-dollar tentacles fed by Wall Street. But Bernanke waved them all away with the statement, "the Fed has the most sophisticated PhD economists in the world and we don't see a problem."

Bernanke, Paulson and Geithner continued to make rosy economic prognostications up until August, 2008 when they fell into a deep state of panic and stayed in that panicked state for a couple of years. Then their story kept changing.

In their latest book in 2020, *First Responders,* the three men now claim they knew there was a crisis coming, but they didn't have the tools and "the powers they needed to fight the panic, nor was there an established playbook." Their book centered on how government can clean up the next crisis, but once again they failed to warn the public about today's growing asset and debt bubbles created by Fed policies. They forgot to mention that conditions are riskier today than they were before the 2008 financial crisis.

The financial crisis was not, as Bernanke claimed, "a surprise event with macroeconomic forces that could not have been foreseen." The housing bubble, the subprime mortgage bubble, the Wall Street securitization bubble, and the credit default swap bubble were growing right there in plain sight.

The men who started and stoked the fires are now claiming to be firefighters and first responders, when in fact they were the arsonists. The 2008 crisis should not have happened and could have been contained if Bernanke, Paulson, and other policymakers would have listened and acted before 2008.

In 2007 and 2008, Congress, politicians, regulators, and the Federal Reserve, through inept policies and actions, turned a cyclical housing downturn into the worst financial crisis in nearly a century. Fed chair

Bernanke admitted to the FCIC that during those panicked days in September 2008, "Twelve of the thirteen of the most important financial institutions were at risk of failure within a week or two." Yet he never explained the true reasons why some banks were cut off from liquidity and others were showered with billions.[2]

In the bleak days at the height of the crisis, our elected and appointed officials turned finger pointing, coverups, and diversionary tactics into a cottage industry. Instead of learning from past mistakes and charting a new, safer course, leaders through overly expansive monetary policies and runaway federal budget deficits have now put us on a path toward a new financial crisis. We believe conditions are currently riskier than they were just prior to the last financial crisis. Our economy is highly leveraged, and negative shocks to the system could propel us once again into the abyss.

This book is about informing the American public about what really happened behind the scenes in the last financial crisis and pointing out what must be done today to prevent the next financial crisis.

Many popular books about the 2008 financial crisis have been written by self-aggrandizing bureaucrats, politicians, and regulators, all eager to justify their actions during the crisis they helped to create and failed to monitor effectively. Their books, such as *Firefighting, Bull by the Horns, The Courage to Act, On the Brink, Stress Test*, and *First Responders* positioned their authors as heroes, justified their lack of action before 2008, but sadly cast a blind eye toward how their actions helped cause the financial crisis. Many economic scholars have published their theories about the crisis, while some writers have authored tales long on drama and light on facts. Many important facts about the last financial crisis have not yet been revealed.

This is the first book to reveal the true behind-the-scenes reality of the 2008 financial crisis told from the perspective of a CEO heading up the sixth-largest bank in the country and his wife, a partner in an international accounting firm, who consulted with banks and thrifts for over twenty years. Washington Mutual was one of the first banks to be significantly impacted by the government's flawed response to the crisis.

Our readers will note throughout our book a shifting of voice from Linda to Kerry to the pronouns *us* or *we*. This reflects the fact that we both lived this experience; we both share an in-depth understanding of the US financial services industry, and our opinions—discussed and debated throughout the research and writing of this book—are united. We have made every effort to be candid and share the behind-the-scenes actions of regulators, politicians, investors, directors, and management.

The financial crisis could have been prevented but was fueled by blunders from the Federal Reserve and other regulators. We discuss how politicians fueled the housing bubble by demanding increased subprime lending, and we uncover the soft underbelly of the multimillion-dollar political contributions from the powerful megabanks.

We show how the politicians, regulators and Wall Street pushed for lower loan underwriting standards, forcing Fannie Mae, Freddie Mac, and subsequently bank portfolio lenders to reduce their lending standards. We describe how government and Congress ignored the dozens of unregulated shadow banks that originated and securitized nearly $2 trillion of substandard subprime loans. We note how a revolving door of regulators and politicians in and out of Wall Street all but assured the demise of thrifts and community banking to the benefit of large Wall Street banks. We show how the financial crisis destroyed trust in government for millions of hardworking people who paid the price in lost housing and wages, while the beneficiaries of the government's actions were large Wall Street banks and wealthy investors. It is no wonder our country is more divided than ever, and our very democracy could be at risk because of the shrinking middle class.

We tell our story through the prism of the Washington Mutual bank. More broadly, we review the history of home lending in the United States and Washington Mutual's growth from a small local thrift to the sixth-largest bank in the country. Founded in 1889, Washington Mutual became a Fortune 50 company with $300 billion in assets, operating twenty-five hundred retail branches in some of the nation's leading markets.

Washington Mutual navigated many housing cycles, including the Great Depression and the banking crisis of the 1980s. However, beginning in 2003, Kerry grew concerned the housing market was becoming overheated and could experience a downturn. He proceeded to take a number of actions over the following four years to reduce the bank's exposure to residential home loans. Measures included diversifying the bank away from residential lending by growing commercial and small

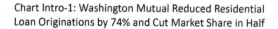

Chart Intro-1: Washington Mutual Reduced Residential
Loan Originations by 74% and Cut Market Share in Half

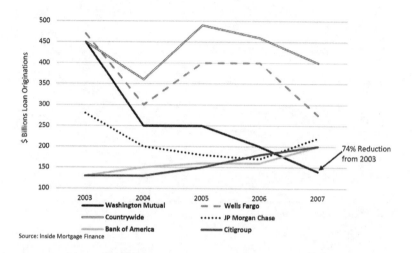

Source: Inside Mortgage Finance

business lending and retail operations, expanding multifamily lending, and acquiring a credit card company.

Kerry is probably one of the few CEOs of a Fortune 50 company who saw a crisis coming and within a couple of years, dropped the core product (residential lending) by 74 percent, replaced the revenue with a diversified portfolio of new products, hired a new management team, and continued to produce record revenue and profits.

Chart Intro-1 illustrates the mortgage lending volumes of the six largest regulated mortgage lenders: Bank of America, JPMorgan Chase, Washington Mutual, Citigroup, Wells Fargo, and Countrywide. The chart illustrates how Washington Mutual cut all forms of residential lending by nearly 50 percent in 2003 and continued to dramatically reduce all mortgage lending through 2008. Between 2003 and 2007, the bank reduced lending by 74 percent, further and faster than the competition.[3]

The bank also made dramatic cuts in subprime lending, finally shutting subprime down in mid-2007. Subprime lending was typically less than 10 percent of the mortgage lending for most of the top six regulated banks, including Washington Mutual. Before the financial crisis, Washington Mutual sold off much of its loan-servicing portfolio, closed down all the home loan branches, laid off fifteen thousand mortgage employees, cut billions in operating costs, and raised over $11 billion in new capital.

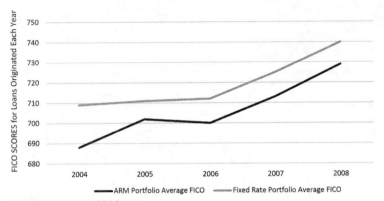

Chart Intro-2: Washington Mutual Continually Raised Their
High Average FICO Scores From 2004 to 2008 [7]

Source: Washington Mutual Risk Reports

In addition, from 2003–2008, Washington Mutual continued to upgrade loan standards and loan performance remained substantially better than the industry. The Federal Reserve (Fed) and other experts agree that the two most important pieces of data that determine the performance of a home loan are the loan-to-value (LTV) ratios and the FICO scores.[4] Historically, research has shown that mortgage loans with an LTV below 80 percent (implying a 20 percent or more down payment) and FICO scores over 660 (prime loans) had the lowest default rates—historically a fraction of 1 percent.[5] Chart Intro-2 shows Washington Mutual loans in 2004 had high average FICO scores and continued to increase the scores through 2008. Over 95 percent of the loans in the bank were to prime customers, and the bank's default rate remained less than 1 percent in the years before the financial crisis.[6]

Independent research by First American Loan Performance and Performance TS Securities found in mid-2007 delinquencies for mortgage loans for the industry had risen to over 3 percent, but Washington Mutual was well below the industry with only about 1 percent; Option ARM delinquencies for the industry had skyrocketed to nearly 4 percent, while Washington Mutual's delinquency rate only rose to about 1.5 percent.[8] The subprime mortgage delinquencies for the industry rose to over 18 percent, but Washington Mutual's rate was less than a third of that after years of delinquencies less than 1 percent.

The research demonstrates Washington Mutual's loans were of much higher quality than the industry.[9] (See Chart 8-1)

Even though Washington Mutual continued to have some of the lowest mortgage loan default rates in the industry, Kerry became very concerned about the unregulated shadow banking system that was producing massive amounts of low-quality mortgage loans. Starting in 2003, Kerry expressed his concerns in public quarterly earnings reports, investor meetings, and even privately with regulators. Kerry was vice chair and incoming chair of the Fed's TIAC Council, which met frequently with the Fed's Board to advise it on the housing industry. He served on this council when Alan Greenspan was chair and again during Ben Bernanke's tenure.

Starting in 2003, Kerry repeatedly expressed his concern to the Fed that the housing market was vulnerable and actions should be taken to reduce the risks. His concerns were repeatedly dismissed by the Fed, even though they had every opportunity to infuse liquidity into the system when the housing downturn began. Instead, it concluded the risk of inflation was greater than the risk of a declining economy. The Fed, of course, was dead wrong and helped create a liquidity crisis that ultimately led to a full-fledged panic and financial crisis.

Between early 2004 and July 2007, the Fed raised short-term interest rates from 2 percent to 6.25 percent, causing homeowners to move away from fixed-rate loans to the lower cost adjustable-rate loans. The Fed's actions were intended to reduce the risks of rising inflation and potential asset bubbles. Unfortunately, the Fed raised interest rates too high and maintained them at levels that seriously impacted housing. Higher interest rates caused mortgage rates to rise and housing prices to fall. This in turn caused loan delinquencies and loan losses to rise in the industry. The Fed had every opportunity to reduce interest rates and provide liquidity during 2007, but it refused. The evidence was mounting that a modest housing price correction was evolving into a major problem. But instead of helping manage a normal cyclical correction, the Fed added accelerant to the fire by withholding liquidity until it was too late.

By July of 2007, Washington Mutual was comfortable it had done everything possible to position the bank for a housing downturn. That month its regulators, the Federal Deposit Insurance Corporation (FDIC) and the Office of Thrift Supervision (OTS), met with the

Washington Mutual Board of Directors to report their findings from a full safety and soundness examination. They told the board the bank was in a strong position. The overall safety and soundness rating was a 2 (1 was the highest and very rare, and 5 was the worst and equally rare). The OTS and FDIC informed the board the rating was stronger than the previous year and they should think of the rating as a solid '2 plus.' The liquidity rating was upgraded to a 1 because of the strong deposit base and other ready sources of liquidity. All other component ratings were a 2. (See Chart 7-1). The regulator's written comments complimented the executives on their responsiveness in completing any recommended changes.

The board and management felt comfortable heading into the second half of 2007, having reported near record revenue and profitability, a strong stock price, excellent customer growth, improved asset diversification, and glowing regulator comments. As documented in the chapters that follow, the bank effectively prepared for the inevitable downturn, but no one could have predicted the late and unprecedented measures taken by the government, which would precipitate the entire banking industry spiraling into the abyss.

The third and fourth quarters of 2007 became increasingly difficult for the financial services industry. Lack of liquidity and panic over the failures of collateralized debt obligations (CDOs) in the market caused mortgage prices to plummet and interest rates to skyrocket. This in turn caused housing prices to fall all over the country. There are often regional downturns in housing prices, but for the first time since the Great Depression, there was a double-digit decline in the price of housing on a national basis.[10] Washington Mutual, like all banks, experienced a pickup in loan delinquencies, but projected loan losses were still within targeted ranges and still far below the industry average.

By the end of 2007, almost one hundred unregulated subprime lenders had gone out of business. Nearly every large bank was experiencing large losses, liquidity and capital issues, and was searching for ways to accommodate massive loan losses. Liquidity is required for our financial system to work. Inject too much liquidity into the system, and prices tend to rise because too much money is chasing limited assets. Remove liquidity, and asset prices tend to fall. Remove significant liquidity in a very short period of time, and capital markets freeze and asset prices plummet.

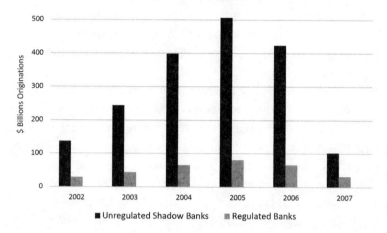

Chart Intro-3: Top 25 Subprime Loan Originators
(85% of Subprime Loans Were From Unregulated Shadow Banks)

Subprime loans have been blamed for much of the problems of the crisis, but the truth is more complex. The majority of foreclosures after the crisis involved loans to prime borrowers. But in the subprime area, most people don't realize that 85 percent of all the subprime loans were created by only twenty unregulated subprime shadow banks. The five largest regulated banks, including Washington Mutual, were not significant originators of subprime residential loans.

Chart Intro-3 reveals that 85 percent of all the subprime loans from 2002 through 2007 were originated by unregulated shadow banks like Ameriquest, New Century, HSBC Finance (UK), Option One Mortgage, First Franklin, and Fremont—nearly $2 trillion over the six year period.[11] The unregulated shadow banks produced the worst of the subprime loans, with loan delinquency rates two to three times that of the regulated banks.[12]

The regulated banks of Wells Fargo, JPMorgan Chase, Washington Mutual, Citigroup, and Countrywide only originated 15 percent of the subprime loans—$300 billion over the six-year period.

The unregulated shadow banks fed their subprime loans directly into the unregulated shadow Wall Street investment banks, insurance companies, hedge funds, and other shadow banks who packaged them into collateralized debt obligations (CDOs). Wall Street's annual sales of CDOs quickly grew from $30 billion in 2000 to around $225 billion by 2006.[13] The FCIC found that Merrill Lynch had the "most spectacular subprime losses at $24.7 billion and the other shadow banks like the hedge funds had losses over $100 billion."[14] The CDOs and other securities were often insured by credit default swaps (CDSs), which grew to an astounding $62 trillion by 2006.[15] No one anticipated this unregulated multi-trillion dollar shadow system would completely collapse in just a few months.

Conditions continued to deteriorate in early 2008, but Washington Mutual took additional actions to weather the storm. While Bear Stearns and the shadow subprime banks collapsed around them, Washington Mutual and most of the other large banks worked on raising capital and liquidity in the toughest market anyone had experienced. Washington Mutual raised $1 billion of new capital in September 2007 and another $3 billion in December 2007. In March 2008, Kerry and the Washington Mutual board concluded raising an additional $4 to $5 billion of capital was prudent to help deal with a deteriorating housing market and the brutal mark-to market accounting requirements.

These capital-raising efforts weren't helped when the OTS director John Reich called Kerry to report JPMorgan Chase was making negative presentations about Washington Mutual to a number of regulators. The FDIC later downplayed the JPMorgan presentation as just a "beef" session trying to pressure the FDIC into thinking Washington Mutual wasn't receptive to Chase's overtures.[16]

Reich told Kerry he believed JPMorgan Chase was trying to create instability by telling regulators, rating agencies, the Treasury Department, and others that Washington Mutual's estimates of lifetime residential loan losses were too low. Washington Mutual used a variety of forecasting models including highly sophisticated models that were stress tested for national housing price declines up to 40 percent. The reality is no one knew for sure how far housing prices were going to fall and how many people would lose their jobs and stop making monthly mortgage payments. Following extensive due diligence, highly sophisticated investor groups including TPG, Cerberus, and Oakhill concluded Washington Mutual's range of loan-loss estimates were reasonable and were willing to provide billions of dollars of new capital to the bank.

With the full support of the OTS and the FDIC, the Washington Mutual Board and its advisors Goldman Sachs and Lehman Brothers advised the rejection of JPMorgan Chase's nonbinding "indication of interest" and the acceptance of TPG's $7.2 billion solid offer of new capital.

The bank became the best-capitalized large bank in the country, with a Tier 1 Capital Ratio of 9.96 percent and a Risk-Based Capital Ratio of 13.93 percent (See Chart 1-1) going into the third quarter of 2008.

By July of 2008, three of the biggest and most troubled banks, Citigroup, UBS (Swiss), and Merrill Lynch, had already suffered a combined $118.2 billion in US mortgage-related losses—nearly half of the losses of the top twenty mortgage lenders in the world. Bank of America, Morgan Stanley, Royal Bank of Scotland, and Deutsche Bank (German) had each suffered about $15 billion in mortgage losses. JPMorgan Chase, Credit Suisse (Swiss), and Washington Mutual had much better results and only posted around $9 billion each in mortgage losses. (See Chart 1-2)

By July 2008, it appeared the worst might be over, but a new set of shock waves hit the industry after a US senator publicly released a letter challenging the financial health of the $32 billion asset IndyMac Bank.[17] Not surprisingly, the bank incurred a large run on deposits and was seized by regulators. This failure cost the FDIC insurance fund an astounding $10.7 billion.

Kerry spoke with FDIC chair Sheila Bair after this episode, and she complimented him on how Washington Mutual was managing the instability in the industry. Kerry told her he was concerned short sellers were targeting banks and thrifts. Many of the other large bank CEOs were complaining about the same problem. The short sellers would take short positions and then incite the media and others with negative stories about targeted institutions. Their motive was to cause a panic and a corresponding drop in a target's stock price. The Treasury Department belatedly realized this was a risk to the system and in July 2008, developed a "do not short" list of financial institutions that would be protected from short sellers.

Inexplicably, Washington Mutual and other non–Wall Street banks, like Wells Fargo and Wachovia, were excluded from the list. Kerry immediately contacted Fed chair Bernanke, FDIC chair Bair, OTS director Reich and Treasury Secretary Henry Paulson in an effort to have the bank included. Bair, Reich, and Bernanke were supportive, but Paulson said he wouldn't help and said the bank shouldn't even worry about short sellers. He added the bank should have sold to JPMorgan Chase and his current priority was to find a solution to the issues with Fannie Mae and Freddie Mac. Behind Paulson's actions was a report he had issued in March of 2008 calling for the elimination of the thrift industry and its regulator, the

OTS, within two years.[18] It seemed clear he wanted Washington Mutual absorbed into Wall Street, despite the bank's favorable financial position.

Working cleverly behind the scenes was JPMorgan Chase, who seemed to be in on Paulson's plan. According to documents referred to in the Washington Mutual bankruptcy examiner's (Examiner) report, during the summer of 2008, JPMorgan Chase developed a "straw-man structure" whereby "West Bank [Washington Mutual] is seized, assets and deposits transferred to a New Bank and a New Bank sold to acquirer [Chase]." Based on these documents, JPMorgan Chase was apparently trying to pressure the FDIC to seize Washington Mutual.[19] It was unprecedented for the FDIC and Treasury to work behind the scenes with a potential acquirer without telling the target bank or its primary regular (the OTS). Washington Mutual was a longtime 2-rated bank with no formal enforcement actions and no need to be seized.

These behind-the-scenes actions began driving a wedge between the OTS and the FDIC. With JPMorgan Chase, Treasury, and the FDIC lining up against the OTS, the regulators began fighting and Washington Mutual was caught in the middle. Despite the challenges of heavy short sellers, inappropriate actions by Treasury and the FDIC, and a formidable competitor working behind the scenes to acquire the bank on the cheap, Washington Mutual was stable and weathering the storm in August 2008. Deposits had returned to previous levels (See Chart 1-3), loan loss provisioning was declining, capital ratios were the highest among the large banks (See Chart 1-1), and there were solid plans to add more liquidity and capital if needed. The executives and board thought Washington Mutual was well positioned to not only weather the storm but to do very well when the cycle improved.

In early September of 2008, the Washington Mutual board decided Kerry should retire. Kerry was still energized about leading Washington Mutual out of this crisis, but he understood the pressures on directors to make changes in executive management when stock prices were down. Over the preceding nine months, most of the CEOs of the major banks had been replaced. At least Kerry left knowing there was plenty of capital, over $50 billion of excess liquidity, a diversified product line and loan-loss performance better than the industry.

In mid-September 2008, the financial crisis exploded when regulators decided to let Lehman Brothers fail. This action accelerated the liquidity crisis, and virtually every major bank suffered deposit and borrowing runs. Panic set in, and the domino effect of bank failures was poised for the fall. Regulators made a major blunder by letting Lehman fail. They may have won some Pyrrhic victory by showing they were letting a major financial institution fail, but they no doubt eventually cost the economy hundreds of billions of dollars and caused millions of people to lose their homes and their jobs. Most economists now conclude letting Lehman fail was a fatal mistake and the tipping point of the crisis.

Like most large banks, Washington Mutual suffered deposit runs for a few days following the Lehman failure, but deposits were stabilizing (Chart 1-3) when the bank was quickly seized and sold for a bargain price to JPMorgan Chase, despite the fact that Washington Mutual had capital well in excess of regulatory requirements and billions available in liquidity. Treasury and the FDIC completely ignored a concrete plan from Washington Mutual to further increase capital and liquidity. The rushed, behind-the-scenes transaction was a result of JPMorgan Chase's rapacious desire to expand its franchise and its successful manipulation of the FDIC, Treasury, and the Fed. This was a great deal for JPMorgan, a terrific outcome for the FDIC because there was no cost to its insurance fund, and a big step for Treasury in its quest to eliminate the thrift and consolidate banking into Wall Street. But it was a devastating deal for Washington Mutual shareholders, bondholders, employees, and the communities it actively supported. We strongly believe the bank was not treated equitably and there was a significant takings and transfer of value. It was especially painful to watch this transpire and not be there to try to stop it.

Years later, the FCIC report stated that in September 2008, "Twelve out of thirteen of the largest banks in the country were ready to collapse," but Treasury, the FDIC and the Fed, acting in a panic, had no discernible logic for which banks would be saved and which would be showered with billions. Within a few days following the seizure of Washington Mutual and the forced sale of Wachovia, all the remaining banks were given capital, deposit and debt guarantees, and other liquidity, which quickly returned the industry to profitability. The unregulated Wall Street investment banks were given full banking charters, which led to huge increases in stock prices. The combined market capitalizations of the five largest megabanks grew from $138 billion at the depths of the financial crisis in March 2009 to over $1.3 trillion at the beginning of 2020.[20]

As it turned out, the winners after the crisis were the large Wall Street banks that funneled hundreds of millions of dollars in political contributions to politicians (See Chart 1-4). Among the large banks, no one benefited more than JPMorgan Chase, whose stock price increased fivefold from 2009 to 2019. As of the beginning of 2020, Chase had the largest market capitalization of any bank in the world—$432 billion with $2.6 trillion in assets.[21]

Before the crisis, Kerry spent time in Washington, DC, serving on various councils and industry trade groups and attending political events so he understood how Wall Street believed it could control its fortunes through influence peddling. However, his Iowa integrity and frugality precluded him from participating in or condoning this type of behavior. Politics had become a very unsavory pay-to-play business, and it was easy to understand why many felt the system had become corrupt.

The Wall Street banks made out very well, but millions of home-owners who lost their homes and jobs did not receive the same level of support from their government. The economy eventually recovered, and unemployment declined, but wages have lagged, and wealth has become concentrated in fewer and fewer people. Our middle class continues to be under siege and politically we seem to disagree on more things than we agree. Confidence in our government and large institutions is still at all-time lows.

Most economists now agree the financial crisis was caused by a speculative housing bubble that quickly morphed into a liquidity crisis when the Fed didn't act. It finally fell into a full financial crisis when the regulators made the fateful decision to let Lehman Brothers fail.

There were other factors that exacerbated the crisis. Greedy Wall Street bankers knew there was a bubble but kept securitizing and originating loans to get their bonuses. Unregulated shadow banks cropped up overnight and originated 85 percent of all the subprime loans—nearly $2 trillion. Wall Street firms packaged poor-quality loans and sold them globally to what were supposed to be sophisti-cated investors. Rating agencies underestimated the layered risks in the loan pools. Global investors seeking higher returns gladly bought higher-yielding but riskier mortgage pools. Congress and the GSE's regulator pushed Fannie Mae and Freddie Mac to increase loans to low- and moderate-income (LMI) borrowers and to lower its underwriting standards. Most banks and thrifts, under competitive pressure from the GSEs and Wall Street, lowered their underwriting standards. Banking regulators, through the CRA rating criteria, pressured regulated banks to increase loans to LMI borrowers, most of which were subprime. Naked short sellers were allowed to earn high returns by fueling panic and pessimism.

Following the financial crisis, politicians and heads of government institutions turned finger-pointing into a cottage industry. There were hundreds of lawsuits aimed at bankers and hearings from the FCIC and the Senate Permanent Subcommittee on Investigations (PSI). These hearings were biased, partisan, and designed to shield Congress from any blame.

Kerry participated in the PSI hearings, and his top Washington DC attorneys revealed that, "The PSI has no standard of care and no rights normally available in an investigation or court trial. It is Kabuki theater, but one that can refer criminal charges. It is not an investigation of the facts of a case; it is made-for-television drama. They will threaten your executives and encourage them to give biased testimony."

They were correct. The PSI ignored the information and facts we presented and developed a false and misleading narrative to support their legislative goals. Kerry was warned not to fight back at the hearings, but he did. He used the hearing as an opportunity to highlight why Washington Mutual was improperly seized and was actually healthier than most of the large banks that were showered with billions. He said that the millions of lobbying funds and the close relationship between Wall Street banks, politicians, and regulators made them "too clubby to fail." This caught some media attention, and the chair of the PSI lashed back by demanding regulators take punitive action against the bank's executives. The PSI wanted to control the drama and didn't like it when Kerry wouldn't roll over for them.

But the PSI drama wasn't over. After the hearings, the PSI chair, Senator Carl Levin made a number of public threats for the FDIC to file suit against the executives. Our attorneys told us the PSI threats were the reason the FDIC quickly filed a lawsuit. The suit was totally without merit but did require time and resources to get resolved. It was clear the lawsuit was designed to get directors' and officers' liability

(D&O) insurance money. The lawsuit was finally settled with no findings of wrongdoing, no fines or bans from banking. This was the same outcome for all the lawsuits filed against Washington Mutual and its executives. Not surprisingly, the lawsuits stopped the minute the D&O insurance money was depleted.

After the federal government bungled its way around before and after the crisis, it did create regulations and changes that were helpful, but much of it has been lobbied away. We believe the current regulated banking industry is better capitalized and capable of withstanding significant financial stress. In spite of this, the entire financial system remains more fragile now than before the 2008 crisis.

Once again behind the scenes, another unregulated shadow banking system has experienced high growth and we don't know how it will perform in the next crisis.

The last few chapters of our book are devoted to the growing risks we see for a new financial crisis. We believe actions taken by the Fed and the US federal government over the past decade produced a highly leveraged and fragile economy vulnerable to a variety of risks. While we were critical of the Fed for withholding liquidity when the system needed it most before the last financial crisis, the Fed has subsequently erred on the side of providing too much liquidity for over twelve years. Instead of returning to neutral monetary policies after the economy recovered, the Fed kept adding excess liquidity and caused both short- and long-term interest rates to remain at unusually low levels.

These actions along with growing US federal budget deficits resulted in a highly leveraged economy built on the back of inflated asset prices and too much debt. Major central banks around the world followed the Fed's lead and exploded their balance sheets to $20 trillion at the beginning of 2020 from less than $5 trillion a decade ago.[22] Excess liquidity via low interest rates and central bank asset purchases led to too much money chasing assets and encouraged countries, individuals, and corporations to borrow heavily.

At the beginning of 2020, we were mostly concerned about six large asset bubbles, including stock prices, housing prices, commercial real estate prices, luxury good prices (especially top works of art), household net worth and Chinese real estate. These asset bubbles were built on the backs of record debt for consumers, businesses, the US government, and China.

Our view is that the US stock market was about 30 percent overvalued at the beginning of 2020 based on its historic relationship to GDP and cyclically adjusted earnings.[23] We similarly view housing prices to be about 10 percent overvalued after more than fully recovering from the depths of the 2008 financial crisis. The Case-Shiller National Home Price Index, for example, began 2020 with a record index of 213, up 15 percent from the 2006 peak and 60 percent above the financial crisis lows.[24] Home prices in many urban markets like San Francisco, Los Angeles, Seattle, Dallas, and Denver rose much more quickly, making them even more vulnerable to a downturn.

We also view commercial real estate prices to be overvalued by 15 to 20 percent in early 2020. Low-cost financing with easy terms over the past decade led to rapidly rising prices. The Green Street Commercial Property Price Index, for example, rose to a record index of 135.5, twice the 63.3 recorded at the bottom of the financial crisis. We believe commercial real estate is especially vulnerable to an economic downturn and changes in patterns of retail sales, commercial office space, and hospitality.

Many luxury items, including art, are being sold at record high prices. Because these assets have no earning, price increases can only be explained by excess liquid assets chasing potential inflated values. The eye-popping report that Leonardo da Vinci's *Salvator Mundi* recently sold for $450.3 million is one thing, but it's the broadening base of expensive art, as *ARTnews* reports, that is more surprising.[25]

Other asset bubbles we are very concerned about are in China, which may have created the biggest real estate bubble in the history of the world. In a concerted effort to grow the economy, build infrastructure, and transition people to urban living, China built about seven million new housing units per year over the past decade. China manipulated housing prices to rise over the past decade despite a growing lack of housing affordability, which resulted in up to sixty-five million unoccupied housing units. The Chinese government will likely continue to manipulate prices, but we believe prices could easily fall by 25 percent or more if free market forces take hold.

While asset prices are a concern, we are even more concerned about the debt bubbles building around the world. In the US, consumer debt is now at record levels with no signs of letting up. Rapid growth in student and auto loan debts (especially subprime) are leaving consumers stretched. Student debt is particularly troubling, as it can't be relieved in bankruptcy and is certain to impact younger adults and their parents, who, in many cases, are guarantors of their children's debt. Corporations have similarly amassed record levels of debt in the past decade to finance acquisitions, share repurchase, and expansion. Most of this debt has been issued by lower-rated companies, which means their risk of default is significant in the next recession.[26]

Particularly troubling is the US federal government debt, which has grown to over 100 percent of GDP—a record peacetime high.[27] Although we have record levels of debt outstanding, the government still hasn't addressed the long-term costs of health care, Social Security, and deferred infrastructure costs. Tax cut legislation in 2017 was supposed to be paid from higher economic growth. However, the economy was already operating at full employment, making further economic growth highly uncertain.

The US economy was operating at full employment early in 2020 when the COVID-19 pandemic struck. In a matter of weeks, the economy fell into a deep recession and unemployment claims reached record levels. Many political leaders view this pandemic as a unique, unlikely-to-be-repeated occurrence. We view it differently. We believe the Fed and the US federal government caused our economy to be highly leveraged and vulnerable to disruptive forces. We view the pandemic as just one of many risks which could strike at any time and affect the fragile backbone of our economy.

New federal programs to respond to the COVID pandemic are necessary, but will increase an already bloated $1 trillion annual US federal budget deficit to new records. The federal government is all but certain to sustain multitrillion-dollar budget deficits over the next few years. Even after the economy stabilizes and eventually recovers from COVID-19, the federal budget deficits will be bloated and debt is already exceeding all-time highs. Our economy will be even more leveraged and vulnerable to future unforeseen shocks to the system.

Another debt time bomb is the unfunded state and local pension liabilities that have grown to $4 trillion. Most of the pension plans assume a 7 percent annual investment return in calculating pension liabilities. We believe it is highly unlikely these plans will achieve those high returns over the next five years. Lower risk investments like Treasury securities are currently earning less than 1 percent and higher-risk investments like common stocks and commercial real estate are fully valued, in our opinion. Poor investment returns could increase the unfunded pension liabilities to $6 trillion or more.[28]

The likely way to pay for these unfunded pension liabilities is by increased property taxes. But raising property taxes would place pressure on housing and commercial property prices. States like Illinois are particularly vulnerable to a vicious cycle of growing unfunded pension liabilities leading to rising taxes, lower property prices, and population outmigration.

Beyond the US, many developing countries—China in particular—have taken advantage of easy money and borrowed heavily. China has amassed debt of 300 percent of its GDP. This debt supported strong economic growth over many years but led to many uneconomic projects, including overbuilding of housing. Other developing countries have also taken on too much debt, and defaults are likely to increase.

It is impossible to predict which of these risks will result in the next financial crisis. But high on our list are an economic downturn and credit crisis in China, uncertain long-term effects from the COVID-19 pandemic, severe correction in the US stock market, a constitutional crisis in the US, rising corporate debt defaults, rising consumer loan delinquencies, potential cyberattacks, trade wars, more worldwide pandemics, and other black swan events.

What we can do is vigorously monitor all risks and address the ones we can control. We believe the Federal Reserve is increasingly assuming the greatest influence over our financial future. The Fed expanded its role when it aggressively undertook its asset purchase and guarantee programs in the last decade. These actions were totally justified in the short term, but they are risky over the long term. We believe the Fed is the agency most responsible for causing the asset and debt bubbles over the past decade. Their actions made borrowing cheap and easy. And their asset purchase programs forced investors into seeking higher returns with higher-risk assets. We believe it is time for the Fed to admit responsibility for building these asset and debt bubbles and initiate actions to gradually unwind some of the bubbles it helped create.

The Fed's actions directly impact the economy, employment, inflation, interest rates, asset prices, and debt accumulation. This power makes the Fed critically important to accomplishing most political and public policy issues. The president and Congress increasingly recognize this power and will no doubt attempt to continue to influence the Fed with selections of the chair and other board positions. This politicization of the Fed has been growing for some time and is likely to follow the direction of the Supreme Court, where justices are primarily picked along party lines or philosophical leanings. We believe the Fed will become less independent and more pressured to support executive and congressional mandates.

Once the economy stabilizes from the pandemic, we believe the Federal Reserve needs to gradually remove excess liquidity from the system and significantly reduce its asset purchase and guarantee programs. We also encourage state and local politicians to fully address their unfunded pension liabilities and for Congress to address health care, Social Security, student lending, and overall government spending. The US federal government needs to bring down spending and fund it in a way that reduces leverage and helps recreate a strong and vibrant middle class.

We view the regulated banking system as fundamentally safe and sound and do not believe additional regulations are required. We do not expect the next crisis to be centered on regulated banks. We are more concerned about unregulated shadow banks that are increasingly engaged in financial transactions. The overwhelming majority of newer financial products, such as ETFs, CDOs, programmed trading, private equity, venture capital, hedge funds, and leveraged transactions, are managed by unregulated shadow banks. We just don't know how these players and their products will perform in the next downturn.

We are also concerned the United States is effectively guaranteeing housing via the dominance of the GSEs of Fannie Mae and Freddie Mac, as well as the Federal Housing Administration (FHA) and Department of Veterans Affairs (VA). Rising home prices and a booming economy in recent years led to very modest loan losses. This in turn made the GSEs more profitable than can be sustained over the long term. Fannie Mae and Freddie Mac were placed into conservatorships in 2008 to stabilize the economy during the last financial crisis, but this was a temporary, ad hoc solution to a crisis and not a carefully planned long-term solution.

Congress needs to take up GSE reform with the goal of creating a viable long-term solution. The GSEs need to build substantial capital cushions during periods of low loan losses instead of allowing profits to flow back into the Treasury. The current approach of maintaining very limited capital in the entities all but assures great taxpayer costs to bail them out in the next housing downturn. Given the federal government is already facing shortfalls to fund Social Security, Medicare, Medicaid, and infrastructure building, the last thing it needs is another bailout of the GSEs.

***

In September 2018, Andrew Ross Sorkin from CNBC interviewed Kerry during the tenth anniversary week of the global financial crisis. The week was filled with exuberant Wall Street executives who celebrated their enormous success and saw only a rosy economy on the horizon. Kerry's interview was different. He warned the viewing audience about the building asset and debt bubbles in the system and predicted a future downturn in the stock market and the economy—just as he had done when he warned Chairman Bernanke and others from 2003 to 2008 about the risks of a housing downturn.

This book explores the massive asset and debt bubbles building around the world and the changing role of another growing shadow banking system. It also shows how the government bungled its handling of the last financial crisis and may be doing the same today as it creates an even more highly leveraged and fragile economy.

We also detail how government actions are leading to an inequitable distribution of wealth, destroying the middle class, reducing trust in government, and accelerating racial injustice.

No institution, government, or country is "too big to fail." This book offers lessons learned from past crises and recommends actions for businesses and government leaders to return our economic system and our democracy to a safer path.

1

"Too Clubby to Fail":
Wall Street Banks Win, Thrifts
and Community Banks Lose

2008

There are days that are uneventful and flow together endlessly. So many days, you can't remember the details. But then there are days that will stay with you forever, days you can never forget, days that will change your life forever. September 25 was always a special day for Linda, because it was the birthday of her only child. She had just given him a brief call. He was busy working as a paralegal, saving money for law school. After the call, Linda and Kerry turned on the TV to watch the news and heard the announcement that was impossible to believe. The sixth-largest bank in the country, Washington Mutual, with over $300 billion in assets, had been seized and sold to JPMorgan Chase for the bargain price of $1.9 billion. The seizure had occurred during the 119th anniversary year of the incorporation of the bank.

This improbable seizure did not fit the facts we knew. Kerry had just retired from the bank three weeks earlier. When he retired, Washington Mutual had over $50 billion of excess liquidity, and over $11 billion of capital had been raised in the last 10 months, so capital was significantly above regulatory requirements. Loan portfolios were

performing better than the industry, and the bank didn't have any formal regulatory directives or enforcement actions. The bank's holding
company had over $30 billion of assets, some of which could have
been down-streamed to the bank. With all those assets and liquidity,
there should have been no reason for the seizure of the bank or the
bankruptcy of the holding company. The bank's residential mortgage
lending had been dramatically decreased in the last few years, and the
growing retail banking operation, credit cards, and multifamily lending
were highly profitable and the bulk of the bank's business.

There are not many CEOs of a Fortune 50 company who have seen
a crisis coming and within a couple of years, dropped the core product
(home lending) by 74 percent, replaced the revenues with a diversified
portfolio of new products, hired a new management team, and continued to achieve record revenue and profits. Kerry felt confident these
actions positioned the bank to face the coming crisis.

However, when the regulators let Lehman fail, most banks, including Washington Mutual, suffered deposit losses. But those losses had
stabilized at Washington Mutual, and the Federal Home Loan Banks
of San Francisco and Seattle offered billions of additional liquidity in
case it was required. The executives at the bank had submitted a plan
to Treasury that would add billions of liquidity and assets to the bank.
They had until Sunday, September 28, to get approval of the plan. It
was only Thursday. We couldn't think of an example when the regulators had seized a 3-rated bank and they had rarely seized a bank on a
Thursday—it was always Friday. What was the rush?

Well-established regulatory protocols appeared to be ignored in an
effort to get a sale completed before additional capital or liquidity
could be brought into the bank. Kerry understood why the board had
asked him to retire earlier that month. Nearly all the large-bank CEOs
in the country had been retired or terminated after all banks experienced record increases in loan losses, record losses in earnings, and
deep plunges in stock prices. After retiring from Washington Mutual,
Kerry had continued on with life, fielding numerous calls from employees keeping him posted on the activities of the bank and also fielding
calls from executives with offers to join their firms or boards.

Hearing that Washington Mutual was seized stunned and scared
Kerry. He knew it meant the entire financial system was about to collapse. Over the past four years, Kerry had repeatedly warned investors,

regulators, and the Federal Reserve that the housing collapse could have a substantial effect on the economy. He pleaded with the Federal Reserve to inject liquidity into the system and was astounded when regulators made the fatal mistake of letting Lehman Brothers fail. Kerry was angry at the continual incompetence of the government officials.

The financial crisis could have been avoided. The seizure of Washington Mutual, the failure of thousands of thrifts and community banks, the loss of millions of jobs and homes should not have happened. Kerry went through his mental trap line—was there anything he could have done differently?

Should he have cut residential mortgage loans even further? Maybe, but he made deeper cuts than any of the large banks and laid off fifteen thousand mortgage employees. Should he have originated any subprime loans at all? Maybe not, but regulated banks were pressured to have substantial portfolios of LMI loans to earn "outstanding" CRA ratings. Washington Mutual's subprime loans averaged about 5 percent of the loan portfolio with loan losses much lower than the industry. Should he have eliminated adjustable-rate loans and only offered fixed-rate residential loans? Maybe, but customers wanted a full range of products and adjustable-rate loans like option ARMs were given to prime customers and had very low default rates similar to fixed-rate loans. Fixed-rate loans made up 70 to 80 percent of Washington Mutual's residential loan originations during the 2000s.

Should he have spent tens of millions of dollars lobbying Congress, like Wall Street did? Maybe, but he felt if you followed the rules and exhibited strong ethics, you didn't need to bribe Congress. That strategy worked for decades because the bank never had any formal regulatory actions, fines, or penalties. Did he always have the right people in the job? Sometimes not, but when that happened, he quickly made changes. Early in the decade, he recruited some of the best and most experienced people in the industry. Should he have converted to a commercial banking charter earlier? Maybe, but large commercial banks were having even more problems.

Should he have raised more capital? He did and in July 2008, Washington Mutual was the most highly capitalized large bank in the country, the first large bank to be Basel II compliant and regulators and experts agreed its $50 billion-plus in liquidity would carry the bank through any serious downturn.

We started getting phone calls and emails from former employees. Nearly all the executives had just heard about the seizure on the news and were shell-shocked. We were very concerned what the seizure meant for the tens of thousands of employees who would lose their jobs and their savings. Between phone calls, Kerry paced the room and carefully reviewed the events of the last nine months, trying to process if there was anything he could have done differently. He looked back to the beginning of the year.

The January 2008 investor conferences in New York City were grim. Nearly all the banks were suffering record losses from their deteriorating loan portfolios, and bank stock values were plummeting and banks were desperately seeking more capital and liquidity. Kerry had been warning the Federal Reserve (Fed) for four years about a downturn and the need for liquidity in the system and was once again using the conferences to warn investors and regulators of the deepening financial crisis. He continued to be frustrated the Fed was so slow to act. He told investors:

> Housing prices were correcting in a fairly orderly manner until the middle of 2007, when the capital markets suddenly froze. In a very brief period, the consumer's ability to obtain financing was severely curtailed. Unfortunately, the Federal Reserve and the [federal] government were very slow to acknowledge deteriorating market conditions, because their economists were forecasting only a brief slowdown in housing followed by a quick recovery.

Kerry continued to be frustrated by the inaction of Fed chair Bernanke. Bernanke was scholarly in an ivory tower way, but he didn't have practical capital market or business experience. As a result, early on, when there were discussions about the housing market, he did not understand what made the mortgage markets work and how sophisticated capital market products would react when liquidity dried up in the system. Bernanke would always respond that he "was more concerned about the potential of inflation than about the decline of the economy."

Fed chair Bernanke and others even ignored warnings by Nobel Laureate economist Dr. Robert Shiller. In Shiller's 2008 book *The Subprime Solution*, he detailed his own efforts to warn Bernanke, the OCC, and the FDIC about the speculative housing bubble. Shiller felt he was viewed as "an extremist who deserved a skeptical response." Shiller, like Kerry, believed if Bernanke had injected liquidity into the system in the fall of 2007, the depths of the crisis could have been avoided.[1]

Most economists and investors understand asset prices will decline when there aren't any buyers. Residential homes are almost always bought with a mortgage because few people have the means to pay cash. If liquidity is restricted, access to mortgage financing will dry up and buyers will vanish. Home prices will fall and the cycle will keep getting worse until liquidity is injected back into the system. Unfortunately, the Federal Reserve and government officials missed this simple concept.

The New York investor conferences in January were the toughest in decades. However, a high point of the week was a dinner at the Morgan Library, hosted by JPMorgan Chase CEO Jamie Dimon. The library is a Classical Revival building tucked into a corner at 225 Madison Avenue, near the Empire State Building. The interior is an Italian Renaissance wonder, with floors covered by thick, warm antique carpets. Well-polished mahogany wood walls are encased by majestic three-tiered bookcases lining the room. The library houses three Gutenberg Bibles, a journal by Henry David Thoreau, a collection of autographed and annotated libretti and scores from Beethoven, Brahms, Chopin, Mahler, Verdi, and Mozart's *Haffner* symphony in D Major. There are Old Master paintings by Rembrandt and Van Gogh. The book *Paradise Lost* is stored there. Certainly, in this storied environment, the conversation would be elevated, refined, intellectual.

There was a scattering of beautifully set tables around the room, ready for the bank CEOs and their spouses. When it was time to be seated for dinner, Linda found her name on a place card next to the host, Jamie Dimon. She froze, a little puzzled. She wondered why Dimon wanted to sit next to her. Kerry had worked with Dimon on industry matters for many years, but she also knew a number of analysts and colleagues had told Kerry in the fall of 2007 that Dimon had been telling people about wanting to steal Washington Mutual for "pennies on the dollar."[2] A number of Chase employees had joined Washington Mutual because they saw better opportunity and a culture that valued people and giving back to their communities. These employees warned Kerry that Dimon would do anything to get control of Washington Mutual. Dimon had made it known that he coveted the extensive branch banking system, the massive online checking platform, and other services that would instantly make JPMorgan Chase the biggest bank in the world.

After Dimon arrived at the table, he started some small talk. He can be exceedingly charming. Linda told him she heard he met his wife at the Harvard MBA program, and he responded by asking where she and Kerry met. She told him they met when they were both vice chairs of their regional Federal Home Loan Banks.[3] Dimon slammed his hands down on the table, looked quickly back and forth around the room, and declared, "The Federal Home Loan Banks are stupid and useless."

Linda defended the banks, stating they are necessary to provide liquidity for community banks. His face turned dark, and he sneered, "Community banks are useless. I don't want them; you can have all of them." He turned away. Linda had been identified as a community bank sympathizer, and Dimon was angry. Normally Linda could debate with the best of them, but this was different. She was concerned about his erratic behavior, and after years of administering the prison and mental health systems in Iowa, she knew the best thing to do was simply disengage and deescalate the situation.

She was somewhat amused at his hotheaded response to community banks, but she wasn't the only one. Years later in 2016, Dimon was at a large televised public meeting where the president and CEO of the Independent Community Bankers of America was describing the unfair advantages of the large Wall Street banks. Dimon publicly called the CEO a "jerk." It was clear Dimon's bullying and contempt for community banking were strong and long-lasting.[4]

Shortly after the investor conferences, President Bush and Congress finally agreed on a $150 billion economic stimulus plan, hoping to prevent the US economy from slipping into recession. Tax refund checks from $300 to $1,200 were sent to over 117 million American families. At the same time, the National Association of Realtors announced 2007 saw the largest drop in existing home sales since the Depression in the 1930s.[5] A check for $300 or even $1,200 did little to help people make their mortgage payments or avoid foreclosure. What really was needed were targeted programs to help people restructure mortgage payments and an injection of liquidity into the system by the Federal Reserve.

Kerry was working overtime communicating with investors, regulators, and the media. He painstakingly detailed the quality of lending at the bank and documented the dramatic reductions the bank had made in home lending over the past several years. The bank was well positioned, but declining home prices were leading to frequent changes in estimates of lifetime loan losses for all the banks. In addition to setting aside money for potential loan losses, the regulated banks were required to "mark to market" certain types of assets—a particularly punitive accounting requirement that was increased after the corporate accounting scandals of Enron and others.

The environment was not only tough for banks, but tough for all businesses looking for liquidity. Analyst Mark Zandi, in his book *Financial Shock*, stated that in 2008 large businesses were immediately scrambling for ways to finance their basic operations. Stock prices had fallen almost 20 percent from 2007. Equity investors realized no business was immune from the fallout of the mounting credit crunch and stock price plunges. Zandi said that, "A string of policy errors [by the Fed and Treasury] had turned a severe yet manageable financial crisis into an inherently unpredictable and even uncontrollable financial panic."[6]

In January, the FDIC released the 2007 fourth-quarter earnings of banks in the country:

The news was the worst since the Great Depression. Bank earnings were only $5.8 billion, a stunning 84 percent plunge from just six months prior.

All banks were hit hard by plummeting housing prices, increasing loan delinquencies, and falling securities prices. Regulators reacted by downgrading the CAMELS regulatory ratings of most large banks. Washington Mutual was no exception and received a letter from the OTS downgrading their composite CAMELS ratings from a 2 to a 3, the first time it had been at this level in over twenty years. Kerry had successfully headed up a 2-rated bank for two decades, so the change was painful. He asked his regulators, the Office of Thrift Supervision (OTS primary) and the FDIC (secondary), the reasons for the downgrade. They responded there were "no associated regulatory directives or orders for Washington Mutual, and the downgrade was also being given to many other large banks because of the precarious economic climate."

In a note to the Washington Mutual board, Kerry revealed:

The downgrade was due to caution in the wake of the near failure
of Countrywide due to liquidity concerns in 2007. Most other
large thrifts and many commercial banks were also downgraded.
The environment is brutal and shows no signs of improvement.
I had meetings with Chairman Bernanke of the Fed, Reich of
the OTS, Bair of the FDIC, and Lockhart of OFHEO last week.
Everyone thinks housing is in free fall, and they don't know what
to do about it. Prices in some markets in California have already
fallen by 25 percent, with more corrections likely. The banking
regulators are worried about credit quality, and the regulator for
Fannie and Freddie expects large losses this year.[7]

In spite of the climate, Fed chair Bernanke and the Fed continued to maintain their position that housing declines presented little
risk to the overall economy. In January, Bernanke said "he expected a
garden-variety recession, which was an acceptable risk."[8] In February,
Bernanke declared, "Among the largest banks, the capital ratios remain
good, and I don't expect any serious problems." Later that month he
publicly stated, "By later this year, housing will stop being such a big
drag directly on GDP. I am satisfied with the general approach that
we're currently taking."[9]

Bernanke may have thought the capital ratios in the banking industry were "good," but the banks had just experienced record quarterly
losses, and all the large banks were searching for more capital to cover
current and future mortgage loan losses and the "mark to market" of the
assets. Bank stock prices were under pressure in the second half of 2007
and early 2008 because of large loan losses and concerns that large
dilutive capital raises would be required. Bank of America, JPMorgan
Chase, Citigroup, and Washington Mutual's stock prices were all down
more than 30 percent, while the Dow Jones Industrial Average declined
by less than 15 percent. In a period of less than a year, most large banks
went from paying high cash dividends and repurchasing stock with excess capital to desperately raising new capital at discounted stock prices.
Investors were naturally not very happy and pressured bank boards to
make management changes. CEOs were replaced at Citigroup, Bank of
America, Wells Fargo, Merrill Lynch, Fannie Mae, and Freddie Mac.

On the first weekend in March, Kerry was scheduled to speak at a
CEO group he belonged to. The group was nearly one hundred years

old and included CEOs and spouses of the oldest and most prestigious corporations in America such as Procter & Gamble, Boeing, General Motors, AT&T, IBM, American Express, and others. Kerry was the only banker in the group, and it was his turn to give a presentation about his business. Kerry told the group the truth—there was a storm coming in the financial world that would likely cause a strong recession. He shared the data he had been revealing at public investor conferences and quarterly earnings reports and mentioned all the measures he had taken to protect his bank and ride out the storm. He advised the group to be conservative over the next couple of years. Years later, some of the CEOs in the group told Kerry they were grateful for his presentation, because they took Kerry's advice and cut costs, allowing their companies to ride out the storm better than most.

In the first quarter of 2008, all types of loans were experiencing delinquency issues. What started off in 2007 as a problem for subprime residential loans quickly spread to prime residential loans, mortgage-backed securities, credit cards, commercial real estate, and small business loans. Falling housing prices caused the overall economy to soften, and even the most carefully underwritten prime loans were experiencing unprecedented delinquencies and loan losses.

Despite declining housing prices, a slowing economy, the failure of nearly one hundred subprime originators in 2007, and declining stock prices, most government officials continued to forecast good times. They simply did not believe a slowdown in housing would materially affect the overall economy. On March 15, 2008, Treasury Secretary Paulson wrote, "The US has the strongest and most liquid capital markets in the world. This strength is due in no small part to the US financial services industry regulatory structure, which promotes consumer protection and market stability."[10] This is a stunning statement, considering nearly every large bank had just experienced record losses and most were desperately searching for more liquidity and capital.

Kerry explored several creative options for dealing with the housing crisis. One plan developed with Goldman Sachs involved spinning out many of the mortgage loans into an off-balance sheet company with enough capital to cover the loans. The remaining assets would create a company with high profitability for the core businesses of retail banking, commercial banking, and credit cards. The home-lending business had already been reduced to a small part of the bank's total revenue and profits, and this would complete the transition. This strategy to split off certain assets worked well in other industries, but they soon learned accounting and regulatory rules made this transaction difficult for banks.

Kerry and the board decided the most prudent way to address the deteriorating economy was by raising additional capital, even though it meant diluting existing shareholders. Their concern was safety first. Goldman Sachs and Lehman Brothers were engaged to seek proposals from leading private equity and other investment groups. But because of the dilution to shareholders, they also sought merger proposals from other large banks. Kerry could have easily left JPMorgan Chase out of the process, but he and the board were open to all options. It was a logical buyer, and despite its past actions, it was appropriate to consider a proposal from them. Both Goldman and Lehman estimated the bank would sell for $15–20 per share in a merger transaction. On March 25, WMI stock was trading at $12.70. They also believed up to $5 billion of new capital could be obtained from private equity investors. The investment bankers told Kerry the sophisticated private equity investors viewed Washington Mutual as a "well-managed retail bank with a unique nationwide franchise."[11]

On March 7, Kerry and the investment bankers contacted Wells Fargo, JPMorgan Chase, TPG, Cerberus, Oakhill, and several others to sign standard confidentiality agreements and then enter into discussions on potential transactions. Kerry also conducted meetings and conference calls with the OTS and the FDIC regarding credit provisions, earnings outlook, and capital-raising alternatives. Both regulators were very supportive.

But trouble was lurking. On March 15, Treasury Secretary Paulson released his little-publicized "Department of the Treasury Blueprint for a Modernized Financial Regulatory Structure," a 218-page manifesto for restructuring the banking industry. He did not sound an alarm about the economy or the dangerous and growing asset and debt bubbles or the current fragility of the banking industry. Nor did he propose any plans to deal with any kind of a crisis. Instead, he only suggested a bureaucratic reorganization.

Alarmingly, Secretary Paulson recommended the elimination of the regulated half-a-trillion-dollar thrift industry within two years, without any public hearings, input from the industry, or detailed research into the companies involved. It was our experience that Paulson, like many titans of Wall Street, had contempt for community banks and thrifts. Secretary Paulson's career on Wall Street no doubt influenced his view of the world, and the financial crisis gave him the opportunity to press his agenda by consolidating thrifts and banks into Wall Street. Not surprisingly, Paulson's report did not recommend any new capital or regulatory requirements for the large unregulated investment banks from which his career and personal wealth were based.

That same month, a global coalition of regulatory agencies including the Federal Reserve and the OCC completed a research project and discovered that the major source of the dramatic losses experienced by the banking industry in the last few months was from losses from collateralized debt obligations (CDOs). They found the worst risk management came from banks with high levels of CDOs and SIVs. Paulson's Blueprint did not mention any concern about this failing multitrillion-dollar system.[12] Also, there was no mention in the report about a plan to deal with the failing investment banks like Bear Stearns or the failing Fannie and Freddie giants.

Even though Paulson claimed to be a "free-market" advocate, he began to personally insert himself into what should have been private-sector matters. In the case of Bear Stearns, when Paulson heard Dimon might walk away, he called Dimon and told him, "We need to figure out under what terms you would do this. Is there something we can work out where the Fed helps you get this deal done?"[13] Dimon then came back with a wish list of government favors he was immediately granted. When Bernanke told Paulson that Dimon was willing to pay $4–5 per share, Paulson jumped on the phone to Dimon to try to convince him to offer only $1–2 dollars. Dimon increased the price to $10 after pressure from Bear shareholders. Under the emergency powers provided by section 13(3) of the Federal Reserve statutes, $30 billion of the most toxic assets in America were taken off Bear's books by a structured investment vehicle (SIV) funded by the New York Fed— of which Dimon was a board member.[14]

Timothy Geithner, in his book *Stress Test*, claimed that one-third of Bear's assets were subprime. He said the New York Fed spent the next three months "locked in brutal behind-the-scenes negotiations, arguing over which Bear Stearns assets the Fed would take and how much they were worth. Dimon wanted to leave as much risk with us as possible, especially now that he had given us a $1 billion cushion against losses. On one occasion, Dimon unleashed a tirade [against a Fed officer] so heated that [the officer] hung up on him; [the officer] then called me to say the New York Fed could no longer negotiate with Dimon." Geithner reported that Dimon's Bear deal "had a lot of people asking for a Jamie Deal."[15]

It's highly unusual for a Treasury secretary and Fed chair to insert themselves in deals that effectively enrich one set of shareholders at the expense of another. Treasury Secretary Geithner admitted in *Stress Test*, "Measures by the Fed [and Treasury] to assist JPMorgan were legally questionable at best. They knew they were crossing a line the Fed hadn't crossed since the Great Depression."[16]

Months later, former Fed chair Paul Volcker told the Economic Club of New York the Fed (with Bear Stearns) had gone to the "very edge of its lawful and implied powers, transcending certain long-embedded central banking principles and practices."[17]

On March 17, Bear Stearns was sold to JPMorgan Chase in a distressed deal that gave little to Bear Stearns shareholders. *New York* magazine reported:

> Jamie's shocking triumph of the agreement brokered by Ben Bernanke, for the pretty-much-laughable price of $2 a share—may have in the process helped avert a financial panic the likes of which hasn't been seen since 1929. Or maybe Dimon will have to settle for the trophy for the best deal ever, spending just $260.5 million for a company whose last reported net worth was $11.7 billion and whose lavish Madison Avenue headquarters alone is estimated to be worth more than $1 billion.[18]

The National Public Radio (NPR) reported the employees of Bear Stearns "owned about 30% of the stock and today those 14,000 employees are worried not only about their jobs, but also their savings."[19] Just three days after the takeover, eight thousand of Bear's employees were laid off. Experian research agency predicted the total tally of financial services job losses in 2008 could hit 180,000.[20]

After the crisis, many analysts felt the sweetheart deal on Bear Stearns almost certainly emboldened Dimon to manipulate regulators into also handing him Washington Mutual for pennies on the dollar. On the same day of the Bear takeover, Kerry received a call from Dimon, assuring Kerry he was still interested in Washington Mutual and could do both deals.

Kerry and the executive team were working around the clock conducting due diligence meetings with potential equity investors Cerberus, TPG, Blackstone, and Oakhill, as well as strategic buyers JPMorgan Chase and Wells Fargo. The acquisition for Chase would provide much needed retail presence in the West Coast and the South; however, the transaction with Wells was not as logical as there were many overlapping branches. The goal was to find the best possible solution for shareholders and to position the bank to weather the current storm. The board was being extremely vigilant, participating in frequent conference calls and special board meetings.

Kerry and the board knew private equity buyers could invest in Washington Mutual without any accounting difficulties. Potential regulated bank acquirers, however, were at a disadvantage because accounting rules required the assets to be written down to current market prices. In 2008 when the capital markets were distressed, most loan and securities portfolios in the industry had market prices significantly below their intrinsic or fair values. An acquiring bank would have to write down all assets to market value and then raise additional capital to cover the difference. Also, the issuance of capital when all the bank stock prices were depressed would be dilutive to shareholders. This is why most banks want to sell or buy when the economy is stable and asset prices fairly reflect their intrinsic value. Kerry was skeptical if any bank could afford to make a fair offer, but he and the board decided it was prudent to include them in the process, even though the banks might just be bottom feeding.

Months earlier, Kerry had scheduled a checkup with his skin doctor for March 23. For years Linda had insisted Kerry get annual skin cancer screenings. Because of the hours he was working to raise capital for the bank, Linda encouraged him to reschedule. However, Kerry never liked to cancel appointments and inconvenience others, so he went.

The doctor found melanoma skin cancer on his leg and performed surgery at the end of the following day. The morning after the surgery, Kerry returned to work with an eight-inch incision oozing under a tight complex of gauze. Kerry had never missed a day of work in his entire career, and now wasn't the time to end his streak.

We were both worried, not only about Kerry's health, but also his father, who was due for cancer surgery in a few days. In addition, two of the potential investors in the bank had told Kerry his presence was key to the deal. If doctors had found Kerry's cancer had spread, he would have to inform the public, and the stock might plunge and possibly kill any deal he could get. For once that year, we got lucky. The cancer had not spread, and Kerry could proceed with the negotiations. But negotiations were about to get more complex.

On March 28, in the middle of the capital raise, John Reich, director of the OTS, called Kerry to inform him JPMorgan Chase's CFO and outside counsel were giving negative presentations about Washington Mutual's loan losses, without informing the OTS.[21] The standard confidentiality agreement clearly restricted disclosure of any confidential information without permission. Reich felt JPMorgan Chase was trying to "create instability by telling regulators, rating agencies, the Treasury Department, and others that Washington Mutual's estimates of lifetime loan losses were too low."[22] OTS director Reich also thought "Treasury may be attempting to influence the OTS's oversight process."[23] Others believed Chase was just trying to get another "Bear Stearns deal." Kerry contacted his attorneys to explore a lawsuit against Chase.

Kerry immediately called Dimon about the OTS reports. Dimon denied that "JPM was saying anything improper to the regulators and would not reveal the contents of their presentations."[24] He told Kerry if his bank "made a bid for Washington Mutual, it would be very low." He went on to say that if it was him, and a good private equity investment alternative was available, he would take it.[25] Contrary to Chase's assertions, Cerberus, TPG, and other investors agreed that Washington Mutual's calculations for the estimated range of lifetime loan losses were reasonable. But the reality is no one knew for sure how bad the economy, unemployment, or foreclosures were going to get, which is why Washington Mutual made a range of estimated losses based on stress tests with up to a 40 percent national decline in housing prices— much more severe than the forecasts of the Fed or most major banks.

Two years later in 2010, the Washington Mutual bankruptcy examiner (Examiner) "found evidence that JPMorgan disclosed confidential Washington Mutual information in meetings with the FDIC, OCC, and [Treasury] in the spring of 2008."[26] The report also revealed documents showing the FDIC had an interesting take on those March, 2008 meetings with JPMorgan Chase. The FDIC later characterized the meeting as just a "beef session in which JPM expressed its frustration that Washington Mutual didn't seem receptive to JPM's overtures."[27]

The Examiner also found that the spring 2008 JPM presentation slide deck prepared for the regulators included confidential information on "Washington Mutual's earnings and capital projections, asset quality metrics, summaries of net charge-offs by portfolio, consumer and real estate losses and a sample Option ARM payment schedule." The Examiner also found the [JPM] slide decks to the rating agencies included confidential forecasts of loan losses.[28]

The FDIC must not have taken JPMorgan's concerns seriously, because neither the FDIC nor the OTS ever approached Washington Mutual with concerns about JPMorgan Chase's calculations of loan losses.

On March 31, the FDIC released its first-quarter 2008 banking profile:

Quarterly earnings were down 50 percent from 2007 to $19.3 billion. Net charge-offs of $19.6 billion were up 139 percent from last year. Noncurrent loans rose 23.6 percent. Banks added $37.1 billion in loan-loss reserves.

The first quarter of 2008 was tough for all banks, but Washington Mutual's $1.14 billion loss was small compared to Merrill Lynch's loss of $2 billion, Citigroup's loss of $5.1 billion, AIG's loss of $7.8 billion, HSBC's loss of $3.2 billion, Fannie Mae's loss of $2.2 billion, and MBIA's loss of $2.4 billion. Even JPMorgan Chase raised $6 billion of new capital to shore up its financial position.[29]

With quarterly earnings of the banking industry plummeting 50 percent, tens of billions of loan losses, and billions in loss of profitability, nearly every large bank in the country was searching for capital and liquidity. The federal government was offering little help and was making noises that there would be no more "Bear Stearns deals." However, Kerry remained calm, and the team was getting positive responses from a number of investors. The management team and board were cautious and wanted the best deal for all the bank's stakeholders.

On March 31, Kerry received a letter from JPMorgan Chase:

We are pleased to provide you with this proposal for the merger of Washington Mutual. JPMorgan Chase is prepared to [make a non-binding] offer of .116 JPMorgan Chase common shares per Washington Mutual common share which currently implies a price of $5 per common share and (ii) a contingent payment that would settle in JPMorgan Chase common stock and that would have a value of up to $3.00 per common share based upon the performance of certain loans in the portfolio.[30]

However, JPMorgan Chase was also demanding a standstill agreement, which would require Washington Mutual reject all the other offers before Chase would make any kind of formal commitment. In addition, Chase was demanding additional highly confidential data the other suitors were not receiving before they would make a commitment. Kerry knew that the Dimon/Weill Citigroup playbook was to make acquisitions during a downturn and give lowball, noncommittal offers that would continually drop in price. Kerry was suspicious. He had a long history of only doing deals with banks with similar ethics and values and with executives showing mutual respect and trust. He didn't see any indication of that with Dimon.

Kerry shot back an email to Dimon, saying that he "continued to be disappointed with the inability to make progress by improving price and terms of a proposal that would allow us to move forward." Kerry responded he was "reluctant to provide their most sensitive, confidential, and competitive information until they had a more detailed view from JPMorgan Chase regarding their pricing and terms. We continue to look for a better way to break this logjam."[31]

Kerry continued, "My team, over this weekend, is doing its best to comply with your extensive due diligence request of Friday. However, to fully comply with your Friday request, I need something from you; your commitment to work to reach agreement on improved pricing and terms. I look forward to discussing this with you."[32] Dimon did not respond.

On April 3, Kerry sent Linda an email:

Jamie is ratcheting up the dirty tricks, so more fires to put out. [CFO] Tom Casey and [COO] Steve Rotella are getting good responses from investors on the east coast. We are negotiating with the private equity people. Need to make our selections tonight or tomorrow at the latest.

Linda emailed Kerry back on the status of his dad's surgery. His dad's bladder cancer had spread into his abdomen. We were relieved he made it through the surgery but knew the road ahead would be difficult. We wanted to be by his side but were thankful other family members were there with him. As soon as we could break away, we would fly to Iowa to see him.

The Washington Mutual Board originally hoped for a $5 billion capital infusion, but investor demand was strong and TPG offered $7.2 billion, with the promise of a quick close. TPG was led by brilliant investor David Bonderman, who had previously served on the Washington Mutual board. TPG was a perfect strategic partner for the bank. It knew the bank well and had carefully vetted the loan portfolio, loan-loss reserves, and operating plans.

The Washington Mutual Board and their advisers, Goldman Sachs, and Lehman Brothers met to carefully consider all the offers. They determined the JPMorgan Chase proposal was "economically unattractive because of its relatively low price and the extreme execution risk to the organization." JPMorgan Chase demanded all other offers should be dropped before it made a commitment, gave a fuzzy valuation of the contingency security, and could easily back out of the transaction at any time. The board, Goldman Sachs, and Lehman Brothers all concluded JPMorgan Chase's nonbinding, tepid "indication of interest" was a "proposition with a per-share price significantly lower than what TPG or Cerberus offered."[33] Cerberus offered a similar proposal to TPG but proposed a complicated merger with one of their portfolio companies that would take a lot of time to execute.

Both Goldman Sachs and Lehman Brothers delivered "commercially appropriate fairness opinions" to reject Chase and accept the best offer from TPG.[34]

For years after the rejection of JPMorgan's "indication of interest," the media continued to quote JPM executives who claimed Washington Mutual should have accepted their eight-dollar-per-share bid for the bank. Even Treasury secretary Paulson believed there had been a legitimate eight-dollar bid. However, that is not what JPMorgan Chase executives told the Examiner in 2010 when they swore they "never submitted a bid to purchase WMI in March 2008 and only gave WM a nonbinding indication of JPMC's interest."[35,36]

A couple of years later, TheStreet.com reported on leaked emails from JPMorgan Chase about a June 2008 meeting between Dimon and the Spanish bank Santander that revealed Dimon did not intend to give a solid bid to Washington Mutual because it would have to "mark to market [the assets] and assign/inject additional capital accordingly."[37]

On April 8, Washington Mutual announced the $7.2 billion capital raise and sale of equity securities to affiliates of TPG Capital and other institutional investors. The bank announced:

> The purpose of the transaction was to maintain capital ratios well above target levels and protect against the rapidly deteriorating economic conditions in the US housing and credit markets. The board of directors also intends to reduce the quarterly dividend rate to 1 cent per common share. This will preserve $490 million of capital annually.

The bank announced plans to expand its retail-focused strategy by investing and growing its retail branches, the online banking and call center production, and closing all the home loan branches. "This substantial new capital, along with the other steps we are announcing today, will position us for a return to profitability."[38]

After the capital raise, Washington Mutual, like most large banks, had an established protocol to close the data room and send a notice for all the participants to return or destroy all the confidential information. The confidentiality agreement also had a standstill provision that signatories could not pursue a merger or acquisition transaction with Washington Mutual in the next eighteen months without the prior approval of WMI (the bank's holding company).[39] At this point, the sale process was closed so all the other offers were rejected and the bidders would not be allowed to continue to use the confidential data. The Examiner determined "the confidentiality agreement asked JPM to promptly destroy all information which has been furnished by WMI." The agreement contained a standstill provision which stated, "For a period of 18 months following the execution of the agreement, the signatory would not pursue a merger or acquisition transaction with WMI without the prior approval of WMI or its subsidiaries."[40]

The Examiner revealed that "JPM continued to use WM's confidential information during the summer of 2008 and relied on that confidential information in preparing and submitting its bid to the FDIC in September."[41] He also found that the FDIC, "agreed to include a $500 million indemnity provision requested by JPM, which indemnifies JPM against future claims of WMI shareholders alleging that JPM breached the March standstill agreement."[42]

Although Kerry heard rumors that JPMorgan Chase was continuing to use the confidential data and was continuing to talk with the FDIC, he dismissed the rumors because regulators would customarily contact a bank if someone were using the confidential data or were talking to the regulators about a purchase. Neither the FDIC nor the OTS contacted the bank about Chase's efforts.

The regulators seemed very pleased about the TPG deal. Kerry and the other Washington Mutual executives were contacted by both OTS director Reich and FDIC chair Bair, congratulating them on the news of the capital raise.

However, not everyone was pleased. Many retired executives and longtime shareholders were extremely upset about the dilution of the new stock issuance and the reduction in the cash dividend. They had experienced over twenty years of increasing cash dividends, stock splits, and a generally rising stock price. There were natural cycles of prosperity and decline, but they didn't know what to expect from this downturn. Many had relied on the constant and lucrative dividend payments, so they were naturally nervous and scared.

The annual stockholders' meeting held in April for the last twenty years was always a very festive affair. The bank had superior returns and made multimillionaires out of thousands of local shareholders and employees. For years it had been held at the Benaroya Hall across the street from the new Washington Mutual office tower in downtown Seattle. Thousands of stockholders gathered every year to celebrate the success of the bank, partake of homemade cookies and other treats, and purchase the bank's branded products in the spacious glass reception room outside the Benaroya performance hall, home of the local Seattle Symphony.

This year was different. People were angry, uncertain, and scared. There was blood in the air. An advisory shareholder ballot to separate the chairman and CEO positions gained a slightly favorable vote. The bank announced a quarterly loss of $1.14 billion because of additions to loan loss reserves. The announcement of excellent performance in the retail bank, card services, and commercial business was barely heard. The $8.1 billion growth of retail deposits and one million net new checking accounts in the past year did not pacify anyone. It did not matter the bank's loan performance was much better than the industry. It did not matter most other large banks were in much worse shape than Washington Mutual. The losses were local, and they were personal.

Kerry and the executives addressed all the shareholder questions. Many questions were emotional and accusatory, but hardworking employees countered with positive comments. After answering questions, Kerry went out in the reception hall to personally thank and talk to as many shareholders as possible. Kerry knew the economy would eventually improve and Washington Mutual would return to strong profitability. This was a long-term journey, and a little patience was required to get through this difficult period.

After the capital raise was completed, Kerry decided to replace the chief enterprise risk officer, Ron Cathcart, with John McMurray, a newly hired risk officer. Cathcart was having a bumpy year and clearly didn't possess the same deep knowledge of residential mortgage lending as McMurray. Analysts and regulators were increasingly complaining about Cathcart's inability to answer their questions and were turning to McMurray for answers. Although Cathcart had done a great job in reining in mortgage lending, the regulators expressed concern to Kerry and the board that CERO Cathcart was not properly overseeing required improvements in the bank's AML/BSA program.[43] Kerry and the board made the decision to replace Cathcart and put McMurray in the CERO position, reporting directly to Kerry.

In early May there was a meeting of the Financial Services Roundtable, a group representing the nation's largest banks and insurance companies. Kerry was vice chair and chair-elect for the group. The theme for the meeting was "Liquidity, Housing, Politics, and the Markets." All members were dealing with difficult conditions, and Kerry was asked to join a panel with Dick Kovacevich of Wells Fargo, Jamie Dimon of JPMorgan Chase, Fred Geissinger of AIG, and Ken Dubuque of Guaranty Financial. Kerry once again warned financial conditions would deteriorate if the Fed didn't infuse the system with substantial liquidity. Other panel members agreed and said they were perplexed by the Fed and Treasury's slow response to the housing downturn.

On May 8, US Treasury Secretary Paulson disagreed with the bankers when he announced he believed the economy was more than halfway through the credit crisis. He pronounced:

> There is still a long way to go in the process of deleveraging the financial system, but the credit crisis is entering its later stages. The better signs involve the large amount of capital that has recently been infused into the banking system through private equity and the purchases of leveraged loans from the balance sheet of the banks.[44]

He was obviously wrong, but consistent in underestimating the growing crisis. On June 3, the Washington Mutual Board separated the chair and CEO positions. A shareholder advisory vote passed by a slight margin, and although it was not a requirement, both Kerry and the board thought it was a prudent move to act on the vote. Steve Frank, longtime lead director and former public utility CEO, became chair. Kerry worked well with Steve and was pleased Steve could spend more time working with him to help get through what Kerry was predicting to be a substantial financial crisis.

In early June, Kerry wrote to the board on a variety of matters, including his concerns about continual destructive rumors about the bank:

> Financial stocks have been under severe price pressure this week. Contributing factors include rising energy prices, rumors of liquidity and capital pressures at Lehman, rising unemployment and rising credit cost assumptions. This has had three impacts on the bank: 1. One analyst increased his lifetime loan loss assumptions. 2. There were [false] rumors we needed to issue more capital. 3. There was a [false] rumor Washington Mutual was operating under a MOU with the OTS.[45]
>
> We decided to issue the following statement: While it is the policy of Washington Mutual not to comment on speculation and market rumors, the company released the following statement to address recurring speculation about regulatory activity. Neither our primary federal regulator, the OTS nor any other bank regulatory agency has taken an enforcement action against

Washington Mutual that we have not previously disclosed. Further, the company is not currently in such discussions with any regulatory agency.

The shareholder approval for the TPG offer was to occur at a meeting on June 24, so Kerry immediately started contacting shareholders to ensure a positive vote for the TPG transaction. Kerry was told by several investors that JPMorgan Chase was fervently working behind the scenes to defeat the vote either by buying out TPG's investment in Washington Mutual or convincing existing shareholders to vote against the transaction.[46, 47]

If true, this would have been in violation of the standstill agreement between the two banks. In 2010 the Examiner reported that a June 18 email exchange between Chase executives revealed that, "To get rid of TPG they would simply have to pay it more than $8.75 a share."[48]

The *New York Times* soon contacted Washington Mutual claiming it had an unnamed source saying the TPG deal was bad for shareholders and should not be approved. Kerry alerted the board:

Gretchen Morgenson is going to write an article this Sunday which attacks the TPG deal. She will say our shareholders would have been better off taking a JPM deal where they could have taken shares in a stronger bank. She will claim management selected the TPG deal because it allowed them to keep their jobs, and the terms of the JPM deal were more attractive. She will say the recent decline in the Washington Mutual share price reinforces why a JPM deal would have been better. Our legal and communication staff are working on comments and responses, but the article is unlikely to change. Based on our past experience it would not be crazy to think JPMorgan Chase has a hand in feeding information to Gretchen.

The new board chair, Steve Frank, emailed back to Kerry, disheartened:

I suppose it's too much to hope she would recognize there was no JPM deal—a tepid lowball response with enough caveats to insure we probably wouldn't have achieved the $5 they offered. I don't have any second thoughts about this, but we're going to have to endure this type of publicity for a while.

The *New York Times* ran the story on June 15 under the headline "Raw Deal for Washington Mutual Shareholders" and ignored the facts provided by the bank. The article read:

> TPG and its fellow investors got a sweet package...Alas for existing Washington Mutual shareholders, the deal is enormously dilutive. Shareholders are also concerned Washington Mutual's Board passed on a better deal with JPMorgan Chase in April. The bank offered to buy the entire company for around $8 a share, according to a person briefed on the discussions who requested anonymity because the talks were confidential.[49]

Only a handful of people knew the details about Chase's nonbinding "indication of interest", so the source of the article was not surprising. Despite the article and the false rumors swirling in the industry, three of the major proxy advisory firms, Institutional Shareholder Services Inc. (ISS); Glass, Lewis and Company; and PROXY Governance Inc., all recommended shareholders vote for both of the company's proposals related to the recent $7.2 billion capital raise at the upcoming special meeting of shareholders.[50]

Years later, the Examiner reported, "JPM continued through the summer to use the confidential data" to prepare a number of options to procure the bank on the cheap. A June 18, 2008 email from a JPM executive described "West [code name for Washington Mutual] as the most financially compelling target at the time. Dimon said that West would provide real earnings over time based on the power of the franchise and the increased earnings would permit them to handle a range of estimated losses. They continued to build slide decks through the summer."[51]

On June 24, the shareholders overwhelmingly approved the $7.2 billion capital raise. Despite any efforts JPMorgan Chase may have made to derail the approval, the new capital was in place. With the shareholder's support, Kerry felt confident the superior capital and liquidity of the bank, along with a loan portfolio performing better than the industry, could steer the bank through the crisis. However, he started hearing more rumors that JPMorgan Chase was pressuring the FDIC to seize Washington Mutual. FDIC rules require the agency to notify a bank when there would be sale or seizure conversations. Kerry checked with the regulators, but they denied the rumors.

The Examiner found JPMorgan Chase had continued to work through the summer of 2008 using the confidential information and "viewed a receivership [assuming FDIC would seize the bank] scenario as having numerous advantages, including no shareholder approval and immediate closing. It would allow JPMC to leave certain contingent and shareholder liabilities behind, as well as put back branches it did not want and reject unwanted contracts and leases."[52] It would also give them the right to the holding company assets like the TRUPS [preferred securities], but not the liabilities. This would save JPM $17 billion they would have had to raise in capital."[53]

In June, Kerry heard from one of Washington Mutual's attorneys, Bruce Fletcher, who had sent a detailed letter with quotes from customers to the general counsel of JPMorgan Chase detailing the wide variety of experiences with JPMorgan Chase employees warning Washington Mutual customers. The customers were reporting JPMorgan Chase employees were telling them, "Washington Mutual is going under, depositors' money will be lost, accounts will be blocked for long periods of time, and lawsuits will be necessary to get your money. You should bring your money to Chase so it will be safe." The latest spark reported by customers was about the manager of a Chase branch on Brighton Beach in Brooklyn telling customers they "should remove all funds from Washington Mutual because their failure is imminent."[54]

Despite these shenanigans, regulators stayed supportive and Kerry focused on the customers to develop programs to modify loan terms, reduce payments and help customers remain in their homes. The $2 billion committed to the program in 2007 was used to help thousands of homeowners avoid foreclosure. Recognizing the need for more support, on June 16 Washington Mutual announced an additional $1 billion to help subprime borrowers. The announcement read, "Eligible borrowers who remained current on their existing loans and anticipated pending payment increases could apply for new discounted fixed-rate loans or other mortgage products available to them." The branch offices worked hard to contact thousands of customers to see if they needed to restructure loans. The bank even offered customers

$100 in cash if they would just come to the branch to discuss lowering the costs of their loans.[55]

By July, 2008 Kerry felt comfortable that Washington Mutual had the proper capital in place, plenty of liquidity and loan performance was better than the industry. Chart 1-1 shows Washington Mutual's capital ratios were higher than all other large banks as of July 1, 2008. While the large banks had capital ratios over 8 percent, the Wall Street investment banks had capital ratios around 3 percent and Fannie and Freddie had capital ratios less than 2 percent.[56]

Chart 1-1: Capital Ratios for the Seven Largest US Banks as of July 1, 2008

Bank	Tier One Capital	Total Risk Based Capital
Washington Mutual	9.96%	13.93%
JPMorgan Chase	9.15%	13.44%
Citigroup	8.74%	12.29%
US Bancorp	8.47%	12.50%
Bank of America	8.25%	12.60%
Wells Fargo	8.24%	11.23%
Wachovia	8.00%	12.74%

Furthermore, Chart 1-2 shows Washington Mutual's residential mortgage losses incurred up to that point during the financial crisis were painful, but much lower than those of most large banks.[57]

The mortgage losses from three of the biggest and most troubled banks—Citigroup, UBS, and Merrill Lynch—totaled $118.2 billion—41 percent of all of the US mortgage losses for the top twenty banks in the world. Even more disturbing was that 51 percent—over half—of the US mortgage losses were from foreign banks, which revealed how deeply embedded the foreign banks were in originating, securitizing and purchasing mortgages in the US.

In addition to all the mortgage losses, many of the large banks held substantial OTC (over-the-counter and unregulated) derivative positions as of June 30, 2008. JPMorgan Chase had $94.5 trillion in notional amounts, Bank of America held $37.7 trillion, Citigroup held

**Chart 1-2 Top Twenty US Residential Mortgage Losses to
Financial Institutions as of June 18, 2008 (Billions)**

Rank	Bank	Losses
1	Citigroup	$42.90
2	UBS (Swiss)	$38.20
3	Merrill Lynch	$37.10
4	HSBC (British)	$19.50
5	IKB Deutsch (German)	$15.90
6	Royal Bank of Scotland	$15.20
7	Bank of America	$15.10
8	Morgan Stanley	$14.10
9	JPMorgan Chase	$9.80
10	Credit Suisse (Swiss)	$9.60
11	**Washington Mutual**	**$9.10**
12	Credit Agricole (French)	$8.30
13	Lehman Brothers	$8.20
14	Deutsche Bank (German)	$7.60
15	Wachovia	$7.00
16	HBOS (British-Lloyds)	$7.00
17	Bayerische Landesbank (German)	$6.70
18	Fortis (Belgium)	$6.60
19	Canadian Imperial (CIBC)	$6.50
20	Barclays (British)	$6.30

Source: *Bloomberg News*[58]

$35.8 trillion, Wachovia held $4.1 trillion, and HSBC (UK) held $3.9 trillion. The unregulated investment banks did not have to report holdings at the time, but when they became regulated bank holding companies in September, 2008, it was reported that Goldman Sachs held $45.9 trillion and Morgan Stanley held $37 trillion of OTC financial derivatives.[59] Most analysts now believe that derivatives, especially the CDOs were the major cause of the financial crisis. Washington Mutual had a trace amount of OTC derivatives.

Years later the Financial Crisis Inquiry Commission (FCIC) reported on the number loans with improper documentation that

Fannie Mae and Freddie Mac turned back to the major banks. Of the delinquent loans and loans in foreclosure sampled by Fannie Mae in 2007–2010, they returned loans to the following lenders: Bank of America, $6.9 billion; Wells Fargo, $2.3 billion; JPMorgan Chase, $2.2 billion; Citigroup, $1.5 billion; SunTrust, $898 billion; and Ally Financial, $838 million.[60]

In a statistical sample in 2009 and 2010, Freddie Mac returned 20 percent of their loan volumes to banks including: Countrywide, $1.9 billion; Wells Fargo, $1.2 billion; Chase Home Financial, $1.2 billion; Bank of America, $476 million; and Ally Financial, $453 million.[61]

From this data it appears that Bank of America, Countrywide, and Wells Fargo had the highest number of returned loans of the large regulated banks. Washington Mutual was not mentioned in this list and had substantially fewer returned loans than most of the other large banks.

On June 25, Kerry had dinner with Fed chair Bernanke at the Thrift Industry Advisory Committee (TIAC) meetings. Bernanke was still not expressing any major concerns, and the Fed was predicting an uptick in the economy through the rest of the year. Kerry once again tried to convince the Fed to push liquidity in the system and/or provide substantial help to the millions of people who were facing foreclosures on their homes.

Only five days after Fed chair Bernanke expressed his rosy view of the economy, the FDIC released the second-quarter 2008 banking profile:

> Quarterly commercial bank earnings had continued to crash and were only $5 billion, an 86 percent drop from a year earlier, the lowest quarterly earnings in over twenty years. Net charge-offs were $26.4 billion, and net residential mortgage loan charge-offs were up 821.9 percent. Noncurrent loans were now over 2 percent of the banks' total assets.

Most of the banks were now reporting dramatic second-quarter losses much worse than Washington Mutual. Merrill Lynch announced $9.4 billion in write-downs and posted $19 billion in losses for the last four quarters. Citigroup announced losses of $2.5 billion and write-downs of $7.2 billion. Wachovia had an $8.9 billion loss. Fannie Mae announced a $2.3 billion loss, and AIG announced a $5.4 billion loss.[62]

In the book *The Shifts and the Shocks*, the author and the economics editor of the *Financial Times*, Martin Wolf stated, "Even two months before the crisis broke upon a largely unsuspecting world, the Chairman of the Federal Reserve had next to no idea what was about to hit him, his institution and the global economy. To be blunt, he was almost clueless."[63]

On July 8, Treasury Secretary Paulson spoke at the FDIC Forum on Mortgage Lending to Low and Moderate Income (LMI) Households. He acknowledged the slowing economy but continued to insist lending to LMI families was appropriate and housing was showing signs of improvement. Paulson didn't mention that the unregulated subprime market that had produced 85 percent of subprime loans had just crashed and left in its wake more than $2 trillion worth of bad subprime loans coursing through trillions of dollars of collateralized debt obligations (CDOs) and credit default swaps (CDSs). Loans originated and securitized in an unregulated shadow subprime system were now bouncing around in the global economy and ready to crash. Despite all the obvious problems in the economy, in July Paulson effused:

> The housing correction and capital markets turmoil has reduced
> the availability of credit for mortgages and other lending. Sub-
> prime and other (LMI) lending has played a critical role in helping
> expand homeownership opportunities. Our responsibility is to
> work through today's issues and do so in a way that preserves and
> protects responsible mortgage lending to (LMI) families. Another
> sign that we are well into the adjustment process is that existing
> home sales appear to have flattened over the past several months,
> indicating that demand may be stabilizing.[64]

The banking system was already fragile enough, but it got a lot worse. On July 11, California-based thrift IndyMac experienced a large run on deposits due to a public statement by a US senator about IndyMac's condition. The OTS had to quickly seize the failing thrift. CNN reported:

> The OTS pointed the finger directly at Senator Charles Schumer
> for the IndyMac failure, accusing him of sparking a bank run by
> releasing a letter that expressed concerns about IndyMac's viability.
> In the following 11 business days, depositors withdrew more than

$1.3 billion from their accounts at IndyMac. Schumer said, "OTS was a weak regulator and I was trying to toughen them up."[65]

However, there had been no evidence the OTS, the thrift regulator, was a weaker regulator than the OCC or the FDIC. Obviously, the OCC had to be a more complex regulator because the commercial banks held more complex and higher-risk banking products than the thrifts. Commercial loans were much riskier than residential loans, and large commercial banks held complex derivative instruments like SIVs, CDOs, and CDSs. The OTS was not involved in the dangerous unregulated subprime companies—that was supposed to be under the purview of other state and federal regulators. The dangerous credit default swaps produced by the insurance company, AIG, was regulated by the state insurance commissioners. Long ago, the CDOs and the CDSs had been exempted from federal regulation.

As far as we know, the OTS had never been investigated by Congress or the government, nor was there any incidence or evidence that would indicate the OTS did not perform as capably as the OCC. However, the OTS and the thrifts were more vulnerable in a housing crisis because they were required by the FIRREA law to keep 65 percent of their assets in residential mortgages and consumer related investments.[66] In March 2007, Senator Chris Dodd held hearings about subprime lending, but the OTS was not singled out as a problem. However, Senator Dodd did single out the Federal Reserve as a regulator who "was asleep at the switch."[67]

Within ten working days after the IndyMac failure, net deposits in Washington Mutual went down about $9 billion, a 6 percent drop in the retail deposits, but neither the OTS nor the FDIC expressed any concern about the losses. Other banks, like Wachovia, also had a similar 6 percent drop in deposits.[68] Through concerted management action, Washington Mutual was able to absorb the deposit losses and make adjustments that significantly increased its liquidity profile in the weeks that followed, gaining back most of the lost net deposits by the end of August.

That same month, we were notified we had both won the Woodrow Wilson Award for Corporate Citizenship and would be honored in a ceremony later in the year. The award was selective and given to executives who had "shown a deep concern for the common good beyond the bottom line." The award recipients had to embody the following characteristics:

> These corporate leaders have inherited Woodrow Wilson's commitment to scholarship, public discourse, and the promotion of knowledge both at home and abroad. They work tirelessly in the service of their belief that private firms should be good citizens in their own neighborhoods and in the world at large. They understand good citizenship can come in many forms, such as promoting renewed growth and vigor in economically disadvantaged towns and neighborhoods, supporting the arts, encouraging ties between different sectors of society, promoting international cooperation and understanding and improving education at all levels. Recipients of this prestigious award recognize the unique, enlightened role they can play in improving society in general, while at the same time advancing the long-term interests of their firms, employees and shareholders.[69]

We sent in all the required information on our biographies but asked them to postpone the award until after the housing crisis. Kerry didn't want any distractions in the mission of guiding Washington Mutual through the crisis.

On July 15, CERO McMurray, head of enterprise risk management, presented his "Quarterly Review of the Enterprise Risk Management Function" to the Washington Mutual Audit Committee and the Board of Directors. He stated that, "risk performance metrics showed loans were still well within risk limits:"

> ERM is supporting eight active projects that are in 'green' [good progress or finished] status. The Basel II program received additional resources and was reviewed by the OTS and we received positive feedback indicating we are on target for Basel II compliance. Washington Mutual continues to strengthen risk management, including improving asset selection processes, investing in credit risk and enterprise fraud management infrastructures, strengthening data governance, and identifying and remediating critical issues.

He also certified the ERM group had sufficient staff and resources and reported the provision for loan losses was appropriate.

That same day, the OTS and the FDIC presented the 2008 exam findings to the Washington Mutual Board of Directors. Every year for nearly twenty years, both the OTS and the FDIC had worked together and made a joint presentation to the board. They had never had a major disagreement or conflict. In fact, earlier in 2008, the FDIC regional director wrote:

> The FDIC and the OTS have a long, cooperative and productive working relationship with respect to the examination of Washington Mutual, which we hope to continue.

Washington Mutual's composite rating remained a 3 for the July 2008 exam, and neither of the regulators expressed concern about the bank's level of loan-loss reserves or the quality of the loans. For the first time ever, the FDIC said it viewed Washington Mutual's condition more negatively than the OTS did, but both agencies still agreed on the 3 composite rating. Once again there were no associated formal or informal regulatory directives or orders for Washington Mutual, and the board was told the 3 rating was due to "the precarious economic climate."[70]

The regulators concluded the bank had more than enough liquidity and capital and agreed with the bank's methodology for establishing loan-loss reserves. Neither Treasury, the FDIC, nor the OTS ever told Kerry during the summer of 2008 that Washington Mutual needed more capital. The July 2008 OTS/FDIC examination report stated:

> Washington Mutual funds its $310 billion balance sheet with a healthy mix of deposits (64%), FHLB advances (21%) and other borrowings of 15% with no significant reliance on capital markets funding sources. After examining all of these funding sources, we conclude *Washington Mutual appears to have adequate liquidity and capital.*[71]

At the July board meeting, CERO McMurray released his second-quarter credit risk management report and informed the board's finance committee:

Washington Mutual's prime delinquencies vs. industry for loans
created in 2004, 2005, 2006, and 2007, were all substantially
better than the industry average. Option ARM loans have an
original LTV of 72%. 1st lien home prime home equity loans had
an average FICO of 738 and original combined LTV of 65%. The
bank has a declining rate of growth in NPAs [nonperforming
assets] and delinquencies.[72,73]

These favorable results reflected the bank's strategy of increasing
underwriting standards from 2003–2008 and reducing the origination
of Option ARMs in 2006 and 2007. Even though Option ARMs were
only originated for prime borrowers and historic default rates were less
than 1 percent, the bank reduced originations because of an uncertain
housing market.[74]

While the board was meeting on July 15, the SEC issued an
emergency order banning naked short selling of only nineteen financial stocks, including Bank of America, Citigroup, Goldman Sachs,
JPMorgan Chase, Lehman Brothers, Merrill Lynch, Morgan Stanley,
Fannie Mae, and Freddie Mac. Even the foreign banks of BNP Paribas
(French), Barclays (British), Credit Suisse (Swiss), Daiwa Securities
(Japanese), Royal Bank of Scotland, Allianz SE (German), Mizuho Financial (Japanese), HSBC (UK), UBS (Swiss), and Deutsche (German)
were protected, but the non–Wall Street banks were not protected.

Noticeably missing were the non–Wall Street banks of Wells Fargo,
Wachovia, and Washington Mutual. The government put a clear target
on them by not giving the same protection given to Wall Street and
foreign banks.[75]

Kerry immediately called Treasury Secretary Paulson, Fed chair
Bernanke, FDIC chair Bair, and OTS chair Reich and sent a letter to
SEC chair Christopher Cox to demand Washington Mutual be added
to the "do not short" list.

FDIC chair Bair, throughout her term, had been very supportive of
Kerry and Washington Mutual and said she would contact Paulson on
his behalf. Kerry emailed the board:

> I had a good call with FDIC chair Bair and thanked her for her pub-
> lic statements in support of deposit insurance. I brought her up to
> date on our capital and liquidity plans, including [down-streaming]

$2 billion of capital [from the holding company] to the bank and in-
creasing our borrowing capacity at the FHLB and the Fed. We talked
about deposit trends and our policies for accepting IndyMac official
checks. I requested the FDIC do more advertising in the northwest
and California where we have seen above average deposit outflows.
She said they would look into increasing advertising in the West. She
will be in San Francisco tomorrow doing public appearances on
deposit insurance. They have hired a crisis management firm to help
counteract the blogs and to help stop unfounded rumors.

She did say she wanted to work with us and felt we ran a good
organization with a strong retail franchise. We agreed to stay in touch.

In addition, Kerry told Bair that nearly all the deposits that had
been leaving the bank after IndyMac were those above the $100,000
insurance level. He recommended to Bair that a lot of panic would
be eliminated if the FDIC insurance limit were raised to $200,000 to
$250,000 per account.

Bernanke, Bair, and Reich were supportive of adding Washington
Mutual to the "do not short" list and said they would call Paulson.

But Paulson told Kerry he shouldn't worry about the short sellers
and said the bank had made a mistake by not selling to JPMorgan
Chase for eight dollars a share. He went on to say he expected significant consolidation in the financial services industry and wanted the
largest banks with diversified business mixes to survive. He said he
wouldn't help Washington Mutual, and his priority at the moment was
to get something done for Fannie Mae and Freddie Mac. Paulson either
didn't know or didn't care that Chase never gave a bid for Washington
Mutual—only a nonbinding indication of interest.

It was clear to Kerry that Secretary Paulson's plan was to become
actively involved in hostile takeovers of banks to reshape the banking
industry to favor large, diversified Wall Street banks and ignore thrifts
and community banks. Paulson was clearly leading the charge; he was
going to be personally involved in influencing or arranging private
transactions and would pressure the banking regulators to follow his
lead. Treasury had a plan to eliminate thrifts, and this was its opportunity to execute that plan.

Historically Treasury was not supposed to pressure the independent regulators. Banks had always assumed the independent regulators

would not succumb to inappropriate advances from Treasury. But times were different now.

Oddly enough, Fed chair Bernanke appeared to be unaware of Paulson's planned takeover of Fannie and Freddie. On the same day that Paulson told Kerry he was focusing on Fannie and Freddie, Bernanke publicly insisted that "Fannie Mae and Freddie Mac are adequately capitalized and in no danger of failing." However, in less than six weeks, Paulson gave those agencies a $187 billion bailout and placed them into conservatorship. Years later, the FCIC revealed that Fannie and Freddie were thinly capitalized by seventy-five to one—a 1.3 percent equity ratio.[76]

After talking with Paulson, Kerry immediately jumped into action and contacted the board, his attorneys, and the regulators. His first step was to engage other banks that had been left off the "do not short" list and encourage them to send a joint letter from the banks' general counsels to the SEC. Then he scheduled a joint meeting on July 31 with his regulators, the FDIC, and the OTS, to give them a full reporting of the bank's condition and ask for their support with Secretary Paulson.[77] Kerry was gathering all his information and developing a presentation for Paulson in early September and was ready to fight hard to protect the bank. He knew Paulson needed to be told the facts quickly or Washington Mutual could be caught up in a political vortex that could threaten its existence.

Kerry's suspicions were correct. Behind the scenes and unknown to Washington Mutual or the OTS, JPMorgan Chase was aggressively pursuing its plan. The Examiner revealed a July 17 email between JPM executives stating they "may soon get some color from regulators on how to structure an assisted transaction [with WMI]." The next day on July 18, "JPM met with the FDIC and OCC."[78] JPM and FDIC executives refused to reveal the contents of the meetings to the Examiner.

On July 26, discussion materials from JPMorgan Chase recommended a straw-man structure whereby "West Bank [Washington Mutual] is seized, assets and deposits transferred to New Bank, New Bank sold to Acquirer [JPMorgan Chase]." A July 26 email stream from JPMorgan Chase executives showed their true feelings about the projected loan losses, "As a result of our work, we believe the most likely range of remaining losses that is the amount of balances that ultimately will be charged off in our [WM] residential portfolio, is between $12–19 billion." These estimates were within the ranges of Washington Mutual's stress tests.[79]

The Examiner also discovered a July 28 "JPM slide deck which reviewed the financial impact of a zero offer [for Washington Mutual]. An analysis circulated on August 1 modeled an out of receivership [seizure] deal with zero cost and assumption of all of the [WM] assets and liabilities. The model indicated that a purchase [of WM] out of receivership [by JPM] would require less capital than a whole bank purchase."[80]

On July 29, Washington Mutual attorneys sent a joint letter with other bank attorneys to the SEC:

> While we applaud the Commission's decision to continue to address abusive trading practices in the marketplace by extending its emergency order suspending naked shorting of 19 foreign and domestic financial institutions, we strongly urge the Commission to move swiftly to expand the scope of the order to include additional U.S. headquartered financial institutions which have been subjected to false rumors and abusive short selling. We believe failure to provide these protections to all institutions with significant mortgage holders has already driven significant naked short activity into those stocks not on the commission's list.[81]

The Wall Street–centric "do not short" order must have been noticed by the rest of the industry, because the SEC Director soon found himself testifying to the Senate Banking Committee and promising that hundreds of banks would soon be added to the list. However, he dragged his feet and this didn't happen until the banking industry collapsed in mid September.[82]

That same week, the *New York Times* ran an article questioning if Hank Paulson could defuse this impeding crisis:

> He has been criticized as having not grasped the threat and severity of the crisis when it began to snowball about 18 months ago. He initially preached against excessive regulation of the financial sector, but he is now presiding over a sweeping governmental intervention in the economy. Critics on the right also accuse Paulson and Bernanke of panicking and over-reaching.[83]

Representative Barney Frank said, "It's fair to say he [Paulson] and almost everybody else failed to anticipate some of these problems. We all underestimated it." Thomas Stanton, an expert on mortgage finance, said, "Once the financial markets showed signs of panic, Treasury had to act. It's almost as if Treasury panicked as well."[84]

Nouriel Roubini, an economics professor at the Stern School of Business at New York University, revealed his concern on the handling of the impending crisis:

It wasn't just Treasury. It was a problem throughout the federal government that everyone was asleep at the wheel. Last fall Paulson repeated often the problem wasn't bad credit, but market fears. He did a low-ball price on Bear Sterns so the public didn't have the impression the shareholders were getting a life raft paid for by Main Street taxpayers.[85]

FDIC chair Bair continued throughout the month of July to publicly pronounce there were no other large banks in any danger. On July 22 she spoke to a group in San Francisco and declared:

Based on the supervisory data and financial data I have, I would be very surprised to see another bank failure the size of IndyMac or larger. Based on what I'm seeing now, I really don't see we will have institutions of that significant size having serious problems.[86]

However, behind the scenes in secret, Bair later reported in her book *Bull by the Horns* that Donald Kohn, vice chair of the Board of Governors of the Federal Reserve, contacted her to let her know Jamie Dimon "had been making the rounds with Hank Paulson, Ben Bernanke and Tim Geithner to let them know of JPMorgan's continued interest in Washington Mutual."[87] Bair also said in her book, after Washington Mutual accepted TPG's bid, she began receiving "gentle inquiries" from both the Fed and Treasury about Washington Mutual, even though the FDIC was not the primary regulator.

Throughout the summer of 2008, the stock prices of Washington Mutual and other large non–Wall Street banks left off the "do not short" list were getting clobbered by naked short sellers and others who were doing their best to spread rumors and create chaos. Government and regulators turned their heads the other way and offered no help. This behavior was unprecedented in banking but consistent with Paulson's plan to consolidate power into Wall Street.

The housing market continued to deteriorate in the second quarter of 2008. New housing starts declined by 25 percent and the Case Shiller National Housing Price Index fell by 8.3 percent from the prior year—an unprecedented decline in national housing prices.[88] The Fed's failure to inject liquidity into the system caused market prices for all mortgage related securities and loans to plummet. This news would continue to panic the market.

In order to make sure the regulators had all the up-to-date and accurate information on Washington Mutual's position, Kerry had arranged a meeting on July 31 with FDIC chair Sheila Bair and OTS director John Reich and staff. Chair Bair brought along John Corston, whom Kerry had never met and who hadn't participated in past audits. Kerry, CFO Tom Casey, and treasurer Robert Williams gave a detailed report on capital, liquidity, asset quality, and earnings forecasts:

> Liquidity remains strong at over $50 billion. The IndyMac failure created an immediate, but manageable outflow of uninsured deposits. Insured accounts have remained resilient and net new account openings have continued. We retain excess liquidity and even with a high stress case plan [a 40 percent drop in national housing prices] we still have over $22 billion in excess cash. $2 billion of additional capital was down streamed from WMI [holding company] on July 21st, bolstering capital ratios. Even without further capital injections, the bank's capital will remain strongly in excess of all regulatory well-capitalized minimums.
>
> Analysts who have modeled the balance sheet over time have generally concluded we have more than sufficient capital even in elevated loss scenarios. In all loss scenarios, both the bank and the holding company maintain healthy excesses to regulatory well-capitalized minimums and actually exceed pre-crisis target levels.[89]

There was a good exchange of information, and the Washington Mutual executives answered a number of questions. The OTS representatives said the plans made sense and they supported the initiatives being taken by the board and management. The meeting had gone well.

Then, out of the blue, FDIC's Corston spoke up and suggested Washington Mutual needed to find a partner like JPMorgan Chase. However, he did not mention a specific reason why, or identify any particular problem with Washington Mutual, other than general concerns about the economy and the mortgage market. Nor did he recommend or demand a formal or even an informal enforcement action. Kerry and his team were stunned. It had been only two weeks since the OTS and the FDIC had given a presentation to the bank's board and nothing was said about finding a merger partner. OTS director Reich, as primary regulator, was equally shocked. Reich correctly indicated such a suggestion from the FDIC was inappropriate and abruptly concluded the meeting.[90]

Shortly after the meeting, the OTS director emailed Kerry:

As you could no doubt tell, I was not happy with FDIC's verbal reaction to your presentation. You and your folks did a good job. I have a 4 pm meeting with Sheila Bair today to express my disappointment with the conclusion of the meeting, and to remind her the OTS is the Primary Federal Regulator, not the Secondary Federal Regulator. We are not subservient or subordinate to the FDIC. The FDIC is a 'back-up regulator' and while we do wish to collaborate with them and will listen to their views, we will make the supervisory decisions concerning the institution.[91]

Kerry immediately wrote to his attorneys and board members:

I received the attached email from OTS director Reich and talked to him on the phone. The OTS is comfortable with our liquidity and capital. He said we did a good job of presenting the information today. The OTS was disappointed and upset about the comments made by the FDIC which they viewed as highly inappropriate and awkward. Reich called *Bair to express his views and she agreed her staff was overzealous.* Reich plans to call Hank Paulson tomorrow to reflect the OTS's comfort with our capital and liquidity.

Several Washington Mutual directors responded they couldn't believe how inappropriately the staff person at the FDIC had acted, especially since neither the OTS nor the FDIC had suggested any type of formal regulatory enforcement action. For over a century, regulators—including the FDIC, the OTS, and the OCC—had generally followed careful step-by-step protocols for a bank. They started with informal enforcement actions and proceeded step by step through formal enforcement actions if the bank didn't correct potential problem areas. The informal actions of commitment letters and MOUs were quite common for banks. Banks that didn't respond to informal actions would then receive formal orders like cease-and-desist orders. The following table describes the step-by-step process followed by regulators as outlined in the OCC manual.[92]

Informal Enforcement Actions are typically given to 1-, 2-, and 3-rated banks and include:
- All nonpublic bank enforcement actions:
  —Commitment letters
  —Memorandums of understanding (MOU)
  —Individual minimum capital ratios (IMCR)
  —Notices of deficiency issued under 12 CFR 30
- Operating agreements
- Conditions imposed in writing within the meaning of 12 USC 1818

Formal Bank Enforcement Actions. If the deficiencies are severe, uncorrected, repeat, unsafe, or unsound or negatively affect the bank's condition, they may use formal enforcements to support the agency's objectives. They are typically given to banks rated 4 or 5.
- All bank enforcement actions include
  —Consent order and cease-and-desist (C&D) orders
  —Restitution orders (a type of consent or C&D order
  —Capital directives
  —Prompt Corrective Action (PCA) directives
  —Safety and soundness orders issued under 12 CFR 30
- Formal agreements
- GLBA (Gramm-Leach-Bliley Act) agreements pursuant to 12 CFR 5.39
- Civil Money Penalties (CMPs)

The primary mission of the FDIC is to preserve the safety and soundness of the federal deposit insurance fund, but during and after the banking crisis in the 1980s, it was our experience that the FDIC and other regulators put a higher priority on working to save community banks that didn't have serious formal enforcement orders or serious misdoings. Washington Mutual, along with virtually all large banks, typically received a few informal regulatory actions, but Washington Mutual had never had any formal enforcement actions. The seizure of the $32 billion IndyMac Bank cost the insurance fund an astounding $10.7 billion, and Kerry knew FDIC chair Bair was panicked about the future of the fund during a crisis. If something happened to Washington Mutual or any other large bank, the entire FDIC fund would be depleted.

Even though there was no indication Washington Mutual should have been seized, Kerry realized there could be a possibility that Paulson's plan to eliminate thrifts, combined with JPMorgan Chase's rapacious desire for Washington Mutual and FDIC chair Bair's deep panic about her deposit fund, could prompt them to conspire to seize Washington Mutual and make a bargain sale to JPMorgan Chase, even though it would be contrary to established FDIC protocols.

However, six days after the meeting in DC, FDIC chair Bair revealed her panic when she emailed OTS director Reich:

I'd like to further discuss contingency planning for W [Washington Mutual] during the call on Friday. Art talked with Scott about making some discreet inquiries to determine whether there are institutions which would be willing to acquire it on a whole bank basis if we had to do an emergency closing and on what terms. I understand you have strong objections to our doing so, so I'd like to talk this through. My interest is in assuring that if we have to market it on an emergency basis, there is multiple bidder interest.

This is a stunning statement because the FDIC has never seized a 3-rated bank, especially one with no formal enforcement actions, $50 billion in liquidity and the highest capital ratios of all the large banks. Oddly enough, only three weeks after Bair's complete support on July 15, she had completely changed her view without giving any specific reason. This was only two weeks after she had publicly declared that "no other banks the size of Indy Mac or larger were having serious problems."

OTS director John Reich immediately shot back an email to FDIC Chair Bair:

> The actions you are talking about could cause irreparable harm to Washington Mutual. If in fact any meetings or discussions have already taken place by the FDIC with either JPMC, Wells Fargo or any other entity, in any capacity in which Washington Mutual was even mentioned, I would like to see a copy of the signed confidentiality agreement signed by the bank, which is required in any resolution scenario before an institution is told the name of a failing bank. This is an OTS regulated institution, we make any decision on solvency, not the FDIC. The FDIC can do whatever internal contingency planning it wishes, but should in no way go outside the FDIC. This is a 3-rated institution. Are you also trying to find buyers for Citigroup, Wachovia, Nat City and others?
>
> *Finally, if Washington Mutual were to learn of the FDIC's actions, there may well be a question as to whether these actions may constitute a disclosable event. That, in of itself, is a reason not to proceed with this approach for a publicly traded institution.* The government should not be in the business of arranging mergers, particularly before they are necessary.[93]

OTS director Reich did not reveal these emails to Kerry for obvious reasons. Reich was absolutely correct. It was outrageous for a secondary regulator to hold secret meetings with potential acquirers without a confidentiality agreement and without informing the primary regulator or the bank. As revealed later in documents released by PSI, FDIC, and the Examiner, JPMorgan Chase over the summer continued its efforts to pressure the FDIC to seize Washington Mutual and sell the remains for a bargain price.[94] These clandestine meetings violated all well-established regulatory protocols and irreparably harmed Washington Mutual.

In spite of all the back-room FDIC antics, August was relatively stable for Washington Mutual. Liquidity was improving as retail deposits returned following the IndyMac failure. Neither the OTS nor the FDIC suggested any formal enforcement actions or other formal actions typically taken on banks with serious issues. Loan quality was substantially better than the industry, the capital ratios remained the highest among the big banks and available liquidity was over $50 billion. Management

and the board were receiving daily reports on deposit flows, and it
appeared the worst might be over.

Even though Kerry did not like to hire a lot of consultants, times
were different, and he continued to elicit advice from key consultants
in the business about the safety, soundness, and management actions
of the bank and was receiving positive reports in all areas. For example,
in August, Goldman Sachs made a presentation to the Regulatory and
Strategy Oversight Committee of the Washington Mutual Board on "liquidity alternatives" and "rating agency observations." Goldman Sachs
gave the bank a full report, declaring, "Washington Mutual has more
than adequate amounts of liquidity available for a deep crisis."[95]

During his long-overdue vacation in the last week of August, Kerry
had devised a detailed plan to confront Paulson on his misguided and
misinformed impression of Washington Mutual. Kerry wanted to make
sure Paulson knew about what was happening behind the scenes and
the dramatic impact that would follow if FDIC chair Bair continued
with her misguided efforts. Kerry had the plans in his hand when he
returned to the office on September 5.

But waiting for him were board chair Steve Frank and director Orin
Smith, who told Kerry it was time for a change and encouraged Kerry
to retire. Kerry could tell this was a hard decision for them, because
they were very sad and emotional in their comments. In many ways,
Kerry was not surprised because nearly all large banks had already
replaced—or were in the process of replacing—their CEOs. Wachovia
was the most recent to replace their longtime CEO, Ken Thompson.
They selected former Goldman Sachs and Treasury executive Bob Steel
for the position. This was a smart move, because Paulson was calling
the shots and Bob Steel was close to Paulson.

Kerry's only concern was the board's choice for his replacement—
Alan Fishman, whom Kerry had known for years. Kerry respected Alan's
operating capabilities. However, Kerry also knew Alan did not have
experience running this large of a bank, did not have strong political
ties to Paulson or Treasury, or the experience to deal with this kind of
crisis. Kerry feared Treasury and the FDIC would use this as an opportunity to make a run at merging out Washington Mutual on the cheap.
This, unfortunately, turned out to be the case in less than three weeks.

The Examiner had discovered that "Dimon had a phone call in
early September with Bair and was talking with Chase about a seizure

of Washington Mutual. They had another meeting on the ninth, but Bair didn't remember the content. The FDIC submission said Bair called John Stumpf [of Wells Fargo] about this same time about an open market acquisition [of WM]."[96]On September 12, JPMorgan Chase's presentation deck for the FDIC described a scenario where it would pay nothing for Washington Mutual, but would be happy to "assume $307 billion in assets, $141 billion in deposits, $8 billion in covered bonds, and preferred securities valued at $4 billion."[97]

On September 6, Treasury Secretary Paulson and the Federal Housing Finance Authority put Fannie Mae and Freddie Mac into conservatorship. The bailout was authorized to purchase up to $200 billion in preferred stock.[98]

Early in September, a number of media outlets reported leaked information that JPMorgan Chase was having ongoing discussions with the FDIC to take advantage of the financial panic setting in and to pressure the FDIC to seize Washington Mutual and hand over the assets to Chase. What normally would be highly confidential and inappropriate conversations continued to show up in the media. The *American Banker* reported the leaked information:[99]

> Sources said negotiations are ongoing at the highest levels of Chase and Washington Mutual for advanced talks for Chase to buy Washington Mutual. Observers have said earlier this week a government assisted transaction may be necessary if Washington Mutual did not recover or find a buyer soon. Knowledgeable sources were optimistic the deal would come together. Sources say JPMorgan Chase has remained interested in buying since their bid was rejected last April.

Responding to these bizarre press reports, Washington Mutual released a mid-quarter update reporting, "third-quarter provision for loan losses would fall by $1.4 billion from the second quarter, liquidity was stable at $50 billion, and the bank was well capitalized." The bank quickly responded to the media that the leaks were false and they were not in negotiations with any bank.

A couple of days after Kerry's retirement, the OTS and the Washington Mutual board agreed to an informal memorandum of understanding (MOU). The matters addressed in the MOU could be addressed in the normal course of business and as expected did not contain any formal enforcement actions. The bank was still rated a 3, and the MOU asked the bank to develop an updated three-year plan—hardly a sign of a failing bank. Things would have proceeded smoothly, but Treasury and the Fed were about to make another bad decision.

On September 12, the American financial system was shaken to its core when Treasury refused to help Lehman Brothers Holdings Inc., forcing it to file for bankruptcy protection. Regulators could have saved Lehman, but they instead chose to let it fail. The bankruptcy of Lehman eviscerated the market's belief of the Bagehot doctrine that in a systemic crisis, regulators would serve as a lender of last resort. This was the straw that broke the financial system's back, and what were previously very difficult conditions quickly disintegrated into a death spiral as all the counterparties started a run in the wholesale funding markets.[100]

The *Wall Street Journal* later that month wrote that Lehman's failure triggered a cash crunch around the globe:

> The bankruptcy sparked a chain reaction that sent credit markets
> into disarray and accelerated the downward spiral of AIG. Richard
> Portes, professor of economics at London Business School
> and the president of the Centre for Economic Policy Research,
> said, 'Letting Lehman fail only exacerbated the central problem:
> nobody knows which financial firms will be able to make good
> on their debts. Spooked that other securities firms could fail,
> hedge funds rushed to buy default insurance on the other firms.
> Those mass moves dramatically drove up the cost of insurance
> on Morgan Stanley and Goldman's debt and created a dangerous
> spiral of fear.'[101]

Later that fall, many of the economists agreed with Alan Blinder, former vice chair of the Federal Reserve, author of the book, *After the Music Stopped*, and a friend of Bernanke at Princeton, who stated:

> After the fact, it is extremely clear that everything fell apart on the
> day Lehman went under.[102]

Many years later, Dr. Laurence Ball, chair of the economics department at John Hopkins University and author of *Money, Banking, and*

Financial Markets, took issue with Paulson and Bernanke's narrative that the Fed was powerless to help Lehman. He said:

> Fed officials have not been transparent about the Lehman crisis. Their explanations for their actions rest on flawed economic and legal reasoning and dubious factual claims. Lehman only needed the kind of well-secured support that the Fed provided liberally to other financial institutions.

The Fed did not rescue Lehman, because the "primary decision maker was Paulson, even though he had no authority over the Fed's lending decisions."[103]

Following the Lehman failure, Standard & Poor's (S&P)—which had just noted Washington Mutual had a sound liquidity profile—downgraded the bank based on "worsening market conditions." However, S&P did not attribute the downgrade to any material change in the bank's actual financial condition, stating, "Washington Mutual's overall liquidity profile is positioned to withstand this weak credit cycle through the end of 2010, *as a result of their conservative and prudent management*."[104]

On the same day Lehman filed for bankruptcy, a triumphant Ken Lewis from Bank of America announced he had agreed to buy Merrill Lynch in an all-stock deal for $50 billion. The price of $29 per share represented a 70 percent premium to Merrill's current share price. Lewis quickly booked a gig on *60 Minutes* and revealed he had conquered Wall Street and declared, "Acquiring one of the premier wealth management firms is a great opportunity for our shareholders." The CEO of Merrill Lynch must have been a consummate dealmaker, because he knew that the collapse of Lehman would make it very difficult for him to get the short term funding he needed to prop up his doomed mortgage portfolio.[105][106] Merrill Lynch was getting saved despite having some of the worst loan and securities losses in the industry.

During the week after the Lehman failure, trust in the financial markets plummeted. Financial institutions lost their belief that the Federal Reserve and the federal government would serve as a lender of last resort. The long-held belief in the Bagehot doctrine was gone. No one felt any fund or bank was safe. Banks were hoarding cash because they were too afraid to make any loans because they didn't know what collateral would be safe. The $62 billion money market Reserve Primary Fund, "broke the buck" because it could no longer maintain the one-dollar share price.

Panicked investors pulled out a record $144.5 billion during the week. They fled to the safest investment they could find—US short term Treasuries and drove that market yield down to near zero. Without the money market fund participation, the $1.7 trillion commercial paper market shrank by $52.1 billion during the week. Treasury started getting panicked calls from the top corporate CEOs in America that they could no longer get short-term loans to fund their operations.[107]

With the stock market in free fall, unemployment rocketing higher, the collapse of the national housing prices, and the collapse of the money market funds and the commercial paper markets, the calm Federal Reserve officials gathered on September 16 at their marbled headquarters to discuss the situation. The transcript for that meeting contained 129 mentions of "inflation" and only five mentions of "recession." Bernanke confidently stated, "I think our policy is looking actually pretty good." Just minutes after the end of the meeting, the Fed agreed to rescue AIG with an $85 billion loan to prevent its bankruptcy.[108]

AIG was getting saved despite its reckless practices in the credit default swap market. A year later it was revealed AIG used some of its bailout largesse by immediately pumping $12.9 billion into Goldman Sachs, $6.8 billion into Merrill Lynch, $5.2 billion into Bank of America, and $2.3 billion into Citigroup.[109] Many observers thought this action was audacious for a number of reasons, including the Federal Reserve and Treasury putting the US taxpayer on the hook for the full cost and full risk of rescuing a failing insurance company—one that was regulated by state insurance departments, not the federal government.

Also, on September 16, "FDIC chair Bair called Dimon to ask him whether JPM would be willing to buy WM out of receivership at no cost to the [FDIC] insurance fund. Dimon told Bair he might be willing to participate. Dimon indicated during the call that a resolution transaction [seizure] would have certain tax advantages for an assuming bank."[110] At the same time, "Chris Spoth, the FDIC Senior Deputy Director of Supervisory Exams, reached out to JPM and other suitors to ascertain whether they were interested in acquiring Washington Mutual on an open bank or private sale." These actions were taken a week before the bidding process was announced.

Also that week, "Citigroup met with the FDIC and expressed interest in acquiring Washington Mutual, but only with government assistance."[111] It was incredulous the FDIC would allow a troubled Wall Street bank to consider this purchase. Citigroup had five times the mortgages loan losses as Washington Mutual and had a history of serious regulatory fines, penalties, and cease-and-desist orders.[112] In 2005 the OCC and the Federal Reserve imposed a moratorium on acquisitions until Citigroup improved its compliance and risk management functions. Citigroup also held $35.8 trillion of risky and unregulated OTC derivative positions.[113] Citigroup was also a 3-rated bank, so it was curious why it was being allowed to even consider such a large acquisition.[114]

On September 16, the FDIC met with the OTS and informed them, "the FDIC had decided to give WMI approximately a week to raise capital or secure an open market transaction or the FDIC would place the bank on the troubled list."[115] Even though the list doesn't identify the name of the banks, they do reveal the asset size and it would have immediately identified and destroyed Washington Mutual. Acting out of full panic mode after the failure of Lehman, Bair was forcing the seizure and sale of banks, without regard to long standing regulatory policies and protocols.

Normally, the protocol stated the FDIC could not seize a bank until its primary regulator declared the bank was insolvent. But Washington Mutual was solvent and the OTS had not informed the bank of any insolvency issues. The FDIC was aggressively moving beyond its established authority. Seizing a 3-rated bank with substantial capital and liquidity, no formal enforcement orders, and loan performance better than the industry, would be a complete abandonment of FDIC protocol.

The OTS was still fighting back against the FDIC, but Washington Mutual dutifully obeyed Bair's orders and hired Goldman Sachs and opened its online data room for any potential buyers. The bank also hired Goldman to develop a stand-alone plan for the bank to recapitalize and increase liquidity for the bank. Management contacted Citigroup, TD, Wells Fargo, Banco Santander, JPMorgan Chase and others. JPMorgan Chase said it wouldn't be making a bid, but it still wanted access to the data room and demanded no one be told of their visits to the data room.[116]

During the banking panic in September, Secretary Paulson and FDIC chair Bernanke continually sent in JPMorgan Chase to assess the situation in other commercial banks, investment banks, and AIG. In his book *On the Brink*, Paulson said, "A number of CEOs expressed concern to us that he [Dimon] was using the crisis to maneuver his bank into a stronger position. Some were convinced he wanted to put them out of business entirely. Jamie assured us JPM was behaving responsibly but pointed out he ran a for-profit institution and had an obligation to his shareholders."[117]

These weren't the only CEOs with concerns. Goldman's CEO, Lloyd Blankfein, was also troubled when he received another message from one of his traders, claiming, "JPMorgan was trying to steal his hedge fund clients by telling everyone Goldman was going under." Dimon claimed no knowledge and sent out a tepid memo to his staff. Other executives were wary because Dimon seemed to be "hanging around the hoop." They knew Dimon's mantra was "Let's make friends with these guys before I eat them."[118] The only people who seemed to completely trust Dimon were Paulson and Bernanke, who were continually asking Dimon to rush in and analyze his competitors.

At this point we were hearing all the false rumors in the media and daily reports from the shocked Washington Mutual executives about the FDIC trying to force the sale of the bank. They were also giving Kerry reports on the deposit outflow after the Lehman failure panic. Kerry thought the deposit outflow wasn't too much worse than after IndyMac and thought the bank deposits would soon stabilize, which they did.

On his last day of work at the bank, September 5, Kerry wrote a supportive note to the new CEO, Fishman, and offered to help during this financial crisis. Kerry never heard from him. Kerry wondered if Fishman really understood what was going on behind the scenes. Kerry found it extremely frustrating not to be there to help the bank—the bank he had meticulously grown over twenty five years into a $300 billion asset bank with twenty-five hundred branch offices. He knew nobody else would have cared as much about the fifty thousand employees who were struggling against unfounded rumors, leaked media reports, confused customers, and panicked regulators.

With all the false press leaks about the FDIC activities, Washington Mutual knew it might not get a fair deal. Based on false and damaging press reports, the banking community was thinking the FDIC was ready to seize the bank. The failure of Lehman was causing deposit runs, liquidity issues, and credit downgrades for most of the major banks. Even though Washington Mutual was highly capitalized, had billions in available liquidity, and deposits were stabilizing, no one knew what other surprises would destabilize the industry. The smart move for all the banks was to continue to add more capital and liquidity. In order to attract new investors to Washington Mutual, TPG waived the antidilution clause in its investment contract, paving the way for a merger or raising new capital at less than $8.75 per share. Washington Mutual management and the board reached out to all potential merger partners and simultaneously reviewed alternatives for raising additional capital and liquidity.

Under pressure from the FDIC, Washington Mutual executives started meeting with a number of banks for a potential transaction. The executives wrote:

> Thirty employees of Wells Fargo have met with the management team and they are interested in following up on specific items and appeared to be very engaged and they have spoken to the OTS. Citigroup has met with the Federal Reserve and the OCC about a potential acquisition. There is also active interest from Toronto Dominion (TD) who may be interested in an option to acquire the branch system. A team of people from Santander have met with the executives.[119]

On September 18, the Dow Jones tumbled five hundred points and Washington Mutual sent out information to the capital markets:

> Capital ratios continue to be well in excess of the levels that regulators require of a 'well capitalized' institution. We also have ample supply of funds on hand to meet the needs of our customers.[120]

On September 18, the board minutes of Washington Mutual revealed:

> "We received a call from the FDIC, who were complimentary of the auction process [the FDIC request to sell the bank or get new capital] and wanted to discuss the timeline. The FDIC indicated Washington Mutual should keep working through Friday or Saturday with their stand-alone proposal and had until Sunday

afternoon, the 28th, to enter into a deal." The executives emphasized the "difficulty of reaching a deal by then and had asked the
FDIC whether they would stop us if substantial progress had been
made and a deal was in the works. The FDIC responded they likely
would listen to their deal and gave them until Sunday the 28th
to finish their negotiations. Shortly thereafter JPMorgan Chase
contacted us and indicated they wanted to start talks but wanted
assurances their participation would be confidential. Chase said
they are fully engaged and wanted to access to a broader range of
people at Washington Mutual.[121]

On September 19, "JPMorgan Chase met with Moody's and gave
presentations about a possible receivership transaction [seizure] with
Washington Mutual. A couple of days later, Moody's downgraded Washington Mutual on September 22."[122] The Examiner found that "those
loan loss forecasts shown to Moody's was considered by Moody's when
it downgraded the financial strength and preferred stock ratings [of
Washington Mutual]."[123]

The data room was opened again, and JPMorgan Chase wanted
access. The Examiner reported, "At one point during this process,
WMI [Washington Mutual] got the impression JPMC was not looking
in good faith at a transaction and terminated JPMC's access to the
data room." Access was later restored but, "JPMC never submitted a
proposal or bid to WMI in September."[124]

According to the executives we spoke with, they still didn't know
the FDIC had been contacting banks and shopping around for buyers during August and early September.[125] They also didn't know the
FDIC had been telling banks Washington Mutual might be seized, and
they weren't told JPMorgan Chase had been working with the FDIC
in the summer and in early September, pressuring the agency to seize
Washington Mutual.

On September 19, Treasury Secretary Paulson announced his proposed $700 billion financial rescue plan. The SEC also issued a ban
on naked short selling of 799 financial stocks. Washington Mutual was
finally added to the list after enduring months of targeting by naked
short sellers.[126] He also announced Treasury set up a $50 billion fund
to guarantee the unregulated and uninsured money market funds.

That same day OTS director Reich and executive Scott Polakoff
went to New York City for meetings with banks interested in acquiring

Washington Mutual. The *Financial Times* broke the news that the bank was in talks with Santander.[127] The *Times* reported that the interest of the banks was unclear because the "suitors were angling for regulatory assistance because of the troubled mortgage portfolio." It was frustrating to see the media claim the bank had a "troubled loan portfolio." The mortgage losses of Citigroup were the worst and five times that of Washington Mutual. Loan losses for Citigroup, UBS, Merrill Lynch, HSBC, Deutsche Bank, Royal Bank of Scotland, Bank of America, Morgan Stanley, JPMorgan Chase, and Credit Suisse all had more mortgage loan losses than Washington Mutual.[128]

Also on September 19, the "JPM board met to review the transactions whereby JPM would acquire some or all of WMI or WMB including a plan to buy assets out of receivership [seizure]. JPM felt the receivership had the advantages of no shareholder approval and immediate closing. It would also allow them to reject any unwanted contracts and leases and the right to holding company assets," including the excess assets in the employee pension plans.[129]

On September 20, Charlie Scharf from JPMorgan told Jim Wigand of the FDIC he wasn't interested in buying Washington Mutual in the open market. Wigand then asked if Chase would be interested in buying the bank after it failed. After that conversation, every bank that called the FDIC and said it wasn't interested was asked if it would be interested in a transaction out of receivership. There was no way Washington Mutual was going to get a fair sale if everyone thought the bank was failing.[130]

On September 21, Treasury and the FDIC announced investment banks Goldman Sachs, Morgan Stanley, and others could become bank holding companies, allowing them to borrow from the Federal Reserve to relieve their liquidity issues. Longer term, it would allow them to better compete with regulated banks like JPMorgan Chase and Bank of America. The shadow, unregulated investment banks that had securitized the worst of the subprime loans—over 85 percent of the total market—were being saved by their alum, Hank Paulson and given nearly unlimited access to liquidity.[131]

September 22 was a busy day. While the "FDIC met with JPM to explain the process of a receivership sale" and the OTS was told to prepare the seizure "S" memo to detail the supervisory reasons for a receivership action, Washington Mutual executives were not aware of what was going on behind the scenes. The FDIC told the banks to turn in their stand-alone recapitalization plan. If the OTS's S memo was turned over to the FDIC, it would allow them to sell Washington Mutual for "pennies on the dollar."[132]

On September 22, *The Wall Street Journal* reported on leaked information:

> There are continuing talks with Washington Mutual about a
> sale including Citigroup, JPMorgan Chase, Wells Fargo, and
> Banco Santander of Spain. Some people close to the discussions
> hope a deal could be struck within days. Some would favor a
> government-assisted takeover, people familiar with the matter said.
> One scenario is that the FDIC would seize control of the Wash-
> ington Mutual banking unit and then sell its deposits to another
> bank. The buyer would have the right to pick the branches and
> assets it wanted to buy along with Washington Mutual deposits.
> But that would leave the government to grapple with the riskier
> leftovers. At the bank, pressure to resolve the uncertainty swirling
> around the company is coming from the FDIC, which has been
> taking an increasingly tough stance with troubled financial
> institutions.[133]

It was a startling event that an S memo was being written, when there were no associated formal or informal enforcement actions and the bank had plenty of capital and liquidity. At the same time, banks in much worse shape were given billions in aid. In Chapter Ten in this book, former FDIC chair William M. Isaac revealed:

> If he had been provided, on a no-name basis, the financial condi-
> tion of a bank that had capital, nonperforming assets, and core
> funding similar to Washington Mutual, he would have concluded
> the bank was likely in good condition and not in any imminent
> danger of failure.

That same day, the FDIC told Washington Mutual it was bringing the sale of the bank in house and giving competitors the opportunity to bid for the bank. The potential suitors were notified on September 23 of the "opportunity to bid on a depository institution" with a link to a secure website for more information. They were given about twenty-four hours to submit their bids. Washington Mutual executives were told they could still submit a plan to raise capital and liquidity and would give them until September 28 to complete their plan. But the FDIC made raising new capital or finding a merger partner impossible by informing potential partners Washington Mutual would be seized.[134, 135] Years later the Examiner found that JPMorgan Chase "relied on Washington Mutual's confidential information when preparing their bid"—confidential information that the other bidders did not have.[136]

On September 23, the minutes of the Washington Mutual board meeting revealed:

> Many of the counterparties are now dealing directly with the
> FDIC to submit bids to acquire the bank's assets. We have devel-
> oped a stand-alone plan that did not involve a third party. The
> plan would take advantage of cash held by the holding company
> and of the REIT preferred at the bank, which was backed by $10
> billion of performing loans as collateral. The plan would provide
> the holding company enter into agreements with the bondholders
> to exchange debt for preferred securities. Following the exchange,
> nonperforming loans would be sold to improve the quality of the
> balance sheet.

Executives were hopeful Treasury would accept their detailed twenty-seven-page stand-alone plan to add liquidity and capital to Washington Mutual. The letter attached to the report pleaded with Treasury not to panic the industry with an unwarranted public seizure:

> We urge you to let us implement this plan. Its completion will
> produce a well-capitalized competitor able to serve the needs of
> ordinary Americans across the country.
>   There is no reason to take the drastic step of effecting the larg-
> est bank seizure in our nation's history when our proposal would,
> quickly and simply, create $19 billion more capital and reposition
> the bank to withstand the current market turmoil—all without
> government assistance. A seizure of the bank would represent a
> further destabilizing event in the financial markets, adversely af-
> fecting the deposit bases and share prices of many other financial

institutions. The seizure by the FDIC of a large, well-capitalized U.S. banking organization is without precedent in the U.S. history and will send a stark message to bank customers and investors.[137]

In their presentation, they mentioned the bank had twenty million customers and was not seeing an erosion in the customer base. It had at least $20 billion in near-term available liquidity, credit costs were on budget, and the deposit base was more stable than before IndyMac.

On September 24, WMI presented its stand-alone plan to the OTS and Treasury. The WMI board minutes expressed hope for its plan:

> We had a call with the Federal Reserve Vice Chairman and staff from the FDIC and the OTS. Questions were asked and answered concerning the proposed stand-alone recapitalization plan. The FDIC mentioned five bidders had participated in the auction process. It appears all bidders were asking the FDIC for assistance and were [only] bidding on certain assets and liabilities. The process appeared to not be going well from the FDIC's perspective. We told the FDIC our stand-alone plan would improve the bank's capital position by $19 billion and its liquidity by $15 billion.

When looking back on the facts, it was clear that Treasury and the FDIC were insincere in considering the stand-alone plan, when behind the scenes they had already told the suitors that the bank was going to be seized.

On Wednesday, September 24, JPMorgan Chase made a presentation to its Board of Directors. It was clear it wanted Washington Mutual badly:

> The FDIC process is contemplating Friday (9/26) receivership for West [code name for Washington Mutual] in parallel with our process seeking an open bank solution. Bidding contracts were made available on Tuesday, September 23rd and bids were due Wednesday, Sept. 24th at 6pm. FDIC will engage in conversation with the highest bidder on Thursday and Friday to prepare for handover of operational control. Winning bidder and FDIC will announce transaction and winning bidder takes control on Friday night.
>
> West provides a unique opportunity to expand the retail banking franchise. Will give Chase nearly a trillion dollars in

deposits and 5,410 branches. Good transaction for Park [Chase] shareholders, immediately accretive to earnings and substantially in the future. Asset write-down reduces risk to volatility in future earnings. Opportunity to grow revenue and realize significant cost savings. West provides significant opportunity to expand business banking and the retail branch presence provides the basis for strong middle market franchise.[138]

On September 24 at 8:23 p.m., a mere two hours and twenty-three minutes after all the bids were due, there was an email from FDIC chair Bair to JPMorgan Chase's Jamie Dimon:

Congrats, you are the high bid. The technical issues you raised in your cover letter can be easily addressed. The board will approve this Friday morning and we will complete the transfer on Friday. The *WSJ* and the *NYTimes* are both on to the 'auction' and we may have to accelerate the announcement.

On the morning of September 25, one of the Washington Mutual executives "received an email from the OTS notifying him of the OTS decision to declare a supervisory event and direct a conditional exchange of the TRUPS [trust preferred securities] for WMI preferred stock. The executive thought it meant a conditional exchange was taking place in order for WMI to implement its stand-alone plan." Instead, the FDIC was secretly initiating the transaction to move the TRUPS over to Chase.[139]

The Examiner reported that he was "unaware of any of the WMI employees having received advance notice on the seizure on September 25." The executives "never received a response from regulators concerning the proposed [stand-alone plan]."[140]

Later in the day on September 25, the OTS informed board chair "Steve Frank that the OTS was closing the bank in approximately an hour or two before issuing the order to seize. Notably the OTS did not close the bank because it was insolvent or not well-capitalized." The reason given was the daily deposit outflow. The Examiner found that "from the regulator's perspectives, WMB was well capitalized on the day of the failure."[141]

Following the Lehman bankruptcy, deposits had dropped at Washington Mutual but by the week of September 22, deposits had stabilized.

This September drop wasn't too much more than the 6 percent drop in July following the IndyMac seizure. Washington Mutual still had other sources of liquidity, including tens of billions of untapped borrowing capacity from the Federal Home Loan Banks of San Francisco and Seattle. Additionally, the Federal Reserve was in position to provide additional liquidity. However, the Federal Reserve, which was providing fresh new sources of liquidity to Wall Street banks, called the Federal Home Loan Banks and inexplicably cut back Washington Mutual's borrowing lines.

It appears Treasury wanted Washington Mutual eliminated and years later we learned from officials of the Federal Home Loan Bank of San Francisco and Seattle that they were more than willing to lend billions of dollars to Washington Mutual, but requests for additional lending were not made. Treasury knew the only way for a strongly capitalized bank to be seized was for a liquidity crisis to be created. Cutting off liquidity would ensure the regulators could quickly downgrade the bank to a 4 and give them the cover to seize the bank.

Chart 1-3 illustrates Washington Mutual's daily deposit balances leading up to the inappropriate seizure. On the day before IndyMac's seizure on July 11, 2008, Washington Mutual had deposits of $144 billion. There was a 6 percent drop in deposits after that seizure, to $135 billion, but the FDIC showed no concern about that drop and deposits quickly rebounded to previous levels by August. On the day before the Lehman bankruptcy, deposits were $140 billion, but decreased about 9 percent until it stabilized on September 23 at $125 billion, where it stayed until October 6.[142]

On September 25, the Federal Reserve Bank "downgraded WM to secondary credit status, which reduced the borrowing capacity and increased collateral requirements even further." The deputy director of the OTS said, "The FDIC could have opted to guarantee additional advances by the Federal Reserve, which might have kept Washington Mutual liquid long enough to find a purchaser, but the FDIC did not."[143]

That afternoon, the FDIC seized Washington Mutual Bank and sold it to JPMorgan Chase for only $1.88 billion. The FDIC bypassed century-old protocols by quickly seizing the bank even though management and the board had the ability to add capital and liquidity alternatives.[144] The Federal Reserve had inexplicably reduced lines of liquidity for Washington Mutual and tens of billions of dollars of Federal Home

Chart 1-3: Washington Mutual Daily Deposit Balance

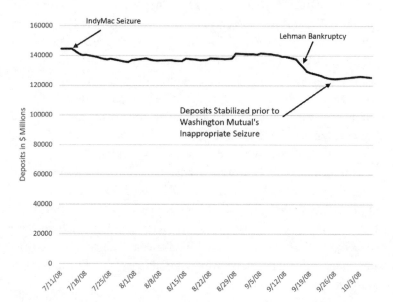

Loan Bank advances were not allowed to be drawn down. Even with these draconian actions, Washington Mutual deposits were stabilizing. It was still solvent and should not have been seized. The Examiner said he was "unaware of any WMI employee having received advance notice of the seizure"—an unprecedented action.[145]

The Examiner said, Washington Mutual "had capital well in excess of regulatory requirements, the only basis on which the FDIC could justify the seizure was concerns for liquidity." In one more punch to the gut, FDIC chair Bair, in an unprecedented action, insisted on a structure that wiped out the bank's bondholders.[146]Treasury Secretary Geithner strongly opposed this move and thought "the US government had sent a message that creditors of US financial institutions were not safe, precisely the wrong message to send at a time of peril."[147]

Shortly after the surprise seizure, we started receiving phone calls from a number of Washington Mutual executives and employees about the stunning takeover. They were also concerned because many of the executives were forced to sign confidentiality agreements swearing they would not reveal the flurry of changes in the FDIC purchase agreement with JPMorgan Chase.

Years later, the Examiner revealed that, "The evidence indicates that JPM and FDIC from September 22–26 negotiated and changed various provisions of the P&A agreement, even though the bidders were told verbally and in writing that the P&A was not negotiable. One of the changes required the FDIC to indemnify JPM for $500 million against future claims of WMI shareholders alleging that JPM breached the March, 2008 standstill agreement," which prohibited JPM from purchasing Washington Mutual for eighteen months, without approval from the bank. Other changes allowed JPM to claim certain assets out of the holding company with a value over $11 billion.[148]

It appeared that JPMorgan Chase had cleverly figured out the most profitable path to purloin Washington Mutual and played the regulators and the media like a fiddle. It apparently pressured Treasury, the Fed, and the FDIC to seize the bank, giving them cherry-picked assets and limited liabilities for a bargain sale price and then reportedly leaked stories about a seizure of the bank to ward off other potential buyers.

The US inspector general's report released in 2010 stated Washington Mutual was "liquid up to the day of its seizure."[149] The bank never ran out of cash or had trouble paying depositors. The Fed and Treasury cut off liquidity sources to the bank in order to have an excuse to seize the bank. Their opinion was no doubt influenced by Treasury's desire to have Washington Mutual and other banks merged into Wall Street, FDIC's panic over their deposit insurance fund, and JPMorgan Chase's desire to get a great bargain.

Washington Mutual's holding company, WMI, had $33 billion of assets, some of which could have been down-streamed to the bank, but the regulators chose to quickly seize the bank rather than requesting the additional capital be down-streamed. The regulators simply seized the holding company's primary asset—Washington Mutual Bank.[150] This was the structure that JPMorgan Chase mentioned in their presentation decks going all the back to July. The seizure "would not require shareholder approval, would give immediate closing, have the ability to reject unwanted leases and contracts and give them rights to the holding company assets."[151]

The seizure of the bank resulted in a bankruptcy filing of the holding company in order to protect and distribute cash to equity holders, employees, and other claimants. The filing reported that Washington

Mutual's holding company assets were $32.9 billion and liabilities were only $8.2 billion. To further add to a great deal, JPMorgan Chase, through bankruptcy negotiations, received billions of dollars of additional assets from the holding company.[152] Unfortunately, FDIC chair Bair insisted that the bondholders of the bank not get paid, which sent shock waves throughout the financial system.

Consistent with Treasury Secretary Paulson's plan to eliminate thrifts, protect investment banks, and centralize banking into Wall Street, Washington Mutual's quick seizure and bargain sale to JPMorgan Chase was a huge win. Treasury wanted to get this done quickly before new legislation passed that would have provided substantial new liquidity and capital to all banks including Washington Mutual.

The repercussions of Washington Mutual's inappropriate seizure and sale were profound. Three years later, the Financial Crisis Investigation Committee (FCIC) agreed:

> Losses among Washington Mutual creditors [when the FDIC
> stiffed the bondholders] created panic among the unsecured credi-
> tors of other struggling banks, particularly Wachovia, with serious
> consequences.[153]

Nobel Prize Laureate economist Dr. Robert Shiller later stated:

> The FDIC had emergency authority that allowed it to guarantee
> the creditors of a bank. In the case of Washington Mutual, however,
> the FDIC chose not to use that authority. This added to the fire,
> accelerating the panic, spreading it to the broader banking system.
> If you haircut creditors in a systemic panic when all firms look
> vulnerable, you risk intensifying the crisis and forcing broader
> interventions to prevent the collapse of the financial system.[154]

Dr. Shiller was accurate. If the FDIC had used its emergency authority, it could have avoided calamity in the market that destabilized Wachovia and the rest of the financial system.

Even though Secretary Paulson was calling for the elimination of thrifts in March of 2008, he later regretted his actions with regards to Washington Mutual. In his 2010 book, *On the Brink*, he admitted his regrets:

I see that, in the middle of a panic, [the seizure of Washington
Mutual] was a mistake. Washington Mutual, the sixth biggest bank
in the country, was systemically important.[155]

Neel Kashkari, former US Treasury official under Paulson and president of the Federal Reserve Bank of Minneapolis, also characterized the seizure of Washington Mutual as "a mistake." He stated:

Questions still remain about whether Washington Mutual's financial condition justified seizure. Documentary and testimonial
evidence suggest Washington Mutual was seized and sold even
though the bank had liquidity and was operating above the well
capitalized levels. Liquidity reports from the date of seizure put
the bank's liquidity in the range of $9.5 billion to $24.5 billion. It
was widely recognized Washington Mutual was well capitalized at
the time of the seizure.

In my judgment that [seizure] was a mistake. At that time, the
economy was in such a perilous state, [not helping Washington
Mutual] was like playing with fire.[156]

Internal memos from Washington Mutual confirmed the bank had
at least $20 billion in liquidity on September 25, 2008. Since deposits
were stabilizing, the $20 billion along with billions in the holding company would have been more than enough to keep the bank going for
another eight days before the passage of TARP.

In his book *Stress Test*, Treasury secretary Geithner felt FDIC chair
Bair failed in her duties by not using her authority to help banks
through the "systemic risk exception." He knew Congress had given
the FDIC that flexibility to protect bank creditors and Geithner later
asked the question, "What was the point of systemic risk authority if it
didn't apply to the worst systemic emergency since the Depression?"[157]

In her book on the crisis, Bair confided the loss of Washington
Mutual was "below the fold if it was even on the front page... barely
a blip."[158] During and long after the crisis, Bair continued to downplay the significance of the Washington Mutual seizure—an action
she knew was not necessary and one that was counter to most of the
FDIC's protocols. A seizure helping to create a global financial panic
she could have helped prevent.

Years later in their books, Paulson, Bernanke, and Geithner made a point of strongly disagreeing with Fed chair Bair and her decision to stiff the Washington Mutual bondholders. Bernanke said Bair "put the fund ahead of the interests of the broader financial system." Geithner had harsh fights with Bair and stated in his book he "was frustrated by what I considered the FDIC's narrow and parochial focus on protecting its fund during a global emergency."[159]

In his insightful book *Too Big to Fail*, Andrew Ross Sorkin mentioned that Geithner, Bernanke, and Paulson felt Bair was "one of their least favorite people in government. They had always regarded Bair as a showboat, a media grandstander, a politician in a regulator's position whose only concern was to protect the FDIC, not the entire system. She was not a team player." Paulson said, "When she is surrounded by her people, when she's peacocking for other people, or she's worried about the press, then she's going to be miserable."[160] They also complained Bair regularly leaked information to the media. They even gave an example of a "confidential" fake story they gave Bair, which immediately showed up in the media. Chair Bair complained in her book that Paulson, Geithner, and Bernanke were not keeping her informed or involved in their decisions. It appears they may have had good reasons for not involving her.

The highly unusual and unprecedented structure the FDIC forced on the seizure and sale of Washington Mutual caused shock waves in the investment community, with bondholders of Wachovia and other banks up in arms.

Wachovia, the fifth-largest US depository bank, became so distressed after these actions that the FDIC arranged for Citigroup to acquire it for only $2.1 billion. Citigroup received forty-three hundred US branches and $600 billion in deposits. Citigroup would be responsible for the first $42 billion in losses, with the FDIC covering any additional losses. The FDIC would provide a cap on losses of Wachovia's $312 billion mortgage portfolio. In return for the cap on losses, the FDIC would receive a $12 billion stake in Citigroup in the form of warrants and preferred shares. Citigroup would assume the company's senior and subordinated debt, which was a huge relief to Wachovia's bondholders. Secretary Paulson defended the move, saying Wachovia's failure would have posed a systemic risk, and its sale prevented a market disruption. Wachovia's shares fell to $1.27.[161]

Ironically, the troubled Citigroup bank, with more mortgage loan losses than any other commercial bank in the world (See Chart 1-2), was allowed to acquire another 3-rated bank.[162]

Years later we were able to get a copy of the Wachovia deposit levels during the 2008 crisis. After the IndyMac debacle in July, Wachovia, like Washington Mutual, experienced about a 6 percent drop in total core deposits. Wachovia, like Washington Mutual, was also downgraded to a 3 in 2008. Both banks regained deposits before the Lehman failure. After the Lehman failure, Wachovia and Washington Mutual had a similar percentage drop and recovery in deposits, yet they were treated substantially different.[163]

In a Wachovia case study on the Stanford University website, the postmortem claimed, "Non-support for Washington Mutual bondholders was the catalyst that brought down Wachovia Bank."[164]

On September 29, the FDIC started the Temporary Liquidity Guarantee Program (TLGP). For a small premium of seventy-five basis points, certain unregulated banks were authorized to borrow from the FDIC with 100 percent insurance. In the past the FDIC had only insured deposits, but now, according to its press release, it was going to insure promissory notes, commercial paper, interbank funding, corporate bonds, and unsecured parts of secured debt. By May 2009, the program had mushroomed to $350 billion, with Goldman Sachs first in line to bag the new goodies.[165] Once again the FDIC and Treasury policies made no sense. There was no defined reason why some banks like Wachovia and Washington Mutual were cut off from funding, but the shadow investment banks, which originated and securitized nearly all of the most toxic subprime loans, continued to be showered with billions.

On October 1, 2008, just six days after the seizure and sale of Washington Mutual, the IRS issued a tax ruling allowing loan losses in acquired banks to be treated as carry-forward losses, making loan losses potentially a valuable tax asset. The ruling also removed the burdensome mark-to-market treatment of loan losses for acquiring banks. Treasury must have known the rule was forthcoming at the time of the Washington Mutual seizure, but it conveniently did not tell anyone at Washington Mutual.

However, Citigroup quickly learned you can't trust panicked government agencies, because within a day the FDIC welshed on its deal with Citigroup for a better offer from Wells Fargo. Armed with the new favorable tax rulings from Treasury, Wells Fargo bid $15.1 billion, without government assistance, for Wachovia's banking operations.[166]

In Charles Kindleberger's highly regarded book *Manias, Panics and Crashes*, he, like many other economists, agreed the haphazard way of handling AIG, Lehman, Washington Mutual, Wachovia, and others caused panics that made the crisis much worse than it needed to be. Kindleberger and others quoted from the well-respected Bagehot doctrine that "a central bank should lend freely—but at a penalty interest rate—to forestall the likelihood that a liquidity crisis would cascade into a solvency crisis."[167] Kindleberger felt if the Federal Reserve, Treasury, and the FDIC had followed the Bagehot doctrine—and provided liquidity to all the banks—much of the depths of the crisis would have been avoided.[168]

On October 3, only eight days after the seizure and sale of Washington Mutual, the US House of Representatives passed the revised bailout bill, TARP, and President Bush signed it into law. The bill gave the Treasury Department the power to purchase $700 billion of assets from banks and gave the government the ability to invest directly in banks to supply liquidity. The bill also increased the FDIC insurance limit on deposit accounts to $250,000 and guaranteed bank bondholders.[169] When asked, Paulson said the bailout numbers "Were not based on any particular data point. We just wanted to choose a really big number."[170]

Shortly after the legislation passed, the US Treasury Department poured nearly $239 billion into 296 of the nation's eight thousand banks. Sixty-seven percent went to the nine largest institutions. The Big Nine that were invited to the Treasury Department on October 12 were Citigroup, JPMorgan Chase, Bank of America, Wells Fargo, Merrill Lynch, Morgan Stanley, Goldman Sachs, Bank of New York Mellon, and State Street Bank. Treasury was going to buy $250 billion of preferred stock in the banks. Secretary Paulson explained that opting out wasn't an option. The standard agreement between Treasury and the institutions did not require the banks to track or report how they planned to use the money or if they would use the capital for investments. The agreement did not put any limits on the banks' compensation programs.[171]

Paulson, Bernanke, and others continue to brag that all the TARP funds have been repaid, however, that is a little misleading. *ProPublica,* an independent investigative media company, continues to track the bailout funds, and as of October 2020, the data show only 62 percent of the $634 billion principal has been repaid. However, TARP has collected interest, dividends, and fees of nearly $365 billion, including the $121.1 billion in profits from Fannie and Freddie. Of all the TARP funds, 38.7 percent was given to banks, 30.2 percent given to Fannie and Freddie, 12.6 percent given to auto companies, and 10.7 percent to AIG. The US government and the taxpayers lost $11.3 billion on the government's investment in General Motors and $1.2 billion on its investment in Chrysler. TARP also gave an additional $9.3 billion to Citigroup, Bank of America, JPMorgan Chase, and Wells Fargo to encourage them to pass on the money to homeowners. That money does not have to ever be paid back.[172]

Months after the crisis, a top executive at the Treasury Department wrote in a paper for the Brookings Institute that there was "Chronic disorganization in Treasury, a broadly haphazard policy process within the administration, and strained relationships between Treasury and White House staff that made it difficult to harness the full energies of the administration in a common direction."[173]

But the worst part of the handling of the crisis was having a small group of Wall Street insiders, in pure panic mode, decide which banks would be abandoned, which would fail, and which would be saved. This was a massive conflict of interest and what many believe was possibly a violation of the intent of monopoly laws.[174]

The Congressional Oversight Panel, which later reviewed the ten largest TARP transactions, concluded Treasury "paid substantially more for the assets it purchased under the TARP than their then current market value." Chart 1-4 illustrates the banks that spent the most on lobbying Congress received the most TARP funding, regardless of their reckless lending policies.

After the crisis the National Bureau of Economic Research (NBER) did a study to determine if the political influence of the financial industry contributed to the crisis. They concluded that banks that spent the most on lobbying were "associated with more risk-taking at mortgage origination, higher securitization rates, and faster mortgage credit expansion. These lenders lobbied more aggressively, took more regulatory risks and had worse [lending loss] outcomes. Finally, they were more likely to be bailed-out than other lenders."

Chart 1-4: Eight Largest Banks:
2008 Lobbying and TARP Funding[175]

Bank	Lobbying	TARP Funds
Citigroup	$5.6 million	$45 billion
JPMorgan Chase	$5 million	$25 billion
Bank of America	$4.7 million	$45 billion
Merrill Lynch	$4.6 million	$25 billion
Goldman Sacs	$4.2 million	$10 billion
Morgan Stanley	$2.4 million	$10 billion
Wells Fargo	$2 million	$25 billion
Washington Mutual	Not much	Nothing

The NBER research recommended that "the prevention of future crises might require a closer monitoring of lobbying activities by the financial industry and the weakening of their political influence."[176]

For example, Citigroup spent $3 million in the first six months of 2002 lobbying against the Predatory Lending Consumer Act of 2001, which would have placed tighter restrictions on lenders. After dozens of successful lobbying efforts, Citigroup ramped up their mortgage lending and CDO production and by June of 2008 had the worst US mortgage losses in the world—$42.9 billion. They were also one of the largest holders of OTC derivatives—$35.8 trillion. Yet in the depths of the September crisis, they were allowed to purchase Wachovia and also receive one of the biggest bailouts of any bank—$45 billion.

Billions in TARP funds were given to the banks with some of the worst loan performance, but that didn't stop the Wall Street bonuses. The top nine firms received nearly $200 billion in taxpayer TARP funds, and within days paid out $32.6 billion in bonuses. Even though bank profits in the fourth quarter were down 94 percent from the previous year, the bonuses still rolled in. In 2008, 1,626 JPMorgan Chase employees received bonuses of more than $1 million; at Goldman Sachs, 953 execs received bonuses of more than $1 million, and 212 received bonuses of more than $3 million. The near bankrupt Merrill Lynch paid the top 149 execs $858 million. Citigroup, who had the worst loan performance in the world still gave multimillion-dollar plus bonuses to 738 execs.[177]

After the crisis, Dimon sent Paulson a quote from one of President Teddy Roosevelt's speeches to comfort Paulson after all his hard work. "It is not the critic who counts; not the man who points out how the strong man stumbles or where the doer of deeds could have done better. The credit belongs to the man who is actually in the arena." In other words, "Thanks, Hank, for everything you have given me!"[178]

But let's not kid ourselves. The men and women who were actually in the arena fighting hard were the thousands of employees in the community banks fighting to save their banks, the millions of small business owners who struggled to survive, and the millions of Americans who lost their jobs and their homes. The millions of main street Americans that Wall Street, Congress, and the federal government barely saw the need to protect.

The FDIC released its third-quarter 2008 banking profile:

> Quarterly earnings were only $1.7 billion, down 94 percent from last year. Net charge-offs of $27.5 billion were up 156.4 percent; noncurrent loans rose to 2.31 percent of total loans. Nine banks failed in the quarter.

The Dow Jones Industrial Average fell below ten thousand for the first time since 2004. Four of the five of the largest unregulated US investment banks, which had securitized the worst of the unregulated subprime loans were bailed out by the government. The GSEs, which had been woefully undercapitalized and directly owned or guaranteed nearly $5 trillion in mortgage obligations, had to be put into conservatorship. The US had now lost over six million jobs since the crisis began in 2007.[179]

On October 15, federal investigators opened an investigation into the seizure of Washington Mutual. They set up a task force that included investigators from the FBI, the US Securities and Exchange Commission, the FDIC, and the IRS criminal investigations unit.[180] We were hoping they would be investigating the stunning and unwarranted seizure of the bank. We never heard another thing about this task force.

In October, Kerry was receiving a number of calls from attorneys around the country who wanted to represent him in the bank's leftover lawsuits and the bankruptcy settlement. Although there were many impressive attorneys who wanted to work with him, the choice was easy for Kerry. He picked who he thought was not only the most brilliant, but who also displayed the Washington Mutual ethics of integrity, hard work, and caring—Barry Kaplan of Wilson Sonsini in Seattle. Even though Linda rarely was at the bank and never got involved in Washington Mutual's business, Kerry asked her to attend all the attorney meetings because of her extensive past experience in banking. We had no idea these intensive, days on end meetings would last for six more years.

On November 8, we flew to Des Moines, Iowa, to attend our charitable foundation's annual Veteran's Day concert at the downtown Civic Center. Kerry's father, Karl, had founded the hundred-piece Iowa Military Veterans Band in 1996. The concert was free, and over three thousand people attended, including Iowa senator Charles Grassley. We were thrilled the concert was in honor of Karl's career, and a short film was produced to highlight Karl's contributions to music.

We enjoyed the time to connect and relax with family, friends, and neighbors, but we also had another meeting in Des Moines. We had prepared detailed information on the inappropriate seizure of Washington Mutual and set up a meeting with Iowa attorney general Tom Miller, who was our friend and Linda's ex-spouse. Tom had led a group of attorneys general in lawsuits against New Century, Ameriquest, and other shadow subprime banks, and he understood the dynamics in the industry. Tom was one of the few government officials who was trying to get at the real truth of the crisis, and he was intrigued with the information we provided. He asked us to keep him posted on our investigation.

After our meeting with Tom, we went back to Kerry's parents' home and prepared for the Iowa Military Veterans Band concert. Karl had grown weaker as his illness had progressed, so we arranged for him to be backstage in a wheelchair to watch the performance before he went on stage to receive his honors and applause for a long career in performing music for Iowans.

Karl came home that night beaming about another successful concert and opportunity to share music with his fellow Iowans. He fell asleep that night and passed away in the morning surrounded by loving family. We stayed in Des Moines the next few days to help make funeral arrangements for a large gathering of friends, former students, fellow teachers, and musicians, who all came to the funeral to pay tribute. We were heartbroken to see him go but so grateful to have had him in our lives. After the funeral Linda sat in the living room in Kerry's parents' home in Beaverdale and just sobbed. She never cries, but Karl's death tipped her over the limit.

During funeral arrangements, Gretchen Morgenson from the *New York Times* called, saying she was writing a story on Washington Mutual and asked for Kerry's comments. She had several questions with the same tone: "When did you decide to pursue a reckless high-risk lending strategy?"[181] We were hoping the media would pursue the unwarranted seizure of Washington Mutual. But instead, behind the scenes, a new and completely false narrative was being promoted.

When we got back to Seattle, we prepared charts and information regarding actions taken to reduce residential lending and prepare for a housing downturn. None of our carefully prepared data and information were used in the article. Instead, it quoted confidential sources pulled from a plaintiff attorney's shareholder lawsuit. Years later, when those confidential sources were deposed, most of them either denied their quotes in the lawsuit and the media or said they were misquoted. By May of 2009, the federal judge rejected key portions of the lawsuit and called it a "verbose and disordered argument that failed to identify specific claims of fraud. The Court remains mystified at the plaintiff's counsel's failure to allege cohesive claims."[182]

In 2010, the Examiner completed his report on the seizure of Washington Mutual. He said, "The FDIC would not give up any of their documents, although the OTS did." The Examiner said, "The FDIC refused requests to interview Bair and two others with knowledge of the meetings about the bank and they were not fully responsive." The Examiner found it was difficult getting any of the JPMorgan employees to testify, and "their attorneys restricted and prevented much of their testimony." He stated the "FDIC may not have understood the value of the assets it's seized [at WMI] and that Chase may have been the only bidder who knew of or understood the value of the trust preferred securities, pension plans [BOLI/COLI], or the tax refunds which had over $11 billion in value."[183]

He also found JPMorgan Chase and the FDIC from September 22 to 26 negotiated and changed various provisions of the Purchase and Assumption agreement (P&A), even though all bidders were told verbally and in writing that the P&A was not negotiable.[184] He found that "it is highly likely a Court would conclude WM was solvent into the summer of 2008. The Equity Committee found no basis that would substantiate the claim that WM was insolvent when seized."[185]

As 2008 wound to a close, our faith in the US government hit rock bottom. Growing up in the Midwest, we were taught to trust institutions like the church, the government, and regulators. What made our country great were people and institutions working hard, doing the right thing, and treating everyone equitably and fairly. But in the past year, we saw political leaders and regulators refuse to listen to warnings about the economy and monetary policy. We saw regulators fighting to further their own agendas. We saw Treasury execute a capricious plan to eliminate thrifts and community banks and consolidate power in Wall Street. We saw major Wall Street banks shower politicians with multimillion-dollar contributions and get back billions in TARP money. We saw a revolving door of politicians, regulators, and Wall Street executives with mounting conflicts of interest. We saw Washington Mutual inappropriately seized just as lifelines were given to the large Wall Street banks who had substantially worse lending losses.

Washington Mutual simply got caught in the Venn diagram where JPMorgan Chase's hostile takeover plan was accommodated by Treasury's goal of eliminating thrifts and focusing power into Wall Street and the FDIC's desire to do any kind of a deal that didn't touch the FDIC insurance fund. The question is whether these cozy relationships, violations of established protocols, and questionable ethics between an exclusive set of Wall Street insiders and government is good for banking or for business and this country generally. We wondered when Washington, DC, would support a banking system that would serve the average citizen, rather than just Wall Street.

The well-connected large Wall Street banks were "too clubby to fail" and clearly won. Thrifts and community banks trying to serve their communities were the losers. More importantly, the biggest losers were the millions of hardworking people who lost their jobs and homes while the large Wall Street banks received billions. No wonder trust

in government and Congress spiraled down and still remains at rock
bottom today.

Most people think the financial crisis of 2008 was created in the
2000s, however, the crisis, ironically, had its roots in the deregulation
movement in the 1970s and the 1980s. The OPEC oil embargo that
caused gas prices to rise, the escalating costs of the unpopular Vietnam
War, and the Watergate hearings that drained much of the faith in the
federal government and unabated inflation gave birth to a whole new
set of economic theories that believed less government might be better.
The next chapter reveals how the deregulation efforts of the 1980s
paved the way for the excesses of the 2000s.

2

Increased Risk Taking Due to Deregulation

The Early 1980s

In October of 1982, President Reagan strode into the Rose Garden to sign the Garn–St. Germain Act and proudly announced the bill was the "First step in our administration's comprehensive program of financial deregulation" that would "cut savings and loans loose from the tight girdle of old-fashioned restrictive federal regulations." He stated, "For fifty years we relied on S&Ls to finance our homes, but regulations prevented thrifts from competing in the sophisticated financial marketplace of the eighties." He summarized the day by saying, "All in all, I think we hit the jackpot."[1]

Not surprisingly, the survival of the thrift industry was a priority for Reagan. Nine of ten of the largest thrifts in the country were located in California, and the executives had been major contributors to Reagan's political campaigns. The California executives, as key board members of the Federal Home Loan Bank Board (FHLBB), their regulator, controlled nearly one-third of the thrift industry assets and were not shy about demanding Reagan help save them. Their interest rate troubles were rooted in the Faustian bargain of the Banking Act of

1933 (Glass-Steagall Act) that gave banks insured deposits but in return set caps on savings and checking account interest rates for banks and thrifts. When the unregulated money market funds in the 1970s began paying more interest than the banks, millions of people moved their accounts away from regulated banks and thrifts.

During the 1970s, the federal government ran up a large debt from the unpopular and costly Vietnam War. The 1973 OPEC oil embargo caused gas prices to escalate, and the Watergate hearings drained much of the public's trust and faith in the federal government. The result was an extraordinary fifteen-year inflationary spiral. The cost of living rose 186.4 percent (7.3 percent annually) between 1968 and 1983.[2]

In order to cure the inflation of the 1970s, Fed chair Paul Volcker raised the fed funds rate to a peak of 20 percent in 1981. The prime interest rate rose to 21.5 percent, which led to a recession with national unemployment over 10 percent. Some economists posed the idea that people may never be able to buy a home again.[3]

Securitization of the mortgage loans of thrifts was limited in the 1970s, so the thrifts—the primary housing lender in the country— found themselves loaded with low-interest, thirty-year fixed-rate home loans that couldn't cover the cost of consumers demanding higher interest on their deposits. The model of 3-6-3 banking—"take in deposits that pay 3 percent, loan out the money at 6 percent, and get on the golf course by 3:00 p.m." was not working in the inflationary spiral of the seventies. But this economic stagnation was about to change by economists who felt raising the fed funds rate would deter inflation.

The volatility of inflation, the rising demand for civil and human rights, and government ineptness gave birth to new trends in economic thinking around the bloated growth of government and its ineffectiveness in solving our problems. The new economic theories centered around the notion that government was too big and ineffective, so smaller government and the deregulation of industry would produce a more effective economic model.

The concept of deregulation gained momentum out of research from the Chicago School of Economics and think tanks like the Brookings Institute and the American Enterprise Institute, all of which held seminars on the need to decrease government regulation. One of the leaders of the movement was Milton Friedman, who won the 1976 Nobel Memorial Prize in Economic Sciences for his ideas about inflation, the money supply, incomes, and pricing. He was also a proponent of privatization and deregulation.[4]

President Ford (1974–1977), President Carter (1977–1981), and many members of Congress on both sides of the aisle all seemed to be swayed by these new economic theories. Ford was the first to support deregulatory legislation, signing into law the 1976 Railroad Revitalization Act, which gave the railroads more freedom in setting rates and service. Ironically, Democrat Carter signed the greatest number of deregulation bills, including acts relating to the airline, railroad, and motor carrier industries. However, an industry that was in dire need of help from deregulation was the banking industry.

Although the federal government created a national charter for a bank, historically it did not interfere with a state's rights to control its own banking industry. However, during the Civil War, Abraham Lincoln signed the National Bank Act of 1863, which allowed him to finance the war by establishing a national currency and a secondary market to sell war bonds and US Treasury securities. The act also established the Office of the Comptroller of the Currency (OCC) within the Department of the Treasury, which became responsible for the regulation and inspection of the commercial banks. However, between 1863 and 1913, there were still a number of major commercial banking crises.[5]

To attempt to prevent these crises, Congress passed the Federal Reserve Act of 1913, creating the Federal Reserve Board system with twelve banks around the country. The purpose of the system was to promote the health of the US economy, set monetary policy, supervise and regulate financial institutions, promote consumer protection, lend money to the bank members to insure liquidity in the system, and serve as a lender of last resort.[6] This was the first time the federal government had stepped into the financial regulatory business. However, this new system did nothing to prevent the biggest run and panic in the history of the world, the crash of 1929.

Before the 1929 crash, thrifts grew rapidly to an all-time high of 12,500 by 1925, but thousands of thrifts failed with the crash and the Depression that followed, leaving only six thousand thrifts by 1945. Commercial banks suffered a similar fate, dropping from thirty thousand banks before the crash to 13,302 by 1945.[7] None of the thrifts or the commercial banks in 1929 had insured deposits, and many people lost everything. These traumatic losses signaled the beginning of a twelve-year Depression that affected much of the industrialized world and instilled a trait of frugality in this country for decades to come.

Home loans before the crash of 1929 were typically originated for only 50 percent of the value of the property and were repaid within three to five years with a balloon payment at the end.[8] That changed with the creation of the Federal Housing Administration (FHA) in 1934. The FHA insured mortgage loans to qualified homeowners and encouraged thrifts to abandon short-term balloon loans in favor of the more affordable, long-term, fixed-rate mortgages. Before and after the 1929 crash, the thrift system was self-funded with savings accounts and remained a very stable system until the rising interest rates in the late 1970s.[9]

The commercial banking industry in America had a more raucous experience before the Great Depression. Before the crash of 1929, banks experienced dozens of major panics and bank runs. Many believed this was because banks couldn't spread their risk since they were regulated by the states and couldn't branch or grow beyond their borders. They also relied on borrowing funds from larger banks on the East Coast in order to have the liquidity they needed to provide more loans to their communities. For decades following the 1929 crash, both the thrifts and the commercial banks enjoyed a relatively stable period, due to conservative lending and generally growing economic activity.

Commercial banks focused mostly on commercial lending, but they also provided savings and checking accounts for retail and commercial businesses. The vast majority of the fourteen thousand commercial banks of the 1970s were community banks, meaning they were locally owned and operated. Regardless of size, a community bank is one that serves its local community and mostly caters to retail customers and small and medium-size businesses.[10] Presidents of local community banks typically understand the needs of the local farmers, families, and businesses, who depend on the local banks to approve their loans and help the community survive. The hundreds of community bankers that Linda consulted with for over twenty years were typically community leaders who served on the local Chamber board, went to church every Sunday, headed up local fund-raising drives, and deeply cared about the growth and prosperity of their communities. They had completely different goals and values than the Wall Street bankers, who mostly concentrated on larger businesses and extremely wealthy clients. Our experience taught us that historically Wall Street bankers looked down on community bankers as unsophisticated and somewhat irrelevant.

Most states did not allow branch banking or interstate banking, so most of these community banks were landlocked, but this was part of the American principle of states' rights and local control of banking. A principle that, since the founding of this country, had been in conflict with those who felt the need for larger centralized Wall Street commercial banks that could finance war and large corporate growth. History buffs will know this is an ongoing argument in the United States, going back to the days of Jefferson and Hamilton.

The thrifts, on the other hand, had been tasked with only two goals over their 140-year existence: take in deposit money and loan it out for home loans. The first home lender or building association in America, the Oxford Provident Building Association of Frankford, Pennsylvania, was established in 1831, during the presidency of Andrew Jackson. It was formed by a group of textile workers who pooled their money to help each other buy homes. They took this idea from similar organizations formed in England around trade groups. Many of the building associations in America were formed by groups of ethnic immigrants who lived and worked in the same town.[11]

By the end of the 1800s, there were thousands of thrifts, or savings and loan associations, which banded together to form the US League of Local Building and Loan Associations. Their motto was "The American Home: The Safeguard of American Liberties." The home lending function was considered a safe investment; thus, the federal government made no attempt to regulate or centralize their activities.[12] Because of their patriotic mission—which aligned well with the goals of their state legislatures—the US League grew to be a very powerful lobbying force, especially after World War II.

After the shock of the crash of 1929, Congress passed a number of laws to protect both the thrifts and commercial banks. Key among them was the Banking Act of 1933, also known as the Glass-Steagall Act, which created the Federal Deposit Insurance Corporation (FDIC) to insure commercial bank deposits and it also separated commercial and investment banking functions. This separation prevented banks from taking federally insured deposits and gambling them on risky investment banking functions. Section 11 of the act, called Regulation Q, prohibited interest payments on demand deposits (checking accounts) and set interest rate ceilings on savings accounts. One of the purposes of this regulation was to protect the thrifts by setting interest rate caps higher for the thrifts than the banks, so the thrifts could have enough funding for home lending.[13] After all, if the thrifts lost customer savings, it would curtail their ability to lend for mortgages, thereby threatening the "American dream."

In 1932, Congress also created a system similar to the Federal Reserve for the thrifts, called the Federal Home Loan Bank Board (FHLBB), with twelve branches, to provide liquidity and central regulation to the thrift system. It also created the Federal Savings and Loan Insurance Corporation (FSLIC, pronounced "fizz-lick") to insure thrift deposits. Both the thrifts and commercial banks paid a fee to each of their deposit insurers—FSLIC and FDIC—to build a fund to pay depositors up to $40,000 per account if a bank failed. If either insurance fund ran out of money, the taxpayers would be on the hook to pay the rest.[14]

These actions all provided a strong regulatory climate that produced a relatively stable financial system that lasted about forty years. However, the federal deficits and rampant inflation of the 1970s created an unstable environment for the six thousand thrifts that now found their balance sheets filled with low-interest fixed-rate mortgages in a dramatically rising interest-rate market. At the same time, they were also facing increasing competition from unregulated money market funds that could pay substantially more than the capped low interest rates in the bank's deposit accounts. At that time, mortgage securitization was not available to the thrifts, so the thirty-year, low-interest fixed mortgage loans languished on the balance sheets of the thrifts during this highly inflationary period.

The crisis was growing and the politicians were only kicking the can down the road. Congress added to the problem by approving the 1977 Community Reinvestment Act (CRA), which forced banks and thrifts to extend more lending to low-and moderate-income (LMI) neighborhoods. Although the motive to fund more LMI housing was a much-needed and worthy cause, it had many unintended consequences. Title VII of the Act required "the appropriate federal agency to use its authority when examining financial institutions." In other words, if the banks didn't receive a strong CRA rating, they would be fined, sanctioned, or not allowed to merge or grow. The goals inspired an entire industry of consumer groups ready to pressure regulators to sanction banks for not committing to large CRA goals.[15]

Making matters worse, the same year the CRA was passed, Merrill Lynch CEO Donald Regan (later President Ronald Reagan's Treasury secretary) introduced the groundbreaking cash management account (CMA), which brought all of a customer's assets under one account and paid more interest than the commercial banks or thrifts could pay.[16] The CMA combined the traditional brokerage margin account with check-writing and Visa card privileges tied to a money-market mutual fund. This allowed small savers to reap the same percentage returns as wealthy savers—although the money-market funds were not insured by the federal government.

Consumers fled thrifts and banks in droves, moving over to Merrill Lynch and other investment firms to take advantage of the higher interest rates. This reached a crisis by 1980, when it was estimated 85 percent of the thrifts were losing money and the industry was thought to be worth a negative $120 to $150 billion. Both Congress and President Carter thought the thrift industry would collapse by the mid-1980s, and there were no other available options for maintaining home lending if all the thrifts failed.[17]

At the end of 1974 there was $2.4 billion in money-market funds, but by 1980 it had skyrocketed to $76.4 billion. The American Bankers Association became so concerned with this new unregulated competition, it submitted legislation to protect the banks from this drain on funds.[18]

The bankers successfully lobbied Congress to pass legislation, and President Carter signed the Depository Institutions Deregulation and Monetary Control Act of 1980 (DIDMCA), which allowed banks to merge, eliminated interest rate caps over a six-year period (Regulation Q), allowed negotiable order of withdrawal (NOW) accounts, increased FSLIC and FDIC deposit insurance limits from $40,000 to $100,000, and allowed the credit unions and thrifts to offer checking accounts.[19]

In 1980 the FHLBB also implemented a series of actions to help save the failing thrifts. It lowered net worth requirements from 5 percent to 4 percent in November of 1980 and then down to 3 percent in 1982. Now thrifts only needed three dollars of their own money at risk for every $100 of assets, while commercial banks were required to have six dollars for every $100 of assets.[20]

There seemed to be opposing forces in regulating and deregulating the banks. The forces for federalization of the banks were seen in three important congressional acts: the Veterans Act, which centralized the mortgage insurance for veterans; the CRA, which prohibited redlining

and forced more LMI lending throughout the country; and the laws
that allowed Fannie Mae and Freddie Mac to set national standards
for lending. President Carter started the movement to deregulate the
banks and thrifts, and it was only going to increase under President
Reagan, who wanted to release banks from even more of the shackles
of federal control.

Shortly after winning the presidential election in 1980, the Reagan
administration probably read an article in a December issue of *Newsweek*, "The S&Ls in Deep Trouble," and worried about how it was going
to solve a financial crisis it didn't create. Of the four thousand thrifts
in the country at the beginning of the 1980s, the FHLBB estimated
only forty or fifty (about 1 percent) were solvent.[21] Runaway inflation
had driven up mortgage interest rates from 7 percent in 1961 to over
19 percent in 1982.[22] This only made it harder for thrifts to write more
mortgages, and new business stalled.

Reagan believed an entrepreneurial and deregulated thrift industry
would expand economic development and be a tremendous growth
engine in his home state of California. Right after he took office, Reagan created the President's Commission on Housing, which came back
in April 1982 with a 320-page report describing how housing cycles
were becoming more severe and housing subsidies were spiraling out
of control. The report held some disturbing data. The Section 8 rental
subsidy program had quadrupled in just six years, from $61 billion in
1975 to over $250 billion in 1981. The monthly mortgage payment on
a typical new home had doubled from about 20 percent of a median
family budget to nearly 40 percent of the family budget in 1980.[23]

The housing report recommended granting new and expanded
powers for the thrifts and encouraged the private sector to develop
new mortgage products, like adjustable-rate mortgages, that would
protect lenders from interest-rate risk. The committee believed home
financing in this country was on the verge of collapse and deregulation
would save the industry. The report laid the groundwork for the Garn–
St. Germain Depository Institutions Act of 1982 and the Alternative
Mortgage Transaction Parity Act of 1982, which preempted state laws
that required banks make only fixed-rate amortizing loans. The new
Parity Act encouraged the development of adjustable-rate (ARM) loans,
balloon payments and interest-only mortgages.

Option ARMs were critical in states, like California, that were
experiencing stratospheric housing price increases. At a time when

fixed-rate mortgage rates were nearing 19 percent, the ARM, with its adjustable rate, made mortgages more affordable. When they first became available, they helped millions of Americans afford homes, and the default rate on these products was similar to that of thirty-year fixed mortgages, which were no longer practical or safe for a bank to hold in an era of rising interest rates.

Shortly after the Garn Act was signed, the thrifts' FHLBB eagerly loosened more restrictions on the thrifts. It eliminated the requirement for four hundred or more shareholders and allowed a single entrepreneur to own and control an entire thrift. To make it easier for an entrepreneur to buy an existing or new thrift, regulators allowed buyers to capitalize the bank with in-kind contributions of land, stock, and other real estate, regardless of their real value.

The FHLBB also encouraged thrifts to raise their deposit rates to attract "brokered deposits" and removed the 5 percent limit on those deposits, allowing thrifts access to unprecedented amounts of cash. Soon both commercial banks and thrifts were inundated with brokers looking for the best rates on their deposits. This opportunity was so attractive, brokered deposits in thrifts increased 400 percent between 1982 and 1984.

Brokered deposits were developed by unregulated, independent "brokers" who would act as commissioned middlemen collecting large deposits from cash-rich clients like credit unions and pension funds. These clients were cash-rich because of the Employee Retirement Income Security Act of 1974 (ERISA) and other related laws that forced companies to set aside money to fund their pensions. These funds ballooned to $1 trillion by 1979.[24]

The brokers would take the pension and other funds and scour the country looking for the thrifts and banks with the highest interest rates at which to park the deposits. The brokers pocketed the lucrative fees, and the thrifts and banks used the newly found deposits to "invest" in things like oil and gas deals, Nevada brothels, wind farms, and ADC (acquisition, development, and construction) loans, sometimes with no money down.

In addition to brokered deposits, the lightly regulated investment firm of Drexel Burnham Lambert created a hot new product called "junk bonds." These bonds were issued by highly leveraged companies and were rated non-investment grade by the rating agencies. Drexel built a large liquid market for junk bonds, which grew from $6 billion in

1970 to $210 billion by 1989. This made it easier for about 85 percent of American companies to raise money with these lower-rated junk bonds. Junk bonds became popular again at the new millennium, when over $600 billion of new bonds were issued by US corporations from 2003 to 2006.[25]

Thrifts were a prime target for Drexel because thrifts had most of their assets in low-yielding thirty-year home mortgages and they held nearly $1 trillion in federally insured deposits. Drexel told them they could package those home mortgages, sell them to investors, and use the proceeds to buy their higher-yielding junk bonds. The thrifts were, on average, earning 10 percent on their mortgages, but they could earn 15 percent with Drexel.[26] By 1988 almost two hundred thrifts would own $14.4 billion in junk bonds.

The FHLBB also eliminated the existing ten-year amortization requirement on goodwill and allowed the thrifts to use a more generous standard to amortize goodwill over forty years, another tool to disguise their financial position.

The Garn–St. Germain Act also allowed the thrifts to practice "forbearance," a method of overstating the actual net worth of a thrift. The FHLBB through FSLIC would issue government notes that thrifts could count toward their net worth. FSLIC would give them a net worth certificate and would promise to pay cash if the institution were ever liquidated. In exchange, FSLIC would get an IOU. A GAO report revealed that in 1987, 508 thrifts were insolvent, and nearly six hundred were barely solvent. All the troubled thousand-plus thrifts were operating with capital levels below the regulatory 3 percent minimum and were receiving forbearance.[27] At the time, Linda was a partner in an international accounting firm and was more than a little horrified at the accounting tricks used to make the thrifts look good on paper. The new rules were counter to Generally Accepted Accounting Principles (GAAP) and were called Regulatory Accounting Principles—RAP. Her accounting partners quickly morphed the term into "CRAP."

Congress and the Reagan administration felt all the new regulations to accommodate the thrifts would preserve homeownership for the American people. It was a quandary: if too many thrifts failed, the FSLIC deposit insurance wouldn't have the funds to cover the deposits, so the taxpayers would have to cover the rest. But if they could hang on with the help of deregulation and funny accounting, they wouldn't cost the government or taxpayers anything. It was a recipe for disaster; accountants all over the country rolled their eyes in disbelief, and housing advocates celebrated. Congress, on both sides of the aisle, had just socialized the debt of thrifts and privatized their profits.

By the end of 1984, more than one-third of the states had given their thrifts investment powers beyond those of the federally chartered institutions. The Nolan Bill in California made it possible for almost anyone to own a thrift and allowed them to invest in anything they wanted. Texas allowed thrifts to invest their entire net worth in any type of lending product. Ironically, many of these new thrift "entrepreneurs" had no intention of lending out money for low-income housing or even regular mortgages. The new entrepreneurial nonbankers preferred the high-risk, high-return industrial and commercial projects.

President Reagan and Congress had the best of intentions when they followed the economic thinking that deregulation of the financial industry would provide a growth engine for the economy. They did not realize, however, that deregulation still required government oversight. Within just a couple of years, there were hundreds of new thrift charters that took their federally insured deposits and invested in casinos, fast food restaurants, ski resorts, brothels, and windmill farms. They populated their balance sheets with junk bonds, arbitrage schemes, and brokered deposits. Most of the assets were used for investments in acquisition, development, and construction loans for apartment buildings, shopping malls, and other commercial developments, with no down payment required. Many of the states, like California, Texas, Oklahoma, Nevada, and others, essentially had created an unregulated shadow banking system. Some of the thrifts were run well by experienced bankers, but many of the new thrifts were run by nonbanker entrepreneurs who thrived on taking big risks.

It wasn't just the thrifts that had a tough time in the 1980s. Between 1984 and 1995, more than five thousand commercial banks insured by the FDIC were closed or merged.[28] By early 1985, the FDIC had 901 commercial banks under special scrutiny, the OCC had 793, and the Federal Reserve wouldn't release its data. Analysts suggested about eighty-one hundred lenders were in fragile condition.[29]

Many of the larger commercial banks were caught in the great wave of new gas and oil drilling projects in Texas and Oklahoma. The new drilling was inspired by the 1973 Arab oil embargo and this country's patriotic response to release itself from the dangerous reliance on OPEC oil. The commercial bank at the apex of the 1980s gas and oil lending was an Oklahoma City bank called Penn Square. Engulfed in the gas and oil fever, Penn Square made hundreds of poorly under-written energy-related loans it sold not only to the eastern banks of Continental, Chase, and Citibank, but also smaller banks like Seattle's First National Bank, Michigan National Bank, and others. Many of the banks, including Continental, used brokered deposits to purchase the gas and oil loans.

Penn Square was the first of 139 Oklahoma banks that failed in the eighties. The final investigation by the FDIC uncovered 451 possible criminal violations in the bank, and the bank's energy lending chief received a two-year prison term.[30]

Continental Illinois National Bank and Trust Company of Chicago, one of Penn Square's top clients, had to write off about $500 million in loans purchased from Penn Square. Continental soon became the larg-est bank failure in US history when a run on the bank led to its seizure by the FDIC. However, because of its size, the FDIC was not willing to let it fail and covered all the deposit accounts and bondholders and infused $4.5 billion to rescue the bank.[31]

Continental had been overly aggressive in its gas and oil lending because Illinois law was particularly punitive if a bank wanted to grow. The state did not allow banks to have branches, and they had a usury ceiling for consumer loans. The Illinois laws were one of the most re-pressive in the nation for consumer lending if a bank wanted to grow, but it allowed investments in any kind of commercial loans at any rate. Chase Manhattan and Continental were also not permitted to have branches that could funnel in customer deposits, so they were forced to purchase most of their funds through money markets, with increas-ingly higher rates of interest. They also relied on short-term borrowing in fed funds and the repo markets, rolling over more than $8 billion every night. They were committing one of banking's riskiest bets: bor-rowing short and lending long.

When the regulators swooped in to clean up the Penn Square mess, they found evidence of loans secured by the same collateral or no collateral, evidence of falsified financial statements, altered notes, and phony credit files. The FBI announced an investigation into charges of misapplication and embezzlement of funds by a bank officer and allegations borrowers made false statements in order to obtain funds.[32]

At the congressional hearings on the Continental failure, Todd Conover, comptroller of the OCC, gave shocking testimony. In an unprecedented acknowledgment of the special place of big banks in the financial system, he said the eleven largest US banks would never be allowed to fail. He stated, "Such decisions should not depend on the whims of the FDIC or the OCC and the pressures of the moment. This rationalization of an inequitable arrangement is likely to take the form of changes in the deposit insurance system where shaky institutions pay more for deposit coverage."[33] It was here the term "too big to fail" was coined.[34]

As the financial system was roiling in turbulence in the early 1980s, we both found ourselves in the banking industry. Linda became a consulting partner in an international accounting firm and quickly grew a business developing strategic plans for commercial banks and thrifts. As the banks and the thrifts failed in the 1980s and early 1990s, the regulators would call her in to develop a strategic plan for troubled institutions. She was in the thick of it, traveling to Oklahoma, Texas, and California and working with bankers to plan a way out of the mess. She learned the protocols of the regulators and understood what constituted a crime.

In 1982, Kerry was an executive vice president and on the board of directors for both the securities broker-dealer Murphey Favre, established in 1888, and the mutual fund management company, Composite Research. The Composite Group of Funds grew rapidly in the late seventies and early eighties, because their money-market mutual funds offered excellent customer service and significantly higher returns than traditional bank deposits. Murphey Favre's president, Lee Sahlin, was a wonderful person with impeccable integrity. He recruited Kerry to manage the mutual funds and chart a growth strategy for the company. Sahlin reported, "In just two and a half years, Kerry helped increase the Composite Group of Mutual Funds from $40 million to $350 million."[35]

At a time when other banks and thrifts were thinking of ways to scam the new financial regulatory environment, Kerry was quietly envisioning the benefits of combining the great products and service of a securities firm with the customer base and capital of a bank. He was looking to merge Murphey Favre with a commercial bank; however, banks were not allowed to buy a broker-dealer or a mutual fund company. His companies were similarly not allowed to buy a commercial bank or a thrift. However, Kerry discovered a provision in Washington State mutual savings bank law that permitted a Washington-chartered savings bank, like Washington Mutual, to acquire a full-service securities and mutual fund management company. In the state of Washington, state savings banks were not thrifts, so they were not part of the FHLBB system and were not insured by FSLIC. Instead, they were regulated by the state and the FDIC, and the deposits were insured by the FDIC.

Kerry studied a number of options and finally contacted Washington Mutual, a financially ailing savings bank in Seattle.[36] Washington Mutual not only suffered from overexposure to thirty-year fixed-rate mortgages, but it also had an unusually large number of nonperforming commercial real estate loans and was losing tens of millions of dollars each year.

Washington Mutual was created after the devastating Seattle fire of 1889, when local businessmen got together and formed the first mutual savings bank west of the Mississippi River and named it the Washington National Building and Loan Investment Association. In February of 1890, the bank made the first installment loan on the Pacific Coast, a $700 loan to a local seaman. The loan was one of the first installment loans, which let the borrower pay in equal monthly installments for seventy-two months, with each payment lowering the balance on which interest was charged. Throughout the years, the bank honored every withdrawal request and paid interest on every deposit, even through the crash of 1929 and the Depression. It launched its first school savings program in 1923. In the next few decades, Washington Mutual led the quiet life of a hometown savings bank.[37]

By 1982 Washington Mutual had about twenty branches clustered around Seattle and eastern Washington. It offered checking and bill-paying services, school savings accounts, student loans, fixed-rate mortgages, mobile home loans, home improvement loans, fixed and variable rate auto loans, and commercial loans.

However, after nearly a century of quiet and productive work, the fabric of Washington Mutual had unraveled by 1982, when the bank became mired in an extensive portfolio of nonperforming commercial real estate loans. Its nonperforming loans had reached over 3 percent of assets with no end in sight. Washington Mutual's 1981 net loss for the year was $32,222,000, and the net loss for 1982 turned out to be $25,645,000. These losses were substantial for a small savings bank with only a couple of billion in assets.[38]

The bank's regulator, the FDIC, informed the board the bank was on their "watch list" and would probably be seized within eighteen months. Under these threats, the board asked CEO Lou Pepper to either find a buyer or develop a plan to return the company to profitability. There were no buyers on the horizon, so Kerry's call to Lou Pepper about merging and creating a new company offering a full range of financial services was well timed and well received.

Kerry's proposal outlined how an acquisition of Murphey Favre and a focused plan to reduce problem assets, lower operating costs, and conversion to a stock company could bring the bank to profitability in a matter of months. New capital from the public offering and the natural growth of Murphey Favre could finance new branch growth and small and careful acquisitions. The board liked the plan and immediately agreed to the proposal; however, Kerry was a very cautious investor. The bank's financial condition was so precarious, Kerry required Washington Mutual to set up a trust account funded with seasoned performing mortgage loans. The trust would pay out to Murphey Favre and Composite Research's shareholders if Washington Mutual declared bankruptcy.[39]

On April 21, 1982, Washington Mutual became the first bank in the nation to own a full-service securities brokerage and investment advisory firm. The merger took place several months before Reagan's Garn–St. Germain Act, so the combination of this type of merger was untested. Not surprisingly the banking trade groups and the Securities Industry Association filed lawsuits challenging the transaction on the basis of Glass-Steagall violations. It was quickly resolved—the transaction was legal. States' rights prevailed. The suits were dismissed, and the petitions withdrawn.[40]

The media were mystified by this first-in-the-nation transaction. *The Seattle Times* wrote, "The coupling is a bit odd. Here is Washington Mutual, bathed in red ink, buying out the moneymaking Murphey Favre."[41] The *Donoghue Money Fund Report* called the transaction a "fascinating development," but it didn't understand why "a successful money fund would put its fate in the hands of a weak thrift."[42]

The Seattle Post-Intelligencer stated, "Washington Mutual has assets of $2.6 billion and deposits of $1.8 billion in about 400,000 accounts as of March 31. Killinger said he had been approached by a number of firms for a merger, but he wanted to join with a bank to cross-sell products. Murphey Favre would be an independent subsidiary of the bank."[43] Another local paper questioned the health of the transaction, because, "Washington Mutual had been plagued by losses for several quarters because of bad quality loans."[44]

Kerry and the management team got right to work implementing the turnaround plan. They immediately established licensed investment professionals in the branch offices, started a plan of cross-selling products to the customers, and then executed the plan to convert the mutual savings bank to a stock savings bank. The stock conversion was a shrewd and unusual move that resulted in the largest mutual savings bank conversion in the history of the country. Washington Mutual changed from being a mutual-owned company (owned by account holders) into an investor-owned company. In the following years, there would be hundreds of mutually owned insurance companies, financial organizations, banks, and thrifts that would follow Washington Mutual's lead and change to stock ownership in order to monetize and grow their business. Back in Iowa, Linda had heard of Kerry's success and actually helped a number of her clients make this conversion.

On March 11, 1983, the bank's conversion was complete, and on August 9, 1983, Washington Mutual's common stock was quoted on the NASDAQ National Market System under the symbol WAMU. This meant securities dealers throughout the nation could now report every transaction in the stock within ninety seconds of execution.

By August 1983, shortly after the first anniversary of the merger, Murphey Favre, the wholly owned subsidiary, had established investment professionals in most of the Washington Mutual branches. The *Seattle Times* wrote that after one year, the "Murphey Favre division had turned around Washington Mutual from a $8.2 million second-quarter loss in 1982 to a $4.9 million second-quarter gain in 1983. After one year, assets were up 19%, deposits were up 15% and loan production had tripled. Net worth went from $144 million in capital to $185 million."[45]

Kerry announced to the staff that a year ago there were only thirty-four investment officers in Murphey Favre, but now there were seventy. Their star product, the Composite Tax-Exempt Bond Fund, increased from $3 million in assets in 1982 to $65 million in 1983. The bank's stock market value doubled from $20 million to $45 million in a year.[46]

Throughout 1985 and 1986, Kerry and the team continued to execute the plan to turn around and grow Washington Mutual. The bank purchased Lincoln Mutual Savings Bank of Spokane, Washington, through the first merger/stock conversion involving an FDIC-insured bank. The bank also issued $60 million in Washington Mutual subordinated capital notes and acquired Benefit Service Corporation, a pension administration and consulting firm.

On February 14, 1986, Washington Mutual paid its first quarterly cash dividend of ten cents per share on its common stock. On July 1, 1986, the board created a three-man Office of the President including Lou Pepper, Kerry, and Lou's nephew Bill Longbrake, who was the CFO. Later that month the team started wholesaling financial services of the Washington Mutual Financial Group to other banks and thrifts across the nation, and on August 15, 1986, it issued its first stock dividend—a fifty-cent stock dividend in addition to the regular cash dividend of ten cents per share. Later that year the company sold and leased back sixteen financial centers through a limited partnership, offered and managed by Murphey Favre Properties Inc., and purchased Mutual Travel, making it the third-largest travel agency in the Pacific Northwest. It also acquired one of Oregon's largest independent securities brokerage firms, and Washington Mutual Life introduced Investor's Annuity, a flexible premium annuity.

A February 1986 *Seattle Times* article told the story of Washington Mutual's success in becoming the third-largest financial institution in the state of Washington. "A few years ago, it was hit with huge losses first from high interest rates and later from bad real estate loans, but now is reporting profit increases worthy of a young technology company. There is so much growth it is rumored to be a takeover target." The bank was "the largest mortgage lender in the state surpassing other giant banks of Seafirst and Rainier. Bad loans declined to 1.57% of assets down from 2.02% last December 31, and 2.95% at the end of 1985. The problem loans that existed when Kerry joined the bank in 1982 had been a drain on profits, and Kerry was not at all satisfied with where they were, but he was confident he could get the losses below 1%."[47] By March 31, 1986,

Washington Mutual had assets of $4.1 billion, and the profit in the last four quarters was $23.9 million.[48]

In December of that year, the *Seattle PI* quoted an Oppenheimer and Company stock analyst in New York as saying, "Washington Mutual, by offering brokerage, travel, insurance, and investment services as well as traditional banking, may become the prototype of a [full-service] financial services company. Though the bank was a 'money loser' in 1982 due to long time bad loans, the bank made substantial progress by 1983 and cleaned up many of the bad loans and posted a profit."[49] Paul Sullivan, partner in the Seattle securities firm of Cable Howse, praised the work of Kerry and his team, saying, "They've done a good job of turning the bank around."

In 1987 Washington Mutual Life, the bank's life insurance company, acquired Empire Life with a license to conduct business in twenty-three states and opened the first out-of-state mortgage lending office in Coeur d'Alene, Idaho.[50] In November of that year, *Bottomline* magazine summarized the reasons for Washington Mutual's success:

> To become profitable again, the bank decided to base its business on a service and sales-oriented strategy that would put the customer's needs first. They first adopted this approach in 1982 when they acquired Murphey Favre. Since 1982 registered investment staff grew from 25 to 150 and funds under management has grown from $350 million to $650 million. They have acquired banks including Shoreline Savings and Columbia Federal and will have a total of 76 financial centers in Washington. Because of this success there are rumors of a buyout. Rumored buyers include Citicorp and First Bank Systems.[51]

The Seattle Times weighed in: "1986 profits of $70.7 million were four times the previous year's net income of $18.9 million. Washington Mutual is building a national reputation for doing that very, very well [attention to customers' needs] and that is the important part of the story."[52]

In early 1989, Kerry was named president and joined the Washington Mutual board. He was thirty-nine years old, and the bank had $6.2 billion of assets and operated seventy-four financial centers statewide. Under a succession plan developed by the board, Kerry would become CEO in 1990 and chair of the board in 1991.

In a *Tacoma News Tribune* article in 1989, Kerry's goals for the company were clarified: "When the board of directors appointed Kerry as president of the entire bank in 1989, he started to articulate his clear message for the company he repeated often: expand the branch offices when appropriate and shut down low-profit branches and businesses."[53]

In his first year as president, Kerry a developed a new five-year plan with an eye toward the future, which scrutinized the profitability and the customer need for every service in the company and eliminated those products that did not meet his stringent tests. Many CEOs have a hard time changing, eliminating, or reevaluating products, but Kerry believed that an organization needed to be reinvented every five years in order to meet changing customer needs.

In a *Seattle PI* article, Kerry stated he was going to streamline the "high costs of too many [product lines]. The cost to support that complexity is fairly high and he was aiming for a ROA [return on assets] of 1%. Hitting this 1% would make Washington Mutual one of the best run banks in the country and with its asset base would produce [annual] profits of $64 million." Kerry was not sentimental about any of the product lines of Washington Mutual or Murphey Favre—if they couldn't meet the profitability, customer service, and growth goals, they would be eliminated.[54]

Kerry had a long history of dramatically pulling back on business when economic conditions or customer needs changed. This would ultimately serve him well in 2003–2007, when he saw the housing crisis coming and dropped mortgage lending faster and further than any other large bank.

An article from the *Seattle Times* in 1989 stated despite the declining economy, "The bank has 2,000 employees, $3.9 billion in deposits, $6.4 billion in assets, and 1988 profits of $38.6 million."[55] In the March 1990 issue of the company newspaper, Kerry outlined nine target areas for the company: "Expand loan originations to $1.7 billion, increase deposits and investment product sales by concentrating on cross-selling and cooperation among members, increase annuity sales to $110 million and Composite Group assets by $30 million, continue to build net interest income by increasing our percentage of retail assets like lending, and decrease the percentage of wholesale assets such as investment securities. This focus will take advantage of our strong local economy and reduce

our exposure to a slowing national economy. It will allow us to operate more efficiently."

But even more important than the financial goals was Kerry's focus on
customer and employee satisfaction. During the 1980s, he often shared:

> We are going to develop a uniform look for retail and reinforce
> excellent customer service as our trademark in advertising and po-
> sitioning. We are going to continue to develop our most important
> asset, our people, by establishing an employee recognition program,
> by broadening the racial and cultural diversity of our employees
> and by introducing an employee stock purchase program.[56]

As soon as he became president of the bank, Kerry wrote and
implemented a new mission statement and a set of corporate values.[57]
The mission of the bank was to create a premier financial services
company by offering the best possible products with outstanding customer service. The set of corporate values emphasized absolute honesty and integrity and demonstrating fairness and respect for everyone.
The bank's success would be measured by a balanced scorecard of
returns for shareholders, growth, customer satisfaction, opportunities
for employees and contributions back to the communities it served.
Before it was popular, Kerry insisted the bank cater to the needs of all
stakeholders, not just making more money for the stockholders. He
insisted employee needs, customer needs, and community needs be
equally important.

In 1990, *The Journal of American Business* announced Kerry became CEO in addition to president of the bank, and the bank had
written $1.3 billion worth of mortgages, up 67 percent from the year
before. Bruce Harting, an analyst for Salomon Brothers in New York,
said, "Washington Mutual will be an exciting pure play on the Pacific
Northwest in the 1990s. It's one of the few hometown companies in a
hometown that is roaring."[58]

Kerry also continued to do his trademark tours of the field, visiting
and talking with employees, customers, and community leaders about
his vision of friendly and convenient full-service financial centers with
good value and honest dealings. He was also hard at work asking everyone for input, ideas, and feedback. He always encouraged employees
to challenge his thinking and bring him the bad news. Throughout

his career at the bank, he continued every year to talk with tens of thousands of employees, customers, and community leaders to pick up any feedback he could. As usual he did a number of talks in towns in his service area, including one reported in the Wenatchee Apple Seed Rotary Club newsletter, which reported Kerry's test for any investment, acquisition, or product offering: "Is it the truth? Is it fair to all concerned? Will it build goodwill and better friendship? Will it be beneficial to all concerned?"[59] Words he continued to live by.

At the same time in the late 1980s, when the government was shutting down hundreds of banks and thrifts, and the FBI and DOJ were indicting hundreds of executives for crimes of embezzlement, theft, forging documents, and flipping loans, Washington Mutual was creating a growing, profitable business providing excellent products with integrity and superior service to its customers.

Presidents Ford, Carter, and Reagan and the members of Congress had good intentions when they celebrated the 1982 Garn–St. Germain Act and other deregulation efforts. They had hoped in an era of dramatic federal deficits, inflationary spiral, and turbulent protests, the deregulation attempts would fuel a growing economy, but it didn't work. Instead of building a strong economy, they built an environment that created a large, unregulated shadow financial system that created junk bonds, brokered deposits, and other instruments that found a home primarily in the newly deregulated thrifts in the states like California, Texas, Nevada and Oklahoma.

The long-overdue meltdown occurred in a four-month period from February to May in 1989, when FSLIC, the thrift deposit insurer, took control of over two hundred thrifts. On August 9, 1989, Congress finally passed the Financial Institutions Reform, Recovery, and Enforcement Act (FIRREA), which increased thrift capital requirements, raised premiums on the deposit insurance, dissolved the FHLBB and replaced it with the Federal Housing Finance Board (FHFB), an independent monitor to oversee the twelve regional Federal Home Loan Banks. The Federal Home Loan Bank system was no longer involved in regulatory issues, but it provided a system of liquidity for the twelve Federal Home Loan Bank regions across the country—much like the Federal Reserve provided for commercial banks.

The Office of Thrift Supervision (OTS) was created under the Treasury Department as the new independent federal regulator for all the thrifts. The FHLBB and the FSLIC were abolished and the OTS became responsible for the supervision, examination, and chartering of the thrifts. This time the thrift presidents would not be their own regulators. The FDIC would now provide deposit insurance to all the thrifts. Because of the acquisitions of a couple of federally chartered thrifts, Kerry was required to add the newly formed OTS as a regulator. The FDIC, OTS, and the Washington State Department of Financial Institutions all subsequently regulated Washington Mutual.

Over the next eighteen years, Kerry would include the FDIC and the OTS in the development of strategic and operating plans and the review of the progress in the quarterly reports to the regulators. Every year the FDIC and the OTS made joint presentations of examinations findings to the Washington Mutual board.

In an overreaction to the overzealous investments in corrupt commercial projects of some of the thrifts, FIRREA forced thrifts to invest at least 65 percent of their assets in home mortgages and other consumer loans. It also required thrifts to increase their capital ratios to 6 percent, and placed limits on how much a thrift could lend to one borrower.[60]

FIRREA also gave both Freddie Mac and Fannie Mae additional responsibilities to support mortgages for LMI families. Government regulators (OTS and OCC) were required to issue Community Reinvestment Act (CRA) ratings publicly and conduct written performance evaluations using facts and data to support the agencies' conclusions. CRA also required a four-tiered exam rating system with performance levels of outstanding, satisfactory, needs to improve, or substantial noncompliance. This exam system increased the pressure on banks to make more mortgage home loans to inner city and rural areas and ignore the 1934 "redlining laws."[61] It soon became very difficult for a bank or thrift to merge or acquire other banks or even avoid fines, unless it acceded to the demands of consumer groups and regulators and make multimillion-dollar commitments to much riskier and often unprofitable lending. (See the growth of CRA commitments on chart 4-1.)

FIRREA also created the Resolution Trust Corporation (RTC) to sweep up all the failed thrifts and auction off their assets, which turned into a $400 billion portfolio of more than three hundred thousand properties. The boondoggle fire sale of the properties turned out to be a gold mine for speculative investors and provided inspiration for the bottom-feeders that existed in the 2008 crisis.[62]

As the regulators investigated the carnage of the thrift crisis, thousands of criminal referrals were made to the FBI and the Department of Justice. They investigated financial crimes: insider loans, illegal transfers of funds to insiders, excessive compensation, the bogus sale of bad loans to get them off the books, trading phony loans to increase their value, kickbacks, and falsifying documents. They found plenty.

The media at the time was giddy with stories about hundreds of thrift executives who brazenly plundered millions from their thrifts and engaged in unbelievable schemes of cash for trash, daisy chains, land flips, kickbacks, and falsification of documents. A cottage industry of dozens of books appeared on the adventures of the S&L bandits.

It was easy to blame the thrift owners, because so many of their acts were obviously criminal. However, as the dust settled, many of the economists and historians also appropriately blamed Congress and government policy that kept the troubled thrifts open, hid their insolvency, enacted legislation that encouraged risky investments, and then failed to implement adequate oversight.[63]

During the early 1990s, the RTC was still shutting down and selling off assets of hundreds of thrifts around the country and there were a lot of bargains. Both the thrifts and the commercial banks were in a rapidly consolidating industry. From 1934 until fifty years later in the mid-1980s, commercial banks had consistently numbered about fourteen thousand, but by 2000, the number of banks had dwindled to 8,315.[64]

Kerry rejected most of the offers to buy these bargain thrifts and banks on the market—he did not want to get involved with troubled institutions. He was disciplined and held tough with his requirements for the acquisitions: they had to be accretive to earnings in less than a year, have the same type of corporate culture and values, a very low rate of nonperforming loans, a disciplined risk culture, similar product lines, and at least a 15 percent internal rate of return. After merging with Washington Mutual in 1982, Kerry had learned his lesson about how hard it was to get rid of nonperforming loans and he was going to do everything he could to avoid that in the future.

In the eight years between 1988 and 1996, Washington Mutual, on the average, completed two small acquisitions each year. Most had only two or three hundred million in assets and nearly all of them were within a couple of hundred miles of Seattle. The acquisition and integration teams were tough and experienced and were able to successfully integrate these acquisitions within a few months. The acquisitions combined with internal growth provided a conservative and well-planned growth to $21.6 billion of assets by 1995.[65]

The crisis in the 1980s not only affected thousands of banks and thrifts, but more importantly hurt the US economy and employment. From 1986 to 1991, new home construction fell from 1.8 million to one million, the lowest rate of new home construction since WWII.[66] There was a dramatic rise in unemployment, seven thousand banks and thrifts either failed or were merged, and the economy struggled. At the end of the thrift crisis, it was determined the cost to taxpayers was over $160 billion.[67]

Twenty-five years later, the Mises Institute studied the 1980s crisis and noted, "Many scholars seemed to uncritically parrot the simplistic explanations of the debacle posited by non-economist reporters, journalists and political leaders, who have self-serving motivations for their opinions. The causes of the market collapse will be an examination of the catalytic role a coalition of special interests played in successfully lobbying for public policies that changed the structure of the S&L industry. The new industry structure, which proved to be unstable, was the major cause of the debacle. Thrift lobbyists were more influential than any other industry."[68]

Robert Litan, a Brookings Institute economist and member of the FIRREA Commission, blamed excessive risk taking and abstract forces for the collapse of the Texas economy after the crisis. He claimed, "The emphasis on fraud and criminal prosecution is a cover-up that panders to the anger of the American people. The real causes are fundamental and far more frightening. This wasn't a bank robbery—it was a fundamental economic failure of the financial system."[69]

3

Deregulation, Politics, and Criminal Prosecutions

The Late 1980s

In the midst of the 1980s deregulation movement, *BusinessWeek* magazine caught the zeitgeist of the era in an article entitled "Casino Society":

> Start an S&L, offer a premium interest rate and watch the deposits roll in. Your depositors are insured by Uncle Sam, so they don't care what you do with your money. You can pile $100 of assets on every $3 of capital and you've built a speculator's dream machine.[1]

Many of the states like California, Texas, Nevada, and other states had essentially created an unregulated shadow banking system around their thrift deregulation. This large group of nearly unregulated thrifts, combined with the billions of unregulated junk bonds and brokered deposits, created this country's first massive unregulated shadow banking system. This was the precursor to the new unregulated shadow subprime system, created in the early 2000s, that would spawn trillions of dollars of defaulting collateralized debt obligations and credit default swaps.

We had both lived through the 1980s banking crisis and understood the rampant crime that existed in a few of the new deregulated states. The decade of deregulation started when President Reagan and Congress celebrated the Garn–St. Germain Act, and proclaimed the bill would "cut savings and loans loose from the tight girdle of old-fashioned restrictive federal regulations."[2] Within three or four years, the federal government was already arresting the new wave of bankers who had been cut free from their tight girdle of regulations but were now confined in a tight girdle of handcuffs.

Aiding and abetting the deregulated banks in the 1980s was an unregulated shadow banking system of junk bonds and brokered deposits that gave nearly unlimited liquidity to commercial banks as well as thrifts. It was this unregulated stash of funds that inspired hundreds of banks and thrifts to leverage these funds into risky projects like gas and oil loans, condo deals, and Nevada brothels, that they hoped would produce higher returns than conservative mortgage lending.

As we stated in Chapter Two, Linda was a consulting partner in a large international accounting firm in the 1980s and 1990s and was called in by the regulators to develop strategic plans for failing banks or thrifts. She accepted her assignments and traveled to the heart of the crisis—California, Texas, Oklahoma, Nevada, and occasionally the Midwest—and stared into the faces of bankers who were losing their banks. It was heartbreaking and frightening. She was there when the regulators took over banks. She was there when one bank president was kidnapped and held for ransom. She was there when bankers lost banks that had been in the family and the community for generations. She was shocked when she discovered one of her clients was keeping two sets of books. She saw bankers hauled away in handcuffs. She knew a bank president who was murdered by a desperate Iowa farmer who thought he was losing his family farm.

If crimes were discovered, the regulators would quickly take control and attempt to sell the remaining assets. Otherwise a plan was developed, and regulators allowed the financial institutions to attempt to implement their plans. Linda found that most of the time the goal for the regulators was to do everything they could to save community banks that were not consumed with malfeasance. Her experience was that most of her bank and thrift clients were run by honest, experienced bankers who were victims of the times, but there were a number of the new non-bankers who were there to take advantage of the unregulated shadow thrift system that was cropping up in the highly deregulated states.

Most of the time criminal activities in the 1980s involved banks who were overly involved with brokered deposits, junk bonds, risky land deals, self-dealing in construction projects, and outright fraud.

The federal bank fraud statutes at the time identified the major types of crimes that would be punished, including kickbacks and bribes (18 USC Section 215); theft, embezzlement, or misapplication of funds (18 USC Section 656); schemes or artifices to defraud (18 USC Section 1344); knowingly or willfully falsifying or concealing material facts or making false statements (USC Section 1001); false entries in bank documents with intent to injure or defraud bank regulators or examiners (USC Section 1005); aiding and abetting and conspiracy (18 USC Section 2371).[3]

We read dozens of books and studies about the S&L crisis but only found one independent research study on crime statistics about the crisis: a 1997 study, "The Savings and Loan Debacle, Financial Crimes and the State," led by researchers Kitty Calavita, Robert Tillman, and Henry Pontell. The authors gathered a group of researchers and criminologists who studied the Resolution Trust (RTC) data on criminal referrals and also the criminal referral data from the Dallas Office of Thrift Supervision in the state of Texas.

The researchers selected a 20 percent random sample from the 1,210 criminal referrals filed between January 1985 and March 1993 in Texas. Of the 241 cases they studied, 193 involved insider fraud, which was consistent with the data the RTC collected. The most common forms of fraud were insider loans, self-dealing, and false documentation. The researchers found much of the crime in the eighties was "collective embezzlement"—a bank owner actually created the thrift as a vehicle for perpetrating crime.[4]

Chart 3-1 illustrates the number of financial crimes and their losses found in the statistical sample of 241 Texas cases.

Some of the thrift owners of the eighties actually created the organization as a way to "loot" and steal resources from the thrift.

Chart 3-1: Statistical Sampling of
1980s Financial Crimes and Their Losses

Crimes	Number	Mean Losses
Insider Loans	56	$5.7 million
Self-Dealing	50	$3.8 million
False Documentation	37	$10.0 million
Land Flips/Daisy Chains	18	$32.0 million
Siphoning Funds/Kickbacks	21	$0.5 million
Misuse of Funds	11	$15.8 million
Misrepresentation	11	$32.7 million
Diversion of Proceeds	9	$1.1 million
Cash for Trash	7	$21.6 million
Other	21	$4.7 million
241		**$7.28 million mean loss**

However, researchers in this study also thought many members of Congress were willing participants in the heavy lobbying for deregulation from the wealthy CEOs and the powerful US League of Savings and Loans. The following outlines the examples of the crimes committed in the 1980s.

Criminal loans to insiders include the following examples of insider loans, self-dealing, looting, and siphoning funds. Insider loans usually involved loans to executives that they never had to pay back. Self-dealing occurs when an employee benefits at the expense of the customer—like insider trading or using company funds with or without a loan. Siphoning off funds occurs when officers divert thrift funds for their own use. Below are some examples:

Don Dixon of the Dallas-based Vernon S&L used depositors' federally insured money to purchase luxury vacations across Europe and a 112-foot yacht for $2.6 million, where he wooed members of Congress and regulators on extravagant boating parties.[5] The 1982 thrift deregulations had removed the 5 percent limit on brokered deposits, and thrift owners like Dixon now had an almost unlimited source of cash at high interest rates. Officials

charged Dixon used his thrift to funnel money from brokered
deposits into his holding company, Dondi Financial Corporation.
When Vernon was finally taken over in 1987, 96 percent of its
loans were in default. FSLIC filed a $500 million lawsuit against
Dixon and his associates for having illegally transferred more
than $540 million from Vernon S&L. Dixon was sentenced to two
consecutive five-year prison terms.

David Paul bought the CenTrust Savings Bank in Miami in
1983 and quickly turned it into a mega thrift with $9.8 billion
in assets, of which $1.35 billion were junk bonds from Drexel.[6]
He spent over $40 million of CenTrust money to upgrade his $9
million waterfront estate and purchased a $7 million personal
yacht, a $12 million Rubens painting, a sailboat, china, and Bac-
carat crystal.[7] The forty-seventh floor of the $170 million CenTrust
tower had a gold inlay ceiling in his private office. The thrift's
failure cost taxpayers $1.7 billion.[8]

Paul was convicted on ninety-seven counts of federal fraud
charges for racketeering and fraud. In December 1994, he was sentenced to eleven years in prison and ordered to pay $60 million
in restitution and a $5 million fine.[9] The town mayor admitted to
taking $35,000 in bribes to help Paul get permits to expand his
home's deck.[10]

Tom Billman, the CEO of Community S&L in Bethesda,
Maryland, was sued for plundering more than $100 million from
his thrift to prop up his failing real estate companies and add
to his personal wealth. He eluded authorities by leading them
on a four-year international chase, traveling the world using
aliases and fake passports and living off the $22 million he had
squirreled away in Swiss bank accounts. He left his wife and got
a new girlfriend to accompany him on his yacht. He was finally
captured in Paris in 1993 and whisked away to trial, where he was
sentenced to forty years in prison and charged with a $25 million
restitution order.[11]

The CEO of Old Court S&L in Maryland, Jeff Levitt, had his
thrift pay for two of his beach condos, three racehorses, apartments in Baltimore and New York City, and membership in a
Florida country club.[12] He pleaded guilty to theft and misappropriation of bank funds and was sentenced to thirty years in prison

but was released in six years.[13] Before he was CEO at Old Court, he was a notorious Baltimore slumlord, convicted of housing violations over five hundred times.[14] Levitt's actions "sparked so much wrath that a tenant once fired a 12-gauge shotgun blast through his window and sent shards of glass into Levitt's buttock."[15] These previous convictions did not stop his state from giving him an S&L charter. On his way to prison for misappropriation of $14.7 million of federally insured deposit funds, Levitt simply said, "I got carried away."[16]

California-based North American S&L's CEO Duayne Christensen used the thrift to make loans to his own real estate project and make land flips through a real estate company owned by his friend, Janet McKinzie. McKinzie used bank funds to charge hundreds of thousands of dollars of clothes from Neiman Marcus along with a $125,000 gold eagle statue, an $18,500 letter opener, and a $500 solid-gold paper clip. She drove around in a $165,000 Rolls-Royce Corniche, paid for by depositors' funds. The bank also paid for a five-course dinner for several hundred friends with Sammy Davis Jr. providing the entertainment.[17] McKenzie was convicted on twenty-two of twenty-six counts of racketeering, conspiracy, bank fraud, and wire fraud. She pleaded not guilty by reason of insanity, but was found guilty and sentenced to twenty years in prison, and ordered to pay $13.5 million in restitution.[18] Christensen died in a mysterious car crash hours before the bank was seized.

Criminal loans involving outsiders of the bank included cash for trash, daisy chains, land flips, misuse of funds, and kickbacks. Cash for trash involved the sale of bad loans to an outsider in order to remove them from the books and thereby enhance the bank's financial position. Daisy chains involved a network of outsiders who helped each other create phony documents—like selling a loan for more than it's worth over and over down the daisy chain, much like a Ponzi scheme. Land flips involved selling a property back and forth until its value had increased many times over. The property can then be used as collateral for a larger loan. Misuse of funds involved using the bank's money to host personal parties or buying yachts. Kickbacks involved getting money for referring business to a bank. Examples include:

California Lincoln S&L owner Charles Keating loaned $129 million to Southmark S&L, vastly exceeding the amount the bank could lend to one borrower. In return, Southmark loaned Keating $35 million and exchanged about $246 million in existing mortgages, booking $12 million in accounting profits from the swap.[19]

Developer Danny Faulkner and his partners hosted weekend brunches at Wise's Circle Grill with guests including officials from Texas-based Empire S&L, investors, appraisers, and politicians who all exchanged millions of dollars of phony or improperly appraised properties.[20] They also had "daisy chain" events, where lines of loan officers would close a sale of a condo and pass the papers to the next guy, who would close another sale at a higher price. Each guy would get a commission and the last guy could use the inflated loan to borrow more money. It wasn't important if someone actually lived in the condos or even if they were finished. Someone taped the event and sent it to the regulators. When they shut down Empire, the local residents could still see rows of unfinished condos "rotting in the Texas sun." Danny Faulkner, Spencer Blain, and two others were convicted in November 1991 of looting $175 million from five thrifts through fraudulent land deals.[21]

California's Centennial S&L CEO Erwin Hansen and his high-flying financier friend Sid Shah regularly used the land flipping techniques. In one example, they bought and sold one property worth $50,000 back and forth until it reached a market value of $487,000, so they could get a loan based on the inflated value.[22] Sid Shah was found guilty of money laundering. He was later convicted of conspiracy in a drug trafficking ring and sentenced to seven years in prison.

Don Dixon at Vernon S&L, his partner Fast Eddie McBirney at Sunbelt S&L in Dallas, and their friend developer Danny Faulkner used land flips and other schemes to finance hundreds of miles of condos on the I-35 corridor of Dallas. Empire S&L financed the land flips to inflate the value of the land and provide rationale for the condo loans. Dixon was sentenced to two consecutive five-year terms, which were later reduced. Fast Eddie was sentenced to fifteen years in 1993, but he was released on parole after serving less than two years in prison.[23]

Donald Mangano, a real estate developer and John Molinaro, a former carpet salesman, bought the California Romano S&L in April 1994 and spent $25 million—or a quarter of the thrift's assets—to build a Palm Springs condo. They found three men to set up four dummy corporations and sign phony documents indicating those companies bought the condo units for $29 million. The three men then transferred the stock to Mangano, making him the new owner of the condo. They recorded a $4 million profit and had the thrift's Board of Directors issue them a $2 million bonus.[24]

When the FBI arrested Molinaro on his way to the Cayman Islands after the collapse of the thrift, the FBI found his notes: "Consider storing gold in Cayman deposit box...write out a plan for depositing Cayman cash and bring some back thru Canada." The two bandits were charged with looting more than $24 million out of the small thrift.[25]

Mangano and Molinaro each faced more than thirty charges in the US District Court. Molinaro was found guilty on five of thirty-three counts of bank fraud, conspiracy, and cooking the books. He served nearly two years in prison after he tried to obtain a passport in 1986 using the birth certificate of a dead man.

Loan broker Mario Renda was so brazen he advertised in the *Wall Street Journal*, the *New York Times*, and the *Los Angeles Times*—"Money for rent: borrowing obstacles neutralized by having us deposit funds with your local bank: new turnstile approach to financing."[26, 27] Renda would place large brokered deposits in a thrift and receive a finder's fee. In return, borrowers with credit "obstacles" automatically received a generous loan from the thrift. Renda would convince unions and pension funds to deposit with his bank clients, and all the bank had to do was agree to make a few loans to Renda's real estate partnership. Borrowers would receive a fee of 2.5 percent to 6 percent, but when the loan defaulted, they were stuck with the liability.[28]

Renda placed a number of his deposits in Indian Springs State Bank near Kansas City, for which he received a hefty finder's fee. Straw borrowers were paid a kickback, then took out loans from the thrift with proceeds going to Renda's partnership. When he was caught, examiners found two sets of lyrics written by employees: "The Twelve Days of Bilking" and "Bilkers in the Night."[29] Renda placed $6 billion of deposits in thirty-five hundred institutions and was arrested in 1987 and charged with stealing $16 million from two union pension funds.

Charles Knapp, the CEO of Financial Corporation of America in Los Angeles, was indicted on eight counts of conspiracy, false statements, interstate transportation of stolen funds, and money laundering. He inspired his employees through twin "motivations of pride and greed." Earnings of the thrift had to be restated, and Knapp received over six years in prison.[30]

Financial crimes of preparing false documents, misrepresenting customer services, diverting funds, and keeping false books were also common:

> Probably the most famous of the thrift owners was Charles Keating, owner of Lincoln S&L in Los Angeles. His thrift sold uninsured, risky junk bonds originated from his shell corporation, American Continental, to over twenty-three thousand bank clients, right in the bank lobby. The clients, many of them elderly, thought if they were buying something inside a federally insured bank, it would be insured.[31] When the customers would come in to renew a large certificate of deposit (CD, federally insured up to $10,000), they would be told the money would be just as safe and earn more by investing in (uninsured) American Continental junk bonds.
>
> When examiners took over Lincoln S&L, they discovered thousands of documents with forged signatures, fabricated information and shredded original documents.[32] Keating was found guilty of seventeen counts of securities fraud by the California Superior Court and was sentenced to ten years in prison and ordered to pay a fine of $250,000. Handcuffed and disgraced, he performed the coveted perp walk that hundreds of media outlets in 2008 were hoping for. He was released after four years and his federal conviction thrown out because the jury improperly concealed knowledge of his earlier state conviction.[33]

Collateral damage included politicians, accountants, and others who aided and abetted the criminals:

Keating became famous because of the $1 million plus he con-
tributed to five senators, who were later called the Keating Five:
Senators Alan Cranston, John Glenn, John McCain, Donald Riegle,
and Dennis DeConcini. The senators were accused of accepting
money and then trying to inappropriately influence regulators on
Keating's behalf. Senator Alan Cranston (Democrat of California)
wrote a letter to the Federal Home Loan Bank Board in September of 1987 and arranged a meeting with the five senators and the
regulator.

As a result of the meeting, the senators were investigated by
the Senate Ethics Committee. Cranston was under investigation
for two years on charges he intervened improperly with the
FHLBB on Keating's behalf in exchange for nearly $1 million in
contributions. Cranston's letter expressed opposition to a rule that
would have required thrifts to value certain assets at market value.
The rule was opposed by many thrifts, which were holding junk
bonds whose value had plummeted.[34]

The Senate Ethics Committee sought a formal rebuke of
Cranston on the Senate floor, but Cranston avoided the disgrace
by deciding not to run again. A powerful DC attorney, Robert
Bennett, pleaded the case of Senators McCain and Glenn and
cleared their charges.

Representative Tony Coelho, chair of the House Democratic
Campaign Committee, also came under Senate scrutiny for his
close relationship with Don Dixon of Vernon S&L. From 1987 to
1991, Coelho was the House majority whip, but he resigned rather
than face an ethics probe.

During this crisis, the elder Vice President Bush also had his
worries. A judge in Colorado had recommended thrift regulators
issue a cease-and-desist order to Bush's son Neil for his alleged
conflict of interest in his role as a director of the failed Silverado
S&L. Bush had arranged a loan from the bank to a friend, who
in turn, provided Bush with a loan Bush allegedly did not have
to repay. The House Banking Committee grilled Neil Bush
extensively on his dealings as the bank's director and accused him
of engaging in "breaches of his fiduciary duties involving multiple
conflicts of interest." Although Bush was not indicted, the regulators initiated a civil lawsuit that was eventually settled.[35]

No one was safe from the 1980s pillage. By 1990, twenty-one certified public accountants had been sued by the federal government, fourteen of whom were in Big Six firms. In one GAO study of eleven failed thrifts in Texas, six involved negligence on the part of accountants, whom investigators referred for formal actions. Arthur Andersen endorsed the bookkeeping of Charlie Knapp of the Financial Corporation of America. Deloitte, Haskins, and Sells approved David Paul's records at CenTrust in Florida, which were artificially enhanced through a series of round robin stock trades. Touché Ross confirmed the viability of the troubled Beverly Hills S&L.[36]

Arthur Young audited the books of Don Dixon's Vernon Savings and reported no irregularities. It also audited the books of Western S&L, that was later found to have fraudulent land flips. The firms all denied the charges but paid $1.4 billion in fines. Laventhol and Horwath, the seventh-largest accounting firm, failed in 1990, partly because of the lawsuits from failed thrifts.[37]

There were similarities and differences between the thrift crisis of the 1980s and the financial crisis of 2008. The similarities involved a massive shadow unregulated banking system that grew out of control because of lack of supervision by government authorities. Both periods also had large bonuses, bubble thinking, and record asset and debt bubbles. However, the 1980s were different in that most of the troubled thrift executives were not professional bankers, but a conglomerate of high risk–takers, developers, and entrepreneurs who did not understand or ignored the rules of professional banking and committed obvious crimes.

In the financial crisis of 2008, the regulated banks and thrifts were tightly controlled by regulators and nearly all executives were professionally trained bankers who understood the laws and were not going to engage in crimes like flipping loans, cash for trash, and illegal self-dealing. There is no question many, if not most bankers made poor decisions before the 2008 crisis, but criminal activity was rare. This is why there were so few criminal referrals made, despite pressure from Congress and the media for more prosecutions.

As the 1980s rolled on, Kerry was quite appalled by the crimes committed in the banking and thrift industry and wanted to make sure all the executives and board members at Washington Mutual understood the ethics important to the organization. He put together an ethics policy that all the executive officers and board members had to sign every year. Kerry, as CEO, did not want to be involved in the approval of any loans and he felt loans should not be granted to any of the executives or the directors. In addition, all larger loans would have to be approved by the full board of directors (excluding Kerry). After Kerry became CEO, he took away typical bank executive perks of company cars, country club memberships, executive dining rooms, and company-owned planes. He sold planes and expensive art of acquired companies and continued his policies of frugality for his two decades as chairman, president, and CEO. He continually stated, "Frugal is sexy."

These actions served Washington Mutual well over the years. Conflicts of interest were not tolerated, and absolute integrity and honesty were required. This corporate culture is one of the reasons neither the bank, nor any board member nor any senior executive, was ever fined, paid civil money penalties, or was subject to a formal regulatory enforcement action.

4

The Four Major Waves
of Change in the 1990s
That Laid the Groundwork for
the 2008 Financial Crisis

At the beginning of the 1990s, the financial services industry was still
reeling from the eighties banking crisis. The industry had shrunk by
half—the number of banks had dropped from 14,400 in 1980 to 8,315
by 2000.[1] Thrifts had shrunk from 3,200 down to about 2,000. But the
decade ahead would present even more challenges. There were four
major waves of change forming in the early nineties that would significantly impact banking and eventually lead to the great financial crisis
of 2008. The first wave was Wall Street's increasing use of complex
financial derivatives; the second wave was a government mandate for
more homeownership for low-income and minority (LMI) populations;
the third wave involved the new Basel II capital standards imposed on
regulated banks, but not imposed on the shadow banking system; and
the fourth wave was another substantial consolidation of the banking
industry, creating powerful Wall Street banks that were deemed "too
big to fail."

The First Big Wave:
Privately Developed Financial Derivatives

The first major wave of change in banking in the 1990s was the explosion in the use of private financial derivative instruments and other synthetic securities. A financial derivative is a contract based on the future value of a stock, bond, or some other asset. The concept has been around for centuries. Airlines hedge their risks on the future cost of jet fuel, banks hedge their interest-rate risks, and currency traders hedge their positions. The Chicago Board of Trade regularly deals with derivatives on the price of agricultural or animal products. These derivatives are regulated by the Commodity Futures Trading Commission (CFTC).

Financial derivatives like mortgage-backed securities (MBSs), collateralized debt obligations (CDOs), and credit default swaps (CDSs) are traded over the counter (OTC) and were not regulated by any federal exchange or regulator in the years before the 2008 crisis. They were typically sold by brokers, who act as middlemen matching buyers and sellers, and dealers, who took a position for themselves as a net buyer or seller.

Financial derivatives are essential for helping businesses hedge risks. But financial derivatives can also be used as speculative tools when speculators use options, swaps, and futures contracts to bet on price changes. Some speculators take positions and then strive to influence future prices by spreading rumors or other destabilizing factors.

The Commodity Futures Trading Commission (CFTC), during the Clinton administration, tried to get OTC financial derivatives regulated, but it was blocked by Fed chair Alan Greenspan, Treasury Secretary Robert Rubin, Deputy Secretary Lawrence Summers and SEC chair Arthur Levitt. They all felt regulation of financial derivatives would stifle valuable innovation, send derivative trading offshore, and create legal uncertainties.[2]

During the 1990s, Fed chair Greenspan believed "the most significant event in finance during the past decade has been the extraordinary development and expansion of financial derivatives. The product and asset price signals enable entrepreneurs to finely allocate real capital facilities to produce those goods and services most valued by consumers, a process that has undoubtedly improved national productivity growth and standards of living."[3]

A few years later, in 2000, under pressure from Wall Street lobbyists, Congress passed the Commodity Futures Modernization Act (CFMA), which formally deregulated the OTC financial derivatives market and eliminated oversight by both the CFTC and the SEC. The law also preempted any state laws that would have made OTC financial derivatives illegal. A Dallas Federal Reserve paper reveals that markets in non-prime residential MBS and CDS soared after the passage of the CFMA.[4]

However, not everyone was convinced of the need to deregulate these instruments. In 2003, Warren Buffett issued a stern warning, "Derivatives are financial weapons of mass destruction, carrying dangers that while now latent, are potentially lethal. There is no central bank assigned to the job of preventing the dominos toppling in insurance or derivatives. Large amounts of risk, particularly credit risk, have become concentrated in the hands of relatively few derivative dealers."[5]

But the horse was out of the barn and the growth of the unregulated financial OTC market was galloping out of control. In 2000, the notional amount of OTC financial derivatives outstanding globally was $95.2 trillion, with a gross market value of $3.2 trillion. By June 2008, outstanding notional global OTC derivatives had skyrocketed to $672.6 trillion, with a gross market value of $20.3 trillion.[6] Much of this growth was accomplished by Wall Street investment banks, commercial banks, hedge funds and other unregulated financial firms.[7]

Back in the 1990s, the Wall Street investment banks focused their work around investment advice including very lucrative initial public offerings (IPOs). For an IPO to work well, the banks typically required a company show profitability three years in a row. However, at the heightened bubble frenzy of the high-tech IPOs of the late 1990s, no history of profitability was required. As a result, the number of IPOs shot up nine times—up to $45 billion—and the bonuses were enormous. The key legacy of the 1990s internet boom was that Wall Street was now driven by the pursuit of enormous personal bonuses. After the crash of the dot-com bubble, Wall Street needed to find a new source of big bonuses—and OTC mortgage securitizations provided the new gold rush.[8]

When both Presidents Clinton and George W. Bush announced their immense programs for affordable housing, Wall Street saw the opportunity and bought up major positions in subprime companies and expanded their mortgage securitization capabilities. In 1997, Bear Stearns was eager to be helpful in this newfound bonanza and quickly

launched the first publicly available securitization of CRA loans into
CDOs. Soon Wall Street was cranking out billions of dollars of MBSs
and CDOs and insuring them with trillions of dollars of CDSs.[9]

Mortgage-backed securities (MBS) have been around for decades
but were initially created by government agencies. For over fifty years,
Fannie Mae was entrusted with securitizing FHA loans and turning
them into MBSs, without any major problems. Freddie Mac started
securitizing mortgages in 1970. However, in 1968, Lewis Ranieri, vice
chair of Salomon Brothers, invented the first privately developed MBSs
and changed Wall Street forever. He helped teach Wall Street how to
securitize assets and inspired the securitization of many different asset
categories.

Chart 4-1 shows the dramatic increase in private issuance of MBSs
leading up to the financial crisis. Private (nonagency) market share,
mostly from Wall Street banks, hedge funds and other unregulated private companies, increased from around 20 percent to nearly 60 percent
in 2005 and 2006. After the financial crisis, nearly everyone turned
back to Fannie and Freddie (agencies) for securitization, and private
securitization plummeted. However, recently there have been signs that
once again unregulated private companies have been increasing the
use of securitizations.

Historically, most MBSs were "pass through securities" where cash
flows from interest and repayment of principal were simply passed on
to investors holding the securities. However, a more complex financial
security called the collateralized debt obligation was developed to better tailor cash flow payments to investor risk and return requirements.

Collateralized debt obligations (CDOs) gather cash flow payments
from residential mortgages and bonds and repackage them into discrete
classes or tranches (French for slices) of securities. Cash flows from the
collateralized assets are prioritized with the highest rated tranches with
the least risk receiving payments first. Higher rated tranches typically
were paid a lower return, but were the least risky and often rated AAA
by the rating agencies. The lower tranches were typically paid higher returns, but were much riskier and often were rated low investment grade
or below investment grade, by the rating agencies.[10]

Throughout the 1990s and into the 2000s, Wall Street continued
to refine and expand assets that could be used in CDOs. Residential
mortgages became the largest class of assets for securitization and

Chart 4-1: Federal Agency (Fannie and Freddie) Versus
Private Securitization Market Share

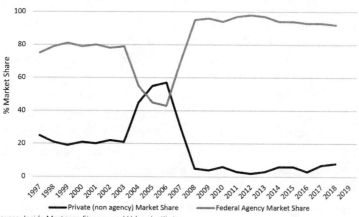

Source: Inside Mortgage Finance and Urban Institute

loan categories were broadened (to include subprime mortgages), and underwriting criteria were generally relaxed. Armed with historic data, the Wall Street wizards outlined how lesser-quality loans would perform in a superior manner by being pooled with other mortgages. They claimed this diversification feature could significantly improve returns and lower risks. After all, Fed chair Bernanke often declared, "There has never been a nationwide decline in housing values since the Depression."

The FCIC said, "Between 2003 and 2007, as housing prices rose 27 percent nationally and $4 trillion in MBSs were created, Wall Street issued nearly $700 billion in CDOs that included MBSs as collateral."[11] Other sources in the Fed and the FCIC report claimed that outstanding CDOs grew from $11 billion in 1984 to over $200 billion in 1994 and over $4 trillion by 2007.[12] Their popularity also fueled the rapid growth of hedge funds, which grew from $30 billion under management in 1990 to over $1.2 trillion by 2005.[13]

The Black-Scholes model developed in the seventies gave banks the comfort they could more effectively calculate the value of complicated derivatives and the hedges needed to protect themselves in the ever-more complicated task of slicing, dicing, and packaging the mortgage securities and selling them all over the world. The Gaussian Copula model developed in the late 1990s, gave additional comfort because it could theoretically calculate the probability that a given set of loans would face correlated losses.[14] From 2004 to 2007, Merrill Lynch, Goldman Sachs, and the securitization arm of Citigroup structured 30 percent of the CDOs. The foreign banks Deutsche and UBS were also two of the top global securitizers of CDOs.[15]

The buyers of CDOs included mutual funds, insurance companies, investment trusts, commercial banks, and pension fund managers, as well as foreign investors. There was a flood of worldwide liquidity in the early 2000s, and global investors were eager to earn higher returns from what were believed to be historically safe mortgage assets. Rating agencies rated each tranche of the securities, and subprime loans were increasingly allowed to be included in certain pools.

Ground zero of the financial crisis came in August 2007, when housing prices started to trend down. The rating agencies made unprecedented mass downgrades of MBSs after two highly leveraged Bear Stearns hedge funds holding MBSs and CDOs collapsed in August of that year.[16] This created a market panic and the Fed did little to help stabilize housing prices or infuse liquidity into the system. By the end of 2008, 91 percent of the CDO securities had been downgraded.[17]

All these new CDOs needed to be insured or hedged, so Wall Street turned to credit default swaps.

Credit default swaps (CDS) were invented by JPMorgan Chase in 1997 when it needed to shift the default risk of loans off its balance sheet. It jiggered together a template to hedge or insure its CDOs. The CDS made it possible to insure MBSs and CDOs with pools of mortgages, auto loans, student loans, or any other debt that had a steady stream of income.

Chase developed a home for the CDS within an off-balance company called a structured investment vehicle (SIV) to hold the insurance contract. The bank paid premiums to the SIV or SPV (special purpose vehicle) to insure the loans, and the premiums backed new bonds issued by the SIV to investors. The SIV would send the premiums to the lightly regulated insurance firm AIG, which in turn offered to pay off the CDS if it failed. So, the actual risk of defaulted loans was transferred from JPMorgan Chase to the SIV or SPV and then on to AIG. By transferring this risk, JPMorgan Chase did not have to maintain the capital reserves for those loans, so it became easier to make more loans. SIVs were created in part as a response to Basel II requirements so a bank would need less capital by moving assets to an off-balance-sheet SIV. Regulators actually encouraged the SIVs because it took risk off the books of the banks.

The CDSs grew like gangbusters. The International Swaps and Derivatives Association estimated the notional value of CDSs outstanding was a mere $919 billion at year-end 2001. By the end of 2007, total CDS volume topped $62 trillion—a compounded growth rate of 102 percent per year for six years. Hedge funds drove nearly 60 percent of CDS trading in 2006 at the height of the bubble.[18]

Most of the Wall Street banks became heavy users of CDSs, and AIG was the leading party issuing those contracts. This credit protection on assets, including MBS and CDOs grew from $20 billion in 2002 to $211 billion in 2005 and $533 billion in 2007, which translated to CDSs with a notional value of $2.7 trillion.[19,20] AIG neither adequately hedged the risks, set aside sufficient capital reserves, nor posted enough collateral. This had to be one of the greatest risk management failures ever. AIG did not have a central federal regulator but was regulated by all the state insurance commissioners. Because credit default swaps were not regulated insurance contracts, there were no requirements to set aside reserves in case of a loss. No one was paying attention. After the crisis of 2008, Bernanke, Paulson, and Geithner all claimed the SEC should have been regulating the AIG credit default swaps. However, before the crisis, all three men were noticeably silent about the impending implosion of AIG or the exploding CDO/CDS market.

In 2005, AIG lost its triple A rating when auditors discovered it had manipulated earnings and had to restate earnings by $3.9 billion over the five-year period.[21] Oddly, the company continued to produce CDSs until 2006. In 2006, the head of the AIG financial products division famously stated, "It is hard for us, without being flippant, to even see a scenario within any kind of realm or reason that would see us losing one dollar in any of those [CDS] transactions."[22] When the panic began in 2007, AIG had $2.7 trillion in notional exposure on derivatives, which unpacked like little Russian *matryoshka* nesting dolls—$527 billion of the derivatives were CDSs that contained $70 billion of MBSs that contained at least $55 billion of the nastiest unregulated subprime loans.[23] From January 2007 through September 2008, AIG lost $32.5 billion—almost entirely from the financial products division that produced the credit default swaps.[24]

Unfortunately, AIG had not put aside sufficient capital to deal with mortgage defaults. This lack of ability to pay panicked the market and stimulated more defaults. Soon AIG owed hundreds of billions of dollars to the Wall Street firms. AIG had to be saved by the government because no one wanted AIG and the interconnected Wall Street firms to all go down. However, when all the dust settled, the traders in AIG's financial products division still received their multimillion-dollar bonuses. In a 2009 ABC interview, former Treasury secretary Larry Summers stated, "There are a lot of terrible things that have happened in the last eighteen months, but what happened at AIG...the way it was not regulated, the way no one was watching...is outrageous."[25]

The growth of CDSs was not just from a normal CDS where the bank placing the bet actually owned the underlying CDO. Soon Wall Street turbocharged the CDS and started betting on everyone else's CDOs and other derivatives, without having ownership in the underlying assets. This is called a "naked CDS," and it is worse than betting in a casino—at least Vegas doesn't allow people to place bets they can't cover. Some analysts alleged there were bankers and investors who would buy insurance on another bank's CDOs and then start rumors, causing panic for a bank. This would be like buying insurance on your neighbor's house, setting it on fire, and then collecting the insurance. Illegal, right? Well, not when it involves Wall Street speculators.

In 2008 the ISDA estimated about 80 percent of the CDSs were "naked"—pure gambling by people who had no ownership in the property.[26]

After the 2008 crisis, the 2010 FCIC revealed that Citigroup and Merrill Lynch reported the most spectacular losses, mostly because of their extensive CDOs, writing down a total of $23.8 billion and $24.7 billion, respectively. Billions more in losses were reported by Bank of American ($9.7 billion), Morgan Stanley ($10.3 billion), JPMorgan ($5.3 billion), and Bear Stearns ($2.6 billion).[27] Insurance companies, hedge funds, and others had mortgage related losses of over $100 billion.[28] Washington Mutual had nominal CDOs or CDSs.

In March 2008, a coalition of world-wide regulatory agencies including the Federal Reserve, the OCC, the Federal Reserve Board of New York, and banking commissions in France, Germany, Switzerland, and the UK prepared a study for the FCIC: "Observations on Risk Management Practices during the Recent Market Turbulence." They found the primary source of bank losses came from the "warehousing, structuring, and trading of CDOs." They said particularly the Wall Street firms found their "aggregate exposure to this risk was larger than they initially recognized." This included "retaining exposures in warehouse portfolios for significantly longer periods of time than expected when firms realized they were unable to find buyers for CDOs and high yield bond exposures." They found the most effective risk management was found in banks that chose to "avoid business lines such as CDO warehousing or SIVs because the perceived contingent liquidity risk outweighed the potential returns."[29]

Most thrifts and community banks, including Washington Mutual, did not participate in the riskiest part of the financial system, which involved complex derivative securities like CDOs and SIVs, highly leveraged loans, and CDSs.

The Second Big Wave:
The Community Reinvestment Act (CRA) and the Presidential and Congressional Mandates That Created The Shadow Subprime System

The second big wave of change involved the efforts of regulators and politicians to address the overwhelming documented evidence of racial injustices in the country that prevented minorities from fully participating in affordable housing. The massive home-building programs after World War II, like the Levitt neighborhoods, catered mostly to homes for whites in suburban neighborhoods. This left many minority populations in crowded, low-income urban areas. The Federal Housing Administration (FHA) further "segregated the neighborhoods by refusing to insure mortgages in and near African American neighborhoods"—a policy known as 'redlining.' In order to follow government mandates, banks also adopted the redlining policies."[30] In the early 1990s, government's solution to this problem was to create massive new programs promoting LMI lending to meet the new CRA goals.

About the same time CRA programs became popular, Congress, under considerable pressure to get Fannie Mae and Freddie Mac out of government ownership and have them privately financed,

approved the Housing and Urban Development Act, which converted
Fannie and later Freddie into private companies with shareholders,
but still regulated by HUD. The support for Fannie and Freddie
ran along party lines. The Republicans wanted them privatized and
taken off the public dole. The Democrats wanted them inside government so they could control LMI lending and other housing policies.
The compromised resolution for the agencies left them with profits
that were privatized but losses paid by the taxpayers. No actual government guarantee existed to bail out Fannie or Freddie in case of a
crisis, but investors believed it was implied. The two agencies began
to serve two masters with different goals: shareholders demanding
increased earnings and returns and government demanding more
affordable housing.[31]

Representative Henry González (Democrat of Texas), chair of the
House Banking Committee and a champion for human and civil rights,
must have felt his blood boil when he read the new 1991 Federal Reserve study on housing. He implored, "The report showed discrimination in lending to be so pervasive, it was inflicting great pain across the
country." González's Mexican-born parents fled their country during
the Mexican Revolution and settled in America for more opportunity
for their family. They probably never imaged their son would become
a US representative and chair of the prestigious House Banking Committee, where he had the power to get something done. The chair of
the Senate Banking Committee, Senator Don Riegle (Democrat of
Michigan), agreed with his colleague and announced, "Banks and their
regulators had not given the issue of discrimination in lending the
attention it deserved." They both held hearings.[32, 33]

The Federal Reserve Bank of Boston also completed a study of
nineteen large cities and found blacks and Hispanics were two to
three times more likely than whites to be denied a mortgage. The
Senate Banking Committee hearings that followed demanded Fannie
Mae and Freddie Mac be more aggressive and convincing in their
efforts to serve LMI families. In 1991 HUD released their study, "Not
in My Back Yard: Removing Barriers to Affordable Housing." It had
a number of federal recommendations including Action #30, which
encouraged fast automated underwriting in order to cut loan pro-
cessing time, and Action #35 for "innovative low-down-payment programs," which encouraged 97 percent loans. Action #37 encouraged

banks to let customers withdraw funds from IRAs and 401(k)s in order to buy a home.[34]

To help with the new affordable housing effort, González informally deputized ACORN (Association of Community Organizations for Reform Now) and other community groups to draft statutory language setting the laws for the affordable housing mandate. The groups successfully lobbied Congress to mandate the aforementioned innovative and flexible lending practices for the LMI population.[35]

In 1992, President H.W. Bush signed the Housing and Community Development Act, which amended the charter of Fannie Mae and Freddie Mac and required them to meet affordable housing goals set annually by the Department of Housing and Urban Development (HUD). The initial LMI goal was 30 percent of their loans. This was increased to 42 percent in 1995 and 50 percent in 2000. By 2008 the main LMI goal was 56 percent, with 27 percent of those loans for borrowers at or below the 80 percent median income of the area. Title VIII of the Act, called the Federal Housing Enterprises Financial Safety Act, encouraged Fannie and Freddie to have a greater number of 5 percent down-payment loans. At this point HUD had supervisory control over Fannie Mae, Freddie Mac, FHA, and the VA, so it was not shy about applying pressure for more subprime and affordable housing loans.[36]

President Clinton, inspired by the affordable housing movement and the recent studies on lack of affordable housing, developed the 1995 National Homeownership Strategy[37] program, which had a goal to generate up to eight million additional homeowners in order to achieve 67.5 percent homeownership within five years. He had a list of one hundred specific actions in the next five years that could achieve that goal but "not cost taxpayers one extra cent."[38] He said the program would make it "easy for people to own their own homes and enjoy the rewards of family life."

All these plans encouraged greater use of adjustable-rate loans to increase home affordability in certain regions of the country. Under product names such as Option ARMs or Pic A Pay loans, these products were first developed following the passage of Reagan's 1982 Garn–St. Germain and Parity Acts. These loans were primarily used in California because of rising costs of homes in that state and the tendency of people to want shorter-term loans because they moved more often. The loans were also helpful to business people with uneven flows of income. These loans were sold to prime borrowers, and for decades the loans performed as well as fixed-rate loans, with less than 1 percent default rates.

Clinton's plan also required Fannie Mae and Freddie Mac employ automated underwriting programs that could process loans quickly and relied mostly on FICO scores, LTV ratios, and computer-generated proof of employment, credit history, and property values. Data from FICO and LTV scores were statistically proven to be the most predictive of whether people will pay their mortgage. Automated underwriting turned out to be a very efficient method of gathering the necessary paperwork for a borrower to close on a loan in a timely manner, replacing the cumbersome need to gather full documentation. Regulated banks and thrifts that sold directly to Fannie and Freddie carefully followed the prescribed underwriting rules, including expanded use of "stated income" loans. However, the unregulated shadow Wall Street banking system that appeared in the 2000s didn't have to worry about CRA or Fannie and Freddie's rules because their loans went directly to Wall Street for the compilation of MBSs and CDOs. Over time, intense competitive pressure led the GSEs and Wall Street to loosen their underwriting standards.

In 1999, HUD secretary Andrew Cuomo took Clinton's program a step further when he announced a directive to force Fannie and Freddie to buy $2.4 trillion in LMI mortgages for 28.1 million families in the next ten years. Cuomo hoped the program would stimulate the construction economy and create jobs. He stated, "It will help ease the terrible shortage of affordable housing plaguing far too many communities and will help reduce the huge homeownership gap dividing whites from minorities and suburbs from cities."[39] The American Homeownership and Economic Opportunity Act of 2000 included reverse mortgages and increasing financial assistance to the poor, elderly, and disabled.

Just a few months later, the vice chair of Fannie Mae told a rapturous crowd at the American Banking Association convention that Fannie had committed to securitizing over $500 billion of CRA loans. He urged all the bankers gathered in the room to send Fannie their CRA loans for flexible underwriting and special financing to produce "CRA Your Way."[40]

Just a couple of years later, President George W. Bush also supported an aggressive affordable housing program in his 2002 "Blueprint for the American Dream," which set a goal of $1 trillion of loans to minority borrowers.[41] Bush proudly announced, "Too many...minorities do not own a home. Part of being a secure America is to encourage homeownership. So, by the year 2010, we must increase minority homeowners by at least 5.5 million. The greatest single barrier to homeownership is a high down payment." He proposed $2.4 billion of single-family affordable housing credits and pushed Fannie and Freddie "to increase their commitment to minority markets by more than $440 billion." Bush's program introduced a Zero Down Payment Initiative that would eliminate the 3 percent down payment rule for first-time home buyers with FHA-insured mortgages.[42]

The gauntlet had been laid down—President Clinton promised eight million more minority and LMI families would have affordable homes, and President Bush promised 5.5 million more homes for minority families. Both presidents wanted their goals reached within a tight time frame, and they both laid most of the responsibility for this explosion of subprime lending on Fannie and Freddie. The pressure to reach these numbers came from presidents and congressional members of both parties, who all felt these goals could be accomplished without a significant increase in risk.

Community groups naturally fully supported these calls for action. Unfortunately, the only way to reach these goals was to lower standards, eliminate barriers, and use fast automated underwriting to accommodate the surge of millions of new home loans. Banks were told by Fannie, "Forget about [low] FICO scores and high LTV levels. Almost everyone evaluating your portfolio assumes that the FICO scores will be low [less than 660] and LTVs will be high [over 90 percent]."[43] We both personally supported increased lending to LMI families but knew these massive programs presented high risks, especially with the quickly growing unregulated shadow banking system lurking in the background, that eventually cranked out $2 trillion of poor quality subprime loans.

Regulated banks of all sizes were pressured by community groups and regulators to adopt large commitments to expand LMI lending as part of merger or growth approvals. Regulators also expanded the complexity and breadth of regular CRA examinations. Time and time again, it has been proven that massive government programs, government guarantees, and political mandates, without proper oversight, lead to dislocations and improper allocation of capital with unintended consequences.

Responding to the pressures to meet CRA goals, hundreds of regulated banks all dutifully pledged to write billions of LMI loans. Between 1977 and 2007, community organizations proceeded with tough negotiations with the banks and produced over $4.56 trillion in LMI loan commitments. [44]

In 2004 JPMorgan Chase announced $800 billion in CRA commitments when it purchased Bank One, Bank of America announced $750 billion in CRA commitments when it merged with FleetBoston in 2004, Citigroup made a $120 billion commitment when it acquired California Federal Bank in 2002. When Citigroup merged with Travelers in 1998, they made another $115 billion commitment. Both Wachovia and Washington Mutual pledged $100 billion when they did acquisitions.[45] There is no question these government actions were one of the causes of the 2008 financial crisis. Chart 4-2 illustrates the rapid growth in commitments, reaching nearly $5 trillion by 2007.

Kerry was on the Fed's TIAC council when it was first considering modifying CRA rules by requiring banks to have a certain percentage of LMI lending. Kerry told the Fed that requiring banks to have a certain percentage of subprime lending made no sense and could lead to unintended consequences. He mentioned banks like Washington Mutual focused primarily on prime borrowers and should not be forced to radically change its business plan to maintain its outstanding CRA rating. Kerry completely supported LMI lending but worried the massive programs would attract unregulated shadow banks to expand quickly if there was no federal government oversight. However, the Fed went ahead and implemented the new CRA test that measured a bank's market share of prime loans versus its market share of subprime loans. A bank's CRA rating could be downgraded if its subprime and LMI loans did not have a similar share of market as their prime loans.

Responding to these political and regulatory mandates, virtually all major banks either bought new subprime originators or expanded their existing operations:

JPMorgan Chase bought Advanta. Lehman bought BNC and Aurora. Citigroup bought Associates First Capital. AIG bought

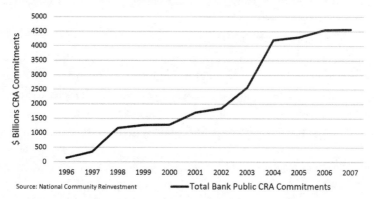

Chart 4-2: Total Regulated Bank LMI Commitments

Source: National Community Reinvestment   ━━━Total Bank Public CRA Commitments

American General Finance. First Union bought the Money Store. Bank of America bought Equicredit. Goldman Sachs bought First Franklin. HSBC (UK) bought Household Finance and Beneficial Mortgage. Capital One bought Greenpoint Mortgage. Morgan Stanley had a special relationship with New Century, and Washington Mutual bought Long Beach Mortgage. Other banks, like Wells Fargo, already had a very large subprime consumer finance operation.[46] However, the Wall Street banks also bought subprime loans from the 300,000 unregulated mortgage brokers and the nearly one hundred independent subprime companies that were popping up all over the country.

The Wall Street banks and the foreign banks typically operated their subprime companies as unregulated shadow off-balance-sheet subsidiaries. Loans were underwritten to Wall Street standards and were sold to Wall Street for packaging and securitizing. Most regulated banks, though leery of the aggressive government goals, were committed to making LMI lending and viewed it as a community service.

Alternatively, the unregulated shadow banking system of Wall Street investment banks and subprime companies like Ameriquest and New Century viewed subprime lending as a tremendous opportunity. They had no mandate to achieve CRA ratings or a moral imperative to increase affordable housing. They simply wanted to get in on the gold rush of millions of new subprime borrowers.[47] A number of public and private companies developed their own unregulated subprime mortgage units, including General Motors, General Electric, H&R Block and AIG Insurance.[48] International banks like HSBC and Barclays also purchased American subprime companies.

While subprime lending was not very profitable for the regulated banks, the new unregulated shadow banking system had much lower operating costs, low regulatory costs, high fees, and excellent profitability.[49] Those companies had a number of characteristics in common that assured the fragility of the subprime system:

- They were willing to finance their operation with expensive short term or overnight funding to originate mortgage loans.
- They quickly sold the loans to Wall Street to gain more liquidity.
- They were not required to have any capital requirements.
- There was a lack of regulatory oversight and lax oversight from the Wall Street banks and the rating agencies.
- There was a lack of barriers to entry in the system and no formal professional training or certification.
- Compensation systems were based on commissions, with few if any checks on the quality of the loans.

Wall Street needed billions of subprime loans to package into securitized bonds, and the dozens of new unregulated subprime companies were happy to gather up subprime loans from the three hundred thousand unregulated mortgage brokers populating our country. Wall Street expressed little concern about loan quality because the loans would be packaged with thousands of similar subprime loans. Diversification was supposed to reduce the risk of any single poorly written loan.[50]

Most subprime originations, servicing, and packaging were done outside of the oversight from federal banking regulators. Unregulated shadow banks are typically defined as financial institutions not regulated by a US federal banking regulator (OTS, OCC, Federal Reserve, FDIC) and not authorized to accept federally insured deposits.[51] Because they do not have the ability to take deposits to finance their operations, shadow banks have to rely on expensive overnight funding or short term loans.

Chart 4-3 illustrates the unregulated shadow subprime system from 2002 to 2007. Over three hundred thousand unregulated independent mortgage brokers fed subprime loans to more than one hundred unregulated subprime companies (e.g., Ameriquest and New Century).[52,53,54] These unregulated subprime companies along with some regulated banks fed subprime loans to Wall Street investment banks, who securitized them into billions of dollars of unregulated CDOs, insured by trillions of dollars' worth of unregulated CDSs. The barriers to entry were low, and little regulatory oversight fueled explosive growth. Because subprime loans needed scale to survive, only twenty-five companies produced 93 percent of the total subprime loans each year.

Between 2002 and 2007, the unregulated shadow companies produced nearly $2 trillion of subprime loans—85 percent of the subprime loans produced in this country. These unregulated loans failed at more than twice the rate of subprime loans from the regulated banks. The large regulated banks of JPMorgan Chase, Citigroup, Wells Fargo, Washington Mutual, and Countrywide, collectively produced less than 15 percent of the subprime loans during this entire period.

As a result of government programs and directives, subprime mortgage originations increased annually from a modest $35 billion in 1994 to a peak of over $500 billion in 2005. As a share of all residential mortgage lending in most large regulated banks, subprime increased from 5 percent in 1994 to nearly 10 percent in 2006. US federal government targets to increase homeownership increased to a peak of 69 percent in 2006. Politicians hailed this accomplishment but said little about the unintended consequences of putting too many people in homes they couldn't afford. Or letting a shadow, unregulated system produce 85 percent of the subprime loans and securitize them into hundreds of billions of dollars in CDOs, helping fuel a financial crisis that would nearly bring down the global economic system.

After the 2008 crisis, the 2010 FCIC report revealed that the bank with the most mortgage loan losses was shadow bank Merrill Lynch with $24.7 billion in losses.[55] In addition, the other shadow banks, like hedge funds and insurance companies, had mortgage losses of over $100 billion.[57] None of them were centrally monitored by the main federal regulators—the FDIC, OTS, OCC, or the Federal Reserve. Most of them appeared to covet the subprime loans that typically had lower starting rates and reset to higher rates after two years. They particularly liked the "cash-out" refinancing, which encouraged borrowers to pull any excess cash from their homes. Cash outs represented as much as

Chart 4-3: The Unregulated Subprime Shadow Bank System 2002–2007[56]

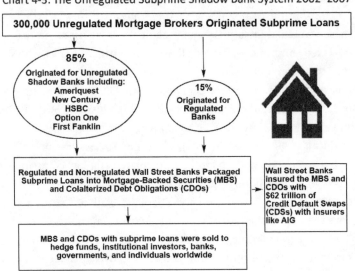

75 percent of subprime originations from the unregulated channels in the early 2000s.[58]

After the crisis, Nobel Laureate Paul Krugman described the run on the shadow banking system as the core of what happened to cause the crisis. He stated: "As the shadow banking system expanded to rival or even surpass conventional banking in importance, politicians and government officials should have realized they were re-creating the kind of financial vulnerability that made the Great Depression possible. Anything that does what a bank does, should be regulated like a bank."[59]

The smaller community banks in the country were not as dramatically affected by the use of complex derivatives or the strict Basel II requirements, but some were deeply affected by the regulators' demands for more CRA lending. Sometimes, even the smallest community banks were required to have CRA goals and prove they were increasing their efforts to extend lending to minority and LMI populations. If they had plans to merge or be acquired, they would first have to establish a satisfactory or outstanding CRA rating. This was a high-wire act for many community banks who were deeply proud of their reputation and low risk profile but still had to participate in the higher-risk CRA market or risked being labeled "unsatisfactory" by the regulators. A rating that would be made public.

The Third Big Wave:
Capital Allocation and Basel II Standards

The third big wave of change was the international effort to impose capital standards on all regulated banks around the globe. The Bank for International Settlements was hard at work at the start of the 1990s trying to develop a worldwide capital standard for the banking industry, called Basel I and Basel II, for holding enough capital to protect a bank with different lending risks. Basel I assigned a risk weighting for each asset type, which had the downside of creating incentives for banks to originate products that required less capital. Also, the complexity of risks with securitizations was not adequately addressed in Basel I. This resulted in the creation of the 2004 Basel II, which allowed banks to create their own internal credit risk requirements. It required banks to quantify and measure operating risk, interest rate risk, and credit risk. Historical loss rates were determined for each asset category, and incremental capital was held in relation to those risks. The European banks were stalling on implementing these standards, but US banking regulators were quicker to try to adopt Basel II. But this made the US banks less profitable and less competitive with the European banks, which didn't have to hold as much capital.

The theory behind Basel II was each type of lending product should have enough backup capital to protect the risk. For example, cash and equivalent instruments didn't need any backup capital because they were very safe. The next safest lending instrument was mortgage loans, which historically had less than a 1 percent default rate, so they needed less capital than the riskier and more profitable commercial loans. Credit cards are even riskier and required even more backup capital. This all seemed harmless, but Wall Street could not wait to "game the system" and quickly went about developing complex "efficient capital allocation models" that fundamentally changed what regulated banks held in portfolio versus assets originated for sale.

In the late 1990s, the executives of the investment banks of Goldman Sachs, Merrill Lynch, Lehman, Bear Stearns, and Morgan Stanley, ironically led by Goldman's CEO, Hank Paulson, wanted out of this Basel system and spent millions successfully lobbying

Congress to reduce their capital requirements. Later in 2010, the FCIC discovered the five largest unregulated Wall Street investment banks had been "operating with extraordinarily thin capital." It found leverage ratios were as high as forty to one, meaning for every forty dollars in assets, there was only one dollar in capital to cover the losses. Fannie and Freddie were also able to lobby Congress to lower their capital ratios, and by the end of 2007, their combined leverage ratios stood at seventy-five to one.[60] The Federal Reserve was supposed to be monitoring the investment banks, but there was no sign of effective control over the shadow system. Even more troubling was the shadow banking system of mortgage brokers and subprime lenders that had virtually no capital requirements. These shadow banks were trying to optimize income and minimize capital retained in their businesses.

Another challenge for Basel II was the assumption that historic loss rates would reflect future loss rates. Historically safe assets like residential mortgages performed well for decades. However, during and after the 2008 crisis, all types of mortgage products, including subprime, prime, adjustable-rate, and fixed-rate, performed poorly when housing prices plummeted and millions of people lost their jobs.

Finally, Basel II led Wall Street regulated banks to "game" the allocation of capital. The banks promptly estimated risk-adjusted returns for every asset category and assigned appropriate capital to those categories. The highest risk-adjusted-return assets would typically be given capital and allowed to grow. The poorest risk-adjusted-return assets would typically be reduced if share repurchase provided a higher return on capital. For asset categories like residential home loans, Basel II required too much capital relative to the modest risk-adjusted returns. This led most banks to shed residential mortgages held in portfolio and replace them with assets having higher risk-adjusted returns. This accelerated the trend away from portfolio lending of residential loans to originating and selling loans to the GSEs or Wall Street for securitizations.

Optimizing return on capital led most Wall Street banks to securitize as many products as possible. Kerry met with one Wall Street CEO who told him the future was securitizing virtually every asset, in the belief there were willing buyers for just about any asset pool. To optimize return on capital, investment banks wanted to maximize fee income by packaging and selling assets versus the traditional approach of holding them on their balance sheets.

Ultimately, efficient allocation of capital and Basel II led regulated banks to reduce residential loans held in portfolio, retain higher risk-adjusted-return assets, sell assets with poor risk-adjusted returns, and repurchase shares when appropriate. The Basel II requirements also encouraged banks to park riskier assets in off-balance-sheet companies, so no additional capital would be required in the bank. In July of 2008, most of the top regulated banks in the country had decent capital reserves, but had unknown assets parked in SIVs. Washington Mutual was the first large American bank to meet Basel II standards and had no exotic off-balance sheet accounts.

The Fourth Big Wave: Gigantic Mergers and Consolidation of the Industry

The fourth big wave of change in the financial industry was a dramatic acceleration of bank mergers in the 1990s. The 1994 Riegle-Neal Interstate Banking and Branching Efficiency Act finally allowed banks to merge across state lines, which inspired a massive consolidation of hundreds of commercial banks and thrifts. The demise of the Glass-Steagall Act at the end of the decade once again inspired the combination of insurance companies, commercial banks, and unregulated investment banks, using federally insured customer deposits, to invest in increasingly risky financial products. Some banking pundits believe that banking mergers in the long run do not increase value. However, the successful Wall Street banks of today were largely created by the massive consolidation of the industry in the 1990s.

For example, the JPMorgan Chase of today was created by a series of multibillion-dollar mergers during the 1990s. Manufacturers Hanover and Chemical Bank merged in 1991 at a price of $1.9 billion and in 1995 merged with Chase Manhattan in a deal valued at nearly $10 billion. In 1999 Chase Manhattan bought the Silicon Valley boutique investment bank Hambrecht & Quist for $1.35 billion. In 1995 First Chicago did a $5 billion merger with National Bank of Detroit to create the seventh-largest bank in America with $72 billion in assets. In 1998 the new First Chicago NBD announced a $30 billion merger with

Banc One. JPMorgan Chase was founded on December 1, 2000, after
Chase Manhattan acquired JPMorgan for $30.9 billion. Soon after,
JPMorgan Chase agreed to buy Bank One Corporation for about $58
billion, creating the second-largest bank in the country with assets of
$1.1 trillion.[61]

In 1991, Bank of America acquired rival Security Pacific in a $4 bil-
lion[62] transaction marking the largest bank merger in US history with
over $200 billion in assets. Then it purchased Montgomery Securities
in 1997 for $1.2 billion in cash and stock.[63] In 1996 NationsBank
acquired Boatmen's Bancshares for $9.6 billion, and the next year
bought Barnett Bank for $15.5 billion and finally merged with Bank of
America in 1998 for $62 billion, forming the biggest bank in America
with assets of $524.72 billion.[64] In 2004 the new Bank of America
bought FleetBoston (which was the result of three mergers in New
England) for $47 billion in stock, creating a bank with nearly $1 trillion in assets, the highest number of retail outlets in the country, and
over 180,000 employees.[65]

Wells Fargo started its merger strategy in 1996, when it finally won
its hostile takeover fight for First Interstate in a deal valued at $11.6
billion. Wells won the fight after a year of failed hostile takeover bids,
a lawsuit from First Interstate claiming Wells violated securities laws
by manipulating its stock price, public hearings by the Federal Reserve
Board to rule on competing proposals, and after the SEC barred First
Bank from buying back its shares with First Interstate. Less than two
years later, Wells Fargo announced a "merger of equals" with Norwest in
a 1998 stock deal valued at $34 billion. The combined banks created
the sixth-largest bank in the country, with $191 billion in assets and
more than ninety thousand employees.[66]

Wachovia was also developed from a series of large mergers. In 1998
First Union acquired CoreStates, creating the sixth-largest banking company. In 2001 First Union won a hostile takeover bid of $14.3 billion
for Wachovia, beating out a rival bid from SunTrust and creating the
fourth-largest bank with assets of $324 billion. Wachovia had been a take-
over target after running into problems with earnings and credit quality
in 2000. In 2006 Wachovia paid an astounding $25.5 billion, or $81.07 a
share, to buy the third-largest thrift in the country, Golden West.[67]

Most of these mergers pretty much "stuck to the knitting" in
combining banks with similar operations and product lines. However,

Sanford I. Weill and his eager young assistant, Jamie Dimon, broke the mold in a string of mergers and acquisitions during the 1990s. Weill started with Commercial Credit, a subprime consumer credit, property, and casualty insurance and credit card company. In 1988, Weill paid $1.7 billion to acquire Primerica, a financial services and direct-marketing company and a parent of the Smith Barney investment firm. In 1993, Primerica offered Travelers insurance a $4 billion deal and then purchased the Salomon Brothers investment firm in 1997 for more than $9 billion in stock, after losing its first choice, Goldman Sachs.[68] Weill's final triumph was the acquisition of Citigroup in 1998, which defied the sixty-five year-old Glass-Steagall Act, but brought the bank's assets up to $698 billion, to become the largest financial services company in the world at the time.[69]

Weill proceeded to cleverly spend millions lobbying Congress and finally got the illegal marriage legitimized in 1999 with the passage of the Gramm-Leach-Bliley Act.

Ironically, the impetus back in 1933 for the Glass-Steagall Act was to force the breakup of the risky behavior of the investment banking division of the National City Bank (precursor to the current Citigroup). With the new deposit insurance laws after the 1929 crash, Congress felt it didn't want risky investment banks gambling with federally insured deposit money. This concept held true for nearly sixty-five years, until Citigroup was once again united with an investment banking partner and became the largest bank in the world. And once again Citigroup became one of the poorest performing and riskiest banks before the crash of 2008.

From 1998 to 2007, the combined assets of the five largest US banks—Bank of America, Citigroup, JPMorgan Chase, Wachovia, and Wells Fargo—more than tripled from $2.2 trillion to $6.8 trillion.[70] The assets of the five largest Wall Street investment banks—Goldman Sachs, Morgan Stanley, Merrill Lynch, Lehman Brothers, and Bear Stearns—quadrupled from $1 trillion in 1998 to $4 trillion in 2007.[71]

The investment banks were also changing and growing radically in the eighties and nineties. They changed their partnership structures and went public. In his book *Finance and the Good Society*, Nobel Laureate economist Dr. Shiller believed, "The decline of the partnership structure on Wall Street may have contributed to the crisis in 2008. It reduced the incentives to manage long-term reputation and long-term risks in favor of a structure that encouraged rapid growth of the firm."[72,73]

While the largest commercial banks were quickly consolidating into mega giants, the largest thrifts on the West Coast were also involved in a number of mergers. The four largest thrifts in the country were the California thrifts of Golden West, American Savings Bank, Great Western, and H. F. Ahmanson.

American Savings Bank, with $30 billion in assets, had been one of the largest thrifts in the country, but in 1989 it was in liquidation, when the Robert M. Bass Group Inc. of Forth Worth purchased it from the government. It quickly made four thrift acquisitions from 1991 to 1994.

Golden West, which primarily held option ARM mortgages, also acquired dozens of thrifts during the 1980s to help its expansion in the state of California and other markets.

Great Western was founded in 1929 and grew to become the second-largest thrift in America. In a five-year period in the late 1950s, it acquired five other thrifts, and in the late sixties and early seventies it purchased six more thrifts. In the eighties and early nineties, it acquired nearly twenty thrifts, most from the Resolution Trust, twelve of which were in Florida. It also purchased branches in Arizona, Washington, and New York.

Great Western loved to use celebrity spokespeople in its ads, including John Wayne, Maureen O'Hara, Barbara Stanwyck, John Huston, Glenn Ford, and others. In 1984, as a tribute to its most famous spokesman, Great Western commissioned a full-size bronze statue of the actor John Wayne to stand guard in front of its Beverly Hills headquarters at 8484 Wilshire Boulevard. The thrift remained mortgage-centric and relatively conservative in its lending and quickly became the country's most profitable thrift with a net income of nearly $300 million with $43 billion in total assets in the mid-1990s. It had 1,150 retail banking, mortgage lending, and consumer finance offices in thirty-one states.

H. F. Ahmanson was the holding company for the largest thrift in the country, Home Savings of America, with assets of over $48 billion in the mid-1990s. It had a large portfolio of mortgages and commercial apartment loans. In the 1980s it completed a series of acquisitions in Florida, Missouri, Texas, Illinois, Arizona, Washington, New York, and Ohio. Many of its branches attracted customers by offering rates as much as 2 percent higher than local competitors. In the 1990s it continued its merger strategy in New York, Connecticut, and California. During the worst of the 1980s thrift crisis, Ahmanson survived through acquisitions, conservative lending policies, and a low-cost structure.

During the 1990s, the major banks made significant contributions to Congress to support large bank mergers and help repeal Glass-Steagall restrictions. From 1998 to 2008, the financial sector spent $1.7 billion on campaign contributions and $3.4 billion on lobbying expenses; the securities industry alone spent $500 million on campaign contributions and $600 million on lobbying. The chair of the Senate Banking Committee, Christopher Dodd, received $2.9 million from the securities industry from 2007 to 2008, more than three times as much as any other senator. Banks were also the top donor to Barney Frank, chair of the House Financial Services Committee. Both were supportive of financial deregulation over the years.[74]

Back in the late 1970s, all the commercial banks together held $1.2 trillion of assets, equivalent to 53 percent of GDP. By the end of 2007, the commercial banking sector had grown nearly tenfold to $11.8 trillion in assets, or 84 percent of GDP. The unregulated investment banks grew one hundred fold from $33 billion, or 1.4 percent of GDP, to $3.1 trillion in assets, or 22 percent of GDP. Asset-backed securities such as CDOs, which hardly existed in the late 1970s, accounted for another $4.5 trillion, or 125 percent of GDP, by the end of 2007.[75]

Meanwhile, Washington Mutual developed a conservative strategy and focused its activities in the Pacific Northwest in the early 1990s. However, some surprising opportunities were in store at the end of the decade.

The four big waves of changes consolidated into a tsunami of destruction emanating from Wall Street and heading directly to the average American consumer. All told, the debt held by the financial sector grew from $2.9 trillion, or 125 percent of GDP, to over $36 trillion, or 259 percent of GDP in 2007, but they soon would be saved by the politicians they were paying.[76]

5

Washington Mutual
in the Age of Consolidation
of the Financial Industry

The Late 1990s

The great decade of banking consolidation occurred in the 1990s, when JPMorgan Chase, Citigroup, and Bank of America put together dozens of mergers to become $1-trillion-asset megabanks. Wachovia and Wells Fargo also staged dozens of mergers and became banks with a national footprint with hundreds of billions in assets. Investment banks also dramatically expanded their assets. In an effort to diversify their portfolios, large commercial banks combined very disparate lines of business, including investment banking, credit cards, global corporate banking, and complex derivative operations with collateralized debt obligations, credit default swaps, structured investment vehicles, and large subprime operations.

The complex Wall Street banks were getting so large and interconnected with the world's businesses, they were viewed by the Washington, DC crowd as "too big to fail." By the end of the 1990s consolidation, the number of commercial banks had dropped by 33 percent, from 14,434 in 1980 to only 8,315 in the year 2000.[1] By the turn of the century, the ten largest banks controlled 50 percent of deposits nationally, up from 40 percent at the beginning of the decade.

During this same time period, the four largest thrifts in the country—Golden West, American Savings, Great Western, and H. F. Ahmanson—had also been buying dozens of thrifts all over the country, with each of the largest thrifts growing to around $40 to $50 billion in assets.

Meanwhile, Washington Mutual entered the 1990s by adopting a conservative five-year plan aimed at growing its franchise in a deliberate low-risk manner. The bank had a much more conservative merger strategy than the fast-growing megabanks. The 1991 Washington Mutual annual report, called "A Conservative Approach," said the bank would concentrate on five key areas: "improving operating efficiency, sustaining high credit quality with conservative underwriting standards, maintaining strong capital ratios, expanding the financial center network, and achieving solid profitability."

To execute the plan, Kerry assembled an executive team of both traditional and nontraditional bankers who each brought their own strengths to the team. Craig Tall, head of corporate development, was not experienced in banking but was an excellent negotiator and capable of searching out growth opportunities. Liane Wilson, an experienced banker, was placed in charge of operations and the important task of integrating acquired bank operating systems. A youthful Deanna Oppenheimer, who had little banking experience but a great ability to innovate and motivate people, was placed in charge of the marketing and branch banking system. Lee Lannoye was placed in charge of corporate administration and credit. Fay Chapman, longtime outside counsel, was brought inside as general counsel. Bill Longbrake returned from a brief stint at the FDIC to be the CFO, and Craig Davis joined from American Savings to head up residential home lending.

The executive team met every morning for informal discussions, met over a working lunch each Monday, and held monthly off-site retreats. Kerry encouraged frank and open discussion of every issue and encouraged the execs to bring in and confront any bad news. Every effort was made to emphasize teamwork, frequent communication, and elimination of bureaucracy. Operating frugally was also always a central message to the team. Kerry was fond of saying, "Frugal is sexy," and gave the management team bottles of wine with the label "Cheap Wine" to display on their shelves.

Before any growth initiatives, Kerry and the team first focused on the basics of improving loan quality and delivering outstanding customer service. Kerry was not only good at financial analysis and shrewd deal making, but he had a talent for understanding customer needs and attracting customers with clever marketing programs. Innovative new products such as free checking were rolled out to customers, and award-winning advertising was developed by the Seattle office of McCann Erickson. Fun and quirky television advertising was developed with themes targeted at everyday consumers. The popular "Friend of the Family" and "Merge With Washington Mutual" campaigns made Washington Mutual part of the community by highlighting unusual Northwest icons like polka-playing log rollers, a precision lawnmower drill team, and the Rodeo Grandmas.

When Wells Fargo completed a hostile takeover of First Interstate, Washington Mutual started a new campaign to reach the disaffected customers. *Washington CEO* magazine reported:

> The highly touted new 'Merge with Washington Mutual' campaign created by McCann Erickson is bringing in 6,000 new accounts a month from retail consumers who are confused by and dissatisfied with the recent surge of bank buyouts and mergers that has created unfriendly and distant service.[2]

With the franchise in a solid and growing position in the early 1990s, Washington Mutual carefully added profitable acquisitions in the Pacific Northwest, including Frontier Federal Savings, Sound Savings, Vancouver Federal Savings, Great Northwest Bank, and Pioneer Savings. *Washington CEO* magazine reported:

> My impression of Kerry Killinger is he's as tough as nails, he's the guy that turned it [Washington Mutual] around. I've got a hunch you don't want to underestimate him. The mission was to attain what only a handful of world-class banks had achieved—a 1% ROA and a 15% ROE.

As part of his careful growth strategy, Kerry had been studying Pacific First Financial, which was a similar size to Washington Mutual and had branches in Washington and Oregon. Pacific First was owned by

Canada-based Royal Trustco and was suffering from poorly underwritten commercial real estate loans in California. Kerry approached Royal Trustco about acquiring Pacific First, and after months of preliminary discussions, Royal Trustco invited Washington Mutual to submit an acquisition proposal. Kerry sent large due diligence teams to dive into every aspect of the business, especially the commercial real estate loans. He was personally involved, sitting on top of boxes of records at the end of the day, to debrief everyone working on due diligence. The team came up with an innovative structure where Washington Mutual would purchase Pacific First but could return a certain amount of higher-risk commercial real estate loans to Royal Trustco. Royal Trustco agreed to the terms, and Washington Mutual doubled its size and extended its branch system to Oregon.

Within a couple of months after the acquisition, it was clear more than enough cushion had been built into the Pacific First loan-loss estimates, and the acquisition quickly became highly profitable. This acquisition was transformational and praised by the investment community and the media. Montgomery Securities analyst Joe Jolson stated, "Washington Mutual controls the most attractive independent consumer franchise in Washington and has recently vaulted to the fourth largest in Oregon." Merrill Lynch analyst Jerry Gitt continued, "The company's capital ratios are among the strongest of the major banks and thrifts in the nation." *Washington CEO* magazine reported:

> Some say Killinger's boundless energy and his ability to communicate a clear corporate vision have helped transform the
> 102-year-old Washington Mutual into a forceful competitor in an
> environment of rapid change and newly created mega-banks.[3]

The Pacific First acquisition greatly expanded Washington Mutual's branching system including convenient branches located inside Fred Meyer grocery and other retail stores. Pacific First was also a sponsor of a celebrity golf tournament called the Fred Meyer Challenge. Washington Mutual continued this sponsorship because the tournament raised millions for local charities, with support from local golf standout Peter Jacobsen as host pro and participating golfers like Arnold Palmer and Jack Nicklaus. Kerry had the opportunity to play with celebrities like Glenn Frey of the Eagles, Jack Lemmon, and Clint Eastwood. Kerry remembers Eastwood's humor—Clint started whistling the "Look for the Union Label" song to another one of the CEOs when an aircraft flew overhead pulling a banner criticizing the CEO's labor policies.

In Washington Mutual's 1993 annual report, Kerry stated:

> We want to be the Premier Consumer Financial Services Orga- nization in the Pacific Northwest. Our dedication to individual consumers sets us apart from the competition and continues to be the foundation of our success. We do not strive to be the big- gest bank, but we do strive to be the premier bank with excellent customer service and friendly, engaged employees.

The annual report emphasized the core values of "making every human contact caring, courteous, dignified and pleasant; conducting all actions with absolute honesty, integrity and fairness; striving to perform every task in an outstanding manner; and constantly seeking better ways to do everything."

The 1993 annual report also highlighted the employee volunteer group that donated ninety-four hundred hours to ninety-nine projects. Employees were given paid time off to volunteer in the communities, and personal charitable contributions were matched with corporate funds. Employees who donated at least $500 or one hundred hours of community service were honored. Kerry was proud Washington Mutual adopted a policy to return 2 percent of pretax profits back into the communities it served. Major areas of focus were K-12 education, affordable housing, health and human services, and helping communi- ties become better places to live and work.

As a point of pride, Kerry was personally involved in most employee volunteer activities. He especially enjoyed participating in the United Way Day of Caring projects, including one where the Washington Mu- tual team cleaned up an overgrown and junk-laden lot in a low-income neighborhood. Unfortunately, United Way gave the employees the wrong lot number. The lot was actually owned by a major oil company rather than a low-income family. Fortunately, the oil company felt so bad about the mistake, it made a nice donation to the United Way.

By 1995, Washington Mutual was doing very well in the Pacific Northwest. Assets reached $21.6 billion, profits reached $191 million, and employee volunteerism rose to seventy-five thousand hours on 150 projects. The bank expanded its affordable housing centers and had 150 loan representatives conducting seminars to educate the public on credit costs, budgeting, and financial planning.[4]

Having completed an extraordinarily successful five-year plan, it was time to create a new five-year plan for the second half of the decade, which included continuing to build and diversify in the Pacific Northwest and researching expansion opportunities in California. Kerry and the management team had been studying the large California market for quite some time. California was the world's seventh-largest economy and growing, but it suffered from cyclical ups and downs, so one needed to proceed with caution.

After reviewing all the options in California, Kerry and the team approached Robert Bass and the investor group who purchased American Savings after it failed in the thrift crisis of the 1980s. Kerry respected their key investors—Robert Bass, David Bonderman, and J. Crandall—and thought a merger made sense for everyone. A merger would keep the investor group involved while creating a $44 billion bank with excellent scale and a platform for continued growth. David Bonderman and J. Crandall joined the Washington Mutual Board of Directors, and Robert Bass attended several meetings as an observer.

It was standard in a merger transaction like this to have all parties sign confidentiality agreements and keep all negotiations confidential. The transaction was a material event to Washington Mutual shareholders, so confidentiality was a must. However, when the Bass Group originally purchased American Savings from the Resolution Trust Corporation, the FDIC received warrants to purchase 10 percent of the thrift. This meant the FDIC was a party to the transaction, and it, too, signed confidentiality agreements.

However, the FDIC decided it needed advice from an investment banker. Instead of quietly hiring an adviser, it put out a public RFP—request for proposal. This action made the transaction immediately public and revealed how naive the FDIC was in capital market matters. That move startled the market, but Kerry's team quickly moved to get the acquisition announced and approved by shareholders and regulators. The media and analysts were universally positive on the bank's prospects. That year, *Fortune* magazine chose Washington Mutual as one of its Top 100 Most Admired Companies. *Washington CEO* magazine reported:

The fragmented banking system in California is ripe for consolidation, which makes the American Savings acquisition right. It received a 96% yes vote and the new goal for Washington Mutual is to be the premier financial services organization in the Western United States.

Under his [Kerry's] technocratic, nose to the grindstone leadership since 1988, Seattle based Washington Mutual has grown from a sleepy, stagnating thrift into a highly profitable franchise. It is now the nation's fourth largest thrift and largest bank headquartered in the Pacific Northwest. The low-key Killinger, regarded by his peers as a master technician and shrewd dealmaker, has brokered the 22 acquisitions since 1983 that have moved the bank to 551 offices in nine Western states. Customers are attracted to their long-term strategy of free checking accounts and McCann-Erickson's clever ad campaign featuring Rodeo Grandmas; four authentic ridin', ropin' grandmothers from Ellensburg.[5]

One of the managers said, "Kerry's kind of a big nerd, but he's a lovable sort of guy. What's fun about him is he is always willing to try something new."

Steve Schroll, an analyst with Piper Jaffray, said, "It's a blockbuster deal. Upon completion and successful integration, this company stands a much better chance of remaining independent." Jay Tejera, an analyst with Dain Bosworth, extolled the merger, "Killinger is a multi-dimensional thinker—the American Savings deal is his masterstroke and catapults them into the big leagues. American Savings is the number two residential lender in California and fifth largest in consumer deposits behind Bank of America, Wells, Home Saving and Great Western Financial."[6]

Not everyone was on board. The vice president of communications for the California Bankers Association, had strong doubts that a friendly thrift from the state of Washington could compete in California. He went on to say, "I read about the [bank's] strategy in the paper and without prognosticating I'd have to say the competition in California is very fierce. It's the biggest state in the country and the seventh largest economy in the world. It is attractive, but it is a challenging environment for a new player with big ambitions."[7]

Investor Robert Bass, former owner of American Savings, who owned 8 percent of Washington Mutual, said, "Mr. Killinger has a very strong record in maximizing the value of a franchise. The investment is a great growth strategy for us and Washington Mutual."[8]

By early 1997, Washington Mutual was performing exceptionally well with a strong stock price and steady profitability. Not to be out-done, in April of that year, H. F. Ahmanson launched a hostile takeover attack on fellow California-based thrift Great Western Financial. Both companies were suffering from mediocre financial performance, and H. F. Ahmanson wanted to take over Great Western to wring out signifi-cant cost savings.

Wells Fargo had just completed a hostile takeover of First Interstate, and the acquisition did not go well. This left investors and analysts gun-shy about large banking mergers. Great Western's board did not support the hostile attack, and Washington Mutual was invited to consider being a white-knight suitor. The regulators—FDIC and OTS—were also concerned about a hostile bid, and they encouraged Washington Mutual to take a serious look at the acquisition.

Even though the timing was challenging because systems were still being integrated from the American Savings acquisition, Kerry told regulators the team would take a serious look at the combina-tion. Great Western would double the size of Washington Mutual and would expand its footprint to Florida. The cost savings from combined systems and duplicative branches would be substantial. After signifi-cant due diligence, it was determined the combination would be im-mediately profitable, would not present significant problem assets, and could be successfully integrated onto Washington Mutual's operating platform. In May 1997, Washington Mutual became the white-knight alternative to H. F. Ahmanson.

The majority of Great Western shareholders were institutional investors who needed to be convinced Washington Mutual's offer was superior. The investor relations team put together a presentation deck showing Washington Mutual had superior long-term stock price per-formance, an efficient operating ratio of 49.1 percent, a strong return on common equity of 19.4 percent, low nonperforming assets of only 0.73 percent of assets, and a proven ability to integrate acquisitions. The combined company would create the nation's largest thrift, the third-largest bank in California, the second largest in Washington, the fifth largest in Florida, and a lender with offices in twenty-four states coast to coast.[9]

Great Western had a strong business line that matched most of the key products of Washington Mutual, plus it had extensive experience in small business banking, which Washington Mutual wanted to adopt across its branching system. The detailed plan presented to investors showed how annual operating costs could be reduced by $340 million by closing duplicative branches and integrating operations onto Washington Mutual's operating systems. The new acquisition would be accretive to earnings immediately.[10]

Over the period of 1990 to 1996, Washington Mutual provided a compounded annual return to shareholders of 34 percent, versus only 14.7 percent for H. F. Ahmanson, 14.2 percent for Great Western, 26.2 percent for Wells Fargo, 24.5 percent for Bank of America, and 15.5 percent for the S&P 500.[11] H. F. Ahmanson's primary advantage was its claim of higher cost savings, but it did not have experience in completing large acquisition integrations, and its stock performance significantly trailed Washington Mutual's.

For nearly three months, Washington Mutual and H. F. Ahmanson were embroiled in a public battle to win over investors. Kerry led the management team into three to five cities a day for investor meetings all over the country. Kerry was often joined by Great Western CFO Carl Geuther to help explain why Great Western wanted Washington Mutual over H. F. Ahmanson. Carl had a good Wall Street following and an easygoing manner. On the other hand, Great Western CEO John Maher, a former investment banker, only lasted for one meeting with investors. Kerry respected and enjoyed working with John, who was known for his blunt and candid opinions. However, when a leading Wall Street analyst said he favored the H. F. Ahmanson offer, John responded by telling the analyst he reminded him of "Bozo the Clown, and he wasn't going to respond to such a stupid comment." Knowing it was going to be a long battle, Kerry politely suggested the best use of John's time was to return to California to attend to important matters and let Carl help with the rest of the investor meetings.

During the battle, H. F. Ahmanson felt compelled to raise its offer, but Washington Mutual held firm. Washington Mutual kept the focus on its low-risk plan and ran full-page ads in the *Wall Street Journal* showing Washington Mutual's superior performance. Gradually, Washington

Mutual won over investors, and H. F. Ahmanson finally withdrew its hostile offer.

Kerry will never forget his relief on the day H. F. Ahmanson dropped out. After working fifteen-hour days for several weeks, he went live on CNBC to review the transaction, which received praise from investors and the media. After a few minutes under intense, hot studio lights, Kerry started to pass out from exhaustion. He fortunately thought to dig his fingernails into his leg to try to stay alert. After drawing blood under his pant leg, the interview continued without interruption.

Regulatory approvals were quickly obtained, and 80 percent of Great Western shareholders voted in favor of Washington Mutual's $8 billion acquisition value. *US Banker* magazine wrote:

> Great Western, the target of a hostile takeover bid by local rival H. F. Ahmanson, played out like a board game in which Killinger usually seemed to have the upper hand. Tirelessly courting Wall Street and ignoring or ridiculing the arrows shot his way by Ahmanson, Killinger kept the offering price within a competitive range for months. Then following a widely hailed analyst meeting in mid-May, he watched his stock climb above the competitors.
>
> As part of his acquisition and integration team, Killinger hired Deanna Oppenheimer and Craig Tall in 1985. A stuffed Energizer Bunny sits in his office, a gift from employees and a recognition of his work habits that symbolize his recent flurry of trips to California and Florida to introduce the bank to its new employees.
>
> Washington Mutual was chosen as the most respected bank in a *Fortune* magazine survey earlier this year. Regulators commented that Kerry's seriousness and commitment to community lending came across to all our members.[12]

Investors and the media were very complementary of the team. However, Kerry revealed, "We had about ten seconds of elation and then the realization the most important part of the journey had just begun. With a deadline of just nine months, there wasn't much time to take a breath before getting started on meeting the post-merger goals, including achieving identified cost reductions and revenue enhancements, attracting new households, increasing residential mortgage and deposit market share, and integrating operating systems."

Robert Bass, Washington Mutual's largest shareholder, complimented the "thrift's demonstrated track record of acquiring and successfully growing financial institutions. Bass added, "As shareholders, we have great confidence in management's ability to undertake and maximize the value of this acquisition."[13]

In the months that followed the Great Western acquisition, the integration was proceeding smoothly when Kerry was asked if he would take a call from H. F. Ahmanson CEO Charlie Rinehart. Even though Kerry and Charlie had fought hard in the Great Western battle, they respected each other. Kerry naturally accepted the call, figuring they would discuss industry issues. The call did not go as expected. Charlie jumped right in, asking Kerry, "We think you have developed a wonderful franchise. Would you be interested in acquiring H. F. Ahmanson?" Kerry was silent for a moment. The timing would be challenging, but he was interested.

Kerry immediately convened his executive committee and asked for a special meeting of the board's merger and acquisition committee. Everyone was concerned about all the work still to do on the Great Western acquisition, but they also knew the opportunity to acquire H. F. Ahmanson was unique. They also knew a major competitor would likely acquire Ahmanson if Washington Mutual didn't. Ahmanson had a strong retail branch system and an outstanding multifamily (apartment) lending unit that were hard to ignore. The multifamily lending unit would aid in Washington Mutual's plan to diversify away from residential home lending.

The decision was made to send a due diligence team in to see if a financially attractive acquisition with low risk to Washington Mutual shareholders was possible. A $10 billion acquisition proposal was developed that identified substantial cost savings and growth opportunities. The transaction included conservative pro forma assumptions and would be accretive to earnings within a year with an IRR (internal rate of return) of 16 percent, which would substantially exceed Washington Mutual's cost of capital and would create a strong low-risk balance sheet. The presentation deck showed that among banking peers, Washington Mutual, from January 1990 to March 1998, had the highest total annual shareholder return of 30.5 percent. Wells Fargo was 19.9 percent and Bank of America was 25 percent.[14]

The proposal was negotiated and then accepted by the H. F. Ahmanson board in October 1998. Once again, the team set out to quickly convert H. F. Ahmanson to the Washington Mutual operating platform and to achieve the cost savings promised to shareholders and the great service promised to customers.

In a short three years, Washington Mutual moved into the state of California and became the largest thrift in the country, with assets exceeding $150 billion. More important than size was achieving the clearly articulated goals in the five-year plan of reaching top-tier performance, growing the customer base with superior service, operating efficiently, providing an engaging workplace and awarding the staff with stock grants, maintaining low problem assets, and achieving high returns on shareholders' equity.

After years of dedicated work, virtually all goals set out in the 1995 five-year plan were achieved by the end of the decade. A key ingredient to achieving these goals was striving to have every employee in the organization committed to achieving the plan. Kerry visited hundreds of branches and delivered countless presentations to employee group meetings all over the country each year to reinforce the company's mission, values, five-year plan, and progress toward achieving the plan. All employees were given stock options or stock grants on several occasions over the years. Kerry wanted everyone to benefit from the hard work it took to achieve the plan.

Kerry also believed a single unified corporate culture needed to be achieved. After each acquisition, the new branch offices were quickly rebranded Washington Mutual, human resource systems and pay programs were unified, and a single operating platform was adopted. Washington Mutual's culture of frugality prevailed when all acquired corporate jets, company cars, country club memberships, and expensive artwork were either sold or donated to local arts organizations.

Following the H. F. Ahmanson acquisition, *Washington CEO* magazine described Kerry as having: "Ample portions of driving ambition, endless energy, excellent management skills and a good dose of lady luck." The article went on to quote executive Deanna Oppenheimer:

> Kerry is a type A personality who times himself while mowing the lawn. He sold a number of private jets owned by executives of the banks he acquired, preferring to fly business class. Kerry is gifted with ceaseless energy and an ability to connect with an audience

while communicating a message. If there is one word people attribute to Kerry, it's vision. He has a great financial mind with a knack for figuring out how to make money and seeing potential financial pitfalls. He is a very bright and very astute guy. He has that Midwest practicality and clear vision that has transformed the company's culture.

Analyst Jay Tejera added, "To sum it up, Killinger made credible with his people the possibility Washington Mutual could become a big profitable national bank."[15]

As the 1990s drew to a close, Washington Mutual was well on its way to achieving its mission of being the premier financial services organization by delivering superior customer service and an outstanding array of products to everyday consumers. The bank had the scale and financial strength to compete, and shareholders, employees, customers, and the communities it served were the beneficiaries. All the complex operating system conversions and branch consolidations from the large acquisitions were completed, and the franchise was performing very well. It was by far the most successful decade in the organization's 110-year history.

Most of the acquisitions in the nineties involved a carefully planned merger of smaller or similar-size banks. The three largest acquisitions were unique opportunities strongly supported by the banking regulators. Regardless, all the acquisitions continued to follow Kerry's rules: they had to have the same corporate culture and values, be accretive to earnings within the first year, have a disciplined risk culture and very low nonperforming loans, a 15 percent or higher return on capital, integration into Washington Mutual's operating systems within a few months, and business lines consistent with the strategic plan.

As the year 2000 approached, Kerry knew much more needed to be done to ensure the bank's continued success. Huge resources needed to be devoted to preparing computer systems for Y2K conversions. More importantly, Kerry knew Washington Mutual's historic roots in residential home lending needed to be diversified with a larger platform in small business, multifamily lending, credit cards, and consumer lending. His long-term goal was to change the bank from a monoline thrift charter to a diversified commercial bank charter.

The residential home lending business was changing and had become more volatile and less profitable over time. Federal government policies effectively nationalized most residential lending standards. Government guarantees on loans made by Fannie, Freddie, VA, and FHA greatly reduced the role of local thrift and bank portfolio lenders. Underwriting standards were increasingly dictated centrally by the Washington, DC bureaucrats rather than determined by local lenders.

Most residential loan originations moved away from regulated bank and thrift employees to unregulated mortgage brokers, who had little regulation and higher commissions. Loan servicing was separated from loan originations, and ownership of mortgages moved away from banks and thrifts to securitizations owned by investors. Efficient deployment of capital and managing to the Basel II capital standards all pressured banks and thrifts, including Washington Mutual, to retain fewer residential home loans on its balance sheet. Furthermore, government directives to expand LMI lending were pressuring all lenders to lower credit standards and engage in riskier lending activities.

For example, in order to receive regulatory and activist group support for the Great Western acquisition, Washington Mutual had to agree to a $75 billion ten-year commitment to expand LMI lending. Most of this lending had to be to lower-income (i.e., subprime) borrowers. The community groups threatened to support the competing H. F. Ahmanson offer and oppose the Washington Mutual proposal if it didn't commit to the high CRA goals. With the H. F. Ahmanson acquisition, the agreement had to be increased to a $100 billion, ten-year commitment. The bank's regulators—FDIC and OTS—encouraged this agreement and fully supported the political pressures to increase lending to low-income and other underserved communities. However, Washington Mutual was very cautious about LMI lending and only approved 40 percent of the applications, as opposed to a much more aggressive Wells Fargo, which approved 71 percent, and Bank of America, which approved 64 percent.[16]

Washington Mutual was primarily a fixed-rate residential portfolio lender for decades, and those low-interest fixed-rate loans nearly bankrupted the bank in the early 1980s when interest rates skyrocketed. The American Savings, Great Western, and H. F. Ahmanson acquisitions brought substantial portfolios and origination capabilities of adjustable-rate residential loans (ARMs), which were being pushed by the regulators, Congress, and presidents of both parties. These ARM loans performed well over the cycle because they were underwritten locally and were made to prime borrowers. They could be retained in portfolio because loan interest rates adjusted to changing interest rates. But by the end of the 1990s, Fannie Mae, Freddie Mac, and Wall Street were eyeing the product for their own use. Under pressure from Congress and government regulators, Fannie and Freddie lowered underwriting standards, decreased documentation requirements and purchased lower quality subprime loans from unregulated shadow mortgage brokers all over the country. A product once dominated by local portfolio lenders changed to a higher-risk product sold by unregulated brokers to Fannie, Freddie, and Wall Street.

Kerry realized these trends would make residential lending less profitable and riskier and he continued to move the bank away from residential mortgage lending.

Although Kerry had a highly successful career, it eventually impacted his personal life. He had always had a strong relationship with his two sons, spending substantial time with them when they were growing up. The three of them bonded over sports and outdoor activities, frequently waterskiing in the summer, snow skiing in the winter, and playing golf, tennis, basketball, and pickleball. Kerry even built a sports court in the backyard of their home and encouraged the boys' friends and neighbors to participate in team competitions. But in the early 1990s, Kerry's youngest son went off to college, and Kerry's travel requirements at Washington Mutual grew dramatically.

The California acquisitions in the late 1990s were especially taxing as Kerry continued to fly commercial to reinforce the frugal culture. Unfortunately, his wife did not enjoy travel, and they were often apart. Kerry noticed over the years how much worse his wife's alcoholism was getting, and he attempted to help her a number of times. He knew something more formal needed to be done when she spent $250,000 on his surprise birthday party in June of 1999. For someone still mowing his own lawn, this extravagance just did not compute. Her family and Kerry arranged an intervention for her, and she eventually agreed to enter the Betty Ford Center in January 2000. After she completed her stay, they agreed to separate and divorce. Kerry was grateful they had a cordial parting of the ways, there were no complications, and the divorce was quickly finalized by December of 2000.

Entering the new millennium, Kerry was looking forward to working on the next five-year plan, both professionally and personally.

6

Record Profits and the Stunning Growth of Shadow Banking

2000–2003

The golden age of banking occurred in the first few years of the new millennium. The industry was poised for success, and the success was universal. The new megabanks of Citigroup, JPMorgan Chase, Bank of America, Wells Fargo, and Wachovia had survived the purge of the 1980s and grew big and tall during the massive consolidations of the 1990s. The 1980s had started out with over 14,400 commercial banks, but in less than twenty years, the number of banks had dwindled down to about 8,315.[1]

Wall Street investment banks had also masterminded an enviable position for themselves. They had convinced the regulators that the sophisticated hedging and derivative products they had created were so safe they only needed minimal capital backup. No one was effectively watching the Wall Street investment banks while they gobbled up trillions of dollars of poor-quality subprime loans from unregulated subprime companies. All of these activities compiled so fast and so stealthily no one had a handle on how massive, intertwined, and fragile the system had become. Meanwhile this untested stealth system was showering billions of dollars of bonuses on Wall Street and their comrades.

The power elite of Wall Street was forming: Hank Paulson, chair and CEO of Goldman Sachs, was the leader of the group of investment bank CEOs that convinced regulators they didn't need much capital. While the regulated commercial banks and thrifts were required to have at least 6 percent backup capital, the investment banks quickly ramped up their leverage ratios up as high as forty to one. Sandy Weill had successfully built Citigroup into a mega–commercial and investment bank, but the bank continued to get into scrapes with the regulators.

Wells Fargo, Bank of America, and Wachovia continued to grow independently from the purview and the protection of the powerful Federal Reserve Bank of New York. They were regulated by less powerful Federal Reserve boards in their geographic location outside New York. The Wall Street commercial and investment banks were the most generous to Congress and therefore had the most power to wrestle Congress to their will.

At the beginning of the millennium, giant credit bubbles were growing as consumers rushed to extend their credit. Credit costs were low, and housing prices were rising. Because of the low interest rates, massive numbers of people were buying primary homes, vacation homes, and investment properties. Some of the most popular shows on TV taught amateurs how to flip houses for quick profits. Everyone got in on the action; no one wanted to be left behind. The media was regaling the public with stories of people with no previous real estate experience buying condos in Miami and other hot markets and flipping them for quick, easy profits.

Presidents Clinton and Bush and both parties in Congress had just put out mandates to increase homeownership and to expand affordable (subprime) lending. Regulated banks were pressured with increased CRA lending requirements, Fannie and Freddie received new subprime mandates, and unregulated subprime lenders grew into massive multibillion-dollar companies within months. Unregulated investment banks entered loan production agreements with the unregulated subprime lenders, and many purchased their own subprime companies, eventually producing 85 percent of all the subprime loans created from 2002 to 2007. (Chart Intro-3).

Large regulated banks limited the number of subprime loans they originated to less than 10 percent of their mortgage production. But unregulated investment banks and subprime companies could originate and securitize any amount and type of loan. Wall Street wrote its own standards, and the shadow subprime companies produced loans to meet those steadily declining standards.

The development of CDOs, CDSs, SIVs, and improved technology for slicing, dicing, and pooling the loans provided the means for Wall Street to leverage up the volume of subprime loans. Fannie and Freddie, mandated by Congress and their regulator, FHFA, similarly provided a growing outlet for loan originations to subprime borrowers.

As a result of government encouragement and strong investor demand, the number of unregulated subprime mortgage originators exploded in the early 2000s. Very quickly, more than three hundred thousand unregulated mortgage brokers around the country were originating subprime loans for over one hundred fast-growing unregulated companies like Ameriquest, New Century, Option One (owned by H&R Block), WMC Mortgage (owned by GE), Freemont General, and BNC Mortgage.

Subprime loans were sold to Wall Street and then resold to investors as whole loans or securitizations. With the development of CDOs and CDSs, investors could select the level of return and risk that best met their needs. Most buyers of these loans and CDOs were sophisticated institutional investors, such as hedge funds, mutual funds, pension and retirement plans, and foreign money managers in their insatiable search for higher yields. Most securitizations were rated by the rating agencies, S&P, Moody's, and Fitch. They all should have known better.

2000

Washington Mutual entered the new millennium a completely changed organization. Kerry and his team took the bank from near bankruptcy in 1982 and grew it to the sixth-largest bank in America, stretching across the country with over $200 billion in assets. Every goal in the last five years had been met—ROE over 15 percent, ROA over 1 percent, and continual recognition for the best place to work and bank. Its large California acquisitions had been integrated and were highly profitable. With the bank doing well, Kerry hoped he could work on his personal plan, but he found he was much too busy to focus on his personal life. However, despite putting his personal life on the back burner, fate had other ideas.

Kerry and Linda first met on October 26, 1999, at a Federal Home Loan Bank meeting in Seattle. They were both vice chairs of their regional Federal Home Loan Banks (FHLBs of Seattle and Des Moines) and had been elected to the National Council of FHLBs. At the meeting in late October, the president of the Des Moines FHLB introduced Linda to Kerry. She told Kerry she knew his father, Karl, who had founded and conducted the music concerts at the steps of the Capitol building every summer. Those concerts were great; you gathered a blanket, hung out on the Capitol steps, and listened to concert band music or music from the Big Band era while gazing at the stars on a warm summer night. We spent a lot of time talking that day, mostly about what it was like growing up in Des Moines, Iowa, a childhood experience accurately captured in Bill Bryson's book *The Life and Times of the Thunderbolt Kid.*

During the year 2000, Linda and Kerry briefly saw each other at a couple of council meetings, and Kerry called her a couple of times that year to ask her advice about the new leadership center he was building near Sea-Tac airport. He knew she had started a leadership school for banks in the Midwest and wanted her thoughts on curriculum. She asked him for advice in her work as chair of Iowa governor Tom Vilsack's housing task force.

It was a busy year for both of them that left no time for a social life. Kerry was gearing up to execute his most complex five-year plan for 2000–2005, which focused on growing the retail banking operations into key cities across the country, diversifying the asset mix away from residential loans, expanding loan servicing capabilities, and growing commercial, multifamily, and small business lending. He also wanted to find a way to develop a safe mortgage product for the LMI communities. He established financial targets for achieving industry top-quartile performance for return on equity, operating efficiency, asset quality, and customer growth. An important part of the new five-year plan was to reduce the bank's concentration in California and diversify into cities with dense and growing populations: New York, Chicago, Dallas, Houston, Phoenix, Atlanta, and cities in Florida.

At the start of the millennium, Kerry wanted to grow the mortgage business, but the major challenge of the business was its cyclical nature. When interest rates were low and housing demand was good, new loan originations, especially refinancing, had high volume and strong profitability. Conversely, new loan origination volumes and profitability fell dramatically when interest rates rose. Kerry wanted to balance the cyclical mortgage business by growing the mortgage servicing area, adding credit card companies and commercial multifamily lending (apartment houses), developing the retail branch system, and becoming a leader in nationwide online banking. He was particularly intrigued with developing the first completely automated online checking account product.

The servicing (collecting payments, etc.) of mortgage loans for others provided good income over the cycle, but the duration of that income was unknown. If a loan remained outstanding for thirty years, the income stream continued for that full period. However, if a loan was quickly refinanced, that income stream would be cut off. Accounting policy required the mortgage-serving stream of income (called mortgage servicing rights—MSRs) to be valued as an asset that had to be continually marked to market. The value of the MSR asset could fall dramatically when interest rates fell and rise dramatically when interest rates rose—just the opposite cycle of mortgage originations.

For this reason, the mortgage servicing business was viewed as a "natural hedge" to the highs and lows of the residential loan origination business. In order to smooth out the residential mortgage loan profitability, Washington Mutual expanded its loan servicing capabilities in 2001 and 2002 through purchases of the loan servicing portfolios of PNC Mortgage, Fleet Mortgage, and Homeside Lending. These purchases were all done on attractive terms, and Washington Mutual gained the added benefit of acquiring loan origination capabilities in new geographic areas.

But that wasn't the only mortgage issue facing all the banks. Congress and the federal regulators were demanding all banks dramatically increase their LMI lending to meet their CRA goals. At the beginning of the millennium, nearly every regulated big bank went out and dutifully acquired a subprime mortgage company to fulfill those CRA goals. It was a challenge for all the regulated banks to figure out how they were going to properly enter this relatively new market.

Kerry had mixed feelings about the pressures to increase lending to millions of new LMI households. He definitely wanted to help more people fulfill the American dream of homeownership, but he was leery of the subprime industry. The industry had only been around for a few years but had experienced rowdy booms and busts. It was not federally regulated, survived on expensive overnight funding, often had sloppy operating systems, charged high interest rates, and had a scurrilous culture. The companies were constantly chased after by the state attorneys general and showed little remorse for its nefarious activities. Fines and settlements were just a cost of doing business. These companies employed high-pressure salesmen who were paid on a commission-only basis. They couldn't be more different than the friendly, engaged employees who greeted customers at the Washington Mutual branches—employees who were paid for great customer service and long-term relationships, not short-term commissions.

Kerry honestly believed he could figure a way to change the subprime industry. What if you could develop a product with low costs, good value, and fair, honest dealings focused on the LMI market?

If Washington Mutual could develop better customer-oriented products and deliver them to borrowers at lower prices, this would be highly beneficial to everyone. Kerry knew this effort would be only marginally profitable because the broker commissions were high and the loan sizes were relatively small. However, he viewed subprime lending as a necessary part of achieving a needed public service and achieving a high CRA rating. To become more familiar with the industry, the bank began buying subprime loans for its own portfolio in 1998. The loans were limited to less than 5 percent of the mortgage portfolio. Performance of this subprime portfolio was much better than the industry average because Washington Mutual re-underwrote all loans purchased and had the right to put back loans not meeting its standards. Returns on this portfolio were adequate, and losses were less than 1 percent—well below industry averages.

The primary products for the subprime industry were 2/28 and 3/27 hybrid adjustable-rate loans. Interest rates were fixed at a lower rate for two or three years and would then reset to higher rates over the remainder of the loan term. These loans worked well for those subprime borrowers who improved their credit scores within the first two or three years and refinanced into lower cost prime fixed-rate mortgages. However, these loans could be expensive for subprime borrowers not able to improve their credit scores.

Based on the success of this portfolio, Washington Mutual decided to purchase a small subprime mortgage originator. California-based Long Beach Mortgage was selected, and the $350 million acquisition was completed in 2000. This was a very small acquisition and only represented a small percentage of the total assets of the bank. Like most of the subprime companies, Long Beach did not originate its own loans but bought them directly from a network of thousands of local unregulated mortgage brokers. The long-term plan was to gradually replace Long Beach's broker origination network with bank employees located in Washington Mutual branches. The plan was also to develop more customer-friendly products and to offer them with lower fees than other lenders. It was hoped both the bank's CRA goals and the public would benefit.

There was never an expectation of more than modest profitability from the subprime unit, because the loans were small and were costly to originate. Independent brokers wouldn't do subprime unless there were higher commissions because of the all the extra work they required.

To help figure out how best to serve the LMI neighborhoods, Kerry developed a partnership with Earvin "Magic" Johnson, who had been working on economic revitalization in urban neighborhoods. Johnson persuaded Starbucks, TGI Fridays, and Lowes Cineplex to locate in urban areas, but supermarkets and banks were missing. Kerry worked with Magic to help rebuild those communities. Both Magic and Kerry believed if it was safe to go to work and walk the streets, if the public education system was solid, and then you add homeownership, you've created an environment where people can live and prosper. Within two years, they had added about twenty-two lending centers to inner-city and underserved communities.[2]

Another key part of Kerry's five-year plan was to diversify away from the bank's heavy concentrations in California. He was looking carefully in the high-growth states of Nevada, New York, Texas, Arizona, and Florida. He proceeded with Texas first.

The bank already had forty-eight branches in Texas, acquired from the H. F. Ahmanson transaction, but a larger presence was needed in Texas to reach operating efficiency and fully participate in the growing Texas marketplace. After reviewing all the alternatives, Houston-based United Savings, run by legendary Wall Street executive Lew Ranieri, was selected. Kerry had met Lew years earlier when Lew was vice chairman of Salomon Brothers, where he created private mortgage-backed securities, which revolutionized the residential mortgage industry. Banks could now take mortgages and other loan products off their books, securitize them and sell them off to investors, without the help of Fannie and Freddie.

The purchase of Texas-based Bank United brought 155 branch offices plus good expertise in small business lending. After a period of negotiations, a mutually beneficial deal was put together, and the transaction closed in February 2001. With that transaction completed, it was now time to look for opportunities in New York City, Florida, Nevada, and Arizona.

Beyond acquisitions, Washington Mutual worked on fine-tuning its retail banking model. Friendly service, free checking, low or no fees, and good value for the dollar were primary themes. Extensive customer research showed average, everyday customers were intimidated by the cold, formal atmosphere of most banks. So the bank created a colorful retail store setting, tore down the teller cages, and allowed employees to roam free, wearing khakis and golf shirts, to help customers with their financial needs. The bank was trying to create a friendly space where families could attend to all their banking or investment needs while their children played in the toy area. This space not only attracted customers but proved to be safer, with far fewer robberies, because money was stored in impenetrable kiosks.

Kerry also felt everyday consumers would be best served by employees with diverse backgrounds who understood the needs and challenges of the diverse group of customers. Washington Mutual promoted and provided a safe environment for large numbers of women, minorities, and the LGBTQ+ community. The bank continually had a high number of female and minority executives and board members compared to the industry. Kerry had a strong compassion for issues facing people from all walks of life, and there are hundreds of examples of his generosity to employees, customers, and people in distress. For example, in the early 1990s, Kerry's concern over the lack of health care for AIDS patients inspired him to lead an AIDS awareness walk in Seattle, which successfully raised over $1 million for the treatment of AIDS patients. The executive team was also deeply involved in affordable housing development, and many weekends Kerry would work with his team to clean up and revitalize distressed neighborhoods and schools.

It was also important to recognize the employees who worked hard to create a great customer experience. Bonuses were not just based on sales, but a balanced scorecard of customer service scores, employee satisfaction, quality of lending, and innovation of service. The bank made stock and stock option grants to all employees to reinforce the importance of long-term performance. The bank also had cutting-edge employee benefit plans, including subsidized wellness, college tuition reimbursement, and child daycare programs.

Kerry also developed a variety of recognition programs for employees, including annual recognition trips. Every year thousands of the outstanding, hardworking employees were rewarded with trips to Hawaii and other tropical places for recognition events and celebrations of their work. Rather than only recognizing front-line salespeople, the branch office, support and operations personnel also participated in recognition events. Many of them had never been on a plane before. They all proudly took a spouse, parent, child, or friend with them on the trip to receive the awards. Every employee got to go up on stage and receive their award. The celebrations were joyous, and Kerry personally greeted and had pictures taken with every one of the thousands of employees who attended the award trips.

Kerry spent a great deal of time traveling around the country to talk with community service groups, civil rights activists, education groups, and advocates for underserved neighborhoods. He encouraged employees and activists to feel comfortable telling him the bad news along with the good news and welcomed an active dialogue. He wasn't a banker who spent his time in the Hamptons or at prestigious country clubs. He saw himself more as a community organizer, a promoter of education, an advocate for human rights. He spent his weekends working on community service projects and home renovations.

Kerry believed compensation should be fair and consistent with achieving long-term objectives. Senior management and executive pay programs were all directly linked to the strategic plan and annual operating plans, and base salaries were set at market averages. Kerry hired Daryl David from Amazon to head up the human resources department and hired Towers Perrin to develop a sophisticated compensation plan based on achieving long-term objectives. Bonuses were tied to a balanced scorecard of growth, customer service, employee satisfaction, excellent loan performance, operating efficiency, asset quality, and profitability. Cash compensation was deemphasized, with most pay tied to long-term performance and denominated in Washington Mutual stock performance. For the top executives, 90 percent of pay was paid in stock and tied to specific operating goals over multiyear periods. This pay approach worked very well by keeping executives focused on long-term results.

Overall, 2000 was a very good year for Washington Mutual. Even though the economy was slowing, Washington Mutual posted excellent results. It had been less than two years since the Ahmanson and Great Western acquisitions, but they were fully integrated and producing record profits. The bank earned a record $496.9 million in the fourth quarter and a record $1.9 billion for the year 2000. The cash dividend on the stock was increased each quarter, and the bank had grown to two thousand branches and $195 billion in assets with a share price trading at forty-five dollars.

2001

In 2001, the economy continued to soften due to a decline in GDP, and Kerry expressed his concern in an interview with the *Seattle PI* in early 2001:

> We are closely watching credit quality and may increase loan loss provisions this year. The company has no credit cards and little unsecured consumer debt, two areas where defaults and delinquencies tend to be higher in slowing economies. We will put off expansion of the commercial lending until the economy improves.[3]

In April *USA Today* released the salaries and bonuses of the top one hundred public company CEOs. Kerry was ranked fiftieth, placing him squarely in the middle, right where he wanted to be. Washington Mutual had outperformed most of the companies in the top five hundred, but Kerry worked hard to make sure the executives and the board of directors were in the middle of the pay scales. He didn't want to be in the group of banks like Citigroup, which awarded its CEO with $301 million in stock that year, or American Express, which awarded its CEO with $48 million in stock.[4]

In the spring, *Forbes* magazine issued its "Super 100" evaluation of big companies based on their sales, profits, assets, and market value. Washington Mutual came in forty-eighth out of the top five hundred companies in the S&P. The bank was nineteenth in assets, sixty-first in profits, 123rd in sales, and ninety-sixth in market value. Even with all those great financial rankings, Washington Mutual still stayed in the midrange in pay.[5]

Business Week also issued its list of "Top Fifty Business Performers of the Year." Washington Mutual was ranked thirty-ninth out of the five hundred S&P companies. Nine ingredients went into performance rankings, including revenue growth, earnings growth, and total returns (stock price movement plus dividends), which are key measures of how well management is performing for shareholders. The top 20 percent were graded A, next 20 percent got B, and so on. Washington Mutual was rated an A and was in the top ten for percentage increase in total return.[6]

After all the success in the business, Kerry was finally ready to move on with his personal life, and he thought he had found the right person. In April of 2001, he called Linda and asked if they could have dinner sometime. Linda was finalizing her divorce, and she had accepted a consulting partnership on the West Coast. She told him she was going on a long-overdue solo eat-pray-love vacation to Italy in May and would be back after two weeks. This did not deter him. Kerry responded he would be in Sweden that week leading a Seattle Chamber visit to sister city Stockholm, and perhaps he could fly to Milan to meet her for dinner.

When it was time to leave Stockholm, Kerry told several Chamber board members he was flying to Milan to have dinner with a wonderful woman. The board members were thrilled to see the normally calm Kerry so excited. Kerry had been separated and divorced for over a year and a half, so everyone was hoping he would soon find someone. During their discussion, one of the board members said, "Kerry, do you know there are two airports in Milan? Linate for European flights and Malpensa for international flights. You two will be at different airports." This was before everyone carried international cell phones, and Kerry didn't know what hotel Linda was staying in, so the entire Chamber group went into problem-solving mode. Maybe a message could somehow be sent to the airline? Kerry thought about it for a few minutes and said he had a plan.

Meanwhile, Linda was waiting patiently in the Milan Malpensa airport after a long coach flight in a foreign country where she didn't know the language. After waiting for Kerry for a while, she gave up and checked into her tiny Milan hotel. She didn't have a personal phone number for Kerry, so the only option was to leave a message on his business line, something like, "Sorry I missed you, I will be back in the West Coast in a couple of weeks." She expected to hear something like, "This is Kerry, leave a message," but instead Kerry's message on his business line said, "If this is Linda, there are two airports in Milan. I am at the other one and I will wait right here until you come." Linda grabbed her suitcase, found a taxi, and went to the Linate airport. Kerry was quietly waiting on a small bench outside the airport. He rented a car and drove her to Lake Como. We sat on the deck of an outdoor restaurant by the lake and talked all night.

We quickly discovered we had lived parallel lives and were surprised by our common experiences. We were born in the same hospital, delivered by the same doctor, only nine months apart. Our fathers had just come back from the war, and our families lived in the same block near Drake University, where they attended the same classes on the GI Bill. Our families had served their country well during the war. Linda's family was especially grateful because her father, four of his brothers, his sister, and two brothers-in-law all returned safely from the war. We had both been raised with the same Iowa values of hard work, integrity, and caring for others and were both committed to a strong activism in affordable housing and human rights—values we learned from our families. We both had worked multiple jobs putting ourselves through public Iowa universities and both had long and successful careers in banking, insurance, and finance.

Kerry's grandfather Henry was a farmer and music teacher in Adel, Iowa. Henry made it a practice to help friends and relatives with personal and home loans. He loaned Kerry money to buy his first home, and he also prided himself on lending money to up-and-coming musicians, including a loan to Karl King, who went on to write and publish more band marches than anyone in Iowa's history. Every summer Kerry would spend months on his grandfather's farm, where he learned construction techniques, completed the farm chores, and learned how to avoid getting zapped by electric fences and which ponds had the best fishing.

Linda came from five generations of Iowa farmers, and her father, Richard, started a heavy construction equipment business in Iowa in the early fifties that was one of the first in the country to provide finance, leasing, and rental options for customers. He noticed many of his customers and employees didn't have the down payment for a business or home loan; many felt too intimidated to approach a downtown banker. Richard offered them down payments and below-market-rate loans. He put his family on a very tight budget and lived frugally in a small house so they would be able to help their customers and employees succeed.

Because they lived in one of the poorer neighborhoods in town, Linda noticed many of the neighborhood kids lived in homes with little indoor plumbing, and sometimes their parents weren't home for dinner. She would regularly gather them up and her mom would cook them dinner. When Linda was in grade school, her mother taught her how to record mortgage payments and amortize loans given to employees and customers. Her father later sold his company and retired early so he could devote all his time to raising money for the regional children's hospital that provided free medical care to handicapped children.

Our families inspired us both to care deeply about helping people achieve their dream of a safe, warm home and created our passion for home lending as a public service. On that night at Lake Como, we realized we had missed an opportunity by waiting so long to spend time together. We needed to make up for lost time.

When Kerry was back in Seattle, he continued to explore retail bank expansion opportunities in the greater New York market. Market research indicated New York customers were dissatisfied with their current banks and would readily switch to a bank with friendly service and low-fee products. New York was the nation's largest banking market at the time, with $500 billion in deposits, 10 percent of the US total. The research concluded Washington Mutual would do very well in New York if it could assemble a sizable branching network.

Kerry researched several smaller and medium-size thrifts in the New York area, but he needed one hundred or more branches to get a solid foothold in the area. The acquisition team finally settled on Dime

Savings as an ideal candidate because of its branch network and solid deposit base of $13 billion. Dime suffered from below-average financial performance, but Washington Mutual could quickly change that with cost savings from integrating operating systems and adding the bank's products and services.

In June 2001, Washington Mutual announced the acquisition of Dime Savings, and the transaction closed in January 2002. Part of Kerry's goal in entering the New York market was getting the attention of Wall Street to realize the bank was going national, and the acquisition did get attention. The *Wall Street Journal* reported:

> Some banking experts say a savvy small bank operator could compete effectively in the New York market, which is dominated by Citigroup and JPMorgan Chase. Industry analysts say Washington Mutual, which has a reputation as a skillful acquirer, has had its eye on New York for some time.[7]
>
> Despite being populated by financial giants, the New York consumer-banking market remains fairly fragmented and analysts expect Washington Mutual to take market share from rivals, much as it has done in California. The bank should reap about $150 million in annual costs savings from the deal.[8]

Money magazine agreed: "Washington Mutual has turned superior service into a potent marketing tool." But the magazine was concerned bank mergers were out of favor with Wall Street. "High profile blowups like First Union's purchase of the Money Store and Bank One's merger with First Chicago have soured fund managers like Henry Cavanna on acquisitive banks. However, even as analysts and shareholders rave about Washington Mutual's earnings growth of 17% a year since 1996 and total shareholder return of 25% annualized over the same period, the bank trades at a modest earnings multiple. With its earnings growth showing no signs of letting up, profits climbed 40% in the first quarter."[9]

The modest earnings multiple was a double-edged sword. The low multiple reflected the general distaste Wall Street held for thrifts, leftover feelings from the banking crisis of the eighties. However, for Washington Mutual, the low multiple meant the bank was undervalued, with potential for growth. Richard Meagley, whose Safeco Equity Fund owned 3.5 million Washington Mutual shares, explained:

The bank has never done a truly bad deal. Killinger's acquisition record is superb. Mortgage lending and branch banking are low margin businesses that need scale to succeed. Other banks responded to this problem by redeploying capital from mortgages into high risk, high margin businesses like venture capital and stock underwriting.

Forbes magazine also weighed in:

.

Washington Mutual now has 2,656 branches and offices up from 39 when he [Kerry] arrived in 1982. The mild-mannered and bespectacled Killinger is fond of tossing off what underlings call 'Kerryisms,' like 'frugal is sexy' and 'check your ego at the door.' The bank is the nation's largest thrift with $247 billion in assets. The stock trades at only 11.6 times forward earnings, compared with an average multiple of 13.8 for nine of its big bank peers. ROA for the bank is 1.2%. Kerry often trots out a slide illustrating the company has produced the third highest five-year earnings growth rate among the ten largest banks. Give Killinger credit for elevating his thrift above a drab peer group and notching a 33.5% annual return as CEO.[10]

Jonathan E. Gray of Sanford C. Bernstein & Co. wrote:

Washington Mutual's management has a history of which Alexander the Great would have been proud and they haven't had problems with integrating their acquisitions, which is amazing.[11]

Many of the articles repeated Kerry's rules for acquisitions: he won't do a turnaround, because he won't gamble with the bank's results. He maintains a target of 20 percent return on common equity and a 14 percent earnings-per-share growth target. New acquisitions must be accretive to earnings within a few months, and they must be a good fit with the bank's core strategies and values. There must be a disciplined risk culture and a low rate of nonperforming loans.

Because of the rise in home lending due to government mandates, Kerry decided to establish his "Responsible Lending Principles," becoming one of the first lenders to create specific principles to guide mortgage origination. The principles stated the bank would only do business with licensed brokers in good standing, would independently evaluate the borrower's ability to repay the loan, would require certain fair pricing and credit grades from brokers, and use foreclosures only as a last resort. The bank started a large Medical and Financial Hardship fund to help borrowers avoid foreclosure and would not refinance a home unless it was a net tangible help to the customer. They would not originate loans where points and fees exceed 5 percent of the loan and did not purchase loans where broker fees exceeded 5 percent. They would not originate or purchase high cost mortgage loans as defined by HOEPA and would not sell single premium credit insurance.

In the fall of 2001, George H. W. Bush's Points of Light Foundation presented Kerry and Washington Mutual with the Award for Excellence in Corporate Community Service. Their award stated:

> At Washington Mutual, making communities better places to live and work is part of the mission. Their charitable giving will total more than $70 million in the form of grants and other assistance with an emphasis on affordable housing and K-12 public education. Additionally, they have made a ten-year $75 [to $100] billion lending commitment for low and moderate communities nationwide.
>
> The bank complements its financial support with hands-on involvement. Employees started volunteering in the 1950s and they now have a structured company-wide program called CAN! (Committed Active Neighbors). The bank provides incentives including four paid hours per month for volunteering, a $100 donation to the nonprofit for every 15 hours of service; coupons redeemable for CAN! merchandise including clothing, book bags and quarterly awards for exemplary projects. Two pages of the company's monthly magazine are devoted to coverage of volunteer efforts across the country.
>
> In housing the company provides major grant support for programs and projects that provide safe, long-term affordable housing for low income individuals and families. Last year, the bank's financial and employee volunteers were the national sponsor of National NeighborWorks Week where an estimated 22,000 families were assisted and 3,500 homes were improved, making

it the most widespread housing and community revitalization campaign in the event's 18-year history. More than 50% of the employees volunteered on thousands of projects ranging from repairing homes to serving food at local homeless shelters. They hold Community Summits around the country to get feedback on community needs.[12]

In the first week of September 2001, Kerry asked Linda to fly to New Jersey with him to meet his son, daughter-in-law, and two grand-children. We had a wonderful visit, two-year-old granddaughter Lexi and Linda developed an immediate attachment, while Kerry had several business meetings in New York. On Monday, September 10, we took a United Airlines flight out of the Newark airport. Linda remembers commenting on the lax security at the gate. The airport security employees were chatting in the corner, and bags went through security unnoticed. We were flying to Omaha to participate in Warren Buffett's annual charity golf tournament. The next day the United flight out of that same gate was hijacked, and the passengers bravely tried to fight off the terrorists. We were all terrified about everything that unfolded in front of us on September 11. We spent that night at dinner with Warren Buffett and his group, extremely concerned about the safety of our country.

Kerry met Warren Buffett in the early 1970s, when Kerry was an equity research analyst with Bankers Life of Nebraska. They were both fans of Ben Graham's value-investing strategies. These strategies helped Kerry propel the growth in his mutual fund company. Buffett knew they had similar approaches and had recently written Kerry a letter, stating, "I have followed Washington Mutual's success and you have done an outstanding job." Linda also knew Buffett from the early 1980s, when he offered her and a friend jobs at his company. They both turned down the offers, because the compensation was based mostly on stock grants, and they didn't know how Berkshire Hathaway's stock would perform over time. This was clearly one of those decisions Linda wished she could redo.

During the time we spent in Omaha waiting for flights to resume, we had a lot of time to discuss living life to the fullest, how family is the most important thing in the world and none of us knew how long we had to enjoy the people we love. We had originally planned to wait a lot longer to get married, but after our experience on September 11, we understood how much we wanted to be together and decided to get married sooner rather than later.

On a crisp fall day in October, Kerry took Linda to their favorite Seattle restaurant, Canlis. After dinner, Kerry got down on one knee and asked Linda to spend the rest of their lives together. We were married over the Thanksgiving holiday on a beach in Hawaii.

That fall Kerry dedicated the new Cedarbrook leadership center near the Sea-Tac airport. With all the acquisitions over the last few years, Kerry wanted a leadership center close to the airport and bank headquarters to get people together to work on common goals and values and continue the culture of community and customer service. He also wanted a central location for continued training on the bank's total quality management program—*Operational Excellence*. The center saved millions each year in travel and hotel expenses, and it was handy to have the center so close to the downtown headquarters.[13] The *Puget Sound Business Journal* reported on the new Cedarbrook leadership center:

> Kerry wanted to teach the same values and culture in an inviting
> corporate center, called Cedarbrook, which resembled a quaint
> mountain lodge surrounded by trees, a calming stream and
> attached hotel lodge. They saved a lot of money and created an
> inviting environment for planning, project development and
> leadership training. Kerry said as they grew, they needed to keep
> the leadership bench strong and deep and continue the common
> culture and values.[14]

As always, Kerry was very busy that fall with a number of projects at the bank and a lot of travel. Kerry came home one night and told Linda the former CEO of Washington Mutual, Lou Pepper, wanted us to drive to his house for dinner so he could meet Linda. Lou had been retired from the bank for over thirteen years, but Kerry and Lou were close, and Kerry continued to provide Lou office space in the bank. After Kerry had become CEO, the rise in Washington Mutual's stock price made Lou financially well off, and he loved giving speeches about Washington Mutual's success. As expected, Lou and his wife, Mollie, hit it off well with Linda, and Lou said he was really happy Kerry had found such a wonderful woman and he fully approved. Lou even gave Linda a manuscript of a small book he was writing and asked her to critique it.

In December 2001, Kerry received the Banker of the Year award from the American Bankers Association. It was the first time they had given the award to a thrift CEO. Kerry was also the only thrift CEO to be asked to join the invitation-only Financial Services Roundtable, whose members were CEOs of the largest banks, insurance companies, and credit card companies in the country. Kerry was on their board, and became vice chair of the group and chair-elect for 2008. In the *American Banker* article announcing the award, the bank's executive vice president, Craig Tall, said, "Kerry was very good at articulating the story to investors and employees." Another officer, Bill Longbrake, said, "When an opportunity presents itself, Kerry doesn't react emotionally. He reacts strategically. He wants as much financial information on the table as possible, but he does have an intuitive capability. When they were working on the Ahmanson deal, they attended close to 200 meetings with investors. Kerry has a long run view; his sense was he was building a company that would have significant value over time."

Phil Erlanger of Lehman Brothers shared:

> He's one of the more driven people I know. He really wants to be a winner in the industry, but he doesn't come across as a grab you by the throat or arrogant kind of guy.

The article continued, "Investor enthusiasm with the concept of a consumer bank/mortgage giant, plus the bank's immunity from commercial loan problems, made it one of the best performing financial services companies. Last year the stock rose 105% and third quarter profits rose 84% to $832 million. Associates say although the bank has changed a lot under Killinger, he has not changed. He has learned to delegate more, but still relies on the group of senior execs who started at the bank when he did. At staff meetings, one is apt to hear Killinger utter such maxims as 'check your ego at the door,' 'frugal is sexy' and 'what can't be measured can't be managed.'"[15]

Lou Pepper added, "There's no ego in the man, he's just the same as when I first met him."

2002

The year 2002 began on a strong note. Profits for 2001 reached a record $3.1 billion, and the Dime Savings acquisition was successfully integrated. New York was an exciting new market for the bank. But there were four challenges to tackle in 2002: straighten out the newly purchased small Long Beach Mortgage company; install the new mortgage origination and servicing system, named Optis; develop a centralized risk management unit; and develop the next generation of executives to take on the added diversification and sophistication of the bank.

The toughest challenges were straightening out the Long Beach Subprime Mortgage company and installing the Optis loan origination and servicing system. Long Beach represented only a small fraction of the bank's assets and it was purchased as an experiment to see if the bank could effectively develop a safe and honest product for the LMI market. The Long Beach employees did not originate loans but purchased them from the unregulated and unpredictable independent mortgage brokers. Immediately after acquiring Long Beach, Kerry had made significant management changes and tightened up the underwriting guidelines and controls.

However, dealing with the independent mortgage brokers proved to be a challenge. Kerry implemented a number of rules to rein in the brokers, including refusing to pay commissions if the loans defaulted within the year. He finally had to completely stop all production and move his general counsel, Fay Chapman, in to straighten out all the legal and administrative issues. Once she gave her okay to resuming production, they would try again. Fortunately, the subprime market was only a tiny fraction of the bank's mortgage business, but Kerry was determined to try to make a difference in the industry, even though the subprime loan business was not profitable.

The other tough issue was the integration of the mortgage servicers PNC Mortgage, Fleet Mortgage, and Homeside Lending into the bank's new loan-servicing platform. A team of technology experts, including Accenture, developed and implemented a new industry-leading loan origination and servicing system called Optis. The bank had always been successful with computer system integrations, but Optis proved a challenge. After continual delays and excessive costs, Kerry became progressively frustrated and concerned about whether the existing management team could execute the complex issues. He decided to change the home loans group management and simplify some of the systems under development. He also hired Deb Horvath from General Electric to be the executive vice president and chief information officer, and she successfully reworked Optis into an effective operations platform.

The other top priorities of developing the management team and consolidating the risk function also proved to be successful. Several executives were nearing retirement age, and others were having difficulties keeping up with the complexities of an expanding company. With an employee base of sixty thousand and operations stretching from coast to coast, skills in managing large work groups were required. Washington Mutual's growth and unique culture and values were a strong draw, and soon dozens of new senior and executive managers were trained up through the ranks at the Cedarbrook leadership center, and executives were also recruited from other large financial institutions. High on the list was a hunt for a new chief financial officer (CFO) as well as a new risk manager with large, complex banking experience. Kerry selected Tom Casey from General Electric as CFO, who would prove to be an extremely valuable asset in the coming years.

Another key addition Kerry wanted to make to the executive team was a chief enterprise risk officer (CERO) to report directly to Kerry and head an industry-leading enterprise risk management (ERM) department. The new ERM department brought all the operating, credit, compliance, and market risk managers into one group. Chief risk officers were set up in each business unit, and the CERO was responsible for risk for the entire organization. Kerry prided himself on the bank's low ratio of nonperforming assets, which had been lowered to a fraction of 1 percent of total assets versus over 3 percent when he first arrived at the bank. Kerry frequently spoke to business units about the importance of ERM, and every month the CERO presented his risk reports to the executive team and every quarter to the finance and audit committees of the board as well as the full board.

Bill Longbrake, former CFO for the bank and for the FDIC, established the original ERM department and quickly turned the job over to Jim Vanasek, who came from risk management at Wells Fargo. When Kerry called Wells Fargo CEO, Dick Kovacevich, for a recommendation for Jim, he was told Jim was very good but was inflexible and would be tough on the lending people. He went on to say Jim preferred making no loans to taking on any risk. Kerry loved that recommendation, because he wanted a tough-minded watchdog. Kerry told Vanasek ERM would always receive priority funding, even during periods when there would be company-wide cuts. Kerry kept his promise, and ERM staffing remained the same up through 2008, even though residential loan originations decreased by 74 percent.

Every quarter, CERO Vanasek presented his risk reports to the executive committee, the board, and the board finance and audit committees. Each quarter he signed a statement that "the department was adequately staffed and functioning effectively, and sufficient resources were being provided across the organization to support critical risk management functions." Vanasek also met privately with the board committees and the regulators so he could be completely candid. He would also regularly give risk reports to the public during frequent investor calls and quarterly earnings calls, certifying publicly to the bank's effective risk controls and very low rate of nonperforming loans.

In January 2002, *Fast Company* magazine interviewed the bank's executives on the success of their acquisition strategy. Executives commented that after an acquisition, the integration team would do presentations to the new employees:

> The new employees would come into the room nervous and cautious, but after we did presentations about the bank, the environment and values, the tension was gone and the new employees would say, 'This sounds like the company I've always wanted to work for, but never knew existed.'
>
> Washington Mutual currently has grown to 4 million checking account holders and the bank stock price has climbed nearly tenfold in the past decade. Executive Vice President Craig Tall said the 'success is more striking because many banks and brokers have a terrible time making acquisitions work.' Tall described the six key rules from the bank's M&A playbook: 'Focus on a few key markets where you can achieve national leadership, work with companies who share the same values, immediately merge the companies into the bank's structure and values, close the deals quickly, go all out to win the trust of your new employees and don't become too dependent on acquisitions—never stop growing internally.'[16]

On February 14, Kerry and Linda held a wedding reception in Seattle and invited a number of people from Washington Mutual and the Seattle community. Our parents and a number of family members also attended the event. We hired a local band that played for a lot of events in Seattle. When Linda hired the band, she talked to the leader and told him she wanted Kerry's father to come up and play with the band at some point. The bandleader gave her a knowing look and said, "Yes, of course, we do that for a lot of family members. We could let him come up and play a song with us. Don't worry, it's a big band and nobody will be able to hear him."

About halfway through the night, the bandleader asked Karl to come up with his trombone. After the first few notes, the band members looked around at each other in shock. Then they asked him to stay and play more songs. By the end of the night, they were asking Karl to go on the road with them. When the bandleader remarked on how well Karl played, Linda quietly shared, "I think I forgot to mention to you, Karl has his own big band and has played with some of the legends of the Big Band era."

It was a great evening, and everyone had such a good time. Linda received dozens of comments from Washington Mutual employees and the community that they had never seen Kerry so happy. The community of Seattle was very welcoming to Linda, and she was quickly asked to join a number of boards of community organizations and for-profit companies. She picked the charities where she had the most experience and ones that met the goals for their charitable giving. One of the personal goals Kerry had was to establish a charitable foundation, but he never had anyone to put it together and manage it.

Before it was popular, Kerry had made the decision to pledge most of his wealth to charity. He asked Linda to start and run the foundation, and soon she had it up and running, and we were very generous to the Seattle community. After a few years, we changed our public foundation to a private donor-advised fund. It still carries the same name, the Kerry and Linda Killinger Foundation, and the mission—to enhance our communities by being advocates for civil discourse, broadening access to the arts, promoting excellence in higher education, and caring for those in need—remains the same, but there is a lot less paperwork as a private donor-advised fund. You can learn more about our foundation on our website, www.thekerryandlindakillingerfoundation.org.

As life got back to normal after the wedding reception, *Institutional Investor* wrote an article about the bank:

> The bank's earnings surged 56% in the fourth quarter (2001) to
> a record $842 million. Earnings for the year rose by two-thirds
> to $3.1 billion, making it the fourth most profitable banking
> company in the country. Over the past 10 years, the bank's shares
> have been among the best performing anywhere, rising six-fold to
> a recent $33.
>
> William Longbrake, longtime CFO, said, 'We have enough size
> and mass and leadership to become a leading player in national
> financial services. It's not just New York or the East Coast, it's
> national. Our goal over the next few years is to be in every major
> metropolitan area in the country.'
>
> In the Dime purchase, SNL Securities reported Chase lost
> nearly 2 percentage points of its New York market share in the
> past year. Washington Mutual targets the mass-market banking
> customer with $30–50,000 in annual income, who are scorned
> by the big commercial banks. They are opening new checking
> accounts nationally at a rate of about 200,000 per quarter and
> their special appeal is service. They give their branch managers a
> good deal of autonomy and much of their pay comes from incen-
> tives [based on customer service, low nonperforming loan rates,
> employee satisfaction, and other metrics].

Another analyst said, "Washington Mutual will perform better than other mortgage shops because it extends both adjustable- and fixed-rate loans. Golden West makes only adjustable-rate loans, which do well when rates are rising, but is sucking wind now because they don't have a quality fixed-rate product. Washington Mutual with 72% of its loans at fixed-rate is competitive in both environments."[17]

In 2002 the *Business Week Fifty* moved Washington Mutual up to a ranking of number twenty-nine from thirty-nine the previous year. The reasons for the ranking included record loan volumes, record earnings, and five announced or completed acquisitions, including the $5.2 billion Dime Bankcorp purchase. "They doubled assets to $242.5 billion since the mid-90s becoming the nation's largest mortgage lender."

The worst-performing bank was Bank One, at 224th, which received an F for total return for three years and sales growth for three years and a D for sales growth in one year.[18] Jamie Dimon was CEO of the bank from 2000 to 2004. Stock analyst Mike Mayo, who continually rated Bank One stock as "a sell" under Dimon's reign, claimed Dimon was very sensitive about Bank One's lack of performance and publicly chastised Mayo often for his "sell" ratings. In his book, *Exile on Wall Street*, Mayo mentioned those stories as an extreme example of the pressures and bullying tactics analysts face from disgruntled CEOs. The *Financial Times* took note and wrote about the Dimon's antics in an article entitled, "JPMorgan Chief in Spat with Analyst Over Stock Picks."[19]

In March, the *NYSE Magazine* had a cover story on Kerry as the Banker of the Year for 2001, and Washington Mutual being selected as one of *Forbes* magazine's five "overachieving companies." Kerry commented:

> One of the key parts of our culture is innovation. We are never satisfied with the status quo. We continually reinvent ourselves and all of our businesses and that brings quality with it. Consistent and constant communication is a high priority for us. As soon as we complete an acquisition our executives visit the company and let them know what our corporate culture is like. We expect everybody to work together in a collaborative way. You develop trust in each other by sharing information and being open about what you're doing. The marketplace changes so quickly that if you're not willing to act quickly you can get left behind. Diverse input means you can better see the changes going on in the industry.[20]

Forbes magazine named Kerry one of the country's "Best Bosses: the CEOs that give the best return to shareholders and while doing so take a reasonable paycheck."[21] Of all the accolades he received, giving the best return to shareholders and taking a reasonable paycheck was very important to Kerry. The other recognition most important to Kerry was the annual awards for best employer, best employer for minorities and women, and best customer service awards.

During an interview with *USBanker* magazine, the reporter was trying to talk to Kerry about the amazing success of Washington Mutual, however:

> Kerry kept talking about his new wet saw from Home Depot. 'It cuts right through rock. Like butter.' Kerry does not wear his

ambition on his sleeve. As the son of an Iowa music teacher, that's not his style. Even though Washington Mutual is huge and returns better earnings per share than Jamie Dimon's Bank One, its stock multiple trails the industry. He is opening branches in Manhattan this summer, with an eye to having 400 up and running in two years.

The bank branches take cues from retail stores' look and feel, ditching desks, donning khakis and roaming the bank floor, the bank is at the vanguard of a new level of customer service. They've really researched what customers are looking for. They changed the way in which people in the branch deal with the customer. There are no tellers and no teller lines. There's no desk in between. The employees wear khakis and three button shirts; they're very approachable. Branches get to profitability very quickly and their average deposits per branch are very high. The bank is as creative as you can get in terms of being different and new. They're really trying for a new customer experience. In fact, when people walk in, they go, 'Wow, I wouldn't even expect this to be a bank.' But what really is making it special is the customer interaction by these people who have a new attitude about serving them as clients.[22]

Jay Tejera, a bank analyst at Ragen MacKenzie, who has followed the bank for fourteen years, said because of these changes, Washington Mutual was "still getting 4 to 6 percent account growth in a one-quarter-percent growth market. They're still taking share."

In the fall of 2002, Kerry received the E. Thomas Medal of Achievement from the NorthWest Industry Partnership award dinner and the Fred Hutchinson Cancer Research Center. He was recognized for his "vision, leadership, and dedication to commemorate a lifetime of achievement with far reaching benefits to humanity." A record fourteen hundred guests attended and brought in a record $1.6 million for cancer research at Fred Hutchinson. Boeing executive Larry Dickenson said, "We certainly admire his hard work and what he's done for Washington Mutual. We also admire him for the leadership he displays in a variety of activities that help make this community an incredibly special place to live."[23]

Although everything seemed to be going well in the regulated banking industry, behind the scenes there was trouble lurking. During the early 2000s, Wall Street and the unregulated shadow banking system had started to pile up their use of more exotic derivatives including CDOs, CDSs, and SIVs. But they weren't the only ones experimenting with the new instruments, and soon Enron, WorldCom, and other companies collapsed. This should have been a warning to all Washington DC regulators that free markets did not prevent fraud or unintended consequences. WorldCom and Enron committed accounting fraud that was missed by its auditors, the banks underwriting its debt, and the credit rating agencies rating the debt.[24]

Enron used special-purpose entities, derivatives, disguised loans, and aggressive accounting to shift revenues forward and backward in time, creating phantom profits and hidden debts. While its intentions seemed to be fraudulent, the financial techniques were so novel it was not clear which were illegal and which were merely innovative.[25] After the collapse, class action lawsuits named JPMorgan, Citigroup, Credit Suisse, First Boston, CIBC, Bank of America, Merrill Lynch, Barclays, Deutsche Bank, and Lehman as its enablers. The claim was Enron's banks were helping it create fake transactions. All the lawsuits were eventually settled.[26]

Congress reacted quickly and passed the Sarbanes-Oxley Act of 2002, which established new standards for corporate financial statements, including the requirement that CEOs and CFOs personally sign off on the 10K and 10Q financial statements, so they could no longer plead they were unware of accounting fraud. This law proved to be effective in deterring executives from obvious fraud and false statements, because few of the regulated bank executives in the 2008 crisis were accused of or convicted of accounting fraud.

The collapses of Enron, WorldCom, and others should have been a warning to Wall Street banks and regulators about the "weapons of mass destruction" they were securitizing. However, Wall Street just doubled down. Realizing that CDOs backed by corporate loans were getting too risky, investment banks moved on to greener turf—securitizing subprime mortgage loans. Most Wall Street investment banks and a number of foreign banks either purchased subprime companies and/or developed close relationships with companies like New Century, Ameriquest, and others. None of them were inspired by helping LMI families, nor were they required to have CRA goals—they were in it for the gold rush.[27] By 2003 the shadow system was securitizing about $200 billion of subprime loans, and by 2005 they had reached an annual volume of $500 billion. Between 2002 and 2007, the unregulated

subprime machine originated and securitized 85 percent of all the
subprime loans—$2 trillion.[28]

At the end of the year, *Fast Company* magazine had an article interviewing six CEOS asking them about their shrewdest move. Kerry said:

> The smartest thing we did was to stay focused on our long-term
> strategic plan, which meant growing the company when many others
> became conservative and [pulling back when the environment gets
> risky]. Our long-term plan is to create the nation's leading retailer of
> consumer financial services. We're always designing new products and
> finding better ways to meet growing demand for financial services.
> But this year, we took three big steps toward that goal. 1. We entered
> the New York market and are doing business the Washington Mutual
> way. 2. We are now America's leading home lender. 3. I visited more
> than 20,000 employees. With the aftermath of September 11th this
> was an important year to do that. I wanted to communicate the core
> values of the company and what our brand stands for.[29]

Washington Mutual ended 2002 with another record year of profitability of $3.89 billion, and the directors increased the cash dividend
each quarter of the year. Return on shareholders' equity reached
19.5 percent, and nonperforming assets remained at a low 0.97 percent.

Washington Mutual, among the *Fortune* 500 companies, was now
twentieth in profits, with $3.89 billion; eighteenth in assets, with $268
billion; thirty-first in stockholder equity; and fifteenth in return on revenues. The bank was listed nineteenth in five-year growth in earnings
per share.[30, 31] When figuring the ten-year compound annual growth
rate as of the end of 2002, Chart 6-1 shows Washington Mutual had
more than double the performance of its banking peers.[32]

Chart 6-1: Washington Mutual Financial Stats
Compared to Banking Peers for Ten Years: 1992–2002[33]

	Washington Mutual	Banking Peers
Net income growth	42%	20%
Asset growth	39%	16%
Deposit growth	38%	14%
Revenue growth	40%	17%

Even more important than the composite growth rates was keeping the loan-loss rates well below 1 percent, as well as continuing to win top awards for customer service and employee satisfaction.

2003

After another record year, Kerry and his team were expecting more mortgage loan growth in 2003, but something was in the air that year. At the beginning of 2003, Wells Fargo, Countrywide, and Washington Mutual were all vying for the top spot in total mortgage originations. They were each originating about $450 billion in mortgage loans— about 80 percent were fixed-rate loans, about 15 to 20 percent were adjustable rate, and only about 4 percent of their production were subprime loans.

However, that year the Federal Reserve began raising interest rates, and it was frightening to see how fast mortgage originations dropped for all the regulated banks. In the previous two years, most of the people who were going to refinance had done so, and the rise in interest rates moved consumers away from long-term fixed-rate loans to the lower-cost adjustable-rate loans available in all the large banks.

Chart 6-2 shows the mortgage originations by the top six *regulated* mortgage originators. Kerry knew at some point interest rates would rise and mortgage production would fall, and he had prepared for this better than most. Kerry also became concerned housing prices were rising too quickly and directed the bank to reduce residential loan originations. In 2003 he cut mortgage loan production in half, and over the next four years, the bank's residential mortgage originations declined by 74 percent—further and faster than any of the big banks. The five-year plan now called for mortgage revenues to be replaced with non-mortgage products like credit cards, retail operations, and commercial lending.[34]

Washington Mutual cut mortgage originations by 50 percent in 2003 by raising loan standards and laying off thousands of mortgage employees. In 2003 there were 22,541 mortgage employees, which were cut to 14,197 by 2004. By June 30, 2008, mortgage employees had been reduced to 7,338. Even with all these reductions, Kerry kept the same number of risk management employees over those years and tried to

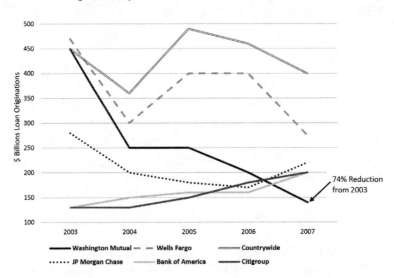

Chart 6-2: Washington Mutual Reduced Residential Loan
Originations by 74% and Cut Market Share in Half

move as many mortgage employees as possible into other positions in
the bank.

In 2003, *Forbes* magazine once again selected Washington Mutual as one of the "Best Big Companies in America." The results were
measured in return on capital, sales growth, and earnings per share
(EPS) growth.[35]

The bank was now ranked number thirteen in the "Business Week
Fifty." The magazine concluded the bank was "fast becoming the bank
for middle America. With sales of $18.8 billion and net income of
$3.9 billion, Washington Mutual ranked number one in the banking
category." In a separate article on "Who will have staying power?" it
listed nine companies, including Washington Mutual. *Forbes* stated the
bank "has been a longtime favorite of such studious stock pickers as
Oakmark Funds' William Nygren. It not only trades at less than eight
times earnings but also pays a dividend healthy enough to make for a
3.5 percent yield."[36]

But those top rankings did not change Kerry's mind about executive compensation. On April 12, 2003, the *Wall Street Journal* reported
a listing of CEO compensation of the top fifty-four financial companies. Kerry ranked right in the middle, at twenty-eighth in total direct

compensation realized, even though the bank's performance was much better than most of the industry.[37]

The March 2003 issue of *Fast Company* magazine identified Washington Mutual as one of the:

> Giant companies that somehow manages to keep costs low and service high and meet the needs of the middle class. The strategy is minting money and the share price is up more than 150% during the past three years. Their strategy is to deliver great value and superior service for the everyday Joe. 'The blue collar, lower white-collar end of the market is either underserved or overcharged,' says a Ragen Mackenzie bank analyst who has been following the bank since 1985. 'Kerry is a slight, quiet man, born and bred in Iowa. He doesn't radiate the charisma of a Steve Jobs or the manic energy of Jeff Bezos, but he wants nothing less than to reinvent how people think about banking.' Kerry said, 'In every retailing industry, there are category killers who figure out how to have a very low-cost structure and pass those advantages on to customers, day in and day out, with better pricing. I think we have a shot at doing that in this segment.'
>
> They are the number one national player in mortgage servicing, with a loan portfolio of nearly $750 billion and it's a close number two to Wells Fargo in mortgage origination. Once the system is in place, the advantage goes to bigger players, who can offer a lower cost and use the relationship to sell additional products. Analyst Tejera says the bank's package of products is irresistible to the middle-class market: 'Checking accounts and mortgages are two of the most important products for Main Street America. Washington Mutual can offer a package of products at better value than you could get by offering those products independently.[38]

Washington Mutual studies showed when customers have multiple products in a bank, retention rates soar. After one year, 96.4 percent of customers with four products were still with Washington Mutual. Part of the reason behind the Dime purchase was to try to get Wall Street's attention. By moving into New York, Kerry wanted to show the capital markets firsthand what Washington Mutual's business model could accomplish. He was convinced that just a couple of years operating aggressively in New York would make an impact on investors. The national magazines were paying attention.

In April 2003, *Fortune* wrote an article about Washington Mutual as the "new bank model":

> The bank is using a creative retail approach to turn the banking world upside down. What is really turning heads is the company's unorthodox retail approach. While banking behemoths like Citigroup and Chase were investing millions to steer customers out of their branches and to faceless ATMs, Washington Mutual courted customers in underserved urban markets by offering free checking and other well-targeted incentives. The thrift's deposits have grown an average of 38% annually for the past ten years, compared with 14% for other banks. Part of what has held Washington Mutual together in its rapid period of expansion is its zealous corporate culture.
>
> The Street gives them high marks for not overpaying [for acquisitions], for quickly integrating technologies and picking acquisition targets that will make them a market leader. They use technology to automate the mortgage underwriting process and promise faster closing time, which is a big lure for homebuyers.[39]

Washington Mutual continued to receive kudos for successful acquisitions and integrations, but some analysts were concerned if interest rates continued to rise, it would squeeze the bank's net interest income. If mortgage rates went lower, there would be another wave of refinancing that would decrease future loan-servicing fees. Analysts were getting concerned that if housing prices fell dramatically, the collateral behind the mortgages would take a serious hit. They admitted investors were still hung up on the shrinking mortgage part of Washington Mutual's business and not focusing on the high growth in the consumer and commercial banking. Analyst Bill Nygren of the Oakmark fund said, "There's a memory overhang of what thrifts used to be like, but Washington Mutual is more characteristic of a growth retailer. It's just substantially undervalued."[40]

In May 2003, *Bloomberg Markets* weighed in:

Like its boss, Washington Mutual is trying to project a folksy image. It uses such slogans as 'More Human Interest' and 'The End of Minimum Balance Oppression.' TV ads broadcast in New York show customers at rival banks, bar coded and shoved down a factory assembly line. Killinger says, '"when every customer comes in, we will try to give them a good level of service, so we earn more business. I would call that a retail strategy rather than a traditional banking strategy.'

Killinger has a backup plan for when the mortgage lending business cools. Being one of the largest servicers of mortgages, it is a business that will counter a decline in new mortgages should interest rates rise. To avoid the pitfalls of a traditional thrift he hired the CFO from GE insurance, Tom Casey [to add more sophistication to the finance function]. The bank also constantly adjusts its loan portfolio to minimize the level of interest rate risk it carries. A Bank of America securities analyst says Washington Mutual is one of banking's most sophisticated users of hedging instruments. The extreme refinancing environment of the mortgage market this past year put both companies to the test and they both passed with flying colors.[41]

In May, Lou Dobbs interviewed Kerry, calling him a banking leader who is "shaping our economy and the world we live in, as well as the best and brightest in business and Wall Street. Good people doing good business and running good companies." He said:

I have a great deal of respect for what Kerry has done taking his company from $12 billion in assets to over $260 billion, creating the seventh largest financial services company in the country. One of the things that impresses me most about Kerry is that he's managed to do it in all sorts of economic conditions. In recognition of his achievements, *American Banker* magazine named him 'Banker of the Year' in 2001. When it comes to our 'good people doing good business' test, Kerry passes with flying colors.

Kerry told Dobbs:

We are going after the average person, underserved market
because most of the commercial banks are targeting both their
commercial customers and upscale individuals. Our internal
plans show refinancing will slow down in the second half of
the year if interest rates remain where they are. I think growth
in the economy is so lackluster it's unlikely to lead to rapid
growth—which typically would drive interest rates up. Consumers
have really fueled this economy in the last two or three years, and
I don't think there is much more the consumer can do. The guys I
talk to in other industries continue to be pretty conservative and
aren't sounding like they're going to have significant expansion
for some time. I wouldn't be surprised if we stay in a GDP growth
range of 2 percent or something fairly low.

When asked about values, Kerry elaborated:

Fortunately, we have always taken the position of having a very
strong independent board that is extremely involved in setting
strategies and engaged in monitoring management. We've always
had a very strong group of independent directors and very strong
corporate governance. The values and ethics you hold yourself accountable to as an organization are very important and we always
had integrity at the top of the list.

We have very clear statements about the corporate values. The
top one is always integrity. We have respect for people, encourage
teamwork, and place value on innovation and excellence. We give
stock options to every full- and part-time employee. If you look at
the last twenty years, a $10,000 investment in Washington Mutual
stock including reinvested dividends would have grown in excess
of a half a million dollars. This works out to about 21.7 percent
or so per year annual return. If you put that same $10,000 in the
S&P 500, it would be less than $100,000, which is about 12 per-
cent over that same twenty-year period.

We haven't had the big write-offs for goodwill where we overpaid
for something, or we had to take big operational restructuring because we mismanaged operations or had unusual credit costs. That
stability of good solid growth of earnings have allowed us to have a
return that relatively few companies have been able to sustain.[42]

Barron's magazine reported on Washington Mutual's success:

> Kerry seeks to do nothing less than revolutionize the delivery of financial services to what he has called the mass consumer market. Washington Mutual has delivered.
>
> Credit quality has been strong and key measures like loan charge offs stack up well vs. major banks. Nonperforming loans are less than 1% of assets and loan loss reserves are almost four times annualized charge-offs, about double the levels [loan loss reserves] of JP Morgan and Citigroup. Killinger told the Lehman conference they have seen very few deals in the last couple of years that could compete with the financial returns of either share repurchase or just growing our own business. The bank has been an active buyer of its own stock, repurchasing 62 million shares for $2.2 billion in the past four quarters, shrinking its outstanding shares to 929 million.[43]

In June, the team was ready to open twenty-eight de novo (new) branches in Chicago in a single day. Not suprisingly, Bank One was threatened by their moves. *The Wall Street Journal* reported on the event:

> The local Chicago Bank One Corp, run by CEO Jamie Dimon, immediately drafted a 29-page playbook for employees on how to fight the interloper from Seattle with a slogan, 'They Want What's Yours, Go Take Theirs.' After Washington Mutual opened its first wave of branches in June, Bank One summoned its 200 Chicago area branch managers to a meeting at headquarters. They were given a playbook entitled 'Five Steps to Victory against Washington Mutual.'

The playbook instructed the Bank One employees to identify customers with the highest fees and offer them a range of discounts. It was interesting they only focused on the top, prime customers, rather than deciding to help all the customers. Dimon's warlike, winner-take-all strategy was the polar opposite of Washington Mutual's strategy of working to meet all customers' needs, offering a good deal for everyone.[44]

The Washington Mutual employees barely noticed the competitive efforts of Bank One—they were too busy courting schoolteachers and sending out employees with free pizza from the "home of free checking." They had a promotional piece stating, "We won't nickel and dime you...use our free ATMs and save $1.50." During the summer in downtown Chicago, the employees handed out over one thousand coin purses with $1.50 inside as a marketing tool. They were having fun and simultaneously winning market share.

Kerry was not surprised by Dimon's warlike stance. Although he barely knew Dimon at the time, his reputation preceded him. Most bankers had heard about Dimon's antics in a number of books and other media reports. Sandy Weil had considered firing Dimon for quite some time after hearing a number of executives complaining about Dimon's continual "belligerent behavior and disrespectful attitude." However, the decision was finally made in 1998 after a Citigroup black-tie dinner where the executives and their wives were engaging in "drinking and dancing" and Dimon got into a physical brawl with another executive.

Weil and John Reed found "Dimon's confrontation totally unacceptable" and Weil decided, "Jamie's got to go." Another book reported that, "In a sign of his lack of empathy and social awareness, Dimon failed to see the incident sealed his fate."[45] In Weill's book, *The Real Deal,* he regretted his mentorship of Dimon. "I brought Jamie along too quickly and in doing so probably gave him a sense of entitlement which discouraged him from building a consensual management style. My real mistake though, was that I repeatedly missed the chance in our early years together to curtail his aggressive behavior and mentor him into becoming a team player."[46]

In the fall of 2003, Kerry wrote one of his regular letters to the board on the progress of the bank and mentioned the overall credit risk profile was lower than any time in the past three years. He relayed the bank's total quality management program, called "Operational Excellence," was progressing well through the bank and had three primary objectives: improving the customer experience, increasing productivity by eliminating redundancy, and stimulating employee development. He said the program was on target for saving $1 billion in annualized noninterest expense by the second quarter of 2005.

He also mentioned the bank had just been recognized as the "Best Retail Bank in America" by the Lafferty International Retail Banking Awards, on the basis Washington Mutual was "noted for trailblazing an innovative brand of retail banking."[47]

Despite the fact Washington Mutual had cut mortgage origination in half, the diversification strategy was working, and the bank reported record earnings of over $3.9 billion for 2003 and achieved a return on common equity of 18.9 percent. Earnings per share increased to $4.21, and once again the cash dividend was increased each quarter. Nonperforming assets to total assets was a low 0.7 percent and plans were in place to reduce that down to about 0.5 percent in the next year.[48]

The 2003 annual report to shareholders revealed a $10,000 investment in Washington Mutual in 1983, when the bank became a public company, would have grown to $585,403 by the end of 2003. The same $10,000 investment in the S&P 500 would have only grown to $127,867 over the same period.

7

Record Banking Profits and Growth, but There Is a Canary in the Mine

2004–2006

2004

Despite all the accolades and accomplishments over the past fourteen years as CEO, Kerry began the new year of 2004 with deep concern about the growing unregulated shadow subprime mortgage banking system. The unregulated subprime lenders, like Ameriquest, New Century, First Franklin, Option One (owned by H&R Block), Fremont Investment, HSBC Finance (UK bank), WMC Mortgage (owned by General Electric), BNC, and about 100 others, were creating hundreds of billions of dollars in subprime loans that were being gobbled up and securitized by the casually regulated hedge funds and the investment banks of Morgan Stanley, Goldman Sachs, Merrill Lynch, Lehman Brothers, and Bear Stearns.

Although Washington Mutual's loss rates on subprime loans were staying low, the default rates on the unregulated shadow industry were rising dramatically. Any mortgage product needed to have scale to survive, so in the critical period between 2002 and 2007, the top twenty-five regulated and unregulated subprime lenders originated about 93 percent of all the subprime loans in the country.[1]

Of the top twenty-five, twenty of the firms were unregulated shadow subprime companies who produced 85 percent of all the subprime loans in the country—nearly $2 trillion. The remaining top five regulated banks (JPMorgan Chase, Wells Fargo, Washington Mutual, Citigroup, and Countrywide) only produced an average of 15 percent of the subprime loans in those six years. The loan-loss rates for the regulated banks increased a little, but the loss rates for the unregulated industry were more than two to three times those of the regulated industry. By 2007, the delinquencies of subprime loans had risen to over 18 percent, primarily because of the shadow unregulated system.[2]

In 2004, the top twenty unregulated subprime players originated nearly $400 billion, and in 2005 they produced over $505 billion—over 85 percent of all the subprime loans. Even more troubling, during those years nearly one-half of the subprime loans in the country were concentrated in just five of the unregulated subprime companies as shown in Chart 7-1.

Chart 7-1: The Top Five *Unregulated* Shadow Subprime Producers 2004–2005 (in Billions) Produced Nearly Half of All the Subprime Loans in the Country[3]

Companies	2004	Companies	2005
Ameriquest	$82.67	Ameriquest	$75.56
New Century	$42.20	New Century	$52.70
HSBC Finance	$33.50	HSBC Finance	$58.60
First Franklin	$28.95	Option One	$40.33
Option One	$25.99	Fremont	$36.24
Total: Top Five Shadow Banks (About 45% of Total Subprime)	$213.31		$263.43
Total: Other Shadow Banks	$185.97		$242.24
Total: Five Regulated Banks (Only 13% of Total) Subprime	$61.54		$73.88
Total Subprime Loans	$460.82		$579.55

The only regulators for these subprime companies were the mixed array of state licensing agencies and the shadow unregulated Wall Street investment banks, which were setting the standards and "monitoring" the quality of the loans. They were packaging these loans into billions of dollars of CDOs and insuring them with trillions of dollars of CDSs. The subprime loans of the unregulated companies had more than two to three times the default rate of the regulated banks.

Even more concerning was the participation in the US mortgage market of foreign banks that were not fully controlled by US federal regulatory bodies. By June of 2008, nearly 50 percent of all the US mortgage loan losses of the top twenty banks were from foreign banks' mortgage lending products sold and securitized in the US (See Chart 1-2.)

By 2004 it became obvious to many in the industry that a euphoric speculative housing bubble had been building as the S&P Case-Shiller US National Housing Price Index rose to record highs. Dr. Shiller who helped develop the index said "speculative bubbles are fueled by contagious optimism, seemingly impervious to facts, that often takes hold when prices are rising. Bubbles are primarily social phenomena; until we understand and address the psychology that fuels them, they're going to keep forming. Financial bubbles are like epidemics—and we should treat them both the same way."[4]

The federal banking regulators did not appear to be concerned by the growth in the massive subprime system, but the state attorneys general (AGs), other state regulators, and the Federal Trade Commission (FTC) were taking notice. Between 2000 and 2004, the FTC received 466 complaints about Ameriquest—about triple what it received about Countrywide and New Century combined.[5] Lawsuits from AGs from California and 20 other states against Ameriquest showed a pattern of fraud, falsification of documents, bait-and-switch sales tactics, and other violations. The Connecticut Department of Banking sought to bar Ameriquest from doing business for charging excessive fees and violating state laws on loan flipping.[6]

The four biggest securitizers of the unregulated subprime loans were Merrill Lynch, Citigroup, UBS (Swiss), and HSBC (UK). In 2002, the FTC concluded its biggest predatory lending investigation of Citigroup, which agreed to pay two class action settlements totaling $240 million, to be paid out to as many as two million people who had taken out mortgages.[7] According to the *New York Times*, Citigroup had lending programs for subprime lenders with credit scores below 450. At the same time, JPMorgan Chase aggressively marketed its "no doc" and "stated income" programs to mortgage brokers, using slogans such as "It's like money falling from the sky."[8]

That spring, Washington Mutual was named by *Fortune* magazine as the seventh-most-admired company in America with a score of 8.43 (the best score of any of the banks) and was again named one of the "100 Best Companies to Work For."[9] The magazine rated Washington Mutual "Number One for Innovation," ahead of Starbucks and Procter & Gamble, and Washington Mutual was voted number three among all companies for social responsibility.

In the spring of 2004, the OTS, the FDIC, and the state of Washington conducted a joint exam of Washington Mutual and issued the bank an informal directive to develop a policy for increasing lending to "higher-risk borrowers" and develop a subprime lending strategy to remix its lending platform. In response to this directive, CERO Jim Vanasek, from the enterprise risk management group, developed the Higher-Risk Lending Strategy that outlined specifically how the bank would manage higher-risk loans like commercial and business loans and credit cards. The board and the regulators approved this plan, which targeted only twenty-five basis points of expected net loan charge-offs and sixty basis points of peak cycle net loan charge-offs.

As was done each year, the Washington Mutual directors held a two-day retreat in June of 2004 to update the bank's strategic plan and approve key business operating plans. The new strategic plan continued to remix assets away from residential mortgages in favor of variable-rate loans such as credit cards, home equity, multifamily, and business loans. The plan noted that "risks were rising from an inflated housing market and competition from unregulated prime and subprime originators." As a result, over 50 percent of earnings were expected to be returned to shareholders via dividends and share repurchases versus growing the loan portfolios. If conditions deteriorated further, loan portfolios would be allowed to shrink, and share repurchases would accelerate.

While Washington Mutual was dramatically reducing its mortgage lending, closing down mortgage operations and laying off mortgage sales staff in favor of non-mortgage lending like small business and commercial lending, not all the analysts and pundits were supportive. Some analysts, like one from Morgan Stanley, was chastising the bank for curtailing mortgage lending. He said, "The mortgage business needs size to compete, the lesson seems to be lost on Washington Mutual, who is firing masses of [mortgage] sales people and closing branches that sell mortgages. Another analyst stated, "This is backwards, they are firing the people who generate assets...a recipe for losing market share. As the bank retrenches, its two main competitors, Countrywide and Wells Fargo, are looking to expand aggressively. Wells Fargo, which already sells more mortgages than any other bank, wants to double its 10,000 strong sales force in the next few years. Countrywide is even treading on Washington Mutual's toes as part of its plan is to triple its sales force by 2008."[10] But Kerry stood strong and was not swayed by their arguments. He was pleased that most of his former sales force would be able to find jobs, but completely mystified why the competition would want to double down on mortgages at this point.

Even though Kerry had chopped mortgages in half, the thirty-year fixed-rate loans were still more than 70 percent of all mortgage loan production. About 25 percent of the production were the adjustable-rate mortgages, and about 5 percent or less were subprime loans. After interest rates started rising, millions of people abandoned fixed-rate mortgages for the more affordable adjustable-rate mortgages. Both the fixed-rate and ARMs had similar default rates, but ARMs were safer for the bank because it could be held in portfolio and good for the customer because it offered flexible payment options. The other top five regulated banks had a similar mortgage loan mix. Option ARMs were supported by Congress and presidents all the way from the Reagan era through to Clinton and Bush.

Even Fed chair Alan Greenspan, in a 2004 speech to the Credit Union National Association, said, "Recent research within the Federal Reserve suggests that many homeowners might have saved tens of thousands of dollars had they held ARMs rather than fixed-rate mortgages during the past decade."[11] It wasn't until after the 2008 crisis that Congress forgot it passed several pieces of legislation to promote ARM loans and decided to politicize them.

Washington Mutual had minimal to no exposure in higher-risk lending products such as leveraged buyout loans, student lending, automobile financing, leasing, corporate lending, shared national corporate credits, international loans, below-investment-grade bonds, unsecured consumer financing, and highly leveraged transactions. Washington Mutual had minimal securities trading operations and had no participation in credit default swaps, structured investment vehicles, collateralized debt obligations, and collateralized loan obligations.

Kerry stubbornly refused to allow pay day loans, student loans, and subprime automobile financing in the bank, because he thought they were not only a bad deal for customers, but presented too much risk to the bank.

Kerry's goal over time was for Washington Mutual to shed its thrift roots and sufficiently remix its balance sheet to become a bank holding company regulated by the Federal Reserve and the Office of the Comptroller of the Currency (OCC). These steps would likely reduce the cyclical impact of housing cycles and improve the company's valuation by Wall Street. This journey toward becoming a commercial bank started with the acquisitions of commercial banks Enterprise Bank and Western Bank. But these were small acquisitions, and larger acquisitions, or mergers, were required. Consistent with this plan, Kerry traveled to London and Europe each year to explore merger possibilities with large banks like HSBC, Lloyds, Santander, BBVA, and BNP Paribas. He also attended the World Economic Forum in Davos, Switzerland, to develop relationships with international bankers.

In the United States, Kerry discussed mergers of equals with banks such as US Bancorp and Capital One. And he was open to merging into much larger banks like JPMorgan Chase, Citigroup, and Wells Fargo if the terms were favorable to Washington Mutual shareholders.

Kerry maintained relationships with other CEOs through the Financial Services Roundtable, the American Society of Corporate Executives, and other informal CEO groups. He also attended the annual international CEO conference organized by Microsoft and Bill Gates. He remembers a humorous exchange between Warren Buffett and Amazon CEO Jeff Bezos at a fireside chat one evening. Buffett told Bezos he just didn't understand the valuation of tech companies like Amazon. Bezos told Buffett, "Warren, you are old and your approaches to valuation are outdated. I have created billions of shareholder value and our stock price is rising." Buffett responded, "Yes, Jeff, that often happens in the early stages of a Ponzi scheme."

That summer we were invited to the home of Bill and Melinda Gates for dinner and a reception for the National Governors Association meeting in Seattle. Kerry accepted the invitation because Washington Mutual operated in most states in the country and he had contacts with many governors through his national education and affordable housing efforts. Linda looked forward to the event because she knew a few governors from her days of political activity in Iowa. We have been in the Gates house a number of times, but it is always inspiring. We have been there for large and small dinners, and every year they have an international CEO meeting and spouses are invited. Many times, guests arrive by boat and enter the house via their large dock on Lake Washington.

The Gates home is a modern, expansive, earth-sheltered home built in the hillside in the Pacific Lodge style. When you enter from the dock on Lake Washington, you notice the first level has a large meeting/dining room on the right, and straight ahead is a long stairway leading to the rest of the house. The second floor has a large dining room and kitchen that eventually lead to personal living areas. Paintings worth tens of millions are casually lined up on the walls. You could reach out and touch them. Most people's favorite area is either the media room or the large room with a built-in trampoline. Our favorite is the library on the top floor. If you are lucky, you will be there when Leonardo da Vinci's Codex Leicester is "home." It is contained in a chest-high steel container with pullout drawers. The Codex is on tour much of the time and is guarded by its very own curator. It is one of thirty scientific journals da Vinci is believed to have authored. The text is written in his famous mirror-image style, and the words are supposed to be read from right to left. The text focuses on his thoughts about the moon, earth, and sun and their relationship with tides, eddies, and dams. We were lucky enough to be in the library when Bill Gates Sr. was there, and he carefully opened the drawers so we could see the precious documents. For library junkies like us, this was the ultimate in adventure.

In August Kerry wrote to the board about the good quarterly earnings, which were 33 percent above plan. He reported the Associated Press just did an article on how most companies are hiding behind excuses for their performance misses, but it cited Washington Mutual as an example of a company that was forthright and candid in explaining its challenges. Kerry reported he'd just met with the regulators in DC, and the meetings were cordial with no problems mentioned.

In the summer of 2004, Kerry concluded it was time to designate a president and chief operating officer so he could focus more attention on strategy, risk management, Wall Street, board relations, and industry matters. After evaluating the internal candidates, Kerry and the board concluded an outside search was required. The executive search firm of Spencer Stuart was hired to search for a president and chief operating officer and Kerry instructed them to find the best person possible with extensive experience in managing large banking organizations.

Throughout the year, CERO Vanasek regularly reported to the board, the finance and audit committees, and the public that the bank was "adhering to the established credit risk limits, thresholds and targets" and also updated the board about other risks the bank was facing, steps to mitigate those risks, and the sufficiency of risk management resources. Vanasek also regularly gave risk reports at public investor conferences and on quarterly earnings calls. He continually certified to the board that he had adequate staff and resources.

By midyear Fannie Mae started to experience some of its first serious problems. Its regulator, FHFA, issued a two-hundred-page public report criticizing Fannie's management and its board for accounting irregularities. The board was forced to enter into an agreement with the regulator to raise significant capital and agree to severe operating and governance restrictions. Fannie had to restate earnings for several years, its stock price dropped dramatically, several class action lawsuits were filed, and rating agencies put it on notice for possible downgrades. The SEC notified Fannie of an investigation, and politicians from both sides of the aisle were calling for hearings and legislative changes. However, no one seemed to notice this was one of the first steps in the unraveling of the subprime crisis. Apparently both Fannie and Freddie had been manipulating their numbers for years in order to mask the increasing numbers of lower-quality loans their regulator had been forcing them to make.[12]

In the fall we attended Hewlett Packard's CEO Leadership Retreat in California. Kerry and Howard Schultz of Starbucks were asked to speak in a panel about innovation. Kerry noticed the audience had an interest in the bank's philanthropy initiatives, and he spent most of his time talking about the bank's program—including its commitment to give 2 percent of its pretax profits to charity each year. Actor and director Robert Redford attended Kerry's session and was kind enough to come up later and mention how impressed he was with Washington Mutual's initiatives to make the communities it serves better places to live and do business.

In December the executive search firm Spencer Stuart uncovered a number of top candidates for the position of president and chief operating officer. Candidates were intrigued with the opportunities for growth at Washington Mutual and its unique corporate culture. Many said the culture was a breath of fresh air from the cutthroat cultures of the major Wall Street banks. Virtually all candidates were on the East Coast, and Spencer Stuart suggested we both travel to New York to meet the candidates and their spouses. Steve Rotella, president of the JPMorgan Chase mortgage group, was selected, and he joined Washington Mutual in January 2005.

Kerry received positive responses on the addition of Rotella to the team. The Mortgage Bankers Association said getting Steve Rotella from Chase was "the coup of the decade. Washington Mutual's gain is Chase's loss." Most analysts Kerry talked with also saw Steve's addition as a positive.

Profitability in 2004 had declined to $2.9 billion as a result of rising interest rates and declining mortgage originations, but the bank did not reduce lending standards to try to get more business. Instead it continued to implement the diversification strategy and added 260 new retail bank branches and eight hundred thousand net new retail banking customers. Nonperforming assets declined to only 0.58 percent, and shareholders continued to do well. A $10,000 investment in Washington Mutual from 1983 had grown to $644,109 by the end of 2004.[13, 14]

2005

In January 2005, as required by the regulators, CERO Vanasek presented his Higher-Risk Lending Strategy report to the finance and audit committees and the full board of the bank and sought approval for the report. He identified the credit risks, compliance risk, financial risks and execution risks and outlined how his department would be monitoring the risks and reporting back the status regularly in board meetings. To double-check on the strategy report, Kerry hired risk management experts Mercer Oliver Wyman to review the asset alternatives and advise on the remixing strategy, and they confirmed that the Higher-Risk Lending Strategy—or more accurately the Remix Strategy—was "appropriate, safe and consistent with remix strategies in other large banks."

At public meetings and board committee meetings, Vanasek relayed:

A strong governance process will be important as peak loss rates associated with this higher-risk lending strategy will occur with a several-year lag and correlation between high-risk loan products. For these reasons, my department will proactively review and manage the implementation of the strategic plan and provide quarterly feedback and recommendations to the executive committee and timely reporting to the board.

Vanasek emphasized to the board:

Increased credit risks are managed prudently and priced adequately. Most of the increase in lending will be multifamily, nonresidential real estate and consumer loans. Subprime was slated to only grow at a maximum of 8 percent a year, but only if market conditions were appropriate.

Lending strategies will be implemented in a careful phased approach, depending upon the economic climate.

He said his department would continue to make sure nonperforming assets were less than 1 percent, net charge-offs less than twenty-five basis, points and the net charge-off (NCO) rate would be capped. Vanasek thought the bank should be Basel II compliant soon to allow sufficient capital to cover the "slight increased risk in lending."

In response to Vanasek's conservative strategy report, the regulators sent reports complimenting Washington Mutual for implementing the new policies. The OTS wrote:

Management developed an Enterprise Asset Allocation Initiative that incorporates not only single-family mortgage and other consumer loans, but the full range of assets on the balance sheet.

Management completed the Asset Allocation Initiative including definitions and concentration limits for higher risk borrowers. Management has completed action items resulting in the closure of this matter.

Kerry's main concern that year was the flat yield curve, which he knew would hurt the net interest margin. CERO Vanasek wrote Kerry in February:

> There is no real problem at the current time on taking on more credit risk and the bank's losses could double from the current rate and we would remain adequately reserved.

However, Kerry and Vanasek agreed that an even more conservative approach was appropriate and put a curb on more lending.

Kerry wrote to the board in March:

> February will be another strong month. Despite a flattening yield curve, we experienced excellent expense management, good MSR performance, low credit cost and above plan gain on sale. Our preliminary plan is February income will come in at about $330 versus $262 million in the plan. But we are cautious about the flat yield curve. We selected Freddie to be our primary GSE partner. They will get 65% of the business and Fannie will get 35%.

The new COO Steve Rotella was just settling into his job when Kerry received a call from JPMorgan Chase CEO Jamie Dimon, registering a complaint that Kerry was hiring too many people from his bank, and it must mean Kerry was targeting them. Dimon said he was not inclined to push the legal front but wanted Kerry to know "he will retaliate in one way or another." Kerry told Jamie he was not targeting JPMorgan Chase, but their employees were the ones contacting the recruiters. Kerry said he would check on the matter and get back to him.

In March, the Alliance for Education's tenth anniversary celebration was held. Kerry was the co-founding chair of the alliance, which was formed to promote excellence in education in Seattle and the state of Washington. In his remarks he said, "A highly competitive economy requires today's students to have more knowledge and skills than ever. Setting high expectations and improving the conditions for student learning at all levels is the best gift we can give to our community's children. That's why we created the Alliance."

Kerry's father was a music teacher, and Kerry devoted a lot of time and resources to improving education locally and nationally. Kerry was chair of the Washington Roundtable, where he focused on education reform in the state of Washington, and he also was chair of the national group Achieve, which was formed by a group of CEOs and state governors to work on national education reform.

That spring Kerry continued to be concerned about the risky housing market and made repeated public and internal warnings that the bank would be very cautious during this period. Kerry emailed CERO Vanasek about the high-risk housing market:

> I suspect the toughest thing for us will be to navigate through a period of high home prices, increased competitive conditions for reduced underwriting standards and our need to grow the balance sheet. I have never seen such a high-risk housing market, as market after market thinks they are unique and for whatever reason are not likely to experience price declines. This typically signifies a bubble.

CERO Vanasek agreed with Kerry:

> I could not agree more. All the classic signs are there and the likely outcome [for the industry] is probably not great. We would all like to think the air can come out of the balloon slowly but history would not lean you in that direction. Over the next month or so I am going to work hard on what I hope can be a lasting mechanism for determining how much risk we can afford to take.

By 2005 more than 85 percent of all the subprime loans were originated by the unregulated shadow banks like Ameriquest and New Century, but the Federal Reserve was not paying attention. Back in 1998 the Federal Reserve Board of Governors had unanimously decided "to not conduct consumer compliance exams nor investigate consumer complaints" from the shadow unregulated banks.[15] If the

Fed had noticed the massive unregulated subprime lending industry in 2004 or 2005 and the billions of dollars of CDOs and trillions of dollars of CDSs, maybe the crisis could have been averted.

In March Kerry warned the board about the growing subprime system and explained how the bank's efforts to scale back had been successful:

> Results look very good and should easily exceed Wall Street expectations of $0.82 per share. Our results are led by excellent MSR performance, good cost controls, good credit performance and continued balance sheet growth. Financial stocks have been under pressure because of rising interest rates. We are down 6% for the year, Fannie down 24%, Citigroup down 8%, Chase down 10% and Wells down 6%. Dimon called to complain about taking so many of his people. Our lawyers are very comfortable we have conducted ourselves appropriately in responding to the many inquires we seem to be getting from employees at Chase.

Later that week, Kerry called Dimon to tell him they had conducted a complete investigation and the recruiters assured him they were not targeting or approaching any particular bank. He also told Dimon they had investigated the pay scales, and the Chase people were not getting premiums (as Dimon had claimed), but only market-rate packages based on a balanced scorecard of performance goals. Dimon replied that he didn't care anymore because "all the former [Chase] executives were just a piece of shit, I don't need them and you [Kerry] could have them."[16] Kerry wasn't too surprised at Dimon's comments, a few months previous, Dimon had told *Fortune* magazine, "What do I think of our competitors? I hate them! I want them to bleed!"[17]

The executive team was not surprised by Dimon's comments, and Rotella responded to Kerry:

> I don't have to rehash anything about JPMorgan Chase, but FYI, apparently things have been unsettled since I left and Jamie/Charlie made it worse when Jamie sent out an email denying sale of the [mortgage] company and expressing full support of the [mortgage] business. They are also offering stock and retention bonuses to

mortgage staff [because employees were concerned about the
bank's commitment to mortgage lending].[18]

Shortly after this encounter, *Business Wire* reported JPMorgan
Chase just committed $800 billion in LMI lending, the biggest com-
mitment ever made by a bank, which would focus on housing, small
business lending, and community development over a ten-year period.[19]
It looked like Chase had just made a huge commitment to the LMI
mortgage market.

In the spring, *USA Today* reported on CEO pay at one hundred of
the largest companies. There were seven financial services companies
that listed 2004 compensation. Washington Mutual tied more pay to
long-term performance than any other bank. Kerry was proud that
nearly all of his pay was long-term-performance based and typically
tied to three- and five-year performance goals. And unlike most of the
large banks, Washington Mutual did not provide country club memberships, executive dining rooms, security teams, multiple private jets, cars
and drivers, or other perks typically provided to bank executives.

First-quarter earnings came in at $900 million, or $1.01 per share,
25 percent above plan. Kerry wrote to the board:

> We had excellent performance in asset growth, expense manage-
> ment, MSR management, credit and gain on sale. I just returned
> from a bank CEO meeting and most are expecting earnings to be
> flat to up 10% this year. Everyone is feeling the pain of a flattening
> yield curve and most are reporting pressure on banking service
> fee income. Many are complaining about subprime results. Our
> efforts over the past year to get our mortgage cost structure
> down and to tighten up our prime and subprime operations
> may position us to do much better than most. Another topic of
> concern at most banks is regulatory aggressiveness in the area of
> the Bank Secrecy Act—AML/BSA compliance. Many CEOs report
> the regulators have been quick to assess fines and seek immediate
> corrective actions. We have not had any problems in this area.
>
> On acquisitions, we talked to a New York bank CEO who is
> willing to sell, and it would be a good fit, but his price is too high
> so we turned him down. We also had a meeting with the CEO of

Providian credit cards. We would like to sell their credit card to all
our banking customers. Preliminary analysis suggests we could do
a transaction with Providian with good IRRs and quickly accretive
to earnings. But we are concerned how the larger losses with credit
cards would affect our balance sheet.

The Corporate Development Committee of the board met and
approved pursuing Providian Financial, visiting with the regulators and engaging the company in negotiations and due diligence.
The regulators gave their support to continue the process and we
visited with rating agencies to get their confidential perspective
on appropriate capital levels.

At the annual shareholders meeting that year, Kerry gave his message to the group:

Our mission is to become America's leading retailer of financial
services by delivering the combination of great value and friendly
service to consumers and small business. We are proud of the individual leadership roles our employees played in their neighborhoods not only by using company paid time to volunteer, but by
volunteering using their personal time as well. Last year our team
volunteered an amazing 187,000 hours to help schools, affordable
housing organizations and other community partners.

Fulfilling our community lending and investment commitment, we pledged $375 billion to low and moderate income and
other underserved communities over a 10-year period. In 2004 we
received word from the OTS that we had again earned a CRA rating of 'outstanding,' the highest possible rating. Magic Johnson so
far has opened 22 inner city loan centers [for Washington Mutual],
enabling thousands of people in those underserved communities
to realize the dream of homeownership. Our new building, the
Washington Mutual Center, will be open in 2006 and will reduce
our occupancy costs by over $15 million per year, getting rid of
the 12 facilities employees are in now.

We have 5 key focus areas: Growth, industry leading productivity, rigorous risk management, commitment to innovation, and
developing future leaders. Key growth areas are retail branch

franchise and the multi-family commercial lending market. In risk
management we currently have high credit quality and we have
improved risk management surrounding our mortgage servicing.
Risk management remains of utmost importance to us. We will
maintain a culture of identifying risk and actively managing it.
Our entire executive committee is involved.

In April, we both received the 2005 "Corporate Class Act" award
from the New York Arts Connection. We were honored by their
statement:

The Killingers personify the spirit of public/private partnerships.
Linda serves on the Board of Trustees of the Seattle Art Museum,
board of the University of Washington Foundation, Board of
Trustees of [the Seattle] Chamber of Commerce, and the Board
of Governors at Iowa State University. She also is teaching at the
University of Washington Graduate School of Business. Kerry's
financial services company has more than $319 billion in assets
and an employment base of more than 50,000 people. Kerry is a
member of New York Stock Exchange listed companies advisory
committee, serves on boards of the Financial Services Roundtable,
Washington Business Roundtable, Washington Financial League,
the Committee to Encourage Corporate Philanthropy, and the
Partnership for Learning. He is a director of Safeco Corporation
and the Green Diamond Resource Company.
    As a corporate mission, the bank has made supporting local
schools a top priority. Last year, they provided $18.7 million in
cash grants to support education, with an emphasis on professional development opportunities for teachers and teacher recruit-
ment programs. The popular WaMoola for Schools programs
ties support for customers' choice of schools based on the points
earned every time they use their Washington Mutual Visa card
to make a purchase. In 2004 customers directed more than $5.4
million to schools throughout the 50 states.[20]

Washington Mutual's success and increased visibility led to offers
for Kerry to join several corporate boards. Kerry declined all offers outside the Seattle area, because his schedule was so tight. Kerry believed

serving on corporate boards helped give executives broader perspectives, but he also believed a CEO's time needed to be quite limited for these activities, particularly with his focus so heavily attuned to what Kerry thought was a looming potential housing downturn.

One of the important activities for a CEO is the development of contingency and disaster planning. As a part of the bank's detailed Disaster Recovery Plan, Kerry and his team had been talking with a number of states about adding computer centers away from the earthquake-prone West Coast. For security reasons it is a good idea to keep computer centers located in different places around the country, and Kerry was looking for the most cost-effective way of creating new data center locations. Texas had offered substantial cash incentives and a very attractive low cost of living for employees. Kerry was impressed with the pro-business attitude of Texas and the low cost of housing. Washington Mutual proceeded to open both a new data center in the Dallas area and a large operations center in San Antonio.

In May CERO Vanasek presented a 2005 strategic planning capital allocation report to the Board of Directors. His recommendations included that Washington Mutual "should allocate much of our economic capital surplus to credit cards, home equity loans, and subprime mortgage lending." He added, "Investors typically value earnings more if derived from well-managed credit risk vs. market (interest) risk and these asset classes have a higher proportion of credit rather than market risk. Portfolio theory shows the benefits of diversifying into asset classes with low return correlations with those from the current mix." He outlined a more optimal asset mix, which over five years would reduce residential home loans from 50 percent to 24 percent while growing home equity loans from 20 percent to 34 percent and multifamily loans from 11 percent to 16 percent.[21] Given Vanasek and Kerry's concerns about a potential housing bubble, underwriting standards were raised on all lending products, and plans for growth were deferred until a more attractive housing market returned.

In June, Kerry and the team made a number of presentations to investors' groups, warning about the risk in the housing market. At the Sanford C. Bernstein Strategic Decisions Conference, Kerry shared his view the United States had a significant above-average risk in housing. He was seeing evidence of investors buying increasing amounts of property, lotteries for new projects, and day trading in real estate—all evidence of a very heated, speculative market. He knew everyone in banking needed to be exceptionally prudent, calculated, and careful.

Also that month, Kerry heard the good news that David Schneider of Citigroup had agreed to accept the offer from Washington Mutual to become president of the home loans group. Hiring both Steve Rotella as president and COO and David Schneider as president of the home loans group significantly strengthened the executive management team. Their additions were part of Kerry's strategy to build the best-run home loan operation in the country. Even though new residential home loan originations were being greatly curtailed because of concerns of an inflated housing market, Kerry knew the housing market would eventually recover.

Kerry had now completed his transition to a more experienced and sophisticated management team with highly experienced new executives in critical roles as president and COO, CFO, president of the home loans group, and the heads of technology, enterprise risk management, retail banking, and human resources. Other long-term senior managers like SVP Scott Gaspard, Chief Administrative Officer Benson Porter, and SVP for Planning Todd Baker completed the team. Scott, Benson, and Todd exemplified the bank's key values of integrity, teamwork, and commitment to employees and customers.

On July 27, 2005, Kerry gave a speech to the National Urban League regarding the importance of education. He said,

> This country has slipped from first to fifth in the percentage of young people holding a college degree. We're now sixteenth among twenty developed nations in the percentage of students who complete high school. We rank near the bottom of the industrialized nations in math and science test scores. We have an unacceptable achievement gap between various ethnic groups, and we need to focus on hiring great teachers. Overall homeownership has grown to 69 percent, but less than 50 percent of African Americans own their own homes. We have teamed up with Earvin 'Magic' Johnson to increase home lending in underserved minority communities in the nation's largest urban centers. We have funded more than $2 billion in home loans to inner-city residents in the past two years. We are working on bringing together a broad forum of key community partners, like the National Urban League

and the Housing Policy Council, to jointly undertake initiatives to strengthen financial literacy especially as it relates to home buying.

In July, CERO Vanasek reported to the board:

The bank had excess capital of approximately $3.2 billion and management has concluded rather than take on additional interest rate risk or operational risk, the shareholder is best served by skillfully adding additional credit risk. Additional credit risk when balanced with portfolio diversification will result in a more effective utilization of this excess capital.

Even though Vanasek noted more credit risk could be taken, Kerry and Vanasek concluded risks were rising in the housing market, so additional credit risk was focused on credit cards and multifamily loans. Excess capital was deployed into share repurchase versus adding residential home loans.

In July, Ben Bernanke, as chair of the Council of Economic Advisers, assured CNBC and the world that the economy was stable. The interviewer asked him, "We have so many economists coming on our air saying the bubble will burst and it will be a real issue for the economy. What is the worst-case scenario...if [housing] prices come down?" Bernanke quickly responded, "I don't buy your premise. It's a pretty unlikely possibility. We've never had a decline in house prices on a nationwide basis. I don't think it's gonna drive the economy too far from its full employment path."[22]

In the fall *FTSE Global Markets* issued a report on Washington Mutual:

[Kerry] announced second quarter earnings had increased 73%. His company is one of the great banking success stories in U.S. history and among its most unlikely. Since [Kerry had arrived in 1982], the bank has achieved a 21% compounded return for its shareholders, compared with 13% for the S&P 500. Cash dividends have been increased each quarter over the past 10 years.

They have a long-term dividend policy of paying out 45 percent of net earnings. Killinger is more worried about the feverish run up in housing prices. He said, 'Certainly we pay very close attention to the rapid escalation in home prices in certain markets. We adjust our loan programs accordingly and monitor our average loan to value ratio and other indicators. This is a high-risk period for residential home lending, but I think we have taken appropriate steps in our underwriting and also our loan loss reserving.'

Kenneth Bruce of Merrill Lynch said, 'I think Washington Mutual will continue to be a potential takeover target because of its attractive footprint on the West Coast and in some other fast-growing markets, it would be attractive to a foreign or domestic bank that does not have overlapping operations. A bigger bank could offer a premium of 25–40%, which is what Bank of America paid for its Fleet Boston Financial takeover. That premium was derided at the time but is widely praised now.'[23]

In October, the acquisition of Providian Financial credit card company for $6.1 billion was completed. Providian was led by longtime credit card executive Joe Saunders, who successfully turned Providian around from previous management missteps and focused the company on middle-market prime customers. Its credit card portfolios were performing well, and growth opportunities centered on providing credit cards to Washington Mutual's vast customer base. Sanders joined the executive committee to continue to run the credit card division. The Providian acquisition greatly aided Washington Mutual's strategic goals of diversifying its assets away from residential home loans.

Both the media and the banking analysts praised the acquisition. The *Seattle Times* called the deal a "coup because the bank could market the new credit card to their 11.7 million customers and encourage Providian customers to move to the bank's checking accounts and other consumer products."[24]

The *Wall Street Journal* said the transaction "plugged a big hole in the bank's consumer business." The paper quoted Richard X. Bove, an analyst with Punk Ziegel & Co.: "I like this deal, it has good fit," and he raised his rating on the bank to a "buy" from "market perform." The *New York Times* said the acquisition "should free up money to bolster Providian's marketing efforts and cross sell to Washington Mutual's existing customers."[25]

Later that month Kerry wrote to the board, "You no doubt saw the acquisition of credit card company MBNA by Bank of America. The price paid in terms of P/E and other measures was considerably higher than what we paid for Providian. This reinforces we were disciplined in our approach and our shareholders should be the beneficiaries. It appears our second quarter earnings will be slightly stronger than I indicated in my last update. MSR performance was good the last week of June and I am not aware of any negative offsets."

In November, Kerry was once again warning the public about the housing market. In his speech to investor conference calls, he remarked:

> Our solid third-quarter 2005 earnings reflected excellent retail banking household growth driven by our long track record of industry-leading customer service, as well as our ability to adjust to a challenging interest rate environment. The results also highlight our continued focus on balanced growth, earnings diversity, and risk management. While we continue to see strong loan demand in all of our key markets, we're keeping a watchful eye on this situation and believe that we may be entering a period of industry shakeout in both the prime and subprime sectors. Given our more cautious outlook, we are continuing to take steps to reduce potential future exposure. We are continuing to sell the vast majority of our current mortgage production, and we are reducing our exposure to loans and residual interests that do not provide adequate risk-adjusted returns.

CERO Vanasek presented his customary quarterly enterprise risk management report to the audit committee:

> The board also recognizes the importance of effectively integrating Providian into our risk management structure and ensuring strong risk controls remain in place through the integration process. The Chief ERM officer will report to the audit committee at each meeting on the progress of the integration with respect to risk management. The Enterprise Risk Management Group is adequately staffed and functioning effectively. Sufficient resources are being provided across the organization to support critical risk management activities. A comprehensive report on the risk profile of the company is prepared semi-annually by ERM and presented to the full board of directors.

At the November Investors' Day conference, Kerry warned:

You have heard my conservative voice on the housing market for several quarters now. We were concerned housing prices appeared overextended in many markets around the country, and we felt the housing market was likely to cool. To prepare for this, we elected to selectively reduce credit risk this year. Now these actions have limited near-term profitability, but they help protect us from a softer housing market if that were to occur. Good credit management is all about what you do before the problem is there.

Kerry not only warned investors and the public about a potential burst in the housing bubble, but he also continued to warn the Federal Reserve and the regulators about the impending problems. Kerry was frustrated the Fed continued to execute moves that added to the fuel of the burning housing market. But Kerry wasn't the only one frustrated with the Federal Reserve.

Nobel Laureate Dr. Shiller, in his August 2008 book *The Subprime Solution*, expressed continued frustration with the acts of the Federal Reserve. He reported:

The Federal Reserve had cut its key rate, the federal funds rate, to 1% in mid-2003 and held it there until mid-2004—roughly the period of most rapid home price increases. The real inflation corrected federal funds rate was negative for 31 months from October 2002 to April 2005. The Fed was excessively focused on preventing recession and deflation because they honestly saw the home price increases as continuing indefinitely, even if they were to implement a monetary policy that would feed the bubble.[26]

Shiller warned the most important element in understanding speculative booms is the social contagion of boom thinking. Shiller said Bernanke revealed his boom thinking often, for example, Bernanke said:

House prices have risen by nearly 25% over the past two years. Although speculative activity has increased in some areas at a national level, these price increases largely reflect strong economic fundamentals including robust growth in jobs and incomes, low

mortgage rates, steady rates of household formation and factors
that limit the expansion of housing supply in some areas.[27]

In November of 2005, the soon-to-be chair of the Federal Reserve,
Ben Bernanke, was questioned by Senate Banking Committee chairman Paul Sarbanes (Democrat of Maryland). Sarbanes told Bernanke
that Warren Buffett had just warned that derivatives are time bombs.
Bernanke responded that he was more "sanguine about derivatives"
and thought they were very valuable. He added that derivatives are
"traded among very sophisticated financial institutions and individuals
who have considerable incentive to understand them and use them
properly." Bernanke added additional comfort:

> The Federal Reserve's responsibility is to make sure the institu-
> tions it regulates have good systems and good procedures
> ensuring that their derivatives portfolios are well managed and do
> not create excessive risk in their institutions.[28]

After the 2008 crisis, Bernanke continued to contradict his previous
statements and declared, "neither the Fed nor Treasury oversaw [the
investment banks or derivatives]. Their only regulator was the SEC."[29]
Kerry wrote to the board in November:

> October financial results were in line with expectations. The
> business is operating pretty well, but we are facing mounting pres-
> sure from rising short-term interest rates and a flattening of the
> yield curve.[30] We just held our annual Investors' Day in New York.
> Attendance was a record at about 250 analysts and institutional
> investors. Response was generally positive; we got good marks for
> our strategy, quality of management team and operating plans
> to execute the strategic plan. Investor concerns centered on the
> interest rate environment and risks of a housing market downturn.

Kerry also wrote to the board that the process of winding down Long
Beach Mortgage was progressing. Kerry outlined how he was not satisfied with progress at Long Beach even though management changes
had been made. Competition from unregulated subprime originators
with reduced underwriting standards made subprime loans much

too impractical and unprofitable to produce. Fraud was growing, and first payment defaults were rising in the entire industry. Kerry wanted the board to know changing market conditions led management to substantially shrink subprime originations even though the original strategic plan called for growth of not more than 8 percent each year.

At the end of the year, *Fortune* magazine produced an "Investors Guide: 2006 Built to Last." It recommended ten sturdy stocks to buy, and once again Washington Mutual made the top-ten list. "It offers the best of all possible worlds," said William Nygren from Oakmark.[31]

In December, the bank's communications director received a call from a *Seattle Times* reporter commenting she had a source at JPMorgan Chase who told her the bank was looking at possible acquisitions in 2006, and Washington Mutual was on its short list. She asked Kerry if he cared to comment. Kerry gave the standard "we don't comment on rumors or speculation" and added the board had "adopted a resolution affirming they believe our business plan can deliver superior returns to shareholders as an independent company."

On December 28, 2005, the *Seattle Times* wrote an article on JPMorgan Chase's interest in Washington Mutual:

> Dimon expects the New York powerhouse to be able to make a major purchase in mid-2006. When Killinger became CEO in 1990, they expanded rapidly from a regional thrift with less than $7 billion in assets to a company with more than 2,000 branches in 15 states and $333.6 billion in assets. The deal would give JPMorgan a solid foothold in California, where it has no retail branches and Washington Mutual has the second-highest market share. It would give them share in Florida, Texas, Arizona, Colorado, Utah and Connecticut. Most of the Washington Mutual branches would remain intact. Seattle could lose another corporate headquarters and its last major financial institution and thousands of bank jobs.
>
> Coveted for its retail banking and mortgage business, Washington Mutual has dodged takeover rumors for years. But Jamie Dimon, the incoming chief executive of JPMorgan, might change that. Dimon expects the New York powerhouse to be able to make a major purchase in 2006. 'The only way JPMorgan can get the West Coast is Washington Mutual,' said Frederick Cannon, analyst

at Keefe, Bruyette & Woods in San Francisco. 'If the bank told JPMorgan quietly it has no interest in selling, shareholders might never know and legally, publicly traded companies must consider buyout offers.'

Headquarters jobs are hit hardest in a merger. JPMorgan slashed 2,000 jobs in Chicago after last year's acquisition of Bank One. If the WM-JPM merger marriage were to take place next year, the merged company would be roughly the same size as Citigroup, the country's largest bank with $1.5 trillion in assets. The deal would give JPM a solid foothold in California where it has no retail branches and where Washington Mutual has the second highest market share at 16.7%. There would also be layoffs in the mortgage area, where both banks have a large presence.

Michael Moebs, CEO of Moebs Services, a research firm in Lake Bluff, Illinois, said a deal would be bad for Washington Mutual employees and customers. He warned:

Somebody like Morgan Chase is stepping in just to fulfill their national geographic strategy goal, that's all they're thinking. They're not thinking about how the people are going to be treated. They'll talk a good line about how they are going to be service oriented and things, but the Dimons of the world are basically interested in only dealing with the upper middle class and beyond. Prices from the biggest four bank buyouts in recent years suggest Washington Mutual would garner something closer to $61/share.[32]

Analyst Frederick Cannon said JPMorgan Chase had planted a story to send a message to the board and investors that Dimon was interested in an acquisition. Dimon might have been hoping board members and investors would either try to do a back-door deal with Dimon or maybe force Kerry into a sale. Kerry kept his board members and investors fully informed and they didn't hear another word from JPMorgan Chase.

If Dimon wanted to do a genuine deal, he could have approached the bank board with an actual offer, and the board would have considered it. But Dimon never approached the bank with any kind of offer. The Washington Mutual board was no longer dominated by people from Seattle, because the board diversified itself to include seasoned executives from all over the country—New York, Texas, California, etc. The board members themselves did not have any particular loyalty to Seattle or to keeping the bank independent. The board was open to any and all offers that would be best for shareholders, employees, customers, and the communities they support. They would not refuse an offer just to protect management—corporate governance was too sophisticated to allow that.

Every year Kerry and the Board of Directors would hire investment banking firms to assess Washington Mutual's strategic and financial plans and give them an assessment of the competitive environment. They would assess whether shareholders were better off with a sale of the company or keeping the bank independent. They would also assess any weaknesses that could make the bank attractive for a hostile takeover. Every year the investment bankers deemed the bank to be at low risk for a takeover, because the bank was good at keeping costs under control. Each year the board would assess the reports and vote on whether to keep the bank independent. This vote would give Kerry permission to tell any suitors the board had voted to remain independent and would also give him permission to seek appropriate merger and acquisition partners.

CERO Vanasek retired at the end of 2005, but before he left, Vanasek wrote a letter thanking the executive committee:

> I will simply say I have been honored to be the head of ERM
> during this formative period, and I wish to express my sincere
> appreciation to each and every one of you for your effort, kindness
> and support.

Before he left, he told Kerry and the board the risk management function was properly staffed, loans were staying well within their limits, and the bank was only taking conservative risks.[33]

Vanasek's replacement as CERO was Ron Cathcart, who had been chief risk officer with Bank One's retail bank and CIBC of Toronto. Cathcart took over as CERO on January 1, 2006.

Despite the bank's dramatic cuts in mortgages, the new diversification plan was working, and Washington Mutual had near record earnings in 2005 of $3.43 billion. Return on common equity was a solid 14.6 percent, and nonperforming assets were only 0.57 percent of assets.[34]

Shareholders continued to do well, with that $10,000 investment in 1983 having grown to $694,016 by the end of 2005. The bank delivered solid performance, achieving a 12 percent earnings per share for the last quarter of 2005 and 14 percent for the year. The board approved a cash dividend increase to $0.50 per share, which represented forty-two consecutive quarters of increases.[35]

The entire regulated banking industry did well in 2005:

The FDIC reported record third quarter earnings of $34.6 billion. There was a record low of only sixty-eight problem banks around the country, and 2005 was the first year with no bank failures. All the regulated FDIC banks were feeling pretty good, so most missed the footnote about the industry-wide increases in loan-loss reserves.[36]

However, out of view of the green eyeshades of the federal regulated banking system, the hundred-plus shadow unregulated subprime companies like Ameriquest and New Century had a banner year, producing over a half a trillion dollars' worth of subprime loans that were securitized by the unregulated Wall Street investment banks, who also had a banner year of bonuses.

2006

By 2006 Kerry had cut mortgage lending over 60 percent—further and faster than any of the major banks. At one point Kerry was proud Washington Mutual had become the top mortgage originator in the country, but that was only because the default rates were very low, and the loan standards were very high. However, Kerry understood that consumers considered mortgage loans to be a commodity—the most important factors were price and ease of getting a mortgage. Many banks, especially the unregulated shadow banks, were dropping standards, reducing documentation, and accepting a higher default rate.

Kerry refused to do that and instead raised standards, took fifteen thousand employees out of the mortgage operation, and built up the retail banking, commercial lending, and credit card operations. He couldn't understand why many of the big banks, like Wells Fargo, Countrywide, and Citigroup were actually adding mortgage staff.

Through the carefully orchestrated transition, Kerry once again reinvented the bank within five years and came out at the end with the bank's most profitable year ever. However, Kerry was still very concerned about the massive shadow banking system and continued to warn the investors, the Fed and the public:

> We expect the operating environment for mortgage banking to
> be much more challenging during the next four quarters. The
> subprime lending environment continues to be challenging with
> narrowing margins and the anticipation of a less favorable credit
> environment. [Our efforts at] increasing FICO scores and LTV
> requirements have strengthened the portfolio over the past year,
> leaving it better equipped to deal with the increased economic
> stresses that may lie ahead.[37]

Unfortunately, the new Federal Reserve chair, Ben Bernanke, had a completely different take on the economy. When he was President George W. Bush's chairman of the Council of Economic Advisers, Bernanke drafted the Economic Report of the President, which claimed, "The economy has shifted from recovery to sustained expansion...and is well positioned for long-term growth." He projected the unemployment rate to stay at 5 percent from 2008 through 2011.[38]

In the first quarter of 2006, home prices were still fairly robust. For the nation as a whole, the Case-Shiller National Home Price Index reached an all-time high of 185 in 2006. But some markets were already starting to recede from the torrid housing price increases of the previous three years.

The unregulated shadow subprime industry had a record year in 2005 by producing over $500 billion of the worst subprime loans in the history of the world. However, the state attorneys general were on to them. The AGs launched thousands of enforcement actions, including 3,000 in 2006 alone. By 2007, twenty-nine states had passed some form of anti-predatory lending legislation.

After months of investigations, a coalition of forty-nine state attorneys general brokered a settlement with Ameriquest for $325 million.[39]

The settlement forbade the outlandish sales quotas for the loan officers and the higher commissions for sticking borrowers with higher prices and prepayment penalties. Attorney General of Iowa Tom Miller, lead attorney on the settlement, was hoping the settlement would convince other subprime companies to improve their practices, but the CEO of Ameriquest seemed to float through these negotiations without pause. Just the cost of doing business. He was one of the major contributors to President Bush's campaigns, and on February 8, 2006—sixteen days after the AGs' settlement—the US Senate confirmed him as ambassador to the Netherlands, without discussion on an uncontested voice vote.[40]

In February 2006, *Fortune* magazine once again ranked Washington Mutual very high in its listing of the "100 Best Companies to Work For." Washington Mutual ranked at the top in three breakout categories: best large company, highest number of female employees, and ethnic diversity. This was a recognition Kerry cared deeply about—he wanted a bank ranked as a great place to work, especially for women and minorities. Washington Mutual continued to consistently have one of the highest percentages of women and minority managers and members of the management teams and the board of directors.[41] Kerry made sure the pay scales for women, men, and minorities were exactly the same.

Later that month Kerry gave another speech at a CEO event about lessons for a successful high-growth company. He emphasized that changing consumer needs, technology, and competition require constant innovation, and he believed a company should reinvent itself every five years to be responsive to customer needs. He promoted a flat organization that continually needed to be reassessed so there are no more than three to five people between the customer and the CEO. He believed winning companies always have a productivity advantage and manage their risks very carefully. He believed you can't manage what you can't measure. His top priorities were to build excellent customer service and motivated employees. He thought executives should always check their egos at the door.

By the end of February, the JD Power retail banking study showed Washington Mutual with top performance, with the added distinction of having the highest customer commitment ranking, which is a combination of satisfaction, loyalty, and the amount of business a customer has with a bank.[42]

In March 2006, we attended a dinner honoring Kerry as the CEO of the year for *Washington CEO* magazine. The magazine drew a parallel between Kerry and the character of Willie Gillis, Norman Rockwell's fictitious WWII veteran and college student portrait that hung in the bank's conference room wall:

> Both men wear comparable expressions of Midwest honesty and confidence that seemed to play off one another. Kerry is the one who pushed hard for expansion, taking the company through two dozen acquisitions that have brought the bank's assets from about $6.6 billion in 1990 to more than $300 billion today.
>
> He is the one who pushed for clear goals and accountability, where progress reports are a mainstay that help make sure daily activity is in line with the company's vision. He makes sure the company values [fair, caring, human, dynamic and driven] are known throughout the organization. Employee surveys provide feedback on company behavior around those values. The surveys are then used as a tool to address the areas of the company where certain values need to be addressed. Kerry is also the primary advocate behind 'disruptive' technology throughout the company. The bank is designed to be more customer friendly with a concierge, a play area for kids and more customer/employee interaction. Until then you stood between the velvet ropes and waited in silence for a teller.

The magazine also addressed Kerry's succession of five-year plans that were successfully completed:

> From 1990–1994 the plan was to expand retail in the Northwest. From 1995–1999 they expanded retail banking into California. From 2000–2004 they had been working on expanding retail banking nationwide in select cities and increasing multifamily and home loans to a national level. That effort took the share price from $17.25 to $42.28. It also made Killinger a business all-star along with his friends Jack Welch of General Electric and investment guru Warren Buffett of Berkshire Hathaway.

The strategy from 2005–2009 is to get deeper into small business banking and credit cards. The plan started last September when it bought San Francisco–based Providian Financial Corp. for $6.5 billion and achieved the goal of getting a small business credit card. Setting goals and seeing them through with discipline are some of the values he instills in the company. The Midwest has a consistency of family orientation: you get ahead in life by working hard. Those things have helped to create values of no-nonsense, absolute honesty, integrity, trying not to take things too seriously and doing the right thing.

His shirtsleeves are buttoned, not cuff-linked. His watch is plain with a plain black band. He works in a roomy but hardly ostentatious office on the 16th floor of the 55-story Washington Mutual Tower in downtown Seattle. He never recognizes himself.

To Killinger, doing the right thing means keeping innovation alive. Kerry said, 'One of the things I tell our people is the company needs to totally reinvent itself within a five-year period. What that does is keep everybody on edge a bit, to not get complacent or stop innovating. It's very easy for larger companies to build bureaucracy and then innovation wanes. The CEO must also set the company's strategy and vision and bring all constituencies along. But most importantly, absolute integrity and honesty have got to be in the forefront.'[43]

Kerry was proud of his frugal ways and plain watch. Every year or so the watch would stop working so he had to run back to Walgreens and buy a new watch. He got all his suits at the basement Nordstrom sale, he drove himself to work in a ten-year-old car and Linda kept them on a strict annual budget. One year she decided to splurge and bought him a better quality watch at a jewelry store for his birthday. He told her to take it back. After all, frugal is sexier.

On April 18, 2006, CERO Cathcart reported to the board, "The bank has control measures in place to manage all of its top five risks," and he told the board he had hired Mercer Oliver Wyman and KPMG to assist him in determining how to further improve Washington Mutual's enterprise risk management department. The resulting reports detailed that the bank had best-in-class controls and risk management practices and the department was adequately staffed by industry standards.

In May, the Federal Housing Finance Agency and the Office of Federal Housing Enterprise Oversight (OFHEO) released a special exam of Fannie Mae and claimed it had overstated reported income and capital by about $10.5 billion. It claimed Fannie had "deliberately and intentionally manipulated accounting to hit earnings targets." The CFO was forced to step down, and Fannie agreed to pay a $350 million civil penalty to the SEC and a $50 million fine to Treasury.[44]

On June 1, 2006, Kerry spoke at the Sanford C. Bernstein Strategic Directions Conference. Kerry once again warned of a worsening housing market:

> At this conference a year ago, I commented I'm very concerned about housing and I've been the resident bear on housing prices and especially the activities I saw going on in the mortgage origination market. As a result, we started taking more conservative actions. In our existing portfolio of option ARMs, our average FICO score is about a 710 and our loan to value (LTV) was 71 percent at origination.
>
> I think it is a mistake for those mortgage companies who are not adjusting their cost structure. The reality is the industry is past its peak. The lending volumes are likely to be constrained and profitability in the industry is under some pressure. On the credit front, we continue to be in excellent shape. Nonperforming assets of only fifty-seven basis points [0.57 percent] is well within our long-term target of 1 percent. We are getting our cost structure down.[45]

In June 2006, the regulators were completing their annual examination process and met with all the top executives. COO Rotella wrote Kerry regarding his meeting with the OTS: "The OTS commented on the progress in home loans and said they thought it was the best cohesion and focusing in that business they have experienced." Once again, the bank received all 2 ratings from regulators OTS and FDIC.

On June 15, 2006, the *Puget Sound Business Journal* developed an entire magazine section on the bank's move to its new headquarters building. It reported there were only fourteen offices in the entire building. The only new artwork was framed photographs of employees and branch offices. No need to buy any expensive artwork. The *PSBJ* reported on the building:

> Each neighborhood [work areas in the building] had groups of people who work together, and each neighborhood had a cafeteria. By consolidating the workers into a single tower and reducing the per employee square footage, Washington Mutual is capturing efficiencies that will enable it to save upward of $15 million a year. The showpiece of the building is a 20,000 square foot patio on the 17th floor that features outdoor seating, a fireplace and a stone walkway through a landscaped garden.
>
> The 17th floor indoor living room will serve beer and wine in the evenings. The executives received a great deal of data from employees on the best way to organize their workflow and had come up with the idea of clusters and neighborhoods. There was also a large employee dining room with discount food and private conference rooms. There was no executive dining room. All facilities were open to all employees. They also arranged to have Starbucks on the mezzanine floor of the building. [46] The City of Seattle guaranteed $65 million in bonds for the new [Seattle Art Museum] in the bank building. The new museum was built with no cost to taxpayers.

Although everything seemed to be moving along very well, trouble was lurking. During the summer of 2006, Kerry was dealing with a growing problem with his predecessor, Lou Pepper. Lou had been retired from Washington Mutual for over fifteen years, but Kerry provided him with an office in the bank and enjoyed visiting with him from time to time. Lou clearly basked in the success and growth of Washington Mutual after his departure and loved to give speeches about the bank's success. But managing a large nationwide organization with sixty thousand employees became increasingly difficult for Lou to comprehend. There were two things deeply bothering Lou: he was not getting an office in the new building, and he didn't get his choice for the chief operating officer position.

Kerry received a growing number of complaints from senior and executive managers that Lou was disrupting their operations and wasting their time. Lou was apparently wandering around the offices and dropping in to give his opinions. Lou became increasingly vocal that he didn't like the updated corporate values statement developed by fifteen senior managers with input from all the employees. Lou was critical of including the word *driven* as a core value and sent long rambling letters to the executives. The problem escalated when Lou showed up at COO Rotella's office, ranting about the definition of the word *driven*.

Kerry met with Lou a number of times to address Lou's concern about the word *driven* and even shared the results of the recent employee surveys, which were the most positive employee surveys the bank ever had. He showed Lou the many awards the bank had recently received for the best place to work. He showed data that revealed the bank had a very low employee turnover and shared the bank's state-of-the-art whistle-blower hotline that had shown no serious concerns from employees. Kerry showed Lou the results of the 360-degree performance reviews. Most of these systems were developed and monitored by outside agencies, to keep the results independent. Kerry even had the outside HR consultant assure Lou about employee satisfaction. But Lou wasn't listening.

The updated core values were written by the employees, approved by the executive committee and board, and were a balanced scorecard of fair, caring, human, dynamic, and driven. The "driven" value was clearly defined: "We are committed to excellence and the achievement of superior longtime returns for our shareholders. We set high, measurable goals and hold ourselves accountable to achieve them. We recognize addressing challenges head-on is a requirement for success. We benchmark from our customers' viewpoint and deliver what is most important to them. We look both within and outside our industry to learn."

The issue escalated when three board members told Kerry that Lou was bothering them and was disruptive. Kerry engaged an outside consultant, who had previously worked with the board and senior managers, to look into the problem. The consultant wrote to Kerry and praised his patience and kindness in dealing with Lou's disruptions, but added:

Lou has strong biases formed from very narrow sources, mostly from one executive who left because she didn't like the new COO. Despite Lou's reservations about 'driven' as a value, after reading the most comprehensive studies about business cultures, the only sure value that distinguishes companies who outperform others is some version of 'performance driven.' I would not respond to Lou's questions about an office in the new building or tell him there are a few visitor offices he can use. These thoughts may seem harsh, but although Lou is concerned about culture, he is unintentionally doing damage to Washington Mutual.

Kerry decided, unfortunately, it was time for his old friend to have his office somewhere else. It was a lesson for Kerry that CEOs should leave an organization when they retire. It is almost impossible for retirees to hang around without becoming disruptive to an organization.[47]

On June 30, 2006, the FDIC released second-quarter bank earnings:

The FDIC reported record bank earnings of $38.1 billion. Non-current loan rates reached an all-time low, capital indicators remained robust, and there were no bank failures for more than two years. What could go wrong?

That summer, CERO Cathcart reported to the board audit committee:

Current risk exposures are within expected and manageable tolerances in our limit structure.

    There have been more Early Payment Defaults (EPD) and the deterioration is across FICO segments [in all the banks in the country]. There are many positive economic drivers: the GDP remains strong, unemployment is close to cyclical lows, Dow Jones returned to pre-2001 levels, and inflation today is lower than in the 90s. The negative drivers: Continuing trade and budget deficits, the auto manufacturing sector is weak, there is a sharp deceleration in housing prices and a negative consumer savings rate.

    Escalating home prices have accounted for about 50% of the GDP growth over the last four years, the long-term average is only

10%. Housing starts are down 26% from the January 2006 peak.
New home and existing home sales are down 17% and 12.6% and
existing home sales month's supply is 7.5 months, the highest
since April 2003. Mortgage purchase applications are down 18.7%
industry-wide. Home prices are decelerating quickly in all markets
with a few exceptions in the central U.S. The CME housing futures
market predicts material declines in housing prices over the next
year in most markets.[48]

Cathcart had several conclusions: the bank's mortgage loan portfolio had significant price appreciation, initial LTVs were conservative, higher risk lending was controlled through concentration limits,
subprime lending was declining, and the bank was well capitalized.
He added to ensure the bank was prepared for a possible decline in
housing, all the business units would be working together to develop
market-based triggers and corresponding action plans.

In July, Fed chair Bernanke went on CNBC and, from his Wall Street
perch, seemed completely out of touch with the average American and
completely unaware home prices were decelerating so quickly. He
stated, "We've never had a decline in house prices on a nationwide
basis. So, what I think more likely is that house prices will slow, maybe
stabilize." He bragged the economy was "robust" and "strong."[49]

On July 18, 2006, the regulators (OTS and FDIC) met with the
Washington Mutual board to deliver their examination findings. They
concluded the bank was again a 2-rated bank. They noted significant
improvement in credit risk management and were pleased to report
a 44 percent reduction in total examination findings, a 75 percent
reduction in criticisms, and 31 percent fewer recommendations. They
further stated, "The overall risk posed by the higher risk lending remains adequately controlled through managed growth, monitoring
of delinquencies and nonperforming loans and the maintenance of
adequate ALL [Allowance for Loan Loss] factors and capital are com-
mensurate with portfolio risk."

Every year regulated banks are given an extensive examination by
their regulators—the OCC if you are a commercial bank and the OTS
if you have a thrift charter. Kerry went a step further and for decades
included the FDIC in the annual audit. For nearly twenty years, both

the FDIC and the OTS worked with each other and the staff to identify and resolve issues the bank needed to address. Every year both the FDIC and the OTS met with the Washington Mutual Board of Directors to discuss the exam and offer any suggestions.

During the nearly twenty years Kerry was CEO, the OTS and the FDIC always agreed on the ratings and praised the Washington Mutual team for their responsiveness to their requests.

Regulated banks were given a composite score called the Composite Uniform Financial Institution Rating or CAMELS score that is based on six major components: Capital adequacy, Asset quality, Management, Earnings, Liquidity, and Sensitivity to market risk. Of lesser importance are the ratings on the IT-information technology scores which consist of four components: Audit, Management, Development and Acquisitions, and Support and Delivery. Banks are rated on a scale of 1 to '5' on each of these ten components with 1 as the top rating and very rare. Banks with an overall composite score of 4 or 5 would be subject to formal enforcement orders.

Chart 7-2 shows Washington Mutual's exam ratings from 2003 to 2008. Every year Kerry was CEO until 2008, the regulators gave Washington Mutual a Composite Uniform Financial Rating of 2. Similar to all large banks, Washington Mutual had numerous audit findings and suggestions each year, but most were immediately corrected. Washington Mutual received a 3 rating in "sensitivity to market risk" in 2003/2004 due to volatile mortgage servicing assets. The regulators encouraged the bank to reduce market (interest rate) and to slightly increase credit risk. At the request of the regulators, ERM developed a "higher risk lending strategy" where caps were placed on credit risk in all loan portfolios. The regulators then changed the rating for market risk back to a 2 at the next exam and credit risk remained a 2 rating.

The first composite overall 3 the bank received was in March of 2008, when the financial markets were collapsing. Regulators told the bank the downgrade was being given to many banks and Washington Mutual was told the downgrade was due to the precarious economic climate. There were no associated formal or informal orders given with the downgrade. This composite 3 remained with the bank until shortly before the seizure.

Chart 7-2: Washington Mutual Regulatory Exam
Composite Ratings 2003–2008[50]

	2003	2004	2005	2006	2007	2008
Composite Uniform Rating	2	2	2	2	2	3
CAMELS **Component Ratings**						
Capital Adequacy	2	2	2	2	2	2
Asset Quality	2	2	2	2	2	3
Management	2	2	2	2	2	2
Earnings	2	2	2	2	2	4
Liquidity	2	2	2	2	1	3
Sensitivity to Market Risk	3	3	2	2	2	2
IT Composite Ratings	**2**	**2**	**2**	**2**	**2**	**2**
Audit	2	2	2	2	2	2
Management	2	2	2	2	2	2
Development and Acquisitions	2	2	2	2	2	2
Support and Delivery	2	3	2	2	2	2

The OTS examiners spent more than thirty thousand hours a year auditing Washington Mutual, and the FDIC was also on site working with the OTS.[51] Regulators always had dozens of findings after an exam. They were divided into observations, recommendations, and criticisms. Observations and recommendations were common and could be corrected in the course of business. If the criticisms were not corrected in a timely manner, a bank would first receive informal regulatory actions, and if those weren't corrected, the bank would be downgraded and then receive formal regulatory actions that were given to banks rated 4 or 5. In 2003 the bank had only twenty-five criticisms, which was reduced to eleven in 2004 and 2005 and then down to three in 2006 and only one criticism in 2007. This is positive evidence that Washington Mutual responded quickly to any exam criticisms.[52]

The bank was able to respond effectively to exam findings because it had an exam-tracking system called ERICS managed by a task force of managers who tracked the progress of all the exam findings and sent a progress report to the board every month. Throughout this time period,

Washington Mutual continued to receive compliments from the OTS and FDIC about addressing criticisms in a very timely manner. The bank also had annual audits from Deloitte that always gave the bank clean opinions, and the bank never had to restate earnings. Deloitte also found no major issues with risk management or other regulatory requirements. In addition, the PCAOB accounting oversight board gave targeted exams on Washington Mutual between 2005 and 2007 and found no major issues.[53]

In July, Kerry told investors:

Second quarter net income reached nearly $1 billion. This was a great accomplishment given greatly reduced profitability from the Home Loans Group. Our actions to reduce all residential lending hurts short term results but will better protect us from a falling housing market. In the meantime, we are improving our operating efficiency, reducing interest rate risk and continuing to grow our highly profitable retail banking, multifamily lending and credit card businesses.

On July 21, 2006, CERO Cathcart sent a note to the executive team:

Congratulations to the entire team for a first half filled with accomplishments. You truly have moved the dial on all these initiatives. The board and executive committee feedback on what has been achieved has been universally favorable. Thanks to all you do for the diligence and energy which you have brought. You truly have made numerous quantum improvements to the credit infrastructure over a very short time.

COO Rotella responded:

ERM is indeed moving the dial and driving initiatives that are helping us improve and build momentum. I noted at the senior leaders meeting I really feel our business lines and the support units, notably ERM, are working more closely than ever before. Thank you for your role in this process and keep up the good work.

Kerry continued to beef up the risk management group. A team of PhDs in economics and experts in home loan modeling and analytics were hired to develop new forecasting models for the bank. The team grew from seven members to over forty in 2007 and over sixty members in 2008. The new modeling was very important in determining projected loan losses and other modeling analytics.

In August, *Bank Director* magazine had an article about the "Washington Mutual Way." Praising Kerry's approach, it reported he "installed a dramatic transformation in the once stodgy thrift, essentially turning it into a trend-setting consumer bank that operates on both coasts. With $350 billion in assets, the bank now ranks as the sixth largest US depository institution, behind Wells Fargo and ahead of US Bancorp." The article continued:

> Kerry stated, 'We want to grow [our retail bank] customer base by about one million per year. We can open de novo stores, make acquisitions or use newer distribution channels like the internet. The de novo stores are getting more expensive so we are having extraordinary success in opening new customer accounts online. We have new technology that allows a customer to electronically open checking accounts and we are getting 1,000 new customers per day.
>
> 'Each year we get the board's judgment of whether we can create superior returns for our shareholders as an independent company. We will go through a process of reviewing and typically come out of the session with a course of action for the company.
>
> 'We have four main business units and we have plans in place we think will achieve double digit growth over the next several years. Our first priority is the retail bank activities. Our second focus is to accelerate Providian's [credit card] growth rate by making them available to our customer base. Third area is the commercial multifamily lending and small commercial real estate. Finally, in the mortgage lending space, we have had to make a major adjustment in our core business model. I would like to continue to diversify our balance sheet away from prime residential loans to a diversified portfolio of consumer and small business and commercial loans.
>
> 'There has been a valuation discount assigned by some investors to the thrift charter over time, and I think there is evidence price to earnings ratios for banks tend to be a little bit

higher. That is a factor we consider in terms of the choices on charters we might operate under. At the same time, I'm seeing a significant shift occur in our shareholder base. We are getting purchased more and more by investors who view us as a bank and see our future as a bank and believe there is an opportunity in the potential revaluation of our company if we're able to make that successful change [from a thrift to a bank charter]. I'd also note we are now being followed by a number of banking analysts, whereas five years ago we were basically followed only by specialty finance or thrift analysts, so there is a major shift going on in the coverage of our company.'[54]

In August, the *Wall Street Journal* carried a story about the rise of subprime mortgage delinquency rates. It included an example of a woman who got a subprime adjustable-rate loan with an introductory rate of 2.35 percent that jumped to 8.75 percent after two years.[55] She was not a client of Washington Mutual, but the primary products offered by all subprime originators were 2/28 and 3/27 mortgages where payments are fixed for two or three years followed by adjustable payments for the balance of the thirty-year loan term. Banks handled this in a variety of ways, but Washington Mutual offered the lower fixed rates upfront to allow the subprime customers a couple of years to straighten out their finances and improve their FICO scores enough to qualify for a prime thirty-year fixed-rate loan. A large percentage of the Washington Mutual customers would improve their scores and move into a prime fixed-rate loan. However, when the economy lagged and housing prices dropped, the delinquencies of the 2/28 and 3/27 loans grew dramatically. Washington Mutual handled this situation by setting up a multibillion-dollar fund to move these loans into fixed-rate products with lower monthly payments.

Although the 2/28 and 3/27 loans were developed by the industry to help subprime customers, prime customers were eligible for a number of adjustable rate products, like option ARM and Pick-a-Pay loans. There has been a tremendous amount of false information about the option ARM loan and negative amortization. Option ARMs were encouraged by Congress in the 1980s Garn–St. Germain bank and parity deregulation acts. They were developed in response to inflationary housing problems in states like California. During times of high interest rates, adjustable rate loans can be more affordable than higher-rate fixed-rate loans. The option ARM had been successfully used by California banks for nearly thirty years and performed similarly to fixed-rate loans with less than a 1 percent default rate. The Option ARMs were sold to prime customers, and the FICO and LTV scores were similar to fixed-rate mortgages.

They were especially valuable for small business and self-employed businesspeople with irregular income. They could make minimum payments during times of low cash flow and then higher payments when cash flow was better. Many customers took advantage of flexible payments, but as shown below in Chart 7-3, the overwhelming majority of customers did not incur large negative amortization as reflected in the total loan balances of negative amortization being a small percent of total loan balances.

Chart 7-3: Washington Mutual Option ARM Performance (millions)[56]

	2005	2006	2007
Loan balance in portfolio	$71,201	$63,557	$58,870
Average LTV at origination	71%	73%	73%
Current average LTV	69%	77%	74%
Total negative amortization	$160	$888	$1731
Total % negative amortization	0.2%	1.4%	2.9%
Loan losses	<1%	.6%	1.5%

Chart 7-3 shows Washington Mutual option ARMs were well-performing prime loans that were originated with an average of almost 30 percent down payment (equity) and maintained strong LTV ratios. The loans performed for decades with less than 1 percent default rate and with less than 1 percent negative amortization—which is the amount the loan balance went up. The rise in negative amortization in 2007 was due to the lower number of option ARM balances combined with a dramatic decrease in housing prices and a slowing economy. Most customers did not build large negative amortization as reflected by total loan balances (including negative amortization) remaining at a conservative 74 percent LTV in 2007.

In September, Washington Mutual held its annual Investors' Day, and Kerry continued to get more vocal about his concerns on housing. He warned the attendees:

> A year and a half ago, I was pounding the table saying the housing market had become very speculative. My view was housing prices had increased too much in relation to inflation and the core fundamentals. A slowdown in housing will lead to higher delinquencies and credit costs. We began planning for this quite some time ago and took a number of defensive actions.
>
> We have lost market share [in mortgages] over the last year as a result of tightening the credit guidelines in our subprime business. We are ahead of many of our competitors and dramatically dropped the subprime business which reflects a more conservative posture. A slowdown in housing will lead to higher delinquencies and credit costs and we factor that into our planning. The Bureau of Labor Statistics shows mortgage industry employment is up 11 percent, but volume is down 26 percent so there is huge overcapacity. Over the same period, 2003 to 2006, we have taken out 70 percent of mortgage staff. But the industry has its head in the sand.
>
> Most economists feel employment will remain firm and a recession is not a high probability. However, in the last two years I have been predicting the economy and housing was going to slow, and probably I have been too conservative. I think the mortgage industry has severe overcapacity and significant problems. Overall our portfolio is very solid, FICO scores at 716 and 69 percent LTV at origination. [This means an average 31 percent down payment]. I get questions about negative amortization in the option ARM, but it is [currently] only two-thirds of 1 percent, a very small fraction of the portfolio.[57]

Kerry also expressed warnings at the Lehman Brothers investor conference:

> In our company I am the resident pessimist on housing. When I was at this conference last year, I said I'm very nervous about the

US housing market, because I felt it was getting into a peak that could present risk for everyone. We are going to continue to be fairly defensive in that we are not going to grow our assets at the rate we normally would. We are decreasing our home lending in every area.

As part of my cautious outlook on the economy, I really felt housing was likely to slow. Beginning two years ago, we started to prepare for a slowing economy. We have reduced staffing by 27 percent over the past twelve months and cut noninterest expenses 21 percent since last year.

Based on Kerry's concerns, the risk managers created stress models that factored up to a 40 percent drop in national housing—much higher than the GSEs or the Federal Reserve was calculating. In October, when the economist Dr. Shiller was a panelist at the Yale Investment Club, he recalled asking a Freddie Mac executive about its stress tests. Freddie had calculated a national housing drop of at the most only 13.4 percent.[58]

That month Kerry attended the Fed's TIAC Council. Kerry was vice chair of the group, and he talked with Fed chair Bernanke and other governors about stresses developing in the housing market. Kerry warned the Fed conditions were worsening and could have a significant impact on the economy. The governors listened but said their economists disagreed. Following the meeting, Kerry sent a letter to the board sharing his concerns on the delinquency trends in the prime and subprime markets and warned of future issues:

> Bernanke said the Fed was carefully assessing the impact of housing deceleration on the overall economy. However, Bernanke was confident he was on top of developments in the housing market and seemed comfortable there wouldn't be a problem.[59]

On September 30, 2006, the FDIC published third-quarter bank earnings:

> The FDIC announced record bank earnings of $38.1 billion. Noncurrent loan rate reached an all-time low. Capital indicators remained robust, with no bank failures in more than two years.

On October 17, 2006, Washington Mutual reported solid quarterly earnings of $812 million and Kerry told investors:

> The housing market is clearly weakening with the pace of housing price appreciation slowing in most regions of the country. We are experiencing somewhat higher delinquencies and loan losses; however, we began preparing for this possibility quite some time ago and took defensive measures.

In response to a question, Kerry noted that "In our underwriting of option ARMS we underwrite to the fully indexed rate, we never underwrite to the teaser rate."[60] Kerry also mentioned to the group that option ARMs had less than 1 percent negative amortization.

In October 2006, federal regulatory agencies including the OCC, OTS, and FDIC released the "Interagency Guidance on Nontraditional Mortgage Product Risks." It recommended lenders evaluate borrowers' income against the fully indexed, fully amortizing payment amount, accounting for any capacity for negative amortization. Washington Mutual was way ahead of the curve, having voluntarily required option ARMs to be underwritten to the fully indexed, fully amortizing payment amount. The regulatory guidance did not prohibit the issuance of option ARMs, even when the market worsened in 2007, although Kerry had the bank eliminate option ARMs early in 2008.

In the fall, CERO Cathcart presented another credit risk deep dive to the board's finance committee and declared:

> The LTVs of the loans are conservative and provide great cushion. Higher-risk lending segments are controlled through concentration limits, and subprime lending has been reduced. The bank is well capitalized and credit reserves are appropriate and have more rigorous analytic underpinnings. To ensure we are prepared for the decline in housing, we are working together to develop market-based triggers and action plans.
>
> Subprime loan delinquency remains in line with industry averages. Washington Mutual has superior credit quality due to re-underwriting and rejection of low-quality assets prior to settlement. The bank's reserves to charge-off coverage ratio is in line with peers.

Low-risk (thirty-year fixed-rate) prime residential real estate
lending continues to be Washington Mutual's most significant
concentration [about 70 percent through 2004–2006]. Our credit
strategy was approved by the enterprise risk management committee and the board. In July 2006 the finance committee of the
board approved a credit risk limit structure to manage significant
risks in lending portfolios. Current exposures are within expected
and manageable tolerances in our limit structure.

CERO Cathcart concluded:

Better risk-adjusted pricing should compensate for additional
credit risk in the market. The bank is well capitalized. Credit
reserves are appropriate and have more rigorous analytical
underpinnings. The executives also put together detailed analysis
of what would happen if the entire housing market collapsed
40 percent. They determined Washington Mutual had enough
capital and liquidity to survive a 40 percent housing collapse.
Most of the other banks were using much more timid models.[61]

At the Merrill Lynch Banking and Financial Services Conference in
November, Kerry warned:

Washington Mutual has been a leader in reducing its
mortgage-related staffing by about 70 percent from 2003 to 2006,
but most competitors in the industry just have not stepped up to
the plate and they haven't rationalized their capacity to the new
environment. The inevitable outcome is severe margin compres-
sion as players try to maintain volume to support their excess
capacity and bloated cost structures. As a result, the mortgage
industry as a whole is not currently earning a satisfactory return.
    Our credit performance has been extraordinarily strong over
the last four years, in part because we've been preparing our portfolios for a more difficult credit environment for quite some time.
Our single-family residential portfolio consists of high-quality
loans performing very well, as exhibited by a very low net
charge-off rate of only four basis points for the first nine months

of the year. [One hundred basis points is 1 percent.] The portfolio
is solid with an average FICO score of 715 and 70 percent loan to
value at origination and current estimated LTV of 56 percent.

Our quality of option ARMS reflects the underwriting which
evaluated the borrower's ability to make the loans fully amortizing
payments, even though they are allowed to make a much lower
initial payment. The amount of negative amortization is less than
1 percent.[62]

At the Goldman Sachs conference in December, Kerry confirmed
the bank's safe portfolio and again warned about the housing market:

Washington Mutual had a return on equity in the high teens,
double-digit earnings per share growth, and an efficiency ratio
under 50 percent. Our nonperforming assets are less than
1 percent of assets.

Two years ago, I was raising my hand here and saying, guys, I
think the housing market is inflated, we have a bubble that has been
created, and we are going to have to unwind this speculative excess,
and it's going to happen with some kind of a deflation process going
on in housing. I have been saying this for some time, there is a total
disconnect in mortgage banking between the realistic levels of production that are going to happen and the level of employment. From
2002 to 2005, the industry went through an extraordinary period of
expansion and profitability. From 2003 to 2006, origination volumes
declined by 35 percent and mortgage employment grew 8 percent.
You can't have volume coming down 35 percent and employment
growing by 8 percent without getting an industry in severe overcapac-
ity. I think mortgage banking is currently a lousy return industry.

Clearly our credit performance has been outstanding in the
last several years. This is in part because we started preparing
some time ago for a more difficult credit environment. If anything,
I can be accused of being too conservative. But we want to stay
ahead of the curve and be a little more conservative.[63]

That fall the media were highlighting Washington Mutual's hard
work and focusing on Kerry's unique approach to banking and business.

In November, *Seattle Magazine* reported:

> Kerry is quiet, unassuming, and thoughtful. Kerry doesn't act like
> a typical CEO but has been the driving force in transforming the
> bank from a little-known regional thrift into the largest S&L in
> the country. He has turned Washington Mutual into the retailer of
> bank services for the middle class by pushing for nontraditional,
> comfortable retail branches, offering inexpensive services [the
> industry standard free checking was initiated by the bank], and
> online innovations (it's the only bank where customers can open
> an account entirely electronically). Kerry said, 'We have built our
> brand through our advertising, which is a little quirky and very
> human and an alternative to stodgy old bankers.'[64]

In December, the bank hired the independent risk-consulting firm
of Protiviti to provide a thorough corporate credit review assessment
of the risk management department. It concluded Washington Mutual
had "a highly experienced [risk management] team overall and they
are very hard working. The total FTEs in the department is within the
range of reasonableness compared to the industry." It observed the
group had spent significant time and effort on establishing appropriate policies, protocols, and methodologies. It had a few recommendations on organizational structure and some protocols but concluded
the risk management department was "competitive with peers."[65]

At the end of the year, CERO Ron Cathcart discussed his presentation on the "Nonprime Plan" in the board meeting:

> Loan volume has decreased due to more stringent credit guidelines
> and actions taken to date in 2006 have improved the loan profile and
> reduced overall losses. Overall 2006 was a good year for Washington
> Mutual with a near record net income of $3.6 billion. A slowdown
> in the housing market caused nonperforming assets to increase to
> 0.80 percent of assets but were still well below the long-term target of
> 1 percent. Reflecting the plan to reduce residential lending and diver-
> sify the asset mix, new home loan originations declined by 24 percent
> in 2006 and loans serviced for others declined by 25 percent
> following a servicing rights sale to Wells Fargo. Retail banking drove
> excellent financial results in 2006 with profits of $2.2 billion. Card

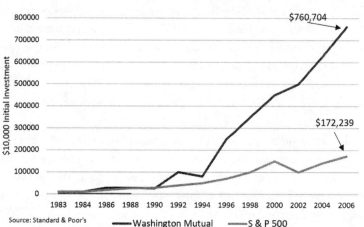

Chart 7-4: A $10,000 Investment in Washington Mutual versus the S&P 500 (1983-2006)

Source: Standard & Poor's

services added $745 million and commercial added $368 million. Home loans contributed a small loss of $48 million in 2006.

Stockholders continued to do well in 2006. Chart 7-4 shows a $10,000 investment in Washington Mutual common stock when the company went public in 1983 would have grown to $760,704 at the end of 2006. The same $10,000 investment in the S&P 500 would have grown to only $172,239 over this same period. The cumulative total includes reinvested dividends for both Washington Mutual and the S&P 500. This outstanding long-term performance resulted in strong support from institutional and individual shareholders.

The FDIC reported the annual earnings for the banking industry in 2006:

The FDIC revealed record earnings of nearly $150 billion. Net charge-offs for loans was down 36 percent that year, and most of the year was at an all-time low for charge-offs. The OTS reported the thrift industry had an all-time record net income of nearly $16 billion. The mortgage loans thirty to eighty-nine days overdue were at a relatively low 0.61 to 0.70 percent of total assets and the ninety-plus-day delinquent loans were around the 0.64 percent all year, a percentage the banks should have been able to handle.[66]

The years 2000 to 2006 were a very good period for most banks, including Washington Mutual. Washington Mutual earned total profits of $22.7 billion over this time period and successfully diversified its geographic footprint. Major new retail banking markets were added, including New York, Texas, Chicago, Atlanta, Las Vegas, Phoenix, and Florida. Its customer base grew to over eleven million, and its business mix changed over time to emphasize retail banking, card services, and commercial lending. As housing market conditions changed, both prime and subprime residential lending were curtailed.

The unregulated shadow subprime companies had a slower year in 2006, but they still created over $490 billion of subprime loans, only about 20 percent less than in 2005. They probably thought their business would still be viable. However, in just a few months, this trillion-dollar unregulated industry would collapse from its own weight. Their world, and the worlds of many others, were about to end abruptly.

8

The Financial Crisis Hits

2007

The regulated banking industry started the new year floating on
a high after the 2006 all-time record earnings—nearly $150 billion.
Non-current loans were at an all-time low, problem banks were at an
all-time low, and there had been no bank failures for nearly three years.[1]
They all knew the housing market was cooling off—housing prices
had reached all-time highs but then decreased. Even the high-flying
multitrillion-dollar mortgage securitization market was cooling off.
But the regulators, Treasury Secretary Paulson and Fed chair Bernanke,
were comfortable the banks would be fine. They suspected there would
be a shakeout in the unregulated subprime companies, but none of
them seemed to realize how tightly the unregulated subprime tentacles
had infested the Wall Street mortar.

The unregulated subprime companies were the first to feel the
heat of the new year. Subprime loan production for 2006 had been
down by about 20 percent, the first downturn all decade. Maybe they
thought it was just a bump in the road, but it was hard to tell what they
were really thinking—they didn't have a federal regulator to monitor

their progress or their problems. It started slowly, and then came the tsunami. The loans from the unregulated shadow subprime companies were being turned back to them. Early payment defaults were rising throughout the industry, and the unregulated subprime originators did not have the financial resources to honor the buyback provisions on their troubled loans. Most of them had relied on expensive overnight funding for their operations, but those loans were now hard to come by.

These companies had minimal capital bases for protection, and their Wall Street liquidity sources were drying up. In the first quarter of the year, they all crashed like an upended line of dominos. Within three months, forty-two of the unregulated subprime originators, including the two giants, Ameriquest and New Century, were gone.[2] By the second quarter of the year, nearly all of them were gone. For six years the unregulated shadow subprime industry had created about $2 trillion of the most toxic loans ever created in the history of the world, and within weeks the companies had vaporized—but their toxic loans still remained embedded in billions of dollars of Wall Street CDOs, insured with trillions of dollars in CDSs.

Federal regulators remained unconcerned about these events. In February of 2007, Fed chair Bernanke told the Budget Committee of the US House of Representatives the housing downturn was not of a "broad financial concern or a major factor in assessing the state of the economy." Bernanke also opined that he "expected moderate growth and the economy should begin to rebound by the end of the year."[3] He added that the "business sector remains in excellent condition."

Treasury Secretary Paulson felt the collapse of the unregulated subprime companies meant "the subprime mortgage problems are largely contained." A month later Fed chair Bernanke told a Fed conference, "We do not expect significant spillovers from the subprime market to the rest of the economy or to the financial system." Neither of them seemed to be aware of or concerned about the trillions of dollars of layered risk created by Wall Street's gigantic shadow subprime system, nor did they seem to be alarmed that the Case-Shiller house price index recorded the first year-over-year decline in nationwide housing prices since 1991.[4]

Even the titans at the 2007 World Economic Forum in Davos were in a cocky and celebrative mood. Any concerns at Davos were mostly focused on the hedge fund and equity titans. One forum about hedge fund transparency carried the subtitle, "Concern is growing the opaque nature of the $1,500 billion hedge fund industry may precipitate a future financial crisis, spurring demands for greater transparency." The participants swaggered on stage as the wealthiest and most unregulated financiers in the world and assured the raptured audience they were too disciplined and brilliant to cause a future financial crisis. They were firm in their belief that any transparency and regulation in their industry would "destroy America as we know it."[5]

Another session entitled "Is Bigger Better in Private Equity?" showcased the participants in the biggest equity deal ever—the $21 billion deal for the hospital conglomerate HCA. They believed few corporations were beyond their reach and "Yes, bigger is better."

Nouriel Roubini, chair of Roubini Global Economics, spoke at a Davos forum where he warned of the increased use of derivatives as financial instruments. He stated, "The amount of leverage in the system is growing at rates that are scary. We don't know if derivatives are diffusing risks or concentrating it. The risk of something happening is rising." However, most of the attendees applauded Thomas Russo, chief legal officer of Lehman Brothers, who disagreed with Roubini and countered, "Risk is spread out in the financial services industry now much greater than ever before."[6]

Kerry traveled to Davos and Europe each year to participate in investor conferences and visit international bank CEOs and investors. His goals were twofold: there was an increasing number of international investors interested in Washington Mutual stock, and a long-term game plan could involve a merger with an international bank. Many of the international banks were looking to expand into the United States, and Washington Mutual, with its well-run branch network and efficient and diversified mix of products, would be a logical merger partner.

After the meetings in Davos, Kerry felt he was the only large bank CEO who had adequately prepared for what he thought would be a substantial implosion in the mortgage industry affecting the entire economy. He had decreased mortgage lending by 74 percent and diversified the bank with retail operations, credit cards, small business lending, and commercial apartment lending. He thought he had done everything he could to protect the bank, and the numbers proved him right. In 2006 Washington Mutual had net income of $3.56 billion

and a record fourth-quarter income of $1.06 billion. During the year
the bank had opened a record 1.23 million net new checking accounts,
added a record 848,000 net new retail households (a household
could have more than one checking account), and experienced strong
cross-sells of the new branded credit card to current customers.[7]

In addition to all the financial success, Washington Mutual had
been the recipient of a number of awards for service, innovation, and
workplace environment. The Reputation Institute named Washington
Mutual the bank with the best reputation in the country. Criteria were
leadership, citizenship, governance, workplace values, innovation, products and services, and performance.[8]

Business Week listed Washington Mutual number fourteen on the
list of the "Top 25 Service Champs"—the only bank to ever make
the list.[9] *Fortune* magazine designated Washington Mutual as a Blue
Ribbon Company—the only bank ever so designated—because of
its inclusion in all of *Fortune*'s lists: *Fortune*'s 100 Best Companies to
Work For, America's Most Admired Companies, the *Fortune 100* and
the Global 500.[10] JD Power announced the bank was number one in
service in the West, California, and the Midwest.[11] *Black Professionals*
magazine named the bank one of the top companies for diversity.

ComScore named the bank first for its online checking application and number two for customer satisfaction on the internet.[12] The
Council on Financial Competition recognized the bank for having two
of the top innovations in financial services for 2006. BAI's Deposit
Benchmarking Study concluded the bank had the highest household
growth rate of any major bank over the past two years.[13]

And most importantly, the results from the 2007 all-employee survey were outstanding, with survey participation rising from 73 percent
to 88 percent and employee engagement rising from 70 percent to 73
percent. They also saw the overall values index rise from 74 percent to
81 percent with particular gains in being *fair, caring* and *human*.[14] Exit
interviews were also showing good results and turnover was low because of strong wages and benefits and good working conditions. Kerry
strongly believed good financial results came from highly engaged and
well-treated employees giving top-notch customer service.

During the first-quarter 2007 investor calls, board calls, and investor
meetings, Kerry once again expressed his concern about the housing
market and repeated all the work the bank had done to protect itself:[15]

I have been pretty pessimistic on the housing market for the last couple of years and felt the market was overheated and likely to be a slowdown. Because of this we have taken a number of defensive actions and have been diversifying our mix of business away from home mortgages into credit card services and commercial and business lending. We tightened underwriting and decreased production volume. Our prime loan portfolio, including option ARMs, has an average FICO score of 710 with a current estimated loan to value of 55 percent. Our home equity loans have average FICO of about 740 and a combined LTV of 67 percent. We have chosen to stop growing our subprime portfolio.

The subprime industry continues to have major problems. Early payment defaults are rising throughout the industry, and some marginal companies do not have the financial resources to honor the buyback provisions on these loans. Asset bubbles are being created around the world. Housing prices are escalating at double-digit rates in many areas. Too much capital is chasing too few assets.

Private equity is displacing public ownership as a preferred financing vehicle. Money continues to flow into hedge funds and private equity firms, which are increasing their appetites for doing very large deals. Ironically many of the private equity firms are considering going public in order to monetize the value of their franchise.

We are in unchartered territory and just don't know if all of the newer financial instruments [SIVs, CDOs, CDSs], increasing use of leverage, and increasing hedge funds and private equity financing, will reduce risks or will cause a massive financial crisis. The whole system is untested, and I do fear layering of risks may be creating some form of pyramid that could collapse if certain variables were to radically change.

Kerry was correct—the layers of Wall Street risk in the system created the largest financial scheme in the history of the world. US households became increasingly indebted with the ratio of debt to disposable personal income rising from 77 percent in 1990 to 127 percent at the end of 2007. Much of this increase was mortgage related. People listened to the media and government promotion of housing and were moving toward low-payment products, housing speculation, and bubble psychology.[16]

In response to Kerry's view of the housing market and the changes in the economy, he not only had dramatically cut mortgage lending, he was starting to close retail branch offices that were not meeting target goals. Kerry felt strongly that the banking industry had put too many branches in the system and in the future, customers would be focused more on online products. In response to this, the team had created the first completely automated online checking product that won awards for ease and accuracy of use and was producing over one million net new accounts each year.

Todd Baker, the bank's prescient strategic planning executive, continued to be concerned about Wall Street, the regulators, and the Fed's failure to predict or prepare for the coming crisis. In February he wrote:

> Housing expansion lasted 15 years, but FICO scores will act differently in the future. Perpetually rising property values and product design have led to false statistical conclusions about default likelihood and loss severity for subprime. Reliance on pooled data driven by underwriting was allowed to override traditional judgment [in Wall Street banks].

In other words, Wall Street, in slicing and dicing all their new complex instruments, was just projecting forward past performance data and ignoring all the layered risk when predicting future financial patterns.

But Fed chair Bernanke was still comfortable. In March he testified to Congress that "The impact on the broader economy and financial markets of the problems in the subprime markets seems likely to be contained."[17]

In March 2007, CERO Cathcart presented his credit risk highlights to the board's finance committee. In his executive summary he reported:

> Overall portfolio risk metrics are contained within board-approved credit concentration limits and are consistent with the company's board-approved strategy to expand credit across asset classes in 2006. There is continued tightening of

higher risk subprime residential lending to higher FICO scores, more documentation, lower LTVs required and lowering of DTIs.

In the spring, Kerry attended the financial roundtable meeting as well as the Fed's TIAC meeting.

We skipped the last dinner at the spring Financial Services Roundtable meeting, because we had been invited to have dinner at the home of the CEO of Capital One, Richard Fairbank, and his wife. Richard and Kerry had been discussing a merger of the two banks, which would combine the strength of Capital One's credit card operations with the strengths of Washington Mutual's retail banking operations. The combined bank would create a powerhouse with a strong national footprint. Both CEOs had similar values and respected each other. After serious discussions they decided to put the idea on hold, because both of them wanted to focus on their own banks until the economy stabilized. They agreed to stay in touch and reconsider at a later date.

In late March, Kerry wrote to the board:

I had dinner with Ben Bernanke and spent over two hours with the Federal Reserve Governors last week. They were very interested in our perspective on housing and developments in the subprime area. I also discussed some ideas as to how they could bring the common equity ratios of the European and US banks closer together. This input appears to have had an impact on this week's open market committee meeting.

Many of the leading subprime monoline companies have gone out of business and subprime lending is front and center with regulators and Congress. David Schneider, President of Home Lending, and his team are doing a good job of responding to changing market conditions and we appear to be making progress on a number of fronts. We have increased pricing, tightened our underwriting, reduced our costs and adjusted to new regulatory guidelines. Despite these and many other actions we undertook in 2006 and 2007, we will have poor results from subprime in the first quarter. The biggest challenge is an unprecedented widening of credit spreads which will require us to write down the value of loans held in the pipeline. This, along with the write down of subprime residuals and additional loan loss reserves for subprime loans will likely lead to a $200 million first quarter loss in subprime lending.

Senator Dodd held hearings on subprime lending yesterday. A couple of Senators attacked the Fed for not being more aggressive in regulating subprime lending but our regulator, the OTS, was not the brunt of any attacks. The challenge for the Fed is the majority of subprime lending is done with nonregulated brokers selling loans directly to Wall Street. Meaningful reform in subprime lending requires getting controls around brokers and Wall Street. This is something we would support as it could improve the industry's image and long-term profitability. Washington Mutual was not mentioned in the hearings.

The FDIC released its first-quarter 2007 bank earnings, which were down slightly to $36 billion. Provisions for loan losses increased 54.6 percent. Year over year residential mortgage loan charge-offs rose 93.2 percent.[18]

Although the quarterly earnings were only down a bit, provisions for loan losses and loan charge-offs were increasing dramatically and taking the banking industry by surprise. According to the April issue of *Money* magazine, "Approximately 13% of all subprime loans are delinquent and financial firms and hedge funds likely own more than $1 trillion in securities backed by subprime mortgages."[19] They didn't know the half of it.

Kerry announced the bank's quarterly earnings were much higher than estimated due to tough expense management, stronger credit card results, improving net interest margin, good fee income, and stability in the valuation of the subprime residuals.

You can see the benefit of diversification and our risk remix strategy. Virtually all [unregulated] subprime monoline companies are severely crippled or out of business. Our stock price has been under selling pressure as some investors are betting we will have a very difficult first quarter. While none of us are happy with current operating results, you can sure see the benefits of diversification. It is easy to see why monolines [companies with only one product] are becoming a thing of the past. This is similar to what happened to monoline consumer finance and credit card companies in the past.

In April, Washington Mutual sponsored another event where employees helped revitalize a neighborhood school in a distressed area in Los Angeles. Both Kerry and Linda, along with employees, students, teachers, and family members, worked all day Saturday to upgrade a local high school. We worked on painting; planting trees, bushes, and flowers; carrying away debris; and other activities. When she was taking a short break from hauling debris and planting, Linda looked in on one of the Washington Mutual classes that was teaching students and their parents financial literacy around budgeting, raising their FICO scores, and saving for the future.

As usual, after the quarterly earnings reports, there was a round of stories about the bank. The *Puget Sound Business Journal* declared:

> Killinger is a down to earth CEO who has been known to come to work in a Halloween costume and who still makes it a point to mingle with the rank and file employees in the company cafeteria.

Kerry shared in the article:

> A couple of years ago, we were very vocal the housing market was growing at unprecedented levels which was becoming a bubble and there needed to be a correction. Our reaction to the subprime problem was to significantly reduce our participation and we dropped subprime 80% last year.[20]

Fortune magazine wrote an article entitled "People Are His Bottom Line" and remarked:

> The maverick exec created not only the nation's sixth largest bank, but also one of the industry's most innovative. Kerry said, 'Coming from a little humbler background, I appreciate the importance of keeping some humility and checking your ego at the door.'[21]

All the articles were saying the same thing: Kerry was still the humble and down-to-earth CEO, the mortgage environment was getting tough for everyone, "but deep cuts in mortgage lending, high lending standards and product diversification were working for Washington Mutual."

That same month we attended the opening of the Seattle Art Museum and the Olympic Sculpture Park. Linda was one of eight members of the major gifts committee of the Board of Directors of the museum, who worked very hard to raise over $100 million for the two projects. We were all thrilled to see the positive reception from the Seattle community. Downtown Seattle didn't have any downtown parks or green spaces, so the sculpture park was a very positive addition. Mimi Gates, director of the Seattle Art Museum, frequently told us the park "would be the only place downtown where you could walk down to Puget Sound and dip your toe in the water." The opening of the museum was an extra special event for us because Washington Mutual's support and cost sharing for the museum were the main reasons the museum and the sculpture park could afford to be built. By combining the art museum with the bank, millions of dollars of construction costs were saved and Washington Mutual gave the museum $5.8 million a year in a long-term lease of some of their space.

In May Kerry wrote to the board:

> I just returned from investor meetings and meetings with major
> bank CEOs in Europe. The investor meetings were generally quite
> positive. Investors were quite complimentary of our progress
> in expense reduction, growing the retail customer base and our
> credit card services growth.
>
> Highly leveraged private equity transactions are being
> announced daily. The abundance of cheap financing is driving
> up asset prices throughout the world. Most stock markets are at
> all-time highs. In short, a bubble is developing which presents
> significant risks.

That year at the Lehman conference, the Sanford Bernstein conference and the second-quarter earnings release, Kerry had the same message:

> Seventy-nine subprime mortgage companies have gone out of
> business so far this year,[22] but we prepared for this crisis. We
> tightened credit guidelines and adjusted pricing, which drove our
> production down 51 percent from the same quarter last year. The
> option ARM products have the same standards as the thirty-year
> fixed mortgage. The average FICO scores are above 700 and the
> LTVs are less than 60 percent.[23]

The trends started dramatically changing after the second quarter of 2007, when people realized the values of their homes had dropped so dramatically that they owed more on the house than the house was worth. The National Association of Realtors reported the inventory of unsold homes was the highest in nearly two decades. In these desperate times, consumers were suddenly changing their behavior. In the past, people would pay their home mortgage first and let the credit cards slide. Now they were doing the reverse, paying off the credit cards and giving the house keys back to the bank—and often times, these were prime customers.

The Center for Responsible Lending, after studying six million recent subprime mortgages, predicted a sharp increase in foreclosure rates.[24] The Joint Center for Housing Studies, using data from the American Community Surveys, found 45 percent of owners and 57 percent of renters were spending more than half of their disposable income on housing.[25] The recommended budget amount should be closer to 35 percent on housing.

Still, there was little concern from the federal government. In April of 2007, the Federal Reserve released a report, "Large Financial Institutions' Perspectives on Risk," which studied the risks in the system's largest banks. The report stated, "There are no substantial issues of supervisory concerns for these large financial institutions. Asset quality across the systemically important institutions remains strong."[26] In May, Fed chair Bernanke assured the world when he forcefully stated, "We do not expect significant spillovers from the subprime market to the rest of the economy or to the financial system."[27] He felt there was evidence that "terrible things could not happen."

Fortunately, Kerry was concerned about industry-wide trends that clearly showed "terrible things could happen." He and his team jumped into the problem and developed a number of programs to help customers stay in their homes. The bank introduced a new type of mortgage called the All in One Mortgage Plus Loan, which had no closing fees and no need to refinance. It combined a first mortgage and a home equity line of credit into a single loan. This new loan could consolidate mortgage and home equity loans into one loan with lower interest rates and more affordable payments.

Another program Washington Mutual announced was a $2 billion grant to reduce payments by subprime customers by refinancing loans at discounted interest rates. The bank set up phone banks to contact customers and sent out letters to thousands of customers offering them $100 in cash just to come and talk about reducing their home loans and getting lower payments. Kerry stated:

> We want our customers to know what's ahead, to avoid surprises and to understand the choices available to them. We set up a team of mortgage professionals focused on providing workout options aimed at keeping borrowers in their home. We have a long history of cooperation with community groups who specialize in borrower education and foreclosure prevention and the bank has joined forces with a number of key partners including the NeighborWorks Center for Foreclosure Solutions and the Home-ownership Preservation Foundation to launch a national effort to avert foreclosures.[28]

In June, Kerry wrote to the board:

> We had a good May. Net income was $331 million vs. $251 million in April. We benefitted in May from larger than normal card securitizations and hedging gains. The flat yield curve and deteriorating housing market conditions continue to put pressure on our results. However, continued outstanding growth in retail banking customers, good fee income growth and improving home loan performance were positives for the quarters. I recently met with several of our largest shareholders who are supportive of our strategies and believe we are executing well in a difficult environment. Our largest shareholder continued to add to their position, bringing their total ownership to 20% of our outstanding stock. They did mention our dividend policy was very important to them.

On June 23, Bear Stearns bailed out some of their loan funds with a $3.2 billion loan, which riveted Wall Street for two weeks because so many firms had investments in subprime mortgages and they didn't know which ones were good and which were bad. Bear thought they had prevented a crisis by providing the loan.[29]

On June 29 Kerry met with the Federal Reserve and Fed chair Bernanke. Kerry wrote back to the board:

I visited at length with Chair Bernanke and other officials. Their position is the housing downturn will be modest and liquidity will not become a major issue for the capital markets. We were told the Fed employs some of the best economic forecasters and they only predict a modest downturn. We warned them our data were showing something much more serious and we have been taking several steps to tighten underwriting and cut staff for almost three years.

They were quite interested in our observations regarding subprime mortgages and our leadership in helping families avoid foreclosures with counseling and loan modification activities. The Fed appears comfortable with keeping interest rates at current levels, so major changes are unlikely for a while.

But Fed chair Bernanke disagreed with any warnings. In July he said:

Employment should continue to expand...the global economy continues to be strong...financial markets have remained supportive of economic growth.[30]

On July 8, Kerry sent a letter followed by a speech to the risk management group to encourage them to continue to tighten lending standards:

There is a lot going on in a volatile market and it's changing daily. The economy seems solid, but there is a developing liquidity crisis in home mortgages. The stock market is near an all-time high, inflation is low, housing prices are falling and credit spreads tightening. Our delinquencies are rising and we have much higher losses and loan loss provisioning than we ever had in the past. Liquidity in the market is getting tight. Widening credit spreads will hurt the value of loans in process and pipelines.

We have three businesses that are doing very well. Retail banking and credit cards both have record growth and commercial loans have record originations with very low delinquencies. Second-quarter 2007 income is up 8% and earnings per share are up 16%, net interest margin is 2.90 and efficiency is 56.4%. ERM is a critical part of our company and our model of pulling risks together into ERM is appropriate and we are a leader. We are still evolving and improving our model, but we are on the right track. Risk management is especially important today because of increased regulatory expectations and oversight, new Basel II capital requirements and increased credit risks, increased liquidity risk, volatility, litigation risk and increased pressure to stretch for profit.

You [ERM] have made good progress in managing market risk and developing operational risk models. As a bank we cannot make adequate returns unless we take market risk, credit risk, and operating risk. But we also know we can fail if we don't properly manage these risks. Enterprise risk management is doing well and audit services continue to improve.

In short, I see ERM as making good progress, but the environment is getting tougher and we need to take our game to a higher level. Remember ERM is not about having us reduce or avoid risk, it is about identifying risks, measuring those risks, and managing risks within a targeted level. You are an essential part of our company and I thank you for your hard work. You have a strong leadership team and we have confidence we will achieve our goals.[31]

At the July 17, 2007, board meeting, the OTS and FDIC regulators were in attendance and presented their annual exam findings. Washington Mutual received an outstanding 2 in each category, and the regulators concluded the "financial position of the company was sound and noted the company had made much progress during the last four years." Both the OTS and the FDIC said the bank should "consider themselves rated a '2 plus' because of the strong liquidity position and the stable loan portfolio." It is common for banks to receive informal exam criticisms and recommendations, but over the years they were declining substantially, for an all-time low in 2007. Regarding the bank's relatively small higher-risk mortgage loan portfolio, the FDIC and OTS told to the board:

The overall risk posed by the higher risk lending strategy remains adequately controlled through managed growth, adequate monitoring of delinquencies and NPAs [nonperforming assets] and the maintenance of adequate allowances and capital relative to portfolio risk.[32]

Washington Mutual had near record earnings of $1.6 billion for the first two quarters of 2007. Loan delinquencies had only minor increases despite the collapse of the unregulated subprime industry.

In July, Reuters reported Secretary Paulson's, SEC's, and OCC's varied insights on the housing decline:

> Secretary Paulson said, the 'US housing downturn is near the end. I don't think the subprime mess poses any threat to the overall economy.' However, the SEC Division of Trading and Markets concluded 'virtually the entire banking sector failed to anticipate the magnitude and scope of the housing decline that is still ongoing.' John Walsh, chief of staff at the OCC, said 'Nobody realized in looking at these bad real estate loans that a tsunami was coming, as opposed to just a tide.' FDIC examiners explained no one could have predicted the precipitous fall in home prices and the complete shutdown of the secondary market.[33]

Just days after Secretary Paulson announced housing wouldn't affect the economy, Bear Stearns sent a letter to investors that two of their hedge funds specializing in subprime deals had lost at least 90 percent of their value.[34] Kerry contacted the board:

> Investors and warehouse lenders immediately pulled back and exited the market due to concerns over the events. The event primarily impacted credit spreads and liquidity in the subprime market, but also impacted prime nonconforming products on concern they too will have lost value. The drop in the value of the securities forced many investors to sell securities in order to meet margin calls. There is virtually no liquidity in the subprime markets.[35]

One day after the Bear Stearns announcement, the Fed was still predicting moderate economic growth of about 2.5 percent for the rest of 2007. However, Fed chair Bernanke finally acknowledged the Fed and other regulators had been too timid in reining in aggressive mortgage lenders. He also announced plans to review the practices of mortgage lenders to see if new rules or enforcement are necessary.[36] They never pursued those plans.

Near the end of July, Kerry wrote to the board:

> The capital markets are extremely volatile. Credit concerns are rising in corporate securities, LBO financings, asset backed securities, and mortgage related securities. The DJIA was down 226 points today and the ten-year treasury rate declined to 4.94% as investors fled to high quality. Our stock declined to $39.09, although it was less of a decline than most of the other financial stocks.
>
> Our pricing discipline has served us well over the years and we have benefited from not overpaying in the frothy environment in the past couple of years. Wachovia is the current poster child for feeling the market's wrath for over-paying for Golden West. Their stock has underperformed the market by 28% since they announced that transaction.
>
> We have been saying for quite some time credit spreads were too tight and there was a likelihood credit spreads would widen as credit risks became more apparent. We accordingly reduced our assets, bought back stock and deferred taking on new higher risk assets. Credit spreads have now widened and we may be able to carefully increase our balance sheet.

Some analysts thought the crash of the unregulated subprime system would provide opportunities for the regulated banks, but Kerry disagreed. He quickly concluded the subprime market would continue to deteriorate, and he completely stopped subprime lending in July. His calculations were accurate, because on August 1, Bear Stearns halted redemptions in the third collapse of its hedge funds, and one of its subprime hedge funds filed for Chapter 15 bankruptcy. Soon after, the French bank BNP Paribas froze $2.2 billion worth of its funds. It cited as the reason, "the complete evaporation of liquidity in certain market segments of the US securitization market has made it impossible to value certain assets fairly." The LIBOR rate leaped over Treasury rates by thirty basis points in just three business days. For three days JPMorgan Chase, Bank of America and Citigroup had not been able to roll over its commercial paper. Fear and panic had grabbed the market by the throat.[37]

In August, David Viniar, the risk officer for Goldman Sachs, said, "We were seeing things with twenty-five standard deviation moves, several days in a row. Three standard deviation moves would cover 99.8 percent of all possible outcomes. The risk management models were wrong."[38] Years later, market analyst Mark Zandi said the Bear Stearns event (August 1) was "arguably the proximate catalyst" for the financial crisis.[39]

Analysts said more hedge funds could collapse—especially those that didn't have enough capital. Reuters reported JPMorgan Chase, the third-largest US bank, said it "tripled the amount of money set aside for loan losses as even borrowers with good credit defaulted on home equity loans. Countrywide, the nation's largest mortgage lender, reported similar problems on prime home equity loans."[40] The market panic was escalating.

In early August, Kerry updated the board:

> As we discussed at our [July] planning retreat, abundant and cheap credit fueled a bubble in housing prices. That bubble started to deflate last year, and price declines are now occurring in many parts of the country. Declining prices are leading to increases in delinquencies and projected loss rates on all housing-backed mortgages, including prime, subprime, alt A, and home equity. Many of these housing-related mortgages were put into securitizations, which were bought on a leveraged basis by hedge funds and other capital market players. The rating agencies badly underestimated the losses inherent in these securitizations.
>
> With delinquencies rising and fears of losses increasing, the market price of these securitizations fell, and those who invested in these on a leveraged basis got hit very hard. This is what happened to the hedge funds sponsored by Bear Stearns. Facing growing uncertainty, investors backed away from purchasing new securitizations. This led to lower market prices and little or no market liquidity for new mortgages being underwritten by mortgage banking companies. Mortgage bankers couldn't sell their new production and had to mark their pipelines to lower market prices. This led to severe liquidity problems for many mortgage bankers, including American Home Mortgage, who was forced into bankruptcy and had to fire over six thousand of its employees last Friday. It also led to market rumors of liquidity problems for Countrywide, IndyMac, and several other mortgage bankers.

Concurrent with these mortgage-related concerns, investors became nervous over the huge funding commitments of the major banks and securities firms for leveraged buyouts. These exposures led to rumors of liquidity challenges for Bear Stearns, Lehman Brothers, and others, which led to extreme volatility in the share prices of many mortgage-related securities companies. For example, in the third quarter from peak to trough, Countrywide fell by 32 percent, Lehman fell by 24 percent, and we fell by 20 percent. Over the past few days, investor confidence has improved, and Countrywide is up 16 percent, Lehman is up 15 percent, and we are up 10 percent to $37.55.

The liquidity scare caused credit spreads for our unsecured debt to widen from a norm of LIBOR[41] plus 35bp to a peak of LIBOR plus 150bp. Today, our spread tightened to LIBOR plus 80bp. Fortunately, we did not need to do unsecured borrowings when the credit spreads reached their peak. Our team has done a nice job of diversifying our funding sources and giving us many alternatives for dealing with tight liquidity.

The fear and panic in the mortgage market caused most bank stocks with mortgage products to drop in price and become victims of unscrupulous short sellers and rumor mongers. Kerry worked hard through the second half of 2007 and throughout 2008 to stop the unscrupulous naked short sellers and educate the investors on the diversified nature of the bank. In the fall he was talking with investors at the fall investor conferences:

Our consumer and small business lending banking model is dramatically different from and much more resilient than the monoline mortgage companies. Many of them have gone out of business over the past two months because they were not as diversified and lacked the adequate capital and sources of liquidity we have. We have taken key actions to further diversify our business, reduce our market risk, and reduce our expenses, all of which has put us in a better position to weather this challenging market environment.

Our top-tier retail bank and card services businesses delivered the bulk of our revenues, and these businesses continue to thrive and have not been impacted by the mortgage-centric problems.

We anticipated a housing market correction and have been very proactive in preparing for it. This will lead to higher nonperforming assets, loan losses, and loan-loss provisioning in the near term. Our portfolio has an average FICO of 722 and an estimated LTV of 63 percent. The credit spreads are improving, and our expectation is to increase our balance sheet with assets at good risk-adjusted returns. Much of the increase in assets was caused by lack of market liquidity to buy loans in our pipelines.

On September 17, former Fed chair Greenspan warned the public of double-digit declines in housing prices as a result of the housing bubble. Bernanke and Paulson remained silent. Nobel Laureate economist Paul Krugman reported this could be the Wile E. Coyote moment—the cartoon character runs off a cliff, and when he finally looks down, he realizes he's standing on thin air and plunges.[42] This rang true for Kerry because for years, he had been trying to convince Bernanke and others that the economy was running on thin air and the coyote was about to crash land. But the times had been so good, no one wanted to listen.

On September 20, the Financial Services Roundtable met with Fed chair Bernanke, and once again Kerry warned the group about the extent of the crisis. Kerry reported to the board:

July and August market disruptions were severe enough to basically shut down the securitization market for nonconforming mortgage loans. Although we continue to originate prime jumbo loans, we have redirected our production of these loans to our balance sheet portfolio. The prime jumbo market is suffering from a temporary loss of liquidity, which will adversely impact the higher-end housing market over the near term. The subprime market landscape has shifted to a great extent, with much of the origination capacity of the industry having been wiped out, and there is lingering uncertainty regarding the extent of potential losses on existing pools of loans. This makes it much more difficult to be optimistic regarding any return to a more normal securitization market environment.

The Federal Open Market Committee convened on August 30, and Nobel Laureate economist Dr. Shiller warned yet again housing would probably fall hard.⁴³ The financial world was experiencing a liquidity crisis, and everyone wanted to get their hands on more cash. At the board meeting in September, Kerry gave a thorough review of credit, which included a matrix for estimated credit costs under various house price change assumptions:

> Washington Mutual is the first and only major bank to adopt Basel II capital requirements. During the third year of our five-year strategic plan, a declining housing environment, a punitive rate environment, mispriced risk spreads, and high prices for potential acquisitions led us to make significant changes to our strategy. Changes included deferring significant balance sheet remixing and economic capital optimization goals due to poor risk-adjusted returns, and we tightened credit guidelines and reduced production of subprime loans due to our negative view on housing prices. There is a decline in housing prices and a shortage of liquidity in mortgage markets. We deviated from our long-term growth strategy by shrinking the balance sheet and stopping subprime mortgages.

In this time of panic, baseless rumors, and merciless naked short sellers, Kerry heard some disturbing news from a surprising source. He was getting a lot of calls claiming JPMorgan Chase's CEO Dimon was telling investors he was going to try to find a way to steal Washington Mutual "for pennies on the dollar." Kerry called him, Dimon denied it, but Kerry was getting too many calls to the contrary. Kerry knew Washington Mutual's twenty-five hundred retail branches and its powerful retail banking and multifamily lending business would make JPMorgan Chase the biggest bank in the world—something Dimon wouldn't be able to resist.

Kerry consulted with attorneys and the board about Dimon's comments, and the board continued to voice its decision to keep the bank independent at this time. Kerry consulted with the regulators (OTS and FDIC) and was told they totally supported Washington Mutual's management and board and would not be supportive of a competitor trying to buy the bank on the cheap.

That fall the bank's strategic planning executive, Todd Baker, continued to warn management about the environment, sharing his belief, "the bank should batten down the hatches in the biggest area of vulnerability, which would be credit cards, home equity loans, and commercial real estate." Baker saw a recession coming, which would be tough on those nonmortgage products. COO Rotella responded it had already exited subprime lending and pulled back hard on prime mortgages and home equity. He said he would approach the head of credit cards to make more cuts. All the executives agreed with the bearish view of the market and decided to make even more dramatic cuts.

At the September Financial Services Roundtable, Fed chair Bernanke finally acknowledged that market conditions had worsened much more than the Fed anticipated and said the Fed would have to take actions to reduce the impact of declining housing markets and freezing credit markets. He made a few moves but did not do what was really needed the most: a large injection of liquidity into the entire financial system, not just Wall Street.

Later at the Roundtable meeting, Dimon asked to meet with Kerry at 5:00 p.m. in the Ritz-Carlton lobby bar. Even though Dimon was difficult during phone conversations, with one-on-one meetings with Kerry, Dimon always acted very respectful, even shy. He politely asked if Kerry was interested in selling the bank. Kerry told him the board had voted to keep the bank independent. The meeting was short, and they went their separate ways. Kerry didn't trust Dimon and didn't think their banks had the same values, so he was hesitant to get too involved in discussions about mergers. Dimon never approached Washington Mutual with any type of an offer.

The next day Kerry met with Al Hubbard at the West Wing of the White House, James Lockhart at OFHEO, and Senator Harry Reid, before departing from Washington DC to Vail for the American Society of Corporate Executives meeting. Kerry was meeting with a number of officials to advise them of the impending housing crisis and also to recommend regulations for the unregulated independent mortgage brokers.

On October 10 Kerry forwarded a news article to his execs regarding Bank of America's and Wells Fargo's increases in mortgage lending and wondered if the risk-based pricing models used by those banks were telling them to produce more higher-risk/higher-return loans. Todd Baker wrote back, "It is pretty clear they all got the risk-based pricing wrong as the backward-looking statistical models couldn't and

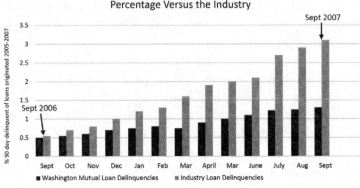

Chart 8-1: Washington Mutual Residential Loan Deliquency Percentage Versus the Industry

Source: First American Loan Performance TS Securities through September 2007

didn't predict what is happening to collateral values or the profound impact product design had on performance and risk," meaning the layering of risks in SIV and CDOs and other instruments.

Washington Mutual did not use the backward-looking forecasting models, but instead developed a more perceptive assessment of the current environment. As a result, the bank's residential loan portfolio performed better than the industry average when housing prices declined and loan delinquencies increased in 2007.

Chart 8-1 shows delinquency rates for single-family residential loans originated in 2005 through 2007 for Washington Mutual versus the industry. While the industry was reaching a combined loss ratio of over 3 percent, Washington Mutual's loans were still performing with only 1 percent loss ratios. The loans were of higher quality and performed better for all loan categories, including fixed-rate, option ARM/adjustable rate, and held for investment subprime mortgages. This positive performance reflected Washington Mutual's tightening of loan underwriting throughout this period. Average loan-to-value ratios of loans held in portfolio remained around 70 percent, and average FICO scores increased throughout this period.

Washington Mutual's excellent loan performance was especially noteworthy given its concentration in housing markets in California, Arizona, Nevada, and Florida, which were hit by extraordinary declines in housing prices in 2007 and 2008. Many of those markets experienced 40 to 50 percent drops in housing prices.

Washington Mutual's loan portfolios were well positioned to benefit from the eventual recovery in these markets because of their conservative underwriting. These markets recovered much faster than the national average, and Washington Mutual's loan portfolios would have benefited greatly throughout the decade following the financial crisis. It is not surprising that an independent study detailed in Chapter Ten shows Washington Mutual's residential loans put into securitizations from 2004 to 2007 outperformed the industry and outperformed JPMorgan Chase and Citigroup, which had nearly twice the loss rates. (See Chart 10-2.)

Washington Mutual also had substantially lower losses in its credit card and commercial loan portfolios.

As fall continued, Kerry became more concerned about the transparency of the three hundred thousand–plus unregulated independent mortgage brokers. He felt most of them were not providing adequate disclosure of the key factors in their sales contracts, like effective interest rates, fees, terms, and broker compensation. Kerry thought that since most of the shadow loan companies had gone out of business that year, it might provide the opportunity to try to rein in the wild practices of many of the shadow unregulated mortgage brokers. Kerry and his team decided to create a one-page mortgage broker disclosure form that spelled out the contract in simple, readable terms the consumer would understand. The execs decided to require a signed form for each mortgage contract and decided to try to make the form an industry-wide standard.

American Banker magazine reported on Washington Mutual's new mortgage broker disclosure form:

> The Washington Mutual ideas have already won the support of James Lockhart, the director of the Office of Federal Housing Enterprise Oversight, which regulates Fannie and Freddie. He said it 'looked like a very good approach, getting the ideas laid out simply was very helpful.' He said his agency would encourage Fannie and Freddie to pass the forms on to lenders, but probably won't require they use it.
>
> The policies Washington Mutual unveiled this week require brokers provide mortgage applicants with a one-page cost summary detailing things like the yield-spread premium, prepayment

penalties and rate resets and broker commission. The bank also
said it would contact all borrowers by phone before closing their
loans to review the terms. Washington Mutual said they presented
the practices to the director of the OTS who 'believes that our
wholesale lending procedures should become the industry
benchmark for all lenders and brokers, to bring about meaningful
change to the mortgage industry.'

John Taylor, the president and CEO of National Community
Reinvestment Coalition in Washington, agreed. 'Lenders in
general have to be made more responsible for the actions of
brokers and I think the first step is informing borrowers.' Washington Mutual said, 'Improved disclosures would benefit brokers
by creating better informed borrowers.'[44] Some industry observers
said wider adoption of the practices are likely with or without
regulatory endorsements.

The mortgage broker disclosure form was becoming even more
important as RealtyTrac reported US housing foreclosures doubled in
September compared to a year earlier.

Rising mortgage loan losses had tumbled bank industry third
quarter earnings by 25 percent. Record levels of foreclosures were
expected to worsen as the industry thought adjustable-rate mortgages
would possibly reset to higher interest rates. There were now $350 bil-
lion in ARMs currently outstanding in the US.[45] Fortunately interest
rates stayed low in the next few years, and most ARM loans didn't
have to reset significantly to a higher rate. However, the 2/28 and 3/27
products sold by subprime originators experienced huge rate increases.
Washington Mutual handled this problem in 2007 and 2008 with a
multibillion-dollar program that restructured subprime customers
into lower cost fixed-rate loans.

On October 17, Washington Mutual reported third-quarter earnings of $210 million. Kerry said, "Q3 net income was down 75 percent
because of a weakening housing market and disruptions in the secondary market. Every time the housing market adjusted, loans held in portfolio and not intended for eventual sale did not have to be revalued.
However, assets originated for eventual sale or securitization had to
be marked down quarterly according to the price it would sell for on
the open market, regardless of its past value." This was a devastating

accounting policy in a period when lack of liquidity drove prices down
well below any reasonable or intrinsic value.

In November, the Financial Accounting Standards Board (FASB)
did not help at all when it increased mark-to-market reporting requirements. Many of the news sources reported, "The new standard
may have had the unintended consequence of exaggerating losses
on assets banks were holding for investment."[46] The *Halbert Wealth
Management* report stated, "The rule change required financial institutions to update pricing of illiquid securities. That led to write-downs
in many financial derivatives including credit default swaps (CDS),
mortgage-backed securities (MBS), etc. Ultimately, some banks became
insolvent, including Lehman Brothers."[47]

Later in 2009, Steve Forbes, publisher of *Forbes* magazine, said he
believed mark-to-market accounting was the principal reason for the
US financial system meltdown in 2008. Economist Brian Wesbury declared, "Mark-to-market accounting rules have turned a large problem
into a humongous one. A vast majority of mortgages, corporate bonds
and structured debt are still performing. But because the market is
frozen, the price of these assets has fallen below their true value."[48]

On October 22, Kerry wrote to the board:

> Bank stock prices fell last week due to weak third quarter earnings
> reports which revealed deteriorating home equity, residential
> mortgage and other consumer credit quality. Investors are
> concerned the housing downturn will be prolonged and lead to
> credit issues. But in spite of this fear in the marketplace, we were
> successful in raising $1 billion in hybrid equity at the end of last
> week, we are pleased this capital will give us more flexibility.
>
> You may have read about the super conduit fund being
> promoted by Treasury, Citi and other banks. [A fund that would
> mostly help Wall Street with its risky securitizations.] This fund
> was initially announced as being $100 billion in size. Washington
> Mutual does not have a direct interest in SIVs or other off-balance
> sheet assets, but any measure that brings improved liquidity to
> mortgage assets would be helpful.

Kerry encountered a number of crises in the twenty-five years in
top management at Washington Mutual. The first crisis was in 1982

when Kerry had to implement his plan to turn the bank's $20 million+ annual losses into profitability within a year. During the 1980s and the early 1990s, he had to develop and implement five-year plans in turbulent environments in which thousands of banks collapsed. In the 1990s, he had to navigate government demands for extensive subprime lending, massive consolidation of the banking industry, and the development of complex derivative instruments that would eventually collapse the economy. In the age of mass consolidations of the 1990s, the bank thrived because the two largest thrifts trusted Kerry and turned to him when they needed to sell their thrifts.

When the Fed started raising rates in 2003 and the unregulated subprime companies started making trillions of dollars in subprime loans, Kerry responded with an industry-leading plan to drop mortgage loan origination and add a diversified group of products to the bank. He achieved this goal over the next few years and still achieved record earnings.

Because of careful planning during two decades of major upheavals in the industry, Washington Mutual thrived. The team not only thrived and executed plans during unexpected crises, but they also had developed specific plans for dealing with more predictable crises: Earthquakes, floods, hurricanes, cyber threats, fraud, breaches of technology, terrorism, robberies, and many more.

The crises plans were built based on the guiding principles of the bank—to create a bank offering a better, fairer deal for the average American family. Principles that matched the values of the bank—integrity, fairness, caring, and a drive to achieve excellence. Kerry and the executive team were in constant communication with major stakeholders during each crisis event—community groups, employees, customers, shareholders, the media, regulators, and consumer advocates.

Because of the careful execution of these plans, the stock performed four times better than the S&P 500 from 1983 to 2007 and the bank had continually received awards for the best reputation of any bank and awards for the best place to work. The bank's careful crisis plans succeeded because during Kerry's term as CEO, the bank never had a single federal investigation, fine, penalty, or formal regulatory order.

But Kerry knew this crisis shaping up in 2007 was going to be different because the entire industry was in full panic mode. He had the planning teams in place and he was ready to continue to focus on his four major principles for working through a crisis:

- Provide constant visible and truthful communication to major stakeholders including investors, regulators, customers, employees, community leaders, and the communities they serve.
- Provide an action-oriented response with decisive and timely decision making through a calm atmosphere that promotes trust, integrity, and civility.
- Provide an experienced executive counselor who would work with the executives privately in order to help them cope with the crisis and lay out plans to guide the stakeholders through the turbulent waters. Lay-offs would be a last resort.
- Promote participative management and embrace change: employee groups at the Cedarbrook Leadership Center would focus on innovative plans to deal with the crisis.

Kerry and the team saw the 2008 crisis coming and developed plans for extensive information sessions with major stakeholders. During past crises, there was usually a certain amount of stress, anxiety, and fatigue, but Kerry knew this crisis was going to be much tougher. Many bank CEOs, including Kerry—during and after the crisis—commented on how difficult the crisis was for their executive team. Execs who used to be independent and decisive now turned to Kerry frequently to help them make their decisions. Some people who used to be open and forthcoming became secretive. Execs who had always focused on the bank's best interests became ever more focused on protecting their own interests. Everyone played out their pain in a different way, and Kerry worked hard to maintain a level head and help his executives through the crisis.

However, Kerry was about to experience one of his biggest disappointments ever.

On November 1, Kerry was in an executive meeting preparing for Investors' Day when he was told the New York attorney general had just held a press conference and announced he was suing real estate appraisal companies for conspiring with banks, including Washington Mutual, to inflate values on appraisals. Kerry and the executives were shocked—they hadn't heard a word about this. The AG's office had never called or contacted them to investigate or confirm any information. They were shocked because there would be no incentive for the bank to want to inflate appraisals. Additionally, Kerry had initiated the process of farming out appraisals to independent companies to avoid any potential conflict of interest. The regulators applauded and approved this change, because having the bank's employees appraise the value of a home was a clear conflict of interest.

Kerry immediately called his longtime general counsel, Fay Chapman, to investigate the allegations and find out what was going on. Kerry had trusted his general counsel for two decades. She was acerbic, thorough, and prickly about looking at every detail. Through the years some of the board members had wanted her replaced because they thought she was too cantankerous and stubborn, but Kerry always defended her. He wouldn't sign a paper, approve a policy, or give a speech without her written legal approval. After touching base with Chapman, Kerry went into full action mode to address the issue.

He immediately called the OTS to ask them to investigate the charges. He contacted the AG's office and offered full cooperation and hired the New York law firm Simpson, Thacher, and Bartlett to conduct a full investigation of the appraisal activities. He also released a statement to the press, opening up about his surprise and disappointment in the allegations:

> We have suspended our relationship with [the appraisal company] and will investigate the situation. We have absolutely no incentive to have appraisers inflate home values. In fact, inflated appraisals are contrary to our interests. We use third party appraisal companies to make sure appraisals are objective and accurate.

Shortly after the New York law firm was engaged, Kerry received a call from Simpson Thacher's senior partner, claiming the bank's general counsel was impeding their investigation. In addition, Washington Mutual's deputy general counsel also called Kerry to deliver the same message. Kerry immediately moved the oversight of the investigation to the board of directors. After thorough investigations from Simpson Thacher and another Seattle-based law firm, the board and Kerry were advised a change in general counsel was appropriate. The board of directors and Kerry immediately decided to replace her, and an interim general counsel was hired. This was difficult for Kerry to do because he respected and liked the general counsel he had worked with for so many years, but maintaining absolute honesty, integrity, and cooperation with governmental agencies superseded any personal relationships.[49]

The New York law firm and the OTS completed their independent reviews of the appraisal allegations and concluded there was no evidence of systemic appraisal inflation. Washington Mutual was exonerated, and the AG's office dropped the investigation, but this distraction could not have come at a worse time, as the market was devolving into the deepest banking crisis since the crash of 1929.

Kerry was also having some issues with CERO Cathcart. Although he was doing well working with the other executives and reining in mortgage lending, he was falling behind in implementing other programs. Both Kerry and the board were upset that the regulators were concerned Cathcart had not addressed all their concerns about compliance with the AML/BSA. Kerry wanted to give him another chance and deferred a decision on Cathcart.

With the investor conferences coming up in November, Kerry decided the market was in such turmoil he would develop even more comprehensive information on the Washington Mutual loan portfolio. He had the managers develop complete statistics on every loan portfolio. At the November 7 Investors' Day conferences, Kerry told several hundred analysts the severe third-quarter liquidity squeeze dried up mortgage financing for nonconforming and subprime borrowers, ultimately causing refinancing to slow, home sales to plummet, housing inventories to soar, and prices to fall. Despite this, Washington Mutual's risk was contained and its underwriting was sound.

At the public conference, CERO Cathcart shared his credit report showing Washington Mutual's mortgage delinquencies were substantially below the industry averages. He stated:

> All single-family delinquencies for the industry were close to 3 percent, but Washington Mutual stayed about 1 percent. Subprime delinquencies in the industry were over 18 percent; Washington Mutual's delinquencies were a third of that. The option ARM's industry average on delinquencies was over 3 percent, but Washington Mutual was only slightly over 1 percent. We have taken dramatic actions to reduce lending and had declared the bank had 'strong capabilities to manage through the environment.'[50]

Cathcart went on to say:

Housing prices will continue to decline and put more pressure in high-growth markets, but Washington Mutual will maintain a strong capital position and continue proactive liquidity management. The bank will have a disciplined balance sheet growth, invest in retail banking, drive profitable growth in card services and commercial group, continue to adjust home loans to market conditions, drive expense management, and proactively manage credit losses. Washington Mutual was proactively adjusting to the housing downturn by aggressively tightening origination criteria in all residential portfolios and shutting down subprime lending. Nonperforming loans and charge-offs remain low and stable.[51]

On November 13, Kerry went back to New York for more meetings with Goldman Sachs, UBS, Lehman, and Morgan Stanley to discuss additional capital raising. There were also investor conferences that week followed by a flight to Baltimore to talk with the NAACP about affordable housing and then to Las Vegas for the American Community Bankers' market expo, where Kerry gave a number of speeches to the group about the imploding housing market.

In the midst of this upheaval, Kerry received the Thurgood Marshall Award of Excellence for decades of efforts in minority hiring, support for minority causes, and affordable housing. Also, J. D. Power named Washington Mutual number one of all companies in customer service—it was the only bank on the list. Washington Mutual was named number one on the West Coast, number one in California, and number one in the Midwest among all the banks. J. D. Power said the bank was managing for best-in-class performance.[52]

On his November 30 board update, Kerry shared:

New housing data released this week were all quite negative. I spoke to Secretary Paulson last week and am meeting on Monday with the director of OTS and will participate in a National Housing Symposium sponsored by the OTS. The severity of the housing correction and the lack of market liquidity is causing our loan-loss provisioning to increase. In our previous planning, we estimated loan-loss provisioning for 2008 would increase to about $5.5 billion. Further deterioration in housing is causing our new provisioning estimates to rise to $7.5 billion. This will put strains on our profitability. We have arrived at a plan to present to the board next week.

On December 6, David Schneider, the president of home loans, announced another proposal aimed at keeping borrowers in their homes. He said:

Washington Mutual has worked very closely with Treasury and the American Securitization Forum to develop what we believe is a positive step for borrowers who are unable to handle an increase in their monthly payment. The proposal establishes a new set of industry best practices making it easier for servicers to modify loans under the existing agreements. We are in the process of implementing the fast-track modification process and expect to have it operational over the coming weeks.

On December 11 Kerry wrote to the board:

We completed the issuance of $3 billion of convertible preferred this afternoon. Because of excellent demand, we were able to price at a coupon of 7¾ percent with a conversion premium of 22 percent. Reactions to our announcements yesterday were pretty much as we expected. The press was tough on us and analysts were generally negative on our prospects for 2008. However, reactions from our major shareholders were generally supportive. As part of the convertible preferred offering, we touched base with most of our large shareholders. They supported our initiatives to build capital and reduce costs. They also understood the challenges we and others are facing from a hostile housing environment. The $3 billion offering would provide sufficient additional capital to sustain us through the losses. The estimated loan loss assumptions and projected capital needs were based upon S&P models and more comprehensive models developed at the bank.

At the end of the year, most of the large banks were reporting record multibillion-dollar write-downs and credit losses.[53] The banking industry, especially the Wall Street shadow subprime system, was collapsing.

- Merrill Lynch reported a loss of $7.8 billion for the year, which was blamed on a $24.7 billion write-down on their investments. CEO Stan O'Neal resigned after the write-down announcement on October 31 and was offered a $160 million payout.[54]
- Citigroup announced it had $23.8 billion in write-downs in the fourth quarter. The bank reported a $9.83 billion loss in the fourth quarter.[55] Citigroup CEO Chuck Prince resigned after the announcement.[56]
- Morgan Stanley announced $10.3 billion in losses and $9.4 billion in write-downs from subprime loans. It received a capital injection of $5 billion from a Chinese sovereign wealth fund.[57]
- HSBC (UK) reported $17.2 billion loss on write-downs of their US mortgage portfolio.[58]
- Barclays Bank (UK) confirmed a $1.6 billion write-down for October on subprime holdings, which could lead to more write-downs in the future.[59]
- Freddie Mac announced a $2 billion loss on mortgage defaults and credit losses. Shares of Freddie dropped 28.7 percent, and shares of Fannie dropped 24.8 percent.[60]
- Fannie Mae announced a 2007 net loss of $2.1 billion and increased its loan-loss allowance to $5 billion.[61]
- Countrywide was downgraded to junk status, faced liquidity issues, and was eventually sold to Bank of America.
- UBS (Swiss) announced a $19 billion write-down in US mortgage holdings in the first quarter of 2008 and announced $10 billion more in subprime write-downs in late 2007. It also had a capital injection of $11.5 billion from the Singapore government and an unnamed Middle East investor to cover losses.[62]
- AIG announced a $5.2 billion loss for the fourth quarter of 2007. In 2008 it lost $99 billion and were on their fourth CEO in a year. The total bailout for AIG was $180 billion. Much of the loss was due to the revaluation of its CDS holdings.[63]
- Bank of America had losses of $9.7 billion and took a write-down for the year of $12 billion.[64]
- Capital One was projecting losses of about $5 billion.
- JPMorgan Chase had losses of $5.3 billion and cut the value of its investments in the subprime market by $1.3 billion.
- Wachovia estimated it would provision $1 billion in excess of charge-offs, doubling its earlier estimates.

- Lehman took a $830 million net write down during the quarter.[65]
- Wells Fargo recognized a $1.4 billion provision as part of its $11.9 billion liquidating portfolio. The bank reported a 37 percent loss in net income for the fourth quarter.[66]
- Bear Stearns reported its first quarterly loss in its eighty-four-year history of $854 million and a write-down of nearly $1 billion in mortgage-related write-downs.[67, 68]

In 2008, Citigroup would take another $63 billion in losses, Merrill $39 billion in losses, Bank of America $29 billion, Lehman $14 billion, JPMorgan Chase $10 billion, and Morgan Stanley $10 billion.[69] Despite these enormous losses, thousands of home foreclosures, and the forty-six thousand jobs per month lost in the first quarter of 2008, the Wall Street CEOs still treated themselves to bountiful bonuses. In 2007 JPMorgan's Jamie Dimon earned $28 million, Goldman's Blankfein's take was $68.5 million, Dick Fuld of Lehman was $34 million, John Thain of Merrill Lynch got $84 million, and John Mack of Morgan Stanley received $41 million.[70] In 2006, the last year he was with Merrill Lynch, CEO Stan O'Neal's package was $91 million. The top employees of the five largest investment banks divided a bonus pool of over $36 billion in 2007.[71]

Most of the banks saw dangers in the market, but few were working to change things. Goldman Sachs CEO Blankfein pointed out later, "In January 2008 there were twelve triple-AAA-rated companies in the world. At the same time, there were sixty-four thousand structured financial instruments...rated AAA. However, when the market demands it, the innovative financial structure supplied it."[72]

Some banks even kept on selling subprime mortgages. *National Mortgage News* reported the top subprime originator in the fourth quarter of 2007 was JPMorgan Chase, with subprime production quadruple what Citigroup and Wells Fargo were selling.[73] Washington Mutual had no subprime loans that quarter.

Washington Mutual was in a better position than most of the banks and reported operating income of $1.6 billion for the year and break-even net income after writing off $1.6 billion of goodwill. Because pay plans were based on multiyear results, Kerry was eligible for a year-end cash bonus, but he decided the right thing to do was decline any cash bonus until the housing crisis had passed. We also continued our practice of giving Kerry's base salary to charity every year.

In the investor conferences in January of 2008, Kerry explained the bank's relatively good position occurred because of a series of proactive steps taken despite the unprecedented conditions facing the entire industry:

> We raised $2.9 billion of convertible preferred stock and reduced the quarterly dividend for the first time in fifty quarters. We dramatically reduced loan production and will have a major expense reduction of $500 million. We shut down subprime mortgages months ago, shut down most of the home loan offices, eliminated over fifteen thousand home loan positions and eliminated 550 corporate and support positions.[74]
>
> The current downturn in housing is acute and deeper than expected. We continue to see declining home prices, elevated inventories of unsold homes, and increased foreclosure activity. Home values are declining nationally, and the downturn has been more severe in larger markets like California. There are measures that could help the market including aggressive easing by the Fed, temporary raising of the conforming limits for GSEs, government economic stimulus actions, and continued efforts by lenders to help borrowers remain in their homes.

The FDIC's fourth-quarter 2007 banking profile showed:

> After a couple of years of record quarterly earnings around $35 billion, the last quarter had plummeted to $5.8 billion, the lowest since 1991. Net charge-offs sharply increased by $16.2 billion. Noncurrent loans rose 32.5 percent, the largest increase over 24 years of reported data. For the first time, noncurrent loans exceeded the reserves in the banks.[75]

9

The Aftermath of the Financial Crisis

2009

As we described in Chapter Eight, the second half of 2007 was difficult for all banks, but Washington Mutual was performing better than most. It appeared the diversification plan to move away from mortgage lending had paid off. Washington Mutual was one of the few banks with operating profits in 2007, and Kerry had little trouble procuring over $11 billion in additional capital to tide the bank over in the turbulent waters of the impending crisis. With a highly profitable retail branch system, credit card operations, and commercial and business lending divisions, Kerry felt he had done everything he could to cushion the bank. In the summer of 2008, Washington Mutual had over $50 billion of available liquidity and was the only large bank that was Basel II compliant with 14 percent total risk-based capital—the highest among the big banks.

Washington Mutual's mortgage loan losses were substantially below the industry average, regulators were supportive, and costs had been cut to the bone. Fifteen thousand mortgage employees had been laid off, all the mortgage offices had been closed, and mortgage loan production had plummeted below any of the other top regulated banks. The July 2007 regulatory exam had given Washington Mutual a 2-plus rating and in July of 2008, the OTS and the FDIC proclaimed the bank had more than enough capital and liquidity to get through a severe economic downturn. However, Treasury Secretary Paulson and Fed chair Bernanke were still not sounding alarms or injecting the system with much-needed liquidity.

But as you read in Chapter One, 2008 held many unpleasant shocks. The economy devolved into the worst financial crisis since the Great Depression. So, what happened? There were many missteps and blunders. The Fed and Treasury ignored warnings from top economists and and completely missed how the breaking of the housing bubble could affect the entire economy. They missed the inherent dangers of the layering of risks in Wall Street securitizations and refused to inject adequate liquidity into the system. Finally, when they were in pure panic mode in September of 2008, they forced capricious and thoughtless mergers and shutdowns that caused substantial damage to hundreds of thousands of investors and employees. Their moves assured the dominance of Wall Street at the expense of community banks and thrifts. Politicians on both sides of the aisle demanded too much subprime lending to LMI borrowers and forced the GSEs of Fannie Mae and Freddie Mac to lower standards to achieve improbable homeownership goals. Naked short sellers were allowed to bet on financial stocks, further destabilizing the banking system.

Congress and the regulators made major mistakes in not federally regulating the investment banks on Wall Street, the three hundred thousand independent mortgage brokers, and the hundred-plus subprime originators. Apparently, no one was noticing the multitrillion-dollar escalations of the complex financial products like SIVs, CDOs, and CDSs. Rating agencies and Wall Street used ineffective risk models that assumed the low failure rate of mortgages in the past would hold true in the future. Regulators were less vigilant because the banking industry was so profitable.

Most banks went along with the decreased lending standards offered by the GSEs and Wall Street. Since most of the new loans were being originated for sale, most banks gradually moved away from using their own underwriting standards to accepting the standards dictated by the GSEs and Wall Street. We all should have fought back more on reduced underwriting standards in the industry.

Most experts now agree the financial crisis was caused by the breaking of a housing bubble, which unfolded into unprecedented housing price declines, putting runaway panic into the multitrillion-dollar complex and intertwined CDO and CDS Wall Street system. Then Treasury, banking regulators, and the Federal Reserve let Lehman fail, which mushroomed into deep panic in the financial system. Top economists also agree the FDIC's move to stiff the bondholders of Washington Mutual caused a further panic because Treasury and the Fed seemed to have no discernable plan.

After the crisis, the Federal Reserve finally injected needed liquidity into the system, and asset prices began to stabilize. Tone-deaf to public opinion, Wall Street executives continued to take home billions in bonuses, which only made the public angrier. This anger is still playing out today in our elections and our daily lives. It took far too long to help homeowners avoid foreclosure, and there were insufficient efforts to revitalize the job market. The FDIC showered hundreds of unwarranted lawsuits on community banks, further destabilizing the industry.

Instead of owning up to all their involvement, the major players developed their own narratives to deflect their responsibility for the crisis. For example, for many years Senator Carl Levin was one of the senators demanding banks and the government provide more loans to subprime LMI households. During the six-year buildup of the unregulated shadow subprime lending system, and the massive multitrillion-dollar derivatives build-up, Levin remained silent. But he became vocal again when he realized there could be some personal political gain to this crisis.

On January 21, 2009, Senator Levin had formed his conclusion about the crisis, even before the Senate Permanent Subcommittee on Investigations (PSI) started its work. He stated, "The subprime crisis is the product of predatory lending practices directed at the less sophisticated borrowers. Those practices included subprime mortgages sold to borrowers who qualified for better loans, use of dishonest appraisals, and the sale of mortgages containing exploding interest rates, unfair prepayment penalties and excessive fees."[1] He failed to point out that most of the troubled loans in the system were created by the unregulated subprime system and the loans were a product of congressional mandates and lack of regulation in the major players. Levin and many members of Congress were trying to establish a narrative that squarely pointed blame away from themselves.

As the year 2009 started, we transitioned into an alternate universe. Job losses were getting to Depression-era levels, thousands of Washington Mutual employees were unemployed and searching for jobs in an impossible economy, mortgage foreclosures were increasing dramatically, and few were being resolved. Every large bank in America was hit with dozens of lawsuits, and hundreds of banks were failing. Congress was in a tizzy trying to figure out how to deflect blame away from their bad policies, and their millions of dollars in political contributions and put much of the blame back on the regulated banks.

Media outlets all over the country were tripping over each other trying to set up interviews and develop their narrative on the causes of the crisis. The frustration from the American public over the massive TARP giveaways, Wall Street bonuses and ineffective government actions was starting to play out in the Occupy Wall Street and Tea Party movements. Attorneys and PR firms in New York and DC were filling their calendars with clients. No one knew what would happen and how all of this would be unwound. Would we ever recover from this, and how would we address the growing homelessness issues?

The country had lost over six million jobs since the crisis began in 2007. In the last quarter of 2008, 651,000 people a month lost their jobs. Through 2009 and into 2010, the job losses scaled to 780,000 jobs a month. This would be equivalent to a state with the population of Idaho or New Mexico losing all its jobs—every month. Millions were losing their homes, and Wall Street banks had not been willing or able to cut monthly mortgage payments to ensure people could stay in their homes.[2]

On February 19, *The Economist* wrote:

> No part of the financial crisis has received so much attention,
> with so little to show for it, as the tidal wave of home foreclosures
> sweeping over America. Government programs have been inef-
> fectual and private efforts are not much better. Up to 9 million
> homes may enter foreclosure over the 2009–2011 period. The
> Hope Now Alliance during the second half of 2007 helped
> 545,000 borrowers, only 7 percent of the outstanding loans.[3]

Analyst Mark Zandi wrote that by 2009 close to 14 million home-owners were underwater, double from the previous year. The Census Bureau claimed that more than 2.2 million homes were vacant at the end of 2008. In early 2009, lenders were selling foreclosed property for 50 percent of market prices. In January of 2009, the stock market plunged from the 2007 high of 14,000 down below 7,000.[4]

Realty Trac announced that there were 1,525,833 foreclosures in 2007 and 2,890,189 foreclosures in 2008. By the end of 2009 the total US foreclosures for those three years were 8,096,845.[5]

Complicating the efforts to help homeowners avoid foreclosures was the new banking structure that had developed in the years leading up to the crisis. In the past, most banks kept their mortgage loans on their books and performed the mortgage servicing themselves. When a homeowner was having problems with their mortgage, the bank could easily restructure the loans for the customers. The entire time Kerry was CEO, Washington Mutual was a national leader in helping homeowners restructure monthly payments to help people stay in their homes when times were tough. Kerry knew it was better for everyone to keep people in their homes rather than go through a foreclosure process.

But with the demands from Congress requiring banks to loan to more LMI households, the system became split. Instead of originating and holding loans in portfolio, it was more economical and safer for banks to sell their loans to the GSEs and Wall Street for securitization. Servicing of those loans was separated and sold to a few large mortgage-servicing companies.

After the crisis hit, there were few portfolio lenders who could re-structure payments to keep people in their homes. Washington Mutual was one of the few banks before the crisis that actually modified billions of dollars of loans it held in portfolio, but the loans sold to the GSEs or Wall Street could not be modified. Unfortunately, those loans had been sold to investors who were very reluctant to allow any reduction in monthly payments. The reality was those investors cared more about their contractual income than they did about doing the right thing for homeowners.

The effort became so complex, the state attorneys general and the DOJ finally had to sue many of the banks to get them to straighten out the system. Treasury eventually gifted tens of billions of dollars in

TARP funds to several of the Wall Street banks and many of the servicing companies to incent them to restructure mortgages.[6]

However, the Wall Street–centric policies of the Bush administration were about to change to the politics of a president who had a completely different view of Wall Street. In January, Linda's son, Matthew, and his father, Attorney General Tom Miller, attended an Inaugural Ball for the new President Obama. Tom had been Obama's campaign chair in Iowa, the state that launched Obama's campaign with an important win, and Obama was appreciative of Tom's help. Matthew called regularly from Washington, DC, about updates on whom he was seeing and what they were doing. The crowds were estimated at 1.8 million as many Americans celebrated the election of our first Black president.[7]

Meanwhile, we were back in Seattle spending a substantial amount of time working with our attorneys, going over millions of pages of public documents about Washington Mutual. JPMorgan Chase was still stalling on giving Kerry his internal documents, so we didn't have the documentation we needed to properly inform the media or work effectively on the lawsuits. Thousands of lawsuits were now bouncing around the country for all the banks, and the legal odometer was spinning out of control.

We had fewer lawsuits than the other banks, but it was still frustrating sorting through them. The attorneys told us the FDIC typically sues all the banks it seizes but had no standing with Washington Mutual, because there was no cost to the deposit fund. The FDIC was now suing hundreds of banks that were failing. We were told the OCC—even though it was the successor agency for the OTS—did not have standing to sue Washington Mutual, especially since the bank had never been served with a formal enforcement order. Plaintiffs' attorneys were filing ERISA lawsuits against nearly every public bank, claiming employees were encouraged to keep pension money in company stock. We had little concern about an ERISA lawsuit, because Washington Mutual had strict policies to educate employees on diversifying their retirement portfolios. The SEC was investigating most of the large banks, looking for statements made by executives about the health of their companies. We were comfortable about Kerry's statements and never heard from the SEC. The DOJ was also investigating every large bank for any kind of criminal or civil actions.

About this time, one of the most prominent law firms in the country sent out a warning to its clients about the government's aggressive investigation tactics they found with some of their clients. The law firm warned the investigators were using "Ambush-type tactics where executives and employees are often confronted by prosecutors and agents who will show up unannounced at their homes, workplaces, or even health clubs or supermarkets. The employees will be caught by surprise, but usually feel some pressure to cooperate and be responsive. There will not be an opportunity for preparation or reflection or to gather facts. Most significantly the individual almost certainly will be without benefit of legal counsel. The statements will be considered as an 'admission' and used to establish corporate and personal liability. Many times, the agents will threaten the employee with criminal prosecution. The employees typically don't understand their legal rights."[8]

We read that and worried that the employees would be ambushed and threatened, but couldn't imagine investigators would find anything important. There were a few outstanding lawsuits with Washington Mutual, but nothing serious. The DOJ was investigating most of the banks, but we felt comfortable it wouldn't find any problems at Washington Mutual. The creditors' committee from the Washington Mutual bankruptcy lawsuits might be the biggest problem, because it was threatening to sue all the executives and prevent them from collecting their employment contracts and pension plans. It was all negotiating tactics. We knew it shouldn't go anywhere because the bank regulators and the Examiner later declared the bank was likely solvent up to the day of the seizure.

Every large bank also had a plaintiffs' lawsuit complaining the price of stock fell during the crisis. The Washington Mutual plaintiffs' lawsuit was the subject of a sensationalized story in the *New York Times* in December 2008, but the lawsuit was not holding up well in the court system. The local federal judge scheduled a hearing on the shareholders' lawsuit for May 1, which would last for three hours. They did not allow testimony or facts at the hearing, but they did send a list of questions. At this point in the legal system, allegations asserted in a lawsuit are assumed to be true and factual, even if they are filled with false and unsubstantiated claims.

The judge allowed our attorney, Barry, to talk for only fourteen minutes at the hearing to state his legal case, but he wasn't allowed to defend the bank, show the facts of the case, or refute any untrue allegations. He gave an eloquent summary for dismissal because there were no credible facts and there was no proof or indication of scienter or intent to defraud. He was pleased with the judge's questions, which indicated her understanding the plaintiffs must document a specific false or misleading statement to show intent to defraud.

A couple of weeks later, the federal judge rejected key portions of the plaintiffs' lawsuit and called the lawsuit a "verbose and disordered argument that failed to identify specific claims of fraud. The Court remains mystified at the plaintiff's counsel's failure to allege cohesive claims." The judge threatened to take the lead lawyers off the case if they could not address her concerns in an amended complaint.[9]

We were relieved with the direction of the lawsuit, but that spring we had even more lawsuits added to our repertoire. In March, WMI, the holding company for Washington Mutual, sued the FDIC for $13 billion for the improper seizure of the bank. The lawsuit accused the FDIC of agreeing to an unreasonably low sale price of $1.88 billion. The suit also sought "the return of $4 billion of trust preferred securities wrongfully transferred down to the bank, $3 billion of tax refunds and damages of $177 million in unpaid loans to the bank unit."[10]

In March, JPMorgan Chase sued WMI, the holding company, and FDIC for the right to retain certain assets of the Washington Mutual holding company, including "$6.5 billion in capital contributions, $4 billion in trust securities and several billion dollars in tax refunds."[11] Getting over $300 billion in assets for $1.88 billion was not a good enough deal—they wanted more.

That same month, JPMorgan Chase announced a $138 million plan to buy two new luxury corporate jets and build the "premier corporate aircraft hangar on the eastern seaboard." The plans included the purchase of two $60 million Gulfstream 650s—the "fastest, widest and most comfortable private jet ever—and an $18 million lavish renovation of the hangar, which included a vegetated roof garden." Nell Minow, editor and founder of Corporate Library Independent Corporate Governance Research, said, "It's a remarkably boneheaded decision. It's completely tone-deaf." JPMorgan Chase responded that none of the $25 billion in TARP money would be used for this. Dimon said, "When I hear the constant vilification of corporate America, I personally don't understand it." His 2008 compensation package was at least $19 million.[12]

In April, seven months after the crisis, the Washington Mutual executives still didn't have their documents from JPMorgan Chase. Our attorney sent letters to the general counsel at JPMorgan Chase as well as Chad Smith, general counsel at WMI:

> We are contacting you regarding our repeated requests to receive
> documents on behalf of Kerry Killinger. For several months, we
> have been requesting Kerry be provided with copies of his files
> and emails for the purpose of allowing us to prepare his defense
> to lawsuits and to prepare to respond, in connection with the pub-
> licly disclosed government investigations involving WMI. We have
> sent repeated emails and phone calls and still haven't received the
> documents. We received consent to receive documents from Chase
> as the current custodian of many of the hard copy and electronic
> documents. We have the approval for expense payment.[13]

The executives and the board decided they would all have to sue JPMorgan Chase to get their documents, which legally should have been released the prior September.

In May, Congress passed the Fraud Enforcement and Recovery Act, which created a ten-person panel, called the Financial Crisis Investigative Commission (FCIC), to "examine the causes, domestic and global, of the current financial crisis in the US." The act was quickly signed by President Obama and was intended to duplicate the Pecora Commission created after the 1929 stock market crash. While initially eager to see the investigation move forward, we were ultimately disappointed. The makeup of the commission alone indicated the newly created panel was not going to investigate the acts of Congress that created the burgeoning subprime market or the lax regulations that produced the overheated Wall Street CDOs, SIVs, and other exotic products. The panel was hand-selected by Congress and was created to find fraud in the regulated banks. It quickly became clear Congress and the regulators were going to be protected.[14]

The press was filled with stories about bankers, very much like the May issue of *Condé Nast Portfolio*. One article showed a picture of the CEOs of Countrywide, Bear Stearns, Lehman, and Merrill Lynch in a prison cell with the caption, "It's the stuff of populist dreams; Fuld clad in a prison jumpsuit, Mozilo bound in shackles and Thain penned in a concrete cell. Very little has been done to address the pent-up rage." It had another set of darkened pictures of five CEOS with signs on the odds of prosecution pasted on their chests. Possible charges included securities, mail, and wire fraud because of statements made before the crisis. Two Bear Stearns hedge fund managers were under indictment for making sunny statements to investors while privately expressing doubts. Federal prosecutors had subpoenaed Lehman execs to appear before a grand jury. AIG faced probes by the FBI, SEC, and the New York AG. The SEC and FBI were probing Countrywide's trading of company stock, and federal and state investigators were probing disclosures related to Merrill's sale to Bank of America, including its bonus payouts. Former New York attorney general Eliot Spitzer was interviewed and commented AIG was the "most likely to face criminal charges because of their deeply problematic structure."[15]

This national mood of anger and frustration with the lack of government action and justice is dangerous and reminded us of a time in our past.

During the 1980s, our home state of Iowa was in the midst of one of the worst financial crises in its history. By 1984 the nation's farm debt was double what it was in the seventies. Net farm income plummeted from $19 billion in 1950 to only $5.4 billion in 1984. When President Carter halted grain shipments to the Soviet Union in 1980 in response to Russia's invasion of Afghanistan, farm prices collapsed. The all-time high for the number of farms in this country was 6.8 million, but by the mid-1980s there were only 2.2 million farms left. This had an impact in small towns all over this country, especially in the Midwest. When farms go broke and disappear, so do small towns, their main streets, and their community banks. This contagion spreads to all agricultural products, manufacturing, and sales.[16]

The falling farm commodity prices, together with the rising debt loads, created the scenes of farm foreclosure auctions nearly every night on television. Iowan Dale Burr had farmed his central Iowa land his entire life, as had his father and grandfather before him, but in 1985 he was over $500,000 in debt, and he could not contain his rage and his sorrow. Driven by grief, he drove to the Hills Bank and Trust near Iowa City with a twelve-gauge shotgun and shot and killed the bank president, John Hughes. He then went home, killed his wife and a neighbor, and then shot himself.[17]

Representative Jim Leach of Iowa, a friend of banker Hughes, said, "No incident could more tragically reflect the brewing violence in the Farm Belt than the senseless killing of John Hughes." At the time Linda was a partner in an accounting firm with a number of banking clients. We all knew and worked with Hughes and knew he was one of the fairest and kindest bankers, and it was reported he had no intention of foreclosing on Burr. We knew he worked hard to help his customers in those challenging times, and he was known throughout southeastern Iowa as a farmer's friend. Linda immediately called Iowa attorney general Miller: "This has to stop. Someone needs to come up with a solution to this crisis."[18]

Miller was already working on a solution. He had teamed up with the Iowa Bankers Association and other local groups to encourage the Iowa state legislature to pass a law requiring mediation between farmers and lenders before foreclosure. He said the goal was to "find a sweet spot in which the farmer could remain on his land and the bank would receive more in payments than it would from a foreclosure, even if writing off a portion of the loan was necessary." The head of the Iowa Bankers Association said, "Some of the banks weren't too thrilled with having to do that at the beginning, but in time everybody gave a little. The farmer could walk away with something to get started again and the institution got the issue resolved." AG Miller was trying to apply some of his ideas of the 1980s when he later had settlement talks with the largest banks on foreclosure practices in 2012.[19]

We were very concerned, because the same anger and desperation was playing out again in the 2008 financial crisis. Our national leaders, the media, and politicians didn't seem to be trying to manage or mediate the grief, but rather they were all trying to agitate, foment, inflame, and provoke more anger.

One of the agreements JPMorgan Chase made with the FDIC is it wouldn't have to honor any of the bank's lease agreements, which caused problems for people all over the country. One of the biggest issues was the Washington Mutual Center that included the Seattle Art Museum (SAM). Washington Mutual was paying SAM $5.8 million a year for office space on a long-term lease Chase wanted to abandon. We heard from sources at SAM that the negotiations were brutal, but Chase finally announced a $10 million gift to the museum that would cover the price of the rent for only twenty-one months. If SAM had to default on the $65 million in bonds, the citizens of the city of Seattle would be on the hook for $4 million a year in bond payments. It was frustrating not being able to do much to help.[20]

One great piece of news was JPMorgan Chase finally agreed to make payouts of the supplemental retirement plans to thousands of Washington Mutual employees. We were grateful and relieved so many of the employees would receive a much-needed payout that was rightfully theirs.

We also received a sizable payment, but we decided to give most of it to charity and keep some to make direct gifts to employees. Given the challenges facing everyone, we felt the right thing to do was give this money back to our communities and help former employees. We didn't make a big deal about this—we knew it was the right thing to do.

On July 3, the *Wall Street Journal* reported most of the causes of the home foreclosures were negative equity and unemployment increases. The Mortgage Bankers Association said 51 percent of all foreclosed homes had prime loans, not subprime, and the foreclosure rate for prime loans grew by 488 percent compared to a growth rate of 200 percent for subprime foreclosures. The steep ascent in foreclosures began in the third quarter of 2006, during which more than 4.3 million homes went into foreclosure.

McDash Analytics produced a report, based on more than thirty million mortgages, that claimed "the popular narrative that liar loans [stated income] were the cause of the crisis appears wrong. Regulation won't do the trick, the most important thing is the amount of skin in the game."[21] However, with the unprecedented 28 percent national drop in home prices rising to over 50 percent in some cities, millions of homeowners who had substantial equity in their homes woke up one day and discovered they no longer had any equity or "skin in the game." Many of them just walked away.

The federal programs offering incentives to loan servicers to change mortgage terms were only providing $1,000 for each loan modified and were only focusing on lowering the interest rates. Wells Fargo data in June showed only 58 percent of modifications involved cutting the payment amount, which proved to be the most effective way to keep people in their homes. The average reduction in June was

$173 per month. In June the data showed almost thirty-two thousand liquidation sales with an average loss of 64.7 percent of the original loan balance.[22]

That summer, former Treasury Secretary Paulson was grilled by Congress about his relationship with Goldman Sachs. According to calendars acquired by the *New York Times*, Paulson spoke with Goldman CEO Blankfein far more frequently than other CEOs. Goldman was given permission at the height of the crisis to convert from an investment firm to a national bank, giving it easier access to federal financing. Goldman further benefited when the SEC changed its rules governing stock trading, barring investors from being able to bet against Goldman's shares by selling them short.[23]

On September 14, 2009, Obama traveled to Wall Street to promise government intrusions would be temporary, but he would push hard to increase government's role in overseeing the financial system to prevent a repeat of the excesses that caused the crisis.[24] We think he probably tried as hard as anyone could to prevent a repeat of the excesses that caused the crisis. However, there were two things he might not have factored into the equation. First, government officials and Wall Street were not going to reveal the true cause of the crisis, and second, no president will be as powerful as the tens of millions of dollars of Wall Street political contributions that roll into Congress each year. Many of the new regulations and protections that were passed after the crisis were later lobbied away by Wall Street. After dealing with the bankers for a few months, Obama changed his tune and started calling them "Wall Street Fat Cats."

In September, there were a number of requests for interviews for the first anniversary and we produced a statement for the media, saying that Kerry "cared deeply for Washington Mutual's many committed and excellent employees and was greatly saddened [to see] so many good people lose their jobs due to the unfair seizure of the bank. Kerry appreciates all the efforts being made to assist those who lost their jobs. He has personally spent countless hours over the last year trying to assist many former employees to find new positions."

Understandably, articles on the anniversary were generally negative. There was a lot of justifiable anger from former employees, shareholders, and the local community about why Washington Mutual was inappropriately seized. With so many lawsuits pending, the attorneys did not want us to talk to anybody about what happened. However, in an effort to get out the truth, we did develop data sheets about the high quality of the Washington Mutual loans and how the bank dramatically reduced lending 74 percent from 2003 to 2007. Although we distributed the data to numerous media outlets and government agencies, none of the data was ever referred to or printed.

As the FCIC, Congress, and numerous government agencies prepared their investigations and the local media ran the one-year anniversary stories, one of the bank's beloved execs, with a long history of depression, took his life at his home. It was another in a long line of tragedies connected to the crisis. We were all devastated that the inappropriate and cruel seizure of a company could destroy so many lives in so many ways. We decided to set up a scholarship fund for the exec's son and started calling and writing the Washington Mutual execs and board members for contributions, and they were very generous. None of the execs or board members who contributed expected any publicity, and no one called the media to get a story on their heroics. They all gave privately out of love.

On the day of the funeral gathering in a restaurant in downtown Seattle, the room was filled with grieving former employees. The widow of our friend greeted us at the door and thanked us for starting and contributing to her son's tuition fund. She walked around the room with us, and we talked to nearly everyone gathered at the event. The former employees were comforted and pleased to see Kerry and others at the gathering. We were filled with love and gratitude and felt blessed to be a part of this group of people, despite the tragic circumstances that brought us together. We encouraged everyone to move on from Washington Mutual, and we offered to help with references, job ideas, or financial help.

In the fall of 2009, FDIC chair Bair was still in pure panic mode when she announced the FDIC deposit insurance fund had a negative balance because of the failure of 165 banks in 2008 and 2009. She decided all the banks needed to immediately prepay $45 billion in insurance premiums to cover the losses.[25] In addition to that idea, Bair had found a second way to fill up the FDIC insurance coffers—she set about suing hundreds of community banks for the troubles they incurred during the crisis.

During the banking crisis in the 1980s, Linda had worked with banking regulators to help banks after the crisis hit. The standard protocol was to shut down or sell banks with fraud or deep deficits, but go out of their way to help other community banks survive. Regulators rarely sued banks that didn't have any criminal activity.

However, during this financial crisis, FDIC chair Bair already had a new playbook she had carefully honed from her work in the summer of 2008: no need to proceed with a careful plan of informal and formal enforcement actions meant to help keep community banks in business. Better to threaten them, seize them, have execs fired, and then sue the banks for their D&O insurance money. And sue she did—hundreds of community banks, regardless of their loan or management quality. Longtime 2- and 3-rated banks that had never had a formal investigation order or showed signs of fraud or illegal activity now found themselves facing seizure, destruction of their careers, and millions of dollars in fines, penalties, and lawsuits that would frighten the boldest of attorneys. The most important thing in the world to FDIC chair Bair was not the preservation of the community banks, but rather the preservation of her deposit insurance fund.[26]

By 2009, the three largest banks that received TARP funds—Bank of America, JPMorgan Chase, and Wells Fargo—were now highly capitalized and controlled half of the market for new residential mortgages and two-thirds of the market for credit cards.[27] The three megabanks were also allowed to be exempted from the federal rule prohibiting any single bank from holding more than 10 percent of all the deposits in the country. They were also exempted from the DOJ antitrust guidelines intended to limit monopoly power in certain metro regions. By the end of 2009, the largest five banks had over 95 percent of the market for derivatives, led by JPMorgan Chase, with a 28 percent share. Megabanks were able to borrow money at rates seventy-eight basis points lower than the smaller community banks, up from an average difference of twenty-nine basis points from 2000 to 2007.[28]

The megabanks were doing well. Not only had they captured the TARP funds, massive market share, exemption from antitrust guidelines, and substantial bonuses, they were also controlling the politics. In his first seven months in office, Treasury Secretary Geithner's calendar showed more than eighty contacts with the CEOs of Goldman,

JPMorgan Chase, and Citigroup. As of October 2009, there were 1,537 lobbyists representing financial institutions.[29]

With all their success, the megabank execs were still a little put out that they weren't appreciated enough. One Goldman Sachs executive commented on the great inequality facing the country, "We have to tolerate the inequality as a way to achieve greater prosperity and opportunity for all." Lloyd Blankfein chimed in that he was doing "God's work because banks raise money for companies who employ people and make things."[30]

One of the year's most interesting stories concerned Bank of America's purchase of Merrill Lynch in September of 2008, days before Merrill was ready to collapse. The sale price was an astounding twenty-nine dollars per share, a 70 percent premium over the stock's closing price. In the spring of 2009, former CEO Ken Lewis testified under oath to the New York attorney general that he had told Paulson and Bernanke in December of 2008 that Merrill's losses were climbing over $15 billion and he wanted to pull out of the deal using a "material adverse clause." Lewis testified the regulatory duo made it clear "they would remove the board and management if we called if off." They had also sweetened the deal by promising more money from TARP to bolster the capital of the combined firm. Allegedly, Paulson and Bernanke forced Lewis not to reveal to shareholders the depths of Merrill's losses or the multimillion-dollar bonuses promised to Merrill's executives. This was a violation of SEC rule 10b-5, which prohibits any act or omission resulting in fraud or deceit in connection with the purchase or sale of any security.[31,32,33]

At first the AG's office was questioning Paulson and Bernanke's activities, but that soon turned into investigations into the Bank of America executives and board. The result was Lewis and the bank were fined millions of dollars. In addition, the SEC sued Bank of America, but the New York federal judge rejected the SEC settlement. The judge wanted more punishment for the bank. It became apparent Paulson and Bernanke would skate through this without any accountability.[34] Six hundred and ninety-six Merrill executives, who had engineered some of the worst loan losses in the world, still received at least $1 million each in bonuses that year, yet millions of people were still unemployed and losing their homes.[35] It became increasingly difficult to understand why the lucky Wall Street crowd, who had originated and securitized the worst of the lending products, felt good about accepting billions in bonuses.

In November, the Bear Stearns execs at the center of their meltdown were acquitted after a three-week trial that was assumed to be a bellwether for other cases. The case was based on email messages prosecutors claimed proved the money managers knew their investments were souring but assured their investors the funds were sound. The jurors, all from working-class neighborhoods, felt there was no clear evidence of fraud.[36] The SEC said it would still proceed with its civil case.[37]

On November 17, the FCIC held a closed session interview with Fed chair Bernanke. He revealed that, "Out of thirteen of the most important financial institutions in the United States, twelve were at risk of failure within a period of a week or two. Fifteen to eighteen major firms were bailed out, rescued, saved by their governments in Europe and in the UK. So, it was very much a global phenomenon. The crisis was caused by macroeconomic events I did not foresee." He also revealed twenty-seven of the banks that received TARP funds had been seized or threatened with seizures by regulators, putting up to $5.1 billion at risk. Bernanke warned credit woes and the job market could restrain growth in 2010.[38]

The next day, President Obama established a Financial Fraud Enforcement Task Force of top federal officials to work with state and local authorities to prosecute cases from the crash of the housing market. Members included Attorney General Eric Holder, Treasury Secretary Geithner, HUD secretary Shaun Donovan, and the enforcement director for the SEC. It had a broad scope and involved state investigators and federal agencies to focus on mortgage and securities fraud. The FBI was currently investigating fourteen thousand financial crime allegations and twenty-eight hundred mortgage fraud cases.[39]

Through all of this, we worked to maintain relationships with family, friends, and former employees. We had managed to get to Des Moines a couple of times in 2009 to see Kerry's mother and were lucky enough to have her fly to visit us during the tough Iowa winter. She appreciated being away from the Iowa snow for a while and was still suffering from the loss of Karl just a few months ago. She was a brilliant woman who spent hours in front of CNBC and other business news shows, catching up on the latest in the financial crisis and calling out any critics of Washington Mutual. She was a devoted champion of Kerry, had no doubts about his complete integrity, and knew Kerry had done everything he could to save the bank and help people save their homes. On one of our last visits, she said, "Kerry, I have been watching those Dimon and Paulson guys on TV and don't think they are nice people. You better be careful if you have any dealings with them. I don't think you can trust them."

We got a call in December that Evelyn was taken ill and in the hospital. We flew to be at her side in the hospital, sat with her during her physical therapy treatments, and spent quality time talking with her and watching old movies. We especially enjoyed her comment "Why can't they make more movies with Betty White? She is the greatest." Soon thereafter, Evelyn passed away, and her family wept by her bedside. She was with Karl now. Friends, relatives, former band students, and neighbors filled the church in Beaverdale to pay their respects to what Linda thought was the world's best mother-in-law. Linda's son, Matthew, and his father, Tom, attended the services and gave us comfort in our grief.

10

Part One:
Investigations and Lawsuits

2010

The investigations of the crisis were now in full force. Both the Financial Crisis Investigation Commission (FCIC) and Senator Levin's Permanent Subcommittee on Investigations (PSI) were planning public hearings for January. They both wanted to control the agenda on who should be blamed for the financial crisis and who would get to write the new financial regulations. There were many in Congress who were hoping to have their names attached to tough new banking regulations. They all wanted their committees to model the Pecora Commission, created after the 1929 crash.

In many ways it was an ironic choice, because the Pecora Commission was not successful in punishing any bank executives. However, it was successful in grilling the Wall Street giants after the 1929 crash and discovering a number of inappropriate activities that spurred public sentiment to support new regulations. The most important change was the Glass-Steagall Act of 1933, which separated the riskier investment banking activities from the normal banking activities that were newly funded with federally insured deposit insurance. In the late 1990s, the

Wall Street investment banks led by Goldman Sachs's Hank Paulson, successfully overturned much of the regulations of the Glass-Steagall Act. In another twist of irony, once again, much of the investigations of the 2008 crisis would center around the unregulated activities of the Wall Street investment banks.

The Pecora Commission was also somewhat of a roadshow. When J. P. Morgan was waiting to testify, circus promoters looking for publicity put a female circus dwarf on his lap. The headlines read, "The world's smallest woman sits on the lap of the world's richest man."[1] Senator Carter Glass remarked the hearings had the atmosphere of "a circus, and the only things lacking now are peanuts and colored lemonade." Charles Mitchell, president of the National City Bank (now called Citigroup) was considered by the commission to have promoted the riskiest activities and was indicted for tax evasion but then acquitted. Utilities magnate Samuel Insull was accused of fraud but fled the country for two years. When he finally returned, he beat the charges. The Pecora Commission ultimately did not put any bankers in prison.

After the banking crisis of the 1980s prosecutors were much more successful. They didn't use any showy lay commissions or Senate hearings to pursue criminal investigations—they relied on the Department of Justice, which put about a thousand bankers in prison.

Back in 2008, Congress created two competing investigations— Senator Levin's PSI committee and the congressionally handpicked FCIC. It was a smoke screen. Neither committee conducted a legitimate criminal investigation. Neither committee investigated the multimillion-dollar political contributions and whether there was any quid pro quo. Neither committee investigated the activities of the Treasury Department and the Federal Reserve before the crisis. Neither committee thoroughly investigated the unregulated shadow subprime system. Both committees seemed to have preconceived ideas about who caused the crisis, with little interest in getting to the true sources of the crisis. But in January of 2010, without knowing why, Kerry was asked to speak before Levin's PSI committee.

With only a couple of weeks before the PSI hearings, the federal judge finally got fed up with JPMorgan Chase's refusal to produce documents for the Washington Mutual executives and subpoenaed Chase to fork over the documents—the same documents they had produced for the PSI over a year earlier. After 457 days of hostage control at

JPMorgan Chase, *some* of the documents were finally released. PSI had over a year to leisurely sort through millions of pages of documents and prepare their offense. We only had a few days to sort through the same documents.

In the middle of a flood of documents, we still had not heard a word from PSI, so we didn't know how to prepare. We only knew Kerry would be interviewed, had to present a paper of defense no longer than twenty pages, and would appear later at a hearing. The hearings were to be televised, and Kerry was allowed only a five-minute prepared comment at the hearing. How could we prepare a twenty-page defense when the PSI would not tell us what the hearing was about or what its concerns were?

Meanwhile we were waiting for the first set of FCIC hearings and hoping they would give us some insight into what was on the minds of the Washington DC crowd. The FCIC consisted of six Democrats and four Republicans handpicked by Congress. It was given the task of interviewing key players in the crisis, preparing a report on the causes of the crisis and referring criminal charges, by December 15, six weeks after the midterm congressional elections. The FCIC had a rather arcane set of rules that made it hard to subpoena people. With the Democrats outnumbering Republicans six to four, the arrangement almost assured a minority report that would disagree with the majority Democrats.

We guessed the Republicans would see this as a chance to finally rid themselves of the traditionally liberal Fannie Mae and Freddie Mac powerhouses. We figured the Democrats would place the blame on greedy and rapacious bankers. We also anticipated the committee members would find no fault with anyone in Congress, because they had just been handpicked by Congress. With the Senate Ethics Committee investigations of the 1980s Keating Five (Senators John McCain, John Glenn, Donald Riegle, Alan Cranston, and Dennis DeConcini) still fresh in their minds, we knew the senators were not going to allow another Keating type of investigation on their watch.

In the coming months, the FCIC panel planned to interview hundreds of people and hold field hearings outside Washington, DC. It had an $8 million budget and a staff of about eighty. We just assumed it would want to interview a number of executives from Washington Mutual, since there were a lot of questions swirling about the legitimacy of the "seizure" of the bank.

The FCIC press release said, "The Commission was instructed to refer to the Attorney General of the U.S. and any appropriate state Attorneys General, any person the Commission found may have violated the laws of the United States in relation to the crisis."[2] If the mission of the FCIC was to see "who had violated laws," it was odd there wasn't one person on the commission who appeared to have extensive experience in complex criminal financial investigations. How could it be qualified to make criminal or even civil referrals?

We both appreciated and admired the FCIC members for their service to their country, and the sacrifices they made to conduct this investigation. They were all exceptional professionals with impressive credentials. Over the years we have both been appointed by many politicians to chair task forces and commissions that served a very positive purpose of listening to all the needs and experiences of citizens involved in a particular issue and making recommendations. However, we never would have joined a committee that expected a group of lay citizens to make criminal referrals. This is a job for professional criminal investigators. All the time and effort and taxpayer dollars should have been given to the Department of Justice to help with its investigations.

Not only were the commission members inappropriate investigators for complex financial crimes, but the witnesses were essentially denied their civil rights by not being able to have their lawyers speak for them, present their own evidence, assess the evidence, or respond to the testimony of other witnesses. Their lawyers could not speak at all. None of the protections of a court trial were available, and their testimony was carried live on television, yet the committee could refer criminal actions. We noticed some of the witnesses had agendas to promote and weren't forthcoming about their responsibility for the crisis. Peter Wallison, a member of the FCIC, wrote in his remarkable book, *Hidden in Plain Sight*, that he found it suspicious the executive director of the FCIC staff was also an executive with the Federal Reserve. This certainly assured none of the actions of the Federal Reserve would be questioned.[3]

Robert John, director of financial reform at the Roosevelt Institute, stated it accurately when he said, "There are an awful lot of politicians who don't want to find out what happened. That unusual structure [of the FCIC] is not there by accident."[4]

There were now twenty-six million people out of work and millions more losing their homes, but everybody in DC was focused on showy TV hearings not aimed at what really happened, but providing drama for the viewing audience. The DC insiders had a lot to lose in this crisis, and it seemed like most of them were thinking not only how they could avoid criticism, but how they could advance their careers. The media were speculating Congress wanted the hearings to "mollify their fears of a public backlash over Wall Street's multimillion bonuses at a time when Main Street still suffered with 10 percent unemployment."[5]

On January 12, we made some popcorn and watched the first televised show of the FCIC. The guests for the first show in the reality TV series were the CEOs of Goldman Sachs, JPMorgan Chase, Morgan Stanley, and Bank of America. The FCIC had previously held private interviews with Geithner and Bernanke. We both wondered, "Why did they get private interviews?"

The four CEOs blamed the crisis on unsound underwriting, lack of capital, mark to market accounting, and lack of adequate reserves for all the other guys, but they professed their own banks were beyond reproach. None of them wanted to discuss the ramifications of having 85 percent of the subprime loans—nearly $2 trillion—originated and securitized by a massive unregulated shadow financial system.

The headlines about the FCIC hearings in the paper the next day were predictable: "Congressional Hearings Grill Banking's Biggest Names." Blankfein bore much of the scrutiny and he offered no regrets for executive pay that is now only likely to increase. All four bankers said they were victims of circumstances."[6]

Blankfein "likened the financial crisis to the fluke of four hurricanes hitting the East Coast in a single year." FCIC chair Phil Angelides shot back the crisis was not caused by acts of God. The *Washington Times* said Angelides "made it clear he already concluded Wall Street investment giant Goldman Sachs, in particular, was one of the primary culprits." The *New York Times* claimed Blankfein "was particularly revealing because he laid bare an essential truth about the Wall Street ethos: if there's a buyer, no matter how sophisticated, there's always a seller."[7]

Other FCIC hearings followed included testimony from a number of government officials including Assistant Attorney General Lanny Breuer and SEC enforcement head Robert Khuzami. When Attorney General Eric Holder testified, he told the panel about the thousands of cases they had filed against small-time defrauders running mortgage scams and investment fraud, but he conceded there weren't any successful prosecutions of crimes by the big firms on Wall Street.

The SEC said year to date it had 634 actions with $1.5 billion of disgorgement and $900 million in penalties. The SEC gave a $94.3 civil fine to State Street for overcharging asset servicing clients.[8] Colonial Bank executives concealed overdraws through a pattern of "kiting." On April 16 of that year, the SEC sued Goldman Sachs for fraud in the structuring and marketing of CDOs tied to subprime mortgages.[9]

The DOJ reported it was using wiretaps and undercover agents and meeting regularly with bank regulators. It had about eighty new agents with plans to hire another seventy. As part of DOJ's investigation, it performed forensic analysis of accounts and looked at patterns, focusing mostly on cases that involved materially false statements. The SEC said it demanded over three hundred clawbacks from bankers for misconduct, and it was proud of the cases it pursued with Countrywide, American Home, and New Century.

In late January, President Obama had a new proposal to ban banks with federally insured deposits from casting risky bets in the markets and resist further consolidation in the financial services industry. In other words, he wanted to bring back Glass-Steagall. He also wanted the creation of a consumer protection agency with oversight over credit cards, mortgages, and other lending products.[10] After Paulson spent all his energy consolidating the banks, Obama apparently wanted to break them up.

At the beginning of the year, Barry arranged for Kerry to be prepped by top Washington DC attorneys who help business executives with Senate hearings. They were high-powered, highly placed political players and attorneys with deep experience with DC politics. Barry had a good experience with them when they helped another client with sage advice in dealing with a Senate hearing. Evidently, one needs a consultant to teach you how to handle a senate hearing. Telling the truth is meaningless in the dangerous shark tank swamp waters of DC politics. One must be schooled in Sun Tzu's *The Art of War.*

Our Sun Tzu guides had spent decades at the highest levels of the White House and Washington politics. They were eager to share their secrets about the dramatic truths of the Levin PSI reality TV series. But it was obvious they were frustrated with the process and what it did to people.

We were eager to have them share with us what Kerry needed to know about testifying in front of Senator Carl Levin's PSI. We were hoping it would be a great opportunity for Kerry to tell the truth about what happened during the crisis. They were surprised by Kerry's behavior and wondered out loud why Kerry wasn't angrier, given what he had been through. Most of the CEOs they had schooled had been very angry. But Kerry is a modest, humble, and measured man—no matter what had happened to him, he wasn't going to change, he wasn't going to get angry now. As anyone at Washington Mutual knew, Kerry always checked his ego at the door.

They started their lessons:

Senator Carl Levin's committee is not an investigation into the facts of a case, it is a made for television drama carefully orchestrated to provide shock and awe to the American people and provide a stage to set himself up as a crusading hero who is going to jail corrupt bankers. He is doing the hearings because he wants the PSI to be the next Pecora Commission.[11] He wants to set the stage for new banking regulations, he wants his name on those regulations and he wants to beat out the FCIC. His hearings will be press worthy and position him as the leader of the restructuring of the financial system. He is looking to find some way to refer criminal charges on bankers. The best outcome you can have in this hearing is to not get a criminal referral.

He has a formula he follows: He has a preconceived notion of what happened in the financial crisis: Greedy bankers sold fraudulent mortgages to unsuspecting people and the bankers should be put in prison. Nothing you say will change his mind. No facts will interfere with his story line. Levin's staff will interview, bully and threaten your former employees with criminal prosecution, but offer them leniency if they will testify and agree to the PSI theories.

Forty-eight hours before the hearing he will contact the media about his framing of the story. He will then have a confidential and closed press conference with the media, and he will hand out thousands of pages of documents that will provide 'evidence' of his findings. You will not see these documents ahead of time, he will not even ask you about them. He loves the element of surprise. You will not be allowed to have a press conference or there will be trouble. He will then produce a report, leak information to the press and possibly refer criminal charges to the DOJ. The media lap up his every word and never question his tactics.

Your tone will be very important; you will be dealing with monumental egos. You cannot win a fight with them. You have to give the impression you have been thoughtful about the impact of the crisis on everyone. We want to surprise them about how caring you are. There has to be more banks he will be bringing in. Your story isn't big enough and he wants a big story.

Levin's mission is to make Washington Mutual emblematic of a broader fueling of the crisis by all banks. He doesn't want to investigate the shadow subprime unregulated banks because people don't know who they are. He wants to get recognizable names in his hearings. His plan is to call for regulations that will prevent a crisis from happening again. He wants to paint a dramatic enough picture so the American people will demand stricter regulations.

You have two stories to tell: the role of the regulators and Congress in pushing for more subprime lending and the role of the FDIC in the inappropriate takeover and fire sale of Washington Mutual. Next week we will learn who else will be there and learn of their theme for the event. You will be allotted five minutes for an opening statement. We will give them plenty of facts in the interview, but they don't care about the facts. They are really just assessing what kind of player you will be in their show. Will you look and act like a merciless greedy banker or are you a sympathetic person?

We need to create a story about how hard you worked to dramatically decrease lending, how you warned the regulators about the coming crisis and how well you protected the bank from the crisis. Kerry has to tell the truth, expressing real feelings for the people who were hurt. We need to try to shatter some of the myths about what happened.

Certain facts can be stated without pointing a finger. FACT... Washington Mutual was not a failed bank, it had surplus capital and plenty of liquidity. FACT...people are afraid of the power of Wall Street. Wall Street was "too clubby to fail" and anyone outside the club was sacrificed.

Your opening statement is very important. Those critical five minutes could change your life forever. People want to know if you are someone who 'gets it.' We have to show you were not out there driven by greed. Your compensation policies prevented that. You were the rare CEO who refused a bonus in 2007 and 2008 and committed to no bonus until the foreclosure crisis was over. You were the rare CEO who gave his entire salary to charity every year and gave 2 percent of the bank's pretax profits to charity. We need to use the charts and graphs you have put together that show you were dramatically cutting loans.

They will frame and leak the story they want, regardless of the facts. How you come across dealing with these huge political egos will be crucial. If you are defensive or combative you will come across poorly. You need a thoughtful demeanor, that you are thinking about this all the time and it weighs on you. You can say, 'with the benefit of hindsight I should have done something else.' You will not likely be invited back for a second day. Levin arrived at his conclusion before the investigation even began.

We were overwhelmed but felt better prepared. After the DC attorneys got to know Kerry better, they commented Kerry had about the best demeanor of any CEO they had worked with. They didn't need to instruct Kerry on how to be kind, humble, and caring. He had been that man his entire life.

At first, they told Kerry he should tell the PSI there were things he should have done differently, like reducing the LTV, increasing the FICO scores, and reducing lending, but when they looked at the graphs and charts we had developed, they saw Kerry did more than any of the large banks and made more public cautionary statements than any of the major lenders.

Their narrative was shocking, especially for someone like Kerry, who during his entire career had never been accused of any wrongdoing, had never been fined or sanctioned or even deposed. Ever. Kerry never even had a traffic ticket. The bank never had a single formal enforcement order and never had a federal investigation or sanction or fines from federal regulators. Despite the Senate's behavior showing us otherwise, Kerry still believed this was his chance to tell the truth to the Senate. Surely, they would listen.

The DC attorneys concluded by saying:

Levin is quite a showman and is looking forward to lambasting
bankers while the television cameras are rolling. Levin wants to
make sure his hearings are more spectacular and newsworthy
than the FCIC and wants to have his report out before the
FCIC so he can eclipse their findings and control the legislative
reforms. Levin is looking to refer bankers to the DOJ and other
agencies.

Kerry will be very frustrated with the superficiality of the
hearing. They will attempt to land punches that are untrue but
fit a stereotype of bankers they want to promote. Kerry needs to
filibuster a bit, there will be limited time for him to talk. Levin will
jab his finger at Kerry and scream and interrupt. The best answer
you can give to any question is 'I don't recall.'

After the session, Linda called Attorney General Tom Miller and
related all the information she had heard from the DC attorneys. Tom
was shocked what the DC legal profession had discovered about the
Senate PSI hearings. Tom had built a successful career as an attorney
general with careful investigations that were fact based and data driven.
He didn't leak information to the press. He didn't engage in showy
press conferences that promoted unproven allegations. He had no desire to prosecute people on TV and violate their constitutional rights.
This was hard for all of us to process.

After the attorneys left, we met with Barry in the same small conference room we had used for two years. As usual he was warm, friendly,
and totally organized. There were dozens of thick white notebooks
standing upright on the table, and everyone had their own copies. The
notebooks were filled with "hot documents," meaning documents or
emails that needed further explanation. If you have sixty thousand
employees and you gather all their emails over a five-or-six-year period,
you are going to see some stupid stuff. The DC attorneys anticipated
there would be emails the PSI would gleefully copy and distribute to
dozens of reporters. The comments would probably not prove anything
or have anything to do with the facts or what actually happened, but
they would be "inflammatory," and Levin would love to pass them out
to the media.

However, after viewing the potential carnage, we were actually
quite proud of the employees. After the crisis, the bank's employees

were poked and probed by the SEC, DOJ, FBI, FDIC, OCC, and IRS for nearly ten years. Washington Mutual was of the few big banks in the 2008 crisis where not one single executive was ever accused of a specific crime; no one was fined or penalized. There were no felonies, no misdemeanors. No one was banned from banking or serving on a public board. Earnings didn't have to be restated.

We patiently went over documents for several ten-hour days. Kerry looked at each item and answered hundreds of questions by the attorneys. *What did you mean when you said this at an investor's conference in the spring of 2003? Does that conflict with what you said in the summer of 2006? How did you tighten lending guidelines? Where's the proof you did that? What decisions went to the board? What does this email mean and why does it seem to contradict this document over here? What were the roles and responsibilities of each of the executives? Why did you make this decision back in 2004?*

Days later, we flew to Washington, DC in February for what we were told would be a two-day session of PSI interviews. After a couple of twelve-hour practice sessions with the DC attorneys, everyone was ready. On Thursday afternoon, February 4, Kerry and the attorneys went off to talk with the staff of the PSI. Linda paced back and forth in the DC law firm, rereading the twenty-page written statement and the five-minute oral statement over and over trying to figure out what else we could have included. She waited, worried, fussed, paced, and waited some more.

Finally, after only a few hours, the doors opened and Kerry walked back in. Linda had to know everything that happened. Kerry said they were immediately hit with Levin's hypothesis: "Washington Mutual aggressively and recklessly ramped up mortgage lending before the crisis. The bank stopped doing thirty-year fixed-rate mortgage in favor of dangerous option ARM and subprime loans. The bank's option ARM loans were mired in negative amortization. The bank's mortgage loans had a high failure rate."

Kerry responded with data and charts compiled from the most respected independent sources on mortgage loan production:

Washington Mutual dropped mortgage production 50 percent in 2003 and continued to drop production 74 percent from 2003 to 2007. Seventy to eighty percent of the bank's mortgage production were thirty-year fixed-rate loans. Option ARM and subprime loans were dramatically reduced—*not* ramped up. Washington Mutual mortgages had some of the highest FICO scores (well over 700) and the lowest LTV rates in the business. The bank's mortgage loan default rates were some of the lowest in the banking industry. Option ARMs were only for prime customers, and negative amortization was historically less than 1 percent of the total balance. Levin's committee had completely misinterpreted data from the annual reports and had not bothered to thoroughly research the bank.

Levin's group continued to confuse the difference between negative amortization and negative equity of a loan. Negative amortization of a loan occurs when a payment doesn't cover the interest. Negative equity occurs when the total loan is higher than the value of a house—over 100 percent LTV. A loan could have several negative amortization payments and still have a tremendous amount of equity in the home. Also, you could have 20 percent or more in equity in a house, but if the price of housing goes down 30 percent—you've got a negative equity loan that is no fault of the customer or the bank. If a customer did fall into negative equity, the bank would often work with them by modifying their payments. The bank had one of the lowest default rates in the industry."

After Kerry showed them the documented truth, the lead PSI staffer slammed his fist on the table and yelled, "That's not what we want, that's not what we want!" The staff of the PSI suddenly realized they couldn't go into a future hearing and rail and scream about how Washington Mutual dramatically increased lending so the greedy executives could make more money. They had lost their narrative, and they were furious. The meeting was over, and Kerry was sent on his way.

Late at night, after thirty or forty rewrites of the statements, we finally got out in the cold night air and walked several blocks to our hotel. There were more interviews tomorrow and Kerry was ready.

On the morning of Friday, February 5 at 8:00 a.m., the attorneys submitted our twenty-page document to the Senate. We were unsure how the PSI would react to the document. We had given startling information about the inappropriate seizure of Washington Mutual. The mood was tense while we waited for word on when interviews would start that day. We had presented them with the facts that completely destroyed their "story line." We waited patiently, and within the hour, we received a phone call from the PSI. "The interviews were cancelled."

The entire legal team froze in horror. They didn't want to talk with Kerry any more than just a few hours? What did this mean? Did we give them so much proof they decided to go after someone else? Were they going to expose the duplicitous Wall Street–DC corridor? Were they going to regroup? We continued to review documents the rest of the day and then left the building.

Heavy snow was falling as we walked past the White House on our way back to our hotel. Linda looked over at the White House and remembered all the wonderful events she had been to over the years. Christmas parties, Easter egg hunts, dinner parties, inaugural parties, the Christmas tree lighting ceremony, visits to the press secretary's office, visits to the Oval Office. All were memorialized in photographs she had carefully pressed into a large scrapbook. This was the Washington, DC, she had known for more than four decades. Parties in the White House for Iowa political insiders, meetings on the Hill for Chamber business, board meetings for the Federal Home Loan Bank, conferences and dinners for the Financial Services Roundtable.

Linda had been involved in Presidential politics for over thirty years—after all, she was from Iowa. She was used to nasty political fights and had built a tough hide over the decades. She used to believe the center of DC was an honorable place. She knew there was no legitimacy to Levin's claims and knew this should turn out all right, but the city felt different. It was harder to get out the truth and there was an elevated level of viral hostility and lack of civility. There was a sea change going on in this country. Liberty, justice, and equality were being threatened and you could feel it emanating from the nation's capital.

This was supposed to be the center of justice for the American people; this was supposed to be the hallmark of our democratic nation. This is what generations of her family had fought for in the Civil War, the World Wars, the Korean War, the Vietnam War. Walking into the White House, the Supreme Court, or the Senate buildings had always felt like entering hallowed ground. It was a place that was supposed to be consecrated to fairness, justice, and helping innocent people. We looked in at the White House with the warm lights and acutely felt the cold, frigid, snowy day. Our thin coats weren't warm enough, and we didn't have any snow boots or mittens. As the heavy, cold snow gathered on big piles on the sidewalk, we realized all of our illusions had been shattered.

That night there was heavy snowfall, and all the flights were canceled for two days. We were stuck in Washington, DC all weekend in a couple of feet of snow, and there was nothing to do but look for snow boots and heavy scarves. The streets were deserted and unplowed. Not a taxi in sight and all the restaurants were closed. We were all alone shuffling through the deep snow as we ventured outside for fresh air while we waited for flights to resume.

In early February 2010, former Treasury Secretary Paulson released his book *On the Brink: Inside the Race to Stop the Collapse of the Global Financial System*. The book chronicled what he described as his heroic and successful attempt to save the financial system. Suspiciously, he barely mentioned Washington Mutual, but he did regret one of the actions:

> I see that, in the middle of the panic, [the seizure of Washington Mutual] was a mistake. Washington Mutual, the sixth biggest bank in the country, was systemically important.[12]

The *Wall Street Journal* correctly observed stages of the housing crisis: "The Federal Reserve's extremely low interest rates from 2001 to 2004 induced consumers to switch from fixed- to adjustable-rate mortgages and drew speculators and flippers into the market. The Fed's increase in rates over the next two years increased mortgage payments and precipitated defaults. Falling prices provided incentives to walk away from homes that were underwater. Unemployment led to more foreclosures."[13]

However, the media soon learned these facts were pretty boring to the American public. None of this mattered when millions of people were losing their jobs and their homes. The news quickly turned to stories calling for the imprisonment of all the bankers.

Many originally thought the crisis was just centered on subprime loans, but the crisis had now taken a toll on every type of mortgage. The *Wall Street Journal* reported, "The Mortgage Bankers Association reported the fastest rising segment of foreclosures in recent months has been traditional prime, 30-year fixed-rate mortgages. Foreclosures are concentrated in four states—Arizona, California, Florida and Nevada."[14] Subprime foreclosures peaked in 2008 and then dramatically declined. Prime loan foreclosures were much higher than subprime in 2008 and then escalated about 40 percent higher until nearly 2011, when they gradually declined.[15]

Shortly after we returned to Seattle, the PSI staff called Barry and said they were surprised the majority (70 to 80 percent) of Washington Mutual mortgage loan originations were thirty-year prime fixed-rate loans, not option ARMS. They demanded copies of our charts on loan production. They had been investigating the bank for over a year and apparently hadn't bothered to get publicly available data on loan production.

The PSI seemed to believe that any loan that wasn't a thirty-year fixed-rate mortgage was subprime and fraudulent. What they did not want to disclose was that adjustable-rate and option ARMs loans for regulated banks were only given to prime customers, not subprime. When fixed interest rates increased in 2003 through 2005, consumers rationally switched to the lower-priced adjustable-rate mortgages, originally promoted by Congress in the 1982 Garn–St. Germain Act and the Parity Act. Lower down payment loans were supported by Congress and required by the regulators and were necessary in order to meet the congressional LMI goals. And for twenty-five years after the Garn Act, Congress and presidents of both parties continued to demand the lowering of loan standards so more LMI loans could be made. Now they wanted to ignore their actions and deflect the blame.

It appeared the PSI and the FCIC were focused on the hypothesis that the top regulated banks abandoned fixed-rate loans and moved most of their lending over to subprime and adjustable-rate loans. The facts proved that hypothesis wrong.

Based on the data from Inside Mortgage Finance, the loan portfolios of the top six regulated banks who originated mortgage loans in 2003—Citigroup, Bank of America, JPMorgan Chase, Countrywide, Wells Fargo, and Washington Mutual—all had about 70 to 80 percent of their originations in thirty-year fixed-rate mortgages, about 5 percent were subprime, and about 10 to 20 percent were adjustable-rate. When interest rates went up, consumers rushed to the lower-priced adjustable-rate mortgages, and the proportion changed accordingly.

Between 2003 and 2007, the large banks still had the bulk of their loans in fixed-rate.[16] Subprime loans were increased slightly but subprime loans for regulated large banks remained less than 10 percent of all their mortgages.

All the attorneys were now sharing with each other what the executives were being asked by the PSI. One of the executives said the PSI was very focused on executive compensation and perks, and at the end was asked how many private airplanes the bank owned and about the bank's private airport. He responded, "What private airport? There was no private airport." Washington Mutual didn't even own a plane. If one was needed, they used a charter service, but even then, the bank was extremely frugal about renting aircraft. After 9/11, security advisors recommended the CEOs of all large banks should fly private because of the number of threats to the banking system, so the board voted to charter a plane as needed. It was clear the PSI wanted a sensationalized version of the bank—and we weren't supplying much fodder for them.

In late February, the PSI notified us there would be a hearing sometime around March 17–27, but we would only be given a couple of days' notice regarding the specific day. The PSI quickly and eagerly released a statement to the press: "On March 25, the PSI will hold the first in a series of hearings that will examine some of the causes and consequences of the recent financial crisis. The first hearing will focus on the role of high-risk home loans in the financial crisis, using a history of high-risk home loans originated and sold by Washington Mutual from 2004 to 2008." The committee demanded a twenty-page written statement by 9:30 a.m. on March 23 and told us to prepare an oral statement no more than five minutes long.

We learned they wanted to discuss Washington Mutual's strategy for the sale of higher-risk and higher-margin loans, including the decision to move to a "Higher-Risk Lending Strategy." We couldn't believe they had taken a document, required by regulators, that was meant to be a plan to diversify the bank into credit cards and commercial and business lending and turned it into a false narrative of dramatically increasing high-risk residential mortgage loans. We were incredulous they had focused on Washington Mutual—which had some of the lowest default rates—and ignored most of the really troubled banks. We were stunned they had completely ignored all the data Kerry had given them.

The DC attorneys weighed in and told us we "have a stout defense and should emphasize not only was the bank solvent and healthy, but it was the apple of JPMorgan's eye. Even Secretary Paulson's book remarked Dimon wanted to 'keep his powder dry for Washington Mutual.'"[17]

Of course, the Senate PSI could hardly wait to leak news and create excitement about its upcoming hearing. One newspaper exclaimed, "They plan to make Washington Mutual, the biggest bank failure in American history, a case study on the causes and consequences of the crisis at the hearing on Thursday."[18]

Kerry was acutely aware anything he said in the hearing would be used against him in a court of law. He was acutely aware he had no rights in the PSI hearing and Barry was not allowed to speak. In fact, Barry wasn't allowed to do anything. He was not allowed to cross-examine witnesses, not allowed to correct or object to false information presented at the hearing, not allowed to see any evidence before the hearing and not allowed to submit any evidence at the hearing. Kerry was painfully aware if he contradicted anything he had said in the last twenty years, it could be cause for a criminal referral. On top of it all, Kerry had been warned by the PSI not to have a press conference or talk to the press and had been told his twenty-page defense paper would probably not see the light of day.

On March 18 we sent a note to the PSI, confirming Kerry's participation:

> Killinger will testify before the PSI at its hearing on March 25th.
> He looks forward to the opportunity to testify about the aggressive steps Washington Mutual took between 2003 and 2007 to dramatically reduce its origination of both conventional and higher risk loan products which he reduced by 74%. He will also testify on the unnecessary seizure and bargain sale of the bank.

A couple of hours after receiving the email, the PSI called and canceled the March 25 hearing. It realized its narrative still didn't fit the facts, they needed a bigger story and it had to regroup again.

On Sunday morning, we had a "red alert" conference call with the DC attorneys, who said Levin had realized Washington Mutual wasn't enough of a story and wanted to add a whole new list of players:

Levin now wants to do a series of hearings and he wants to give an extended opening statement about what caused the financial crisis, and how his series of hearings will address each of the causes. It will be important that we rebut Levin's thesis. They are interviewing potential witnesses from Goldman Sachs, the regulators and possibly the GSEs. Levin will dominate the hearings and most of the senators will not object and let him run the show. The books *Big Short* and *13 Bankers* have gotten everyone on the hill in a tizzy. Senator Levin seems to be enamored with the anecdotal stories in the books.

The hearings were rescheduled for April, and a couple of days before the event we again flew to DC, to prepare.

Barry asked local reporter Kirsten Grind of the *Puget Sound Business Journal*—who had flown in to provide live blogging of the event— to interview Kerry before the hearing. She had previously written a favorable story about the inappropriate takeover of the bank and said she was supportive of the bank's actions. Kirsten spent about an hour and a half interviewing Kerry and his attorneys at their offices before the hearing. Kerry showed her the charts with the decrease in lending and the high quality of the loans and the low default rate. Kerry mentioned all the public warnings he had given. She said the information confirmed her thinking about the unfair seizure. Our attorneys told her Kerry would testify the bank was solid enough to work its way through the crisis and had a long history of loans that performed better than the industry. She told Kerry and his attorneys her blog would "be a great vehicle to convey Kerry's ideas and defenses."

With the interview over, Kerry and all the attorneys packed up their bags and went off to the PSI hearing. The attorneys warned Kerry to be very careful of Levin and temper his statements, reminding him Senator Levin would retaliate if Kerry didn't play his game. But Kerry was only interested in telling truth to power. He also knew the risk managers would be at the hearings, and we heard they had been threatened to ignore all the signed statements they made to the SEC, the public, and the Washington Mutual board certifying to the strength of the loan portfolio and the adequacy of the risk management activities.

Kerry learned that morning that Levin had held a secret press conference with a substantial number of media and handed out hundreds of pages of documents that Levin claimed proved his narrative about the bank. Kerry had not seen these documents ahead of time nor did he have a chance to comment on them, but when they were released to the public months later, he noticed they were either not relevant or completely misinterpreted. It was clear the PSI did not know how to interpret a 10-Q or 10-K of a large financial institution.

Think about this. After interviewing Kerry for just a couple of hours over a month ago, hiding their key documents from Kerry, and holding a secret press conference, Levin was ready to ambush Kerry and the other executives live on TV in front of the media.

Once again Linda sat in the attorneys' offices watching the hearings on TV, taking notes, and holding her breath. Kerry was allowed five minutes before the hearing to fully explain everything they did to protect the bank. He said:

> In 2003, four years before the crisis hit, I was publicly and
> repeatedly warning of the risks of a potential housing downturn.
> We didn't just talk about it; we did something. We dramatically
> reduced our mortgage originations by 74 percent and cut our
> home loan staff by [two-thirds] between 2003 and 2007. Most
> of our growth and our business was providing checking, savings,
> investment, and credit card services to millions of customers in
> our twenty-five hundred branch offices. Ninety percent of the
> loan portfolio had an LTV at origination of 80 percent or less.
> Higher-risk residential products, like home equity, option ARMs,
> and subprime were not new or exotic and were successfully offered
> to customers for many years with less than a 1 percent loss ratio.
> Regulators consistently assigned us the highest CRA rating of
> outstanding and employees were expected to practice our core
> values (on loan originations) and any violations led to reprimands
> and terminations.

Kerry reviewed all the capital raising and other measures taken to position Washington Mutual for a housing downturn. He reviewed the capital levels, excess liquidity, and better-than-industry loan performance. Kerry was adamant that Washington Mutual was inappropriately seized by the FDIC. At the end of his statement, Kerry said the bank "was excluded from hundreds of meetings and telephone calls between Wall Street executives and policy leaders that ultimately determined the winners and losers in this financial crisis. For those who were part of the inner circle and were 'too clubby to fail,' the benefits were obvious. For those of us outside of the club, the penalty was severe."

The hearing continued as expected.

Levin fired at Kerry:

It is without dispute that Washington Mutual and others certainly made some irresponsible decisions that helped fuel this crisis. Did the GSEs ever reject your loans? Did they agree to buy your loans that are by today's standards considered risky? Discuss the underwriting standards at the GSEs.

Kerry responded:

I respectfully disagree Washington Mutual made irresponsible decisions that fueled the crisis. We took significant measures to adjust to changing market conditions. In 2003 I started making public and repeated warnings of the risks of a housing downturn. From 2003 to 2007 we cut originations by 74 percent. The GSEs set their own underwriting guidelines and purchased loans that conformed to them.

Levin continued with his banter and then proudly revealed one of the major findings of his investigation: a crude pencil-drawn line indicating the rise of Washington Mutual securitizations from 2003–2008. Levin had hoped to use this chart to illustrate how the bank had increased lending, but he unwittingly only showed how the bank had reduced its loan portfolio by securitizing and selling the loans. The bank's sale of securities was a minor fraction of what Wall Street was producing and the loans sold in securitization were high quality compared to the industry. (See Chart 10-2).

But Levin wasn't finished. Near the end of the hearing he blasted up to the major finding of his investigation: Another crudely drawn set of five pie charts representing the years 2003 to 2007. Levin proudly declared, "Here is a pie chart we have here which shows the percentage of your inventory which is high risk compared to low risk."

Kerry explained the inaccuracies in the pie charts. He detailed how loans to prime customers represented 95 percent of the loan portfolio and tried to correct Levin's confusion between loan originations, loans held in portfolio and loans sold to the GSEs. Levin was doing his best to create a made-for-TV drama, but it wasn't working.

Kerry remained even-keeled, but he knew the committee didn't really care about facts or data or logic. They were there for a show. Levin poked, prodded, interrupted, and misstated the facts. He called adjustable-rate loans no-doc liar loans to subprime customers. In fact, those products performed well and were given to prime, not subprime customers.

Despite Levin's continued outbursts, the DC attorneys were very pleased with Kerry's testimony and the press that followed. The main stories in the media were dominated by Goldman Sachs, and most of the stories carried Kerry's quote about Washington Mutual's inappropriate seizure and the "too clubby to fail" banks who benefited.

The *Wall Street Journal* reported:

The former CEO [Kerry] held his ground, insisting the Seattle thrift seizure could have been avoided if regulators had offered the same capital infusions. Levin said Washington Mutual tolerated fraudulent lending, knowingly dumped problem loans on investors and did too little, too late to stem problems once they threatened to sink the thrift.[19]

Killinger said the seizure could have been averted and scoffed at lawmakers who blamed him for the largest bank failure. The thrift's seizure in September 2008 could have been avoided if regulators had offered the same help given to other battered banks. Killinger was confrontational with the legislators who accused him of repeatedly ignoring warnings when he knew the bubble was about to burst.[20]

The next day Attorney General Tom Miller called and said he thought Kerry did a great job and thought the risk managers who spoke at the hearings were probably pressured to get immunity. He thought it was "strange there were so many documents the risk managers gave to the public over many years that proclaimed the lending was appropriate and safe, but there was *no* documentation to back up what they said at the hearings." Tom always gets to the heart of the matter.

That week OTS director Reich spoke before the PSI and testified, "Washington Mutual was a liquidity failure, not a capital failure, brought on because of a $16.4 billion run on deposits during the ten-day period preceding September 25 with zero cost to the deposit insurance fund or to taxpayers. A majority of the bank's mortgages were in California and Florida, two states hit with the most severe price declines. Thrifts were more vulnerable to home price decreases because of the QTL [qualified thrift lender] rule that 65 percent of all thrift assets have to be in residential loans."

Director Reich also attempted to correct Senator Levin on several misstatements. Reich said, "I think it is important to point out that although Washington Mutual has been referred to as the largest bank failure in American history, in fact, the largest failure in American history was Citi[group]. But it was not allowed to fail. It was bailed out with billions of dollars of taxpayer money. Washington Mutual was not deemed to be systemic and was not bailed out."

FDIC chair Bair testified the FDIC "had difficulty in gaining access at Washington Mutual because of a requirement in our interagency agreement." She apparently didn't know or remember FDIC staff were on-site frequently for decades at Washington Mutual, and her managers attended quarterly meetings with the bank's executives and fully supported the bank's lending policies and strategic plans. Every year for over thirty years, the FDIC met with the board of directors to go over the results of the annual exam ratings. There are minutes of these meetings. There is documented evidence that neither her nor her staff approached Kerry or anyone on the executive team to say they disagreed with the OTS or had problems with access.

We heard later that Senator Levin was furious with Kerry's performance at the hearing. Kerry clearly refuted all of Levin's claims and destroyed his sloppily patched-together, false narrative. Levin became even more furious when most of the media seemed to think Kerry stole some of Levin's thunder when Kerry's declaration that Wall Street banks were "too clubby to fail" received a substantial amount of press. Our attorneys felt Levin seemed determined to hold a grudge, and for years after the hearings, he demanded revenge on Kerry by pressuring the FDIC and the OCC to file lawsuits against the Washington Mutual

executives and threatening civil money penalties and bans from banking, even though there was no hint or evidence of wrongdoing.

Right after we flew back to Seattle after the hearings, Linda was at
the vet to pick up the dog and ran into Doug Beighle, the longtime
chair of the audit committee for the Washington Mutual board, a Harvard lawyer, and a past chief administrative officer at Boeing. Doug
and his wife were good friends, and we went to dinner together often.
He had always been supportive and kind and confided to Linda the
directors thought Kerry did a great job at the hearing. However, he was
astounded at the testimonies from the risk managers. He said, "For
years those guys were giving presentations showing the loan portfolios
were performing well and certified to us that enterprise risk management was effective and appropriately resourced. We even hired outside
experts to confirm the ERM function was effective. All I can figure out
is someone must have threatened them."

Jamie Dimon must have been worried Kerry's testimony on the inappropriate seizure was gaining traction. Not to mention the testimony
of regulators and others who said Washington Mutual was well capitalized, solvent, and liquid up until the day it was seized. Shortly after the
PSI hearings, Dimon quickly flew to Seattle to speak with about 120
executives at the Rainier Club. He made a point of telling the group
Washington Mutual was "broke and needed to be taken over."[21]

Also, that month Dimon complained that he needed to have more
influence on "ignorant politicians so he could give them the right facts."
He lashed out at Congress for their "unnerving ignorance of fundamental principles of market economics" and said it was "time for the
grown-ups to step in."[22]

Days later, the Washington Mutual bankruptcy judge appointed an
examiner (Examiner) to determine how the nearly $33 billion left in
the WMI holding company should be assigned to each of the claimants
and to determine the financial status of the bank at the time of the seizure. This report would then be used as a backdrop for the future tense
negotiations between all the interested parties in their protracted fight
for the $33 billion.

After the hearings, FDIC chair Bair continued her war on the
community banks. In July, the American Association of Bank Directors' newsletter reported that the FDIC was laying the groundwork for
potentially years of lawsuits against bank executives and directors:

The FDIC has sent hundreds of demand letters warning D&Os of possible civil charges, announced formal investigations and subpoenaed directors' [personal] financial statements and other documents.

David Baris, partner of Buckley Sandler and executive director of the American Association of Bank Directors, remarked, 'If there is insurance, there is money to go after and the FDIC is trying to go after it, whether there is a good case or not.'

The FDIC refuted they are sending out demand letters without cause. Their bluntly worded letters, which include the amount of potential damages. [She claimed they were] required by the insurance carrier to begin the claims process.[23, 24]

The FDIC projected failures would peak in 2009, and it only had a three-year statute of limitations from the date of failure to sue management and board members. Since the start of 2008, more than 250 banks and thrifts had failed, and experts predicted that figure could double in the next year or two.[25]

During the summer the local reporter, Kirsten Grind, contacted our attorney about her plans to write a book about Washington Mutual. She wanted to have several days of interviews alone with Kerry. She said she wanted to produce a fair, truthful, and balanced account of the bank and implied she would be supportive. She added that she wanted a very dramatic book, creating a Shakespearean tragedy about the bank. We had been reading her tweets over the summer and received a lot of reports about her activities. Based on what she wrote and said, it seemed clear she was going to develop a book short on facts and long on gossipy drama.

Our attorney called her back and told her—based on what we had read in her tweets, blogs, and interviews—we didn't think she was going to be fair or balanced. She replied that she could write her book without any of Kerry's help. Our attorney said fine but asked her to call him back to verify any of her data. She said she would, but she never called back. Unfortunately, a substantial number of inaccuracies in the book were never corrected. Fortunately, when she did release her book, sales were sparse.[26]

In September, the *Wall Street Journal* reported JPMorgan Chase sued the FDIC again, seeking billions in additional assets:

The takeover of Washington Mutual gave JPMorgan Chase $188 billion in deposits and a coast-to-coast presence with 2,207 additional branches. The bank recorded a $2 billion gain with a fair market of much higher value. They said they may be able to earn as much as $25.5 billion in interest from its Washington Mutual loans and could receive as much as $6.9 billion in assets as part of a proposed settlement from the bankruptcy of Washington Mutual holding company. Bondholders had holdings wiped out when the bank and the FDIC decided not to honor the senior and subordinated debt holders.[27]

On the second anniversary of the improper seizure of Washington Mutual, Kerry received hundreds of supportive emails and messages from former employees. They all had the same theme that former COO Steve Rotella conveyed in his email to Kerry:

Despite the tragic and uncalled for ending and the residue it has left on many of us, Washington Mutual was a great place to work and a great place to bank. All the people I talk to realized that back then but feel it even more now. I know I do.[28]

After the PSI hearings, our attorneys hired the highly respected consulting firm of Navigant to do an independent research report to assess the risk management function of Washington Mutual. During the PSI hearings, Senator Levin had inaccurately claimed that "instead of strengthening risk management in 2005, when weaknesses in the housing market began to emerge, the bank weakened its risk management practices in order to increase loan volume." A ridiculous statement to make when they knew the bank cut lending by 74 percent and continued to increase lending standards. Navigant assessed each of the PSI statements and refuted every one of the PSI assertions. Navigant reported:

Deloitte issued clean financial opinions and clean controls opinions. There was no indication Deloitte thought the risk management environment was materially deficient. The risks associated with the external economic environment were greater than the internal management risks. Deloitte assessed a bank's risk controls deficiencies with one of three ratings: Normal, greater (worse) than normal or much greater (worse) than normal. Each year Deloitte assessed Washington Mutual's internal management risks with a 'normal' risk rating. Each year they concluded the 'company has implemented, and we have observed in our walkthroughs, processes and controls to ensure compliance with regulatory agencies and bodies.'

Each year Deloitte concluded the 'company has an established process of monitoring its exposure to commercial and consumer borrowers and its system of internal controls related to both monitoring the portfolios and underwriting has been reliable in prior years and is expected to continue to be reliable. Additionally, the company has not experienced significant charge-offs.'

"The bank took steps to reduce credit risk as evidenced by increasing FICO scores and declining LTV at origination. Washington Mutual established a set of credit risk concentration limits, including establishing a limit on high risk lending as a percentage of capital that it did not exceed. The regulators FDIC and OTS allowed those concentration limits."

Navigant also found no basis in PSI's allegations the bank ignored repeated warnings and exhibited unsafe and unsound practices:

The OTS (and FDIC) never reported to the bank's board that the institution exhibited unsafe and unsound practices. This would have been done by giving the bank a composite score of '4' or higher. Washington Mutual had been a long rated '2' bank and was for the first time ever downgraded to a '3' in March 2008. The most significant measurement that the regulator uses to evaluate 'safety and soundness' is capital adequacy. Washington Mutual was above the thresholds of an adequately capitalized institution. The OTS (and FDIC) consistently noted Washington Mutual entity-wide risk management practices were satisfactory.

The National Bureau of Economic Research and the Booth School of Business at the University of Chicago prepared a study for the FCIC in 2010 on "Lessons from the Financial Crisis on Risk Management." Their study found that the most effective bank chief risk managers had four characteristics: they were one of the five or six top paid officers in the bank, they reported directly to the CEO, the percentage of mortgage backed securities to total bank assets were low and the bank had a low ratio of total gross notional amount of derivative contracts held for trading relative to total assets.

They found these four characteristics correlated directly with the success of a bank. Washington Mutual met all four of those criteria. Their CERO was one of the top paid officers, he reported directly to the CEO, the bank had a very low rate of MBS to total bank assets and zero notional amounts of derivative contracts.[29]

After the third quarter of 2010, serious mortgage delinquency rates were skyrocketing for all the banks—every type of loan was experiencing dramatic failures. The delinquency rate for Florida was 19.5 percent; Nevada, 17.8 percent; Arizona, 10.8 percent; and California, 10.3 percent. None of the programs developed to help people were working, and foreclosures were epidemic.[30]

On July 21, 2010, the Dodd–Frank Act was enacted, which created the Consumer Financial Protection Bureau, the Financial Stability Oversight Council with the Office of Financial Research, gave the Federal Reserve new powers to regulate, required that CDOs and other financial derivatives had to be cleared through an exchange, expanded the whistleblower programs, and required more capital in regulated banks. After many years of lobbying efforts, much of the bill has not been implemented or enforced.[31]

In November, Iowa attorney general Tom Miller testified before the Committee on Banking, Housing, and Urban Affairs for the US Senate in a session called "Problems in Mortgage Servicing From Modification to Foreclosure." Miller reported:

> Starting over a decade ago, the attorneys general and our partners in the state banking departments began numerous enforcement efforts regarding fraudulent behavior by lenders in the origination of subprime mortgages. They begin with the First Alliance Mortgage Company, followed by the $484 million settlement with Household Finance, and finally the $325 million settlement with

Ameriquest Mortgage Company, at that time the largest subprime
lender. My staff began to explore servicing and foreclosure issues
in the spring of 2007. In July 2007 my office put out an invitation
to every attorney general in the country to attend a summit on
foreclosures. The purpose was to warn our colleagues that a tidal
wave was coming and they needed to begin to prepare.

Tom helped put together a working group of state attorneys general
and state banking regulators to look at subprime lenders. They set up a
meeting of the top ten servicers in September 2007 and another meeting with the next ten largest in November 2007. (Washington Mutual
was not one of the top mortgage loan servicers.)

Many of the servicers assured the AGs they were well staffed and
prepared for what was coming. We also made it clear to the states
we wanted to base our decisions on empirical data, not anecdotal
stories. In October 2007, the working group became the first
governmental entity to collect data on the servicers' loss mitigation efforts and results. We used the data to publish five reports,
which provide analysis and commentary on a variety of issues. The
reports were published in February 2008, April 2008, September
2008, January 2010, and August 2010. The Office of the Comptroller of the Currency forbade national banks from providing loss
mitigation data to the states.[32]
    The servicers are no longer the people who originated the loan,
so they are not equipped to deal with the amount of foreclosures.
Because servicers are overwhelmed, loss mitigation requests are
often delayed and stretched out over long periods of time. No
matter how many times the borrowers have previously submitted
their paperwork, if the borrower fails one time, the loan modification is denied.

Miller concluded:

All fifty AGs and a committee of state banking regulators formed
a multistate group to address this problem. Our past work and
the contact that we have with consumers allowed us to mobilize
our group very quickly. The outrage over robo-signing is about

due process, protection of private property rights, and the rule of law. The multistate group intends to look at issues regarding the accuracy of the information used by servicers in the foreclosure process, as well as issues such as the imposition of various servicing-related fees and force placed insurance as well as proper chain of title.[33]

It took Linda until now to build up the courage to go back to their old Washington Mutual branch bank to close their safety deposit box. It had always been fun to enter the colorful family-friendly retail experience. There were no teller lines behind bulletproof cages, because the employees were allowed to roam free to help the customers. A friendly person in khakis and a polo shirt would greet you at the door with a helpful smile. There were round, colorful towers that dispensed money and took deposits. Some of the new branches had attached Starbucks. There was a play area with toys and tables to keep children occupied while the parents worked with the bankers. This branch concept was a result of extensive research to find out what kind of environment the customer preferred, and the concept was very successful.

As Linda entered her old branch office, she gasped with sadness. The colorful towers and walls were gone, and the children's play area was replaced with an enclosed office with a large sign stating, "Private Banking Only." There were two tall men in expensive suits with New York accents behind the bulletproof glass with iron bars, doing their best to avoid her. She was wearing blue jeans and a sweatshirt and obviously was not their desired private banking client. She finally caught their attention and asked to close down her safety deposit box. They shot her a nasty look and pushed her a set of keys and muttered, "Go ahead and go in and leave this key in the box when you are done." She entered the room alone and found nearly all of the safety deposit boxes were open and empty, with keys dangling in the doors. Hundreds of cold, empty steel boxes, a metaphor for the atmosphere of the entire branch.

Her heart was broken. Thousands of employees had lost their jobs and savings. They had all worked so hard to create and nourish a family-friendly organization with superior customer service, free checking, low or no fees, and banking with integrity. It was all gone, and now there was only room for private banking for high-net-worth executives. Once again, the average family had lost out in the aftermath of this crisis.

One of the most troublesome aspects of this journey inside the crucible was the bankruptcy settlement group, formed to negotiate who gets the remaining assets left in the holding company. Typically, a bank doesn't have much money in the holding company, so if a bank gets seized, the holding company quietly goes away. However, in the case of Washington Mutual, the bank was solvent at the seizure, but the holding company (WMI) had to enter bankruptcy to determine who got the nearly $33 billion in assets remaining in the holding company. Obviously, there were thousands of people wanting to lay claim to the WMI assets as well as the remaining funds in the directors and officers insurance policies. Those seeking assets included JPMorgan Chase, the FDIC, the bondholders, the shareholders, the employees, the insurance companies and other creditors who all hired attorneys to fight for the remaining assets.

On November 4, 2010, the Examiner released his report, the purpose of which was to determine who had the best legal claim to all of the assets. The Examiner did not evaluate why the bank was seized or the quality of the lending. He recommended that JPMorgan Chase receive an additional $4 billion of the TRUPS (trust preferred securities), $5 billion of the life insurance BOLI/COLIs , and over $2 billion of the tax refunds.[34] He concluded Washington Mutual was solvent during the summer of 2008 and probably solvent until the day of its seizure. The report said: "The Equity Committee found no basis in the information made available to it, that would substantiate the claim that Washington Mutual was insolvent when seized. The collapse of much of the financial sector seemed a possibility in September 2008," which he felt explained much of the panicked behavior of the regulators. He did comment that the debtors and the OTS were very cooperative, but JPMorgan Chase "aggressively preserved its attorney-client privilege and prevented witnesses from answering questions. The FDIC responded selectively to requests and interviews...and refused to make Chairman Bair available." The FDIC employees with the most knowledge of the Washington Mutual dealings were prohibited from giving interviews.[35]

The report also confirmed there was a confidentiality agreement in place between Washington Mutual and JPMorgan Chase and the Chase executives admitted that "JPMC never submitted a bid to purchase WMI in March of 2008." Rather it "submitted a...nonbinding indication of interest."[36] The Examiner also mentioned the FDIC had indemnified JPMorgan Chase for $500 million in case anyone questioned its violations of the confidentiality agreement.

But the release of the Examiner's report was only the beginning of negotiations. The interested parties were all suing each other, and everyone was hoping to get some money out of WMI as well as the remains of the funds in the D&O insurance policies. A bankruptcy settlement group was developed that consisted of at least seventy-three attorneys representing all the claimants on the WMI funds. Twenty-five of the attorneys were defending the board, execs, and employees. These were all attorneys making hundreds dollars an hour—all paid for by the dwindling D&O insurance policy. The group had hired a highly respected former federal judge as mediator, who would lock each party in a different room in a hotel and then walk back and forth hearing their arguments and claims. The mediator happened to be the father of one of the actors in the TV series *The Good Wife*, and we soon were "thrilled" to see a mediation enactment in one of its episodes.

One of the first mediation sessions was in New York in November. The seventy-three lawyers spent the long weekend session locked in little rooms while the mediator walked around trying to figure out the pressure points on all the players. The session ended in chaos on that Sunday when one of the insurance company attorneys got mad and walked out. We thought the mediation was about truth, justice, and contractual rights, but it turned out to be pure game theory, and the winners were the attorneys who put up the biggest fight, hid their true intentions and bottom line, and worked behind the scenes to sabotage, threaten, and bully. This exercise in brinksmanship continued unabated for the next four years. Toward the end of this process, the mediator told us that after this experience he was ready to negotiate peace in the Middle East.

The FDIC must have heard about the settlement meeting, because we soon received a call from a Chicago law firm that was working with one of FDIC's Washington DC, attorneys. They said the Washington Mutual executives were not going to be charged with any misdoings, but they wanted the executives' help in getting the FDIC into the settlement meetings. They said they hadn't realized how quickly the D&O insurance money was being depleted and wanted to make sure they got their share, to the tune of $40 million. Our attorneys told them we would be happy to cooperate, but the FDIC did not have a legitimate claim because there was no loss to the insurance fund. The Chicago law firm said they didn't care. As far as they were concerned, they were going to get the money anyway.

The FDIC was not playing by any discernible rules. By now the FDIC had filed personal civil lawsuits against over eighty bank executives around the country and was seeking to recoup about $2 billion in bank losses. Since January of 2008, the FDIC had shut down or seized 311 banks at a cost of around $77 billion to the deposit insurance fund. It desperately needed money to restore the insurance fund by soaking as much money as possible out of the lawsuits. In many cases, the FDIC was not only suing the banks but personally suing the executives and the boards of directors—even when there was no evidence of any wrongdoing.[37]

FDIC chair Bair continued to up the ante on all these lawsuits and had decided bank directors all over the country had no right to receive any bank documents to help with their defense and promptly sued the attorneys who were defending bank directors. This must have terrified bank directors everywhere, because soon Bair received a letter from the American Association of Bank Directors:[38]

We are writing in regard to the FDIC's recently expressed policy that bank directors have no right to possess bank documents in their defense of a potential suit by the FDIC as receiver. The FDIC has aggressively sought to enforce this previously undisclosed policy by filing a lawsuit against lawyers representing bank directors in the defense of proceedings by the FDIC aimed at recovering losses from their clients. This policy is shortsighted and counterproductive.

Allowing directors access to documents relevant to transactions that might have occurred many years ago would allow the FDIC to obtain critical information regarding whether to proceed with a potentially ill-advised suit. The AABD requests that FDIC announce publicly that:

(1) Once the FDIC issues a demand letter to a director of a failed bank, it will advise the director that he or she is entitled to

obtain copies of or review bank files from the FDIC under any
appropriate confidentiality restrictions.

(2) Bank directors may at any time obtain, possess and retain
copies of any bank records under appropriate confidentiality
restrictions and may retain such bank records following
the closing of their bank, subject to such confidentiality
restrictions."

At the end of the year, Mark Zandi, chief economist at Moody's and
cofounder of Economy.com, gave testimony to the FCIC. He stated:

The FDIC closed 135 institutions in 2009 and another 550
institutions are on the FDIC's troubled list. Most of these institutions have rising losses on commercial real estate loans and are
likely to fail. The National Federation of Independent Businesses
stated the number of businesses who say credit is hard to get is
the highest it's ever been.

The number of bank credit cards in circulation has plunged by
nearly one hundred million, more than 20 percent. Commercial
and industrial loans have declined by $165 billion, or 20 percent
since the peak in 2008. The number of unemployed workers receiving some form of unemployment insurance is ten million workers.
Many who lost jobs at the start of recession two years ago are now
beginning to run out of benefits. Employment has plunged by 2.2
million in the past six months. Unless hiring resumes soon, more
workers will join the twenty-six million plus—17 percent of the
workforce—who are unemployed or underemployed.

Based on credit file data, at the end of November, there were
2.8 million mortgage loans in foreclosure and an additional 1.6
million loans ninety days or more past due. Eight percent of the
fifty-two million first mortgage loans are in deep trouble. Loss of
household net worth has fallen by $17.5 trillion, or more than
25 percent. Tax revenues are off 9 percent for fiscal 2010, throwing
many cities and states into a budget crisis.

The most difficult fallout to gauge from the financial crisis
is the impact on the collective psyche. People are in a dour
mood. The very poor fiscal situation reflects the expected final

taxpayer cost of the crisis to more than $2 trillion, or 14 per-
cent of the GDP.

One in five Americans owe at least 125 percent of the current value of their home. Federal officials estimate five hundred
thousand to 1.5 million borrowers were underwater as of June
30, 2008, which was 23 percent of all households with a mortgage.
The large banks have shown little enthusiasm for helping people
restructure their loans.[39]

More than two years post–financial crisis, was our federal government focused on helping the tens of millions of people out of work
and homeless? Nope. They were focused on the battleground of Senate
hearings, lawsuits to replenish their coffers, and fights to determine
who will hold power in the next financial crisis.

10

Part Two:
Investigations and Lawsuits

2011–2014

2011

In late 2010, the FDIC had approached us declaring it was not going to pursue the executives of Washington Mutual, but it did want our help in getting them into the "global settlement" meetings that would divide up the $33 billion in assets still held in the WMI holding company as well as what was left of the $250 million D&O insurance policy. After a couple of weeks of civil discourse between the attorneys and the FDIC, discussions went dark. US Senator Levin was publicly pressuring the FDIC to sue and fine the execs at the bank, but the FDIC had no charges. Because of Levin's pressure, discussions were getting more frenetic, and suddenly the FDIC threatened a lawsuit against the executives. Kerry offered to travel to the FDIC for an interview, but the FDIC attorney said, "It would not make any difference, we have already decided."[1]

After a couple of months of wrangling with the FDIC, the Washington Mutual execs' requests for the list of charges still fell on deaf ears. Tensions escalated until the FDIC attorney screamed at our attorneys,

"We have to sue you. I will do whatever it takes not to have to end up in one of Levin's hearings." We felt bad for the FDIC attorney. He was relatively new at the FDIC, and from what we could discover, didn't have any experience dealing with complex financial investigations for large banks. We did not fault him for his outburst. Not only was he being bullied by Senator Levin's office, he was also dealing with a fractured, capricious FDIC board that continually changed its directives. If he was hauled into Levin's Kabuki court, he feared it would end his career.

As time went on, the FDIC attorney was getting even more theatrical. He claimed the FDIC "had spent $20 million investigating Washington Mutual" and he had "read ninety-three thousand emails and knew more about this case than anyone in the world." He dug in further adding, "I am not going to be called in front of a Senate investigation hearing. I am not going to lose my job over this."

Because of his continual emotional outbursts, our attorneys in Seattle decided we needed to contact a Washington DC litigator who would defend us in a lawsuit against the FDIC. We had had enough of the FDIC's shenanigans and wanted to sue the FDIC for the illegal seizure and the continual harassment. The Chicago attorney for the FDIC seemed a little nervous about the FDIC attorney's remarks and told us the "FDIC has been asleep at the switch...but now they will make your global [insurance] resolution difficult."

We asked Attorney General Tom Miller for his advice for a top DC litigator, and he arranged a phone conference for us with one of the most famous, toughest, and most highly regarded litigators in the country, Brendan Sullivan, from the prestigious Williams and Connolly law firm. Brendan didn't waste time. He told us:

> I have looked over all the information and Kerry is in an excellent
> position to avoid any charges and has a good case against the
> FDIC. It will take months to do a mediation with the FDIC so we
> should get started with a counter lawsuit against the FDIC. The
> PSI is putting huge pressure on the FDIC to do something to the
> Washington Mutual executives. The FDIC almost has to acquiesce
> to the PSI and go ahead with a lawsuit, but it will affect the entire
> [bankruptcy] mediation process. The lawsuit will be vague, but
> they have to go with something in order to appease Levin.
>
> If they do file a lawsuit, put out a simple statement that says
> you did nothing wrong and you will fight these false allegations.

This is really outrageous—even Paulson and Bernanke admitted all the major banks were ready to fail and the crisis was caused by unpredictable changes in the business climate. Why isn't the FDIC personally suing any of the other large bank executives? But don't worry about this. This whole process is pure psychology and will take years to solve. I am giving you permission to put this behind you and live your life—don't read the newspapers or the news, just live your life. I am going to fight for you because you are innocent. You are not going to get any good coverage in the news so just accept that and move on. If you respond to the press you just create a story and it will never be good and it will never be fair.

We set up what we called a "good cop, bad cop" situation. Our Seattle attorneys from Wilson Sonsini—the good cops—would continue to negotiate the global bankruptcy settlement with the insurance companies and the creditors. But behind the scenes, Brendan Sullivan from Williams and Connolly—the bad cops—would proceed with the lawsuit against the FDIC.

The FDIC had standard procedures for suing a bank. In the past it only sued banks that were a cost to the deposit fund or had serious enforcement orders or crimes, but the case with Washington Mutual was entirely different. The bank was a longtime 2-rated bank that had never received a formal enforcement order, and the seizure of the bank didn't cost the deposit fund a dime. A move to sue the officers would be unprecedented, but we were getting used to unprecedented actions.

On January 28, the final report of the FCIC, "National Commission on the Causes of the Financial and Economic Crisis in the United States" was published, and we clamored to get our online copy as soon as possible. There were over seven hundred interviews and dozens of public meetings and roundtable discussions. There were public hearings with top economists, Wall Street CEOs, regulators and investigators, subprime companies and the GSEs. There were sessions on the shadow banking system with Bear Stearns execs, the SEC, Federal Reserve and Treasury officials, and other bankers. There were sessions on the credibility of credit ratings and the role of derivatives with testimony from AIG execs, Goldman Sachs and regulators. They had public hearings on the impact of the crisis on local communities and banks as well as the state of Nevada, the city of Miami, and the city of Sacramento.

Surprisingly, Kerry was not interviewed, contacted, asked to testify, or verify any information. Washington Mutual was barely mentioned in their report.

The FCIC report said the crisis was "fueled by low interest rates, easy and available credit, scant regulation and toxic mortgages." It reported, "trillions of dollars in risky mortgages had become embedded throughout the financial system, as mortgage related securities were packaged, repackaged and sold to investors around the world."[2]

After reading the report, we felt the blame was spread around to almost everyone, but the FCIC didn't seem to blame Congress for years of irresponsible legislation or the presidential and congressionally inspired push for higher LMI lending or the lack of regulation in the shadow subprime system.

The hearings revealed twelve of the thirteen major banks would have failed within days had Treasury not come to their defense.[3] But they never fully explained why some banks with low capital, the worst of the lending, and billions in dangerous derivatives exposure were showered with billions and other, safer banks were cut off from liquidity.

The report noted five major investment banks—Bear Stearns, Goldman Sachs, Lehman Brothers, Merrill Lynch, and Morgan Stanley—were operating with extraordinarily thin capital. They reported:

Leverage ratios were as high as forty to one. At the end of 2007, Bear Stearns had $11.8 billion in equity and $383.6 billion in liabilities, and was borrowing as much as $70 billion in the overnight market. That is equivalent to a small business with $50,000 in equity borrowing $1.6 million with about $300,000 of that due each and every day. By the end of 2007, Fannie and Freddie's combined leverage ratio including loans and guarantees stood at seventy-five to one.

By 2003 the top twenty-five subprime lenders made 93 percent of the loans. The big banks had gained their own securitization skills and didn't need the investment banks to structure and distribute the loans. The investment banks moved into mortgage origination to guarantee supply of loans. Lehman purchased six different domestic lenders between 1998 and 2004; Bear Stearns acquired three subprime originators, as did Merrill Lynch and Morgan Stanley. Lehman and Countrywide pursued a vertically integrated model, involving itself in every link of the mortgage chain: originating and funding the loans, packaging them into securities and finally selling the securities to investors.

Independent brokers with access to a variety of lenders, worked with borrowers to complete the application. Using brokers allowed fast expansion with no need to build branches. This lowered the costs and extended geographic reach. Compensation for brokers was up-front fees, so the loan's performance mattered little. Consumers didn't always understand the fee came out of the proceeds, so the brokers were incented to choose the highest fees.

Bernanke told the FCIC:

He and Paulson "had underestimated the repercussions of the emerging housing crisis. You know, the stock market goes up and down every day more than the entire value of the subprime mortgages in the country."

It looks like neither Bernanke nor Paulson factored in the securitization of the toxic shadow subprime system and how it infested billions of dollars of collateralized debt obligations insured by trillions in notional value of credit default swaps.

The FCIC found in a sample of loans by New Century, mortgage brokers received more than $17.5 million in fees for the 3,466 loans in the sample. Herb Sandler of Golden West told the FCIC, "Brokers were the whores of the world." Dimon testified to the FCIC that his firm eventually ended its (subprime) broker-originated business in 2009 after discovering the loans had more than twice the losses of the loans JPMorgan Chase itself originated.

The FCIC had several conclusions. The financial crisis was avoidable for a number of reasons: failures in regulation of the banks, excessive borrowing, lack of transparency, an ill-prepared government with inconsistent responses, systemic breakdown in accountability and ethics, collapsing mortgage standards, over-the-counter derivatives, and failure of the credit rating agencies. It made several criminal referrals to the Department of Justice, but no charges came out of the referrals.[4]

As the report went to print, there were twenty-six million Americans who were out of work, could not find full-time work, or had given up looking. About four million families had lost their homes to foreclosure, and another four and a half million had slipped into the foreclosure process or were seriously behind on their mortgage payments. Nearly $11 trillion in household wealth had vanished, with retirement accounts and life savings swept away.[5]

The media was not complimentary about the FCIC report. An article in the *Economist* said the report was "breezily written, despite its bulk."[6] The *New York Times* wrote, "Republicans called the final 545-page report a political exercise whose findings were mostly inevitable, while Democrats defended its main conclusion: Wall Street risk-taking and regulatory negligence combined to produce an avoidable disaster."[7] Other articles in the *New York Times* said the report was a "confusing and contradictory mess, part rehash, part mishmash, as impenetrable as the collateralized debt obligations at the core of the crisis."[8] Another article stated, "Synthetic C.D.O.'s both extended and amplified the crisis, because they made it possible for Wall Street to bet on particularly toxic tranches of mortgage-backed securities over and over again."[9] SEC chairman Christopher Cox added, "Discomfort about the capital cushions at the big investment banks, the decision to rescue Bear Stearns and then to place Fannie and Freddie into conservatorship, followed by its decision not to save Lehman Brothers and then to save AIG, increased uncertainty and panic in the market."

In 2016, five years after the FCIC report was released, some analysts revealed that "The real agenda of the FCIC was to deal with the politics of the financial crisis. The Democrats wanted the narrative for the cause... greedy bankers rigged the game in Washington and imposed this crisis on the American people. It is completely wrong but it still has a phenomenal amount of resonance with the American people."[10]

The media circus after the FCIC report emboldened Senator Levin to put immense pressure on the FDIC to do something big before the PSI report was released, and the FDIC quickly acquiesced. On March 16, we were stunned to receive a short four-page civil lawsuit from the FDIC suing the executives for $1 billion for vague and unsubstantiated reasons. The FDIC had promised it would wait until after the March 22 mediation session before it filed a lawsuit, but responding quickly to Levin's threats was more important than keeping its word.

Before filing a lawsuit, the FDIC and other regulators are required to privately and confidentially contact a prospective defendant, present specific actions they believe to be unlawful, and elicit reasons why they should not sue or attempt to reach a settlement before filing a lawsuit. Such an approach was established protocol and is also required by President Clinton's executive order on civil justice reform. The FDIC also has a rule requiring it to interview someone before it files a lawsuit, present specific charges, and allow the person to respond to the charges. Its rulebook specifically states, "Directors and officers are always notified on a decision to sue prior to filing a complaint, which affords the individual the opportunity to settle."[11]

The FDIC publicly released the lawsuit without interviewing Kerry before the lawsuit, without identifying any specific wrongdoing or reason for a lawsuit, or without the opportunity to respond to any allegations.

Senator Levin wanted his PSI report out before the FCIC, but finally released his report in April—three months late. The *New York Times* said, "The [660-page PSI] report focuses on an array of institutions with the central roles in the mortgage crisis: Washington Mutual, an aggressive mortgage lender that collapsed in 2008, the Office of Thrift Supervision; the credit ratings agencies and the investment banks Goldman Sachs and Deutsche Bank." Levin said, "The report pulls back the curtain on shoddy, risky, deceptive practices on the part of a lot of major financial institutions. The overwhelming evidence is that those institutions deceived their clients and deceived the public, they were aided and abetted by deferential regulators and credit ratings agencies who had conflicts of interest."[12]

The next day the *New York Times* had another article bemoaning the fact no banker had been sent to prison. "The financial crisis was caused by reckless lending and excessive risk taking, no senior execs have been charged or imprisoned, and a collective government effort has not emerged. Many officials said regulators failed in their crucial duty to compile the information that traditionally has helped build criminal cases." Other sources warned time was running out on the FDIC's three-year statute of limitations to sue and punish the bankers.[13]

In May we flew to Washington, DC, to meet with Brendan Sullivan and his team to pursue the lawsuit against the FDIC. We were looking forward to taking the FDIC to court for the illegal seizure and unwarranted harassment, with one of the best attorneys in the country pleading our case.

Our strategy meeting kicked off with one of Brendan's attorneys, who said the FDIC was centering their case around their false claim it had warned the bank about the risky lending strategy. She said the lawsuit reminded her of a scene in the movie *My Cousin Vinny*, when Joe Pesci proclaims, "Everything that guy just said is bullshit." Brendan said he didn't understand why the FDIC was pursuing the lawsuit, but he figured Levin must have been putting political pressure on them. He continued, "With all the precautions and the care the bank executives exhibited, it would be impossible to prove negligence. Especially since there was no self-dealing, no bad faith or bad loyalty." He gave us the bad news that trial costs would be at least $1.5 million a month and could easily exceed $25 million.

Linda asked Brendan how Kerry would come across to a jury in these times when everyone hated bankers. Brendan looked at her and said confidently, "No problem—Kerry is the Dr. Welby of banking.[14] He will be great as a witness. We couldn't ask for anyone better."

Even with the huge cost, we wanted to proceed with the lawsuit but decided the most responsible course of action would be to try to settle the case first. The global settlement mediator was a sophisticated negotiator who had successfully handled dozens of very complex mediations. We asked him to work with the FDIC, and after several days, the FDIC agreed on a settlement of $40 million of D&O insurance instead of their outrageous claim of $1 billion personally against the executives. We were relieved it was all over and relieved the FDIC decided not to pursue Levin's threats. It was clear they had filed the lawsuit to appease Levin and to get national media attention.

However, a couple of days later, the FDIC general counsel called and said he wouldn't do the deal because the FDIC attorney did not have authority to agree to a settlement and he was reprimanded. The mediator canceled the meeting he had with the insurers, and the entire global bankruptcy settlement was dead. The FDIC said it would start pursuing personal fines and bans from banking for the executives. The mediator said he was livid and dumbstruck the FDIC would do this. He said the FDIC willfully ignored a well-known rule not to send anyone to mediation who doesn't have the authority to decide. The mediator thought the $40 million was a good deal for the FDIC and its actions were "amateurish and incompetent."

On August 5, the Department of Justice announced it had closed the investigation of Washington Mutual with no criminal or civil charges. It said it had conducted an extensive investigation, which included hundreds of interviews, and reviewed millions of documents. It also reviewed reports by the PSI, the Treasury, and the FDIC. Participating in the investigation was the Department of Labor, the FDIC, the Office of the Inspector General, and the Washington State Department of Financial Institutions. Nobody asked to interview Kerry.[15]

This was good news, because the DOJ would only talk to the top executive if it had found anything of concern. We knew Kerry and the execs had not done anything inappropriate, but in this tense climate, it was good to know we would not have to spend time or money with the Department of Justice.

However, the closing of the DOJ investigation terrified the FDIC and immediately brought them back to the negotiating table. They had been hoping the DOJ would find some charges they could apply to the FDIC lawsuit. Brendan and his team spent the summer and the fall in an attempt to subpoena the FDIC for all the correspondence between the FDIC and JPMorgan Chase during 2008 and any correspondence or internal reports the FDIC had concerning Washington Mutual for the preparation for a potential trial. The attorneys believed we could get the documents because the federal judge believed in complete transparency. The FDIC appeared to be terrified about turning over all their documents and emails from JPMorgan Chase and refused to cooperate. We looked forward to having those documents because they would not only help our FDIC case but might be beneficial to Washington Mutual shareholders in their case against the inappropriate seizure of Washington Mutual.

The mediator spent the rest of the fall wrangling with the FDIC and fielding its threats of fines and bans in order to negotiate a fair settlement. Finally, on December 7, nearly one year after talks had started, the mediator managed to get the FDIC's signature on an agreement. The FDIC got its $40 million in D&O insurance, and the mediator resumed the global bankruptcy settlement. This time, the FDIC did not renege on the deal, and the FDIC's board approved it.

None of the Washington Mutual executives would be fined, banned from banking, or sanctioned in any way. The bankruptcy judge seemed to be inclined to approve the settlement. Our only regret is we never got to see the FDIC's internal memos and emails. The FDIC clearly didn't want anyone to ever see them. We were exhausted but glad Kerry stood up to Senator Levin during PSI's Kabuki theater hearing and to the FDIC with their empty threats.

We heard Senator Levin was very upset the FDIC settled their lawsuit and didn't force civil money penalties or any other action against the executives. After the settlement, Levin once again publicly threatened the regulators to take action against the executives in the December 17 issue of the *New York Times*:

> Mr. Levin noted the OCC could still act against Washington
> Mutual's former executives. [Levin said], 'There are some real
> possible enforcement actions they can take to go after civil money
> penalties. They have the ability to go after securities violations
> for securities issued that were defective or misleading, unsafe and
> unsound practices, breach of fiduciary duty, general disregard for
> banking regulations—there's still a way to get more accountability.'

Asked whether the OCC would pursue such actions, a spokesman declined to comment.[16] In December, *American Banker* magazine weighed in with their frustration on all the overreach actions taken by the FDIC. It stated, "Receiverships actions [by the FDIC] are simply salvage operations intended to try to reduce the bank's [FDIC's] losses. Whether punishment is to be sought it [should be] the business of other agencies [like the DOJ]."[17]

Business Insider magazine reported, "[Senator] Levin did a lot of things when he was investigating banks, but showing deep knowledge of any financial institution's practices was not one of them."[18]

2012

As we rolled into 2012, it had been nearly four years since the financial crisis, and nothing seemed to be settled. The Campaign for a Fair Settlement, a coalition of labor unions, consumer advocates, and political activists including MoveOn.org, called for a full investigation into bank mortgage lending and the creation and sale of the mortgage-backed securities. Obama quickly created another unit to investigate mortgage misconduct by banks and put New York attorney general Eric Schneiderman in charge of the probe. The New York AG sent out nearly a dozen subpoenas to JPMorgan Chase, Bank of America, Citigroup, Ally Financial, and Wells Fargo.

Meanwhile, in early February, after nearly two years of negotiations, the National Association of Attorneys General announced that the five largest mortgage servicers, Bank of America, JPMorgan Chase, Wells Fargo, Citigroup, and Ally Financial had agreed to a landmark $25 billion settlement with a coalition of state attorneys general and federal agencies that would provide substantial relief to borrowers who were victims of foreclosure fraud and abuse. Iowa Attorney General Tom Miller, lead attorney in the state's efforts, said, "Our goal has been to hold these banks accountable while providing urgently needed relief to homeowners who are struggling because of the banks' misconduct. This agreement will help transform a badly broken system into one that protects borrowers."[19]

2013

We started 2013 grateful the FDIC matter had been successfully negotiated and the DOJ had announced the end to their investigation, and we were hoping the PSI matter was closed. We were working through the complex bankruptcy settlement but still monitoring Senator Levin's threats in the media. We were also still connecting with many former employees, but most of them had found jobs and were content in their new lives. We now had more time to devote to our charitable foundation and our venture capital companies and began to make plans on how we could continue to contribute to our communities and regain our life back.

On January 18, the five-year-old Federal Reserve Transcripts were released, which offered some interesting insight into the Fed's deliberations during the 2007–2008 housing crisis. The transcripts revealed the Federal Reserve entered 2007 still deeply complacent about the housing market. After millions of people had lost their jobs and millions of homeowners were in the process of foreclosure, Bernanke seemed unconcerned about the impact to the average American. Fed chair Bernanke in March of 2008 said:

> The impact on the broader economy and financial markets of the problems in the subprime market seems likely to be contained. There is a certain amount of panic, a certain amount of markets seizing up, with good credits not being able to be financed, and a good deal of concern there is a potential for some downward spiral in the markets that could threaten or harm the economy.

But the Fed's response was still relatively modest—cutting the interest rate on loans from the discount window.[20, 21] It seemed curious how the subprime market could affect the wider economy but still was not motivated to inject needed liquidity into the system.

In March, CNBC News revealed a US Senate report claimed JPMorgan Chase misled both regulators and investors about the nature and size of the losses in their "London Whale" trade, and their derivatives still posed a significant threat to the financial system. The nine-month investigation spearheaded by the Senate PSI committee concluded by declaring an abundance of evidence that JPMorgan was too big to manage. In response, Dimon ordered his staff to not send the bank's daily P&L statement to the OCC because "he believed it was too much information to provide to the OCC." He was upset about leaks in the reports and concerned about the confidentiality of the information being provided to the OCC. At one point, Dimon "raised his voice in anger" at his CFO when the CFO reinstated reports to the OCC.[22]

On April 29, Kerry received a surprising email from one of the bank's executives, who said he had just been interviewed by the OCC to discuss Washington Mutual's lending practices. He said the OCC was doing an investigation of Washington Mutual and wanted to know if we had received a notice and if we knew what this was about. We remembered the December *New York Times* article that quoted Senator Carl Levin's threats to the OCC to bring additional charges against the executives. There was also something recently in the media about Levin applying pressure on the OCC. Could this really be happening again?

The *Wall Street Journal* soon reported that Jamie Dimon was scheduled to meet in May with dozens of bank examiners from the OCC. The town hall–style meeting in New York would include junior examiners who wouldn't normally interact with a CEO. Three weeks earlier, a smaller team of senior examiners from the OCC and the Federal Reserve told Dimon and his board that regulators didn't trust JPM management and cited a series of compliance and risk problems.[23]

On May 7, our attorney told us he had just spoken with the OCC, and it wanted to interview Kerry over the course of one or two days near the end of June. The OCC said as the successor to the OTS, it was investigating the bank's residential lending practices and was considering potential enforcement actions and civil money penalties (CMP) against the executives.

Our attorneys believed we needed to get an expert OCC attorney, but most of them were busy with hundreds of cases around the country. Many of the attorneys we talked with were telling us the same story: "This is an unprecedented move by the OCC, and they have all the cards. The OCC is in complete disarray now because of all the bank failures, the transfer of the supervision of the OTS thrifts to the OCC, and pressure from the politicians and the media to bring lawsuits against bankers. No one is going to question the OCC's authority, because they have draconian powers." We were not hopeful.

A recent *New York Times*/CBS poll had shown nearly eight out of ten Americans believed "not enough bankers and employees of financial institutions were prosecuted for their roles in the financial crisis."[24] With this kind of pressure from the American public, of course the regulators were going to try anything to sue or punish bankers.

We talked with Attorney General Tom Miller again for advice on attorneys with OCC experience. Tom remained curious as to why Senator Levin continued to threaten government regulators to punish Washington Mutual executives. Tom recommended John Villa, a senior partner with Williams and Connolly.

We arranged a phone call with John, during which he shared:

> The OCC does not have much trial experience, and most of their cases are small. They are getting enormous political pressure from the PSI. They hold all the cards. It doesn't matter if they

don't have standing. It doesn't matter they don't have any charges.
They have political prowess now, and not much is standing in
their way.

Despite this bleak assessment, John was intrigued. He thought our
case was an overreach by the OCC, which would be a bad precedent
for all banks.

On May 25, we learned the D&O insurance would pay for the initial defense of the OCC case, and JPMorgan Chase surprisingly said it
would immediately provide all the documents we needed. On a phone
call with John, we asked him how the OCC could do this—it had never
been involved in the bank's exams, there was no evidence of wrongdoing, the statute of limitations had expired, neither the FDIC nor
the DOJ had any charges, and the bank had never received a formal
enforcement order. John said that didn't matter—the OCC had draconian powers to assess steep civil money penalties and bar executives
from banking. To make matters worse, if we lost, our only appeal would
be to the in-house administrative law judges, who sided with the OCC
about 90 percent of the time.

But John wanted to pursue the case. He said, "A win on this fight
with the OCC would not only help us but help other banks in the
future. If the OCC were successful in this effort, it would provide a
startling precedent for the banking industry." A US senator would
be able to publicly threaten an independent regulatory agency into
enforcement actions against bank officers when there were no formal
enforcement actions by the regulators and no charges found by the
DOJ or the FDIC. This would open up a Pandora's box of politicizing the regulatory process in order to further a US senator's personal
political agenda.

We traveled to Washington, DC, on June 5 to meet with John in
person. We could immediately tell he was experienced, brilliant, and
the right person to help us. He had done his homework and knew all
about the case. He was several steps ahead on what he would do, and he
had serious contacts and credibility with the regulators.

John organized conference calls three times a week and periodic
meetings in Washington, DC, spending that time to prepare all the
information for the defense. He understood how to approach the
delicate balance of encouraging the OCC to ignore the pundits and

the congressional threats and do the right thing. He was confident he could appeal to the OCC's better angels. Kerry was eager to fight hard in this battle, because if he lost, the OCC could come after the other executives and possibly the bank's board.

John chose two highly respected former regulators to provide an independent review and report back on their findings. Michael A. Mancusi was an eighteen-year veteran of the OCC and served as senior deputy comptroller of the currency. William M. Isaac was the former chairman of the FDIC. Both of them had reviewed all the data on Washington Mutual and said the execs did not violate any laws or regulations and there was no evidence of wrongdoing. They were prepared to write up their findings and testify in any hearings or court battles.

In July, *Super Lawyers* magazine named our chief Seattle attorney, Barry Kaplan, one of the Super Lawyers in the country, and we felt the honor was very well deserved. Barry told the magazine he still represented Killinger, who he believed was unfairly maligned by the media and Senate investigators. He said, "I have come to know Kerry as an incredibly hardworking, ethical, and honest person. He worked hard to protect the bank from the housing downturn." Barry declined to comment on Michigan senator Carl Levin's tough questioning of Killinger, other than to say with a grimace, "The questions we got weren't responsive to the information we provided."[25]

In late June, we again flew to Washington, DC, to meet with John and his staff, spending several days preparing for the interview with the OCC. John believed our position to be very strong and guided Kerry to aggressively challenge every one of the OCC's assertions with the true facts of the case. John was impressed with the bank's stress tests that showed Washington Mutual had more than sufficient amounts of capital and liquidity to survive a national housing price decline of over 40 percent. Very few of the larger banks had stress tested to that level.

John had a plan for Kerry's interview with the OCC. He wanted to give the OCC enough factual cover to be able to rebuff Senator Levin's assertions. He arranged for the interview at 1:00 p.m. on Friday, and he figured the meeting would be over by two thirty. They would have a car pick Linda up at the hotel at about 2:00 p.m. and have her waiting in the car outside the OCC offices to pick up Kerry and whisk them away to the airport. No hanging around—get out of town. Linda was picked up at the hotel and waiting patiently outside the OCC at two thirty. She was staring at the door waiting for Kerry to come out. Three o'clock rolled around, and the doors remained closed. At three thirty, she remained outside alone.

At four o'clock, they finally came out of the building. She was looking for any signs of despair, happiness, or relief, but she couldn't tell. John turned and walked away. Kerry jumped into the car, and we headed for the DC airport. We decided not to say anything until we were in a private setting at the airport.

We finally arrived at the airport and went over to a corner to talk. Kerry described the interview and why it took so long. The meeting took place in a small conference room with three OCC staff. The format of the meeting was typically for the regulators to ask questions and make statements about their allegations. However, John quickly took command of the meeting and asked Kerry a number of questions in front of the regulators. "Kerry, what was your composite exam score for 2007?" Kerry answered, "2." "What was your composite exam score for 2006?" Kerry answered "2." "What was your composite exam score for 2005?" Kerry answered, "2." "What was your composite exam score for 2004?" Kerry answered, "2."

John questioned, "Between 2003 and 2007, what were the individual scores for capital adequacy, asset quality, management, earnings, liquidity, and sensitivity to market risk? Kerry answered, "With a couple of exceptions, they were all 2." "Kerry, how many formal enforcement actions did the FDIC and the OTS give the bank?" Kerry responded, "None."

This line of questioning continued for a while. John then reviewed the major points of his research and legal findings and listed the top regulatory witnesses who were prepared to testify on Kerry's behalf. John warned the OCC we were prepared to fight very hard against these vague charges. John did this with tremendous respect for the reputation of the OCC.

Kerry said John was masterful and respectful. He was comfortable with the documents presented, and now we just had to wait. We flew back to Seattle, drove up to our marina, and jumped into our little boat to head for the islands north of Seattle. The weather was perfect, the oceans were calm, and we were escorted by a pod of playful dolphins.

We played our favorite album from Earth, Wind, and Fire, and the sky was so blue and clear we could see the snow-capped Mount Baker on the far horizon. We had a large group of friends waiting in the islands for us, and we were grateful for our friendships and grateful for our life together.

The following Monday, John called and told Kerry he did a terrific job and skillfully answered all the questions. John also mentioned JPMorgan Chase had offered to assist with the defense costs. Linda was stunned that after all the years of lack of cooperation, it was willing to finally help. John shared that Chase finally realized getting the true facts out about Washington Mutual and achieving a good outcome in the OCC case would help everyone, especially JPMorgan Chase. John anticipated we would hear back from the OCC in just a few days.

However, later that day, John called back and said he had just received the four-page OCC Notice of Potential Initiation of Formal Enforcement Action letter. The OCC letter said, "For the foregoing reasons, we believe a formal enforcement action against you is warranted. Please send your written response to this letter within 21 days." The reasons given were vague and suspiciously taken directly from the PSI report. Even after Kerry had given them all the factual information about the bank, the OCC still initiated the investigation. John wasn't surprised and started to lay out a plan to respond to the letter. We asked John why the OCC was doing this. He responded, "It is politically motivated— they want a scalp, they want a trophy. They are under pressure from Senator Levin and the PSI." No regulator wanted to get subpoenaed and then grilled in one of Levin's televised Kabuki court hearings.

Once again, the action by the OCC was leaked to the press—a violation of the OCC's protocols to not release a potential action before the banker had the chance to respond to the charges and negotiate a resolution. Our attorneys suspected that once again Senator Levin had released confidential information to the press. The OCC investigations were always kept strictly confidential until it evaluated all the evidence and issued a formal order. To release an investigation before a ruling would destroy a banker's or a bank's reputation.

On July 23, 2013, only twenty-one days after receiving the OCC's potential action letter, John submitted our 126-page defense to the Office of the Comptroller of the Currency. The OCC had years to prepare their action, but we only got twenty-one days to develop our complex response. John's report emphasized:

> If the OCC pursues a formal enforcement action against Mr.
> Killinger, we intend to call the following regulators as witnesses,
> who will testify on behalf on Kerry and Washington Mutual
> including the former Chair of the FDIC, the former top executive
> of the OCC, the director of the OTS, the senior deputy director of
> the OTS, several regional directors and lead examiners of the OTS,
> and several lead examiners of the FDIC.

The conclusion of John's report listed the twelve factors usually considered by a regulatory agency in initiating civil money penalties and the bank's defense. John's comments said, in summary:

> There was no evidence or even an allegation the executives
> breached a fiduciary duty or acted in disregard of consequences.
> During the entire 18-year term of Kerry as CEO, there was never
> a single enforcement action, fine, penalty or a formal order of
> investigation from any state, local or federal agency.
>
> Washington Mutual has frequent documentation of OTS and
> FDIC repeatedly praising the progress in responding to criticisms
> and recommendations. There is extensive written documentation
> of regulators commenting about the bank's consistently trans-
> parent communications. The losses suffered by the bank were
> primarily a result of the financial crisis and the 28% decline in the
> national housing market. The regulators testified at the PSI that
> the bank did not fail because of loan quality. At the time of seizure,
> the bank was well capitalized, had available liquidity and $125
> billion in cash retail deposits.
>
> There was no accusation or evidence of inappropriate financial
> gain of the executives. Until March 2008, the bank had consis-
> tently received a CAMELS rating of 2. The regulators consistently
> gave written confirmation management had effectively managed
> the risk management program. There is no evidence or allegation
> the executives engaged in violations of law—one of the few large
> banks who hasn't.

The attorneys concluded their report by saying the "OCC cannot establish the executives engaged in any misconduct, they cannot establish the executives received any improper financial gain, and they cannot establish the executives acted with scienter."

John was thorough. Attached to the legal research were investigative reports developed by the former chairman of the FDIC and the former senior deputy of the OCC. They had extensively reviewed all the appropriate documentation and stated, "There was no loss or risk of loss resulting from reckless, unsafe, and unsound activities or breach of fiduciary duty by the executives. Washington Mutual's condition was due to the significant, unexpected, and unprecedented downturn in the housing market and home prices nationwide."

William Isaac, the former chairman of the FDIC, wrote:

Based on my review of the record in this matter, I hold the opinion, and I am prepared to testify, Mr. Killinger did not breach his fiduciary duties, violate any law or regulation, act with reckless disregard to the consequences of his actions or inactions, or otherwise engage in unsafe or unsound conduct.

If I had been provided prior to the 2008 financial crisis, on a no-name basis, the financial condition of a bank that had capital, nonperforming assets, and core funding similar to Washington Mutual's, I would have concluded the bank was likely in good condition and not in any imminent danger of failure. Indeed, in my experience, an institution with Washington Mutual's examination ratings and financial ratios has never before been seized by the US government.

Nothing has been brought to my attention, including the OCC's 15-day letter, to indicate Mr. Killinger did not act in absolutely good faith and try his utmost to further the interests of the bank. This fact alone sets this case apart from virtually every other enforcement action the OCC has taken against individuals over the past decade. There is no suggestion Mr. Killinger acted illegally, deceived regulators, or engaged in self-dealing to benefit himself at the expense of the institution.

The Asset Remix (AR) strategy [ie. The famous "High Risk Lending Strategy"] the bank's management proposed in 2004–05 and the board of directors approved was an appropriate business strategy for a savings association. The AR strategy as implemented by the bank was not a headlong plunge into greater credit risk but was instead a strategy that required and received constant reexamination and analysis of risk adjusted returns for higher yielding assets. The bank's AR strategy was adopted with a number of important safeguards and caps to control risks. These safeguards were monitored and the reports from regulators confirmed the bank indeed followed them. The overall AR strategy was suspended when the bank realized the housing market might be softening. This reflects vigilance and concern for the safe and sound operation of the institution.

The former FDIC chair continued:

It is fundamentally unfair to blame Mr. Killinger for allowing the bank to make stated income loans. Such loans were widespread at the time and other large banks and thrifts participated in them to a significantly greater extent than Washington Mutual. Regulators did not prohibit stated income loans or treat them as being unsafe or unsound lending practices.

My review of the Enterprise Risk Management function showed they had the resources necessary to conduct its functions adequately. There was no indication in my review of these reports, from the CERO or any other source, the ERM function did not have sufficient resources and independence or was not functioning effectively.

The oversight and discussion of Washington Mutual's risks were clearly important to Mr. Killinger. He developed a risk governance structure that was aligned with best practices in 2006 and made sure the directors were fully informed about risk exposures and the effectiveness of the risk management processes at the company. As CEO he also focused on ensuring the management-level ERM function was well-structured, well-resourced, independent of the business units and with leading ERM practices in the financial services industry.

Some 546 banks and thrifts failed from 2000 through 2013. Altogether I found just twenty institutions where CMPs (civil money penalties) were asserted after failure of a bank or thrift for safety and soundness infractions that took place prior to failure. I reviewed each of the twenty CMP cases and found none that could be fairly compared with the CMP contemplated against Mr. Killinger. Virtually every one of the twenty CMP cases involved fraud, personal dishonesty, criminal activity, inappropriate personal benefits, and/or violations of law—none of which is present in the circumstances involving Mr. Killinger.

In the case of Mr. Killinger, the record does not support a charge of personal dishonesty, criminal activity, inappropriate personal benefits, or violations of law. The FDIC brought a civil proceeding against Mr. Killinger and others and alleged none of these activities, much less proved them. In this conclusion, I hold the opinion, and I am prepared to testify, it would be a serious miscarriage of justice to impose civil money penalties on Mr. Killinger under the facts and circumstances of this case.

Michael Mancusi, former senior deputy comptroller of the OCC, also completed a full examination of all the regulatory reports and other documentation on Washington Mutual, as well as the testimony and written submissions to the PSI related to the bank. Mancusi wrote:

> I am prepared to testify Mr. Killinger did not act in a reckless manner, did not breach his fiduciary duties, did not violate any laws or regulations, and did not engage in unsafe and unsound practices. The losses were due entirely to the significant, unexpected, and unprecedented downturn in the housing market and home prices nationwide. Without the unprecedented levels of government intervention, many more financial institutions would have failed. The severity of the housing downturn was not forecasted with any reasonable accuracy by any experienced economist or market participant, including Federal Reserve Chairman Ben Bernanke.
>
> Again, Washington Mutual was rated 3 [until hours before the seizure], suggesting the regulators did not have a major safety/soundness issues with the bank leading up to its seizure.[26]

Former top OCC executive Mancusi also mentioned because the thrift industry was *required to hold 65 percent of its assets* in residential products like mortgages and mortgage-backed securities, the thrift industry was more vulnerable in the housing crisis. He did an analysis of 810 thrifts and found in 2008, thrifts had 57.4 percent of their assets in mortgages and MBSs, but an analysis of 8,305 commercial banks during the same time period showed they only had 29 percent of their assets in housing products.

Mancusi included in his report a 2013 independent research study by Lewtan, a sophisticated UK independent financial research firm. It analyzed a random sample of 3.5 million loans securitized from the six largest regulated bank lenders, including Citigroup, Countrywide, Bank of America, JPMorgan, Wells Fargo, and Washington Mutual. This sample analyzed loan characteristics and loan performance of the 3.5 million loans that were used in 1,114 securitizations in the calendar years 2004 to 2007.

This is one of the few research studies that have been performed to show the comparative quality of mortgage loans from the largest regulated mortgage originators. The performance data analyzed how each loan performed for five years after loan origination. Underperforming loans were defined as having at least one foreclosure notice, placement in the REO (real estate owned), or having been liquidated within the first sixty months after origination.

Chart 10-1 below identifies the issuer of the loans, the number of loans and the number of deals in the random sample. Only 10 percent of the loans were from Washington Mutual, which is a statistical indicator of the low level of Washington Mutual loans in securitizations in comparison to other banks.[27]

Chart 10-1: Random Sample of Bank Loans in Securitization

Bank Issuer	Number of Loans	Number of Deals
Countrywide	1,917,021	523
Wells Fargo	381,349	157
Washington Mutual	373,073	136
Citigroup	272,202	72
JPMorgan Chase	259,853	79
Bank of America	253,947	147
	3,457,445	1,114

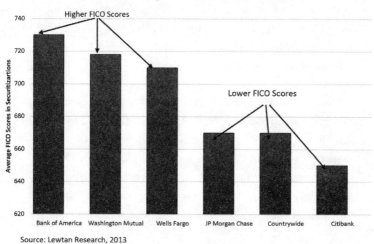

Chart 10-2: Average FICO Scores in Securitizations[28]

Source: Lewtan Research, 2013

The research showed Washington Mutual, Wells Fargo, and Bank of America had the best overall loan characteristics, with an average LTV around 72 percent and average FICO scores of around 720. Citibank had the poorest record, with average FICO scores of 645, and JPMorgan Chase had average FICO scores of around 670. Subprime is usually defined as having a FICO score under 660. Chart 10-2 shows the average FICO scores of loans in securitization from each of the banks.

The researchers measured the five-year performance of each of the loans in the sample. The best loan performance was again from Washington Mutual, Bank of America, and Wells Fargo, which all had a range from 12 to 18 percent of portfolios with underperforming loans—about half the rate of Countrywide, Citigroup, and JPMorgan Chase, which had the worst performances, with nearly 30 percent of their loans underperforming.

The research also measured the loan quality characteristics of low-doc or stated income loans. "Out of the entire set of loans analyzed, about half (1.8 million loans) were low-doc loans." This shows how prevalent low-doc or stated income loans were in all the large banks. Low-doc loans had approximately the same FICO scores and LTVs as the other half of the loans with full documentation. Again, JPMorgan Chase and Citigroup had the worst FICO scores at 680, and the best were Washington Mutual, Bank of America, and Wells Fargo, with FICO scores on stated income loans between 720 and 740 and LTVs of around 70 percent for low-doc loans—about the same scores they had for thirty-year fixed-rate loans.

The research concluded:

> All large banks were major players in the stated income lending market and the quality of Washington Mutual's low documenta-tion loans [stated income] was comparable to all of the large issuers. Washington Mutual cannot be accused of having worse performance on its low documentation loans than that of most if not all issuers. Again, there is no basis to single Washington Mutual out based on its stated income lending activities.

The full report of our defense was sent to the OCC on July 23, 2013, and we waited for a response.

In late fall there was a series of stories that Attorney General Eric Holder was nearing a decision on a number of probes involving large financial firms, and he planned in the coming months to announce new cases stemming from the economic meltdown. The 1989 FIRREA law had given the US attorney general up to ten years to investigate civil actions in banks. Nobody was out of the woods. While Holder was criticized for overstating past efforts, Holder said his marching orders to prosecutors around the country had been clear and forceful, and he "remains aggressive and will pursue these cases." Holder had been criticized in the press because he hadn't brought any criminal charges against bankers.[29] However, it was clear Holder would have done any-thing to have found any kind of a crime in the big banks.

Also, that fall, the DOJ and the US attorney for California shared with JPMorgan Chase's Dimon a draft of a ninety-two-page civil complaint they were prepared to file in federal court. The complaint documented the alleged role Chase had in underwriting fraudulent securities in the years leading up to the 2008 crisis. It was speculated the threat of the lawsuit forced Chase into a $13 billion settlement, at the time the largest ever for the DOJ.[30]

A couple of years later the media reported what they called the Jamie Dimon "Bastile Day screed" when Dimon ranted that "Some-how in this great American free enterprise, we no longer get it. We have become the most bureaucratic, confusing, litigious society on the planet. It's almost an embarrassment being an American citizen traveling around the world and listening to the stupid shit we have to deal with in this country."[31]

We started to add up all the fines some of the major banks had paid for their nefarious activities:

According to the website for the Office of the Comptroller of the Currency, JPMorgan Chase from 2011 to 2015 had a record number of civil money penalties (CMP)—more CMP fines and consent orders than all the other large banks COMBINED. Fines totaled over $1 billion for improper marketing and sale of credit protection products, bid rigging on financial products, improper debt collections, improper trading activities, unfair billing practices, violations of the Bank Secrecy Act, and unsafe practices in foreign exchange trading.[32]

In addition, JPMorgan Chase was fined more than $3 billion from the SEC and other regulatory bodies for "manipulative schemes to transform money-losing power plants into a powerful profit center, manipulating the bidding process for municipal securities, charging credit card customers for identity theft products they never received, and manipulating mortgage backed securities." The largest fine for nearly $1 billion was for the London trading debacle where the bank admitted it "violated banking rules by not properly overseeing its trading operations."[33] At the time the bank was also in talks with federal prosecutors who claimed the "bank turned a blind eye to the Madoff scheme."[34] The US AG's office for the Eastern District of California prosecutors found JPMorgan flouted federal laws with its sale of subprime mortgage securities from 2005 to 2007. The prosecutors had "preliminarily concluded the bank violated certain federal securities laws."[35]

None of the above fines and penalties involved any activities at Washington Mutual.

Citigroup also had its share of troubles with nearly $2 billion in fines, including ones from the Federal Trade Commission for predatory lending conduct and the Japanese authorities for manipulating bond prices and helping clients launder money and manipulate stock prices. The Fed issued a cease-and-desist order and fined them for forcing people to cosign loans when it wasn't necessary, and in 2005 the Fed and the OCC imposed a moratorium on any further large acquisitions until Citigroup cleaned up its risk management functions. The SEC twice imposed large fines for securities violations and the bank also paid fines for certifying FHA loans that didn't qualify.[36]

From 2009 through 2015, the six largest US bank holding companies paid about $130 billion in settlements, fines, and other costs related to the financial crisis. Bank of America paid $73.5 billion, JPMorgan Chase paid $26.4 billion, Citibank paid $13.1 billion, Wells Fargo paid $9.5 billion, Morgan Stanley paid $4.5 billion, and Goldman Sachs paid $4.1 billion.[37]

Despite hundreds of billions of dollars in fines and penalties from the Wall Street banks, none of their executives were personally fined, banned from banking, or penalized by the OCC, FDIC, DOJ, or any other federal agency. How could the OCC possibly now be thinking of fining and penalizing Washington Mutual executives, when neither the bank nor any of its executives had ever received a single fine, penalty, or formal enforcement order from any regulator?

During the fall, the OCC came back twice and asked for a tolling agreement to extend the life of their investigation. We didn't know how many years this would drag on. However, on December 3, nearly six months after Kerry's meeting with the OCC, we had a call from *Bloomberg News* about a rumored settlement with the OCC. They asked for our comments, but we didn't know what they were talking about. We hadn't heard from the OCC in weeks. The OCC had not even attempted to make a settlement. John was very surprised by this leak, because this would be a high-risk move for the OCC to leak this information. John believed this was again likely leaked by Senator Levin's office and advised us not to respond to *Bloomberg*. Within a couple of hours, *Bloomberg* printed a story on the rumor of a settlement, quoting Senator Levin.

A number of newspapers, including the *Seattle Times*, carried the *Bloomberg* article without calling us for confirmation. Their story said, "The OCC is weighing a settlement with Killinger, according to a person who was briefed and spoke on the condition of anonymity because the talks aren't public. The person who said the talks have entered the final stage didn't describe the terms being discussed." Senator Levin was quoted in the article saying the bank executives needed to be punished.[38]

The only other call we received from the media was from Dan Fitzpatrick of the *Wall Street Journal*. He wanted help with background about the *Bloomberg* story. He hoped for confirmation that "Kerry and two other ex–bank execs [were] in settlement talks with the OCC. It sounds like this may be premature based on our early reporting...we thought you could set us straight." These proceedings were supposed to be confidential, and we were again advised by our legal team to not respond to his call. Fitzpatrick called later and told us he couldn't get another source to confirm the OCC story, so they would not be printing the story. We were both relieved and impressed with his thoroughness and professionalism.

The next day, John left us a message:

The OCC has decided not to proceed against any of the Washington Mutual executives. [There was no settlement. The OCC decided to drop the case.] The OCC said if they are asked by the press about this, they will say no comment and encouraged us to do the same. They did not know where the press leaks came from. We strongly suspect they came from Senator Levin's office, who was probably upset when the OCC decided against proceeding.

We were impressed the OCC had courageously made the right decision, even though the political pressure from Levin must have been severe. We later heard Levin was furious no action was taken against the bank. His PSI report was not gaining traction, no major bill was going to have his name on it, and none of his false accusations panned out. He would soon retire from the senate.

2014

During 2014 we continued to work on the global bankruptcy settlement. Some of the creditors filed a rather flamboyant "Hail Mary" lawsuit, suing all the officers and directors, in an attempt to open up the $250 million 2008–2009 D&O insurance policy, but they had limited success. After six years of wrangling over the assets of the D&O insurance policies and the assets of the holding company, the global settlement was finally signed in late 2014 and the federal judge approved the $33 billion dispersion of the assets of the WMI holding company. The settlement put an end to all the lawsuits against the executives and board members.[39]

In January of 2014, the *Wall Street Journal* ran an op-ed piece on the legacy of Fed chair Bernanke.

> Mr. Bernanke was the board's intellectual leader in its decision to cut the Fed funds rate to 1% in June 2003 and keep it there for a year despite a rapidly accelerating economy and soaring commodity and real estate prices. The Fed's multiyear policy of negative real interest rates produced a credit mania that led to the housing bubble and bust. His record before the crisis was a clear failure. The Fed transcripts also make clear Mr. Bernanke underestimated the degree housing impacted the financial contagion, but so did most others.
>
> Less forgivable is Bernanke's refusal to acknowledge the Fed made any mistakes in the mania years.[40]

In the years following the financial crisis, more than 850 banks, hedge funds, financial corporations and associations hired over 3,000 lobbyists to eviscerate the reform bills according to the Center for Public Integrity. In financial services, 175 companies ranging from Goldman Sachs to the Private Equity Council hired lobbyists to weaken or eliminate reform proposals aimed at banks and the capital markets. They spent a total of $1.3 billion during 2009 and the first quarter of 2010.[41]

As 2014 came to a close, we were grateful to leave the hearings, mediations, and lawsuits behind. We had been living in the crucible for over seven years, so we were eager to finally be able to concentrate on our charitable foundation, our venture capital companies, and—most importantly—our friends and family. We have a large number of loyal and faithful friends and family that were always there for us and are blessed to have ten perfect grandchildren.

11

The Fast Buildup of the Next
Shadow Banking System

In the last century, this country has seen a number of serious financial crises—the 1929 stock market crash, the S&L crisis in the 1980s, the dot-com crash in the late 1990s, and the housing crisis in 2008. They all had similar causes: congressionally mandated federal deregulation that produced unregulated shadow financial systems, a bubble euphoria with the public, new unregulated financial products, and overheated asset and debt bubbles with lack of government oversight. Chances are the next financial crisis will also have those components.

The crash of 1929 occurred after a period of deregulation from Congress with presidential support. President Calvin Coolidge said, "The chief business of the American people is business," and President Hoover's Treasury secretary, Andrew Mellon, felt government should "keep its hands off business." So, when the president of National City Bank (now Citigroup) lobbied Congress for freedom to open dozens of foreign offices and engage in risky investment projects, his wishes were granted. The bank added 350 sales associates, and soon regulators discovered the associates were faking orders to inflate their bonuses. The bank developed a large portfolio of risky loans to European countries, especially Germany, that were suffering immensely after World War I.[1]

The economy in the 1920s was switching dramatically from the old industries of coal, railroads, and textiles into the new economy of manufacturing trucks, cars, radios, and consumer appliances. Cars were increasingly equipped with radios. In 1927 there were so many radio stations in operation that the Federal Radio Commission was formed to issue licenses and assign airwaves. Masses of people moved from the farm to the cities to work in the new factories and participate in city life.

The new consumer product manufacturers cleverly hooked up with the burgeoning New York industry of ad men, and soon newspapers were carrying attractive ads urging readers to buy all the hot new consumer products. In 1925 the first Sears retail store opened showcasing a number of new consumer products. In 1927 the first of two Norman Rockwell paintings appeared on the cover of the Sears catalog featuring a couple looking for engagement rings. The banner, "Satisfaction Guaranteed or Your Money Back," appeared on the catalog. In 1928, the first Craftsman tools were introduced in the stores and the catalogs.[2]

Banks got in the action by offering flexible loans with favorable payment plans. Most Americans could now afford to buy clothes, jewelry, appliances, cars, and vacations on credit. The rise of the new manufacturing climate produced overheated stock prices. General Motors' stock went up twentyfold and RCA went up seventyfold, and now everyone wanted to trade stock and look for the next GM and RCA. Women were not allowed to trade on the NYSE floor, but that didn't stop them. They started up an estimated five thousand women-only investment clubs around the country, and they were serious. One of the top groups in Manhattan met regularly at a suite in the Waldorf Astoria hotel, just down the street from the brand new Saks Fifth Avenue store. Some of the women did so well, it was determined there were more women than men paying taxes on incomes over $100,000. The banking house of Lawrence Stern and Company concluded women possessed 41 percent of the total wealth of the nation and did 85 percent of the spending.[3]

There wasn't much regulatory oversight over the banks, the stock market, or the new consumer product companies, and soon there were a number of shady players with questionable corporate ethics. Nobody suspected they would pay kickbacks to journalists to write favorable stories about their questionable companies.

The brokerage house of E. F. Hutton and others encouraged people to buy stocks on the margin and engage in naked short selling. Amateur and ill-informed speculators were betting on rumors. The number of brokerage houses doubled to over sixteen hundred in 1929. Right before the 1929 crisis hit, sixty of the top bankers in the country had purchased so much stock on the margin, they became deeply indebted to JPMorgan. Everyone was on a euphoric high. Joseph Kennedy knew it was time to get out of the market when he heard a shoeshine boy giving stock tips to strangers. The Federal Reserve asked Wall Street banks not to loan money to speculators, but nobody listened. The stock exchange was at record levels—out of proportion to the rise in corporate earnings. It now cost $500,000 to get a seat on the NYSE. Asset bubbles and debt were at record levels. However, employment was good and people were happy. It was the Jazz Age.[4]

Just weeks before the crash, President Hoover said, "The fundamental business of the country...is on a sound and prosperous basis." Then all of a sudden, consumers stopped feeding the system, the shaky corporations failed, and stock prices plummeted.

Then the system caved...fast. Bank deposits were not insured, so millions of Americans lost their savings. Half of the banks in the country closed, manufacturing slowed down, millions of jobs were lost. Germany and other countries were overleveraged and could no longer get credit or pay back their loans. Some historians posed the idea that the lack of credit and financing in Germany was one of the chief causes of the rise of the Nazi Party.

Congress convened a commission run by the Senate to investigate the crash, but nothing got done until an experienced New York assistant district attorney named Ferdinand Pecora took over the group. Although the commission was able to suggest appropriate legislation and more regulation for the banking industry, no one was sent to prison for their deeds leading up to the crisis. Pecora said, "Legal chicanery and pitch darkness were the bankers' allies." Congress passed a number of new regulations it thought would prevent future crises.

The crash caused a profound psychological impact on consumers, because they were so emotionally invested in the new economy and they lost so much. People became more interested in socialist and communist ideas. In 1932 the *Saturday Evening Post* asked economist John Maynard

Keynes if there had ever been anything like this before. He replied, "Yes. It was called the Dark Ages, and it lasted for four hundred years."[5]

Move forward about fifty years, and we are deep into the impending S&L crisis of the 1980s. The new deregulation movement of the 1980s was supported by presidents and members of Congress on both sides of the aisle. Bankers had spent millions lobbying Congress and President Reagan, so when the top executives of the big S&Ls came to President Reagan for help with deregulation, their wishes were granted. Reagan declared, "This is the first step in our comprehensive program of financial deregulation."

The states of California, Texas, Nevada, Oklahoma, and others quickly further deregulated their thrift charters, and hundreds of new, barely regulated shadow thrifts populated their states. Most of the banks and thrifts were run by professional bankers who took fewer risks, but states that allowed nonbanker developers and promoters to own thrifts ran into problems. The nonbank shadow system took its FSLIC insured deposits and invested in wild schemes of land flips, insider loans, daisy chains, kickbacks, and false documentation. The economy was booming; and everyone was happy and wanted to get in on the action. The unregulated business of brokered deposits and junk bonds supplied an endless supply of cash. Even the big commercial banks got in on the action, accepting brokered deposits and junk bonds to fund large investments in gas and oil drilling. Nobody suspected there would be kickbacks and commissions in the lightly regulated system. One thrift sold shaky junk bonds in its lobby, convincing people to trade their insured CDs for uninsured higher-interest junk bonds.

Just weeks before the crash, politicians were still extolling the virtues of the deregulated financial system.

The FHLBB finally intervened and shut down the worst players. The Department of Justice was called in, and over a thousand bankers were sent to prison. Millions of Americans lost their jobs and their savings. Thousands of banks and thrifts were shut down. Congress passed new regulations it thought would prevent future crises. All the big banks were infused with cash and were saved.

Moving forward another twenty years, the 2008 housing crisis occurred after presidents and congressional leaders of both parties imposed millions of new LMI loans on the banking system. President Clinton declared the loans would make it "easy for people to own their own homes and enjoy the rewards of family life." President George W. Bush proudly announced, "Part of being a secure America is to encourage homeown-ership." Fannie, Freddie, and all the regulated banks were expected to dramatically increase their LMI lending to meet presidential goals.

However, soon an unregulated shadow system of over three hundred thousand unregulated mortgage brokers originating subprime loans for over one hundred unregulated shadow subprime companies with shady ethics grew up overnight. These loans were sold to the lightly regulated Wall Street investment banks. The investment banks had spent millions lobby-ing Congress and regulators for deregulation and low capital requirements, and they got their wishes. The shadow subprime system grew unnoticed and between 2002 and 2007 originated and securitized 85 percent of the subprime loans that had the worst performance and became embedded in trillions of dollars of the unregulated CDOs and CDSs.

The unregulated shadow system combed the countryside looking for vulnerable customers to partake in a range of predatory loans, with high interest rates and questionable terms. No one suspected there would be kickbacks and high commissions. Popular TV programs heralded the rise of "flipping" properties, and the media wrote hopeful stories of people making it big with flipping.

Everything was going well—the stock market was at record levels and rising out of proportion to the rise in corporate earnings. Asset bubbles and debt were growing. Only weeks before the crash, Treasury Secretary Paulson and Federal Reserve chair Bernanke were repeatedly making statements that the worst was over and the economy was healthy.

Then the system caved...fast. Nearly all the major banks were on the verge of failure, but the Wall Street crowd was saved. Millions of Ameri-cans lost their homes and their jobs. Countries around the world were over-leveraged and had to take drastic steps to save their economies.

Congress convened two investigative groups run by the Senate to investigate the crash, but few people were satisfied with the results. Some legislation was enacted, but Wall Street managed to lobby the legislation into oblivion.

The crash of 2008 caused a profound psychological impact on con-sumers, because they were so emotionally invested in the economy and lost so much. Citizens became more politically active with left-wing Oc-cupy Wall Street movements and the right-wing Tea Party movements. Presidential candidates extolled the virtues of socialism on one end and conservative protectionism on the other end. We are still living with the results of these movements.

Decades ago, economist John Kenneth Galbraith believed many of the lessons of the 1929 crash, having been digested in the past, were in danger of being forgotten. He was right.

We have lived through a number of banking crises and have not forgotten the lessons learned in each crisis. We wrote this book to identify the behind-the-scenes causes of the 2008 financial crisis that didn't get much attention during the crisis and warn the public that many of the same asset and debt bubbles before the last crisis have become even bigger now. We are hoping our government can be better organized and much more transparent in the future than it was in 2008.

We are generally hopeful optimists but believe it is wise to continually assess risks that might lead to the next financial crisis. Since the last financial crisis, we have enjoyed a period of generally improving economic growth, record low unemployment, low inflation, extraordinarily low interest rates, a booming stock market, and a strong housing market. Some refer to this period as a "goldilocks economy," but the boom has increasingly benefited the top percentile of families, leaving the majority of US families saddled with an enormous amount of debt and struggles with their budget dollars.

Before we can move forward, we have to understand just how pervasive the shadow banking industry can be. The last financial crisis was severe and impacted regulated banks as well as the unregulated shadow banking system. It also dramatically affected the average family, who lost a substantial part of their net worth and after over ten years still haven't caught up.

Much of the shadow banking system collapsed during the depths of the financial crisis. The unregulated subprime mortgage originators were completely wiped out. However, investment banks, mutual funds, and mega–insurance companies like AIG were given billions in government bailouts. Thousands of thrift and community banks were eliminated. Wall Street banks were especially well positioned because they controlled nationwide branch banking networks and were showered with billions of dollars of new capital.

Most regulated banks had strong profits and stock price performance over the decade following the financial crisis. Chart 11-1 shows the market capitalization of the five largest regulated banks (JPMorgan Chase, Bank of America, Citigroup, Wells Fargo, and US Bank), increased more than ninefold from $138 billion at the market bottom on March 2, 2009, to nearly $1.3 trillion at the beginning of 2020. This

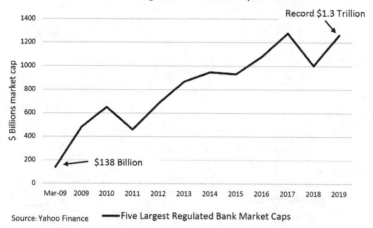

Chart 11-1: Five Largest Bank Market Capitalization

Source: Yahoo Finance ━━━Five Largest Regulated Bank Market Caps

easily outpaced gains in the overall stock market. JPMorgan Chase particularly benefited over this period from the addition of Washington Mutual's outstanding retail branching network, solid credit card operations, and industry-leading multifamily lending business. It also benefited from the dramatic increase in housing prices and the positive impact that had on Washington Mutual's loan portfolios. By the beginning of 2020, JPMorgan Chase's market capitalization had risen to $440 billion from only $60 billion in March 2009.

Banking regulators, armed with new legislative powers after the 2008 crisis, kept regulated banks on a short leash by demanding high levels of capital, stringent lending standards, and limited risk taking. Banks were required to pass stress tests, which showed they could withstand just about any economic crisis. Banks also benefited from sharply declining credit costs and reversing out some of the outsized loan-loss reserves taken at the height of the financial crisis. If Washington Mutual had remained independent, there is no question profitability would have snapped back as housing prices in its key markets of California, Florida, and Washington recovered quickly and increased to record levels. Chart 11-2 shows how residential loan losses declined following the financial crisis for regulated banks. Washington Mutual's portfolio would have performed even better given how quickly housing prices recovered in its key markets.

Regulatory oversight of banks continues to be strong, and we believe the industry is currently operating in a safe and sound manner. On a cautionary note, some banks are once again relaxing lending

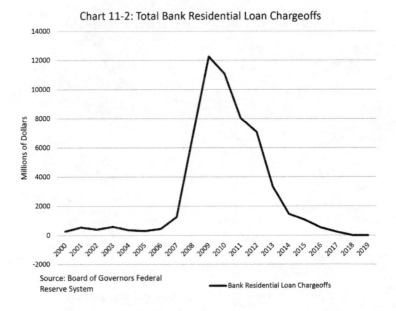

Chart 11-2: Total Bank Residential Loan Chargeoffs

Source: Board of Governors Federal
Reserve System

standards as competition from the unregulated shadow bank system intensifies. We also note Wall Street has been successful in lobbying Congress and the regulators to roll back some of the restrictions and oversight enacted following the financial crisis. Overall, though, we view regulated banks as financially strong and well positioned to withstand an economic downturn.

We believe the regulated banks will likely increase their assets in line with GDP growth but will continue to lose market share to the quickly growing unregulated shadow banking system. Regulated banks have the advantage of being able to accept insured deposits, but they are restricted by regulatory oversight and are limited to permissible business activities. As shown in Chart 11-3, the current shadow bank system's assets as a percent of GDP are larger and growing faster than regulated banks' assets. We expect this trend to continue and encourage policy makers to monitor developing risks from the quickly growing shadow banks.

The Shadow Banking System

There is not a universal definition of shadow banks, but most data sources define shadow banks as those financial institutions not regulated by a US federal banking regulator and not authorized to accept

Chart 11-3: Shadow Bank System Asssets Are Larger and Growing
Faster Than Regulated Bank Assets

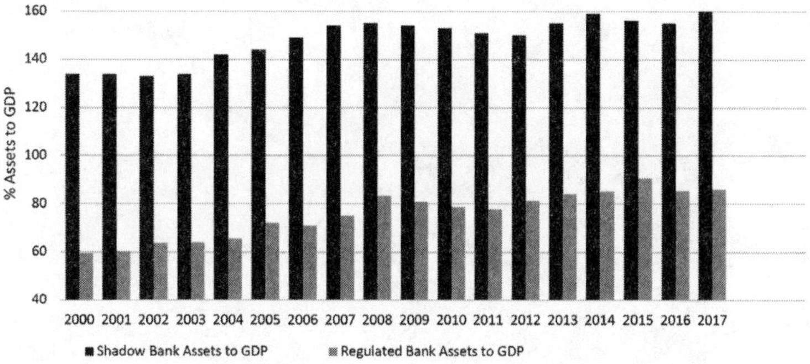

Shadow Bank Assets to GDP   Regulated Bank Assets to GDP

Source: World Bank and Federal Reserve Board of Governors

federally insured deposits. In the US, shadow banks include investment banks, mortgage brokers, money market funds, ETFs, mutual funds, insurance companies, hedge funds, private equity funds, venture capital funds, payday lenders, online lenders, and tech companies offering payments and other financial services.[6]

The shadow banking system of 2002–2007 originated and securitized 85 percent of all the subprime loans and was a major contributor to the last financial crisis (refer to Chart Intro-1). The shadow banking system also developed a significant number of the CDOs and was involved in substantial creation of the multitrillion-dollar naked CDS market. As the financial crisis unfolded, federal banking regulators, Treasury, and the Federal Reserve seemed to have little knowledge of the scope or condition of the shadow banking system, which led to poor decisions and little progress in correcting the deteriorating situation.

Shadow bank activities declined immediately after the financial crisis but have now grown to surpass previous peaks. Some of the growth of shadow banks no doubt grew out of regulatory restrictions on regulated banks. Currently, the majority of all residential mortgage originations are made by unregulated shadow banks such as Quicken Loans, United Shore, Fareway Independent Mortgage, Loan Depot, and Caliber Home Loans. Many regulated banks have concluded the low profit margins, regulatory costs, and legal risks associated with originating residential mortgages made that business unattractive. Chart 11-4 shows shadow banks filled the void and in 2019 originated the

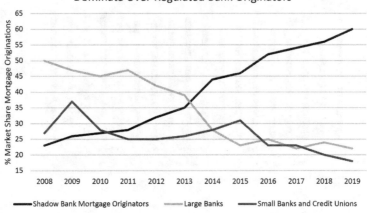

Chart 11-4: Shadow Bank Mortgage Originators now Dominate Over Regulated Bank Originators

Source: Mortgage Bankers Association

majority of all new mortgage loans, while regulated banks and credit unions have declining market shares.[7]

Other areas currently providing rapid growth for shadow banks include student lending, leveraged lending, corporate lending, residential mortgage lending, and consumer lending. Investor demand has also returned for collateralized debt obligations, collateralized loan obligations (CLOs), and various exotic instruments at the center of the last financial crisis. More and more asset categories with ever relaxed underwriting standards are once again being packaged and sold as CDOs and CLOs to investors in both the US and around the world.

Another rapidly growing shadow banking activity is exchange traded funds (ETFs), which are investment funds traded on stock exchanges. They hold assets and operate with an arbitrage mechanism designed to keep shares trading close to its net asset value. They have grown dramatically over the past decade when liquidity was ample and financial asset prices were increasing. As shown in Chart 11-5, ETFs have grown eightfold from $531 billion in 2008 to $4 trillion at the beginning of 2020. ETFs are an attractive, low-cost way to execute investment strategies and are on a trajectory for continued rapid growth. However, we simply do not know how ETFs will perform under stress conditions.[8]

Other shadow banking assets, such as hedge funds, doubled from $1.4 trillion in 2008 to $3.1 trillion at the beginning of 2020. Meanwhile, private equity assets grew from $1.4 trillion to $2.5 trillion over

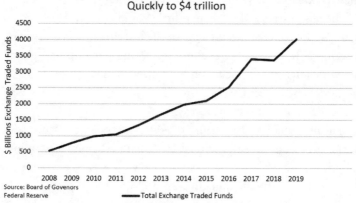

Chart-11-5: Total Exchange Traded Funds (ETFs) Growing Quickly to $4 trillion

Source: Board of Govenors
Federal Reserve   ━━━Total Exchange Traded Funds

this period. Of special note, total private market instruments, which include private equity, closed-end real estate, private debt, natural resources, and infrastructure, grew from $2.5 trillion to $5 trillion since the financial crisis. Just as with ETFs, we simply don't know how these vehicles will perform under stress conditions.[9]

An important issue facing many shadow bank lenders and investors is the valuation of privately held companies. Rapidly growing private companies often require several rounds of financing before they become publicly owned. There are incentives for investors, managers, and sponsors to have valuations rise on each round of financing. Is this rise in valuation legitimate or just another daisy chain where investors sell assets back and forth at ever increasing prices? In several cases the private valuations exceeded the valuations placed on the companies by the public market. So-called unicorn companies are those private companies valued at $1 billion or more. In June of 2020, 600 companies with a total valuation of $2 trillion were classified as unicorn companies. There is a significant risk that valuations of these unicorn companies will need to be written down if economic conditions soften or the stock market declines.[10]

In spite of the above potential risks, we view the shadow banking system as an important and essential part of the financial system. Many innovative ideas are developed and grown by shadow banks. Less regulatory oversight fosters innovation and flexibility to adapt products and services to customer demands. ETFs, private equity, hedge funds, and CDOs are a great example of products that revolutionized how investments could be tailored to very specific investor needs. Most of these products have performed as expected over time. However, under conditions of stress, when there is little liquidity, these products could perform poorly. This was the case in the last financial crisis, when the freezing of liquidity led to subprime mortgage loan prices plummeting, with a magnified impact on both prime and subprime CDOs and credit default swaps. This in turn helped lead the US and many parts of the world into the Great Recession.

The deregulation that occurred before the 2008 crisis caused many of the problems with the unregulated shadow system. The hundred subprime unregulated shadow banks that wrote 85 percent of the worst of the subprime loans quickly grew and quickly imploded. Federal regulators need to watch the growth and the integrity of the quickly growing new unregulated shadow system. If someone had been watching the integrity of the shadow system before the 2008 crisis, many of the problems could have been averted.

Most of the unregulated instruments like ETFs, CDOs, and CLOs are collectively much larger today than subprime mortgage loans leading up to the last financial crisis. ETFs in particular have not been tested under stress conditions. Their phenomenal growth the past decade has been during a period of excess liquidity and generally rising asset and debt prices. We are not particularly concerned with ETFs tied to large liquid equity or fixed-income markets. However, many ETFs are tied to illiquid or leveraged instruments, which may someday experience conditions where pricing is unknown and liquidity is impossible. We just don't know how ETFs would perform if some catastrophe hit and hundreds of billions of dollars of ETFs needed to liquidate positions because of investor selling. It is possible this could lead to instability and contribute to the next economic downturn.

Big Techs and Banks

An exciting but potentially destabilizing development is the growth of financial services products by large tech companies. Big technology firms such as Amazon, Facebook, Google, Alibaba, and Tencent have grown very quickly over the past twenty years. They all developed new business models that captured enormous data about their large customer bases. Use of that customer data led to massive revenue from product sales and advertising.

The major American big tech companies of Facebook, Amazon, Alphabet (Google), Apple, and Microsoft had a combined market capitalization of $7.1 trillion by November 2020. By comparison, the five largest US banks had combined market capitalization of only $900 billion.[11] The large tech companies have large customer bases, high consumer trust, little regulation, excellent technology, and continual R&D investment in new products. Banks, on the other hand, are highly regulated, have lower customer satisfaction, and invest relatively little in new products. Over a period of time, we believe big tech companies are likely to focus more and more on using their extensive customer database to continue to market more financial services to their customers.

While the business is still in its infancy, big tech companies are beginning to roll out financial products to their customers. Examples include Amazon, which launched a credit card with 5 percent cash back on Amazon purchases to its prime customers. Apple launched a credit card branded as an Apple product, rather than branded by the bank that provided the back-room services. Google launched a checking account product. Facebook is working on a global currency with blockchain technology.[12] PayPal operates a worldwide online payment system as an alternative to regulated banks. PayPal's Venmo provides a digital platform for forty million people making over $27 billion of payments each quarter, growing at a 64 percent annual rate.[13]

Regulations require a banking partner for some of these services so JPMorgan Chase provides the back office for Amazon's card, and Goldman Sachs does the same for Apple's card. But in the future, the big tech companies will be in position to control the customers and take more and more of the economics away, relegating the banks to low-margin back-office activities.

Smaller companies embracing technology are also making inroads. Online real estate and mortgage originators like Redfin, Zillow, and Quicken Loans are capturing increasing market share at the expense of traditional licensed Realtors and regulated bank residential mortgage originators. Peer-to-peer lenders like Prosper, Sofi, and Lending Club are capturing substantial market share from regulated banks.

It will be intriguing to watch new product development and marketing approaches by the unregulated tech companies. They have enormous capital and the ability to quickly make acquisitions and acquire talent to bring new products to market. It is easy to visualize a suite of financial services offered by many of the large tech companies that meet most financial-services needs for most Americans. We believe regulated banks will find it increasingly difficult to compete and may increasingly become the low-margin back offices for products requiring the involvement of regulated banks.

Most regulated banks have relatively high cost structures, including large networks of physical bank branches and ATMs. These physical facilities were a big competitive advantage in the past but will increasingly become costly burdens as technology evolves and customer needs change.

We are reminded of the impact Amazon had on Main Street retailers as it developed superior services at lower costs for consumers. We could not have imagined twenty-five years ago how we would make purchases online with same-day delivery. We couldn't imagine prices would be a third less than charged by our neighborhood stores and there wouldn't be any shipping charges. And we couldn't have imagined we would get 5 percent cash back by using Amazon's credit card. Even if we had imagined this scenario, we might have thought somebody like Sears would have been the one who pulled it off. After all, Sears had the most extensive experience in catalog sales and could have put the catalog online with better deals for more products. The winners were clearly those that didn't have to protect their existing business models and didn't have an extensive network of physical stores. Amazon had nothing to protect and could develop a better model from scratch.

Also, worth watching very carefully are the payment system models in our future. Modern payment systems are dominated by debit cards, credit cards, electronic funds transfer direct credits and debits, and e-commerce payment systems. Checks are rapidly declining as a source of payment. The key for payment systems in the future will be low-friction (transaction) costs, convenience, speed, and trackability. For many people—especially the young—mobile devices will be the preferred method for making payments. Mobile payment volume is growing in excess of 50 percent per year and is expected to grow at this rate for the foreseeable future.[14] For example, China and South Korea are the two top markets leading the way in mobile payments. China already has 92 percent of large city dwellers and 47 percent of the rural population using WeChat Pay or Alipay on their mobile devices.[15]

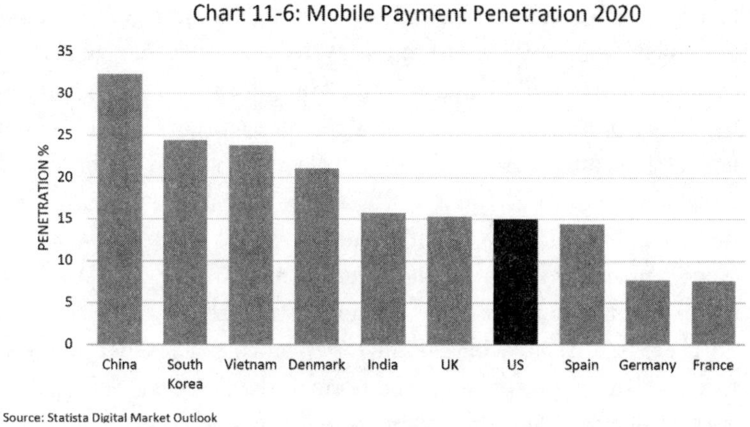

Chart 11-6: Mobile Payment Penetration 2020

Source: Statista Digital Market Outlook

Chart 11-6 illustrates that in 2020 in China, 35 percent of all the payments were from mobile devices, while the US lagged with less than 15 percent penetration.

The US is behind China and South Korea, but we expect the mobile device penetration rate to grow dramatically in the US over the next few years. It is unclear what the long-term role of regulated banks versus big tech companies will be in future payment systems. It is highly likely the large transaction costs currently charged by credit card companies will come down substantially. It is also likely blockchain technology will be implemented to allow faster and more secure settlements.

It is possible some form of digital currency will become widely accepted for payments around the world. To be used as a serious currency, a stable exchange rate is required. While Bitcoin is the most well-known form of digital currency, it is unlikely to ever be significant because its price is so volatile. We think it might be possible for a company or group of companies with trillions of dollars of combined market cap to issue and essentially guarantee a stable digital currency value. We believe worldwide demand for a cybercurrency (aka, cryptocurrency) with a stable price and low transaction costs is massive enough that even Facebook wants to get involved. Regulated banks, banking regulators, and central banks will no doubt do whatever they can to limit development of new cybercurrencies, but many people want an alternative to the current payments system.

Some people want to be off the grid, so to speak. Others trust their personal data in the hands of big tech companies more than in the hands of big banks or the federal government. Trust in regulated banks plummeted following the last financial crisis, with less than 30 percent of people saying they "had a great deal or quite a bit of confidence in banks," according to a 2018 Gallup poll. The same goes for trust in our federal government. As highlighted in Chart 11-7, trust in our federal government continues on a downward trajectory. A poll by the Pew Research Center in 2019 revealed that a historic low of 17 percent of Americans say they can trust the government in Washington, DC, to do what is right "just about always or most of the time."

There is a narrative developing for cryptocurrencies that may lead to broader acceptance than would normally be expected. Nobel Laureate Dr. Robert Shiller in his recent book, *Narrative Economics*, discussed Bitcoin as a membership token in the world economy.[16] Although we don't think Bitcoin will be a winning currency because of its volatility, cybercurrencies with stable values will make their owners citizens of the world and participants in exciting technology capabilities without borders. We totally understand the need to rein in the use of cybercurrencies for illegal activities, but we expect government attempts to stop cybercurrency development will be futile over time.

To frame what could happen between big tech companies and regulated banks in the US, it is instructive to examine what is happening in China. Big tech company Ant Group, formerly known as Alipay, was originally formed by e-commerce giant Alibaba. In addition to its Alipay payment systems, Ant Group originates microloans, savings accounts, mutual funds, small business and personal loans, insurance-like products, and credit scores to its Alipay customers. Ant Group claims to serve over 1.3 billion customers including 900 million people in China. The company plans to expand its customer base to two billion over the next decade and to "dramatically grow its customers outside China," according to Douglas Feagin, president of Ant Group's international business group.[17]

Ant Group is currently a private company with an estimated value exceeding $300 billion, making it the most highly valued private fin-tech company in the world. The company announced plans to go public and list its shares on the Hong Kong and Shanghai Stock Exchange. So far, the US has restricted Ant Group's expansion to this country. Protectionism in the US, however, will not stifle Ant's continued development of technology and lower transaction costs. Ant

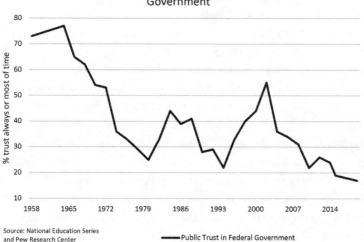

Chart 11-7: Declining Public Trust in US Federal Government

Source: National Education Series and Pew Research Center

━━━ Public Trust in Federal Government

Group's leadership in taking customer information to develop credit scoring systems will also give them a competitive advantage.

Ant Group's Sesame Credit has developed a comprehensive credit/social scoring system that is much more encompassing than credit scores recorded in the US.[18] Sesame compiles a large range of financial and social behaviors. People with high scores can rent cars without a deposit, skip hospital waiting lines, and enjoy special waiting rooms in rail stations. We recently toured China and talked with a number of citizens and guides about the new Chinese facial recognition system. They told us hundreds of thousands of cameras surround the large cities and the government collects data on people's behavior to create "social scores" for their citizens. If you jaywalk, rob, harm people, have a car accident, or other "violations," the cameras recognize your face and record your violations. We were told if your score is low, you could lose jobs or educational opportunities or even the ability to travel. Nearly all the Chinese people we talked with thought the system was good, because it would help the government maintain peace and order.

We envy the Chinese people's faith in their government, however, the advances in facial recognition, combined with advanced techniques in financial behavior and social analysis of data, hold Orwellian warnings. Private companies or the government could eventually control our behavior more than we may want. How can we promote advances in technology and still maintain our privacy? Will security, safety, peace, and order become more important than privacy? We will be wrestling with these questions for years to come.

From a big-picture standpoint, the US has traditionally been the world's leader in technology. However, in the area of financial technology, our country appears to be a laggard. Protecting the high cost structures of retail bank branches, ATMs, high credit card interest rates, high credit/debit card transaction fees, and high bank regulatory costs may limit regulated bank competitiveness. Said another way, large regulated banks with the help of Secretary Paulson's plan to eliminate thrifts and community banks created a big economic moat around their core businesses. This moat may become less valuable as new competitors enter the field.

The Financial Stability Board was established in 2009 by G20 leaders to identify and address vulnerabilities in the global financial system. This group has identified the growing presence of high-tech and other shadow banks as key concerns moving forward. It notes Alibaba and other high-tech companies, in terms of assets, are catching up to China's largest bank, the Industrial and Commerce Bank of China. It also notes competition from big tech companies could reduce profitability and stability of funding sources for regulated banks.

We expect shadow banks and big tech companies to capture large and growing market shares in many areas of financial services. Regulated banks will continue to be important players, but these banks will be saddled with high cost structures, limited capital, and heavy regulatory oversight.

We expect regulated banks to continue to dominate commercial lending, credit cards, investment banking, and payments for the foreseeable future. However, shadow banks like asset manager BlackRock, with $7.8 trillion of assets under management, will probably continue to dominate the asset management business.[19] The same goes for the management of hedge funds, mutual funds, ETFs, private equity, and venture capital. As big tech companies gear up in payments and other services targeted to consumers and small businesses, regulated bank market shares may come under pressure.

12

The Makings of the Next
Financial Crisis

Human nature and bubble thinking lead us to think the longer the good times roll, the more likely they are to continue forever, but history teaches us periods like this are always followed by major corrections. Sometimes risks that are clearly in front of us are glossed over because they haven't yet caused major problems. We are reminded of the 2007 World Economic Forum in Davos Switzerland when we joined a sparsely attended session on growing systemic risks and then went to a highly attended session on growth opportunities in private equity, hedge funds, and highly leveraged transactions. The first session on growing systemic risks was insightful, but nobody wanted to hear it. Humans tend to have a viral case of confirmation bias—if we believe something is true, we won't even recognize the facts that would disprove our bias.

We see several problems developing today that could lead to the next financial crisis. We were very critical of the Federal Reserve's role in the last financial crisis. Instead of infusing liquidity and containing a cyclical downturn in housing, it withheld liquidity and fueled a dramatic fall in asset prices, especially housing prices. Declining housing prices and rising unemployment led to skyrocketing loan delinquencies and poor performance of both prime and subprime mortgage loans. This loss of faith and panic about mortgage products led to poor performance of collateralized debt obligations and synthetic instruments such as credit default swaps. Poor performance, along with the huge mistake of letting Lehman Brothers fail, led to a total freezing of the capital markets and a cascading deflation of asset prices. Housing prices, stock prices, mortgage-backed securities prices, and secondary loan market prices all tumbled to values significantly below their intrinsic values.

There is no question a housing bubble was inflating in the early 2000s. Beginning in 2001, the Case-Shiller National Home Price Index (Chart 12-8) rose at a rate substantially above the trend line and well above the rate of inflation. It is reasonable to expect housing prices to rise modestly faster than the rate of inflation over the long run, but from the end of 2000 to the middle of 2006, the Case-Shiller National Home Price Index rose by 70 percent, versus about a 15 percent cumulative increase in the consumer price index. Even factoring in scarcity of land, building restrictions, changes in square footage, and amenities, housing prices were rising much too quickly to be sustainable over the long run. Housing prices in many urban centers grew even faster than the national average. Our analysis shows housing prices were overvalued nationally by about 15 to 20 percent at the peak in 2006.

To deal with an inflating housing bubble, the Federal Reserve (Fed) appropriately tightened monetary policy in 2004 and 2005 when it raised the fed funds rates by about three hundred basis points.[1] If it had stopped there and allowed those restrictive actions to take hold, we believe housing prices would have corrected in an orderly manner. However, the Fed incorrectly feared inflation was likely to increase and decided to increase the fed funds rate by another 125 basis points in 2006 and 2007. This move choked off liquidity and triggered a more severe correction in housing prices. We believe the Fed's miscues caused a manageable housing downturn to devolve into a chaotic downturn never before seen in our country's history.

Even during the Great Depression, the Case-Shiller National Home Price Index (retroactively developed) declined by only 4.7 percent from peak to trough. But during the 2008 crisis, national housing prices declined by nearly a third. The Case-Shiller 20-City Composite Home

Price Index declined by 33.9 percent while the Case Shiller-National Housing Price Index declined 27.4 percent from peak to trough. Several markets, such as Los Angeles, Phoenix, Las Vegas, and Miami, suffered declines of 40 percent or more.

To the Fed's credit, it finally recognized its mistake and infused the system with massive liquidity in late 2008 and 2009. Its actions, along with important legislation to stimulate the economy and bail out the financial system, stabilized the economy and asset prices. By early March 2009, common stock prices bottomed out at 6,470 for the Dow Jones Industrial Average. Housing prices similarly began to bottom out by mid-2009. The Case-Shiller 20-City Composite Home Price Index stabilized at 140.8 in May 2009, but it took nearly three years for most regions of the country to stabilize. The housing bubble was most pronounced in major cities, so the decline in prices was generally greater in the major cities and less in the rural areas.

There is a very simple relationship between asset prices and liquidity. If you withhold liquidity, fewer buyers have cash to pay for assets and prices tend to fall. Provide adequate liquidity and asset prices tend to perform closer to historic norms and closer to their intrinsic values. Provide excess liquidity and more buyers will tend to drive prices up much higher than historic norms. Whenever asset prices rise quickly or to unsustainable levels, there is the risk of an asset bubble.

There are many examples of past asset bubbles. Some of the better known are the tulip bulb mania of the 1600s and the South Sea bubble of the 1700s. In the past one hundred years, we had the Florida real estate bubble of the 1920s, the stock market bubble of the late 1920s, the Japan asset price bubble of the mid-1980s, the dot-com bubble of the late 1990s, and the US housing bubble of the mid-2000s. All of these bubbles were accompanied by speculation brought on by buyers loaded with cash chasing limited assets.

When asset prices are rising, just about everyone is happy. Rising asset prices increase consumer confidence, generate more tax revenues, create new jobs, lead to increased consumer and business spending, and increase consumer net worth. Politicians are usually the first to take credit for rising asset prices. Wall Street will do anything to keep it going and have testified they will "keep dancing till the music stops."

The challenge, of course, is asset prices cannot increase at high rates forever. When an asset price exceeds its intrinsic value, price declines or underperformance almost always occur. Each of the bubbles noted above were followed by periods of severe price corrections. Sometimes those price corrections occurred quickly, and other times they extended over a period of years. Corrections from the stock market bubble of the late 1920s and the bursting of the dot-com bubble were quick and severe. Correction of the Japanese asset price bubble of the late 1980s was severe and led to twenty-five years of underperformance.

Central Banks Flood the System With Liquidity

The Fed's actions in 2008 and 2009 were bold and somewhat innovative. Instead of just expanding the money supply, it stepped up and also guaranteed bank debt and money market funds and purchased unprecedented amounts of treasuries, mortgage-backed securities, and other high-quality debt obligations. These actions simultaneously drove short-term interest rates to near zero and long-term interest rates down. The Fed historically focused its policies on managing short-term interest rates, but this time its actions directly impacted long-term interest rates and helped shape investor decisions about where to invest.

The Fed has decades of experience in managing short-term interest rates through its monetary policy. However, it has little experience in managing multitrillion-dollar portfolios of purchased debt securities over long periods of time. Fed actions to purchase low-risk assets drove those prices up and yields down. This in turn encouraged investors to purchase other higher-risk assets such as common stocks, corporate

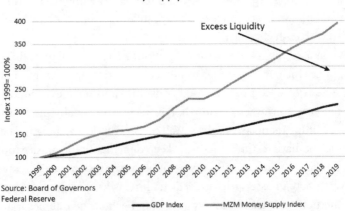

Chart 12-1: Money Supply Grows Faster than GDP

Source: Board of Governors
Federal Reserve

bonds, real estate, and other assets. We simply do not know all the ramifications from supplying excess liquidity and maintaining low short- and long-term interest rates for over a decade.

Chart 12-1 illustrates how the Fed accelerated money supply growth from 2007 through 2019. Over that period, money supply as measured by MZM Money Stock grew by 9.1 percent per year, while the GDP grew by only 4.0 percent per year. MZM is a preferred measure of money supply because it includes money market funds in addition to the conventional measure of M2—cash and equivalents less time deposits.

Excess liquidity by the Fed led to extraordinarily low interest rates over the past decade. The fed funds rate, which is typically above the rate of inflation, fell below the rate of inflation throughout most of this period. As illustrated in Chart 12-2, the fed funds rate averaged only 0.7 percent versus an average of 1.8 percent for inflation as measured by the CPI. When the Fed funds rate is below the rate of inflation, the real interest rate is negative. Many economists believe negative real interest rates in the early 2000s caused the housing bubble just a few years later. Once again, we are now experiencing negative real interest rates which are leading to growing asset and debt bubbles. These low interest rates enticed corporations, consumers, and governments to borrow heavily. This resulted in an explosion of debt, which has led to a very leveraged situation with consumers, corporations, and governments taking on more debt than ever before.

After the 2008 crisis the Fed augmented its easy money policy with unprecedented asset purchases. The Fed's goal was to reduce long-term interest rates and to encourage investors to shift into higher-risk assets.

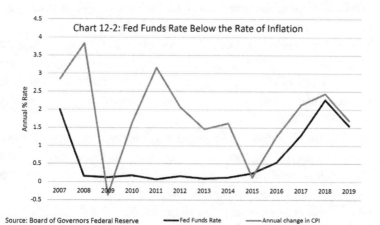

Chart 12-2: Fed Funds Rate Below the Rate of Inflation

Source: Board of Governors Federal Reserve   ━━━Fed Funds Rate   ━━━Annual change in CPI

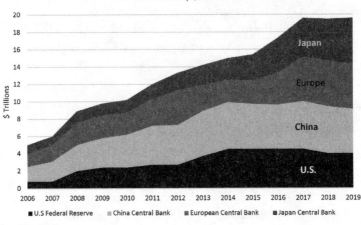

Chart 12-3: Central Banks Grow Their Balance Sheets From $5 Trillion to Nearly $20 Trillion

Source: Haver Analytics

The program, known as quantitative easing, began in late 2008 when the Fed's total bond holdings were only $800 billion. By March 2009 the Fed's bond holdings had increased to $1.75 trillion. In November 2010 the Fed announced a new program to expand purchases by $600 billion, and a third round of purchases was announced in September 2012. By 2014, the Fed's balance sheet had ballooned to $4.5 trillion and remained between $4 trillion and $4.5 trillion through early 2020.[2]

Chart 12-3 illustrates how other central banks around the world followed the US Federal Reserve's lead. Both the Bank of Japan and the European Central Bank increased their balance sheets from less than $2 trillion in 2006 to over $5 trillion by the beginning of 2020. The Bank of Japan was particularly aggressive in its asset purchases by including higher-risk common stocks and ETFs in its portfolio.

Not to be outdone, the Central Bank of China expanded its balance sheet from $2 trillion to over $5 trillion. Combined, the four largest central banks of the US, Japan, Europe, and China increased their balance sheets from $5 trillion in 2006 to nearly $20 trillion by the beginning of 2020.

The world has never experienced a ten-year period when all major central banks provided so much excess liquidity. Excess liquidity for over a full decade is almost guaranteed to produce unintended consequences. We believe those unintended consequences are likely to include potential asset and debt bubbles, which could easily become the catalysts for the next serious economic recession and possibly new financial crises. We believe the economies in many parts of the world, including the United States, have become overleveraged and are vulnerable to disruptive events such as trade wars, natural disasters, pandemics, and terrorism.

We have identified six asset bubbles and six debt bubbles that are so large they are worth particular attention, as the bursting of one or more of these bubbles could easily lead to an economic downturn and possibly the next financial crisis.

Asset Bubbles

1. Common Stock Bubble

In the last decade, stock prices have benefited from strengthening corporate profits plus investor willingness to pay higher prices for those earnings. Expansive central bank policies flooded the system with liquidity, and investors responded as expected. Flush with low-cost cash and looking for alternatives to low-yielding Treasury securities, investors poured trillions of dollars into a limited supply of common stocks. The natural outcome was a decade of rising stock prices. From its low of 6,470 in March 2009, the Dow Jones Industrial Average rose four-fold to 28,538 by the beginning of 2020. This increase significantly outpaced the growth of earnings and the overall economy. Chart 12-4 shows the dramatic rise in stock prices over the past decade to record levels. The question, of course,

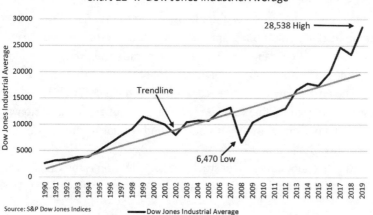

Chart 12-4: Dow Jones Industrial Average

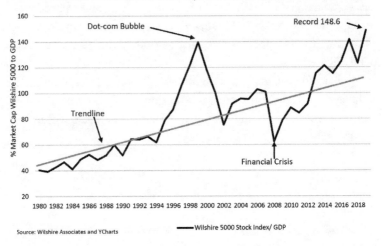

Chart 12-5: Total U.S. Market Capitalization to GDP: Buffett Ratio

Source: Wilshire Associates and YCharts — Wilshire 5000 Stock Index/ GDP

is are stock prices fairly valued or are they approaching the bubble status experienced in the late 1920s or the dot-com bubble of the late 1990s?

There are two measures of stock market value that have been reasonably accurate over the years. The first measure is the ratio of the total US stock market capitalization to the GDP of the US as shown in Chart 12-5. This measure is sometimes referred to as the Buffett ratio, because well-known investor Warren Buffett has referred to it over the years as a good measure of value. At the beginning of 2020, the total market capitalization of the US stock market was $34 trillion, which is a record 148.6 percent of the US GDP.

We believe corporations are gradually becoming more profitable due to technology and efficient use of capital, so it is understandable investors would pay more for stocks as a percentage of the GDP over time. This is why we show a gradually rising trend line. We include a trend line in many of our graphs to show our best estimate of a normal or intrinsic value over time. These are not statistical averages and are subjective because we factor in many variables.

The ratio of the US market capitalization to GDP is well above our estimate of a trend line value. At the beginning of 2020, this ratio was about 30 percent above the trend line and similar to the peak of the dot-com bubble in 2000.

Another good measure of stock market valuation is the CAPE ratio developed by Nobel Laureate economist Dr. Robert Shiller. The CAPE

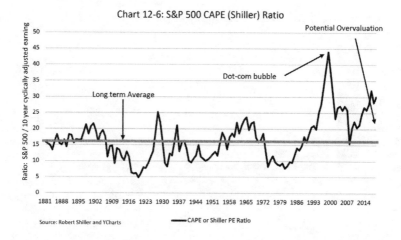

Chart 12-6: S&P 500 CAPE (Shiller) Ratio

Source: Robert Shiller and YCharts — CAPE or Shiller PE Ratio

ratio shown in Chart 12-6, is the measure of stock prices to cyclically adjusted earnings. Rather than simply taking current earnings, this measure attempts to smooth out the effects of economic cycles by including inflation-adjusted earnings over a ten-year period. We believe this is a better measure of long-term value versus traditional measures of price earnings ratios. Historically, stock prices have fluctuated between a low of 4.8 times and a high of 43.9 times cyclically adjusted earnings. The median ratio has been 16.2 times over the past one hundred years. At the beginning of 2020, the CAPE ratio was at 30 times, well above the historical average.

The US stock market outperformed most other stock markets around the world over the past decade. The combination of expansive policies by the Fed plus deficit spending by the federal government led the US economy to recover more quickly from the financial crisis than European or most Asian economies. At the beginning of 2020, the total world market capitalization of stocks reached $85 trillion.[3] Chart 12-7 shows the US was by far the largest contributor, at $37.7 trillion, over three times the next closest—China and Hong Kong at $11.7 trillion. It is interesting to note how the Asian countries of China and Hong Kong, Japan, India, and South Korea have grown to a combined stock market capitalizations of $21.8 trillion while European markets of the UK, France, Germany, and Switzerland total only $12.2 trillion. Clearly the balance of economic power in the world has shifted to the US and Asia and away from Europe.

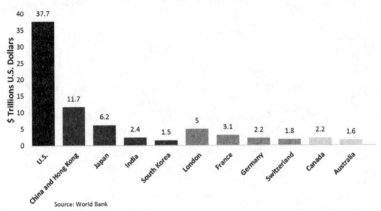

Chart 12-7: World Stock Market Capitalizations 2019

Source: World Bank

Virtually all stock markets benefited greatly from expansive central bank monetary policies over the past decade. Stock prices grew much faster than country GDPs, and valuation levels grew to levels well above historic norms. Our conclusion is stock prices were selling about 30 percent above normal or intrinsic values at the beginning of 2020. We believe the chances are very high that stocks will not perform well over the next five years and could easily experience a 20 percent or more sell-off at any time. In the past, each time the CAPE ratio or the market cap to GDP ratio reached the levels at the beginning of 2020, it was followed by significant price corrections. We believe history is likely to repeat itself.

2. Housing Bubble

There is no question a housing bubble developed in the mid-2000s and subsequently burst fueling the 2008 financial crisis. Expansive central bank policies stabilized housing prices following the 2008 financial crisis and recently propelled housing prices back to record levels. From the peak of housing prices in 2006 to the trough in 2011, prices fell nationally by around 27 percent. But expansive central bank actions in both the US and around the world propelled housing prices to new record levels. In the US, Chart 12-8 shows the Case-Shiller National Home Price Index increased by 59 percent from a financial crisis low of 134 to a record high of 213 at the beginning of 2020. Housing prices nationally have not only fully recovered from post–financial crisis lows but may again be returning to levels above their intrinsic values.

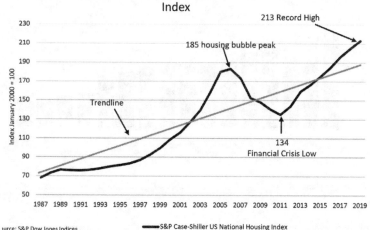

Chart 12-8: S&P Case-Shiller US National Housing Price Index

Source: S&P Dow Jones Indices   ━━━S&P Case-Shiller US National Housing Index

While we view housing prices nationally as about 10 percent over-valued, prices in some communities may be especially vulnerable to a pullback. Examples of metropolitan areas where prices rose much faster than the national average include the Northern California areas of San Francisco and San José and the Northwest communities of Seattle and Portland, Oregon. West Coast markets generally performed very well, while many central and East Coast markets lagged. Underperformance was especially apparent in high-tax states where population outmigration is taking place. Chart 12-9 shows housing price performance for several major communities following the financial crisis lows. Some have experienced hyper price growth while others have not performed well.

A number of factors determine housing prices—land scarcity, building costs and standards, zoning requirements, and supply versus demand. But the most important determinant of housing affordability is the monthly mortgage payment. Most buyers today, especially those under the age of sixty, purchase homes on credit. Currently, the median down payment on home purchases overall is 12 percent and for first time home buyers is only 6 percent.[4] When the Fed lowered interest rates, it made housing much more affordable to millions of people.

We have identified six general concerns about housing prices and future trends. The first concern is affordability. For buyers capable of making a 10 percent down payment and a $1,000 per month mortgage payment, a house costing $185,000 was affordable when mortgage

Chart 12-9: Major City Price Changes From Financial Crisis Lows

Source: S&P Dow Jones Indices   ■ Price Change from bottom to 2019

interest rates were 6 percent. When mortgage interest rates declined to 3 percent, the same buyer could afford a house costing $265,000 and still be able to have $1,000 per month mortgage payments. As interest rates fell, affordability improved, and more and more buyers bid up the prices of existing housing. New home construction did not keep up with demand, and existing home prices soared in many communities.

Unfortunately, rising housing prices shut out an ever-growing number of Americans from being able to afford to purchase homes. Many communities are suffering from lack of affordable housing and increases in homelessness. Incomes for most Americans did not keep up with rising housing prices.

It is fair to conclude housing prices nationally have fully recovered from financial crisis lows and are reaching new heights, but we are concerned housing prices could come under pressure from a variety of forces. The economy at the beginning of 2020 was at full employment, and any slowdown could lead to job loss and limit growth in discretionary income.

A second concern is interest rates are at historic lows and any increase in mortgage interest rates could decrease affordability and put downward pressure on home prices. The reverse of what happened the past ten years could easily happen again. To quantify this, each 1 percent increase in mortgage interest rates reduces the affordability of a house by 10 percent. Put another way, the buyer who can only afford a $1,000 per month payment would need to pay 10 percent less for a home if interest rates increased by 1 percent.

A third concern is rising property taxes in certain markets, which make affordability more difficult. A good example is the northern suburbs of Chicago. Decades of underfunded pension liabilities for state and local employees are leading to large property tax increases in order to fund the pension plans. According to *Crain's Chicago Business*, "Longtime homeowners have seen property tax bills double, triple or even quadruple over the past couple of decades."[5] From an affordability standpoint, most buyers have limited resources, so higher property taxes means less is available for mortgage payments. When less is available for mortgage payments, house prices tend to fall. This is currently taking place in the northern suburbs of Chicago, where housing prices are falling and foreclosures are rising despite low interest rates and full employment.

A fourth concern is demand for housing may change over time. Technology and lifestyle changes may decrease the size of housing required by many buyers. The birth rate continues to decline in the US, and prime-age home buyers may require fewer bedrooms. Technology is also changing how we live. Large kitchens, dining rooms, and storage for physical records are all in less demand in an age of electronic records, take-out eating, and increased time with electronic games and entertainment. So-called McMansions—which were popular in the 2000s—may be less desirable and less affordable in the future.

A fifth concern is tax legislation that limited deductibility of state and local taxes from federal income taxes. These provisions particularly impacted the deductibility of property taxes in higher-cost East and West Coast markets.

A sixth concern is how the country will address affordable housing and homelessness in the future, without causing overbuilding or the euphoric bubbles we experienced before the financial crisis. Household wealth and income inequality are creating near-hopeless conditions in many high-cost housing markets. Many people simply can't afford housing, and there are unfortunately too many people also dealing with mental health or substance abuse issues. Tent cities and thousands of homeless people living on the streets in many urban areas is a problem that will not go away on its own, and we believe solutions are best developed at the local level instead of relying on massive federal programs.

From a pure investment standpoint, we believe housing will not do particularly well over the next decade. It is hard to say if there will be catalysts to cause housing prices to fall, but the risks of increased interest rates and increased property taxes (to address underfunded pension liabilities in certain communities) are high. We believe the risks noted need to be monitored very carefully.

3. Commercial Real Estate Bubble

Commercial real estate prices fully recovered from the financial crisis and were overvalued by 15 to 20 percent at the beginning of 2020. Fed policies of driving down interest rates greatly benefited commercial real estate prices because lower financing costs resulted in higher net income for most properties. Lower interest rates also led investors to reduce the capitalization rates used in establishing property values. The net result was a rising trend in commercial property values over the past decade. Chart 12-10 illustrates the Green Street Commercial Property Price Index, which measures unleveraged retail, office, apartment, health care, industrial, lodging, and other commercial real estate property values over time. As shown in this chart, property values more than doubled from the financial crisis lows and were at a record high of 135.5 at the beginning of 2020.

Commercial real estate prices over the past decade increased much faster than GDP or the rate of inflation. As noted earlier, common stock prices benefited from a substantial increase in price earnings ratios. Commercial real estate investors similarly benefited from a declining capitalization rate. Most commercial properties are valued on a capitalization rate (or cap rate) that is the ratio of net operating income divided by a property's value. The inverse of the cap rate is the multiple of net income investors are using to value properties. As of the beginning of 2020, cap rates were near historic lows, meaning the multiple of earnings paid was very high.

Since commercial real estate was selling at an all-time high in the United States at the beginning of 2020, risks for price corrections are high. Our primary concerns include the impact of a slowing economy, potential rising interest rates and cap rates, and reduced demand for many types of commercial real estate properties. Each type of commercial real estate is impacted by industry-specific issues such as changing demand for retail space due to e- commerce or changing demand for office space as technology permits more remote and home-based

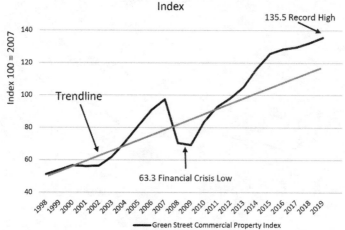

Chart 12-10: Green Street Commercial Property Price Index

Source: Green Street Advisors

workers. Apartment prices may also be impacted by a surge in new construction in certain markets.

It is difficult to forecast if prices will correct slowly or go through a severe correction, but it does appear commercial real estate prices are more extended at the beginning of 2020 than they were before the 2008 financial crisis.

4. Art and Luxury Items Bubble

There is not great data available, but the Fed's policy of easy access to money and low interest rates produced rapid escalation in the price of many collectibles, luxury goods, and fine art. Since most of these items produce no income, changes in their prices are instructive because they solely reflect buyers having a lot of cash to purchase limited assets. Chart 12-11 illustrates the trends in the Artprice 100 Index, which measures the prices of the 100 top-performing artists each year. Sale prices of top works of art have appreciated much faster than the stock market. However, lower-priced art by lesser-known artists did not perform as well as the top one hundred artists. Scarcity value and the growth of mega-rich people no doubt played into the extraordinary performance of this index.

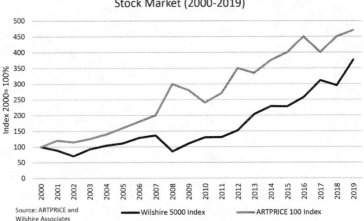

Chart 12-11: Percentage Change in Art Index versus US Stock Market (2000-2019)

Source: ARTPRICE and Wilshire Associates

Wilshire 5000 Index   ARTPRICE 100 Index

The Artprice 100 Index has performed better than the stock market since 2000 as measured by the Wilshire 5000 Total Market Capitalization Index. Considering how strongly stock prices performed over this period, it is obvious that worldwide investors have extra cash to invest considerably in assets such as art, which have no cash flows.

However, it is interesting to note that even the top art market has a wealth division. In 2019, the global art market shrunk 5 percent, but there still was record sales in the very top ranks. Sotheby's had a record sale for impressionists when they sold Claude Monet's *Meules* for $110.7 million and Christie's had a record sale for a living artist, when they sold Jeff Koons's *Rabbit* for $91 million.[6,7]

Luxury retail goods also performed very well over the past decade. Luxury autos, yachts, fashions, and unique luxury properties are at all-time high prices and sales. A slowing economy, rising interest rates, and declining stock prices all present risks to prices of art and luxury items. This risk is magnified by increasing use of debt to purchase art. In 2019 over $24 billion of debt was used to purchase art, more than double from a decade ago.

5. US Net Worth Bubble

With housing, stocks, bonds, commercial real estate, and collectibles all selling at very high prices, US households were wealthier than ever at the beginning of 2020. Chart 12-12 illustrates that the net worth of US

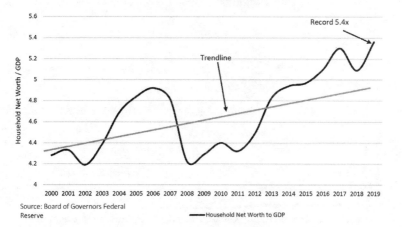

Chart 12-12: US Record Household Net Worth to GDP

Source: Board of Governors Federal
Reserve

households grew much faster than the GDP over the past decade and is currently at a record of over five times GDP. According to the Fed, the average household net worth was $692,100 at the beginning of 2020, which was an all-time record. But that is misleading because nearly all the increase in net worth went to the top 10 percent.

Record household net worth can be a good thing, but it also highlights how a bursting of the stock market, housing, commercial real estate, bond, or collectible bubbles would likely lead to reduced consumer confidence and spending. How these bubbles play out will have a direct effect on the economy and should be of great concern to the Fed and its management of monetary policy.

Another serious issue for the US is the increasing concentration of wealth in the top 10 percent of households. In the past century, the US successfully created a large middle class, which benefited from economic growth over many decades. The past three decades, however, saw an ever-increasing share of net worth concentrated in the top households while the bottom 90 percent of households did not benefit. The government's response to the 2008 financial crisis only exacerbated the problem, because most resources went to bailing out financial institutions and other corporations rather than helping families stay in their homes.

Chart 12-13a shows at the beginning of 2020, the top 10 percent of households controlled 68.5 percent of household net worth, while the bottom 90 percent controlled only 31.3 percent. The trends since

Chart 12-13a: Household Net Worth Share
Concentrated in Top Households

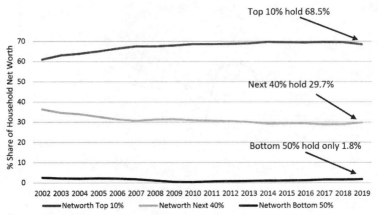

Source: Board of Governors Federal Reserve

1990 show the rich getting richer and the poor getting poorer. This uneven distribution of net worth is a risk to the continuance of our democracy and will be a hotly debated topic for politicians that will impact fiscal, regulatory, and monetary decisions in the future. Even though the average US family net worth was $746,821, the median US family net worth is only $121,411. This clearly shows how the average is skewed by the super wealthy.

Chart 12-13b illustrates that US household net income is reaching all-time highs in inequality. In the last century, this country has experienced only two times when the income inequality has become this extreme. The first time was right before the 1929 stock crash and we are nearly close to that level now. The Gini Index is a measure of income inequality in this country. The index scale goes from zero to one hundred, with zero representing total equality and one hundred representing extreme inequality. It is enlightening to review how the Gini Index peaked during the build-up to the 1929 stock market crash to reflect the mega-rich families who benefitted from the rise of the stock market and the growth of consumer products. The Index plunged after the crash, but settled into an era in the 1950s through the 1970s when income equality created a strong middle class in this country.

However, beginning in the 1980s, federal government policies favoring deregulation, easing of trade restrictions and the decline of union

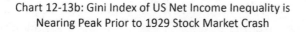

Chart 12-13b: Gini Index of US Net Income Inequality is
Nearing Peak Prior to 1929 Stock Market Crash

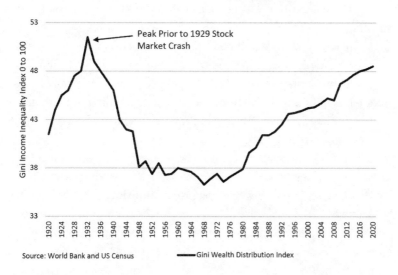

Source: World Bank and US Census   ●——●Gini Wealth Distribution Index

wages led to sharp increases in both net worth and income inequality. We believe these continual expansionist policies have threatened the middle class and our democracy.

6. Chinese Real Estate Bubble

China may have created the largest real estate bubble in the history of the world. To support the government's long-term plan to move hundreds of millions of people to urban centers, to increase standards of living, and to achieve GDP growth of 7 percent or more, China undertook massive infrastructure, commercial, and residential construction projects. Construction accounted for about 25 percent of total GDP for China. China's share of global crude steel production has risen to 53.3 percent at the beginning of 2020. The US was fourth at only 4.7 percent of the total. In the last three years, China used more concrete than the US used in the entire twentieth century.[8]

Infrastructure building in China has been impressive. We have visited the country twice in the past few years and were awestruck by the bridges, dams, rail, and other infrastructure projects built throughout the country. We were also impressed with initiatives taken to decrease dependence on heavily polluting coal-fired electric plants and other efforts to improve air quality. A commitment to phasing out fossil fuel transportation in favor of electric vehicles is important and necessary, as acid rain has been a health and environmental issue in China.

Chinese commercial and residential construction grew at a torrid pace over the past decade as the country added about seven million new housing units per year. For perspective, the US typically adds about 1.3 million housing units per year.[9] The building of these new housing units kept the GDP growing and was a source of pride for the Chinese government.

The real estate boom in China was financed by a combination of consumer savings, government funding, government-controlled corporations, and a huge shadow banking system. Individuals in China were permitted to buy homes at discounted prices beginning in the late 1990s. Most citizens took advantage of these opportunities, and 90 percent of Chinese citizens now own homes (or more accurately—own apartments).[10]

Unfortunately, prices rose so high that currently new homes are not affordable to most citizens. In Beijing, for example, new housing units cost about twenty-three times the average annual earnings of most people. This mismatch between new housing prices and affordability resulted in massive numbers of unoccupied housing units. We saw ghost cities throughout China, which had finished office and housing towers that stood completely vacant. It is estimated over 20 percent of all housing, or more than fifty million housing units, were unoccupied at the beginning of 2020.[11]

Despite this huge number of unoccupied housing units, real estate prices rose substantially over the past decade. Chart 12-14 shows the rise in the residential property price index over the past several years, reaching record levels by the beginning of 2020 . Residential property prices rose faster than inflation and were greatly influenced by the Chinese government. Unlike the US, where market forces primarily determine property prices, the Chinese government manipulates the price of housing. Whenever it determines prices are rising less than it would like, it implements massive programs to accelerate growth. Similarly, it often takes actions to reduce price rises when it determines prices are rising too quickly.

Chart 12-14: Residential Property Prices in China

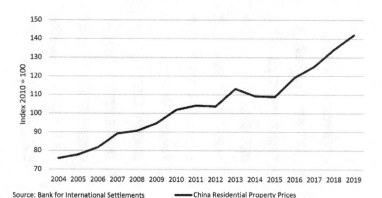

Source: Bank for International Settlements ▬▬China Residential Property Prices

While we were in China we visited the Shanghai Urban Planning Exhibition. It holds an auditorium-sized 1/500 scale model of the ten-year building plan for Shanghai. The plan is developed by the central government and presented to the Chinese people. There is no input from the community. The plan we saw is near the end of its term and we could see the hundreds of apartment buildings that had been recently built. The people we spoke with seemed very excited to see the new ten-year plan that is due soon.

Interestingly, the Chinese savings rate is a robust 36 percent versus less than 10 percent in the US. Strong savings rates and government encouragement to invest savings in real estate led Chinese citizens to purchase more and more real estate. It is estimated 80 percent of Chinese household net worth is invested in real estate, which would make it very vulnerable in a crisis.[12] Chart 12-15 shows how many housing units are owned by those purchasing homes in China. Most buyers now own two or more housing units. This is eerily similar to what happened in the US in 2005 and 2006, when millions of people purchased second and third homes as investment properties.

By allowing residential real estate prices to increase faster than the rate of inflation, the Chinese government virtually guaranteed above-average returns on savings invested in real estate by Chinese citizens. High returns on savings meant Chinese citizens could invest an ever-increasing amount of savings into new properties at

Chart 12-15: Chinese Are Buying Multiple Homes

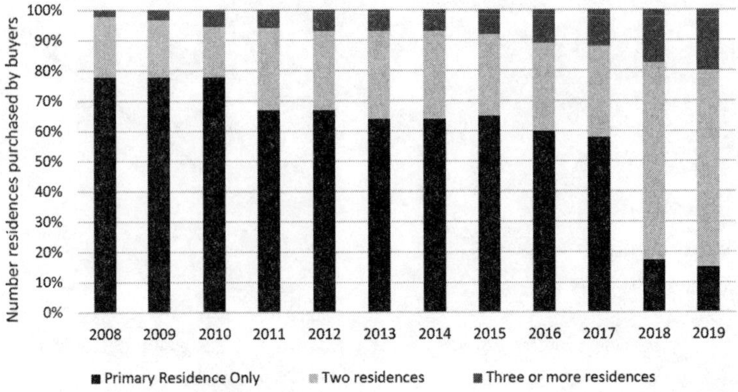

Source: Survey and Research Center for China Household Finance

ever-increasing prices. Chinese citizens reacted as expected, by purchasing second and third properties as investments.

As more and more savings were invested in real estate, Chinese citizens increased household debt to pay for real estate purchases and to support increased consumer spending. Total household debt accordingly grew at 27 percent annually over the past three years and grew to 60 percent of GDP by 2020 versus only 25 percent a decade earlier.[13]

It is possible the Chinese government will be able to manage residential real estate prices to continue to rise faster than the rate of inflation or the GDP. However, the more real estate prices rise faster than a reasonable measure of intrinsic value, the risks of the major breaking of a bubble increase. We understand the Chinese government has every incentive to keep its citizens happy by manipulating real estate prices higher. However, if trade wars, pandemics, terrorism, or limitations on sources of new capital limit the government's ability to continue these actions, market forces could take hold. In this scenario, normal market forces would likely lead to substantial price declines that could destabilize both China and worldwide financial markets. Because of the sheer size of the real estate bubble and the 1.4 billion people involved, this bubble needs to be very carefully monitored. We believe real estate prices in China could fall by up to 20 percent if normal market forces rather than government interference were to determine prices.

Debt Bubbles

1. Global Debt Bubble

Massive infusions of liquidity by central banks all over the world led to huge increases in worldwide debt. Borrowers took advantage of low interest rates, easy access to money, and favorable loan terms. Financial corporations, governments, businesses of all sizes, and average citizens all got in on the action. Total worldwide debt at the beginning of 2020 exceeded $255 trillion, according to the Institute of International Finance. Chart 12-16 shows which regions of the world were responsible for these increases.

China and the US drove the increase in total global debt over the past few years. For China, the debt was used to support aggressive GDP growth initiatives, especially the real estate boom. For the US, growth in debt was led by large federal government budget deficits and sharply increasing consumer and corporate debt. For both the US and China, total debt as a percent of GDP rose to unprecedented levels for peacetime activities.

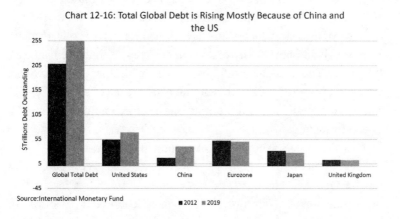

Chart 12-16: Total Global Debt is Rising Mostly Because of China and the US

Source: International Monetary Fund

2. US Consumer Debt Bubble

Major areas of consumer borrowing in the US include residential mortgage loans, auto loans, credit cards, and student loans. In total, consumer debt totaled more than $14 trillion at the beginning of 2020, which was an all-time record. Of this total, residential mortgage loans were about $10 trillion.[14] Given higher housing prices and somewhat tighter underwriting standards over the past decade, we do not expect a repeat of the severe problems experienced in the 2008 financial crisis. However, if housing prices were to fall, mortgage delinquencies and foreclosures will no doubt rise. Also, if the newly created unregulated shadow banking system starts to dramatically securitize its own loans without supervision or if Fannie and Freddie are privatized without supervision, there could be serious problems. With residential housing loan underwriting primarily set by government-backed institutions, we do expect a sharp increase in FHA and VA problem loans, which typically have higher LTVs and lower FICO scores. We are also concerned that Fannie Mae and Freddie Mac relaxed underwriting a few years ago, which led to 10 percent of their loans having LTVs of 95 percent or more at the beginning of 2020. These loans will be very vulnerable to any reduction in home prices or rise in unemployment.

In addition to housing-related debt, consumers held $4.2 trillion of other debt primarily from credit cards, auto loans, and student loans. More than 128 million American households have credit card debt, averaging about $8,400 per household. As shown in Chart 12-17, total credit card debt of $1.1 trillion has been growing in recent years after declining following the 2008 financial crisis.[15] Credit card debt is extremely costly, and Americans have difficulties paying off this debt. The overwhelming majority of consumers keeps rolling the balances on forever. This is highly profitable for the banks but a heavy cost to the average family. Credit card delinquencies are once again rising and will be greatly impacted by a downturn in the economy and a rise in unemployment.

Chart 12-17 also shows auto debt totaled a record $1.2 trillion at the beginning of 2020, up 75 percent from a decade ago. The US has invested more in highways and roads and relatively less in rail and mass transit systems in most regions of the country. It is estimated 86 percent of Americans drive to work each day, so it is not surprising the demand for autos has been high.[16]

However, readily available credit at low interest rates and extended loan terms led Americans to purchase autos with ever-increasing amounts of debt. In order to keep monthly payments as low as possible, loan terms were extended to seven years or more. The problem is the value of many autos declined much faster than the repayment of the

Chart 12-17: Growth in Auto and Credit Card Debt

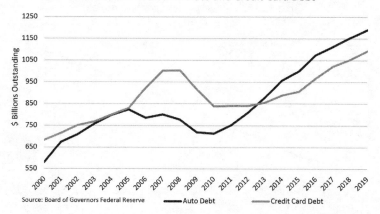

Source: Board of Governors Federal Reserve   ━━━Auto Debt   ━━━Credit Card Debt

debt. This resulted in millions of underwater loans, where the value of the auto was less than the outstanding loan balance.

Lenders responded by allowing people to trade in used autos for new autos and roll the underwater loan balance into the loan on the new auto. Current estimates are a third of all autos being traded in have negative equity loans, which are being rolled into the new loan balance.[17] This presents a growing risk as millions of borrowers are amassing levels of debt that exceed the collateral value and may become increasingly difficult to repay.

It is not surprising auto loan delinquencies were rising even though unemployment was at record lows and the economy was strong in early 2020. Many of the loans were subprime and given to families in the bottom 50 percent of our economy that did not benefit from the overheated economy. Over seven million Americans were ninety days or more behind in their auto loan payments at the beginning of 2020. Subprime auto loans made up about 21 percent of all auto loans and were particularly prevalent for loans made through shadow bank dealers and auto finance companies.[18]. We see large risks for subprime auto loans when the economy and employment soften. We also see risks of declining collateral values as technology progresses and electric vehicles gradually replace gas engine autos.

Chart 12-18 illustrates that student debt is a large and rapidly growing problem. Student debt outstanding totaled an all-time record of $1.6 trillion at the beginning of 2020, up from only $600 billion

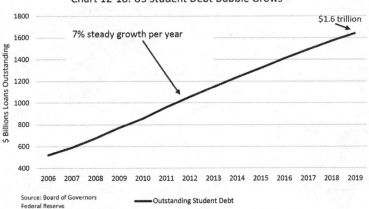

Chart 12-18: US Student Debt Bubble Grows

Source: Board of Governors
Federal Reserve

━━●Outstanding Student Debt

a decade ago. At current growth rates, student debt could exceed $3 trillion within the next ten years. In an effort to help more people attend college, the US government developed student lending programs and made it very easy for millions of prime and subprime borrowers to amass large debts and defer payments into the future. While these programs helped millions to further their education, they also created enormous problems that need to be addressed.

The US government could reasonably be accused of being a subprime student loan predatory lender. It thrust millions of loans on subprime borrowers who were not adequately informed about the costs and long-term impacts those loans might have on their future. In many cases the government and frankly the college system showed little interest in assessing the ability of a borrower to ever repay the loan.

Easy availability of student loans with low costs and deferred payments led to logical actions. Increased demand for college educations led public and private universities to expand their programs, facilities, staffing, and cost structures. The demand also led to the rapid growth of for-profit unregulated colleges, many of which were eventually chased out of business by the DOJ and the state attorneys general. To pay for these costs, tuition and other fees doubled at many universities over the past decade.

An astonishing forty-four million students took advantage of easy access to student loans, and now two-thirds of all college graduates are saddled with student debt. In many cases, these loans made it possible for students to extend their time at a university, and sometimes they

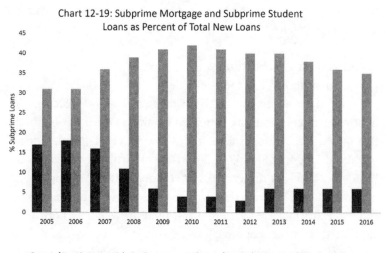

Chart 12-19: Subprime Mortgage and Subprime Student Loans as Percent of Total New Loans

■ Percent of New Mortgages to Subprime Borrowers   ■ Percent of New Student Loans to Subprime Borrowers

Source: Equifax and Wall Street Journal

did not critically assess the long-term earnings potential from their field of study. In many cases, parents and grandparents were required to cosign the student loans. Unfortunately, many young people did not fully understand the terms of the loans and the impact those loans would have on their long-term financial position.

More than one-third of all student loans made in recent years were to subprime borrowers. As Chart 12-19 shows, the percentage of student loans made to subprime borrowers exceeded the percentage of mortgages made to subprime borrowers during the peak of the housing bubble.

Substantial numbers of student loans made to subprime borrowers have resulted in millions of Americans saddled with debts they cannot repay. Official delinquency rates exceed 10 percent, and it can be argued real delinquency rates are much higher if all restructured and loan forgiveness initiatives are included. The African American community is especially hard hit by these policies, because the delinquency rates are four times those of whites. Student debt led many young people to defer purchasing homes and starting their families and impacted millions of senior citizens who found themselves liable for student loans in their retirement years. We are reminded the US government was at the center of the 2008 financial crisis when government-backed entities reduced underwriting standards to support increased homeownership. That strategy backfired and hurt millions of people, especially minorities and low-income homeowners. We feel the government has already repeated itself with student lending.

3. US Corporate Debt Bubble

Corporations took full advantage of easy money and low interest rates following the 2008 financial crisis. Chart 12-20 shows US corporate debt of large corporations increased to over $10 trillion by the beginning of 2020, which is a record 48 percent of GDP. A decade ago, corporate debt was only $6.6 trillion. Debt of smaller and medium-size businesses also grew to a record $5.5 trillion by the beginning of 2020.

Corporations borrowed heavily to support common share repurchase, acquisitions, and various growth initiatives. These borrowings supported stronger economic growth, rising stock prices, and rising corporate profits. Leverage is a good thing when asset prices and economic activity are rising. The risk, of course, is the servicing of debt and repayment of debt can become burdensome in the next recession. Combined, all US businesses have debt of $15.5 trillion, or 74 percent of GDP.

The segments at greatest risk are lower-rated credits and the financing of highly leveraged transactions. There are currently $1.3 trillion of highly leveraged loans, $1.2 trillion of below-investment-grade bonds, and $3 trillion of corporate bonds rated one notch above junk status.

We are also concerned ETFs and CDOs that own some of these seldom traded bonds may perform poorly when the financial system is

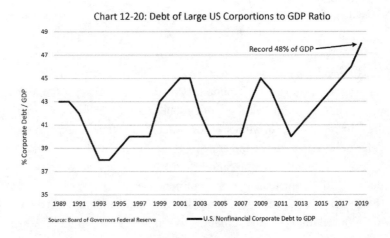

Chart 12-20: Debt of Large US Corportions to GDP Ratio

Record 48% of GDP

% Corporate Debt / GDP

Source: Board of Governors Federal Reserve   U.S. Nonfinancial Corporate Debt to GDP

stressed. Poor performance of CDOs invested in subprime mortgages contributed to the last financial crisis. We just don't know how ETFs developed since the last crisis will perform the next time the financial markets are stressed.

4. The Chinese Debt Bubble

China has created a massive debt bubble over the past decade. Easy access to borrowing along with low interest rates allowed China to amass record debt. Chart 12-21 shows at the beginning of 2020, China's total debt had risen to a staggering $23 trillion, which is 300 percent of its GDP. Because China's economy is controlled by the central government, China's total debt has to be looked at from a combination of household, state-owned enterprises, local governments, private enterprises, and central government debt. China is less transparent than most economies, so we may not know if these numbers show all of the country's debt.

However, when we analyze China's debt, it is huge and growing. This debt fostered outsized economic growth the past decade and supported rising real estate prices. As we stated before, China may have created the largest real estate bubble in the history of the world, and this bubble was built on the back of a huge debt bubble.

China's government is a lender, borrower, and regulator. The government simultaneously owns or controls banks, corporations, shadow banks, investment savings, real estate, and virtually all parts of the

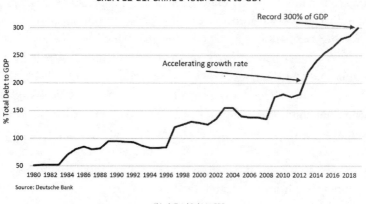

Chart 12-21: China's Total Debt to GDP

financial services industry. The government decides which loans are good, which should be written off, and which should be ignored. The checks and balances we have in the US are not present in China. Because the government manipulates the price of real estate and its currency, financial results often defy normal economics. That is why real estate prices have marched ahead while over fifty million new housing units remain vacant.

China used its borrowing power to further its geographic influence by financing infrastructure projects in many developing countries. China's "New Silk Road," has financed $1 trillion of projects in Central Asia, the Middle East, and Africa. China's government says it may ultimately lend as much as $8 trillion for infrastructure projects. China has signed up one hundred and fifty seven countries to build roads, power plants, rail lines, and shipping terminals that have saddled those countries with massive debts that will be hard to pay back in a recession. China's strategy is to limit spending on the military and emphasize lending on infrastructure projects to further its international interests. However, that strategy is dependent on China's ability to borrow heavily from investors around the world. We believe investors will become increasingly skittish as China continues its borrowing spree. If there is another global finance crash that impacts global tourism and trade, China could find itself the owner of hundreds of failing global infrastructure projects.[19,20]

5. The US Government Debt Bubble

The US federal government annual budget deficit is large and growing. To fund this growing budget deficit, federal government debt outstanding grew to a record $23.2 trillion at the beginning of 2020. This exceeded the nation's annual GDP for the first time since World War II, as shown in Chart 12-22. Of this debt, $17.2 trillion was held by the public and $6 trillion was held by intragovernmental agencies.

The annual federal government budget deficit has increased because of stimulus programs following the 2008 financial crisis. Unfortunately, politicians got hooked on deficit spending after the economy stabilized. This resulted in a rapidly expanding US federal government debt. We are very concerned this lack of fiscal discipline made our economy highly leveraged and fragile.

Chart 12-22: US Federal Government Debt to GDP

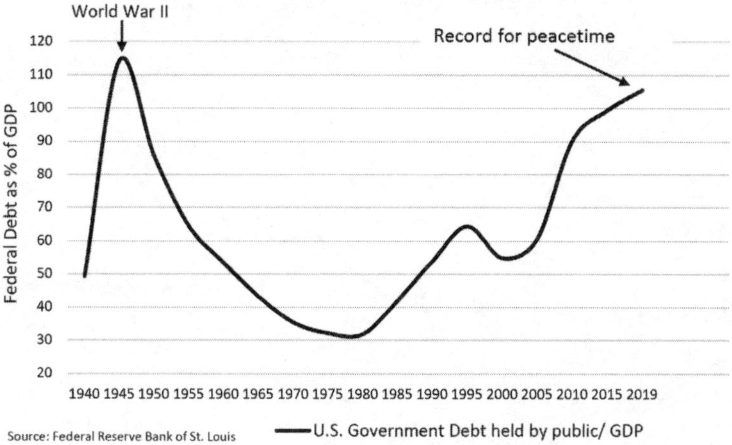

Source: Federal Reserve Bank of St. Louis ——U.S. Government Debt held by public/ GDP

6. State and Local Government Debt and Unfunded Pension Liabilities

The US state and local governments have been more fiscally prudent than the federal government over the past decade. Its total debt remained unchanged at $3 trillion. Much of this discipline includes fresh memories from the 2008 financial crisis plus the requirement of most state budgets to be balanced. One troubling area, however, is the underfunding of many state and local government pension plans. Unlike most corporations, which recognized these growing liabilities and transitioned to pay-as-you-go 401(k) and similar defined-contribution plans, most state and local governments continued with defined-benefit plans.

Defined-benefit plans are expensive and present huge risks to their sponsors. Since benefits are guaranteed, the plan sponsors are on the hook if life expectancy exceeds forecasts or investment returns fall short of plan assumptions. There is an added risk that politicians can capriciously decide to increase the guaranteed benefits for all participants. For example, in the late 1990s, California made what may become a fatal mistake by increasing guaranteed benefits at the height of the dot-com bubble when it had surplus investment returns. The surplus, of course, vanished when the dot-com bubble broke, but the plan will be forever saddled with increased guaranteed benefits.

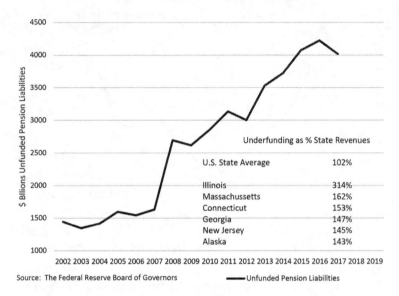

Chart 12-23: State and Local Unfunded Pension Liabilities

Underfunding as % State Revenues	
U.S. State Average	102%
Illinois	314%
Massachussetts	162%
Connecticut	153%
Georgia	147%
New Jersey	145%
Alaska	143%

Source: The Federal Reserve Board of Governors   ▬ Unfunded Pension Liabilities

Chart 12-23 shows the growth in unfunded pension liabilities. The sharp increase in 2007 and 2008 was primarily the result of poor investment performance during the financial crisis.

It is troubling that unfunded pension liabilities have grown despite a solid economy and extraordinary investment returns over the past several years. Collectively, state and local pension funds are estimated to be underfunded by about $4 trillion, and this could grow to $6 trillion or more if actual investment returns fall short of plan assumptions. At the beginning of 2020, most pension plans assumed long-term investment returns of 7 percent or more. To achieve higher investment returns, most pension plans invested the majority of their assets in higher-risk investments such as common stocks, private equity funds, hedge funds, venture capital funds, commercial real estate, and junk bonds. These investments performed well in the past decade when excess liquidity drove most of these asset prices to record highs, but that could change quickly.

Our concern is that a 7 percent plan for investment return assumptions appear to be too high and actual returns are likely to be much less over the next few years. With the fed funds rate and the ten-year Treasury bond yields currently at less than 1 percent, 7 percent investment returns would require taking on substantial risk. As noted earlier, common stock and commercial real estate prices have been rising much faster than earnings growth over the past few years. This could easily reverse itself leading to poor price performance over the next several years. Another risk is the potential for bond prices to fall if long-term interest rates rise in the coming years. Marking bond holdings to declining market prices could further pressure pension plan returns.

Many state and local governments will be pressured to materially increase funding of their pension plans. This will require reallocation of funds away from essential services like education, police and fire protection, and a whole range of health and human services. The alternative will be to raise taxes. When property taxes are materially increased, housing and commercial real estate prices typically fall. Some state and local governments will not be greatly impacted by funding their retirement plans. On a per capita basis, it appears states like Tennessee, Indiana, Nebraska, Florida, and Idaho are in reasonable shape. On the other hand, as shown in chart 12-23, Illinois, Massachusetts, Connecticut, Georgia, New Jersey, and Alaska are heavily underfunded in relation to their state revenue.

Our biggest concern is for states that already have high income and property taxes and simply can't raise taxes further. These communities will need to curtail essential services, making the quality of life in those areas less appealing. People and businesses are increasingly mobile and will relocate to areas giving the best balance of taxes, housing prices, and quality of life. For those communities on the short end of this stick, mass exodus of businesses and people is a real possibility. In the West, people and businesses are migrating from high-tax California to low-tax Texas, Washington, and Nevada. In the Southeast, high-tax Kentucky is facing outmigration to low-tax Tennessee. In the Midwest, low-tax South Dakota has in-migration while high-tax Illinois, Wisconsin, and Iowa face outmigration. On the East Coast, high-tax Massachusetts and Connecticut face outmigration while low-tax Florida faces strong in-migration. Future funding of pension liabilities will further highlight differences between regions and help accelerate the relocation of businesses and people.

Other Debt Bubble Considerations

In addition to China, many developing countries took advantage of easy money and low interest rates over the past decade. Those countries with the largest national debt to GDP include Japan (237 percent), Venezuela (214 percent), Sudan (178 percent), Greece (174 percent), Lebanon (158 percent), and Italy (133 percent). We recently traveled throughout Southeast Asia and to several port cities in Spain and Portugal. In addition to the many large, empty residential projects, we were amazed to see huge new port facilities in small cities that appeared to be underutilized. We could see the results of easy money and low interest rates, but we wonder if many of those projects made economic sense. Any reduction in international trade or tourism would seriously impact those countries.

At the beginning of 2020, investors were not concerned about the financial health of most developing countries' debt. However, despite all the spending on their infrastructures, many of these countries have made little or no improvements to their financial health since the 2008 financial crisis. Credit spreads tightened dramatically during the decade when the central banks were flooding the system with liquidity. Even Greece—which is BB- rated—issued a ten-year bond with a yield of only 1.4 percent in 2019.

Easy money, low interest rates, and central bank asset purchases have led to a highly unusual condition of negative interest rates in some areas of the world. There were $17 trillion of bonds issued with negative interest rates outstanding in late 2020. Historically, investors demand a return for lending their money to governments that approximates or exceeds the rate of inflation. But there was so much money chasing a limited supply of bonds that yields were not only below the rate of inflation but were negative. From an issuer standpoint, this was an excellent time to lock in low or negative interest rates for as long as possible.

For investors, we just don't see why it makes sense to buy these bonds, which have little to no returns. We believe the price of bonds is in a bubble that will eventually deflate. Prices of long-term bonds are sensitive to changes in interest rates. For example, a thirty-year bond yielding 2 percent today would fall in price by 20 percent if interest rates rose by 1 percent in the future. The central banks of the world have infused so much liquidity into the system that we are all getting used to living in a bubble, but that bubble can't last forever. The bigger the bubbles grow, the greater the chance they will burst.

What Could Trigger the Next Financial Crisis

We believe the risks of a significant downturn are greater today than they were prior to the 2008 financial crisis. That financial crisis was triggered by the bursting of the US housing bubble, which was magnified by the use of exotic financial instruments and poor regulatory and monetary decisions. Conditions in early 2020 were quite different. Instead of the risks of breaking a single bubble, there were many asset and debt bubbles that could break at any time.

Let's summarize the potential bubbles we see early in 2020 versus conditions that existed in early 2007 before the housing bubble burst. First, we look at potential asset bubbles:

- The stock market, as measured by the Dow Jones Industrial Average, was 129 percent higher at the beginning of 2020 than in early 2007. A key measure of value, the CAPE ratio, which measures price to cyclically adjusted earnings, was thirty times cyclically adjusted earnings versus twenty-seven times in early 2007. A second key measure of value, the ratio of total stock market capitalization to GDP (the Buffett Ratio) was 149 percent versus 103 percent in early 2007.
- Housing prices, as measured by the Case-Shiller National Home Price Index, were 16 percent higher at the beginning of 2020 than in early 2007. Housing prices in hot urban markets like San Francisco, San José, and Seattle were 40 percent higher than in early 2007. Home prices could easily fall if interest rates rise, unemployment rises, or property taxes increase (to pay for unfunded pension liabilities).
- Commercial real estate prices were 49 percent higher than in early 2007. Low interest rates and improved operating income led investors to reduce cap rates and pay higher multiples of earnings. But prices could easily correct 15 to 20 percent if the economy softens or if interest rates and cap rates rise because of rising economic uncertainty.

- Prices for top works of art as measured by the Artprice 100 index were 160 percent higher than early 2007. These price increases are a direct reflection of easy money chasing limited assets and driving up prices.
- Household net worth in the US was at a record 5.4 times GDP versus 4.9 times in early 2007. Household net worth is primarily determined by stock and housing prices, which have risen to record levels. However, most gains in household net worth went to a small fraction of the population. Any significant reduction in stock or housing prices would likely lead to a decline in household net worth and a corresponding reduction in consumer confidence and spending.
- Real estate prices in China were 74 percent higher than in early 2007. China's government manipulates housing prices to increase despite over sixty-five million unoccupied housing units and serious affordability issues. It is uncertain if China will be able to continue to manipulate prices or if normal market forces will take hold.

There are also growing potential debt bubbles:

- Total world debt was $255 trillion at the beginning of 2020 up 100 percent from early 2007. Households, corporations, and governments all took advantage of easy and cheap debt. For the major economies, total debt grew to the largest percentage of GDP ever.
- US non-mortgage consumer debt, led by explosive growth of student debt, increased to $4.2 trillion versus $2 trillion in early 2007. Rising subprime and underwater auto loans and student debt are particularly troubling.
- US corporate debt increased to $10 trillion versus $6.6 trillion in early 2007. Highly leveraged debt and debt to below-investment-grade credits will be stressed with a softening economy.
- The US federal debt increased to $23.2 trillion versus only $8.5 trillion in early 2007. As a percentage of GDP, total federal debt increased to 106 percent versus only 62 percent in 2007. Debt is almost certain to rise unless new fiscal restraint measures are enacted.
- State and local governments face unfunded pension liabilities of $4 trillion, which could grow to $6 trillion or more if pension plans experience poorer-than-assumed investment returns.

- China's total debt increased to $23 trillion versus only $7 trillion in early 2007. As a percent of GDP, total debt increased to 300 percent from 138 percent in early 2007. A bursting of China's real estate bubble or a disruption in trade could create a debt crisis.

Risk of one or more of these bubbles popping is real and growing. Just as with the bursting of the housing bubble in 2007, the severity of the downturn will be determined by how well governments and regulators manage the crisis. In 2007, the Fed had plenty of firepower to infuse the system with liquidity. The fed funds rate was over 5 percent, and several rounds of rate cuts were possible. The Fed and the federal government had good flexibility to stimulate the economy with increased federal spending in 2007 and 2008. However, in early 2020 the federal government was incurring $1 trillion budget deficits and total debt outstanding grew to $23.2 trillion. The capital markets could easily decide to pressure the federal government to restore its financial discipline before rolling over that debt.

It is impossible to pinpoint what will trigger the next downturn and possible financial crisis, but high on our list is a real estate or a debt crisis in China. We realize the Chinese government has unique control over its economy and asset prices. However, in order to keep growing, China needs continued massive borrowings, and investors could become concerned if tariff wars, unrest in Hong Kong, or other disruptions to its economic system take place. China is so massive that any bursting of its bubbles would quickly impact the entire world.

We also believe the risks of a correction in the US stock market are high. After a decade of rising prices and valuation levels well above historic norms, a bear market correction of 30 percent could easily take place. The explosive growth of programmed trading and ETFs may magnify any downturn in common stock prices. We know how ETFs perform over a decade of rising stock prices with relatively low volatility, but we don't know how they will perform in stress conditions when prices are declining and investors are fleeing.

Also high on our watch list is an economic downturn that devolves into a serious recession because of heavy debt leverage currently imbedded in the system. Massive increases in borrowings by consumers, corporations, and governments have levered the system to new heights. Defaults on student loans, credit cards, autos loans, and lower-rated corporate loans could be significant in the next downturn.

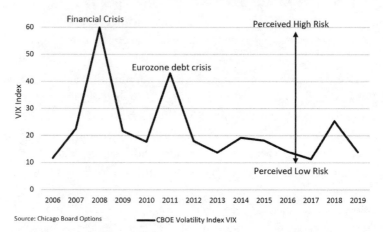

Chart 12-24: The "Fear Index" (CBOE VIX Index)

Source: Chicago Board Options ▬▬CBOE Volatility Index VIX

Asset and debt prices had very low risk premiums built into their pricing at the beginning of 2020. Similar to conditions just prior to the 2008 financial crisis, investors at the beginning of 2020 did not perceive risks to be high. Chart 12-24 illustrates the Chicago Board of Option Exchange Volatility Index, which measures the market's expectations of near-term volatility. It is sometimes referred to as the "fear gauge" or "fear index." When this index is high, investors are focused and concerned about risk. When it is low, they tend to worry less about risk.

In May 2007, just before the financial crisis hit, this index was at a low 13.05. Investors weren't worried about risks and assumed the good times would go on forever. When the financial crisis hit, this index rose to 59.89 in October 2008. It rose again in September 2011, when the Eurozone debt crisis was taking place. Since then it has traded in a range of 9.5 to 28.4 and at the beginning of 2020 stood at 13.9, which is at the low end of the range. With asset and debt prices at historic highs and investors perceiving risks to be very low, there is little margin for error. Any unexpected bad news could change everything, just as it did in 2007 and 2008.

Despite the capital markets assigning very low risks at the beginning of 2020, the Global Economic Policy Uncertainty Index, shown in Chart 12-25, reached a record high. This index measures the relative frequency that newspaper articles discuss economic policy uncertainty in twenty major countries around the world. We find it fascinating that there is such a disconnect between risks being discussed around the

Chart 12-25: Global Economic Policy Uncertainty Index

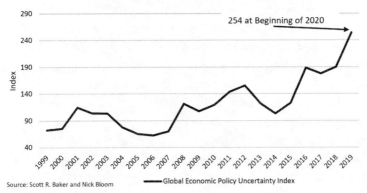

Source: Scott R. Baker and Nick Bloom ■— Global Economic Policy Uncertainty Index

world and investor sentiment that risks in the system are very low at the beginning of 2020.

In addition to the risks associated with asset and debt bubbles, we believe risks of cyberattacks, terrorist attacks, pandemics, wars, and natural disasters are real. Our world is interconnected with trade, technology, and a financial system that relies on quick, efficient transactions. Breaks in that system create risks that are hard to quantify but could be substantial.

We also see risks in the UK from their exit from the European Union. While Asia and the US are far more important in total economic terms, changes in Europe would be disruptive. Many European countries are not doing well, and a recurrence of the Eurozone debt crisis is a possibility.

Risks are also growing in the US for some type of constitutional crisis. The United States is extremely polarized along political party lines. Working toward bipartisan solutions and compromise have given way to partisan winning at all costs. Our political leaders don't seem to be able to even agree on facts, let alone agree on some version of the truth. Congress is hopelessly deadlocked on most issues, the executive branch is exerting more and more power, and the Supreme Court is starting to make decisions along political lines. These issues, along with the wealth, income and racial inequality building in our country, present an unclear picture of how politics will play out over the coming decade.

The final risk we are watching is how much longer the Federal Reserve and other central banks will try to stimulate the economy with easy money and asset purchases. It appears efforts to stimulate the economy with easy money policies are becoming less effective. Easy money in Europe resulted in negative interest rates and continued subpar economic performance. We may be entering a new era when expansive monetary policies produce little economic benefit and substantial downside risks from potential asset and debt bubbles.

Despite all these potential problems, we remain optimists and believe that this country has a history of solving our challenges if we face our problems and work together to resolve the issues. Our conclusion, however, is risks are substantial and asset prices were ignoring many of these risks at the beginning of 2020. We believe the inevitable outcome will be for major corrections in asset prices. It is possible these corrections will lead to a significant economic downturn and possibly the next financial crisis. Rather than just accepting this inevitable outcome, there are actions that can be taken today to reduce the risks of the next financial crisis.

13

Recommendations to Avoid the Next Financial Crisis

As we have highlighted may times in this book, we believe actions taken by the Federal Reserve and the US federal government over the past decade created a highly leveraged and fragile economy that is vulnerable to a variety of risks. We believe chances are very high that unexpected events will trigger a sharp rise in unemployment and a recession, which would be magnified by the current massive debt structures of individuals, corporations, and the government.

The Federal Reserve

The agency with the greatest influence over our long-term financial well-being is the Federal Reserve. By withholding liquidity when it was needed most, it helped create the 2008 financial crisis. After the crisis, its massive infusion of liquidity and purchase of bonds stabilized asset prices. However, the continuation of these policies for over ten years created enormous asset and debt bubbles. This excess liquidity created an unnatural and very risky condition where short-and long-term inter-est rates were lower than the rate of inflation and too much money was forced into higher-risk investments such as common stocks, junk bonds, and real estate. The Fed's actions have added to these issues by inspiring other central banks around the globe to similarly create excess liquidity.

The debt and asset bubbles can be unwound slowly by Fed actions to significantly reduce its holdings of bonds and gradually increasing interest rates and inspiring the rest of the globe to do the same. If this is not accomplished, bubbles will continue to grow, and the popping of those bubbles could be catastrophic. With central banks all over the world following the Federal Reserve's lead, the size of the bubbles and the impact of the unwinding of those bubbles is magnified.

Former chair of the Fed William McChesney Martin once described the "Federal Reserve as a chaperone who has ordered the punch bowl removed just when the party was really warming up." Unfortunately, the Fed has not only kept the party going, but has grabbed a bigger punch bowl and spiked the punch. It has done this through an increasing variety of asset purchases and guarantees. The result is asset and debt bubbles have overflowed the punch bowl. Even though the party-going politicians want to supply endless quantities of spiked punch, the Fed must be the adult supervision in the room.

We know business and political leaders from both parties will pres-sure the Fed to keep the party and the dancing going as long as possible. With federal elections coming up every two years, the pressure is enor-mous to maximize short-term economic growth and employment. This short-term thinking has grown as the political divide in our country intensifies. We believe the Fed must somehow rise above these pressures.

We believe the Fed's long-term inflation target of 2 percent should be reasonable. The economy operates well with modest inflation, and businesses prefer stable inflation so they can plan accordingly.

We support the short-term asset purchase and guarantee programs that helped stabilize the economy, but we also believe the Fed and other central bankers must gradually unwind these portfolios. Otherwise, we risk a return to building bigger and bigger asset and debt bubbles.

It is also possible that the capital markets will respond differently to future Fed actions. In the past decade, we could count on increased

Chart 13-1: Long-Term Normalized Interest Rates with 2% Inflation

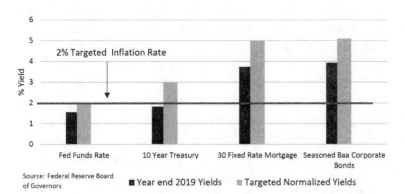

Source: Federal Reserve Board of Governors

■ Year end 2019 Yields   ▦ Targeted Normalized Yields

economic activity and rising asset prices when the central banks flooded the system with liquidity and asset purchases. However, excess liquidity in many countries has recently led to negative interest rates and many are still experiencing poor economic growth. The same thing could happen in the US, where additional liquidity harms even short-term economic growth.

We recognize the relationship of interest rates and inflation can vary greatly over time. But the Fed's policies of driving both short-and long-term interest rates below the rate of inflation is highly unusual and dangerous.

Chart 13-1 shows interest rates at the beginning of 2020 compared to typical normalized interest rates. Assuming a 2 percent inflation rate, historic norms would imply a 2 percent fed fund rate, long-term treasury yields at 3 percent and residential mortgage and investment grade corporate bond yields around 5 percent to reflect prepayment and credit risks. However, by keeping interest rates so low, the Fed is encouraging heavy borrowing and is subsidizing borrowers at the expense of savers, who earn little on low risk assets like CDs or treasury bonds. This has been especially hard on retirees who are forced into risky investments or accept interest earnings below the rate of inflation.

Over the past decade, the Fed has greatly expanded its tools to address its mandates. But the broader use of these tools now directly impacts the fed funds rates, long-term Treasury yields, corporate bond prices, ETF prices, mortgage yields, stock prices, housing prices, and other equity and debt prices. In many respects, the Fed is the agency with the most influence over the setting of prices for virtually all equity and debt vehicles. We believe the Fed has taken on the role of manipulating asset and debt prices and thus has the responsibility to help manage asset and debt bubbles, whose piercing can be devastating to the economy and employment.

Historically, the Fed has shied away from taking accountability for building and piercing asset and debt bubbles. But it is now directly in its purview. If it is going to directly impact asset and debt prices, it must be held accountable for its actions. We believe the Fed's mandate should evolve to include limiting risks from bursting asset and debt bubbles as well as managing inflation and employment.

The Fed has also migrated away from being an independent central bank to an integral player in setting public policy. Like it or not, the Fed has taken on a growing public policy role with significant pressures from both political parties. We expect future Fed actions, as has happened to the US Supreme Court, to be highly influenced by political or ideological views of appointees to the Federal Reserve Board of Governors. The politicizing of the Fed has grown dramatically in recent years, and we expect this trend to continue. The executive and congressional branches of our government know the Fed is perhaps the most powerful influencer over our economic futures, and they will pressure it accordingly to support their priorities and initiatives.

Politicians often argue the US economy should grow faster than 2.5 percent and have pressured the Fed to support higher long-term growth targets. However, growth of GDP in the US is primarily driven by population growth and productivity. Population growth in our country has fallen to only 0.6 percent per year because of an aging population, declining birth rates, and limitations on immigration. Productivity gains normally range between 1 percent and 2 percent per year. Even though the US is a global leader in technology, it is unlikely productivity gains will exceed 1.5 percent per year over the long run. As a result of population growth of 0.6 percent per year plus productivity gains of under 1.5 percent per year, we believe long-term economic growth will average between 2 and 2.25 percent per year. We note the Congressional Budget Office lowered its long-term GDP growth estimates to 1.9 percent in October of 2020 as a result of US federal government deficits and debt burdens, which are becoming a growing part of the GDP. We do not believe it is appropriate for political leaders to pressure the Federal Reserve to support long-term growth above these realistic targets.

US Federal Government

The US federal government is on a spending spree. Federal debt grew to $23.2 trillion in early 2020, and budget deficits exceeding $1 trillion per year are all but assured over the next few years. Even though the economy was at full employment and we were not fighting a large war, total government debt as a percent of GDP grew to over 100 percent at the beginning of 2020. This was simply unprecedented for peacetime.

Both political parties are currently supporting continued large budget deficits. We understand both parties' desire to increase necessary spending and reduce taxes. These are popular positions to take when elections are held every two years. We normally expect the capital markets and investors to be voices of reason and discipline by driving up interest rates on federal government bonds when fiscal irresponsibility is of concern. But with the Fed pumping so much liquidity into the system and actively buying Treasury bonds, this discipline has faded.

US Treasury yields are at historic lows and prices are at historic highs, even though our country's financial health has eroded. We think of this similarly to a family's use of a credit card. In this instance, each time the country hits the max on its credit line, the credit line is extended with no requirement to make payments. Plus, the interest rate charged is reduced because the Fed has lowered interest rates. It is not surprising the response is to keep borrowing as heavily as possible until someone says, "No!"

We believe there is a significant risk the capital markets will wake up one day and tell the US federal government the party is over and it needs to get its financial house back in order. This happened several times in the past when the budget deficit and federal debt were in much better shape than they are today. The one silver lining in the current situation is the US government has the opportunity to issue new long-term Treasury bonds at record low interest rates. We strongly encourage the US federal government to issue as many long-term bonds as possible to lock in these attractive interest rates, which are highly likely to be below the long-term rate of inflation.

We are increasingly concerned political voices calling for fiscal restraint are falling by the wayside. Political leaders appear to be more focused on how many new social programs should be added and how many tax cuts should be implemented, with little concern for how to pay for them. Unfortunately, discussions about returning to balanced federal government budgets are no longer in vogue.

Inequality and Social Justice

In Chapter Twelve we showed how wealth and income are being concentrated in fewer and fewer hands. A large middle class with shared values and common purposes is being replaced with huge inequities as reflected in the Gini Inequality Index rising from thirty-five in 1980 to nearly fifty in 2020. Furthermore, the top 10 percent hold 68.5 percent of US household net worth, while the bottom 50 percent hold only 1.8 percent today. These inequalities are helping to fuel sharp divides along racial, gender, and political lines. This divisiveness creates instability, a lack of shared values, and threatens our very democracy.

We believe US federal government policies and Fed actions helped fuel the decline of the middle class. For example, tax policies favored the wealthy and those benefitting from rising asset prices, while middle income Americans experienced a decline in real wages. Fed policies also disproportionately benefited the wealthy because the asset bubbles they created are primarily owned by the top 10 percent.

Inequalities are especially apparent for Black and Hispanic households where median family income is only 59 percent and 73 percent respectively of white family incomes. This inequality along with many other concerns has led to growing demands for social justice and reforms in government, taxing, and policing policies.

We believe our government must change policies to rebuild a strong middle class. We recognize many good paying manufacturing jobs that helped fuel a large middle class in the 1950s through the 1970s are unlikely to return. However, growth in technology, new business models, and services should help fuel growth of well-paying middle class jobs in the future.

We support government policies and actions that improve access and effectiveness of K–12 and higher education. The majority of well-paying jobs in the future will require higher skills with continual upgrades. With advancements in technology, universal access to the internet, and a new generation of workers fluent in the use of handheld devices and computers, lifelong learning will be easier than ever. The government needs to support actions that improve access and decrease the cost of all types of education. This is especially important for the Black and Hispanic communities. Average earnings for all workers with a bachelor's degree are 67 percent higher than those with just a high school diploma.[1] But in 2020, only 28 percent of Blacks and 21 percent of Hispanics had college degrees versus 40 percent for whites and 57 percent for Asians.[2]

Government investments in education can have huge returns because they can decrease racial inequality and are likely to result in higher future tax revenue from higher wage jobs. It is especially important to support education in high demand fields such as computer science, information technology, cybersecurity, the sciences, and engineering. Investments in higher education may be the most important thing the government can do to reduce income inequality.

Another major way to reduce income and net worth inequality is to change federal tax policy. Tax policies over the past few decades have clearly increased inequality. We believe the federal government should increase capital gains, estate, and income tax rates for the very wealthy and reduce certain deductions. We applaud commitments of many mega rich to donate most of their net worth to charities, but we question if there should be a better balance between donating their assets to charities versus paying more capital gains, estate, and income taxes.

We also believe government policy should provide good safety nets for those unable to work or lack the skills for good paying jobs and support some form of minimum wages or basic income. But the programs must be designed to encourage people to work and not become unduly dependent on the government. Our country is moving in a direction of ever increasing entitlement programs. We risk losing the entrepreneurial spirit and work ethic that made our country so great. There is a need to continually assess the aggressive competition from China and Asia rather than emulating the socialistic policies of many developed European countries.

The current highly partisan political divide is creating inequality. In the past, political leaders of both parties often worked together to come up with policies to address our many challenges. The devolution of politics into winner-take-all extreme positions, has left our country deeply divided with fewer shared values and less willingness to listen to all points of view. Civil discourse, which was once a hallmark of our country, has been replaced with name calling, misinformation, shouting, and highly partisan reporting of the news.

People just don't know who or what to believe and are retreating back to their own cluster of people who share the same views. This clustering of America makes it difficult to attack inequality in a meaningful way. It seems that recently the American people have tolerated political and business leaders who are uncivil, divisive, and have dubious ethics, in the hope that these "leaders" will deliver what we think we need. Instead they have delivered more unrest and corruption. Let's all start demanding that our business and political leaders exhibit the same values that we try to teach our children. Humility, compassion, civil discourse, integrity, kindness, and gratitude.

State and Local Governments

State and local government spending has been much more prudent than federal government spending over the past decade. Aided by fresh memories of the 2008 financial crisis and requirements for most states to have balanced budgets, their financial health overall is sound. However, the major issues facing many state and local governments are pension liabilities, which are underfunded by $4 trillion, and could easily increase to $6 trillion or more if investment returns are poor in the coming years. Trying to address the trillions of dollars of underfunded pension liabilities could have huge impacts on many of these budgets. We are concerned that many state and local governments will need to take resources away from education, police, fire, and human services or significantly increase taxes to address these underfunded pension plans.

We believe state and local governments need to step up and begin to wipe out their pension deficits. A troubling scenario would be for poor investment returns to trigger a required boost in pension funding during an economic downturn. State and local governments in Illinois, for example, are already in a serious deficit. Just imagine where Illinois will be if pension investment returns are poor and the economy is in a deep recession.

Another recommendation is for state and local governments to take a hard look at the design of their pension plans. Defined-benefit plans are expensive and can create huge liabilities for state or local government plan sponsors. Most retirement plans in the US have changed to defined-contribution plans such as 401(k)s, which are paid for on a current basis. We believe state and local governments would be far better off to convert to defined-contribution plans even if cash compensation to employees is increased to reflect this change. We understand the pressure from state and local government employees to maintain these plans. But these plans may simply not be affordable, and employees might prefer to have higher cash compensation as a trade-off for a reduced retirement plan benefit.

Finally, we believe state and local pension plans should reduce their higher-risk investments. In an effort to achieve higher investment returns, pension plans increased investments in higher-risk private and public common stocks, hedge funds, private equity, commercial real estate, and other less liquid investments. Recent studies show public pension plans are more heavily invested in higher-risk equities and alternative investments than comparable private plans. We believe many of these asset categories are currently valued too highly and accordingly believe investment returns over the next several years will likely be significantly below the past few years. We worry that pension plans will continue to increase exposure in these assets at exactly the wrong time.

Student Debt

We view student debt as a huge and growing problem that requires resolution. The federal government's guarantee of student debt led to a number of unintended consequences. Easy access to borrowing led to a surge in students attending private and public universities. Student debt financing was eagerly promoted by universities, which quickly expanded their programs, facilities, salaries, and tuition. State governments reduced their funding of public higher education because universities could survive on voluminous increases in tuition income funded with growing student loans. The system incented the students to extend their time to achieve their degrees and take on fewer part-time jobs because they had easy access to student loans. And there was less critical focus on the cost of degrees versus the earnings potential from those degrees.

The result of easy access to borrowing plus motivations for all parties to participate led to the creation of $1.6 trillion of debt. This is one of those runaway government programs with no checks and balances on its growth. Unfortunately, many people are now saddled with debt that will be very difficult, if not impossible, to repay. Without significant changes, we expect student debt to continue to march right up to $3 trillion over the next decade.

We believe a number of things can be done to slow the growth of student debt while still achieving our nation's goal of providing assistance to people desiring higher education. Some of these measures are currently being implemented, but we believe rather than extending massive forgiveness programs with no restrictions, there should be incentives to make the student loans more effective.

- Total new student debt should be capped to an agreed-upon budget with appropriate underwriting and allocation criteria established.
- College students should be fully educated on the costs and burdens that student loans will have on their future ability to service debt, buy homes, and raise their families.
- College students need transparent information as to the costs of achieving degrees versus the likely earnings potential from those degrees.
- Universities should be required to offer lower-cost degrees by fully embracing technology and freely transferring credits between all accredited public and private universities.
- More students should be able to earn credits in high school and community colleges that can be transferred to all accredited public and private universities.
- Companies and other employers should be encouraged to include tuition payment and student debt repayment help as part of their compensation programs.

- State, local, and federal government employees should be able to earn student debt repayment help in certain types of community-service jobs: police, fire, social work, and medical positions, and science and math teachers.
- Student debt should be able to be discharged in bankruptcy under certain circumstances.
- There should be incentives to encourage people to pursue degrees that will add the most to this country's future economic viability: engineering, computer science, medicine, and scientific research.

The evidence is clear: college degrees generally lead to higher lifetime incomes and better standards of living. There is also clear evidence that a better-educated population is good for our democracy and helps foster our world leadership in technology. We support the use of federally subsidized student debt to help more students achieve college degrees that add to the economic viability of our economy. But it is time to refine the program and to rein in the unproductive parts of the system. It we don't address this soon, we fear there will be a heavy cost to bailing out the program and students in the years to come.

Fannie Mae, Freddie Mac, FHA, and VA

Housing finance in the United States is dominated by Fannie Mae, Freddie Mac, FHA, and VA. Backed by the full faith and credit of the United States, these entities have huge competitive advantages over private lenders. In recent years, government-backed mortgages accounted for more than two-thirds of all mortgage originations. Housing finance in the US evolved from being dominated by local regulated portfolio lenders to being dominated by unregulated shadow mortgage brokers originating loans for sale to the government-backed entities.

Underwriting standards are now primarily set by government-backed entities. This concentration of decision making fosters standardization but also magnifies problems when poor underwriting approaches are utilized. Poor underwriting policies by the government-backed entities contributed heavily to the 2008 financial crisis.

Government-backed entities tightened underwriting standards following the 2008 financial crisis, and standards generally continue to be good today. However, standards are once again being relaxed with approval of high LTV and lower-FICO-score loans. We recently observed a first-time home buyer in the suburbs north of Chicago, where no appraisal was required. There was a 20 percent down payment requirement, but that was coupled with a built-in home equity loan that could immediately draw down funds that would increase the LTV to 90 percent. Those same suburbs are currently experiencing falling home prices, so we wonder if underwriting standards are being loosened to encourage home purchases in a tough market.

The government-backed entities are still pressured by their regulators and Congress to maintain dual goals: safety and soundness, but more LMI lending. These entities have leaned on the side of safety and soundness over the past ten years as memories of the 2008 financial crisis were fresh. But over time, we expect new initiatives to expand lending in low- to moderate-income neighborhoods will emerge.

Fannie Mae and Freddie Mac were temporarily placed in conservatorships during the last financial crisis, but it has now been over ten years. Part of the reason for keeping them in conservatorships was their strong profitability, which is feeding the US Treasury. The federal government put up $187 billion to bail out Fannie Mae and Freddie Mac in 2008 but has already taken out $300 billion, making the bailout a good return on investment. The federal government would like this cash train to keep running.

There are proposals to return Fannie Mae and Freddie Mac to private ownership. If these government-backed entities are returned to private ownership, we believe it is important they first build a significant capital cushion. The housing market has been doing great and credit costs have been very low the past few years, but the cycle will turn. These companies need very large capital cushions to absorb future losses so taxpayers will not have to bail them out again. We also worry private ownership will return the companies to divergent and potentially competing objectives. Consumer activists will want to lower the cost of mortgages and relax underwriting standards to promote affordable housing, but shareholders will want strong profitability and lower-risk assets. Once again, Fannie and Freddie may find themselves attempting to serve two masters.

There were advantages when portfolio lenders dominated residential lending and local underwriting diversified credit risk around the country. Portfolio lenders were also able to easily modify customer loan payments when economic conditions warranted. We now have a system that centralizes underwriting decisions making it an increasingly politically motivated Washington DC system.

The 2008 financial crisis was caused in part by poor underwriting by the government-backed entities and was hurt further by their inability to easily modify customer loan payments because loans were securitized and owned by investors. As we noted earlier, we believe millions of people should have been able to stay in their homes following the 2008 financial crisis rather than being forced into foreclosure. The government-backed entities should have authority to modify customer loan payments under certain economic conditions. Investors are naturally reluctant to automatically give this power to the government-backed entities. However, over the long run, investors as well as borrowers are better off if foreclosures can be held to a minimum. The primary winners in this scenario are the homeowners and the primary losers are the Wall Street investors who love buying distressed foreclosed properties in a crisis and flipping them for high returns.

Regulatory Oversight

The regulated banking industry is safe and sound today. Strong regulatory oversight, memories of the 2008 financial crisis, and strong capital positions the current regulated banking industry should be able to weather economic downturns.

Risks are much higher, however, for unregulated shadow banks, where capital cushions are often low and newer products untested in stress economic conditions. Many shadow bank providers of financial services are regulated by state regulators or licensing bureaus or are not regulated at all. Assets in these institutions are growing much faster than regulated banking assets, and we believe the next financial crisis will again involve shadow banks.

Shadow banks—insurance companies, hedge funds, finance companies, asset management, investment banks, private equity, venture capital, money funds, mutual funds, ETFs, and pension plans—all played a role in the 2008 financial crisis and have rising risks today. We need to monitor these activities in order to help the

Fed make informed monetary decisions and to help all regulators manage risks.

Nobel Laureate economist Paul Krugman said, "As the shadow banking system expanded (before 2008) to rival or even surpass conventional banking in importance, politicians and government officials should have realized they were recreating the kind of financial vulnerability that made the Great Depression possible and they should have responded by extending regulations and the financial safety net to cover these new institutions. Anything that does what a bank does, anything that has to be rescued in crises the way banks are, should be regulated like a bank."[3]

It is tempting to suggest more regulations for shadow banks, but we just don't think that is always practical. Instead, we believe the Financial Stability Oversight Council (FSOC) created by Congress should be reinvigorated and charged with closely monitoring the growth of shadow banking. We need to find a balance of monitoring the shadow banking system for building risks without becoming bureaucratic and burdensome to shadow banking companies that are creating important new technologies. Of course, the shadow subprime companies that existed before the 2008 crisis should have been closely monitored and should have been shut down earlier.

The regulatory hammer of being designated "systemically important" turned many industry participants against the FSOC. There is an important role for the FSOC to identify all the growing risks that might lead to the next financial crisis. It should approach its work from the perspective of helping other regulators identify risks rather than trying to become a new super-regulator. If someone was closely monitoring the rise of the hundred-plus subprime lenders and the massive multitrillion-dollar CDO and CDS market, the depths of the 2008 financial crisis could have been avoided.

As we now know, many shadow banking activities today are closely tied to technology. Among the things that made our country successful are innovation and entrepreneurism. We do not believe a new regulator is required for the rapidly growing and exciting presence of major tech companies in financial services. We are fortunate that Amazon didn't have to go through regulators at each step to develop its retail platform or Apple to develop the iPhone. Tech companies often create entirely new business models, but we still need to be watchful of privacy and security. We believe large tech companies will radically change some areas of financial services and regulations will have to be shaped to those new business models.

However, the mortgage industry is the *bête noire* of consumerism and regulation. Nothing impacts an average family more than the loss of their home. Special regulatory vigilance is necessary in the mortgage market.

Accounting Policies

Mark-to-market accounting contributed to the 2008 financial crisis. Most financial institutions are still required to continually mark their assets to market. This makes great sense for mutual funds, where investors need to know a price each day so they can buy or sell shares. It also makes sense for securities trading operations, where prices are transparent and reflect all appropriate information. For other financial institutions, mark-to-market accounting makes less sense. Many financial institutions are leveraged and have longer-duration assets funded with shorter-duration liabilities.

During periods when there is little liquidity, asset and liability prices can be volatile and not reflect any reasonable estimate of fair or intrinsic value. This occurred in 2008, when loan and mortgage-backed securities fell below their intrinsic values due to a freezing of the capital markets. These distressed prices rippled through the system, helping to drive billions of dollars of reported losses, which in turn led to dilutive new capital raises and merger transactions. Following the financial crisis, mark-to-market accounting rules were relaxed to allow more flexibility. We believe mark-to-market accounting should be limited in its use and should be augmented with reasonableness tests. Accounting guidelines should reflect some flexibility during periods when market values vary widely from intrinsic values.

Accounting for loan losses is another very important topic for financial institutions. Safety and soundness are best served when institutions can build strong loan-loss reserves during periods when the economy is strong. The combination of capital and loan-loss reserves should be as strong as possible during good times so pressures to raise new capital during periods of stress are lessened. Current accounting standards make it difficult to build reserves during good times and often require the addition of loan-loss reserves during periods of stress. Additions to loan-loss reserves during the 2008 financial crisis led to further destabilization and requirements for most banks to raise highly dilutive new capital.

Accounting for loan losses has once again been changed. The Financial Accounting Standards Board (FASB) is requiring adoption of Current Expected Credit Loss (CECL) accounting by 2020. It is unclear what the long-term effects of the new accounting will be on banks. We are generally supportive of any change that helps to build loan-loss reserves during periods of economic prosperity.

Short Sellers

In a normal economy, short sellers can play an important role in our capital markets and investors should be able to short stocks they think are overvalued. However, we also believe short sellers can help destabilize the economy and need to be monitored and regulated. During the 2008 financial crisis, naked short sellers (who did not own the underlying stock) bet against the housing market by shorting financial institutions with exposure to housing. To help drive the prices of those stocks down, they helped spread rumors, hoping to create panic conditions. These actions helped foster deposit runs and the freezing of the credit markets, which created big wins for short sellers at the expense of the economy, homeowners, and shareholders. The naked short sellers are not heroes or particularly prescient. They were greedy speculators that helped drive the economy into the abyss for their own personal gain.

The government totally bungled the regulation of short sellers in the 2008 financial crisis. Basic sense dictates you treat all institutions the same. However, they initially restricted short selling in stocks of mostly large Wall Street and international banks and inexplicably didn't include other financial institutions. This was a misguided action because it focused all the short sellers on a few unprotected institutions. Washington Mutual certainly felt the wrath of this government blunder.

Short sellers—especially naked short sellers—present a risk and should be banned for all financial institution stocks whenever the economy and capital markets are under any stress. Hopefully, government officials learned from the huge mistakes they made in the financial crisis.

Political Finance Reform

Financial institutions are some of the largest contributors to congressional and other political campaigns. The Center for Responsive Politics found that from 1998 through 2020 over $61 billion was spent by industry for political parties, campaigns, and lobbying. The industry that had one of the highest expenditures was the finance/insurance/real estate industry which gave over $9.2 billion in that twenty-two year period. Currently, the top twenty lobbyist payouts in that category are mostly companies that are not centrally regulated by the federal government.[4]

Based on what we experienced in the 2008 financial crisis, the system is corrupt and needs a major overhaul. We saw firsthand how political contributions, personal agendas, and incestuous relationships determined which institutions were saved and which were destroyed. We saw politicians favor their former employers, and we saw politicians and regulators inappropriately insert themselves in the middle of private company merger discussions and hostile takeovers.

Americans are correctly viewing the political system as broken, corrupt, and needing a major overhaul. A 2019 Gallup poll showed only 20 percent of Americans approve of the job Congress is doing. A Pew Research Center study showed only 17 percent of Americans trust their federal government. These reasons, among others, are why the battle cry of "drain the swamp" was so popular in the 2016 presidential election.

We believe political finance reform is appropriate. We favor further limits on direct and PAC contributions from corporations and wealthy donors. We support further restrictions on people moving in and out of private, political, and regulatory positions. We support the elimination of congressional hearings that are designed to be Kabuki theater for the benefit of the television cameras. We support taking civil and criminal proceedings away from Congress and the regulators and returning them to the DOJ and the state attorneys general, which are experienced in these complex financial investigations. We support initiatives to improve civil discourse, so all citizens start focusing on the truth rather than winning at all costs. We also believe Congress should not form handpicked lay commissions that don't have experience in criminal investigations and expect them to identify and refer criminal charges. History shows us successful criminal investigations involve the use of experienced professional criminal investigators.

China

China's real estate and debt bubbles present substantial risks to the US and other global economies. These bubbles need to somehow be deflated slowly over time or their quick piercing could become very destabilizing. We encourage our political leaders to help China work toward a soft landing. This entails encouraging its government to gradually reduce its GDP growth targets and to use our trade policy pressures very carefully. China is a strong export nation, and tariffs are very disruptive. We understand our nation's desire to create a fairer balance of trade and to reduce the theft of intellectual property and forced transfer of American technology to China. But we need to make the necessary reforms in a way that doesn't destabilize China and the global economy.

We view China similarly to a highly leveraged borrower in a house whose value would decline substantially if it went into foreclosure. Our goal should be to keep that borrower in their home and to help them get through a tough period. It would be prudent for China to continue to grow at a moderate rate, to slowly deflate its property bubble, to gradually improve the standard of living for its 1.4 billion people, to continue to make its debt payments, to stop stealing our technology and intellectual property, and to avoid a revolution. On this latter point, China has a long history of revolution and regime changes. Its leaders are fully aware of these risks and will likely control uprisings, such as in Hong Kong, much more aggressively than we might expect.

Summary

Economists Hyman Minsky and Charles Kindleberger said in a climate of excessive optimism, people tend to take full advantage of a strong economy instead of protecting themselves from the possibility of a major correction. In the 1932 book, *The Great American Land Bubble*, historian Aaron Sakolski argued that an atmosphere of speculation dates back to the beginning of US history. The Protestant work ethic in America is easily replaced by hopefulness of the speculative bubbles.[5]

Those of us in the United States are fortunate to be living in the greatest country with the strongest economy in the history of the world. We have many strengths, which position us well for decades to come. But much of the recent economic growth and building of speculative asset values has been built on an ever-increasing tower of debt promoted by the Federal Reserve and the US federal government. Debt can be very helpful during good times but can be devastating during the hard times.

Our biggest hope is we acknowledge the risks of excessive debt and begin a process to deleverage our financial system before it is too late. We need the Federal Reserve and US federal government to take the lead and help businesses and consumers to follow suit. We need to return to the premise that hard work and innovation are the keys to long-term success rather than leveraged returns from speculation. We simply want to find the best balance of employment, quality of life, and stability for all our citizens.

We are fortunate to have had great careers and can now focus on helping our communities become even better places to live and work. We want our ten perfect grandchildren, Lexi, Haley, Alyssa, Aaron, Olivia, Jack, Jake, Ellie, Hailee, and Mason, to enjoy the benefits of a strong and stable economy and to hopefully avoid living through another financial crisis.

Afterword

COVID-19 Strikes

Just as we completed this book in 2020 and submitted the manuscript to our publishers, the COVID-19 pandemic broke out in Wuhan, China, and quickly spread throughout the world. In a matter of six months, the virus spread to over eighteen million people in nearly two hundred countries worldwide. To fight COVID-19, most countries adopted lockdown measures to reduce the number of people exposed to the virus. These measures radically changed people's activities and led to the most dramatic reduction in economic activity and rise in unemployment since the Great Depression. In the US, over fifty million people filed for unemployment benefits within a few months following the outbreak of the virus. For comparison, according to the US Department of Labor, job losses totaled 1.2 million within the first two months following the 2008 collapse of Lehman Brothers and 6.5 million over the twelve months following Lehman's collapse. Similar to the last financial crisis, people hardest hit by job losses in 2020 were the most vulnerable of our citizens.

COVID-19 was a warning shot that illustrated how vulnerable our highly leveraged economy is to unforeseen shock events. The virus is just one of many possible disruptive forces that could strike at any time. Shocks to our system could easily come from more pandemics, wars, civil unrest, terrorist attacks, cyberattacks, and other so-called black swan events. Instead of identifying and developing plans to deal with potential shock events, the Federal Reserve and the US federal government actually increased risks in the economic and financial system by increasing debt and incurring sizable annual budget deficits over the past decade. We encourage policy leaders to not view COVID-19 as a one-off occurrence but to learn from the outbreak and become even more serious about adopting policies to reduce the leverage and fragility of our economy. We simply do not know if there will be repeated outbreaks, other mutations of this virus, or other disturbances that will affect the fragile economy.

It will take quite some time to fully assess the impact of the virus on the economy, employment, financial systems, asset and debt bubbles, political and societal norms, health care, and Federal Reserve and US federal government policies. But we think the impacts are likely to be significant, and we summarize below our thoughts on potential long-term effects of COVID-19.

Economic Activity

The governmental policies of locking down the economy in response to COVID-19 produced a sharp reduction in economic activity in the US and all over the globe. The International Monetary Fund (IMF), in its base case projections, estimated the virus will reduce global GDP by $9 trillion in 2020 and 2021, and GDP could drop even further if the virus is not contained by the end of 2020. The IMF projects the world GDP to decline by 4.9 percent in 2020 with declines in the US by 8 percent and 10.2 percent for the Euro area. China's GDP is projected to fall from 7 percent annual growth to about 3 percent growth.[1] Given the magnitude of GDP declines in 2020 and uncertainty regarding how quickly the virus can be fully contained, it is quite possible it will take two or more years to return to the economic activity levels of early 2020. Politicians are hopeful for a quick V-shaped recovery, but this is far from a certainty.

We expect economic recovery from COVID-19 to be slow and uneven. Some companies, especially in the technology area benefitted from the pandemic and continued to report record profits. Other companies in industries like travel, retail, personal services, hospitality, restaurants, sporting events, and concerts were gravely impacted and their recovery is problematic. Some economists expect a K-shaped recovery where some businesses would continue to grow like the upper part of the K, while other businesses would suffer for quite some time, reflecting the lower part of the K.

Unfortunately, most small businesses, the backbone of this country's employment growth, are likely to experience poor growth for years. As we will explain later, we are very supportive of government prioritizing funds for helping small businesses and distressed populations during the pandemic.

COVID-19 significantly disrupted global trade in 2020. The World Trade Organization projects a greater than 13 percent reduction in international commerce in 2020.[2] Anti-globalization sentiments are growing as political leaders assess risks of being dependent on other countries for critical supplies and trade. The US, Japan, and many European countries are calling for reduced dependence on other countries such as China. Over the past two decades, China was the major beneficiary of a growing global supply chain because it had attractive labor costs, excellent ports, and leading manufacturing capabilities. China became the world's largest export economy, and the US was its largest trading partner. The virus will significantly impact China, but China has the advantage of being the first major economy to reopen after the shutdown.

We are concerned that reduced global trade will negatively impact many developing countries. Many of these countries borrowed heavily to build new port facilities and other infrastructures to handle an expected increase in trade and the cruise/tourist business. We believe many of these ports may not be economical and will operate at a fraction of their capacity. Many of these facilities were financed with large amounts of debt, which will become burdensome in a period of low economic growth.

Federal Reserve Actions

The Fed responded to COVID-19 with unprecedented actions to infuse liquidity and stabilize rapidly declining asset prices. We believe

the financial system was on the verge of collapsing in the spring of
2020 when the Fed reduced the fed funds rate to near zero, aggressively
bought Treasuries, mortgage, and corporate bonds, and helped back-
stop money market funds, ETFs, municipal bonds, commercial real
estate, and other assets suffering from lack of liquidity. In that period,
the Fed ballooned its balance sheet from $4 trillion to $7 trillion. The
Fed clearly learned from its mistakes in handling the last financial
crisis, and its recent actions prevented a serious economic downturn
from spiraling into a full financial crisis.

We applaud the Fed's short-term actions but also believe the actions will inflate existing asset and debt bubbles and further leverage a
fragile economy. So, it is important that once the economy is stabilized,
the Fed should gradually increase the Fed funds rate closer to the rate
of inflation and unwind its balance sheet back to below $4 trillion.

Since its creation in 1913, the Federal Reserve has primarily
influenced the economy through the management of the fed funds
rate and the money supply in order to accomplish its mission "to
foster the stability, integrity, and efficiency of the nation's monetary,
financial, and payment systems so as to promote optimal macroeconomic performance."[3] However, after the September 2008 financial
crisis, the Fed added a new major tool to its arsenal when it purchased
trillions of dollars of low-risk assets like Treasury securities and mortgage securities backed by the GSEs. These purchases drove prices of
Treasury securities and mortgage securities up, which in turn lowered
longer-term interest rates. The massive purchases of these low-risk
assets also encouraged the rise of asset and debt bubbles. When
COVID-19 hit, the Fed not only continued to aggressively purchase
Treasury securities and GSE-backed mortgage securities, but it purchased or guaranteed a whole new array of significantly higher-risk
assets: commercial real estate backed securities, ETFs, municipal
bonds, corporate debt, small business loans, and commercial paper.
The purchase of these higher-risk assets has been previously viewed as
off-limits for any central bank.

Whenever the Fed or the US federal government influences capital
flows through subsidies, guarantees, or asset purchases, dire unintended consequences can occur. US federal government guarantees of
residential mortgage loans plus policies to increase homeownership
helped foster the last financial crisis. The Fed's actions after September

2008 may have saved Wall Street, but they encouraged other investors to move away from low-interest government-backed securities toward much higher-risk investments. This caused the prices of many risky asset categories to increase, and many industries were targeted as beneficiaries while many other industries were excluded.

We understand the short-term benefits of having the Fed purchase riskier assets, but they should be liquidated as quickly as possible after the economy stabilizes. Long-term ownership of these assets by the Fed will distort capital flows and prices. We believe the Fed should return to its historic role of managing the money supply and the fed funds rate and leave the setting of asset prices and capital flows to the free market system.

We have recently had a lot of people ask us if there are limits as to how much money the Fed can create. Since the US dollar is not tied to hard assets like gold, the Fed can and does literally create new money out of thin air. All the Fed has to do to create money is purchase Treasury and other securities or create bank reserves issued to commercial banks. The Fed has complete authority to issue as much money as it thinks is appropriate, as there are no statutory or legislative limitations.

As we explained in Chapter Twelve, since 2008 the Fed has increased the money supply much faster than GDP growth. These actions led to low interest rates and solid economic growth, but they also led to asset and debt bubbles and a highly leveraged economy. To deal with COVID-19, the Fed doubled down on the policies of growing the money supply and purchased a massive and ever-expanding array of securities.

We were hopeful these actions would be temporary, but the Fed has signaled its intention to keep interest rates near zero until the economy reaches full employment and inflation runs moderately above its 2 percent goal for some time. This means interest rates could remain extraordinarily low for several years. We fear this will make the economy even more fragile and leveraged.

The Fed is the most powerful force in the world determining the economic and financial stability of the United States and other developed countries. The Fed historically occupied a unique position of being somewhat independent from the executive and congressional branches of government. Actions taken in the response to COVID-19 moved the Fed to a much more expansive role of determining money supply, interest rates, asset flows and pricing, credit guarantees for selected industries, and support for state and local governments.

In many respects, the Fed has emerged as a fourth branch of government with powers much more extensive than ever envisioned when it was created in 1913. The executive and congressional branches recognize the Fed's enormous power and are increasingly pressuring the Fed to act in concert with their priorities. We believe the Fed's independence was already under attack, and the virus only accelerated this trend.

US Federal Government Actions

The US federal government responded to COVID-19 with record stimulus packages designed to soften the effects of the economic downturn on individuals and targeted businesses. As a result, the projected annual budget deficit in 2020 will skyrocket to $3.7 trillion, 17 percent of GDP. For comparison, stimulus programs developed in the last financial crisis produced a 2009 budget deficit of only $1.4 trillion—9.8 percent of GDP.[4]

Unlike the 2008 financial crisis, when most of the spending was targeted at large banks, the GSEs, AIG, and the auto companies, the spending this time was much more balanced between individuals, small businesses, and targeted large companies like the airlines. We support the targeted initiatives, especially those to small businesses, but are wary of broad brush spending programs that create inequities, waste, and fraud. Some individuals and businesses not otherwise impacted by COVID-19 received windfall benefits, while many individuals and small businesses received little in relation to lost income. It was particularly unsettling to see a large percent of the original allocation of small business relief programs given to large clients of the large Wall Street banks instead of going to the targeted main street small businesses. We were pleased to see the second round of small business relief going primarily to small businesses, with community banks playing a much more active role. This is one of many reasons why community banking is so important to our economy. Community banks are much more focused on the needs of their communities versus large fin-tech companies or the large Wall Street megabanks.

As we mentioned earlier, the US federal government was already running a huge $1 trillion annual budget deficit prior to the COVID-19, but now we are faced with a $3.7 trillion deficit. To finance this budget deficit, the US federal government will need to increase the total US federal government debt to record levels. At the beginning of 2020, total US federal government debt was $23.2 trillion, but now it is projected to rise to $27 trillion in 2020 and $30 trillion by 2021—a record 125 percent of GDP.[5]

COVID-19 also exposed the fragility in our health care system, which was stretched to its limits and facing hardships in assembling the necessary tools like testing kits, masks and gowns, and ventilators. It was gratifying to see how health care workers tirelessly attended to victims of the virus, often putting their own health at risk. It became clear there was no national policy or playbook for dealing with a pandemic. We believe it is likely that health care costs will be permanently higher as a result of the virus, which will only increase the long-term costs of Medicare, Medicaid, medical insurance, and other health-care programs. We certainly hope the government will learn from this crisis and develop a solid playbook and policies for dealing with future pandemics.

In 1992, the business tycoon Ross Perot ran for US president with the sole mission of reducing the burdensome national debt of $4 trillion. Perot is probably turning over in his grave at the projected record national debt of $27 trillion in 2020 and projections of $30 trillion by 2021. Because the burden to pay off this debt largely falls on future generations, it is instructive to understand the burden on our children and grandchildren. In 1992, Perot was very concerned that the national debt burdened every child under age eighteen with $59,880 of future debt.

But by the year end 2020, each one of our children and grandchildren under the age of eighteen already has a crushing US federal debt of $364,865 looming over their heads. In addition, these young people are likely to be saddled with student loan, car, and credit card debt during their working careers. These young people may find it highly challenging to buy homes or achieve a standard of living surpassing that of previous generations. We fear the American dream, where each person has the opportunity to pursue their own version of success in a society where upward mobility is possible, may be much more difficult to achieve.

Political leaders must somehow find the courage and resolve to reduce spending and increase taxes to return the US federal government to fiscal prudence. The federal government expects its citizens to operate in a financially prudent manner. Citizens should expect the same from their government.

To make the looming national debt even more frightening, issuing new US debt in the future could become more expensive. New treasury securities are continually issued to replace maturing debt and to finance annual budget deficits. About 25 percent of the total US federal government debt is owned by intragovernmental agencies like the Social Security trust fund, federal retirement plans, and Medicare. The balance of the US federal government debt is owned by the Federal Reserve, foreign investors, mutual funds, private and public pension plans, individuals, and institutional investors.[6] Over the past decade, issuing new US federal government debt was cheap and easy because the Federal Reserve was a huge buyer of US Treasury securities and investors were flush with liquidity looking for investments.

In December 2020, ten-year Treasuries were yielding 1.7 percent, while thirty-year Treasuries were yielding 1.4 percent.[7] These yields are near historic lows and are likely to be well below the rate of inflation over the next few years. We believe the US federal government should extend the maturities of Treasury securities and lock in low interest rates for as long as possible. By doing this, the US federal government would reduce the risks of annual federal budget cost increases when interest rates eventually rise. This action would also reduce the amount of debt maturing each year requiring the issuance of new Treasury securities. We note there have been periods in the past when rating agencies downgraded the US federal government debt and issuance of debt became difficult. It would be wise to lock in low rates and reduce future risks of issuing new treasury securities.

Asset Bubbles

The six asset bubbles discussed in Chapter Twelve were heavily impacted by COVID-19.

US stock prices as measured by the Dow Jones Industrial Average plummeted 36 percent the first month following the COVID-19 outbreak in the US. Stocks of businesses most directly impacted by the virus fell 50 to 75 percent in price. As we pointed out earlier, we believe US stock prices were in a bubble and were about 30 percent overvalued at the beginning of 2020. With the initial decline in prices following the virus outbreak, we viewed the US stock market as out of bubble status and close to our estimate of fair value.

Aggressive actions by the Fed to infuse liquidity and to purchase and guarantee assets in early 2020 resulted in an immediate and sharp rally in stock prices. The major stock market averages recovered most of the previous declines and several large cap technology stocks quickly rose to record levels. Stock prices of Amazon, Facebook, Alphabet (Google), Apple, Microsoft, and Tesla, for example, rose an average of 70 percent over the first seven months of 2020.

The US stock prices snapped back so quickly that they could easily go through another major correction. The reality is no one knows how long it will take for the economy to fully recover, but corporate profits are likely to be under pressure for quite some time. We accordingly believe stock prices have returned to bubble status and could easily correct 20 percent or more if corporate earnings do not recover as quickly as investors expect. We are especially concerned about the valuation levels of many large technology companies. We continue to believe stock prices will not perform as well over the next five years as they did the previous five years.

We have recently been concerned by the explosive growth in speculative day trading by small investors since COVID-19 hit. With new no-cost trading platforms available, small investors became aggressive traders of stocks and options. Many believed this helped fuel the phenomenal price increases for Tesla, Amazon, and other technology stocks. ETF's available to small investors were even developed for the so-called blank check companies designed to finance mergers and acquisitions, which can be very risky investments. Expanding investment opportunities for small investors can be good, but increasing speculation by unsophisticated investors has not ended well in the past. We are reminded how small investors flocked to the stock market prior to 1929 and the dot-com bubbles, and suffered tremendous losses.

US housing prices were at record levels in the beginning of 2020. When COVID-19 hit, home sales plummeted as potential buyers were abiding by shelter-in-place restrictions. Sharp increases in unemployment and economic uncertainty caused many potential buyers to hold off on purchases, according to the National Association of Realtors.[8] But offsetting these negatives was improved housing affordability due to extraordinarily low interest rates. In December 2020, thirty-year fixed-rate conventional mortgage interest rates were about 3 percent, making affordability very good.

We expect housing prices to remain steady and not repeat the sharp 27.4 percent national decline experienced in the 2008 financial crisis. However, we expect many people to reassess preferences for housing, especially in densely populated urban areas. We would not be surprised to see housing prices in densely populated high-cost urban areas like New York City suffer declines. Conversely, prices of homes in suburbs and less populated cities may rise due to increased demand.

US housing prices overall are about 10 percent overvalued and will remain the same after the pandemic. The largest longer-term risks to housing prices are reduced affordability if interest rates rise and the risks of significant property tax increases. Property taxes could increase dramatically in states and local governments that need to address unfunded pension liabilities and budget deficits spurred by the virus.

Commercial real estate prices were at record levels in early 2020 with the Green Street Commercial Property Price Index at an all-time high of 135.4. By October 2020, that index declined to 121.7. We believe COVID-19 will have a significant impact on commercial real estate prices. Shelter-in-place restrictions caused a surge in employees working from home and a dramatic falloff in retail store, restaurant, travel, and hotel spending. Many employers were pleasantly surprised to see a rise in productivity from employees working from home, and we believe this will lead to reduced demand for office buildings. We also expect consumers to continue to increase their online purchases and expect many large retailers to liquidate or file for bankruptcy, as have Neiman Marcus, Barneys, J. Crew, Pier 1, JCPenny, Brooks Brothers, Lord & Taylor, and many others.

It may also take quite some time for restaurants and the hospitality sector to recover. This all means a shift in demand that will pressure prices of many types of commercial real estate. Prices of shopping centers, strip malls, office buildings, hotels, and nursing homes may be particularly fragile. With so many small businesses going out of business, vacancies are likely to remain very high for quite some time. Our view is it will take a few years to sort out permanent shifts in demand and lease rates. Because most commercial real estate is encumbered by debt, changes in net income and cap rates can have a magnified impact on commercial real estate prices. We believe government mandates and competitive pressures to defer or reduce property rents will eventually be fully reflected in lower-income and commercial property values in 2020 and 2021.

Prices for luxury items including top works of art were at record levels in early 2020. Low interest rates and plenty of liquidity will continue to fuel demand, but declines in stock prices and economic uncertainty may reduce discretionary spending for luxury items, including art. Most auction houses around the world postponed live auctions in the first half of 2020 and pivoted to online auctions and sales. It will take a couple of years to assess the full impact of COVID-19, but we believe the combination of economic uncertainty and declining stock prices will negatively impact art and luxury prices.

US household net worth reached a record 5.4 times GDP at the beginning of 2020. This increase was primarily the result of record stock, housing, and commercial real estate prices. Reactions to COVID-19 caused most of these prices to fall, and average household net worth declined accordingly. We expect this decline, along with rising unemployment and falling economic activity, to result in a flat to declining household net worth over the next few years. Because household net worth is concentrated in fewer and fewer families, we unfortunately expect the bottom half of households to continue to have a smaller piece of the pie.

The Chinese real estate bubble was briefly negatively impacted by COVID-19, but quickly returned to growth by the middle of 2020. Their housing bubble now greatly exceeds the US housing bubble prior to the 2008 financial crisis. In the twelve months ending June 2020, $1.4 trillion was invested in Chinese housing vs. $900 billion at the peak of the US housing bubble in 2006.

As highlighted earlier, there were more than sixty-five million unoccupied housing units in China at the beginning of 2020. Despite the glut of unoccupied housing units, housing prices continued to increase during the year. The Chinese government manipulated prices higher and citizens responded with increased speculative purchases with ever increasing amounts of debt. It is estimated that Chinese residential property values hit a record $52 trillion in 2020, which is twice the size of the total US residential housing market and larger than the entire US stock market.[9] We stated earlier that China may have created the largest real estate bubble in the history of the world. That bubble continues to grow and we believe it needs to be monitored very carefully.

Debt Bubbles

The six debt bubbles discussed in Chapter Twelve are also impacted by COVID-19.

Total global debt increased to $270 trillion at the beginning of 2021. We expect this total to grow as the US, China, Japan, and the Eurozone have had to issue massive debt in order to deal with the pandemic. Virtually all governments increased spending to help jumpstart their economies without any significant offsetting tax increases. The IMF estimated COVID-19–related government direct spending, loans, and guarantees totaled over $9 trillion by August, 2020.[10]

Just prior to the COVID-19 outbreak, residential mortgage debt had increased to $11.1 trillion and US consumer debt outstanding jumped to a record $4.2 trillion.[11] Consumers were already stretched to their debt limits when a staggering fifty million people filed for unemployment benefits over March to mid-August.[12] The inevitable outcome of heavy debt burdens and lost jobs led to an immediate sharp increase in loan delinquencies for residential mortgage, auto, credit card, and student loans. Analysts project these loan delinquencies could spike to $1 trillion before the end of 2020.[13] Regulators and politicians encouraged lenders to offer grace periods and fee waivers and allow delinquent loans to be restructured without classifying the loans as being in default. These actions, along with various government stimulus programs, were designed to keep people in their homes and to minimize unnecessary repossession of collateral. We are pleased the banking regulators learned from their mistakes before and after the 2008 financial crisis, when they were inflexible and forced banks to write down loans and raise new capital. We expect delinquencies to be especially troubling for lower-income (subprime) auto, credit card, and student loan borrowers.

Total US corporate debt increased to a record $15.5 trillion at the beginning of 2020. Debt of large corporations totaled $10 trillion, and debt to small and medium-size businesses totaled $5.5 trillion.[14] The Organization for Economic Co-operation and Development (OECD) stated, "Today's trove of outstanding corporate bonds is of lower credit quality, with higher payback requirements, longer maturities and weaker investor protection."[15] The OECD warned that "the pile of low quality corporate debt rendered corporate bonds especially vulnerable to the negative effects of an economic downturn." COVID-19 was the catalyst to sharply increase credit agency downgrades and spike the number of corporations facing losses, liquidation, and bankruptcy. Industries especially vulnerable included airlines, energy, cruise operators, retailers, hotels, and restaurants and the entertainment industry. We expect corporate debt delinquencies to sharply increase in 2020 and 2021, which could slow the pace of economic recovery. Many highly leveraged companies borrowed heavily from the unregulated shadow banking system over the past decade. We expect many of these shadow banks to reduce their access to credit, and the environment could become very challenging for highly leveraged businesses.

Chinese debt increased to over 300 percent of GDP at the beginning of 2020. COVID-19 led to a rapid slowdown in GDP growth and brought front and center the systemic risk of its banking and financial systems, which are saddled with heavy debt. However, China was first to reopen its economy and quickly returned to economic growth. By the second half of 2020, China's manufacturing, employment and consumer spending had returned to pre-COVID-19 levels. Economists project GDP growth of about 3 percent for 2020, significantly outperforming the US and the Eurozone. However, we continue to view the Chinese debt bubble as massive and worthy of close monitoring.

The US federal government debt bubble exploded to record levels as a result of COVID-19. As we indicated earlier, the US federal government debt is expected to increase to $30 trillion by the end of 2021. As a percentage of GDP, the US federal government debt is expected to exceed previous peaks when the US was fighting World War II. But unlike that period, when government expenditures were quickly reduced following the completion of the war, this period won't bounce back so quickly, because a substantial part of our annual budget is for permanent entitlement and safety net programs. The likely outcome is continued annual federal government budget deficits and ever-expanding US federal government debt. We believe this debt bubble is not prudent and increases the leverage and vulnerability of the economy and financial system.

State and local government debt will be greatly impacted by COVID-19. Tax revenues fell due to lower economic activity while expenditures increased as unemployment benefits and other safety net programs were expanded. As we highlighted before, we are also very concerned about the unfunded state and local government pension liabilities, which could grow to $6 trillion or more if investment returns are poor over the next few years. These financial difficulties are likely to pressure the federal government to bail out state and local governments. But disagreements along political party lines and between states with widely varying financial health makes a complete bailout unlikely. We accordingly believe there could be municipal bond downgrades and some local government and agency bankruptcies. We continue to believe the unfunded pension liabilities will be a large and growing concern for many state and local governments.

Because COVID-19 struck all over the world, developed and developing countries alike were negatively impacted. The European Union, which was already stressed by the exit of the United Kingdom and poor financial health of many of its members, faced the greatest decline in GDP since its formation in 1993. All European economies were negatively impacted by the virus, but the financially strong Germany, the Netherlands, Austria, and Finland will fare better than the highly indebted and poor-performing countries such as Italy, Spain, Portugal, and Greece. Many of the uneconomic projects funded by easy money and low interest rates over the past few years will now become burdensome and place additional fiscal pressures on these countries. We expect debt of many developing countries to be downgraded and defaults to increase.

Political Divisiveness and Inequality

National tragedies often pull people together, and political and other differences are put aside during periods of uncertainty. But with COVID-19, our political leaders did not seem to pull together on a national level but generally split along political and economic divides. From a political perspective, Democrats generally supported those scientists and politicians who projected larger losses of lives and longer stay-at-home orders. The Republicans generally supported those scientists and politicians projecting lower fatalities and opening the economy sooner. Both political parties were initially supportive of unprecedented government spending and programs to help individuals and businesses impacted by the shutdown of the economy.

Decisions on how to deal with the virus were delegated to individual states, which resulted in a patchwork of inconsistent approaches around the country. Some states emphasized limited shutdowns of the economy even if higher loss of life was possible. Other states were more restrictive on economic activity in an attempt to limit loss of life as much as possible. Further complicating matters was that most states issued rules at a state level, even though the risks were quite different in densely populated urban centers versus low-density rural areas. These inconsistencies were showcased on the nightly news and the internet, which further divided people along political lines. News coverage continually reinforced their divergent political points of view, and most people became confused about what was really taking place.

The divide between people with substantial financial means and those living paycheck to paycheck also surfaced. Some well-to-do people were able to ride out the virus without much impact on their lives and financial well-being. Some mega rich people and Wall Street investors even found ways to financially benefit from COVID-19. But the overwhelming majority of people, especially those living paycheck to paycheck, became stressed and angry when they had to stay at home and lost their jobs and what little savings they may have accumulated. This anger is not unlike the impetus for the Occupy Wall Street movement experienced in the last financial crisis. It is also troubling that this virus disproportionately impacted minorities and lower-income people. This impact combined with anger over racial injustice led to protests and demonstrations in many communities.

By and large, most people abided by government directives to stay in place, practice social distancing, and wear face masks when the virus first hit. However, as time passed and there were substantial differences in how states and local communities responded, civil disobedience increased. People increasingly protested the right of state and local governments to restrict activities they felt were not high risk. Most people simply wanted to get their lives and financial well-being back to normal as soon as possible.

It will probably take years to gather the research that will reveal which practices will limit loss of life over time. It appears the most effective deterrents to the virus were simply wearing facemasks and practicing social distancing. Sweden and other countries believed over-all deaths would be lower by exposing more people to the virus sooner rather than strictly imposing stay-in-place orders. So far, South Korea appears to have achieved the best balance of controlling COVID-19 and maintaining good economic growth. Time will tell which approaches are most successful. Until the scientific theories are proven with hard data, we expect arguments to continue along the lines drawn by the political parties.

Long-term changes

We believe COVID-19 exposed the fragility of our highly leveraged and fragile economy. Within a period of three months, the pandemic moved the US from record economic activity to the greatest falloff in GDP and rise in unemployment in our history. Measures taken to flatten the pandemic's curve such as shelter in place and social distancing could have a permanent impact on how people work and socialize.

We expect larger companies to consider permanently allowing more workers to work from home and to have more workers in remote loca-tions rather than being concentrated in large office complexes. We are involved with a company that provides software to help companies measure productivity of their employees working at home. A surprising finding is that some companies experienced a 20 percent improvement in productivity and a reduction in employee turnover when employees were allowed to work from home. The virus led more companies to utilize Zoom and other technology to facilitate collaboration without the need for travel and in-person meetings.

The virus hit densely populated urban centers especially hard. For many people, the model of living in densely populated high-rise apartments and taking tightly packed mass transit to large office com-plexes may come under scrutiny. We believe this may lead to many people preferring to live in less densely populated areas and work from home or in smaller office complexes. If employers become more comfortable with employees working remotely or from home, this could lead to a major shift in demand for housing, office buildings, and modes of transportation.

The virus negatively impacted higher education in a number of ways. The National Student Clearing House revealed that fall 2020 enrollment in colleges was down 2.5 percent. International student enrollment was down 11.2 percent. Robert Zemsky, a professor at the University of Pennsylvania, projects two hundred of the nation's one thousand private liberal arts colleges will likely close over the next five years.[16] Virtually all colleges and universities will experience revenue shortfalls from reduced enrollment, competitive pressures to reduce tuition, reduced revenues from major sporting events such as football, fewer foreign students attending US universities, and reduced investment returns on endowment funds.

Most colleges and universities will be required to cut costs, including significant staff reductions. We expect smaller liberal arts colleges to suffer more than state universities and large well-endowed private universities. Over the long term, we expect lower-cost online courses and local community colleges to increase their market share as students critically assess the costs and benefits of all forms of higher education. We also expect the growth of student loan debt to slow as college enrollment is pressured for a couple of years. We unfortunately expect student loan delinquencies to remain very high because of unemployment, despite federal government assistance programs.

The virus disrupted normal close-quarters activities like travel, hospitality, dining, concerts, sporting events, conventions, and other large group meetings. We expect people to prefer some level of social distancing and be more resistant to being put into close-contact situations like large cruise ships, sporting events, or live concerts.

Major disruptive events like COVID-19 often impact how people view life for decades to come. The Great Depression in the 1930s ushered in an era of fiscal prudence and conservative attitudes toward borrowing and risk taking that lasted for decades. The September 11 attacks ushered in a new era of security protection for travel and vigilance against risks of terrorism. With COVID-19, millions of young people were homeschooled or participated in online and Zoom-type learning experiences. These young people were also exposed to stay-at-home directives and spent extended periods of time with their immediate family. Many young people also saw their parents experience record job losses while government safety net programs were expanded. Because of all the effects of the virus, we believe the country is at an inflection point where the role of the federal government is likely to be permanently expanded. The country will be searching out a new balance of free enterprise capitalism and government-directed programs and safety nets. With the majority of our population continually devastated and angered by these financial and economic disruptions, the country may move more dramatically toward socialistic protections.

Risks of a new financial crisis

We believe COVID-19 increased the risks of a future financial crisis because of the massive increase in US federal government debt. Extraordinary actions by the Federal Reserve and the US federal government prevented the virus from spurring on a new financial crisis, but the monetary and fiscal policies led to an even more leveraged and fragile economy. Deficit government spending and expansive Fed monetary policies were great short-term medications to fight the virus. But their long term use can lead to addiction with severe negative effects. With unprecedented levels of debt and declining fiscal health, future shocks to the financial and economic system could be devastating. The Federal Reserve and the US federal government have pretty well spent their firepower to counter the virus and are ill prepared to address a new black swan–type event.

Following COVID-19, we continue to be concerned about risks that could lead to a new financial crisis. Risks high on our lists include the piercing of the Chinese real estate bubble, a stock market selloff, a sharp depression in commercial real estate prices, a slow and uncertain recovery of the economy, a potential financial crisis in China, poor financial stability in the European Union, poor fiscal discipline by the US federal government, and expansive Fed monetary policies, which could further inflate asset and debt bubbles.

In this country we have always looked up to our government leaders for guidance and inspiration. General Washington and other leaders inspired a nation to fight for its independence. President Lincoln inspired a nation to fight for racial equality and the continuation of a strong union, despite our differences. President Roosevelt inspired a national works program to take us out of the Depression, and when we entered into a massive and destructive world war, he reminded us that "the only thing we have to fear is fear itself." President Kennedy inspired a generation to public service when he challenged us to "ask not what your country can do for you, ask what you can do for your country." Martin Luther King Jr.'s "I Have a Dream" speech inspired hope for a nation struggling with civil unrest and racial inequality.

But when we look up to the stars now, we rarely find the inspiration from our leaders to face our great challenges. Instead we look the nurses, doctors, emergency crews, police, firefighters, and even regular citizens unselfishly risking their lives to help people survive a worldwide pandemic. When you see this level of self-sacrifice, community service, and compassion for others, you know that there is hope for this nation. We are hoping our leaders will once again set aside their differences and become worthy of the people they are serving.

OUR MISSION

TO BE the nation's leading retailer of financial services for consumers and small businesses by delivering products and services that offer great value and friendly service for everyone.

By achieving our mission and adhering to our core values, we will deliver superior long-term returns for our shareholders.

OUR CORE VALUES

FAIR
- Ethics of absolute fairness, honesty, and integrity guide everything we do.
- Our actions match our words.
- We balance the expectations and earn the trust of our customers, employees, communities, and investors.
- We offer our customers products and services which fit their needs and provide great value.

CARING
- We ensure that every human interaction is caring, courteous, and respectful.
- We expect leaders to make difficult decisions, and to carry them out in a way that allows all involved to maintain dignity.
- We value and respect diversity of background, thought, and style and know they are a competitive advantage.
- We speak candidly and listen openly.

HUMAN
- We are positive, energetic, and committed to achieving our objectives and living our values.
- We celebrate our successes and learn from our failures.
- We keep our egos in check and maintain a sense of humor.
- We believe in the power of talented, committed individuals — working as a team — to make an extraordinary difference.

DYNAMIC
- We are never satisfied with the status quo and know that we must continually reinvent our organization and ourselves.
- We break down silos and bureaucracies in order to serve our customers efficiently as one company.
- We continuously drive operational excellence to innovate our products, processes, and services.

DRIVEN
- We are committed to excellence and the achievement of superior long-term returns for our shareholders.
- We set high, measurable goals and hold ourselves accountable to achieve them.
- We recognize that addressing challenges head-on is a requirement for success.
- We benchmark from our customers' viewpoint and deliver what is most important to them.
- We look both within and outside our industry to learn.

ʬ Washington Mutual

Kerry believed all employees needed to know and practice the company's core values which were summarized on a laminated card.

Acknowledgments

After the 2008 financial crisis, we planned to spend more time with our family and friends and focus our energies on our venture capital companies and helping build our communities through our charitable foundation. We knew the press and politicians were spewing out false narratives about the causes of the financial crisis, but we figured it was best to focus on the future rather than dwell on the past. But then we saw the US government and the Federal Reserve implement policies that hurt everyday people in favor of Wall Street banks. We believed those policies were leading us down a highly risky path of reckless government spending on the backs of record debt and asset bubbles and we were reminded of philosopher George Santayana's quote, "those who cannot remember the past are condemned to repeat it."

So about six years ago, Linda began the journey of collecting all the relevant information she could find regarding the evolution of banking in the US and lessons that should have been learned from past economic and financial crises. She studied hundreds of books and economic research papers on financial crises and researched hundreds of thousands of pages of public documents on banks and an extensive collection of Washington Mutual emails, notes, reports, correspondence, telephone calls, and communications to investors, boards of directors, regulators, and politicians. She talked with hundreds of people impacted by the crisis.

From her research, it was clear that the real facts of the 2008 financial crisis had been covered up and replaced with an inaccurate narrative that supported political agendas. She concluded a careful and balanced analysis of the financial crisis was necessary and she began to document her findings. Her goal was to get all the facts on the table so that maybe policy makers in the future would not be condemned to repeat the same mistakes.

Throughout Kerry's career, he was involved in analyzing major economic and investment trends. For four decades he successfully managed mutual funds, investment portfolios, and banks by identifying major undervalued and overvalued market conditions. For over four years prior to the 2007–08 crisis, he repeatedly made public warnings of a dangerous housing bubble. But his warnings were dismissed by policymakers until they began to panic in September of 2008. Their last-minute bungled actions ultimately led to a financial crisis which had to be dealt with through massive monetary and fiscal stimulus programs.

Kerry understood why the US government and Federal Reserve needed to take aggressive actions to help the economy recover from the last financial crisis, but he became increasingly alarmed when those emergency policies remained in place for over a decade. He concluded policies of large federal budget deficits along with unprecedented easy money policies by the Fed are now leading us into us into unchartered risky territory. Multiple asset and debt bubbles are growing and their bursting could be devastating to the economy and millions of citizens.

Kerry began to carefully research how the Fed's and other central bank's easy money and asset purchase policies were leading to growing asset bubbles such as stocks, commercial real estate, housing, art, and real estate in China. These bubbles were built on the back of extraordinary levels of debt. Kerry gathered data and charts to support his conclusions and wrote the sections of this book dealing with growing bubbles and recommendations for public policy reforms to reduce risks for a new financial crisis.

Kerry and Linda brought their work together in this book in order to document what was learned from the last financial crisis, to identify growing risks today, and to propose actions to be taken now to avoid a new financial crisis. Our goal is to get all the facts on the table so better policy decisions can be made.

We are most grateful for input from our Seattle and Washington DC legal, regulatory, and political team: Barry Kaplan, Jack Quinn, Brendan Sullivan, John Villa, and their teams are outstanding professionals. We appreciate their support during our six-year legal battles and their insights about the legislative, legal, regulatory, and political processes were most valuable.

We also thank our book editing and publishing team of Gregory Shaw, Barbara Bonner, and Nicholas Kerr in Seattle and Arthur Klebanoff, Brian Skulnik, and Michelle Weyenberg in New York for their careful editing, encouragement, and support. When the first response to our manuscript was "I read the book and wow," we knew we had the right team. We are deeply grateful of their knowledge of the publishing process and thank RosettaBooks, Clyde Hill Publishing, and Simon & Schuster. We are also grateful for our publicist, Lisa Linden and our New York publishing attorney, Neil J. Rosini.

We especially want to thank the thousands of Washington Mutual employees who worked tirelessly to create the nation's leading bank for everyday consumers. They helped millions of people own homes, reach their financial goals, and contribute back to their communities. They did a wonderful job and should not have been undermined by inappropriate government policies and actions during the last financial crisis.

Also thanks to the charitable foundation team at Fidelity Investments and our wonderful Seattle-based charitable giving advisor Heather Tuininga. Net proceeds from sales of this book will be donated to charity with the help of these advisors. We look forward to working with them on this project.

Finally, we thank our friends and family for support during and following the financial crisis. We write this book in hopes lessons learned from the last financial crisis will help policymakers make better-informed decisions so our children and grandchildren do not have to experience a new financial crisis.

Kerry lovingly thanks Linda for spending countless hours on her extensive research and having the passion to drive this book forward. Linda lovingly thanks Kerry for his thoughtful analysis and perspectives. We are fortunate to have had twenty years of love and happiness together enjoying family, friends, travel, business projects, charitable giving, and now writing a book together. What a great journey!

The Killinger family learned early how to entertain Iowans with their music. Performing here are Kerry's father, Karl, Uncle Keith, and Aunt Wanda. A few years later, they formed the Killinger Big Band.

Kerry's mom and dad ready to get on the Killinger Big Band Bus following World War II.

Linda's father, Richard, with his widowed mom in Bode, Iowa before he shipped out to a carrier in the Pacific during World War II. His mom had six of her thirteen children serving in the war at the same time.

Kerry's parents, Evelyn and Karl, during World War II. Karl was an officer in the Navy on a LST in the Pacific.

Linda and Tom Miller attend one of many events at the Clinton White House. They were both very active in their re-election efforts.

Linda and Tom attended a number of events at the home of Vice President Al and Tipper Gore. Tom was Iowa Chair of Gore's presidential campaign and both Tom and Linda were actively involved

Linda and Governor Robert D. Ray co-chaired fundraisers for an endowed chair at Iowa State University for Mary Louise Smith, the first female chair of the Republican National Committee. Attending one of the events are Linda, President George H. W. Bush, Mary Louise, and Linda's father, Richard.

Kerry met Warren Buffett in the early 1970s when Kerry was an equity research analyst with Bankers Life of Nebraska. Kerry was invited to participate in Buffett's charitable golf tournaments.

Kerry was chosen by *American Banker* as Banker of the Year. During the 2000s, Washington Mutual was continuously chosen as one of *Business Week*'s Top 25 Service Champs, the only bank ever listed. The Reputation Institute chose us as "the bank with the best Reputation." JD Power named the bank #1 in customer service. *Fortune* magazine named the bank a Blue-Ribbon Company for ranking high on all their lists: Best Companies to Work for, America's Most Admired Companies, Fortune 50, Global 500, Top Innovation Companies, and Top Socially Responsible Companies.

President George H.W. Bush presented Kerry with his Points of Light Foundation's Award for Excellence in Community Service for Kerry's charitable giving and work in affordable housing and building neighborhoods.

In October of 2000, the city of Des Moines received the designation as a federal "Brownfield Showcase Community" by the EPA. Senator Tom Harkin commended Linda, vice chair of the Federal Home Loan Bank, for her "leadership role in the project to turn a former industrial area into a new urban neighborhood."

Kerry formed a partnership with Earvin "Magic" Johnson, to work together on economic revitalization in urban neighborhoods. Kerry also received the Thurgood Marshall award for his work to improve racial and social justice.

Kerry put together a number of charitable fundraising events like the AIDs walk in the early 1990s to raise money for AIDs patient care. At many of the events, he would play for donations.

On Valentine's Day, the Washington Mutual Financial Center would be lit up to show support for the community.

Seattle mayor Norm Rice congratulating Kerry and Linda for receiving an award from the Fred Hutchinson Cancer Research Center. The Killingers also endowed a chair in diversity studies at the University of Washington, funded the Kerry and Linda Killinger gallery at the Seattle Art Museum, and are founding sponsors of the Crosscut Festival.

The Kerry and Linda Killinger Foundation sponsored the Civility Summit for the Iowa State University School of Journalism. Kerry introduced the guests for one of the events, Iowa attorney general Tom Miller, former White House press secretary Mike McCurry, and moderator Kevin Cooney.

Glossary

Following the 2008 financial crisis, there was great confusion among politicians and the media regarding loan and other financial definitions. Those not familiar with mortgages often mischaracterized all adjustable-rate loans as subprime loans. This simply wasn't the case. Most adjustable-rate loans were given to prime borrowers. Below are generally agreed upon definitions for key loan products, terms often used in loan underwriting, the government agencies involved in mortgages and bank regulations and important capital markets products.

Key Residential Loan Products

Fixed-Rate Mortgages: Loans with fixed interest rates and the same payments for the term of the loan (often fifteen- to thirty-year terms).

Adjustable-Rate Mortgages (**ARMs**): Loans with interest rates that periodically reset based on an index. Adjustable-rate loans are often tied to indexes such as the cost of funds index, the London Interbank Offered Rate or the one-year constant maturity treasury yield. Reset periods can range from monthly to up to ten years. Adjustable-rate loans were authorized and promoted by Congress in the 1982 Garn Act in order to help thrifts avoid a portfolio full of fixed-rate loans that are harmful in a rising interest rate environment. ARMs were used extensively by banks until the crisis hit in 2008. ARM loans typically have lower interest rates than fixed-rate loans.

Hybrid ARMs: Loans starting with a fixed-rate for periods of two to ten years followed by an annual reset of interest rates tied to an index. Common products for prime customers included 5/1, 7/1 and 10/1 (five-, seven-, and ten-year fixed-rate loans with annual variable rates after that). Hybrid ARMs for subprime customers were typically 2/28 and 3/27.

Interest Only ARMs: Loans where interest-only is paid for three to ten years followed by larger payments of interest and principal amortization for the balance of the loan term. These loans were primarily offered to prime borrowers.

Option ARMs or Pick-a-Pay Loans: Adjustable-rate loans offered to prime borrowers who have several payment options including making a minimum payment or fully amortizing payment. Loan balances could increase for borrowers making minimum payments. However, most borrowers paid their balances down and negative amortization for regulated banks was typically less than 1 percent of total loan balances.

Conforming Loans: Loans meeting the loan size caps and underwriting standards for purchase or securitization by Fannie and Freddie. Underwriting and documentation standards are determined by Fannie and Freddie and they can be either fixed-rate or adjustable-rate loans.

Jumbo Loans: Loans above the loan size caps of Fannie and Freddie. These loans can be fixed-rate or adjustable-rate loans.

Alt-A Loans: Loans to prime borrowers that have some combination of limited documentation, non-standard product structure or more liberal underwriting guidelines. These loans are viewed as slightly riskier than prime loans but less risky than subprime loans.

Subprime Loans: Fixed-rate and hybrid ARM loans made to individuals with poor credit scores. There is not a clear line of demarcation between prime and subprime borrowers, but most lenders define subprime borrowers as those with FICO credit scores below 640. Some lenders define subprime borrowers as those with credit scores below 580. Washington Mutual was more conservative and defined subprime borrowers as those with credit scores below 660. Subprime loans were typically only 5 percent of the bank's loan portfolio. Between 2002–2007, over 85 percent of subprime loans were originated by unregulated shadow banks.

Home Equity Loans: Fixed-rate or adjustable-rate loans with an identified term and set monthly payments. These loans are often used to finance major expenses like home repairs, medical bills, or college expenses. These loans are secured by the equity in the home.

Home Equity Lines of Credit (HELOC): A revolving line of credit secured by the home. Borrowers have great flexibility of drawing down funds as necessary and making payments based on their actual borrowings. Similar to credit cards, borrowers typically are not required to pay off principal and loans can remain outstanding for up to ten years.

Reverse Mortgages: Reverse mortgages are secured by residential properties and enable borrowers to access the unencumbered equity of the property. The loans are typically given to older homeowners and do not require monthly mortgage payments. The FHA has a government guaranteed reverse mortgage program.

Loan Underwriting Terms

FICO Score: A score derived from five key factors to determine creditworthiness: payment history, indebtedness, types of credit, length of credit history, and new credit accounts. FICO scores range from 300 to 850 and are continually updated. Most lenders rely heavily on FICO scores as good predictors of credit risk. FICO is named for the men who created it in 1956: Bill Fair and Earl Isaac of the Fair Isaac Company.

Loan-to-Value Ratio (LTV): This is a ratio of the loan balance divided by the estimated or appraised value of a home. Historically, LTVs of 80 percent or less were deemed to be very safe with 20 percent equity in the home. However, during the 2008 crisis, many communities experienced home values decreasing up to 50 percent. The national average of home price decline in the 2008 crisis was 27.4 percent, thereby plunging millions of homeowners into negative home equity.

Combined Loan to Value Ratio (CLTV): This is the ratio of all loans secured by a home (first and second mortgages, etc.) divided by the estimated or appraised value of a home. This ratio is relied upon for underwriting home equity and home equity line of credit loans.

Appraisal: Lenders require some form of appraisal to estimate a home's value. Appraisals range from full appraisals by licensed appraisers to statistical appraisals based on comparable home sales.

Full Documentation Loans: Fannie and Freddie set the requirements for full documentation loans. Requirements change over time but usually include verification of sources of income, tax returns, checking and savings account statements, credit card statements, and copies of alimony or child support payments.

Limited Documentation Loans or Stated Income Loans: Limited documentation loans were encouraged by Congress in the early 1980s in order to allow Fannie and Freddie to underwrite LMI loans much faster. Most lenders before the 2008 crisis offered limited documentation loans for borrowers with high FICO scores and/or low loan to value ratios. Fannie and Freddie used stated income loans in their automated underwriting systems. FICO scores, appraisals and loan to value ratios are always required for all limited documentation loans, but income verification or tax return documentation may be waived. An updated SEC study found that "FICO scores and combined loan-to-value (LTV) are the strongest determinants of historical loan performance."[1] Some have incorrectly referred to limited doc loans as no doc loans. This simply is not the case because there are substantial documentation requirements for all loans.

Redlining: The 1934 National Housing Act implemented the "redlining" policies that prevented federal agencies from insuring loans in certain minority or distressed neighborhoods. This policy formalized racial segregation in housing. For many decades, regulated banks who wanted their loans insured would have to follow the redlining policies. Subsequent legislation in the 1980s and 1990s tried to eliminate redlining through expanded LMI lending.

Negative Amortization and Negative Equity: Negative amortization occurs when a payment is less than the interest accrued over a payment. Negative equity occurs when the balance of all mortgage debt (first, second, etc.) exceeds the value of the property. Negative equity was common following severe housing price declines when the housing bubble burst.

Government Housing Agencies

Government Sponsored Enterprises (GSEs): Before the 2008 crisis, GSEs were public stock companies with government charters and implied backing of the federal government. Currently Fannie and Freddie are under conservatorship of the federal government.

Fannie Mae and Freddie Mac: These are the dominant purchasers of home loans in the US. Backed by the full faith and credit of the US, these entities are able to offer subsidized interest rates which assures them dominance over portfolio lenders. Before the 2008 crisis, poor performance of their Alt-A and subprime portfolios led to massive losses and the agencies were placed in conservatorship. These entities continue to set the underwriting and documentation requirements for most home loans in the US.

Federal Housing Administration (FHA): FHA loans are designed for low to moderate income borrowers with low down payment requirements and subprime credit scores. FHA accepts LTVs of 96.5 percent for borrowers with FICO scores of 580 and above, and accepts LTVs of 90 percent for borrowers with credit scores of 500 to 579. Their portfolio is much riskier than Fannie and Freddie as reflected in their high delinquency rates.

Veterans Administration: VA loans are insured by the VA and made to eligible military personnel. The VA guarantees the loans and offers 100 percent LTV loans to both prime and subprime borrowers. VA loans require lower down payments, less documentation, lower FICO scores and underwriting flexibility. This leads to a portfolio which is much riskier than Fannie and Freddie and VA delinquency rates are often higher than the FHA.

Bank Regulatory Agencies

Federal Reserve (Fed): The Federal Reserve is the central bank of the US. It conducts monetary policy, promotes the safety and soundness of the financial system, promotes the safety and soundness of individual financial institutions, fosters payment and system safety, and promotes consumer protection. The Fed has direct regulatory authority for bank holding companies.

Office of the Controller of the Currency (OCC): The OCC regulates and supervises national banks, federally licensed savings associations, and federally licensed branches and agencies of foreign banks doing business in the US.

The Federal Deposit Insurance Corporation (FDIC): The FDIC insures deposits in US banks and thrifts. It is a secondary regulator for larger banks and thrifts and is the primary regulator for small state-chartered banks and savings associations.

National Credit Union Administration (NCUA): The NCUA insures deposits for federal credit unions and is their primary regulator.

Capital Markets Products

Mortgage Securitizations: Mortgage securitizations involve the pooling of residential or commercial mortgages and distributing their related cash flows to investors through bonds, pass-through securities, and collateralized debt obligations.

Collateralized Debt Obligations (CDO): A CDO is a collection of pooled assets such as mortgages, auto loans, or corporate bonds that generate income. The assets are pooled and divided into tranches with cash flow prioritized for each tranche. Most CDOs have AAA rated senior tranches, junior tranches, and residuals.

Collateralized Loan Obligations (CLO): Collateralized loan obligations are securities where payments from multiple middle sized and large business loans are pooled and passed on to different classes of owners in various tranches.

Credit Default Swaps (CDS): Credit default swaps are agreements between financial institutions where one party is compensated in the event of a debt default or other credit event. They are basically derivatives acting as an insurance policy. One party typically receives a premium and takes on the responsibility for making a large payment in the event of a default. Credit default swaps can be tied to the insuring of defaults of country debt, municipal bonds, corporate bonds, mortgage-backed securities, and collateralized debt obligations. These were at the center of the 2008 financial crisis when defaults skyrocketed and AIG, the largest writer of CDSs, was unable to meet its contractual obligations. Naked CDSs involve entities who don't own the debt or the CDOs, but still place insurance bets on their possible defaults. They were used extensively by speculators betting against the US housing market before the financial crisis.

Credit Rating Agencies: Moody's, S &P, and Fitch are the largest credit rating agencies. These companies assign credit ratings to issuers of debt such as government bonds, corporate bonds, municipal bonds, CDs, preferred stock, and collateralized debt obligations. Ratings range from AAA (highly rated) through D (poorly rated). BBB- is usually viewed as the lowest investment grade rating. The agencies were criticized for rating many collateralized debt obligations too high prior to the 2008 financial crisis.

Timeline for
Residential Home Lending

1831 The first home lender or building association in America, the Oxford Provident Building Association of Frankford, Pennsylvania, was established during the presidency of Andrew Jackson.

1863 During the Civil War, President Lincoln signed the National Bank Act of 1863, which allowed him to finance the war by establishing a national currency and a secondary market to sell war bonds and US Treasury securities. The act also established the Office of the Comptroller of the Currency (OCC) within the Department of Treasury, which became responsible for the regulation and inspection of commercial banks.

1889 The Washington National Building and Loan Investment Association (later called Washington Mutual) was created after the devastating Seattle fire of 1889.

1892 The US League of Local Building and Loan Associations was formed to popularize the benefits of thrifts and home ownership. Their motto was "The American Home: The Safeguard of American Liberties."

1913 Congress passed the Federal Reserve Act of 1913, creating the Federal Reserve Board with twelve banks around the country. The purpose of the system was to set monetary policy, regulate commercial banks, promote consumer protection, lend money to member banks, insure liquidity in the system, and serve as a lender of last resort.

1918   World War I ended and twhe Spanish flu pandemic began. After everyone recovered, the Roaring Twenties began.

1929   The Wall Street crash of 1929. Within a few years after the crash, over half the commercial banks and thrifts had failed. It was estimated around 25 percent of Americans lost their homes.

1932   The Pecora Commission was created by Congress to investigate the cause of the crash and make any criminal referrals. There were substantial changes in bank regulation, but no bankers went to prison after the crash.

   The Federal Home Loan Bank Board (FHLBB) was created with twelve regional banks around the country to regulate and insure the thrifts (savings and loans). The Federal Savings and Loan Insurance Corporation (FSLIC) was created to insure thrift deposits up to $40,000.

1933   The Banking Act of 1933 (Glass-Steagall Act) created the Federal Deposit Insurance Corporation to insure commercial bank deposits and also separated the commercial and investment banking functions. Regulation Q of the act set interest rate ceilings for the banks and thrifts. The Homeowners Loan Act (HOLA) was created to provide mortgage assistance to homeowners in danger of losing their homes and introduced fifteen-year amortizing loans.

1934   The National Housing Act established the Federal Housing Administration (FHA) to insure mortgage loans to qualified homeowners. It convinced the thrifts to abandon their traditional short-term balloon loans in favor of long-term fixed-rate loans. The Act also implemented redlining policies in the country.

1938   As a part of the New Deal, the Federal National Mortgage Association (Fannie Mae) was created to borrow in the capital markets, buy FHA-insured mortgages, and securitize them in the secondary market.

1944   The Servicemen's Readjustment Act (GI Bill) provided low-cost mortgages, unemployment compensation, and tuition payments for returning GIs.

1962   President Kennedy signed Executive Order 11063, which prohibited lenders using federal guarantee programs (VA and FHA) from discrimination on the basis of race. In 1963 the Congress for Racial Equality (CORE) started taking action against builders, developers, and lenders who they believed were discriminating.

1965   The Housing and Urban Development Act expanded federal housing programs and added new programs for the elderly and disabled, veterans, and public housing.

1968   Congress, under pressure to get Fannie Mae out of government ownership, approved the Housing and Urban Development Act, which privatized Fannie and created HUD to regulate Fannie. The government didn't explicitly guarantee the debts of Fannie and Freddie, but investors believed the guarantee was implied.

1970   Fannie Mae received a baby brother, Freddie Mac (the Federal Home Loan Mortgage Corporation), which was conceived to develop a secondary market for conventional loans—thirty-year fixed-rate loans.

1977   Congress enacted the Community Reinvestment Act (CRA) to encourage banks and thrifts to reject redlining rules and extend more lending to the low- and moderate-income (LMI) neighborhoods.

Merrill Lynch, started the groundbreaking cash management account (CMA). The CMA combined brokerage accounts with check writing and Visa card privileges tied to a money market account with much higher interest rates than the banks and thrifts could pay. Regulated bankers protested and lobbied Congress to protect them.

1980   Congress passed the Depository Institutions Deregulation and Monetary Control Act, which allowed banks to merge, eliminated interest rate caps, allowed the popular NOW account to compete with CMAs, and increased FSLIC and FDIC insurance caps from $40,000 to $100,000.

1982   President Reagan signed the Garn–St. Germain Act, which loosened restrictions on thrifts so they could be more competitive with the money market funds. Some states deregulated the thrifts even more, which opened a Pandora's box of an unregulated shadow banking system of thrifts that acted more like entrepreneurs than bankers.

The act preempted state laws restricting banks and thrifts from only making thirty-year fixed-rate loans. Most thrifts in the country were near insolvency because the costs of rising interest rates for savings accounts could not be paid with the low interest income from long-term fixed-rate loans. The Parity Act, part of the Garn Act authorized the use of adjustable-rate ARM loans, balloon payments and interest-only mortgages.

Kerry Killinger, from the successful securities and mutual fund management firm Murphey Favre, was looking to merge his firm with a bank or thrift. He approached the financially ailing Washington

Mutual with a proposal to combine firms to cross-sell products. Within months the combined company was profitable and became the largest savings bank to change from a mutual company to an investor-owned savings bank. Linda, his future wife, became a partner in an international accounting firm specializing in financial institutions.

1980/90s From 1971 to 1999, most of the large investment banks went from a partnership structure to public stock companies. Merrill Lynch changed in 1971, Lehman Brothers in 1984, Bear Stearns in 1985, Morgan Stanley in 1986, and Goldman Sachs in 1999. Many economists feel the move to an investor-owned structure reduced incentives to manage long-term reputation and favor rapid growth.[1]

1986 The Tax Reform Act of 1986 dramatically encouraged homeownership by allowing a tax deduction on interest for mortgages on primary and secondary homes.

1989 Kerry Killinger was named president of Washington Mutual and joined the board of the bank. He became CEO in 1990 and chair of the board in 1991.

   The Federal Home Loan Bank Board finally shut down hundreds of the thrifts, which were accused of aggressive lending activities. Congress passed the Financial Institutions Reform, Recovery, and Enforcement Act (FIRREA), which increased capital requirements, raised premiums on deposit insurance, and created an independent federal regulator for the thrifts—the Office of Thrift Supervision (OTS). FIRREA also gave more responsibility to Fannie Mae and Freddie Mac to buy mortgages for LMI families. Government regulators were required to issue CRA ratings for banks. The FDIC began insuring thrift deposits.

1992 Congress enacted Title XIII of the Housing and Community Development Act to provide LMI borrowers better access to mortgage credit through Fannie Mae and Freddie Mac. Congress initially specified that 30 percent of the GSE's mortgage purchases had to meet LMI goals. This was increased to 42 percent in 1995 and 50 percent in 2000. By 2008 the LMI goal was 56 percent, and 27 percent of the loans had to be for borrowers at or below 80 percent of the area median income. Fannie Mae and Freddie Mac met those goals nearly every year between 1996 and 2008.[2] By 1995 CRA regulations required banks and thrifts to use "innovative or flexible lending practices"—like flexible subprime, Alt-A, and option ARMs—to increase their level of LMI loans.

1994   The Riegle-Neal Interstate Banking and Branching Efficiency Act allowed banks to merge across state lines, which inspired massive mergers in the banking industry.

The Home Ownership and Equity Protection Act (HOEPA) authorized the Fed to prohibit unfair or deceptive mortgage lending, regardless of the type of regulator they have.

1995   President Clinton developed the National Homeownership Strategy, which had a goal to generate up to eight million additional homeowners in order to achieve 67.5 percent homeownership within five years.[3] The strategy also called for more 97 percent LTV loans and the use of automated underwriting (stated income loans) to slash paperwork and decrease loan-processing time.

HUD amended the CRA to allow securitization of CRA loans into mortgage-backed securities.

1997   Washington Mutual wins its white knight battle for Great Western in California, and the next year H. F. Ahmanson approached Kerry to purchase their bank. The resulting mergers grew Washington Mutual to the country's sixth-largest bank with over $200 billion in assets.

Bear Stearns launchwes the first private securitization of CRA loans into collateralized debt obligations.

JPMorgan Chase pioneers the use of credit default swaps (CDS) to shift the default risk of loans off its balance sheet.

Late 1990s   The age of banking consolidation. JPMorgan Chase, Citigroup, and Bank of America put together dozens of mergers to become $1 trillion–asset megabanks. Wachovia and Wells Fargo also had dozens of mergers to increase their size to over $500 billion. They quickly become the top five banks in the country and had to dramatically increase their CRA goals in order to get acquisition approval from the regulators.

Wall Street investment banks, led by Goldman Sachs CEO Hank Paulson, successfully lobbied Congress to reduce their capital requirements. Later the FCIC report found that most of the investment banks leading up to the 2008 crisis had capital leverage of about forty to one.

Fannie Mae and Freddie Mac also successfully lobbied Congress to lower their capital requirements. The FCIC report showed their capital ratios coming into the crisis were seventy-five to one.

1999   The Glass-Steagall Act is abolished and replaced with the Gramm-Leach-Bliley Act, which allows commercial banks and investment banks to merge. The act failed to give the SEC or any other financial regulatory agency the authority to regulate large investment banks. An amendment to the act prohibited any bank from mergers or acquisitions if it had a less than satisfactory CRA rating.

Fannie heavily invests in subprime loans, buying loans with FICO scores as low as 620 to 640 and LTVs of 100 percent.[4]

1999–2001   Nearly all of the large banks purchase subprime companies to help them with the mandated CRA requirements and federal LMI goals. Kerry is skeptical of the subprime industry, so he developed a partnership with Earvin "Magic" Johnson to help the bank develop safe products for economic revitalization in urban neighborhoods.

2000   Kerry develops the bank's five-year plan, which emphasizes growth in retail branches in New York, Texas, and Florida. He also expands commercial and small business lending and credit card operations.

The Commodity Futures Modernization Act of 2000 (CFMA) clarified the law so most OTC financial derivatives would not be regulated as "futures" under the Commodity Exchange Act of 1936 or as securities under the federal securities laws. This left the CDOs and CDSs unregulated and production soared.

2001   Kerry received the Banker of the Year award from the American Banker Association—the first time a thrift CEO won the award.

2002   President Bush produced the "Blueprint for the American Dream," which set a goal of $1 trillion of loans for minority borrowers to increase minority homeownership by 5.5 million by the end of the decade.

The Sarbanes-Oxley Act was enacted after the failures and financial irregularities of Enron, Worldcom, and others. The act required CEOs and CFOs to sign off personally on the 10-K and 10-Q financial statements.

The 2002 Commodity Futures Modernization Act deregulated the over-the-counter (OTC) derivatives market and eliminated oversight by the CFTC and the SEC. This left the multitrillion-dollar OTC market unregulated.[5]

2003   Kerry becomes more skeptical of the new shadow subprime system developing with unregulated mortgage brokers, over one hundred unregulated subprime companies and the Wall Street mega–investment banks, which were gathering these loans and securitizing and selling hundreds of billions of CDOs into the system. As a result, he cut all mortgage lending in half in 2003 and between 2003 and 2007 cut mortgage lending by 74 percent, replacing revenues with credit card operations, commercial and small business lending, and additional retail branch offices.

Fannie and Freddie purchase $81 billion in subprime mortgage-backed securities.[6]

Fannie's regulator (OFHEO) examined the bank and found improper accounting.

The Federal Reserve begins raising interest rates from 2 percent to 6.5 percent, encouraging homeowners away from long-term fixed-rate loans to lower-rate adjustable loans (ARMs).

2004 The OTS, FDIC, and state of Washington conducted a joint exam of Washington Mutual and issued the bank an informal directive to develop a plan to increase lending to "higher-risk borrowers." In response, the bank's enterprise risk management department developed a detailed plan to place strict limits on all lending products.

Fannie and Freddie purchased $175 billion in subprime mortgage-backed securities.[7]

US homeownership rate peaks at 69.2 percent.[8]

2004 As vice chair of the Federal Reserve's Thrift Industry Advisory Council (TIAC), Kerry started to warn the Federal Reserve, investors, and the public about the overvalued housing market.

The five largest investment banks—Goldman Sachs, Bear Stearns, Lehman Brothers, Morgan Stanley, and Merrill Lynch—were granted exemptions to leverage limitations. They soon increased leverage to nearly forty times.[9]

2005 Fannie and Freddie purchase $169 billion in subprime mortgage-backed securities.[10]

2006 The unregulated shadow subprime system produced 85 percent of the subprime loans in the country between 2002 and 2006 and quickly folded in 2007. (See Chart)

Between 2002 and 2006, the insurance company AIG's Financial Products division sold nearly a half a trillion dollars in credit default swaps but failed to adequately hedge the risks, set aside capital reserves, or post collateral.

The state attorneys general, led by Iowa attorney general Tom Miller, investigated the activities of many of the unregulated subprime companies, like Ameriquest and New Century, and charged them with outlandish sales quotas, prepayment penalties, and other violations.

The Federal Housing Finance Agency and the Office of Federal Housing Enterprise Oversight (OFHEO) released a special exam of Fannie

Mae and claimed it overstated income and capital and had "deliberately and intentionally manipulated accounting to hit earnings targets."

Washington Mutual opened their new building in downtown Seattle. By consolidating workers from about twenty buildings into one, the bank saved $15 million a year. Employees developed the concept of neighborhoods to work in, and all facilities, cafeterias, and conference rooms were open to all employees. There were no executive dining rooms.

Fannie and Freddie purchased $90 billion in subprime mortgage-backed securities.[11] Freddie was fined $3.8 million for illegal campaign contributions.

The FDIC reported annual earnings for the regulated banking industry at a record of nearly $150 billion. There hadn't been any bank failures for nearly three years.

2007 Even though subprime loans typically averaged less than 5 percent of Washington Mutual's mortgage loan portfolio and performed substantially better than the industry, Kerry shut down the subprime loan originations because of his concerns about the housing market.

The FDIC and the OTS gave their annual exam to Washington Mutual in July and said they "rated the bank a '2' plus" because of the strong liquidity, capital, and lending performance. They stated, "The overall risk posed by the higher risk lending strategy remains adequately controlled through managed growth, adequate monitoring of delinquencies and nonperforming assets (NPA) and the maintenance of adequate allowances and capital relative to portfolio risk."

In April, Washington Mutual announced a $2 billion grant to lower payments to subprime customers. The bank adds another $1 billion grant in 2008 to continue to help customers avoid foreclosure.

In late July Bear Stearns sent a letter to investors saying that two of its hedge funds specializing in subprime deals had lost at least 90 percent of their value. With delinquencies rising and the collapse of many of the unregulated subprime companies, panic had set in. Liquidity in the secondary markets had dried up. Naked short sellers saw an opportunity and started targeting any banks with mortgage portfolios.

Loan delinquencies in the industry rose to well over 3 percent, but Washington Mutual losses were one-third of that. (See Chart 8-1.)

Kerry promotes his new mortgage broker disclosure form to the banking industry. It requires mortgage brokers to provide all customers with a one-page summary revealing their prepayment penalties, loan costs, rate resets, and broker commission.

In December, banks report record loan losses, write-downs, and corporate losses. Washington Mutual's loan losses are much lower than the other banks', and the bank shows a slight operating profit for the year. Kerry starts to build a cushion by adding $3 billion in new capital to the bank. The entire industry only reports only $5 billion in quarterly earnings.

Kerry is the only large bank president/CEO to announce he will not accept his bonus in 2007, 2008, and other years until the housing crisis is over. He continues to give his annual salary to charity every year.

2008   In March, Bear Stearns fails and is purchased by JPMorgan Chase.

Treasury Secretary Paulson releases his "Blueprint for a Modernized Financial Structure." He doesn't sound an alarm but rather proposes a bureaucratic reorganization and a startling proposal to eliminate the regulated thrift industry within two years. He declared, "The US has the strongest and most liquid capital markets in the world."

During the spring and into the summer, both Treasury Secretary Paulson and Federal Reserve chair Ben Bernanke continue to make public statements claiming the economy is recovering. They declare: "The credit crisis is entering its later stages. We are well into the adjustment process, because home sales appear to have flattened."

In April, the Washington Mutual board, with the recommendation from Goldman Sachs and Lehman Brothers, accepts the TPG bid for a $7.2 billion capital raise for the bank. Shareholders approved the decision in June 2008.

Washington Mutual became the highest-capitalized large bank in the country with a Tier 1 capital ratio of 9.96 percent and a total risk-based capital ratio of 13.93 percent. (See Chart 1-1.) In addition, public filings showed that Citigroup, UBS, and Merrill Lynch had the worst mortgage losses, with a combined total of $118.2 billion—41 percent of all the mortgage loan losses of the top twenty banks. In addition, JPMorgan Chase, Bank of America, Citigroup, Wachovia, and HSBC had a combined total of $176 trillion in notional amounts of over-the-counter derivatives.

FDIC reported national quarterly regulated bank earnings of only $5 billion—a drop of nearly 90 percent from the previous year.

On July 12, California-based thrift IndyMac experienced a run on deposits and was quickly seized. FDIC Chair Bair publicly announced that she knows of no other large bank in danger of failure. Privately Bair panics on the thoughts than any more failures would wipe out the FDIC insurance fund. Most large banks lose substantial deposits, but most banks, including Washington Mutual, recover by the end of August.

On July 15, the SEC issues an emergency order banning naked short selling of nine large American banks and ten foreign banks.

Inexplicably, it leaves off non–Wall Street banks like Wells Fargo, Washington Mutual, and Wachovia. Kerry and the attorneys work with the other banks to contact the SEC and protest the move.

On September 4, Kerry retires from Washington Mutual.

On September 6, Fannie Mae and Freddie Mac were put into conservatorship by the Treasury Department and FHFA. The bailout was authorized to purchase up to $100 billion in preferred stock.[12]

On September 12, the American financial system is shaken to its core when Treasury refused to help Lehman Brothers, forcing them to file bankruptcy protection. "The bankruptcy sparked a chain reaction that sent the credit markets into disarray and accelerated the downward spiral of AIG."

On September 14, Bank of America agrees to buy Merrill Lynch in an all-stock deal for $50 billion. The price, twenty-nine dollars per share, is a 70 percent premium from the current share price.

On September 16, the Federal Reserve extends an $85 billion loan to AIG to prevent its bankruptcy. Eventually the bailout to AIG rose to $182 billion.[13]

Most large banks continue to have deposit withdrawals and declining stock prices after the haphazard response of the Federal Reserve and Treasury as to who would be abandoned and who would be showered with billions.

On September 21, Treasury and the FDIC announce that investment banks Goldman Sachs, Morgan Stanley, and others can become bank holding companies, allowing them to borrow from the Federal Reserve to relieve their liquidity issues.

On September 25, the FDIC, in an unprecedented move, seizes Washington Mutual and sells it to JPMorgan Chase for the bargain price of $1.9 billion, even though the bank had a reasonable stand-alone plan in place. The bank still had enough liquidity and was highly capitalized. The holding company of the bank, WMI, with nearly $33 billion of assets and only $8 billion of liabilities, was forced into bankruptcy because it lost its key asset—the bank. The FDIC also stiffed the bondholders of the bank, which sent the market into a deeper panic.

Treasury Secretary Paulson later admitted the seizure of the bank "was a mistake. Washington Mutual, the sixth-biggest bank in the country, was systemically important."

On September 29, the ensuing panic causes more deposit runs and Wachovia becomes so stressed that it is sold to Citigroup—without a seizure, bankruptcy or stiffing the bondholders.

On September 29, the FDIC starts the Temporary Liquidity Guarantee Program with lending insurance for promissory notes, commercial paper, interbank funding, corporate bonds, and even unsecured parts of secured debt. The program mushrooms to $350 billion.

On October 1, the IRS issues a tax ruling allowing loan losses in acquired banks be treated as carry-forward losses, making loan losses potentially a valuable tax asset. Wells Fargo quickly offers more for Wachovia and takes the transaction from Citigroup.

On October 3, the TARP bill passes Congress and is signed by President Bush. It gives $250 billion to the top nine banks.

2009   The country lost over six million jobs since the crisis began in 2007, and millions of homeowners have lost their homes.

In January, Senator Carl Levin, chair of the Permanent Subcommittee on Investigations, announces his investigation into the causes of the crisis. In his speech, he announces his conclusion before he even starts the investigation.

In May, the Fraud Enforcement and Recovery Act passed by Congress and signed by the president forms the ten-member Financial Crisis Inquiry Commission (FCIC), to "examine the causes of the current and financial and economic crisis in the United States." Even though no one on the committee had extensive experience in investigating financial crimes, the committee is tasked with giving criminal referrals to the Department of Justice.

2010   There are now twenty-six million American who are out of work, but Congress seems mostly focused on showy TV hearings and investigations.

In January, the first of the FCIC hearings begins, starting with the CEOs of Goldman Sachs, JPMorgan Chase, Morgan Stanley, and Bank of America.

In February, Treasury Secretary Paulson releases his book, *On the Brink*, in which he barely mentions Washington Mutual but does admit seizing the bank was a mistake.

In April, Senator Levin and the PSI start their hearings into the crisis. We are told by a number of Washington, DC, attorneys that Levin's hearings are short on facts and long on drama. Kerry testifies at the hearings and discusses his efforts to warn the regulators and dramatically decrease mortgage lending. He states what most people are thinking: Wall Street was "too clubby to fail" and there was no logic to who was abandoned and who was showered with billions.

In December, the FDIC contacts our attorney and says it will not pursue the executives, it just wants help in getting at the directors and officers (D&O) insurance policies—to the tune of $40 million.

In December, analyst Mark Zandi reveals that FDIC has closed 135 banks, and another 550 banks are on "their watch list." Employment has plunged by 2.2 million in the past six months, and 17 percent of the workforce is unemployed or underemployed. At the end of November, there were 2.8 million mortgage loans in foreclosure and an additional 1.6 million loans ninety days or more past due. Because of declining housing prices, one in five Americans owed at least 125 percent of the current value of their homes.

2011 In January, the FCIC releases its report. It interviewed over seven hundred people but did not interview any Washington Mutual executives or call to verify data. Washington Mutual is barely mentioned in the report. The hearings reveal that twelve of the thirteen major banks would have failed within days had Treasury not come to their defense.

In March, Senator Levin pressures the FDIC to sue the executives at Washington Mutual, and FDIC capitulates. In an unprecedented move, the FDIC sues the executives for $1 billion without interviewing them first and without detailing specific reasons for the lawsuit. The executives prepare to file suit against the FDIC.

The Senate PSI releases its five-volume investigation of the crisis. Neither the report nor the chairman's longing to create his own new financial regulations gain any traction.

In August, the Department of Justice announces it closed the investigation of Washington Mutual with no criminal or civil charges.

In December, Washington Mutual executives settle with the FDIC for the $40 million from the insurance fund. No executive was fined or sanctioned in any way. Senator Levin publicly threatens the OCC to go after the executives.

2013 A US Senate investigation finds that JPMorgan Chase misled both regulators and investors about the nature and size of the losses in its "London Whale" trade, and its derivatives still posed a significant threat to the financial system. The bank was fined $920 million. In addition, the OCC continues to assess fines and civil money penalties to the bank. By 2015, JPMorgan Chase has more civil money penalties, fines, and consent orders from the OCC than all the other banks combined. None of these actions involved any activities at Washington Mutual.

In May, under pressure from Senator Levin, the OCC capitulates and says it wants to investigate Washington Mutual. It asks to interview Kerry for a couple of days.

In July, the OCC decides to pursue a formal enforcement action against the executives. The short letter lists vague reasons for the action. We are given twenty-one days to provide a full defense.

Twenty-one days later, Kerry and his attorneys provide a response to the OCC, which includes research reports from former chair of the FDIC William Isaac and former senior deputy comptroller of the currency Michael Mancusi. Both Isaac and Mancusi say they were prepared to testify that Kerry "did not breach his fiduciary duties, violate any law or regulation, act with reckless disregard or otherwise engage in unsafe or unsound conduct."

Former FDIC chairman Isaac adds, "In my experience, an institution with Washington Mutual's examination ratings and financial ratios has never been seized by the US government." An independent study analyzing loan performance of securitizations of the largest banks reveals Washington Mutual's loans performed as well as or better than the competition. (See Chart 10-2.)

In December, the OCC calls to say it "decided not to proceed against any of the Washington Mutual executives."

2014   The Washington Mutual bankruptcy settlement is finally finished, the assets of the holding company and the remainder of the insurance policies are distributed, and the lawsuits immediately stop.

2018   Andrew Ross Sorkin from CNBC interviews Kerry during the tenth-anniversary week of the global financial crisis. The week is filled with exuberant Wall Street executives who celebrated their enormous success and saw only a rosy economy on the horizon. Kerry's interview is different. He warns the viewing audience about the building asset and debt bubbles in the system and predicts a future downturn in the stock market and the economy.

2020   Kerry writes to investors that the Federal Reserve and the US government actions over the past decade have created asset and debt bubbles that make the US economy highly leveraged and fragile. He warns the piercing of these bubbles could result in a significant economic crisis and potentially a new financial crisis.

The COVID-19 pandemic hits and exposes the leverage and fragility of the global economy. Economic activity plummets, job losses mount, and bubbles burst. Kerry warns risks will continue and the coronavirus is just one of many unpredictable factors that could lead to a new financial crisis.

The authors of this book propose recommendations for changes in public and Federal Reserve policies to reduce risks from a new financial crisis.

Notes

Introduction

1. Financial Crisis Inquiry Committee (FCIC), page 3.
2. Financial Crisis Inquiry Committee (FCIC), page 354.
3. Data obtained from *Inside Mortgage Finance*'s 2009 Mortgage Market Statistical Annual Volume I. According to the notes of *IMF*'s "Top Mortgage Originators" tables, "lenders were asked to report 1–4 family residential mortgage originations. Wholesale purchases, including loans closed by correspondents, are counted. Lenders are instructed to include only HELOC amounts that are actually funded."
4. Federal Reserve, "Credit Risk, Credit Scoring and the Performance of Home Mortgages," July 1996.
5. FICO: Fair Isaac and Company is a data analytics company founded by Bill Fair and Earl Isaac in 1956. The FICO score is a measure of consumer credit risk, and the first FICO score was released in 1989. The scores range from 300 to 850.
6. Washington Mutual annual reports and quarterly risk management reports 2004 to 2008.
7. Washington Mutual risk reports.
8. First American Loan Performance, "Washington Mutual Relative to Industry Benchmarks," December 2007.

9. See Chart 8-1 Washington Mutual Residential Loan Delinquencies vs. Industry. First American Loan Performance, TS Securities through September 2007.
10. See Chart 12-8: S&P Case-Shiller Home Price Index.
11. The top twenty-five subprime lenders originated 93 percent of all the subprime loans from 2002 to 2007.
12. Inside Mortgage Finance, *Inside B&C Lending*. Data acquired by author in November 2019. FCIC report said, "Loans made by CRA regulated lenders were half as likely to default as similar loans by independent mortgage originators not subject to the law."
13. International Swaps and Derivatives Association (ISDA), FCIC, page 130.
14. FCIC, page 256.
15. Ibid.
16. Email stream between OTS director John Reich and Kerry in March 2008. The signed confidentiality agreement required JPM to inform Washington Mutual and/or the bank's primary regulator—OTS—before it gave any information to anyone. Comments from FDIC were taken from the Hochberg Bankruptcy Examination Report (Examiner), page 273.
17. CNN Politics, "Schumer: Don't Blame Me for IndyMac Failure," July 13, 2008.
18. "Department of Treasury Blueprint for a Modernized Financial Regulatory Structure," March 15, 2008.
19. Email exchanges and presentation decks between JPMorgan and FDIC in July and August of 2008, detailed in the Hochberg bankruptcy exam.
20. See Chart 11-1, Five Largest Bank Capitalizations.
21. S&P Global Market Intelligence, April 7, 2020.
22. Chart 12-3, Central Bank Balance Sheets, Haver Analytics.
23. Chart 12-4, S&P Dow Jones Indices Chart.
24. Federal Reserve Bank of St. Louis, "Federal Economic Research," Source of data is the S&P Dow Jones Indices LLC.
25. *ARTnews*, "Leonardo da Vinci's 'Salvator Mundi' Sells for $450.3 million at Christies," November 15, 2017.
26. See Student Debt and Auto Debt, Charts 12-17 and 12-18.
27. Chart 12-22, US Government Debt.
28. Chart 12-23, Unfunded Pension Liability as Percent of GDP.

Chapter 1

1. Robert Shiller, The Subprime Solution: How Today's Global Financial Crisis Happened, and What to Do About It, 2008.
2. In the fall of 2007, Kerry received a number of reports that Dimon was telling people he "wanted to find a way to get Washington Mutual for pennies on the dollar." JPMorgan also planted a story in the *Seattle Times* in December of 2006.
3. Linda was vice chair of the Federal Home Loan Bank of Des Moines, and Kerry was the vice chair of the FHLB in Seattle. They both had been elected to the National Advisory Board of the FHLBs.
4. *American Banker*, "Here's Where Jamie Dimon and I Disagree," May 20, 2016.

5.   *New York Times*, "Home Prices Fell in '07 for First Time in Decades," January 24, 2008.
6.   Mark Zandi, *Financial Shock*, 2008.
7.   Note to Board of Directors, March 3, 2008.
8.   Lightfromtheright.com, "Fed Transcripts From 2008 Reveal Experts to be Clueless and Confused," March 21, 2014.
9.   www.sanders.senate.gov, "Bernanke: In His Own Words," compiled on December 3, 2009.
10.   Department of the Treasury, "Blueprint for a Modernized Financial Regulatory Structure," March 2008.
11.   Email exchange between Goldman, Lehman, and Washington Mutual, March 2008.
12.   Senior Supervisors Group, "Observations on Risk Management Practices during the Recent Market Turbulence," March 6, 2008.
13.   Henry M. Paulson Jr., *On the Brink: Inside the Race to Stop the Collapse of the Global Financial System*, 2010, page 110.
14.   Phillip A. Wallach, "To the Edge: Legality, Legitimacy, and the Responses to the 2008 Financial Crisis," 46–49. *New York Times*, "JPMorgan Raises Bid for Bear Stearns to $10 a Share," "The Central Bank had directed JPMorgan to pay no more than $2 a share for Bear to assure it would not appear that Bear shareholders were being rescued," March 24, 2008.
15.   Timothy Geithner, Stress Test: Reflections on Financial Crises, 2014, Chapter 4.
16.   Ibid.
17.   *Wall Street Journal*, "Volker at Edge," April 8, 2008. *Bloomberg*, "Volcker Shuns the Blame Game," April 10, 2008.
18.   *New York*, "The Heist," March 21, 2008.
19.   NPR, "Bear Stearns Collapse Costly to Many," March 17, 2008.
20.   *The Guardian*, "Bear Stearns to Axe 8,000 staff," March 22, 2008.
21.   All potential parties in the capital raise signed confidentiality documents that required them to contact Washington Mutual and/or their primary regulator, the OTS, before they shared any documents or information about the bank. The bankruptcy examiner Hochberg also verified the FDIC indemnified JPMC $500 million for any charges that they violated the confidentiality agreement. Page 208.
22.   Email exchange between OTS director Reich and Kerry, March 2008.
23.   Permanent Subcommittee on Investigations, April 16, 2010, Exhibit 59.
24.   Hochberg, "Final Report of Examiner", November 2010, page 37.
25.   March 2008 notes and emails detailing conversation between Dimon and Kerry.
26.   Hochberg, page 230–235.
27.   Hochberg, page 273.
28.   Hochberg, page 218–235.
29.   Financial data taken from each bank's quarterly earnings release/annual reports.
30.   Email from JPMorgan Chase to Killinger on March 31, 2008.
31.   Hochberg, page 38.
32.   Ibid.
33.   Hochberg, page 41.

34. Washington Mutual Board of Directors minutes.
35. Hochberg, page 37 and 213.
36. Eric Dash and Andrew Ross Sorkin, "Government Seizes WaMu and Sells Some Assets," *New York Times*, September 25, 2008.
37. TheStreet.com, "Is JPMorgan Chase Guilty of Antitrust Violation?" April 13, 2010.
38. Washington Mutual press release, April 8, 2008.
39. FCIC, *Financial Crisis Inquiry Report*, January 2011, page 208–9.
40. Hochberg, page 34.
41. Hochberg, page 37 and 216.
42. Hochberg, pages, 34, 216, 235, and 303.
43. The Bank Secrecy Act (BSA) also known as the Anti-Money Laundering Law (AML) required financial institutions to report suspicious activity that could indicate money laundering or other crimes. The Feds got particularly prickly and punitive about this after 9/11. Most large banks had received formal enforcement orders on implementing these requirements.
44. www.ft.com/cms
45. A MOU is a memorandum of understanding from a bank regulator that outlines exactly what a bank needs to do to correct certain activities. It is an advisory, not a formal regulatory order.
46. Gregg Gunselman, email exchange re: West, June 18, 2008. Hochberg report.
47. Hochberg, page 34.
48. Ibid.
49. *New York Times*, "Raw Deal for Washington Mutual Shareholders," June 15, 2008.
50. Letters from the three proxy firms.
51. Hochberg, page 217–218.
52. Hochberg, page 223.
53. Hochberg, page 222–223.
54. Email from attorney Bruce Fletcher to Kerry Killinger, June 2008.
55. *HousingWire*, "Washington Mutual Nixes Option ARMS, Adds $1 Billion to Borrower Assistance Fund," June 19, 2008.
56. Data obtained from each bank's public filings. Tier 1 ratio is defined as a bank's Tier 1 capital amount divided by risk weighted assets, and total risk-based capital ratio is defined as a bank's total risk-based capital divided by risk weighted assets. The higher the ratios, the better. Data on investment banks and Fannie and Freddie was found in the FCIC report, which stated that Fannie and Freddie had asset ratios of 75:1 and the investment banks were up to 40:1.
57. In the data prepared by *Bloomberg News*, Countrywide numbers were included in Bank of America.
58. http://www.bloomberg.com/apps/news?pid=newsarchieve&sid=a5GaivCMZu_M
59. FCIC, page 300.
60. FCIC, page 225.
61. FCIC, page 225. Data from the Bingham Letter: "Repurchase Collection by Top Ten Sellers/Servicers," September 14, 2010.
62. Bank press releases on earnings and annual reports.
63. Martin Wolf, *The Shifts and the Shocks: What We've Learned—and Have Still to Learn—From the Financial Crisis*, 2014.

64. FDIC Forum on Mortgage Lending to Low-and-Moderate-Income Households, July 8, 2008.

65. *CNN Politics*, "Schumer: Don't Blame Me for IndyMac Failure," July 13, 2008.

66. In 1989, Congress passed the FIRREA Act, which required thrifts keep 65 percent of their assets in residential mortgage products. This was an over-reaction to the nearly unregulated thrifts in many states in the 1980s, which weren't required to have any mortgages on the books.

67. *New York Times*, "Senate Questioning on Mortgages Puts Regulators on the Defensive," March 23, 2007.

68. FDIC daily deposit records for Washington Mutual and Wachovia.

69. Woodrow Wilson Foundation Corporate Citizenship Award.

70. FDIC and OTS annual exam report, 2008.

71. FDIC and OTS 2008 annual exam report, July 15, 2008.

72. CERO John McMurray, "Washington Mutual Quarterly Review of Enterprise Risk Management Function," July 15, 2008.

73. "Washington Mutual Quarterly Credit Risk Management Report." Industry average loan performance data supplied by Inside Mortgage Finance, Loan Performance TS Securities through April 2008.

74. *Inside Mortgage Finance*, 2009 Mortgage Market Statistical Annual Volume I.

75. Willkie Farr & Gallagher, "SEC Emergency Order on 'Naked' Short Selling," July 18, 2008.

76. www.sanders.senate.gov, "Bernanke: In His Own Words," compiled on December 3, 2009. Statement was made on July 16, 2008.

77. Email stream between FDIC, OTS, and Washington Mutual execs shows Kerry instigated the meeting and OTS asked FDIC to join the meeting.

78. Hochberg, pages 220 and 279.

79. Email exchange from JPM employees and July emails between execs from the PSI and the Examiners Report.

80. Hochberg, page 219.

81. Letter to SEC, July 29, 2008.

82. *Mortgage Daily News*, "Banks, Trade Groups Say SEC Order Does Not Go Far Enough", July 22, 2008.

83. *New York Times*, "Can Hank Paulson Defuse This Crisis?" July 27, 2008.

84. Ibid.

85. Ibid.

86. *Market Watch*, "FDIC Chief Doesn't See Bank Failure as Big as IndyMac," July 22, 2008.

87. Sheila Bair, *Bull by the Horns: Fighting to Save Main Street from Wall Street and Wall Street from Itself*, 2012, page 86.

88. The Case Shiller National Housing Price Index was 181.5 in June, 2007 and 166.5 in June 2008.

89. Washington Mutual presentation deck for the FDIC and OTS, July 31, 2008.

90. Exhibit 64 on the 2010 "Hearing on the Wall Street and the Financial Crisis: The Role of Bank Regulators." Also Exhibits 59, 60 and 66. Hochberg, "Final Report of Examiner", page 210.

91. Email exchange between Kerry and OTS director Reich, 2010 Hearing on Wall Street and the Financial Crisis: The Role of Bank Regulators, Exhibit 64. See also exhibits 59, 60, and 66.

92. Office of the Comptroller of the Currency, Policy and Procedures Manual, PPM 5310-3.
93. Series of emails with OTS director Reich and FDIC chair Bair, August 2008. Senate Investigations Subcommittee, Wall Street and Financial Crisis: Role of Bank Regulators, Exhibit 64, page 262.
94. Hochberg, "Final Report of Examiner."
95. Goldman Sachs report, "Liquidity Alternatives and Rating Agency Observations," August 2008.
96. Hochberg, pages 48, 281–283.
97. FCIC, JPMorgan Chase presentation deck for the FDIC, September 12, 2008.
98. *Investment News*, "Government Seizes Fannie and Freddie," September 2008.
99. *American Banker*, September 12, 2008.
100. Neil Shenai, *Social Finance: Shadow Banking During the Financial Crisis*, 2018.
101. *Wall Street Journal*, "Lehman's Demise Triggered Cash Crunch Around Globe," September 29, 2018.
102. *New Yorker*, "Anatomy of a Meltdown," November 23, 2008.
103. Laurence M. Ball, *The Fed and Lehman Brothers: Setting the Record Straight*, 2018
104. S&P report on Washington Mutual, September 2008.
105. CNBC, "Bank of America to Buy Merrill Lynch for $50 Billion," September 14, 2008.
106. *The Atlantic*, "The Final Days of Merrill Lynch", September 2009.
107. Wall Street Journal, "Shock Forced Paulson's Hand", September 20, 2008.
108. New York Times, "Fed Misread Crisis in 2008, Records Show", February 21, 2014.
109. *New York Times*, "AIG Lists Banks It Paid With US Bailout Funds," March 15, 2009.
110. Hochberg, page 284, 222.
111. Hochberg, page 283.
112. See Chapter Ten, part two.
113. FCIC, page 300.
114. *Wall Street Journal*, "Filing Favors JPMorgan's Washington Mutual Bid Over Citi's," April 23, 2010.
115. Hochberg, page 281, 222–224.
116. Hochberg. Refer to JPMorgan Chase presentations to the FDIC showing they would not pay for the bank.
117. Henry M. Paulson Jr., *On the Brink: Inside the Race to Stop the Collapse of the Global Financial System*, 2010.
118. Andrew Ross Sorkin, *Too Big to Fail: The Inside Story of How Wall Street and Washington Fought to Save the Financial System—and Themselves*, Chapter 17.
119. Washington Mutual September 2008 Email chain.
120. Washington Mutual, press release, September 18, 2008.
121. Minutes of the directors' meeting, September 18, 2008.
122. Hochberg, page 225.
123. Hochberg, page 243.
124. Hochberg, page 51.
125. Hochberg. JPMorgan Chase presentation deck, September 19, 2008.

126. *Wall Street Journal*, "Administration Is Seeking $700 Billion for Wall Street," September 20, 2008.

127. Hochberg, "Final Report of Examiner." *Financial Times*, "Washington Mutual Suitors Line Up for Talks," September 23, 2008.

128. *Bloomberg News*, see Chart 1-2.

129. Hochberg, page 222.

130. Hochberg, pages 284–294.

131. *New York Times*, "As Goldman and Morgan Shift, a Wall St. Era Ends," September 21, 2008.

132. Hochberg, page 284–294.

133. *Wall Street Journal*, "WaMu, Under U.S. Pressure, Scrambles for Deal or Capital," September 22, 2008.

134. Ibid.

135. Hochberg, page 230–231.

136. Ibid.

137. Letter from Washington Mutual to the Treasury Department, September 23, 2008.

138. Hochberg.

139. Hochberg, page 131.

140. Hochberg, pages 56–57.

141. Hochberg, page 304.

142. FDIC Daily Deposit Reports, July through September 2008. See Chart 1-3.

143. Hochberg, pages 298–299.

144. Referring to the Washington Mutual plan submitted to Treasury on September 23, 2008.

145. Hochberg, page 57.

146. Hochberg, "Final Report of Examiner," page 57.

147. Timothy Geithner, *Stress Test*.

148. Hochberg, pages 17, 303, 320.

149. Inspector general's report. Office of Inspector General, "Evaluation of Fed Regulatory Oversight of Washington Mutual Bank," April, 2010.

150. SEC Form 8-K, Bankruptcy and Receivership Report, September 26, 2008. Associated Press, "Wamu Lists Billion Debt Bankruptcy Filing.

151. Hochberg, page 222.

152. Hochberg, pages 6, 8. Office of Inspector General, "Evaluation of Fed Regulatory Oversight of Washington Mutual Bank," April, 2010. Bankruptcy Receivership Report.

153. Alan S. Blinder, *After the Music Stopped: The Financial Crisis, the Response, and the Work Ahead*, 2013. FCIC.

154. Dr. Robert Shiller's comments on Yale University course Financial Markets and the Global Financial Crisis that the authors attended.

155. Henry M. Paulson Jr., On the Brink: Inside the Race to Stop the Collapse of the Global Financial System, 2010, page 293.

156. FCIC report, page 366, congressional testimony and Yale Program on Financial Stability Case Study 2014-3a-v1, "Guarantees and Capital Infusions in Response to Financial Crises: Haircuts and Resolutions," July 30, 2015.

157. Timothy Geithner, *Stress Test: Reflections on Financial Crises*, 2014, page 214.

158. Sheila Bair, *Bull by the Horns: Fighting to Save Main Street from Wall Street and Wall Street from Itself*, 2012.

159. Timothy Geithner, *Stress Test: Reflections on Financial Crises*, 2014.
160. Andrew Ross Sorkin, *Too Big to Fail: The Inside Story of How Wall Street and Washington Fought to Save the Financial System—and Themselves*, Chapter 18.
161. *Forbes*, "Citigroup Swallows Wachovia," September 29, 2008.
162. See Chart 1-2. Citigroup had $42.9 billion in mortgage loan losses by July, 2008—the highest losses of any of the banks.
163. FDIC, "Total Core Deposit Reports."
164. Wachovia deposit levels were found in an internal Federal Reserve Board document, "Wachovia Case Study," released to the public by the Financial Crisis Inquiry Commission (FCIC) and cited on page 304 of the FCIC report. The case study can be found at fcic-static.law.stanford.edu/cdn media/fcic-docs/2008-11-12.
165. FDIC press release and website. September 9, 2008.
166. Federal Reserve, "The Acquisition of Wachovia Corporation by Wells Fargo & Company," September 1, 2010.
167. Charles Kindleberger, *Manias, Panics, Crashes: A History of Financial Crises*, 2011, page 263. The Bagehot doctrine was an accepted doctrine that in a crisis, a lender of last resort should lend freely at a penalty rate to banks that can offer good securities as collateral.
168. Ibid.
169. NPR, "Bush Signs $700 Billion Financial Bailout Bill," October 3, 2008.
170. *Forbes*, "Bad News for the Bailout," September 23, 2008.
171. *New York Times*, "Drama Behind a $250 Billion Banking Deal," October 14, 2008.
172. *ProPublica*, "Bailout Tracker," last update was October 2, 2019.
173. Brookings Institute, "The Financial Crisis: An Inside View", *Brookings Papers on Economic Activity*, No. 1, 2009. brookings.edu/wp-content/uploads/2009/03/2009a_bpea_swagel.pdf.
174. Simon Johnson and James Kwak, *13 Bankers: The Wall Street Takeover and the Next Financial Meltdown*, 2010, Chapter Six.
175. US Senate Office of Public Records, Lobbying disclosure reports. Compiled by *USA Today*, "Level of Bank Lobbying Disclosed." Authors updated TARP funding for Citigroup and Bank of America, who both received $45 billion in TARP funds.
176. National Bureau of Economic Research, "A Fistful of Dollars: Lobbying and the Financial Crisis," Working Paper 17076, May 2011.
177. Karen Freifeld, "Banks Paid $32.6 Billion in Bonuses Amid US Bailout," Sanders.senate.gov, July 30, 2009.
178. *American Banker*, "BankThink," "Dimon: Wait! There is a Silver Bullet," March 12, 2009.
179. Margaret Chadbourn, Bloomberg.com, "Five Banks Are Seized." October 15, 2008.
180. Reuters, "Feds Investigate Washington Mutual Failure," October 15, 2008.
181. Notes from Nyhus Communications regarding questions from the *New York Times*.
182. *Seattle Post-Intelligencer*, "Massive Washington Mutual Shareholder Lawsuit Lacks Substance, Federal Judge Says," May 14, 2009. The lawsuit was settled

in 2011 with an amount substantially lower than they claimed and far less than the settlements from other large bank shareholder suits.

183. Hochberg, pages 6–15.
184. Hochberg, pages 268–270.
185. Hochberg, page 24.

Chapter 2

1. Stephen Pizzo, Mary Fricker, and Paul Muolo, *Inside Job: The Looting of America's Savings and Loans*, 1989.
2. Bureau of Labor Statistics, Monthly Labor Report, "One Hundred Years of Price Change and the American Inflation Experience."
3. Federal Reserve data.
4. Edward Nelson, "Friedman's Monetary Economics in Practice," Federal Reserve Board, Finance and Economics Discussion Series, Divisions of Research and Statistics and Monetary Affairs, April 13, 2011.
5. Senate.gov, "The Civil War: The Senate's Story."
6. FederalReserve.org.
7. Federal Reserve, pfabankapi.app.cloud.gov/api/summary.
8. Senate.gov, "The Civil War: The Senate's Story."
9. HUD.gov, Federal Housing Authority history.
10. In 2020, the Office of the Comptroller of the Currency defined community banks as having less than $1 billion in deposits. The GAO and the Federal Reserve Board broaden the definition to banks having up to $10 billion of assets. We are defining community banks as banks that serve their local communities, regardless of size.
11. Philadelphia Area Consortium of Special Collection Libraries (PACSCL), Historical Society of Frankford Building Association Records.
12. Ibid.
13. FederalReserveHistory.org.
14. St. Louis Federal Reserve Economic Research, "Failures and Assisted Transactions of All Institutions by Federal Savings and Loan Insurance Corporation," Updated February 2020.
15. www.ffiec.gov/CRA.
16. *Business Wire*, "Donald T. Regan, Former Board Chairman and Chief Executive Officer of Merrill Lynch & Co., Dies at 84," June 10, 2003.
17. *National Review*, "Heads I Win, Tails You Lose," March 29, 2012. (The FHLBB estimated $120 billion, and the NCFIRRE estimated $150 billion losses.)
18. *New York Times*, "Merrill Lynch CMA Boom," May 18, 1981. *Forbes*, "Save Our Money Market Funds," March 29, 2012. (Other number was $230 billion by 1982—Markham Financial History of the US). *Wall Street Journal*, "Shock Forced Paulson's Hand," September 20, 2008.
19. R. Altono Gilbert, "Requiem for Regulation Q: What it Did and Why It Passed Away," Federal Reserve Bank of St. Louis, February 1986.
20. Martin Mayer, *The Greatest-Ever Bank Robbery: The Collapse of the Savings and Loan Industry*, 1990.
21. *Newsweek*, "The S&Ls in Deep Trouble," December 29, 1980.

22.   HUDuser.gov, "The Report of the President's Commission on Housing," April 29, 1982.
23.   President's Commission on Housing Report, April 1982, Figure 6.3, page 76. "Initial Monthly Mortgage Payment Burden for a Constant-Quality Housing Unit."
24.   Georgetown Law, "A Timeline of Evolution of Retirement in United States", 2010.
25.   Jerry W. Markham, *A Financial History of the U.S., From the Age of Derivatives Into the New Millennium*, 1970–2001, 2002.
26.   *Business Week*, March 2, 1998, page 28.
27.   GAO/GGD-91-24, "Implications of Stricter Qualified Thrift Lender (QTL) Test," Table 2.1, April 1991.
28.   FDIC data on bank deposits, numbers, and net income.
29.   Wessels Farming 1970s to Today, Foreclosure and Bank Failures.
30.   Mark Singer, *Funny Money: The Wondrous Tale of the Penn Square Bank,* page 188.
31.   Daniel Yergin, *The Prize: The Epic Quest for Oil, Money, and Power*, 1991.
32.   Philip P. Zweig, *Belly Up: The Collapse of Penn Square Bank*, page 389.
33.   Ibid, page 445.
34.   Gary H. Stern and Ron J. Feldman, *Too Big to Fail: The Hazards of Bank Bailouts*, Brookings Institute Press, 2004.
35.   Lee Sahlin, "A History 1888–1987: The First One Hundred Years of Murphey Favre," 1987.
36.   Washington Mutual was a state-chartered savings bank, which acted the same as a thrift, but state law allowed it to buy any type of business. The bank's regulator was not the FHLBB, but the FDIC and Washington State. This means its deposits were federally insured by the FDIC, not FSLIC. This transaction was completed before the Garn–St. Germain Act and other state governments allowed thrifts to purchase any type of business.
37.   Murray Morgan, *The Friend of the Family: 100 Years With Washington Mutual*, 1989.
38.   Washington Mutual Savings Bank, 1985 annual report.
39.   The trust was dissolved when the bank went public in 1983.
40.   Lee Sahlin, "A History 1888–1987: The First One Hundred Years of Murphey Favre," 1987.
41.   *Seattle Times*, April 22, 1982.
42.   *Donoghue's Money Fund Report* and Money Market Ratings, April 1982.
43.   *Seattle Post-Intelligencer*, "Washington Mutual and Murphey Favre Merge," April 22, 1982.
44.   *Spokesman Review*, April 22, 1982.
45.   *Seattle Times*, August 1983.
46.   Washington Mutual newsletter, August 1983.
47.   *Seattle Times*, July 10, 1986.
48.   Washington Mutual 1986 annual report.
49.   *Seattle Post-Intelligencer*, "This Bank Is Blazing a Trail," December 8, 1986.
50.   Washington Mutual 1987 newsletter.
51.   *Bottomline* magazine, November 1987.
52.   *Seattle Times*, April 19, 1987.
53.   *Tacoma News Tribune*, "Washington Mutual Trying New Strategy," July 8, 1989.
54.   *Seattle PI,* "A Sharper Focus for State Bank," July 10, 1998.
55.   *Seattle Times*, July 25, 1989.

56. Washington Mutual in-house newsletter, March 1990.
57. Washington Mutual 1987 newsletter.
58. *Journal of American Business*, "Washington Mutual Names New CEO," March 21, 1990.
59. Wenatchee Rotary Club newsletter, August 1990.
60. National Commission on Financial Institution Reform, Recovery, and Enforcement (FIRREA). Origins and Causes of the S&L Debacle: A Blueprint for Reform: A Report to the President and Congress of the United States. Washington, DC, 1993.
61. FDIC.gov, Financial Institution Reform, Recovery, and Enforcement Act of 1989.
62. GAO/GGD-91-24, Implications of a Stricter Qualified Thrift Lender (QTL).
63. *Fortune*, "Where Did All Those Billions Go?" September 10, 1990.
64. FDIC data on number of banks.
65. Washington Mutual annual reports and SEC filings.
66. Fannie Mae, "Housing Finance in Developed Countries: An International Comparison of Efficiency, United States," 1992.
67. Government Accounting Office report on the cost of the thrift/banking crisis in the 1980s.
68. Mises Institute, *Quarterly Journal of Austrian Economics* 17, No. 2 (summer 2014), "The Savings and Loan Debacle Twenty-Five Years Later: A Misesian Re-Examination and Final Closing of the Book," pages 154–178.
69. Ibid

Chapter 3

1. *Business Week*, "Casino Society," September 16, 1985.
2. Stephen Pizzo, Mary Fricker, and Paul Muolo, *Inside Job: The Looting of America's Savings and Loans*, 1989.
3. R. Tillman, H.N. Pontell, K. Calavita, "The Savings and Loan Debacle, Financial Crime, and the State," *Annual Review of Sociology*, November 2003.
4. K. Calavita, R. Tillman, H.N. Pontell, "The Savings and Loan Debacle, Financial Crimes and the State," 1997.
5. Stephen Pizzo, Mary Fricker, and Paul Muolo, *Inside Job: The Looting of the America's Savings and Loans*, second edition (New York: Harper Collins, 1991).
6. Ibid.
7. Martin Lowy, *High Rollers: Inside the Savings and Loan Debacle*, 1991, page 152.
8. Martin Mayer, *The Greatest-Ever Bank Robbery: The Collapse of the Savings and Loan Industry*, 1990, page 77; Martin Lowy, *High Rollers: Inside the Savings and Loan Debacle*, 1991, page 152–153.
9. *Washington Post*, "Former Chairman of CenTrust Gets 11-Year Prison Sentence," December 2, 1994.
10. *New York Times*, "11-Year Sentence for Chief of Failed S&L," December 2, 1994.
11. *Washington Post*, "Billman Gets 40 Years in Thrift Fraud," June 22, 1994. *Baltimore Sun*, "Billman Convicted of S&L Fraud," April 4, 1994.
12. Michael Binstein, *Regardie's*, "A Confederacy of Greed," July 1989, page 27.
13. AP News, "Levitt Gets 30 Years, $12,000 Fine for $14.7 Million S&L Theft," July 2, 1986.
14. *Baltimore Sun*, "Jeffrey Levitt's New Life: Survivor," March 16, 1997.
15. Ibid.

16.   Michael Binstein, *Regardie's*, "A Confederacy of Greed," July 1989.

17.   *Los Angeles Times*, "McKenzie Guilty of Looting Savings and Loan," March 30, 1990.

18.   *Los Angeles Times*, "Two Who Defrauded North American S&L Avoid Jail Terms." September 25, 1990.

19.   Stephen Pizzo, Mary Fricker, and Paul Muolo, *Inside Job: The Looting of America's Savings and Loans*, 1989, page 400.

20.   James O'Shea, *The Daisy Chain: How Borrowed Billions Sank a Texas S&L*, 1991, page 32.

21.   Kathleen Day, S&L *Hell: The People and the Politics Behind the $1 Trillion Savings and Loan Scandal,* 1993, Chapter 40.

22.   Stephen Pizzo, Mary Fricker, and Paul Muolo, *Inside Job: The Looting of America's Savings and Loans*, 1989, page 66.

23.   James O'Shea, *The Daisy Chain: How Borrowed Billions Sank a Texas S&L, 1991*, page 217–218.

24.   *Los Angeles Times*, "Trial Underway in Ramona S&L Fraud Case," July 21, 1989.

25.   Stephen Pizzo, Mary Fricker, and Paul Muolo, *Inside Job: The Looting of America's Savings and Loans*, 1989, page 39.

26.   Ibid.

27.   AP, "Suit Filed to Recover $50 million from Failed S&L", January 3, 1986.

28.   Stephen Pizzo, Mary Fricker, and Paul Muolo, *Inside Job: The Looting of America's Savings and Loans*, 1989, Chapter 9.

29.   K. Calavita, R. Tillman, H. N. Pontell, *Big Money Crime: Fraud and Politics in the S&L Crisis*, 1999.

30.   *Los Angeles Times*, "Knapp Gets Six ½ Years for S&L," December 15, 1993.

31.   Most of the S&Ls were insured by the Federal Savings Lending Insurance Corporation, not the FDIC. FSLIC was controlled by the Federal Home Loan Bank Board, and the board was made up entirely of S&L CEOs. The S&L industry was self-regulated. At this time Washington Mutual was regulated by the FDIC and the state banking regulators. Their deposits were always insured and regulated by the FDIC.

32.   Stephen Pizzo, Mary Fricker, and Paul Muolo, *Inside Job: The Looting of America's Savings and Loans*, 1989, page 430.

33.   Kathleen Day, *S&L Hell: The People and the Politics Behind the $1 Trillion Savings and Loan Scandal,* 1993, Chapter 40.

34.   *Los Angeles Times*, October 6, 1991.

35.   *New York Times*, "FDIC Sues Neil Bush and Others at Silverado," September 22, 1990.

36.   Martin Mayer, *The Greatest-Ever Bank Robbery: The Collapse of the Savings and Loan Industry*, 1990.

37.   Ibid, pages 295–296, and accounting firm references found in the research study "Big Money Crime: Fraud and Politics in the Savings and Loan Crisis," Calavita, Pontell, Tillman, 1999.

Chapter 4

1.   FDIC, report on numbers of banks each year.

2.   CFTC.gov, Testimony of Brooksley Born, Chairperson, Concerning the OTC Derivatives Market, July 24, 1998. FederalReserve.gov, Testimony of

Greenspan on Regulation of OTC Derivatives, July 24, 1998. *Wall Street Journal*, "CFTC Chief Refuses to Take Back Seat in Derivatives Debate," November 3, 1998. Reuters, "Why US Banks Hid Billions in Derivatives Trades from CFTC," August 21, 2005. Federal Reserve, "The Regulation of OTC Derivatives," Alan Greenspan, July 24, 1998.

3.   Federal Reserve speech, March 19, 1999.

4.   Dallas Federal Reserve, "Shifting Credit Standards and the Boom and Bust in US Housing Prices", Fed Working Paper 1104, Duca, Muellbauier and Murphy, December 2012.

5.   Berkshire Hathaway Annual Report, March 8, 2003.

6.   FCIC, page 48and 299; data from the International Swaps and Derivatives Association (ISDA).

7.   Notional value is nominal or face value used to calculate payments. It is the total value a security controls through the derivative contract like a CDO. The market value is the current price a derivative can be sold for.

8.   Matt Taibbi, *Griftopia: Bubble Machines, Vampire Squids, and the Long Con That Is Breaking America*, 2010, Chapter 7.

9.   *Forbes*, "Financial Reform Doesn't Go Far Enough," June 11, 2010.

10.   Initiative on Business and Public Policy at Brookings, "The Origins of the Financial Crisis," Baily, Litan and Johnson, November 2008.

11.   FCIC, ebook page 465 based on the Asset Securitization Report, "CDO Machine? Managers, Mortgage Companies, Happy to Keep Fuel Coming."

12.   Federal Reserve Flow of Funds, Note 13, Table L.126. FCIC report, page 129.

13.   Center for International Securities and Derivatives Markets, "The Benefit of Hedge Funds," May 2006.

14.   *Wall Street Journal*, "Slices of Risk: How a Formula Ignited Market that Burned some Big Investors," September 12, 2005.

15.   FCIC, page 131.

16.   *Reuters*, "A Dozen Key Dates in the Demise of Bear Stearns," March 17, 2008. *New York Times*, "Bear Stearns Staves off Collapse of Two Hedge Funds," June 21, 2007.

17.   FCIC.

18.   *Brookings Institute*, "Initiative on Business and Public Policy at Brookings," November, 2008. Data from the International Swaps and Derivatives Association.

19.   FCIC, page 140–141.

20.   Matt Taibbi, *Griftopia: Bubble Machines, Vampire Squids, and the Long Con That Is Breaking America*, 2010. Reuters, "How AIG Fell Apart," September 18, 2008. Federal Reserve of Chicago, "AIG in Hindsight," October 2014. Initiative on Business and Public Policy at Brookings, Ibid., FCIC, Page 140.

21.   AIG form 8K, 2005.

22.   *New York Times*, "Behind Insurer's Crisis, Blind Eye to Web of Risk," September 27, 2008.

23.   Congressional Oversight Panel, "The AIG Rescue, Its Impact on Markets, and the Government's Exit Strategy," June 10, 2010.

24.   *Washington and Lee Law Review*, "The AIG Bailout," Volume 66, Issue 3, Summer 2009.

25.   ABC interview of Treasury Secretary Larry Summers by George Stephanopoulos, March 15, 2009.

26. ISDA, "Single Name Credit Default Swaps: A Review of the Emperical Literature," September 2016.

27. FCIC, page 256, data taken from *Bloomberg Professions*, "Write-downs and Credit Losses vs. Capital Raised," data reported for the second half of 2007. Write-downs are for losses to holdings in structured finance and mortgages.

28. Roy C. Smith, *Paper Fortunes: Modern Wall Street; Where It's Been and Where It's Going*, 2010, page 341.

29. Press release from the Federal Reserve Bank of New York, Senior Supervisors Group, "Observations on Risk Management Practices during the Recent Market Turbulence," March 6, 2008.

30. NPR, "A Forgotten History of How the US Government Segregated America," May 3, 2017.

31. HUD.gov.

32. Edward J. Pinto, "Government Housing Policies in the Lead-up to the Financial Crisis: A Forensic Study," draft November 4, 2010.

33. *New York Times*, "Racial Gap Detailed on Mortgages," October 22, 1991.

34. HUD, "Not in My Back Yard: Removing Barriers to Affordable Housing," July 8, 1991.

35. *Wall Street Journal*, "Acorn and the Housing Bubble," November 12, 2009.

36. FHA came under control of the HUD in 1965.

37. US HUD, National Homeownership Strategy: Partners in the American Dream, May 1995.

38. *Washington Post*, "Clinton Pushes Homeownership Strategy," June 6, 1995.

39. US Department of Housing and Urban Development, "Cuomo Announces Action to Provide $2.4 Trillion in Mortgages for Affordable Housing for 28.1 Million Families," July 29, 1999.

40. American Bankers Association Meeting, 2000. *New York Times*, "Fannie Mae Eases Credit to Aid Mortgage Lending," September 30, 1999.

41. Press release, "President Calls for Expanding Opportunities to Home Ownership, Remarks by the President," June 17, 2000. HUD.gov, "Blueprint for the American Dream."

42. President George W. Bush, "President's Remarks to the National Association of Home Builders," Columbus, Ohio, October 2, 2004.

43. "Government Housing Policies in the Lead-Up to the Financial Crisis: A Forensic Study," page 92. Edward J. Pinto, November 4, 2010.

44. National Community Reinvestment Coalition, "CRA Commitments", September 2007

45. Federalreserve.gov, announcements of CRA commitments and the FCIC report

46. Found in bank press releases, company reports, and newspaper searches.

47. Although the unregulated shadow subprime banks were not required to have CRA goals, sometimes activist organizations or state governments would impose CRA goals on them as punishment for predatory activities.

48. The OTS regulated the AIG thrift, but not the insurance or Financial Products division.

49. *Inside Mortgage Finance, Inside B&C Lending*, data prepared for author in November 2019.

50. Bethany McLean and Joe Nocera, All The Devils Are Here: The Hidden History of the Financial Crisis, 2010.

51. Definition of shadow banking found: International Monetary Fund, "What Is Shadow Banking." New York Fed, "The Shadow Banking System: Implication for Financial Regulation," 2009. St. Louis Fed, "Is Shadow Banking Really Banking?" October 2011. *The Economist*, "How Shadow Banking Works," February 1, 2016.

52. Occupational Employment Survey and the National Delinquency Survey of the Mortgage Bankers Association of America 2007, Kleiner and Tod.

53. A 2008 study for the FTC claimed that independent unregulated mortgage brokers grew to a high of around 550,000 with an 70 percent share of all mortgage originations. Morris M. Kleiner and Richard M. Todd, "When Does Mortgage Broker Regulation Matter?", Federal Trade Commission, May 29, 2008.

54. Actually only thirty-two of the subprime companies and six of the regulated banks produced 93 percent of all the subprime loans between 2002–2007. The thirty-two subprime companies produced 85 percent of all of those loans.

55. FCIC. Data ordered by the authors in November 2019.

56. Inside Mortgage Finance, Inside B&C Lending. Data ordered by the authors in November 2019.

57. FCIC, page 256.

58. FCIC.

59. Paul Krugman, *The Return of Depression Economics and the Crisis of 2008*, 2008.

60. Financial Crisis Inquiry Commission report, conclusions.

61. *CNN Money*, "$58 Billion Bank Deal Set," January 15, 2004.

62. *New York Times*, "BankAmerica in $4 Billion Deal to Acquire Rival Security Pacific," August 13, 1991.

63. *Los Angeles Times*, "BankAmerica Takes Over at Security Pacific: Acquisitions: The Merger Becomes Official Today, Creating the Nation's Second-Largest Banking Company," April 22, 1992.

64. *New York Times*, "Nations Bank Drives $62 Billion Merger: A New BankAmerica: Biggest of U.S. Banks," April 14, 1998.

65. *CNN Money*, "BofA Nabs Fleet for $47 Billion."

66. *Stanford Business*, "Wells Fargo and Norwest, 'Merger of Equals,'" June 8, 1998.

67. *CNN Money*, "First Union Buys Wachovia," April 16, 2001.

68. *New York Times*, "A Wall Street Behemoth: The Deal; Travelers to Buy Salomon, Making a Wall Street Giant," September 25, 1997.

69. *New York Times*, "Citicorp and Travelers Plan to Merge in Record $70 Billion Deal: A New No. 1: Financial Giants Unite," April 7, 1998.

70. FCIC report, page 53.

71. FCIC report, page 53, data from SNL Financial.

72. Robert Shiller, *Finance and the Good Society*, 2012.

73. Charles R. Geisst, Wall Street: A History From Its Beginnings to the Fall of Enron, 1997.

74. Simon Johnson and James Kwak, *13 Bankers: The Wall Street Takeover and the Next Financial Meltdown*, 2010.

75. Federal Reserve Flow of Funds, Tables L.1, L.109, L.126, L.129. Nominal GDP from Bureau of Economic Analysis. Data compiled by authors of *13 Bankers*, page 59.

76. Simon Johnson and James Kwak, *13 Bankers: The Wall Street Takeover and the Next Financial Meltdown*, 2010.

Chapter 5

1. Pfabankapi.app.cloud.gov and FDIC's report on numbers of banks in the system.
2. *Washington CEO,* "Tough as Nails," October 1992.
3. Ibid.
4. Washington Mutual annual report 1995.
5. *Washington CEO,* "Checking Into Hotel California," February 1997. *US Banker,* "Taking Aim at California," September 1997..
6. Ibid.
7. Ibid.
8. Ibid.
9. Washington Mutual's Great Western presentation deck. Data was compiled by Bloomberg and included on page 7, May 22, 1997.
10. *High-Growth Consumer Banking,* "Washington Mutual, Inc., Merger with Great Western Financial Corporation.," May 22, 1997. *Washington CEO,* "Banking on Killinger," April 2000.
11. Ibid.
12. *US Banker,* "Taking Aim at California," September 1997.
13. Ibid.
14. Presentation deck of Washington Mutual acquisition of H. F. Ahmanson & Company, March 17, 1998, page 35.
15. *Washington CEO,* "Banking on Killinger," April 2000.
16. *USBanker,* "Breakthrough for Washington Mutual," October 2002.

Chapter 6

1. FDIC statistics on bank numbers.
2. *Fast Company,* "Bank of Middle America," March 2003.
3. *Seattle Post-Intelligencer,* "Washington Mutual on a Roll," January 17, 2001.
4. *USA Today,* "CEO Salaries," April 6, 2001.
5. *Forbes,* "The Super 100," April 16, 2001.
6. *Business Week,* "Top Fifty Business Performers of the Year," Spring 2001.
7. *Wall Street Journal,* "Washington Mutual May Buy Dime in a Deal Valued at About $5 Billion," June 22, 2001.
8. *Wall Street Journal,* "Washington Mutual Reaches Agreement to Acquire Dime Bancorp for $5.2 Billion," June 25, 2001.
9. *Money,* "Restless in Seattle," June 2001.
10. *Forbes,* "The Tallest Midget," July 23, 2001.
11. *American Bankers Association Journal,* "Not Your Father's Savings Bank, Kerry Killinger Builds His Dream Bank," August 2001.
12. The Points of Light Foundation brochure on the Awards for Community Service, 2001.
13. *Puget Sound Business Journal,* "Leadership Center in Cedarbrook," September 21–27, 2001.
14. *Puget Sound Business Journal,* "Full Retreat," July 4, 2003.
15. *American Banker,* "The Best in Banking," 2001. "The Man Behind Washington Mutual," December 2001.
16. *Fast Company,* "Lessons From Washington Mutual's M&A Playbook," January 2002.

17. Institutional Investor, March 2002.
18. *Business Week*, "The Business Week Fifty," Spring 2002.
19. Mike Mayo, *Exile on Wall Street: One Analyst's Fight to Save the Big Banks from Themselves*, 2011; Financial Times, "JPMorgan Chief in Spat with Analyst over Stock Picks", February 9, 2006
20. *Forbes*, "Five Overachieving Companies," March 2002. *NYSE Magazine*, "Washington Mutual Millieu," March/April 2002.
21. *Forbes*, "The Best and Worst Bosses," May 13, 2002.
22. *USBanker*, "Breakthrough for WaMu," October 2002.
23. *Qwest*, Fred Hutchinson Cancer Research Center, Fall, 2002.
24. SEC.gov. Report of Investigation by the Special Investigative Committee of the Board of Directors of WorldCom Inc., March 31, 2003, page 1: "Inadequate audits by Arthur Andersen."
25. Bethany McLean and Peter Elkind, *The Smartest Guys in the Room: The Amazing Rise and Scandalous Fall of Enron*, 2003. Simon Johnson and James Kwak, *13 Bankers: The Wall Street Takeover and the Next Financial Meltdown*, 2010.
26. University of California press release, "Banks, Law Firms Were Pivotal in Execution of Enron Securities Fraud," April 8, 2002.
27. Although the subprime companies were not required to have CRA goals, sometimes the goals were forced on them, like Ameriquest, as part of legal settlements for poor customer protections.
28. Chart Intro-3. Top 25 Subprime Loan Originators.
29. *Fast Company*, "Shrewd Move," December 2002.
30. *Fortune*, "Fortune 500," April 2003.
31. *Forbes*, "America's Top 500 Companies," May 26, 2003.
32. *Fortune*, "A New Banking Model," April 2003.
33. Ibid.
34. Data obtained from *Inside Mortgage Finance*'s 2009 Mortgage Market Statistical Annual Volume I. According to the notes of the *IMF* "Top Mortgage Originators" tables, "lenders were asked to report 1–4 family residential mortgage originations. Wholesale purchases, including loans closed by correspondents, are counted. Lenders are instructed to include only HELOC amounts that are actually funded."
35. *Forbes*, "The Best Big Companies in America," January 6, 2003.
36. *Business Week*, "The Business Week Fifty," Spring 2003.
37. *Wall Street Journal*, "Executive Compensation in Top 500 Companies by Business Type," April 12, 2003.
38. *Fast Company*, "Bank of Middle America," March 2003.
39. Ibid. *Fortune*, "A New Bank Model," April 1, 2003.
40. Ibid.
41. *Bloomberg Markets*, "Washington Mutual Reality Check," May 2003.
42. Lou Dobbs Money Letter, "Washington Mutual Stability + Growth=Big Profits," May 2003.
43. *Barrons*, "A Giant Bargain," June 2008.
44. *Wall Street Journal*, "As Banks Elbow for Consumers, Washington Mutual Thrives," November 6, 2003.
45. Monica Langley, *Tearing Down the Walls*, 2003 and Duff McDonald, *Last Man Standing: The Ascent of Jamie Dimon and JPMorgan Chase*, 2009.

46. Judah S. Kraushaar and Sanford Weill, *The Real Deal: My Life in Business and Philanthropy*, 2006
47. Letter to the Board of Directors, Fall 2003.
48. WM Press Release for 2003 earnings. Chart WM-14, January 20, 2004. Non-performing loans were further reduced to .58 percent in 2004 and .57 percent in 2005.

Chapter 7

1. Between 2002–2007 there were 31 unregulated subprime companies that produced 85 percent of all the subprime loans in the country. These banks, in order of originations include Ameriquest, HSBC/Finance, New Century, Option One, First Franklin, GMAC/Res fund, Fremont, WMC Mortgage, Aegis Mortgage, Accredited Home/Lone Star, BNC Mortgage, American General, NovaStar, Equifirst, ECC Capital, Decision One, Finance America, Fieldstone Mortgage, Ownit Mortgage Solutions, Key National Home Equity, EMC Mortgage, Aames Capital Corporation, ResMae Mortgage, Encore Credit Corp, Saxon Mortgage, Nationstar Mortgage, Mortgage Lenders, Cit Group, Delta Financial Corp, Equity One, Peoples Choice. Nearly all them were out of business by the end of 2007.
2. Washington Mutual Risk management reports, 2004 and Inside Mortgage Finance.
3. Inside Mortgage Finance/B&C Lending—mortgage data compiled for authors in November, 2019.
4. *The Atlantic*, "Shiller, Infectious Exuberance", July/August 2008
5. *Los Angeles Times*, February 4, 2005. Federal Trade Commission lawsuit against Ameriquest. File 042-3082.
6. *Los Angeles Times*, "The Regulators Weren't Even Watching," March 27, 2009.
7. Federal Trade Commission, "Home Mortgage Lender Settles Predatory Lending," March 21, 2002.
8. JPMorgan Chase marketing flyer. *New York Times*, "Subprime and the Banks, Guilty as Charged," October 14, 2009.
9. *Fortune*, "100 Best Companies to Work For," February 16, 2004. *Fortune*, "Most Admired Companies," March, 2004.
10. Economist, "Double WaMu", August 19, 2004.
11. Federal Reserve Board speech file, Chair Alan Greenspan to the Credit Union National Association, February 23, 2004.
12. Office of Federal Housing Enterprise Oversight—Report to Congress 2004. FHFA.gov, "Report of the Special Examination of Fannie Mae," May 2006. OFHEO, "SEC Reach Settlement With Fannie Mae, Penalty Imposed," FHFA.gov, May 23, 2006. "Fannie Mae Stipulation and Consent Order," May 23, 2006, FHFA.gov.
13. Washington Mutual 2004 annual report, 10-K, 10-Q.
14. WM Press Release 2004 Earnings. Chart WM19. January 19, 2005.
15. Francisco Louçã and Michael Ash, *Shadow Networks: Financial Disaster and the System That Caused the Crisis*, 2018.
16. Phone conversations between Kerry and Jamie Dimon; summaries were written in emails.
17. *Fortune* magazine, "The Jamie Dimon Show", July 2002.

18. Email exchange between Steve Rotella, Kerry, and other execs, March 2005.

19. *Business Wire*, "Chase Commits to $800 Billion," April 15, 2005.

20. New York Arts Connection Award Ceremony for the "Corporate Class Act," April 28, 2005.

21. Jim Vanasek's "2005 Strategic Planning Capital Allocation Report," delivered to the Board of Directors on May 19, 2005.

22. CNBC interview with Bernanke, July 1, 2005.

23. *FTSE Global Markets*, "Outperforming to an Indifferent Audience," September 2005.

24. *Seattle Times*, "Providian Credit Coup for Washington Mutual," June 7, 2005.

25. *New York Times*, "Washington Mutual to Buy Providian for $6.45 Billion," June 6, 2005. *Wall Street Journal*, "Washington Mutual Has Deal to Buy Providian for $6.45 Billion," June 6, 2005.

26. Robert Shiller, *The Subprime Solution: How Today's Global Financial Crisis Happened, and What to Do About It*, 2008.

27. Ibid.

28. November 2005 Senate Banking Committee meeting minutes.

29. Ben Bernanke, *The Courage to Act: A Memoir of a Crisis and Its Aftermath*, 2015, and *Firefighting: The Financial Crisis and Its Lessons*, 2019.

30. A flattening yield curve is defined at the narrowing of the yield spread between short- and long-term interest rates. Sometimes when the Fed raises short-term rates, the long-term rates also increase. When the long-term rates don't increase, there could be a very small difference in the two rates—that makes it hard for banks to make money.

31. *Fortune*, "Investors Guide: 2006 Built to Last," November 2005.

32. *Seattle Times*, "New Year May Bring Suitor Knocking on Washington Mutual's Door," December 28, 2005.

33. Email from Vanasek to the executive committee and others, December 2005.

34. WM Press Release of 2005 Earnings, Chart WM19, January 18, 2006.

35. Washington Mutual annual report, 10-K and 10-Q.

36. FDIC Quarterly Report on Bank Earnings, third quarter 2005.

37. Letter to Board of Directors, January 2006.

38. Economic Report of the President, Council of Economic Advisers, Ben Bernanke, chair, February 2006.

39. Iowa state attorney general's website, January 2006.

40. Iowa Department of Justice, Office of the Attorney General, "Ameriquest Will Pay $325 Million and Reform its Lending Practices," January 23, 2006.

41. *Fortune*, "100 Best Companies to Work For," February 2006.

42. JD Power Retail Banking Study, March 1, 2006.

43. *Washington CEO*, "Kerry Killinger Chosen CEO of the Year," March 2006.

44. Federal Housing Finance Agency, "Fannie Mae Façade: Fannie Mae Criticized for Earnings Manipulation," May 23, 2006. FHFA.gov, "SEC Reach Settlement with Fannie Mae; Penalty Imposed." FHFA.gov, "Fannie Mae Stipulation and Consent Order," May 23, 2006.

45. Killinger comments to the Sanford C. Bernstein and Lehman Brothers Conference, and the meetings with the Federal Reserve Board.

46. *Puget Sound Business Journal*, "Washington Mutual New Tower," June 15, 2006.

47. Authors have a file of over forty email exchanges between Kerry, the board, the outside consultant, Steve Rotella, and the HR director reporting on

the issues involving Lou Pepper. After the crisis hit, Pepper claimed he was complaining about subprime lending, but there is no evidence of that in the email exchanges. By 2006 subprime lending had fallen dramatically and was finally discontinued in mid-2007.

48.　CERO Cathcart, July 2006 board report.

49.　Bethany McLean and Joe Nocera, *All the Devils Are Here: The Hidden History of the Financial Crisis*, 2010.

50.　Office of Inspector General, "Evaluation of Federal Regulatory Oversight of Washington Mutual Bank," April 2010. Page 18 publicly reveals all the regulatory ratings for Washington Mutual from 2003 to 2008.

51.　Ibid, page 17.

52.　Ibid, page 19.

53.　The Public Company Accounting Oversight Board (PCAOB) is a private-sector nonprofit corporation created by the Sarbanes-Oxley Act of 2002 to oversee audits of public companies and other issues in order to protect the interests of investors and further the public interest in the preparation of informative, accurate, and independent audit reports. The PCAOB audits are selected on a statistical sampling basis.

54.　*Bank Director*, "The Washington Mutual Way," third quarter 2006.

55.　*Wall Street Journal*, "Homeowners Start to Feel the Pain of Rising Rates," August 10, 2006.

56.　Washington Mutual annual report 2007 and Form 10-K, page 57. Negative amortization is calculated by dividing total negative amortization by total loan balance.

57.　Lehman Brothers investor conference, New York, September 2006.

58.　Robert Shiller, *The Subprime Solution: How Today's Global Financial Crisis Happened, and What to Do About It*, 2008.

59.　Federal Reserve Board meeting, September 22, 2006.

60.　Investors' Day Conference, September 2006.

61.　Ibid.

62.　Merrill Lynch Banking and Financial Services Conference, November 16, 2006.

63.　Goldman Sachs Financial Services CEO Conference, December 13, 2006.

64.　*Seattle Magazine*, "Washington Mutual Guru," November 2006.

65.　Protiviti, "Washington Mutual Corporate Credit Review Assessment," December 2006.

66.　FDIC fourth-quarter 2006 banking profile, December 13, 2006.

Chapter 8

1.　FDIC quarterly earnings reports, 2006.

2.　Wells Fargo report on subprime bank closings, 2007

3.　*Investment News*, "Oops! Bernanke Admits to Subprime Miscues," November 24, 2008.

4.　www.standardandpoors.com.

5.　Notes at Davos sessions taken by author, January 2007.

6.　Author's notes taken at Roubini's session. *New York Times*, "A Look at Davos Through the Years," January 19, 2020.

7.　Washington Mutual 2006 annual report.

8.   *BusinessWire*, "WaMu Named Bank With Best Reputation in US by Reputation Institute," May 22, 2007.

9.   *Business Week*, "Top 25 Service Champ," March 2007.

10. *Fortune*, "Blue Ribbon Companies," Spring 2007.

11. JD Power is a global market research company that measures customer satisfaction.

12. ComScore is a global leader in cross-platform measurement of audiences, advertising, and consumer behavior.

13. BAI Deposit Performance Benchmarking Study, October 2007, a Chicago consumer benchmarking firm that produces twice-yearly reports to analyze consumer data like retail deposit growth, peer performance, branch performance, and other data.

14. Most of the information in a March letter from Kerry to the board.

15. Report to the board, January 17, 2007, page 11.

16. Department of Statistics and Operations Research, "The Subprime Mortgage Crisis," 2010.

17. www.sanders.senate; Bernanke, "The Economic Outlook," prepared testimony of the Joint Economic Committee of the 110th Congress, First Session, March 28, 2007.

18. FDIC first quarter 2007 bank earnings.

19. *Money*, Vol. 36, No. 4, April 2007. money.cnn.com/magazines/moneymag/moneymag_archive/2007/04/01/toc.html

20. Puget Sound Business Journal, April 2007.

21. *Fortune*, "People Are His Bottom Line," April 16, 2007.

22. Wells Fargo report on banks failed banks, 2007

23. The June 1 Sanford Bernstein 23rd Annual Strategic Decisions Conference, the May 16 Lehman Brothers Annual Financial Services Conference, and the second quarter earnings calls.

24. *Wall Street Journal*, "Does the Subprime Index Amplify Risk?" February 27, 2007.

25. Joint Center for Housing Studies 2006, Table A-6, page 36.

26. Federal Reserve, "Large Financial Institutions' Perspectives on Risk," April 2007.

27. www.sanders.senate.senate.gov.

28. Reuters, "Washington Mutual Commits $2 Billion for Subprime Help," April 28, 2007.

29. Wall Street Journal, "Bear Stearns Bails Out Fund with Big Loan of $3.2 Billion", June 23, 2007.

30. www.sanders.senate.gov/newsroom/recent/bernanke-in-his-own-words. December 3, 2009.

31. Speech and note to the ERM department from Killinger, July 8, 2007.

32. Joint annual exam from FDIC and OTS presented to the Board of Directors, July 2007.

33. Reuters, "Paulson Sees US Housing Downturn Near End," July 2, 2007.

34. Uiowa.edu/lifebook/timetable

35. Killinger letter to the board, July 17, 2007.

36. *New York Times*, "Federal Reserve Chairman Bernanke Says Fed Has Reduced 2007 Growth Forecast," July 19, 2007.

37. Reuters, "BNP Freezes $2.2 Billion of Funds Over Subprime," August 8, 2007.

38. *Financial Times*, "Goldman Pays the Price of Being Big," August 13, 2007.

39. Mark Zandi, Financial Shock: A 360° Look at the Subprime Mortgage Implosion, and How to Avoid the Next Financial Crisis, 2008.

40. Reuters, "Bear Stearns Halts Redemptions in Third Hedge Fund," August 1, 2007.

41. LIBOR is the London Interbank Offered Rate, the benchmark interest rate for many adjustable-rate mortgages, business loans, and financial instruments traded on the global financial markets. Bankrate.com. (BP is basis points; 100 BP is equivalent to 1 percent.)

42. New York Times, "The Conscience of a Liberal," September 20, 2007.

43. Dr. Shiller's speech to the Federal Open Market committee on August 30, 2007

44. American Banker, "Washington Mutual Shops a Standard," October 5, 2007.

45. www.ft.com, www.uiowa.edu

46. LewRockwell.com, "Market Failure? Try Yet Another Government Failure," October 1, 2008.

47. www.advisorperspectives.com, "Did Mark-to-Market Rules Cause the Financial Crisis?" September 18, 2018.

48. Harvard Business Review, "Is It Fair to Blame Fair Value Accounting for the Financial Crisis?" November 2009.

49. Internal emails between the board and top executives, November 2007.

50. Loan Performance TS Securities, Cathcart's investor day report

51. Investors' Day conference report, enterprise risk management, November 7, 2007.

52. J. D. Power, November report.

53. Reuters, "US European Bank Writedowns, Credit Losses," September 24, 2009.

54. Business Wire, "Merrill Lynch Reports Full Year 2007 Net Loss from Continuing Operations of $8.6 Billion," January 17, 2008.

55. "Citi Reports Fourth Quarter Net Loss of $9.83 Billion, Loss Per Share of $1.99," January 15, 2008. https://www.citigroup.com/citi/news/2008/080115a.htm.

56. Moneycentral.msn.com, November 5, 2007.

57. www.ft.com/cms.

58. HSBC 2008 annual report and Accounts, March 2, 2009.

59. News.bbc.co.uk, "Barclays Bank Confirms $1.6 Billion Writedown on Subprime Holdings," November 15, 2007.

60. www.ft.com, November 21, 2007.

61. Fannie Mae news release, February 27, 2008.

62. Simon Kennedy and Marketwatch, "UBS Plans $19 Bln Write-Down, Capital Injection," Marketwatch, April 1, 2008. marketwatch.com/story/ubs-takes-further-19-bln-in-write-downs-plans-capital-boost.

63. Kellogg Insight magazine, "What went wrong at AIG," August 3, 2015.

64. Reuters, Factbox, "US European Bank Writedowns, Credit Losses," September 24, 2009.

65. Ibid.

66. www.ft.com.

67. New York, "The Fall of Bear Stearns: A Quickie Guide," March 18, 2008.

68. Mortgage losses were also extracted from Factbox, "US European Bank Writedowns, Credit Losses," Reuters September 24, 2009, and the FCIC report, page 256.

69. Ibid.

70. New York Times, "Executive Pay: The Bottom Line for Those on Top," April 5, 2008. Reuters, "JPMorgan CEO Dimon's 2008 Compensation Falls,"

March 18, 2009. Simon Johnson and James Kwak, *13 Bankers: The Wall Street Takeover and the Next Financial Meltdown*, 2010, see Figure 3.1 on real corporate profits. FCIC report, page 63.

71. Carmen Reinhart and Kenneth Rogoff, *This Time Is Different: Eight Centuries of Financial Folly*, 2009. FCIC report, page 63, and also in the 10-K and 10-Q bank reports.

72. CEO Blankfein, remarks to the Council of Institutional Investors, April 2009.

73. *National Mortgage News*, "Top Subprime Originators 4th Quarter, 2007."

74. Washington Mutual investors' presentation, January 17, 2008.

75. FDIC fourth quarter 2007 bank earnings report.

Chapter 9

1. Homeland Security and Government Affairs Committee, "Where Were the Watchdogs? The Financial Crisis and the Breakdown of Financial Governance," January 21, 2009.

2. FCIC.

3. *The Economist*, February 19, 2009.

4. Mark Zandi, *Financial Shock*, 2018.

5. Realty Trac press release of US Foreclosure Market Report, July 2009.

6. *ProPublica* data on funds distributed by the TARP program.

7. ABC News on January 25, 2017, said, "There were 1.8 million people who attended Obama's inauguration in 2009 and close to one million who attended his second in 2013, according to DC officials."

8. K&L/Gates letter, "Companies Need to Prepare for Aggressive Government Tactics," Aug. 11, 2011.

9. *Seattle Post-Intelligencer*, May 15, 2009. Years later the plaintiffs' lawsuit was settled for a fraction of their asking price.

10. Reuters, "Washington Mutual Sues FDIC for over $13 Billion," March 21, 2009.

11. *The Street*, "JPMorgan Chase Sues WaMu, FDIC," March 25, 2009.

12. *Wall Street Journal*, "JPMorgan Chase Spends Millions on New Jets and Luxury Airport Hangar," March 22, 2009.

13. Letter from attorneys of Washington Mutual to the general counsel of JPMorgan Chase, April 2009.

14. National Archives, press release, March 11, 2009.

15. *Condé Nast Portfolio*, "We the Jury," May 2009.

16. Iowa Public Television, "The Farm Crisis," July 1, 2013.

17. *Chicago Tribune*, "A Farming Legacy Wiped Out," December 11, 1985. *Time*, "He Couldn't Manage Any More," June 24, 2001.

18. *New York Times*, "4 Dead in Rampage in an Iowa Town," December 10, 1985. *Time*, "He Couldn't Manage Any More," June 24, 2001.

19. *Washington Post*, "In Mortgage Crisis, a Lesson from Iowa Farms," May 10, 2011, discussing Iowa attorney general Tom Miller's testimony on Capitol Hill in May 2011.

20. The SAM dilemma was resolved through charitable contributions, and the additional space was eventually rented. In 2014 Seattle planned to sell $45.3 million in revenue bonds to refinance the existing debt on the Seattle Art Museum, backed by the rent on museum owned office space leased to Nordstrom.

21. *Wall Street Journal*, "New Evidence on the Foreclosure Crisis," July 3, 2009.

22. *Wall Street Journal*, "So Many Foreclosures, So Little Logic," July 4, 2009.

23. *New York Times*, "Paulson Calls to Goldman Tested Ethics During Crisis," August 9, 2009.

24. *New York Times*, "Text of Obama's Speech on Financial Reform," September 14, 2009.

25. FDIC website: Banking Crisis and Response: "Deposit Insurance: Fund Management and Risk-Based Deposit Insurance Assessments"

26. Letter from the American Association of Bank Directors, November 2009. Also, from comments in books by Paulson, Bernanke, and Geithner that FDIC chair Bair's major concern was the preservation of the deposit fund.

27. *Inside Mortgage Finance* top originator ranking for 2009.

28. Center for Economic and Policy, research issue brief, "Value of Too Big to Fail Big Bank Subsidy," September 2009. *Washington Post*, "Banks Too Big to Fail Have Grown Even Bigger," August 28, 2009.

29. Roberto De Vogli, Progress or Collapse, The Crisis of Market Greed, 2013.

30. Reuters, "Goldman Sachs Boss Says Banks Do God's Work," November 8, 2009.

31. *The Atlantic*, "The Final Days of Merrill Lynch," September 1, 2009.

32. *Wall Street Journal*, "Ken Lewis Testifies That Paulson Told Him 'We Do Not Want The Public Disclosure,'" April 23, 2009.

33. *Financial News*, "Cuomo Urges Probe of B of A Deal Pressure," April 24, 2009.

34. *NACD Directors Daily*, "Cuomo Subpoenas Five B of A Directors, September 17, 2009.

35. *The Nation*, "Letting the Banking Rats Out of the Bag," August 12, 2009.

36. *NACD Directors Daily*, November 11, 2009.

37. *Wall Street Journal*, "Two Bear Stearns Fund Leaders are Acquitted," November 11, 2009. The case was eventually settled.

38. *NACD Directors Daily*, November 17, 2009.

39. *NACD Directors Daily*, November 18, 2009.

Chapter 10, Part One

1. Smithsonian.com, "The Man Who Busted the Banksters," November 29, 2011.

2. Financial Crisis Inquiry Report, page 18 of 2,418, electronic version.

3. Peter Wallison, Hidden in Plain Sight: What Really Caused the World's Worst Financial Crisis and Why It Could Happen Again, 2015.

4. *USA Today*, "Panel Starts Inquiry on Financial Meltdown," January 2010.

5. NACD Directors Daily, Los Angeles Times, January 13, 2010.

6. *NACD Directors Daily*, January 14, 2010, The Guardian, January 13, 2010

7. *Washington Post*, "The Opening Meeting of the CEOs," January 14, 2010.

8. SEC.gov, "State Street Settles SEC Charges for Bidding Markups."

9. SEC website, "Goldman Sachs Pays Record $550 Million to settle SEC Charges Related to Subprime Mortgage CDO." "Largest Ever Penalty Paid by a Wall Street Firm," July 15, 2010. Also mentioned in the FCIC report.

10. *NACD Directors Daily*, January 22, 2010.

11. The Pecora Commission of 1932 was a US Senate Committee on Banking and Currency to investigate the causes of the Wall Street Crash of 1929. The commission made no progress until the fourth and final counsel, Ferdinand Pecora, a seasoned investigator, took control of the group.

12. Henry M. Paulson Jr., On the Brink: Inside the Race to Stop the Collapse of the Global Financial System, 2010, page 293.

13. *Wall Street Journal*, "Complex Loan Didn't Cause the Financial Crisis", February 9, 2010

14. Ibid

15. National Bureau of Economic Research, "A New Look at the US Foreclosure Crisis: Panel Data Evidence and Subprime Borrowers from 1997 to 2012", June 2015.

16. Data obtained from *Inside Mortgage Finance*'s 2009 Mortgage Market Statistical Annual Volume I. According to the notes of IMF's "Top Mortgage Originators" tables, "lenders were asked to report 1–4 family residential mortgage originations for Total Mortgage Originations, Subprime, Conventional and Adjustable Rate Mortgage Originations."

17. Henry M. Paulson Jr., On the Brink: Inside the Race to Stop the Collapse of the Global Financial System, 2010, page 110.

18. *Huffington Post*, "Senate Inquiry to Open With Probe of Washington Mutual," March 17, 2010.

19. *Wall Street Journal*, "Ex-WM Chief Puts Blame on Club," April 14, 2010.

20. Additional quote from *Wall Street Journal* on April 15, 2010, taken from the National Association of Corporate Directors Newsletter, "Former WaMu CEO Killinger Testifies That Seizure Could Have Been Avoided."

21. *Puget Sound Business Journal*, "Chase CEO Dimon Q&A: WaMu Layoffs Nearly Done," March 2009.

22. Reuters, "JPMorgan Chief Warns of Overregulation," April 18, 2010. *Huffington Post*, "JPMorgan Chase Memo Sneers at Ignorant Senators, Time for Grownups to Step In," May 4, 2010.

23. Actually, the insurance policies didn't expire—they must have meant "until the policy limits are exhausted."

24. Letter from the American Association of Bank Directors to members, November 2009.

25. FDIC website on bank failures.

26. Email exchange between authors and their attorney.

27. *Wall Street Journal*, "JPMorgan Targeting Funds for Washington Mutual Claims," September 28, 2010.

28. Email message from Rotella to Kerry on September 1, 2010.

29. National Bureau of Economic Research, the Booth School of Business at the University of Chicago, "Lessons From the Financial Crisis for Risk Management", Anil Kashya, February 27, 2010. Prepared for the FCIC.

30. CoreLogic delinquency data, 2010.

31. CFTC website.

32. Tom Miller testimony on "Problems in Mortgage Servicing From Modification to Foreclosure" before the Committee on Banking, Housing, and Urban Affairs for the US Senate, November 16, 2010.

33. Ibid.

34. Hochberg, "Final Report of Examiner," November 4, 2010, page 17.

35. Hochberg, "Final Report of Examiner," pages 14–16, page 24.

36. Ibid, page 37.

37. FDIC website on bank seizures.

38. Letter from American Association of Bank Directors, November 2009.

39. *Wall Street Journal*, "Fannie, Freddie Pressed on Mortgages," December 8, 2010.

Chapter 10, Part Two

1.   *New York Times*, "Slapped Wrists at WaMu," December 17, 2011. *American Bankers*, "Ex-WaMu CEO Killinger Said to Be Near Settlement in Bank Failure," December 3, 2013.
2.   The Financial Crisis Inquiry Report, January 2011.
3.   Ibid
4.   FCIC, PBS Frontline: "Phil Angelides Enforcement of Wall Street is Woefully Broken", January 22, 2013. The Hill, "Warren Demands Answers on Lack of Big-Back Prosecutions", September 15, 2016.
5.   Ibid
6.   *Economist*, "The Official Verdict," February 3, 2011.
7.   *New York Times*, "A Political Divide Over the Inquiry of the Financial Crisis," February 17, 2011.
8.   *New York Times*, "Washington's Financial Disaster," January 30, 2011.
9.   *New York Times*, "Inquiry is Missing Bottom Line," January 28, 2011.
10. R Street Institute, "Sizing Up The FCIC Report Five Years Later", March 2016
11. www.fdic.gov/bank/individual/failed/pls/index.html, President Clinton Executive Order No. 12988, February 5, 1996. Financial Services Alert, "Liability considerations for O&D of failed FDIC Insured Institutions, May 2010."
12. *New York Times*, "Naming Culprits in the Financial Crisis," April 13, 2011.
13. PublicIntegrity.org, "FDIC Slow to Pursue Failed Bank Directors, Recover Tax Dollars," March 15, 2011.
14. *Marcus Welby, M.D.*, was a TV medical drama in the early 1970s. The title character was a brilliant old-fashioned doctor with a kind bedside manner who made house calls and was on a first-name basis with his patients and always had the right diagnosis.
15. FBI website, "Department of Justice Closes Washington Mutual Investigation With No [civil or] Criminal Charges," August 5, 2011.
16. *New York Times*, "Slapped Wrists at WaMu," December 17, 2011.
17. *American Banker*, "Whose Job Is It to Punish Executives," December 19, 2011.
18. *Business Insider*, "Gretchen Morgenstern's Disastrous Attack on Latest Washington Mutual Settlement," December 19, 2011.
19. National Association of Attorneys General website, "State Attorneys General, Feds Reach $25 Billion Settlement with Five Largest Mortgage Servicers on Foreclosure Wrongs", February 2012.
20. Federal reserve transcripts.
21. *New York Times*, "Days Before Housing Bust, Fed Doubted Need to Act," January 18, 2013.
22. CNBC, "Senate Report Blasts JPMorgan Executives, Including Dimon, Over Whale," March 14, 2013. *Wall Street Journal*, "For Dimon, Unfamiliar Heat," May 4, 2013.
23. *Wall Street Journal*, "For Dimon, Unfamiliar Heat," May 4, 2013.
24. *New York Times*, "Preet Bharara: Sheriff of Wall Street or Pragmatic Showman?" March 14, 2017.
25. *Super Lawyers*, July 2013.
26. The regulatory report on the seizure of Washington Mutual stated the bank was a 4-rated bank. However, the regulators gave the bank a 3 rating on

September 15. It is speculated that the regulators may have reduced the bank's rating shortly before the seizure.

27. Lewtan, a unit of Daily Mail and General Trust (DMGI), a UK firm, offers and supports a securitization data management tool called ABSnet.

28. Lewtan Research, 2010.

29. *The Atlantic*, "Eric Holder Is Planning More Bank Fraud Cases," December 5, 2013.

30. Vanity Fair, "Jamie Dimon's $13 Billion Secret—Revealed", September 6, 2017.

31. Vanity Fair, "The Real Reason Jamie Dimon Went Berserk About America's Stupid Shit", July 17, 2017.

32. OCC Website under CMP and consent orders

33. CNN, "JPMorgan Fined $920 million in London Whale Trading Loss", September 19, 2013.

34. New York Times, "JPMorgan's Legal Hurdles Expected to Multiply.", September 23, 2013; Wall Street Journal, "Five Takeaways From JPMorgan Settlements, September 19, 2013.

35. *New York Times*, "JPMorgan's Legal Hurdles Expected to Multiply," September 23, 2013.

36. *American Banker*, "Citi Moving Fast to Put Associates Suits to Rest", December 13, 2002. "Citi Exec on FTC Settlement", September 20, 2002. Board of Governors of the Federal Reserve, May 27, 2004. *Wall Street Journal*, "Moving the Market: Citigroup Faces a Fine in Britain for Lapses Linked to Bond Trade, ", May 23, 2005. "Citigroup to Take $25 Million Hit in Dr. Evil Case", June 29, 2005. Federal Reserve board docs and press orders. *American Banker*, "A Bet Vertical Integration Still Has Legs", September 13, 2007. *Houston Chronicle*, "Citigroup Agrees to Pay $2 Billion to Settle Class Action Lawsuit", *Business Standard*, "Citigroup Whistleblower Says Bank's Brute Force Hid Bad Loans for US, "January 21, 2013. *Kellogg Insight*, "How Citi Culture Allowed Corruption", January 12, 2015.

37. *Wall Street Journal*, "JPMorgan Is Haunted by a 2006 Decision on Mortgages," November 21, 2013.

38. *American Banker*, "Ex-WaMu CEO Killinger Said to Be Near Settlement in Bank Failure," December 3, 2013.

39. Wall Street Journal, "Judge Approves $37 Billion Washington Mutual Bankruptcy Settlement", December 24, 2014.

40. *Wall Street Journal*, "The Bernanke Legacy," January 27, 2014.

41. Publicintegrity.com, "Five Lobbyists for each Member of Congress on Financial Reforms", May 21, 2010 updated May 19, 2014.

Chapter 11

1. Gordon Thomas and Max Morgan-Watts, The Day the Bubble Burst: A Social History of the Wall Street Crash of 1929, 2014.

2. Searsarchives.com, Chronology of the Sears Catalog

3. Gordon Thomas and Max Morgan-Watts, The Day the Bubble Burst: A Social History of the Wall Street Crash of 1929, 2014. Liaquat Ahamed, Lords of Finance: The Bankers Who Broke the World, 2009. James Freeman and Vern McKinley, Borrowed Time: Two Centuries of Booms, Busts, and Bailouts at Citi, 2018.

4.   Gordon Thomas and Max Morgan-Watts, *The Day the Bubble Burst: A Social History of the Wall Street Crash of 1929*, 2014. Liaquat Ahamed, *Lords of Finance: The Bankers Who Broke the World*, 2009.

5.   Liaquat Ahamed, *Lords of Finance: The Bankers Who Broke the World*, 2009.

6.   International Monetary Fund, "What Is Shadow Banking?" New York Fed, "The Shadow Banking System: Implications for Financial Regulation," 2009. St. Louis Fed, "Is Shadow Banking Really Banking?" October 2011. *The Economist*, "How Shadow Banking Works," February 1, 2008.

7.   *Inside Mortgage Finance*. Lenders were asked to report their 1–4 family residential mortgage originations. Wholesale purchases, including loans closed by correspondents, are counted.

8.   ETF.com, "ETFs and Shadow Banking," April 28, 2011.

9.   The Financial Stability Board Global Monitoring Report, January 19, 2020.

10. Intelligize, a LexisNexis company, "Analysis of 2019 Unicorn IPOs",

11. Data as of November 1, 2020.

12. Blockchain technology is growing list of records, called blocks, that are linked using cryptography. Each block contains a cryptographic hash of the previous blocks, a time stamp, and transaction data that are difficult to modify; therefor maybe resistant to fraud.

13. Statista: Venmo Q3 2019 payment volume.

14. Statistical Digital Market Outlook.

15. Ibid.

16. Robert Shiller, *Narrative Economics: How Stories Go Viral and Drive Major Economic Events*, 2019.

17. CNBC interview, November 19, 2019.

18. *Time*, "How China Is Using 'Social Credit Scores' to Reward and Punish Its Citizens," December 18, 2019.

19. BlackRock year-end press release, January 15, 2020. Market Watch, "BlackRock Assets Top $7 Trillion for First Time", January 15, 2020.

Chapter 12

1.   The federal funds rate is the target interest rate set eight times a year by the FOMC at which commercial banks borrow and lend their excess reserves to each other overnight. The effective federal funds rate (EFFR) is calculated as a volume-weighted median of overnight federal funds transactions reported in the FR 2420 Report of Selected Money Market Rates. The New York Fed publishes the rate on its website for the prior business day every morning at 9am.

2.   Federal Reserve Board of Governors statistics.

3.   Bloomberg Finance LLP, December 31, 2019.

4.   National Association of Realtors, November 7, 2019.

5.   *Crain's Chicago Business*, "Defuse the Property Tax Bomb," July 23, 2019.

6.   Business Wire, "Christies Global Auction Channel Sales Total $5 Billion for 2019", September 20, 2019.

7.   Artsy.net, "What You Need to Know From Art Market 2020 Report."

8.   Forbes, "How China Used More Concrete in Three Years Than the US Used in the Entire 20th Century.", December 14, 2014. Written by Niall McCarthy who is a statistical data journalist who writes about trends.)

9. Statista 2019 and US Department of Housing and Urban Development.
10. *South China Morning Post*, "China Property: How the World's Biggest Housing Market Emerged."
11. *24/7 Wall St.*, "China Has 65 Million Empty Apartments," January 8, 2019.
12. *Wall Street Journal*, "Less Savings, More Debt: How Chinese Manage American-Style, in 17 Charts," October 30, 2019.
13. *Financial Times*, "China Central Bank Warns Over Rising Household Debt Levels," November 15, 2019.
14. Board of Governors of the Federal Reserve System.
15. Ibid.
16. Brookings Institute, "America's Commuting Choices: 5 Major Takeaways from 2016 Census Data.",
17. Debt.org.
18. *Auto Finance News*, "State of the Subprime Auto Lending Market," October 22, 2019.
19. World Economic Forum, "China's $900 Billion New Silk Road. What You Need to Know", a series of articles.
20. Bloomberg, "China's New Silk Road," April 15, 2019.

Chapter 13

1. US Bureau of Labor Statistics.
2. Digest of Education Statistics.
3. Paul Krugman, *The Financial Crisis: Who Is to Blame*, 2010. Erik Banks, *See No Evil: Uncovering the Truth Behind the Financial Crisis*, 2010.
4. Center for Responsive Politics, Open Secrets.org., Influence and Lobbying Studies.
5. Robert Shiller, *The Subprime Solution: How Today's Global Financial Crisis Happened, and What to Do About It*, 2008.

Afterword

1. International Monetary Fund, August 2020.
2. World Trade Organization, April 2020.
3. Board of Governors, Federal Reserve System.
4. Congressional Budget Office.
5. Congressional Budget Office, April 2020.
6. The Department of Treasury: April 2020.
7. Board of Governors, Federal Reserve.
8. National Association of Realtors, April 2020.
9. Wall Street Journal, "The $52 Trillion Bubble: China Grapples with Epic Property Boom", July 16, 2020
10. International Monetary Fund, August 2020.
11. Board of Governors, Federal Reserve.
12. US Department of Labor.
13. UBS research report, April 2020.
14. Board of Governors, Federal Reserve.
15. Organisation for Economic Co-operation and Development, February 2020.
16. Wall Street Journal, May 2020.

Glossary

1.   SEC, "Qualified Residential Mortgage: Background Data Analysis on Credit Risk Retention", August 2013, updated February 2015.

Timeline

1.   Robert Shiller, *Finance and the Good Society*, 2013, Chapter 25.
2.   1992 Title XIII of the Housing and Community Development Act. FCIC Dissenting Statement, Wallison and Burns, January 2011, pages 452–454.
3.   HUD, "The National Homeownership Strategy: Partners in the American Dream," May 1995.
4.   *New York Times*, "Fannie Mae Eases Credit to Aid Mortgage Lending," September 30, 1999.
5.   FCIC report, page 48.
6.   *Washington Post*, "How HUD Mortgage Policy Fed the Crisis," June 10, 2008.
7.   Ibid.
8.   Census Bureau on residential vacancies and homeownership.
9.   *Barrons*, "Memo Found in the Street," September 29, 2008.
10.   *Washington Post*, "How HUD Mortgage Policy Fed the Crisis," June 10, 2008.
11.   Ibid.
12.   *Investment News*, "Government Seizes Fannie and Freddie," September 2008.
13.   FCIC report, page 350.

Index

Page numbers with *c* refer to charts, those with n refer to notes.

Abbreviations:
WM   Washington Mutual
JPMC JPMorgan Chase
KK   Kerry Killinger

About the Authors

Kerry Killinger was the chairman, president, and CEO of Washington Mutual Bank, the sixth-largest depository bank in the country prior to the financial crisis of 2008. He graduated with a BBA with honors and an MBA from the University of Iowa. He is a chartered financial analyst (CFA) and a fellow in the Life Management Institute. He was chair of the National Education Summit of Achieve and *American Banker*'s Banker of the Year, received President George H. W. Bush's Points of Light Award for his philanthropy, was vice chair and chair-elect of the Financial Services Roundtable, vice chair and chair-elect of the Federal Reserve's Thrift Industry Advisory Council and vice chair of the Federal Home Loan Bank of Seattle. He was elected to the American Society of Corporate Executives.

Linda Killinger has a bachelor of science from Iowa State University and an MBA from Drake University, and completed additional graduate work at the Kellogg School of Management. She was appointed by Governor Robert D. Ray as the director of administration for the Iowa Department of Human Services, which included the prison system, mental health hospitals, AFDC, and other human service programs. She then became a consulting partner in an international accounting firm specializing in strategic planning and merger/acquisitions for financial institutions. She was the publisher and editor of *Oversees Business* magazine. Linda was vice chair of the Federal Home Loan Bank of Des Moines and chair of its audit/finance committee. She was appointed by Governor Tom Vilsack to chair his Committee for a Comprehensive Housing Strategy for Iowa.

Currently Kerry is CEO of Crescent Capital and Linda is CEO of Olympic Consulting Partners. They are very active in their communities and have served on dozens of nonprofit and for-profit boards. Their priorities in life are their charitable foundation, the Kerry and Linda Killinger Foundation, their venture capital companies, and their ten amazing grandchildren.

All proceeds of this book will be donated to charity to aid in criminal and social justice, government reform, civil discourse, and community building.